WILLIAM H. YOUNG

The University of Wisconsin

OGG & RAY'S

Essentials of

AMERICAN
NATIONAL
GOVERNMENT

Tenth Edition

734 - 325

APPLETON-CENTURY-CROFTS
EDUCATIONAL DIVISION
New York *MEREDITH CORPORATION*

PREFACE

In this edition of *Essentials of American National Government* a number of important additions and revisions have been made. For instance, a chapter on government and the economy has been added which deals with the strategies for maintaining a healthy and growing economy—now a firm commitment of the national government. My wife, Sara, a conservation educator, has provided a wholly new chapter on conservation, summarizing the tremendous progress that has been made as well as the enormous problems we have yet to face in this dynamic field of national activity. The chapter on foreign affairs has also been extensively rewritten to change its emphasis from the bipolar Cold War to the multiplicity of policies and commitments in the modern world.

Those portions of *Essentials of American National Government* which in previous editions discussed the relations among the states and the limitations on state authority imposed by the national Constitution have been removed from the chapter on the federal system of this edition. Instead, they have been incorporated into a new volume, *Essentials of American State and Local Government*. The revised chapter on the federal system emphasizes the relationships between the national government and state governments and examines the evolving dominance of the central government.

All of the material has been brought up to date as of January 1, 1969.

William H. Young

CONTENTS

ILLUSTRATIONS

I The Foundations of Government in the United States

A The Constitutional Basis

1

THE SETTING

The American system of government is now nearly two hundred years old.

The great experiment

It has outlived virtually all the systems of popular government in the recorded history of this planet. Conceived as a great experiment in self-rule, it has survived a terrible ordeal by combat, progressively widened its popular base, deployed its strength about the globe as a world power of the first rank, and now stands as leader of the free world and model for many heretofore subject peoples striving for self-expression and self-rule. We might, therefore, be justified in taking its future for granted.

The history of political systems suggests, however, that popularly-based government is one of the most fragile of all. Whereas two or three

Can our system survive?

generations ago the ultimate triumph of democratic government was considered by enlightened Westerners to be merely a matter of time and education, the rise of continental and Asiatic dictatorships, red and black, the prolonged economic stagnation of the thirties, the ever-mounting pace of technological change, and the determined rejection of Western tutelage by the masses of Asia and Africa, have combined to cloud the future and shake our optimism. In the present posture of world affairs, the American nation has undertaken staggering commitments to preserve Western society. It has equipped itself and witnessed the equipment of its leading rival with explosive power capable of devastating most of the earth's surface and the people who live upon it. For these new responsibilities, it is ill-prepared. Can our system survive the stresses of racial conflict and cold war uncertainty? Can it bear the frustrations of guarding the Pandora's box of nuclear explosives? Can it stand a prolonged period of military involvement in Asia without real hope of victory nor fear of defeat? What would happen to our economy

3

if disarmament could actually be achieved or military expenditures be sharply curtailed? Is it capable of promoting creativity amidst the pressure for conformity? Depending as it does on an enlightened populace, can it be subverted by the irrational, the tension-hounded, the spectator-oriented? No one can be certain.

A mixture of democracy and constitutionalism

The American governmental system is neither simple to understand nor easy to operate. We have come to call it a democracy but only in this century and not because it altogether resembles the classical model. It is, in truth, a mixture of elements from constitutional models as well as democratic ones. From the constitutional traditions of Western, mainly English, civilization, it has incorporated the concepts of limited public authority, divided power, regional and local autonomy, and respect for legality. It has adapted from this same tradition, the institutions of civil rights, due process of law, representative legislatures, and separated and mutually antagonistic institutions of political decision-making. From the democratic ideal it has gathered esteem for the individual, granting to him the dignity and worth of the Christian tradition and the equality of spirit and the freedom of thought, utterance, and conscience consistent with this faith. To the democratic spirit it also owes its respect for majorities and their right to govern and it has embodied these ideals in its institutions of voting, political parties, organized associations of interests, and its deference to public opinion. Each of these great ideals—democracy and constitutionalism—has influenced the development of the American system and each has reacted to and influenced the other in such a way as to produce the unique blend which we cherish as our governmental system.

The pluralistic society

Government is, we believe, but one aspect of a larger whole—the American society or the American nation. It is, perhaps, the major institutional embodiment of that larger entity, but it is expected—in large part because of our constitutional tradition—to share influence with the family, the church, and various economic, fraternal, charitable, educational, recreational, and cultural associations of which the society is composed. Ours is thus a pluralistic society with many centers of influence, prestige, and validly exercised authority. The government we regard as the servant of the people and of their interests as manifested by the other associations through which they pursue happiness. It is entirely fitting, therefore, to begin the study of the American government with an analysis of the people by whom and for whom it is operated and of the society which it is intended to serve.

THE AMERICAN PEOPLE

The population of the U.S.

There are 202 million American residents of a continental and island area of 3.6 million square miles endowed with an abundance of natural advantages unmatched by any area of comparable size. These people are responsible for the lives and fortunes of another 2.6 million people in 4,500 square miles of American lands and other territorial areas. The attempt to practice self-government over an area so vast and among so many people is without parallel in history. In fact, many of the wisest minds of Western culture had supposed it to be impossible. Probably the revolution in the technology of transportation and communication accompanying the rise of the American nation, and the spread throughout it of democratic processes has made it possible to unite such an area in a single system of popular political institutions. Even so, the centrifugal pull of regional and local interests and ambitions has repeatedly threatened the unity of national political and social institutions. Our constitutional arrangements allow, if they do not require, the accommodation of regional pressures to achieve a national consensus. We have not as yet found a workable arrangement for bringing all of our island possessions or our national territories such as Washington, D. C., into full participation in our institutions and continue to control them by processes from which the residents are partly or wholly excluded.

The Constitution of the United States was written for a nation of 4 million people occupying an area of 890,000 square miles. The rapid growth of our population by immigration and by natural increase and of our territory by purchase and conquest placed a severe strain on our political system *National growth*

U.S. POPULATION GROWTH, ACTUAL AND PROJECTED 1790—1980

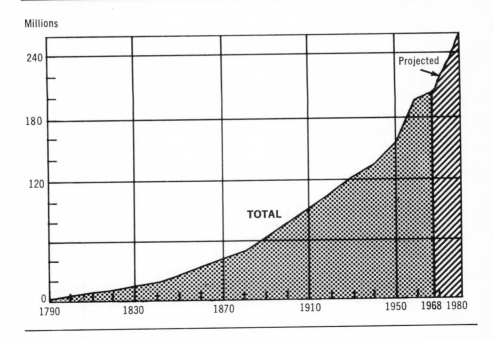

SOURCE: U.S. Bureau of the Census.

BIRTH AND DEATH RATES IN THE UNITED STATES, 1915–1966

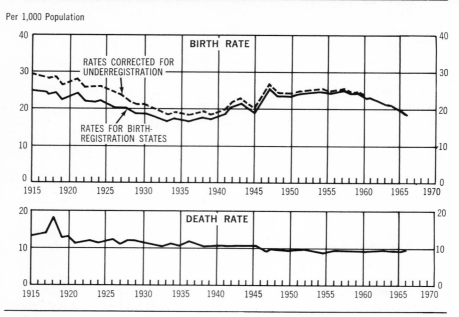

Per 1,000 Population

SOURCE: U.S. Bureau of the Census, *Statistical Abstract of the United States,* 1966.

and has modified it in many important respects. In virtually every decade until World War I our population increased by 25 percent or more. The natural increase was achieved in part by a falling death rate attributable to an abundant natural environment and to the conquest by sanitary engineering and modern medicine of most of the dread scourges of the human species. As the nation became urbanized the birth rate fell rather steadily until World War II. Thereafter, it took a sharp upturn but is now slowly declining again. A major consequence of these fluctuations has been a slowly aging population unsettled by a startling post-World War II increase in children, both taxing heavily the public education and welfare services supported by a relatively smaller productive population.

Immi-
gration   Until 1920 a major factor in population growth was immigration. In a little more than a century, 40 million Europeans came to this country to make their homes—a migration unparalleled in history. At first the newcomers were from the United Kingdom, then from Germany, and Scandinavia, and after 1880 from Italy and the Slavic countries of Central and Eastern Europe. This great movement of peoples of diverse cultures and ethnic stocks is responsible for many of the unique qualities of American civilization. The public schools and the urban political organizations were

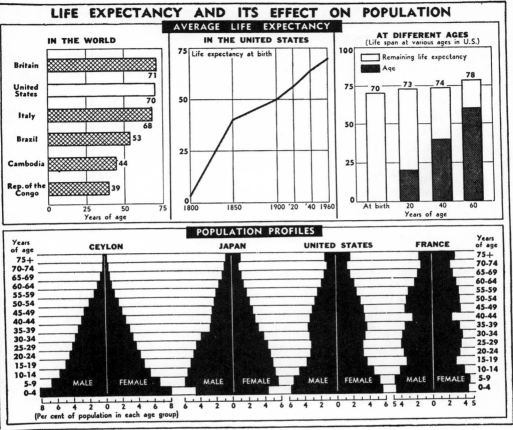

LIFE EXPECTANCY AND ITS EFFECT ON POPULATION

AVERAGE LIFE EXPECTANCY

SOURCE: *The New York Times,* Jan. 15, 1961.

the major transmitters of the American heritage. Urban politics until quite recently was largely influenced, if not dominated, by ethnic considerations, and the large city party machines were built, in part, around appeals to the needs of the newcomers for recognition and acceptance. American citizenship and thus national loyalty was for a nation of immigrants an act of choice not an accident of birth. As such it has aroused intense dedication to the American way accompanied by misunderstanding of and contempt for those of the world whose national loyalty was otherwise acquired. The idea that valid political power is based upon the consent of the governed has always seemed to Americans both natural and obvious. Assimilation into American culture through the public schools was achieved by the children at the expense, typically, of repudiating their parents; peer group rather than familial tradition set the standards of conduct and fashioned the goals by which achievement has been measured. Many experts believe that the permissiveness of child-raising, the pressures for conformity, and the mother-oriented family style of American life may be traced directly to the influence of the immigrant.

The door is closed   "Give me your tired, your poor, your huddled masses," was the American policy until 1921. The closing of the land frontier in the eighteen-nineties, the rise of organized labor, the antipathy toward central Europeans aroused by the spread of communism among them, all contributed to the closing of America's front door. When various restrictions against paupers, contract laborers, criminals, orientals, and others failed markedly to reduce the tide, a quota system was instituted. It remained until 1965 the basis of our admissions policy and under it, migrants from Europe, Asia, and Africa were authorized annually on the basis of quotas allotted to each nation or group of peoples in accordance with the relative contribution of that nation or people to our national population as it stood in 1920. The ostensible purpose of this program was to admit a group of persons each year ethnically equivalent to those already here. In practice the total quota was never used because there was no longer any important migration from Great Britain and Ireland, whose people were entitled to a large share of the quota allotments. Pressure to abandon the preferential treatment of Northern Europeans built in to the quota system brought Congress in 1965 to re-fashion the policy, modify the national origin basis of quotas, and improve the procedure. The most recent law—effective July 1, 1968—established an annual ceiling of 170,000 on migrants, excluding those from independent

THE IMMIGRATION PICTURE, 1820–1966

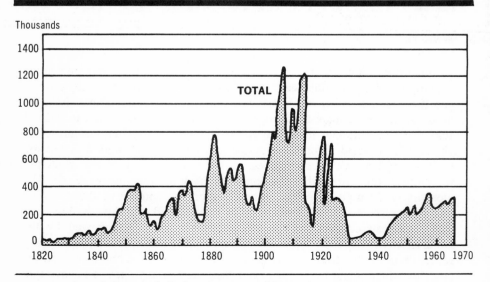

SOURCE: *Annual Report of the Immigration and Naturalization Service.*

nations of the Western Hemisphere and immediate relatives of persons in the United States. Permission for admission is granted on the basis of close family relationship to resident aliens and citizens, work skills and U. S. employment needs. Unused national quotas are made available to nationals of countries whose quotas are exhausted. About 300,000 immigrants are now (1967) entered annually—about 100,000 under the quota system and 200,000 close relatives or Western Hemisphere nationals.

The urbaniza-tion of America

Of the 4 million who founded the nation more than 90 percent were farmers. The philosophy of the self-reliant freeholder expressed so compellingly by Thomas Jefferson dominated the nation for generations. It still has a strong hold upon the outlook and affections of large numbers of our people. Today, however, more than 94 percent of our people live in cities, villages, or small towns; fewer than 6 percent live on farms and this percentage is declining. More than 60 percent live in the central cities or the suburbs of the more than 200 major metropolitan areas of the country. We are now a preponderantly urban people, dependent, huddled-together, insecure, and more highly dependent upon governmental services for our comfort as well as our survival than ever before in our history.

The city vs. the small town

The growth of the modern pervasive state may be traced directly to the industrialization and urbanization of our society. It is the urbanite who

PROPORTIONS OF RURAL AND URBAN POPULATION, 1860–1960

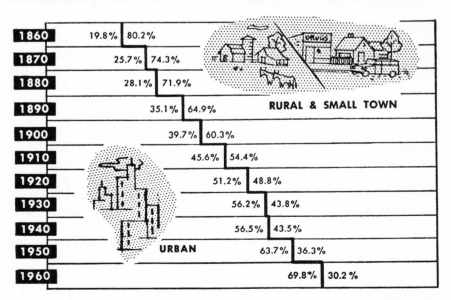

1860	19.8%	80.2%
1870	25.7%	74.3%
1880	28.1%	71.9%
1890	35.1%	64.9%
1900	39.7%	60.3%
1910	45.6%	54.4%
1920	51.2%	48.8%
1930	56.2%	43.8%
1940	56.5%	43.5%
1950	63.7%	36.3%
1960	69.8%	30.2%

RURAL & SMALL TOWN

URBAN

SOURCE: U. S. Bureau of the Census. Since 1910 the Census Bureau has broken down the rural category into farm and nonfarm.

requires the ever-widening concern of the government in his daily life to shield him from germs, loss of wages, and the consequences of aging, and to provide him with education, recreation, and congestion-ameliorating services. Compared to that of rural and even small-town society, urban culture is dynamic, competitive, and anonymous. The rural and small-town outlook, however, yields grudgingly to the demands of the so-called "mass society." Legislative apportionment systems, the federal character of the United States Senate, the organizational arrangements of county, town, and village governments all combine to accord it a larger influence than strict majoritarianism warrants. To many spokesmen for the rural–small-town point of view, the great city means, as it did to Jefferson, wickedness, greed, corruption, charismatic leadership, and decadence. Somewhere in many of the major political controversies of modern America, in the Congress, the state capitols, the party apparatus, and the huge interest groups, the conflicts of outlook between the large city and small town may be found. The constitutional fabric of American government was designed for a rural people; the processes of democracy support the growing influence of the urban masses. Adjusting the one to the other has required and will continue to require the highest order of statesmanship.

Negroes

The first census of the American people (1790) revealed that among the 4 million inhabitants were 757,000 Negroes, more than 90 percent of whom were slaves. According to the census of 1960 there are now more than 18.5 million Negroes in the United States. Assimilating the African slave into American democratic culture has proved one of the most difficult of all national problems, and Negroes are still far from achieving a place consistent with their numbers or with the democratic ideals of the nation. For some decades before and after freedom, the Negro was largely an adjunct to the Southern plantation system of agricultural production. In this century and especially during and after the world wars, Negroes have been moving in great numbers to the large metropolitan centers of the North and Middle West. There, like other streams of immigrants before them, they have sought recognition through political participation and have become active and assertive members of the big urban party organizations. From this vantage they have pressed their claims for greater governmental exertion on behalf of themselves and their southern brethren. Since World War II colored peoples everywhere in the world have been casting off the chains of white colonialism and demanding recognition of their own aspirations. The combination of these domestic and international challenges to "white supremacy" has thrust the race question more vigorously into our national politics than at any time since the crusade of the abolitionists and has and will test our faith in equality, our pretensions to democratic forms, and our commitments to self-determination.

Other minorities

Elsewhere—in the Southwest and on the Pacific coast—the Mexicans and the Chinese and Japanese resident minorities present similar if not quite such dramatic challenges to the political and cultural handicaps long imposed upon them. There were, in fact, 1.6 million members of other non-white races in our national population in 1960.

The virtual cessation of immigration from outside this continent has *A mobile* not meant a halt to the constant ebb and flow of people within our con- *people* tinental area. Our population is probably the most mobile in the world. Internal migration continues at a spectacular rate in three directions: (1) from the east to the west; (2) from the farm to the small town to the city; and (3) from the central city to the suburbs. California, for example, is now the most populous state in the Union whereas only fifty years ago it ranked twelfth. The center of population has moved steadily westward and is now (1960) located in south–central Illinois. Despite the rapid urbanization of the nation, the central cities of Chicago, Cleveland, Detroit, Minneapolis–St. Paul, New York, Philadelphia, Pittsburgh, St. Louis, San Francisco, Washington, D. C., and many others actually lost population from 1950–1960, while the suburban areas of these same cities recorded huge gains. Mobility on this scale has many political as well as social consequences. A vast portion of our people at any time have no real attachment to the local communities in which they reside. Roots in local traditions and self-conscious community loyalties are not easily formed nor very durable. In every election, further, people are disqualified from voting because of their too recent settlement in the state and voting district. Appeals to local sentiment, state pride, and regional autonomy are relatively ineffectual to those on the move.

AMERICAN SOCIETY

Under the impact of urbanization, industrialization, and migration the *The family* American family has been undergoing a thorough reconstruction. In the family farm culture of yesteryear the family was a major unit of production. Each member contributed important and specialized labor, and children could become economic assets almost as soon as they could walk and talk. Patriarchal in organization the rural family was held together by the strong claims of the soil and the job of wresting food and fiber from it. In urban culture, the family is a consuming unit not a producing one; children are an economic liability until well into their teens, and the high cost of housing, the congestion of living areas, the demands of factory and office all exert unremitting pressure on the traditional family relationships. The first shock of urban environment is revealed in falling birth rates, rising crime rates, rising divorce rates, raising emotional disturbances among the newest recruits to the cities. The father is torn between the demands of his home and those of his work. The mother takes charge of the children's moral education, and the school becomes the chief transmitter of the cultural heritage. The urban family is small, isolated from the relatives of the parents, consumption-oriented, and fragile. The immigrant family has suffered the most painful dislocation—the father's authority repudiated, schoolmates fixing the goals for dress, taste, and achievement. More recently, the flight to the suburbs of middle-class families, the spread of public housing for lower-income groups, the recapture of open space for recreation, the decline in the work-week, the increase in job security, the transfer of entertainment from cinema to home television are all recreating a new family environment. The birth rate for a short time took a sharp upward turn. Home ownership is increasing. Status is now acquired more by standards of consumption than by position. Although the divorce rate continues to be high and women continue to enter the labor market in large numbers, the family is nevertheless recapturing some of the functions it had lost. Concern is still widely manifested, however, for the permissive, cooperative, non-authoritarian and success-oriented, child-rearing practices of the American urban family. The pressure for higher and higher consumption standards takes a heavy toll of the breadwinners; the demand for more and more education for the children is placing great strains on all systems of higher education in the land; the rise in the number of unemployed, in some cases unemployable, youth—high school dropouts—is giving city authorities constant concern.

Protestant America

In the main this nation is composed of Protestants. Approximately 60 percent of all those who profess some religious faith are members of one of the Protestant sects. About 30 percent are Roman Catholics. We are thus largely inheritors of the spirit of the Reformation—individualistic and antiauthoritarian. Religious exercises, on the whole, occupy a declining place in our national culture. The separation of church and state to which our constitutional tradition binds us and the pervasive influence of the rigidly nonsectarian public-school system make the family the chief transmitter of religious beliefs. We have observed that the modern urban family is changing its character. It may not, therefore, be as effective as the patriarchal, agricultural family in inculcating strong religious feelings. The school system continues to be the arena of struggle among the faiths for influence over the young.

The modern American enjoys a standard of living not rivaled nor even closely approximated in the rest of the modern world. This prosperity has been achieved by a combination of rich natural resources, widely shared technical facility and willingness to experiment with new methods, and a strong preference for privately owned and operated economic institutions. While our achievements in art, literature, music, and fundamental science may not have been outstanding, our technology of production of all sorts of material goods is unsurpassed.

The economics of affluence

The preferred method of organizing production is the joint-stock corporation, characterized, at present, by widely distributed stock ownership (20 million stockholders in 1965) and small tightly-knit directorates. Some of our corporations have grown to such size, wealth, and power that they overshadow many of our local and regional institutions of government.

Our economic system is characterized by a high degree of competition and great deference to the marketplace as the determinant of corporate effectiveness. The competition, however, is rather closely managed in many sectors of production and rarely extends to prices charged. The economic and political power of corporate management has been challenged for the past two generations by the spread of labor unions among the factory workers. Twenty-two percent of those gainfully employed are now members of some labor organization, and the labor of several key industries (e.g., steel, automotive, transportation) is unionized throughout the nation. However, the increasing application of technology to productive processes and the substitution of capital for manpower are reducing the demand for semiskilled and unskilled factory hands, contributing to the rise of unemployment and to the demand for more technically-trained operatives, and, perhaps, limiting the growth potential of the industrial labor unions. American productive capacity is stimulated and supported by a huge enterprise for which there is nothing quite comparable elsewhere in the world: advertising. Symbolized by Madison Avenue, New York City, American advertising persuades the consumer to want what American factories can produce.

A mixed economy

Although the American economy is predominantly a private enterprise economy, it is by no means a pure system of capitalism of the nineteenth-century model. Every variation of governmental intervention has been or is now being practiced, and a substantial amount of public enterprise (postal service, electric power production, credit supply) exists alongside of private enterprise. Government regulation of the private sector of the economy has been steadily growing in scope and impact. The huge defense establishment, the efforts to penetrate outer space, and the use of goods and services in our diplomacy have important, if not decisive, influence on substantial areas of domestic private enterprise. The corporate income tax is also a prime regulator of corporate conduct. Many of the major political controversies of our national history have stemmed from efforts to mitigate alleged disadvantages of unrestrained private decisions in the production and distribution of wealth. In no other modern industrial nation, nevertheless, has such free play to private initiative and personal acquisitiveness been allowed.

Groups in American life

Much of the stimulus to political controversy in America is provided by economic groups—corporate, union, or agricultural—as each seeks to advance its interests in the political arena. Our system encourages the organization of interests of all types and rewards concerted efforts of this kind with influence over governmental and political decisions. The clash of group interests, notably but not exclusively economic interests, is a very large part (some would say all) of the dynamics of American politics. One of the major lessons of the American experience is that separate individuals are relatively ineffectual in giving direction to the machinery of government unless they associate together to promote common aims. Our democratic processes, combined with constitutional separation of decisive authority, invite organizations of many kinds to struggle for advantage.

Almost from its origin American society has been free from the rigid class distinctions of European society. The southern plantation aristocracy fell before the free-farmer and the factory owner and operator. The great appeal of Marxist ideology to the proletariat, enthusiastically received by many European workers, has been largely rejected in America. More than 80 percent of our people think of themselves as members of the middle class. Nevertheless, sociologists perceive that our society is in truth divided (although not very rigidly) into classes on the basis of living style, attitudes, and belief systems, and that it is characterized by a considerable degree of upward and downward mobility. The very rich and the very poor seem to be the most class-conscious members of American society and together they are a distinct minority of the population. Our productive genius, further, can turn out cars, clothes, homes, appliances, and food in such volume and at such low costs that the ordinary family lacks little except servants that the rich family can afford. The difference between going on horseback and going on foot was after all, a whole world, while that between a Cadillac and a second-hand Ford is but a few steps.

The urban style of life

Perhaps the most significant division of social organization in America is that between urban society and small-town society already alluded to. Urban society is diffuse, hectic, competitive, bureaucratic, consumption-dominated, anonymous, noisy, overstimulated, and highly dependent. The small town is neighborly, compact, unadventurous, closed, immobile, and where intimately related to the countryside, relatively independent. Since, however, urban culture dominates the mass media of communication, and volume production supported by nationwide advertising is the predominant system of creating and supplying consumer wants, the independent or family farm and the small town are slowly but surely giving way to the tastes, styles, and distribution systems of the cities. The automobile allows the urbanite to penetrate ever deeper into the hinterland for living space as well as recreation. Furthermore, the farm and village are constantly exporting their ablest youth to the cities. It seems virtually certain that the subculture of rural America will soon be swallowed up in the mass culture of the metropolis.

Debate continues as to whether it is divine benediction, superior ethnic origins, the frontier, economic abundance, the absence of aggressive neighbors, the religious convictions of the early settlers, the small freehold farm system of land tenure, the assimilation of the immigrant, the addiction to private enterprise, or some other factor which has molded the American character and given it a unique stamp among the peoples of the earth.

The American credo

There is a considerable, although not perfect, agreement, however, that there is a uniquely American belief system and that it is compounded largely of individualism, equalitarianism, antiauthoritarianism, and materialism, and that our political system to a large degree reflects these attitudes. The American is an individualist in the sense that he believes in the worth of each separate soul. Each man is entitled to respect, to pursue his salvation, and to make such contribution as he is able because he is a man not because he is a member of some larger entity—the folk, the chosen tribe, or the proletariat. The heroes of much of the greatest American imaginative literature are lonely adventurers, alienated from society, fighting their desperate struggles for redemption unaided and uncomforted. Americans are the most optimistic people on earth in their belief in rejuvenation by self-will. We bedevil ourselves constantly with improving instruction and exhortation designed to strengthen the will to succeed. We do not, on the whole, believe that men are or should be perfectly equal in intelligence, wealth, ability, or influence, but we do aspire to equality of opportunity. Man should have the chance to move upward, to improve upon the situation into which he was born. The most popular programs of public benefit are likely to be those aimed at improving a man's chances to compete successfully. This attitude, of course, requires that men accept the responsibility for their own situations. Since most of us do not achieve all that we hope for and many stumble and falter on the path, this is a hard and a tension-inducing faith. It drives men to despair as well as to high achievement. The roots of the American's distrust and dislike for authority are deep. Puritan conscience, the rebellion against England, the second-generation immigrant's repudiation of patriarchal authority, the frontier, all have contributed. We are neither a deferential nor a law-abiding people and are capable of exploding in more lawless violence in one month in one city (Chicago, for instance) than the people of all England in one year. The materialistic orientation of American culture is notorious throughout the world. Goods, goods, and more goods! We produce and we consume. Success is measured as much by what we consume as by what we produce, and money is the yardstick of accomplishment. Appliances rather than abstractions excite our enthusiasm and our pride. We are desperately determined to make life here and now more pleasant, more comfortable, and more hygienic. For this, by the rest of the world, we are occasionally despised, frequently patronized, and universally envied. And yet this is not the whole story. About our material possessions we are not miserly; owning them satisfied our desire for esteem. As a people we have probably given more of our wealth away at home and abroad than any other. And paradoxically, we frequently state our international aims in the most idealistic terms—"making the world safe for democracy."

OUR ENGLISH POLITICAL HERITAGE

Each of the mainstreams of migrants from Europe has made important contributions to American life and those who came in the period 1840–1920 have had an enormous impact on the family, economy, and politics of urban society. Our main lineage, however, is undoubtedly English, and it is to the English traditions that we owe the basic forms and concepts of our system of government. The fathers of the American Constitution and

English experience as the basis of our political system

of the War of Independence were inseparably linked to centuries of English institutional development. The triumph of the Revolution separated our people from the English government of that day; it did not, fortunately, sever all ties of memory or shared experience between them and their English forebears. Our political institutions did not emerge suddenly and in complete form in 1776 nor yet in 1787, but had been long abuilding in the colonies and in the mother country as well. Our people lived in the British Empire for almost as long before independence as they have lived outside of it since.

1. The theory and practice of representative government

The Englishmen who settled this land brought with them, among many other concepts, the idea that the powerful parts of any government ought in some sense to represent those who are governed by it. The English Parliament had been in existence for several centuries when this nation was founded and had come to represent the major classes of English society even if it had not achieved effective representation of the great mass of peasants and artisans. The period of setttlement of America coincided with a constitutional revolution in England in which the representative branch of the government successfully wrested power from the despotic or monarchical branch. Although settlers sympathetic to both sides came to America, those favorable to Parliament were especially influential throughout New England.

The colonies were established under various auspices—private proprietors, trading companies, and monarchical endowment—but whatever their origin, a representative assembly was established sooner or later in every one of them to share power with, occasionally to dominate, the executive agents of the sponsors. The members of these legislatures were everywhere elected by vote of a limited number of their fellow citizens (property owners or taxpayers mainly) under better proportioned schemes of representation than in the mother country. There was no need in America to represent an almost nonexistent landed aristocracy in an upper house, for example. These colonial legislatures proved the training grounds for colonial politicians and provided this nation with more than a century of experience with elected representative assemblies before we struck off the ties with the English crown.

In our long colonial history something very like the contest between Crown and Parliament occurred. These representative bodies proved their ability time and again to keep the imported English executives under close control. The idea that the legislature ought to represent the people—or at least the better (richer) part of them—that it ought to control the public treasury and determine major public policy was, therefore, firmly established in practice when the constitutions for a new nation were written. It should also be added that most of the colonial assemblies formed the lower house

2. The idea of limited government

of a two-house legislature, the upper house being a governor's council. Bicameralism was thus well established in America before 1776.

The essence of constitutional government is that power is limited by law and that these limits are enforced upon rulers by established procedures.

Our English forefathers, for the most part, brought with them a firm attachment to the idea that this kind of government is both wise and practicable. The citizens of a nation, they believed, had certain rights which were beyond the power of any government to impair. As Englishmen, they claimed a sphere of personal freedom and asserted that fair procedures must be observed by executive officials. These conceptions linked them with hundreds of years of English constitutional development. The English settler brought tangible records—some old like the Magna Charta and some new like the Petition of Right—to support and illuminate these assertions. In the contest with the mother country, the colonists repeatedly claimed that the English government was trampling upon their rights as Englishmen. There is no more lucid statement in the literature of Western civilization of this English idea of human rights than the opening paragraphs of the Declaration of Independence. Every constitution written for the newly organized states during the Revolutionary period contained guarantees of individual liberty and requirements for fair procedure. In at least seven of these charters these safeguards against undue power were grouped in bills of rights.

That the ultimate source of all legitimate public authority is the people themselves is an idea which our forefathers took for granted. To most of them government came into being by agreement of the governed (social contract), found its justification in protecting their liberties, and received only as much authority as the people felt it necessary to grant. The great English philosopher John Locke, who in the late seventeenth century formulated these views for all time, was speaking for the Englishmen in America as well as for those in his own country. The practice of colonial America—illustrated by the Mayflower Compact, the self-written charters of Connecticut and Rhode Island, and the state constitutions drafted by the colonists at the time of separation—more nearly approached his theories than did any experience of European or English history. When the colonists became their own masters, they conferred power upon their own governments in the most grudging and distrustful manner. Frequent elections, short terms of office, and specific limitations on power characterized every one of the first state constitutions. It should not be assumed, however, that the idea that power rested upon consent included the notion that all or even most of the governed were qualified by merit or by right to participate in the processes of selection or decision. The right to vote was not one which either practice or theory attributed to all adult citizens. In other words, our English political heritage was constitutional government, not democratic government; popular sovereignty was a theory about the origin of power, not about its exercise or its organization. Coupled with the tradition of human rights, however this theory of government by consent laid the foundation for the ultimate triumph of democratic ideals.

3. The idea of popular sovereignty

Perhaps the most complete institutional transfer from England to the New World was that of the English system of jurisprudence. From the beginning of our history to the present day, the English common law has been

4. The common law

the basis of our legal system. Deeply imbedded in it at the time of its transportation were conceptions like "due process," "trial by jury," "freedom from arrest except for demonstrable cause," "equity," and many others which constituted important and specific elements in American bills of rights and in our ideas of limited governmental authority. The common law is largely judge-made law, built up over centuries by the application of traditional legal doctrine (precedents) to new situations. The slow and deliberate adjustment of the laws to the changing fabric of life, which adherence to the common law of England encourages, has been and is now one of the major conservative influences in our national life.

5. The institutions of local government

English institutions of local government, evolved over centuries, were also transplanted almost intact to America. The county was established in 1634 in Virginia and in 1643 in Massachusetts. The town dates almost from the landing of the Pilgrims; the chartered municipal corporation from 1686. The borough took root, however, only in the middle colonies like Pennsylvania. Local officials like the sheriff and the justice of the peace continue to this day to remind us that the history of our political institutions reaches backward without interruption into Anglo-Saxon England. The states of the new nation made no important modifications in these agencies of local government.

The American contributions

Upon this heritage of English ideas and institutions the American system of government was established, overlaid, one must add, by a strong belief, especially among the Puritans, in the wickedness of man and the corroding effects of power. To the stock of English political wisdom with which our ancestors launched this nation as an independent unit in the world of nation-states, the American contributions have been: (1) the democratization of the entire system; (2) the practice of written constitutions and the ultimate interpretation of their meaning by an independent judiciary; (3) the practice of separation of powers among the principal branches of the state and national governments; and, most important of all, (4) the achievement of federal union of the 13 independent states.

Since studies of contemporary public attitudes suggest that the great mass of Americans do not understand very clearly nor appreciate very deeply the lineaments of our political heritage or the modifications made in it by our own experience, it might be concluded that the concepts and institutions outlined above have been submerged in the changing fashions in ideas. Similar studies, however, reveal that the politically active citizens who staff our parties, occupy public offices, and articulate views on public policy, although a minority of the population, are the keepers and transmitters of our political culture. In the main, they understand and appreciate the institutional and ideological bases of our system and so long as they are entrusted by the mass of citizens with the keys to power are likely to operate within the framework of constitutional democracy for which these concepts provide the foundation.

REFERENCES

R. G. Adams, *The Political Ideas of the American Revolution* (Durham, N. C., 1922).

C. Becker, *The Declaration of Independence: A Study in the History of Political Ideas* (New York, 1922).

————, *The Eve of the Revolution* (New Haven, Conn., 1918), Chaps. II–IV.

J. M. Blum, *The Promise of America: An Historical Inquiry* (Boston, 1966).

Bureau of the Census, *Historical Statistics of the United States, Colonial Times to 1957* (Washington, D. C., 1960).

————, *Statistical Abstract of the United States,* Annually.

J. F. Dewhurst and associates, *America's Needs and Resources* (New York, 1955).

E. Dumbauld, *The Declaration of Independence and What It Means Today* (Norman, Okla., 1950).

G. Gorer, *The American People: A Study in National Character* (New York, 1964).

E. B. Greene, *The Provincial Governor in the English Colonies of North America* (New York, 1898).

J. F. Jameson, *The American Revolution Considered as a Social Movement* (Princeton, N. J., 1926).

A. H. Kelly and W. A. Harbison, *The American Constitution; Its Origins and Development* (New York, 1948), Chaps. I–IV.

P. Olson (ed.), *America as a Mass Society* (New York, 1963).

D. M. Potter, *People of Plenty: Economic Abundance and the American Character* (New York, 1964).

2

THE CONSTITUTION OF THE UNITED STATES

THE ACHIEVEMENT OF FEDERAL UNION

The Continental Congress

Fearful of the consequences of concerted colonial action, the English government never gave ideas of colonial unity much encouragement. Scattered proposals like Franklin's Albany plan and experiments like the New England Confederation (1643–1683), looking to solidarity, had captured little loyalty. Growing controversy with the mother country, after the defeat of the French removed the compelling need for English support, stimulated the idea of union, and events after 1770 gave the idea of cooperation new impetus. Still, the colonists seemed more aware of their differences than of their common purposes. As they became more deeply involved in bold and hazardous resistance to English authority, the creation of at least some intercolonial consultative and directive machinery became a matter of the most obvious common sense, and in the autumn of 1774 the First Continental Congress assembled in Philadelphia. It brought together irregularly chosen delegates from every colony except Georgia. For seven weeks the Congress devoted itself to considering the common peril, planning cooperation, adopting a "declaration of rights," and formulating resolutions for consideration by the colonial legislatures. It concluded with a call for a similar congress to meet the following year unless in the meantime the emergency became war. When the Second Continental Congress convened in May, 1775, it found itself obliged, in the absence of any other common authority, to step into the breach, take measures for raising armies and funds, and in effect transform itself into a government. Moving from place to place as the exigencies of hostilities required, this body served as the country's sole organ of national authority until March, 1781.

Need for a central government

Without some such unifying authority as the Continental Congress, the War for Independence could hardly have been carried to a successful conclusion. As an agency of government, however, the body left much to be desired. Starting as only a voluntary intercolonial conference, it remained to the end a revolutionary assembly, resting on no basis of law and exercising powers only by virtue of having assumed them with the tacit consent of the governments and peoples of the newly established states. To meet a temporary emergency, makeshift arrangements such as these might, and did, serve. But the war gave promise of lasting many weary years; if successful, it would leave the country confronted with the problem of a permanent national government. In any event, finance, commerce, and foreign relations, to say nothing of military and naval operations, called for management by a government resting on some regular basis, endowed with definite powers, and assured of some degree of permanence. Out of this practical necessity arose the idea of a genuine and enduring union of the states under a national constitution—in other words, that concept of American nationality which gradually broadened and deepened until it found expression in the Articles of Confederation, the Constitution of 1787, and eventually the vast and complicated mechanism of national authority and management which we know today as the government of the United States.

The first constitution for a union of states was adopted in 1781 and was called the Articles of Confederation. It originated in a resolution offered to the Continental Congress in 1776 by Richard Henry Lee, at the same time that he moved for a declaration of colonial independence. A committee appointed by the Congress quickly drafted a plan of union. It was not, however, approved by the Congress until November 15, 1777, and was not approved by every participating state until three and one-half years later. When this new form of government finally was put into operation, the war that had evoked it was nearly at an end. *The Articles of Confederation*

Under the Articles, the United States at last achieved a government resting on a written constitution and with functions and powers defined therein—a government which, it must in fairness be remembered, was considerably superior to the extralegal Continental Congress, even though it in turn eventually was replaced. Three main features characterized it. The first was the recognition of the practice under the Continental Congress of state sovereignty, expressly asserted in the document's second "article." The states, it is true, relinquished important powers to the new central establishment, but on the whole the union remained a loose confederation or league. In this respect as in others it closely resembles the General Assembly of the United Nations. *Sovereignty of the states*

A second feature was the concentration of all national powers in a Congress of one house, meeting annually and composed of delegates appointed in each state for a single year as the legislature might direct. Each state paid its own delegates and could recall them and appoint others at any time; and no person might serve more than three years out of any six. Voting was by states, and each state had a single vote regardless of the number of delegates it sent. Committees might, of course, be set up and sub- *A Congress of delegates* ordinate officers appointed. There was no separate executive branch and no national system of courts.

Powers
and
limitations
In the third place, powers and functions conferred on the national government were few and severely restricted. Far from being a general law-making authority like our present Congress, the Congress of the Confederation was only a grand committee of the states charged with executive and managerial functions, such as looking after foreign relations, declaring and conducting war on land and sea, building and equipping a navy, carrying on dealings with the Indian tribes, borrowing money, issuing bills of credit, regulating weights and measures, and making requisitions upon the states for soldiers and for funds. It could not reach down past the state governments to control the people in any effective way. It could adopt resolutions and issue commands, but it had only limited means of enforcing them—none at all through judicial process except by resort to the courts of the states. And some of the most important powers entrusted to it—for example, making treaties and coining and borrowing money—could be exercised only if the delegations of as many as nine states concurred.

Contro-
versy
over the
Articles
Even before the Articles took effect, several leading statesmen of the new nation—Washington, Hamilton, Madison, Jay, among others—felt that the power of the central government was inadequate to its tasks. The Confederation period was thus marked from the outset by controversy over the fundamental law itself, and as the years passed the controversy grew in intensity and scope. On the one side were the nationalists—including many of the officers of the Revolutionary army, the merchants, the holders of certificates of public debt, and the manufacturers—who felt the new union cut but a sorry figure internationally, inviting abuse if not invasion by the boastful and aggressive nations of Europe. Only a strong central government could muster cash, soldiers, and armaments sufficient to compel respect abroad. This group was skeptical of the competence and disillusioned by the behavior of the state legislatures which were the centers of political power in the nation. Distrustful of too much democracy, they disdained the frequent elections, short terms of office, and the agrarian biases of the state lawmakers. Only a central authority, they argued, could establish the public credit, restrain state imposition on trade, deal with foreign nations, and stimulate the development of national rather than regional loyalties and ambitions. On the other side there was a numerous group, largely of freehold farmers and without the brilliant leadership of the nationalists, who supported confederation and opposed granting any more power to the central government. Central governments are far removed from the immediate problems of domestic life and are apt to be despotic, they said. We have not thrown off the chains of a transoceanic monarch only to fetter ourselves to a home-grown one. The states are the important units for the exercise of power. Their governments under new constitutions are everywhere close to "the people" and sensitive to their needs. In this way did one of the enduring issues in American politics originate. These two conceptions ultimately con-

tributed to the formation of political parties and under the new Constitution of 1787 continued to clash for generations thereafter.

The powerful arguments of the talented nationalists tended to minimize the significant achievements under the Articles. A new national domain was created by the cession to the central government of the claims of the states to lands west of the Alleghenies. In a series of acts culminating in the famous Northwest Ordinance of 1787, the Congress laid the foundation for the development of five republican institutions in this vast area and their ultimate admission to the Union as states. Executive departments were created and staffed with a permanent bureaucracy: the Post Office, Treasury, War, and Foreign Affairs agencies were created under individuals designated by Congress. The vast debt created by the war was brought into manageable form by the settlement of accounts and was substantially reduced. New loans were rather readily negotiated with Dutch bankers. The country successfully weathered the economic depression following victory, and signs of recovery were everywhere apparent at the end of the Confederation period. *Achievements under the Articles*

The nationalists were, however, able to point to the lack of an independent income and the inability of the Confederation government to meet all of its fiscal responsibilities, either to foreign or domestic creditors, as a serious flaw in the United States government. Without dependable income, the government could not meet its past obligations and it could not prepare the nation to defend itself from hostile European powers. The nation could do little to compel obedience to its mandates; it was wholly dependent upon the states for execution as well as for income. *Weaknesses of the Articles*

The immediate impetus to reform of the Confederation was interstate controversy over commerce. Successful negotiations between Virginia and Maryland, held under the auspices of George Washington, led to another conference on tariff barriers to which Virginia, at the suggestion of Washington and Madison, invited other interested states. To the convention in Annapolis in 1786 came representatives of only five states, but among them were Madison and Hamilton, leaders of the nationalist cause. They induced the delegates to invite all the states to send delegates to a new convention in 1787 in Philadelphia at which all of the defects of the Confederation could be considered, together with proposals for the reform of the Articles. Congress added its weight by formally "calling" the conference, specifying that it be held for *A revision convention called*

. . . The sole and express purpose of revising the Articles of Confederation and reporting to Congress and the several state legislatures such alterations and provisions therein as shall, when agreed to in Congress and confirmed by the states, render the federal constitution adequate to the exigencies of government and the preservation of the Union.

The nationalist leaders threw their full influence behind the conference, and out of it came the Constitution of the United States.

THE CONVENTION OF 1787

Member-
ship

The convention thus called finally got under way on May 25 in what is now known as Independence Hall. Though characterized by Jefferson as "an assembly of demigods," the convention contained men of widely differing temperaments, abilities, and aptitudes. Lawyers predominated, and several of the delegates were reasonably well acquainted not only with the history of English law and politics but with the governmental systems of continental Europe. About half were college graduates. Most had been active in the government and politics of their respective states. Many had helped frame constitutions, sat as members of legislatures, or held executive or judicial offices. Thirty-one had served in Congress. Men of age and maturity were included, notably Franklin, who was almost 82. But a large proportion of the most active and influential delegates were comparatively young: Madison, the master-builder, was 36; Gouverneur Morris, 35; Hamilton, 30; and Charles Pinckney, 29.

Conserva-
tive
temper

Furthermore, the men who now held the country's political destinies in their hands were not ardent supporters of the Confederation. Many of the great leaders of the movement for Independence were absent. Patrick Henry "smelt a rat," and refused to attend. John Hancock was not there; nor were Richard Henry Lee, Samuel Adams, and Thomas Paine. Almost to a man, the delegates were drawn from the professional and propertied classes, chiefly in the tidewater areas where such wealth as existed was largely concentrated. Not one was a frontiersman or a wage earner, and only one had a small farmer background. Few were as conservative as Hamilton, who wanted to see a highly centralized and more or less aristocratic political system set up. But few, also, could be classed as democrats, in the sense of springing from and speaking for the small-propertied or propertyless elements of the population. They were more concerned with order and stability than with liberty and equality.

Common
objective

Plenty of disagreements were bound to arise, once the delegates had started their discussions. Upon the objective chiefly to be aimed at, however, there was, first and last, little difference of opinion—namely, a government of sufficient strength not only to take care of national defense and to discharge national obligations, but to withstand agrarian-debtor agitation typified by Shays' Rebellion in Massachusetts, preserve social order, and keep the country on an even keel. And although the resulting Constitution provided for a more popular plan of government than could at that time have been found in any other important country in the world, it is not surprising that, motivated as it was, it should have been purposely shaped—by means of checks and balances, indirect elections, perpetuation of suffrage limitations in the states and presidential veto—to prevent democratic majoritarian elements from capturing control of affairs. Yet it did not close the doors against more democracy later on, and therein lay one of its principal merits.

Although 74 delegates in all were appointed, only 55 ever attended, and the average attendance seems not to have exceeded 30 or 35. At the opening meeting, Washington was unanimously chosen to preside, and this prevented him from taking an active part in the debates. Indeed, so far as is known, he addressed the convention only twice, on the opening and closing days. With the possible exception of Franklin, he, however, was less dependent on speech-making than any other delegate. He performed his duties as moderator in a manner to allay strife; in private conversation and informal conference, his opinions and advice were always to be had; and it is doubtful whether, on the whole, any member exerted greater influence.

Organiza-tion and procedure

Having full power to make its own rules, the convention early decided that each state, regardless of number of delegates, should have one vote, as in the contemporary Congress. In order to enable the members to speak freely and plainly and to protect them against outside criticism and pressure, the convention further decided that the sittings should be behind closed doors, and that nothing should be put into print or otherwise made public until the work was finished. This injunction of secrecy was observed with remarkable fidelity. A secretary was appointed and a journal kept. When, however, in 1819, this official record was printed by order of Congress, in the hope that it would throw light on the way in which various provisions of the Constitution then in controversy should be interpreted, it proved to be only a bare and not wholly accurate enumeration of formal motions and of votes by states. Happily, Madison, one of the most vigilant and efficient delegates, sensing the importance of what was being done, kept a record of his own. Fragmentary memoranda were left by a few other members, and something can be learned from letters written by certain delegates to their friends. But what we know today about the convention's discussions, as distinguished from its formal actions, comes mainly from the clear and candid *Notes* laboriously compiled by the learned and methodical Virginian.

THE CONSTITUTION FRAMED

> We, the people of the United States, in order to form a more perfect union, establish justice, insure domestic tranquility, provide for the common defense, promote the general welfare, and secure the blessings of liberty to ourselves and our posterity, do ordain and establish this Constitution for the United States of America.—Preamble to the Constitution

Deliberations had not gone far before the delegates were brought face to face with a truly challenging question. Should they merely revise the Articles of Confederation, or should they make a new constitution? There

The con-vention's main problem

was no getting away from the fact that their instructions looked only to revision. On the other hand, many thoughtful persons agreed with Washington when he confessed the hope that the convention would "adopt no temporizing expedients," but would "probe the defects of the constitution [i.e., the Articles] to the bottom and provide a radical cure, whether they are agreed to or not." Both points of view were strongly represented in the convention, and a plan based on each was quickly presented for consideration.

The Virginia plan

The first scheme to appear came logically from Virginia, the state that had taken the initiative in bringing about the convention. Governor Edmund Randolph presented it, although Madison was its principal author. It embodied the best thought of the convention's ablest student of political, and especially federal, institutions. The plan did not explicitly repudiate the Articles. But it looked to a general reconstruction of the system of government existing under them; and after it was submitted, the fiction that a mere revision was intended was soon dropped. A national executive was to be established; also a national judiciary; and, finally, a legislature, with a lower house elected directly by the people and an upper one chosen by the lower from persons nominated by the state legislatures. Thus reconstructed, the national government was to have greatly increased powers, among them those of levying taxes, vetoing state legislation when considered contrary to the national constitution or to a treaty, and calling forth the militia against any member of the union "failing to fulfill its duty." Presented on May 29, in the form of 15 resolutions, this plan gave the convention something to go to work on at once.

The New Jersey plan

One feature of the plan strongly objected to by members particularly sensitive about the "rights" of their states was the proposal to substitute for the existing equal voting power of the states in Congress an arrangement under which, in both branches, such power should be apportioned in accordance with numbers of free inhabitants or perhaps contributions to the national treasury. To forestall such an innovation, a counterplan based on a "purely federal" principle was laid before the convention on June 15 by William Paterson of New Jersey. It went far toward meeting the demands of the delegates for a drastic change. It allowed Congress power to raise money from duties on imports and from stamp taxes, and to regulate commerce, and it invested acts of Congress with the character of "supreme law of the respective states." It even envisaged a national executive in the form of a council chosen by Congress and a national judiciary composed of a "supreme tribunal." Congress, however, was still to consist of but a single house, with all states retaining an equal voice.

Compromise the only solution

Advocated ably by Paterson and other interested members, the New Jersey plan enlisted the support of many delegates. Its introduction, indeed, split the convention sharply into two factions or groups; one representing the nationalist view, the other the federationist view. One wanted political power proportioned to the ability of the states to aid in bearing the public burdens; the other wanted the states to retain the full equality they had enjoyed since independence, and argued that on any other basis the less populous ones would be placed at grave, and even ruinous, disadvantage. Happily, it was not necessary that either element have its way completely. The delegates were, after all, not dogmatic theorists and were accustomed in their business relations and in their state politics to the saving principle of give and take. They expressed their widely differing views freely, sometimes acrimoniously. Having done so, most of them were not averse to compromise. The constitution upon which they finally agreed became, clause after clause, a product of mutual concession.

Fortunately, however, a majority of the delegates were essentially united on matters of decidedly larger significance than those on which they differed; and compromise was resorted to only after certain vital decisions had been reached. The most important of these was to cast aside the Articles and to establish a government resting on a more truly national basis. Some delegates were of the opinion that the instructions given by the states were binding literally, and that if the convention wanted to do more than merely revise the Articles, its members ought to go back to their states and ask for appropriate authority. But the majority were, as Randolph later put it, "not scrupulous on the point of power," and felt, as he further testified, that "when the salvation of the public was at stake it would be treason to our trust not to propose what we found necessary." Within five days after the convention began work, a resolution was adopted in committee of the whole "that a national government ought to be established consisting of a supreme legislative, executive, and judiciary." Madison, Hamilton, and other delegates made it perfectly clear that this meant a government embodying one supreme power, with "complete and compulsive operation." The federationists protested, saying at first that they would have no part in such a union; the nationalist delegates declared they would accept nothing less. The federationists, as we have seen, brought forward the New Jersey plan, yet at the final test only three states voted for it. From first to last—sometimes at grave risk of driving the convention on the rocks—the initial determination was wisely adhered to. *Decision in favor of a strong national government*

From the key decision mentioned flowed certain great corollaries: (1) the powers of the national government should be sharply increased; (2) the machinery of government should be expanded, as indeed was proposed in all of the plans offered; (3) the national government, equally with the state governments, should operate directly on the people, through its own laws, administrative officers, and courts; and (4) the new constitution should be the "supreme law of the land," enforceable in the courts like any other law and paramount over all other constitutions, laws, and official actions, national or state. *A national government resting upon the people*

Adoption of the third principle, in particular, meant that the national government was to be put on a wholly new basis. Instead of resting upon semi-independent states, and having little control over the people except through the medium of state authorities, it was thenceforth to be a government of a single body politic, with power to levy and collect taxes and to make and enforce laws by its own direct action. Thereafter, as James Wilson explained, over each citizen were to be two governments, both "derived from the people," both "meant for the people," and both operating by an independent authority upon the people. And, as Madison subsequently wrote to Jefferson, in adopting such an arrangement the convention deftly divested itself of one of its most delicate problems. If the experience of the Confederation indicated anything, it was that states might fail to live up to their obligations; and every plan thus far presented to the convention had embraced or assumed some arrangement for coercing states proving delinquent. The nature and method of such coercion would, however, have stirred grave differences of opinion; and members must have been relieved to find that in providing for a national government endowed with power to enforce its authority directly upon *people,* they had—so, at least, it was supposed— made the coercion of *states* unnecessary.

The great compromises:

1. The Connecticut compromise

2. The three-fifths clause

These fundamentals settled, the nationalist forces were ready to make concessions; and the first and most notable one related to voting power in Congress. The nationalists wanted representation, and with it voting power, proportioned to population; the federationists wanted voting power to be equal; delegates on both sides threatened more than once to withdraw unless their demands were met. At a very critical point in the proceedings, the delegates from Connecticut brought forward a proposal for equal representation in the upper house, combined with representation in the lower house in proportion to numbers; and after heated debate the deadlock was broken and the compromise adopted. This eminently sensible disposition of the matter was casually suggested quite early in the deliberations and did not originate with the Connecticut delegation. Franklin, indeed, was probably its actual author. Dr. Johnson and his colleagues deserve credit, however, for putting it formally before the convention with an array of unanswerable arguments; and the agreement has ever since been known as the "Connecticut compromise." It removed the greatest single obstacle to harmony.

The decision in favor of proportioned representation in the lower house, however, made it necessary to determine how population should be computed; and difficulty at this point was produced by the existence of slavery. Should slaves be regarded as persons or as chattels? If the former, they ought to be counted in; if the latter, they ought to be left out. With a view to increasing their quotas in Congress, the southern states wanted slaves included; the northern and middle states, having few slaves, wanted them disregarded; and much lively discussion ensued. A possible solution was, however, already in men's minds when the convention met. When asking the states for additional funds in 1783, Congress had proposed changing the basis of requisitions from land values to numbers of population, so computed as to include three-fifths of all slaves. This "federal ratio" was early incorporated in the Virginia plan as an amendment; it found a place also in the New Jersey scheme; and, notwithstanding initial differences of opinion, it was ultimately adopted by the convention as being, in the words of Rufus King, "the language of all America." There was no defense for it in logic. But it represented the closest approach to a generally satisfactory arrangement that a body of practical-minded men could discover. The slave states received less representation than they thought their due. They found compensation, however, in a provision that direct taxes laid by Congress should be apportioned on the same reduced basis as representation—although, in point of fact, direct taxes were actually imposed by the national government only four times before slavery was abolished.

Still another compromise pertained to the powers of Congress over commerce. The delegates north of the Potomac were keenly interested in commerce and wanted Congress to have full power to regulate trade and navigation. The four states farther south, however, were agricultural, and their delegates feared that Congress would levy export duties on southern products and in other ways discriminate against the noncommercial section. Furthermore, there was the question of the slave trade. The northern states would have been willing to see the traffic abolished immediately, and Maryland and Virginia, being well stocked, had no great interest in it. But Georgia and the Carolinas wanted it to continue, and the convention was told firmly that these states would never accept the new plan "unless their right to import slaves be untouched." The outcome was an agreement which pacified all elements. Congress was to have broad powers to regulate navigation and foreign trade, including power to lay duties on imports. But national taxes on exports were forbidden, and the importation of slaves might not be interfered with by the national government (except to the extent of a head-tax not exceeding $10) prior to the year 1808.

3. Commerce and the slave trade

Many other important matters claimed the attention of the delegates through the sultry midsummer days during which the convention patiently pursued its labors. The nature and powers, and especially the mode of selection of the executive absorbed much time and thought, the more by reason of the fact that plans gradually took form for a chief executive different from any the world had ever known. The manner of electing senators—whether by the people, by the state legislatures, or by some agency especially devised for the purpose—proved difficult to decide. The appointment and status of the national judiciary provoked ardent discussion. The broadened powers to be vested in Congress, the mode of admitting new states, the control of the national government over state militia, the manner of amending the new constitution—these and a score of other topics required painstaking consideration; and the convention, as Franklin testified, spent a great deal of time "sawing boards to make them fit." From first to last, the Virginia plan, as progressively amplified, formed the main basis of discussion. First, the essentials of this plan, embodied in the Randolph resolutions, were thrashed out in committee of the whole. Then, after being reported back to the convention considerably altered, they were again debated in full. Next, the growing document was turned over, after a couple of months, to a com-

The Constitution completed

mittee of detail which worked it into a balanced constitutional text. The convention spent upwards of six weeks more in discussing this draft. Finally, Gouverneur Morris, aided by his fellow Pennsylvanian, James Wilson, wrote out with his own hand the completed fundamental law, putting it into the lucid English for which it has ever since been notable among great documents; and on September 17, 39 delegates, representing 12 states, signed it.

The test ahead

Franklin, whose contributions had been chiefly those of wise suggestion and quiet conciliation, remarked to a group of delegates while the signatures were being affixed that "often and often" during the session he had looked at a sun painted on the president's chair without being able to tell whether it was rising or setting. "Now, at length," he added hopefully, "I have the happiness to know that it is a rising, and not a setting, sun." The actual test, however, was yet to come. The convention had ignored the instructions given most of its members and, instead of patching up the Articles, had prepared a new and very different frame of government. Would the people of the states approve what it had done? Even the delegates were not very enthusiastic about the results of their labors. Three of those present when the document was signed refused to put their names to it. Of 13 who were absent, at least four are known to have been critical if not actually hostile. Few, if any, were entirely satisfied: Franklin had many misgivings which he willingly submerged in the interests of unity; Hamilton admitted that he signed mainly because he felt that the proposed scheme of government could not possibly prove worse than the existing one.

THE CONTEST OVER RATIFICATION

Procedures

A decade earlier, adoption of the Articles had been held up for three and one-half years awaiting ratification by every one of the states. To ease matters this time, the Constitution provided in its closing article that it should take effect when ratified by nine states only. To give it a more popular basis, action was required to be taken in each state not by the legislature, as in the case of the Articles, but by a convention chosen for the purpose by the voters. Assenting to both procedures, Congress, on September 28, formally transmitted the proposed instrument to the states without recommendation or other comment.

Objections to the new plan

The controversies that had stirred the convention were now transferred to the country at large. From New England to Georgia, the new frame of government was circulated and discussed, dissected, explained, praised, denounced. Objections arose in many quarters; scarcely a feature of the plan, indeed, escaped attack. There were men who, like Patrick Henry and Samuel Adams, were so imbued with the Revolutionary concepts of liberty that they took instant offense at any proposal looking toward a centralization of authority. On the other hand, some people thought that the new plan did not provide for as much centralization as was needed. The debtor elements were aroused by the clause which forbade the states to issue bills of credit. Many northerners considered that too much was conceded to the slave-holding interests; many southerners felt that these interests had been dealt with unfairly. Large inland elements—small farmers, backwoodsmen, pioneers—feared the effects of the commercial powers given to Congress; men of property, although generally favorable, wondered how freely the new taxing powers would be used. Everywhere the complaint was voiced that the document failed to take any notice of numerous fundamental rights and liberties, for example, freedom of speech, freedom of the press, freedom of assembly, right of petition, and religious liberty, so carefully guaranteed in the bills of rights prefixed to a majority of the state constitutions, and likely to need protection even more, popular elements thought, against a strong central government. No single group of dissenters could have prevailed by its own efforts; but in most states the various hostile elements tended to merge into an opposition extremely difficult to convert or overcome.

Ratification by nine states

In the Philadelphia convention, the interests hardest to satisfy were the delegates of less populous states. The conclusions arrived at were, however, on the whole favorable to those states, which accordingly became the first to ratify. In Massachusetts, Virginia, New York, and other states, time was required to rally support. There was grave danger lest some state indispensable to the proposed union because of its location or general importance should remain obdurate. By cleverly appeasing Samuel Adams and John Hancock, to whom the "anti-Federalists" of the interior looked for leadership, the supporters of the pending plan won in Massachusetts by a close vote, and only after agreeing to a series of suggested amendments aimed at reducing the power of the central government. Ratification in New Hampshire after a hard contest brought the number to the required nine. But no one supposed that the new government could be launched successfully on this minimum basis. Even after Virginia gave a favorable decision, following an exceptionally bitter fight, the battle was not yet won. New York was still outside, and New York was a pivotal state without which the union would be a mere caricature.

Ratification in New York: The Federalist

Moreover, the opposition in New York, especially in the rural sections, was very formidable; and, realizing this, the friends of the Constitution made every effort before the state convention met at Poughkeepsie to convince the people that the proposed plan of government was moderate, safe, and workable. Most active in this was Hamilton, who, after having been "praised by everybody but supported by none" at Philadelphia, now came into his own as a leader in the campaign for ratification. It was he who conceived the idea of printing in the leading newspapers of the state a systematic explanation and defense of the Constitution in the form of a series of brief public letters, associating with himself for the purpose another able New Yorker, John Jay, and also the most convincing expounder outside of New

Ratification of the Constitution of 1787

STATE	DATE	VOTE
Delaware	Dec. 7, 1787	Unanimous
Pennsylvania	Dec. 12, 1787	46–23
New Jersey	Dec. 19, 1787	Unanimous
Georgia	Jan. 2, 1788	Unanimous
Connecticut	Jan. 9, 1788	128–40
Massachusetts	Feb. 6, 1788	187–168
Maryland	April 28, 1788	63–11
South Carolina	May 23, 1788	149–73
New Hampshire	June 21, 1788	57–46
Virginia	June 25, 1788	89–79
New York	July 26, 1788	30–27
North Carolina	Nov. 21, 1789	184–77
Rhode Island	May 29, 1790	34–32

York, Madison. The result was the remarkable group of papers, 85 in number, appearing over the pen name "Publius," but known ever since to students of American history as *The Federalist*. The letters were prepared in haste and published in New York City newspapers at the rate of three or four a week, as campaign documents. But their authors—all young and vigorous—were full of their subject and knew how to write. Taken as a group, the papers, though frankly propagandist and presenting only one side, have never been surpassed as examples of direct, lucid, and convincing exposition. Better than anything else—unless possibly Madison's *Notes*—they reveal what the Constitution meant to the men who made it.

The Constitution put into effect   Either won over by Hamilton and his collaborators or unwilling to see the state remain outside of the Union after all but two of the others had joined, the New York convention finally ratified on July 26, although by a margin of only three votes. Meanwhile, on July 2, it was officially announced in Congress that the ninth state had ratified, and attention was turned to preparations for putting the new government into operation. The states were instructed to choose presidential electors, senators, and representatives, and New York City was fixed as the temporary seat of government. Then the old Congress, already incapacitated by lack of a quorum, disappeared, leaving the field clear for its successor. The new House of Representatives was organized on April 2, 1789; the Senate came together three days later; and on April 30, Washington took the oath of office as President. Seven months afterwards, North Carolina, appeased by a decision of Congress to submit a series of constitutional amendments guaranteeing civil liberties, and threatened with being treated commercially as though a foreign country, ratified the new fundamental law; and similar action by Rhode Island in the spring of 1790 made the union complete.

THE CONSTITUTION'S CHARACTERISTICS AND SOURCES

"This paper," wrote Gouverneur Morris in commending the Constitu-
tion to a friend, "has been the subject of infinite investigation, disputation, *stitution*
and declamation. While some have boasted it as a work from Heaven, others *as a*
have given it a less righteous origin. I have many reasons to believe that it is *document*
the work of plain honest men, and such, I think, it will appear." Herein lies
the reason why the instrument, once adopted, succeeded and survived beyond the hopes of its most ardent advocates. As constitutions go, it is a brief
and simple document. Even with the later amendments, its approximately
6000 words fill only 12 or 15 pages of print; one can read it through in
leisurely fashion in half an hour. Second, its contents are organized according to a clear and logical pattern. Following a brief preamble (significant as
a statement of general purpose, but having no legal force), three main
articles are devoted to the legislative, executive, and judicial branches, respectively. Four shorter articles deal, in order, with the position of the states,
the modes of amendment, the supremacy of national power, and ratification.
Finally come the amendments, appended at the end and numbered serially.
Third, thanks to the committee of detail, and especially to Gouverneur
Morris, the document's language is clear, direct, and concise. To be sure,
some clauses, for example, those touching citizenship, or that authorizing
Congress to "provide for . . . the general welfare of the United States,"
lend themselves to more than one interpretation; and the conflicts and decisions arising out of resulting differences of opinion make up a considerable
part of the country's constitutional history in the past 174 years. Nevertheless, our greatest constitutional controversies are traceable rather to omissions than to provisions of doubtful meaning.

Yet it is its omissions, at least as truly as its actual provisions, that *Signifi-*
stamp the document as "the work of plain honest men." If theorists had *cance of*
written it, very likely it would have been filled with high-sounding phrases *its*
out of touch with reality. Even "practical" men might have made the mis- *omissions*
take of overloading it with details. Instead of merely authorizing Congress
to regulate interstate commerce, they might have undertaken to define
"regulate" and "commerce." Instead of simply empowering Congress to
lay and collect taxes to provide for the general welfare, they might have
undertaken to specify the kinds of taxes to be employed and even to indicate what they meant by "general walfare." If they had done such things,
however, they would at once have tied the hands of the new government,
and would either have forced a long line of later amendments or permanently thwarted the freedom of interpretation, experiment, and decision that
has been the very lifeblood of the nation in later days. What the framers
wisely undertook was simply to apply practical remedies to the defects of an
existing political system. In doing this, they did not hold back from strong

measures. Aware, however, that their judgment and foresight were not infallible, they deliberately omitted from the resulting basic law everything that could safely be supplied by generations faced with new problems and blessed with even richer experience.

Its sources

It follows that the framers did not go out of their way to invent political forms. Nor did they borrow far afield. Some of them were students of Vattel, Montesquieu, and other continental writers; some had read history and could cite the failures of ancient confederacies or draw illustrations from the experiences of France and other continental states. But, as an earlier writer has remarked, this knowledge taught them rather what to avoid than what to adopt; and insofar as they drew upon European sources at all, such sources were the Common Law, the principles of Magna Charta, and the Bill of Rights, the writings of Locke and Blackstone, and other characteristic products of their English motherland. In the main, however, this monumental heritage had passed to America far back in colonial days, and, at the time when the national Constitution took form, was already deeply embedded in the constitutions, laws, and usages of the states. In a literal sense, therefore, the new instrument grew out of the political life of Americans themselves in the colonial and Revolutionary periods. "Experience," said John Dickinson, "must be our guide; reason may mislead us." Fortunately, our forefathers had accumulated enough political experience by 1787 to serve as a rich and adequate resource.

Great principles embodied

All of the great ideas and institutions of our English heritage were embodied in the Constitution as adopted in 1788 and amended by the First Congress and the states. The government established by it was limited in power, representative in character, and based upon the people. By leaving the prescription of voting qualifications to the states it opened the door to the spread of the voting privilege throughout adult America, and thus paved the way for the democratization of American government which has so strikingly modified the entire machinery provided in 1787. By providing a written instrument self-designated as the "supreme law of the land," the framers stimulated the innovation of judicial review, that is, the ultimate and authoritative interpretation of its provisions by an independent national judiciary. The system of separation of powers and of checks and balances which it contains, although directly traceable to colonial and state experience, marks one of the major departures from both the tradition and evolving practice of the British government. The greatest achievement of the framers, however, was unquestionably the federal union—the creation of a strong national government side by side with strong and effective state governments. The Constitution, finally, provides for orderly change, and by legislation, custom, executive action, judicial interpretation, and formal amendment it has proved adaptable to the revolutionary changes in the life of our people since it was adopted. Despite all of the modifications and adaptations, the great principles of the Constitution have endured.

THE PROCESS OF CONSTITUTIONAL DEVELOPMENT

> The Congress, whenever two third of both houses shall deem it necessary, shall propose amendments to this Constitution, or, on the application of the legislatures of two thirds of the several States, shall call a convention for proposing amendments, which in either case shall be valid to all intents and purposes as part of this Constitution, when ratified by the legislatures of three fourths of the several States, or by conventions in three fourths thereof, as the one or the other mode of ratification may be proposed by the Congress, . . .—Art. V.

Actual Constitution is more than a document

The moment the new instrument became effective, executive officers, congressmen, and judges began to interpret and apply its provisions and thus to build up year by year in accumulating practice and precedent the flesh of government that covers the skeleton. The constitutional system of our own times, therefore, embraces the whole fabric of documents, practices, and conceptions, and hundreds of pages are required to expound its operations. It is appropriate that we examine the ways in which the Constitution, thus conceived, expands and adjusts itself to the never ending flux of American society. The first method to be considered is that of formal amendment.

The amending process

Desiring that the new fundamental law should neither be impossible to amend, as the Articles had been, or yet capable of too easy change, the framers devised a difficult but not prohibitive procedure. The only restriction placed upon the free operation of the procedure (aside from a temporary one relating to the slave trade) is that no state may be deprived of its equality in the Senate without its consent.

Stages in the process:

Although two methods of initiating amendments and two methods of ratifying them are provided, all thus far adopted have been proposed in the same way: by joint resolution of the two branches of Congress. All except the Twenty-first (repealing national prohibition) have likewise been ratified in the same manner: by action of the state legislatures. Any amendment receiving a two-thirds vote, that is, at least two-thirds of a quorum, in both House and Senate, is transmitted by the head (administrator) of the General Services Administration to the governors of the several states, to be laid before the legislatures or conventions. The President can interpose no veto. Not being legislative acts, amendments are not officially submitted to him at all.

1. Initiation

The national convention an unused device

This does not mean that there have been no attempts to launch amendment proposals by the alternative method of a national convention. In fact, at one time or another the legislatures of considerably more than two-thirds of the states have called upon Congress to convoke a convention for the purpose. For example, under the auspices of the Council of State Governments, a concerted drive was launched in December, 1962, to get the states to memorialize Congress to call a convention for consideration of three

84TH CONGRESS
1ST SESSION
H. J. RES. 214

IN THE HOUSE OF REPRESENTATIVES

FEBRUARY 14, 1955

Mr. JOHNSON of California introduced the following joint resolution; which was
referred to the Committee on the Judiciary

JOINT RESOLUTION

Proposing an amendment to the Constitution of the United States
providing for the election of President and Vice President.

1   *Resolved by the Senate and House of Representatives*

2   *of the United States of America in Congress assembled,*

3   *(two-thirds of each House concurring therein),* That an

4   amendment is hereby proposed to the Constitution of the

5   United States which shall be valid to all intents and purposes

6   as part of the Constitution when ratified by three-fourths

7   of the legislatures of the several States. Said amendment

8   shall be as follows:

THE BEGINNING OF AN AMENDMENT TO THE CONSTITUTION

amendments aimed at reducing the power of the Supreme Court and
strengthening the power of the states. One of these amendments was aimed
at the amending process itself and would authorize two-thirds of the state
legislatures to initiate amendments without Congressional approval. Although this effort did not attract sufficiently widespread support, another
effort launched in 1963 to authorize states to apportion at least one house
of their legislature on a basis other than population had by early 1968
gained the support of 32 states—just two short of the necessary two-thirds.
Legislation to implement this part of Article V is under consideration.
Petitions designed to convoke a convention for a broad reconstruction of
the Constitution had been sent earlier by the states. They were especially
numerous at the time of the nullification controversy of 1832 and again in

1859–1860 when civil war was imminent. The opinion has sometimes been advanced that every request for a convention made at any time by a state is to be regarded as pending indefinitely, and that whenever two-thirds of the states are found to have made such a request, Congress ought forthwith to call a convention. This "cumulative" view, however, is not generally accepted. Even though there never has been any official determination of the length of time a request from a state shall be regarded as remaining "alive," it is hardly conceivable that Congress would call a convention unless petitions were received from the necessary number of states within a sufficiently limited period to create an appearance of concerted demand. If a convention were once convoked, it presumably could go as far as it liked in proposing amendments, and might even put before the country a completely rewritten fundamental law.

Whether a given amendment shall be acted upon by state legislatures or by conventions especially chosen for the purpose is determined by Congress. Although the original Constitution was ratified by conventions, the legislative method was adhered to uniformly for amendments until the Twenty-first was submitted in 1933. Conventions, although more costly, are likely to give quicker results, and they have the further advantage of being chosen by the people with reference solely to the proposal upon which they are to act. Although ratified by legislatures, the Eighteenth (prohibition) Amendment came to be looked upon as more appropriate for action by conventions, which therefore were employed in repealing it. Whichever plan is used, reports of actions taken are sent by the governors to the General Services Administration, which, if the necessary three-fourths majority is attained, proclaims the amendment effective as part of the Constitution.   *2. Ratification*

Until fairly recently, a proposal failing to get the requisite majority was never officially announced as rejected, and accordingly was looked upon as remaining before the states indefinitely. By their own terms, however, four out of the last six amendments were to become operative only if ratified within seven years. How long an amendment with no time limit shall be considered pending is, the Supreme Court has said, a political question and therefore one for Congress alone to decide. No decision on the matter has ever been made; and a child labor amendment submitted in 1924 is regarded by some as still "alive." Congress has gone so far as to decree that while a state which has rejected an amendment may change its mind and ratify, a state, once having ratified, cannot reverse its action. Finally, under judicial interpretation of Article V, ratification must be literally by state legislatures or conventions, as Congress may ordain, and not by the people acting directly. In 1918, Ohio amended her state constitution to provide that after her legislature should have ratified an amendment the voters should be given an opportunity through a referendum to confirm or reverse the decision. A test case being tried, the United States Supreme Court held this procedure invalid.

The states were not yet safely gathered under the "new roof," as the

Constitution was popularly termed in early days, before proposals began to be made for "extension of the eaves." Altogether, more than 5000 drafted amendments (many of them duplicates, of course, or relating to the same matters) have been introduced in Congress from 1789 to 1968. Nowadays, anywhere from 40 to 60 proposals are presented in the House or Senate (or both) during an average session, referred to the appropriate judiciary committee, filed, and mostly forgotten. The total number of amendments actually endorsed by the two houses is only 30, and the number ratified by the states only, 25. Indeed, it would hardly be erroneous to say that the Constitution really has been amended only 15 times, because the first ten amendments were, to all intents and purposes, part of the original plan promised to many state ratifying bodies.

THE AMENDMENTS

The successful use of the amending process has been episodic: a few years of intense effort separated by long periods of quiescence. In the first twenty years of its life, 12 amendments were added to the Constitution: ten as a result of promises given to ratifying conventions and two as a result of practical difficulties encountered in applying certain provisions. The first ten amendments comprise the Bill of Rights, the absence of which from the original document was widely criticized in the contest over ratification. Madison and others solemnly promised to introduce the desired changes at the earliest opportunity and in the first year of Congress, seventeen amendments were voted by the House, 12 endorsed by the Senate, and 10 later ratified by the states. The Eleventh Amendment added in 1798 reversed a decision of the Supreme Court and provided that thereafter a state could not be sued by a citizen of another state or nation in the national courts. The Twelfth changed the method of voting for President and Vice-President by the electoral college, after a tie vote between Jefferson and Burr threw the election of 1800 into the House of Representatives. Henceforth, the electors were required to ballot separately for President and Vice-President.

Not until the Reconstruction era after the Civil War was the Constitution again changed, despite numerous efforts to postpone or delay the crisis of 1861 by constitutional revision. The Republican majority, after victory, attempted to protect and define the rights of the emancipated Negroes by three amendments aimed at prohibiting slavery, preventing discriminatory state actions against the freedmen, and forbidding the denial of the vote to them because of their color or previous condition of servitude. The southern states were required to approve these amendments as a condition of their readmission to the Union as equal partners.

The next reform era coincided with the administration of Woodrow Wilson. Four amendments were added in this period. The most far-reaching of these was that (16th) authorizing the taxation of incomes without apportionment. It was also aimed at reversing a Supreme Court decision of 1894 which had held such taxation to be direct and, therefore, subject to the apportioning requirement of the Constitution. Two others aimed at widening the democratic aspects of our system by providing for popular instead of legislative election of Senators and by removing discriminatory barriers against woman suffrage. The final amendment of this epoch embraced the ill-fated effort to banish the manufacture and sale of alcoholic beverages.

The New Deal Era Amendments

The reformist New Deal of Franklin Roosevelt achieved most of its goals by procedures other than formal constitutional change. However, during this era the old constitutional calendar was modernized and the traditional "lame duck" session of Congress from December to March after a new election was made unnecessary. The effort to achieve national prohibition was abandoned and the Eighteenth Amendment repealed. As an aftermath of the New Deal and the long tenure of Roosevelt, the Constitution was again changed in 1951 to limit presidential tenure to two terms.

Amendments of the nineteen-sixties

The most recent use of the amending process stems from continued efforts to spread democracy through our system. The Twenty-third, proclaimed in 1961, grants residents of Washington, D. C., the right to vote in presidential elections and the Twenty-fourth, proclaimed in 1964, is aimed at tax-paying qualifications for voting in national elections and is primarily intended to get rid of the poll-tax requirements of five southern states. The Twenty-fifth adopted in 1967 and in the aftermath of President Kennedy's assassination at long last makes adequate provision for succession to the presidency in case of inability and provides for filling the office of Vice-President when it becomes vacant.

Observations on the amendments as a group

Looking over the 25 adopted amendments as a group, one observes certain significant facts. (1) In the main, they deny powers rather than confer new powers. Sometimes (as in the first eight) it is only or chiefly the national government that is restrained; sometimes (as in the Civil War group) it is only or chiefly the state governments. But in any event, most of the number are restrictive rather than otherwise. (2) The amendments are to only a slight extent responsible for the remarkable growth of governmental functions and activities in the last few decades. The phenomenal extensions of national power associated with the New Deal and World War II came without any major change in the written fundamental law. From a somewhat earlier amendment, it is true, the central government derived the exceedingly important power to tax incomes and this has been an important factor in financing the new programs. How could so much happen without more resort to amendments? There has been frequent, indeed ceaseless, resort to fresh and broadened interpretations of words, phrases, and clauses happily chosen a century and a half ago to allow precisely such flexibility. (3) While, however, the amendments have not conferred many express powers on the national government, they have imposed enough restrictions upon the states to have augmented national supremacy indirectly, and hence may be said to have had a nationalizing tendency. Finally, (4) the amendments, while introducing relatively few changes in governmental machinery and procedures, have contributed materially to the advancement of democracy. The first eight defined and guaranteed civil liberties; the Fifteenth, Nineteenth, Twenty-third, and Twenty-fourth removed barriers to universal suffrage; the Sixteenth shifted the burden of government costs in the direction of the well-to-do; the Seventeenth definitely placed the election of senators in the hands of the people.

Proposed amendments

Of proposing new changes in the Constitution there is, of course, no end. And in recent years Congress has repeatedly been urged to adopt amendment resolutions: (1) granting equal rights to women; (2) changing the method of counting the electoral vote in presidential elections; (3) straightening out the tangle of marriage and divorce laws in the 50 states; (4) forbidding national intervention in state schemes of legislative apportionment; (5) limiting the amount of income that may be taken by taxation; (6) changing the treaty-making procedure by making it easier to ratify treaties, by increasing congressional control of executive agreements, and by limiting the subjects on which treaties might be negotiated; and, (7) creating a Court of the Union made up of the 50 state chief justices to hear appeals from certain decisions of the Supreme Court of the United States.

Criticism of the amending process:

1. On the ground that it is too slow and difficult

Madison believed that the modes of amendment agreed upon by the framers guarded "equally against that extreme facility which would render the Constitution too mutable and that extreme difficulty which might perpetuate discovered faults." On the whole, history has sustained his judgment. Chief Justice Marshall, however, characterized the amending machinery as "unwieldy and cumbrous." During the long periods between effective use of the amending process, notably those from 1870–1913 and from 1920–1933, reformers have strongly attacked the process as unnecessarily difficult and have made numerous proposals for lowering the vote in Congress requisite for submitting amendments (usually to simple majorities), or the number of states required for ratification (commonly to two-thirds), or both.

2. On the ground that it is too easy

Hamilton devoted almost an entire number (85) of *The Federalist* to arguing that the amending process could not have been made any easier without inviting constitutional instability. The speedy ratification of the Eighteenth Amendment by legislatures of states in which, both before and after the advent of national prohibition, the people in statewide referenda voted against the plan led many persons to believe that in point of fact the amending process was easier than it ought to be. For some years, therefore, proposed changes looked chiefly in the direction of making it more difficult. This particular complaint died with the repeal of prohibition.

3. On the ground that it is not sufficiently democratic

There has been the criticism, also, that in the absence of any provision for direct popular initiation of amendments or for submission of amendments to popular vote, the system is not sufficiently democratic. In 1912, the elder Senator La Follette brought forward a now forgotten plan designed to meet the objection. Since his effort, several similar proposals have been made. On the whole, however, little is heard in this vein any longer.

The amending process has been occasionally criticized also because of the possible consequences of giving all states, regardless of population, an equal voice in ratification. Any combination of 38 states can make an amendment effective; and 38 can readily be found which among them will contain not much more than one-third of the country's population. Conversely, any 13 states can defeat an amendment; and 13 could be listed which together would have hardly one-twentieth of the total population. Such alignments have not arisen and are quite unlikely to arise. *4. On the ground that minorities may control*

The most recent criticism is of a wholly different nature from any of these. Congress, the President, and the Supreme Court acting together or separately may and do conspire to enhance the power of the central government at the expense of the state, say the critics (mostly state legislators). Unless the states can find a way to change the Constitution without national approval, they may be doomed. And, the argument goes, the national authorities are really subverting the federal system contrary to our traditions and must be halted by allowing the states to initiate amendments. Although subscribed to by a majority of state legislative representatives at a conference of state legislators, this view has as yet been endorsed by only a dozen states. *5. On the grounds that Congress controls the process*

Any change in the amending procedure in the foreseeable future is highly improbable. We have found that it is workable but usually only in great emergency. More than this, we have found that by other procedures the Constitution can be subtly accommodated to changing conditions without the necessity for formal amendment. It seems most unlikely that Congress will consent to reducing its own role in constitutional change. Finally, the so-called "undemocratic" features of the process are part of the whole scheme of American government and will not lightly be thrust aside. *Any change unlikely*

OTHER METHODS OF CONSTITUTIONAL GROWTH

The secret of the endurance of the Constitution will be found not in the formal amending process but in the other processes of constitutional elaboration: legislation, executive action, judicial interpretation, and custom. Illustrations of each of these are found throughout this volume, but a general comment is here appropriate.

Desirous of avoiding what one of them called "a too minutious wisdom," the framers of the Constitution outlined clearly enough the general framework and functions of the new government, but wisely left a multitude of matters to be taken care of, as need might arise, by Congress, and even at certain points by the state legislatures. For example, they provided for a Vice-President to take over the duties of the Presidency in case of necessity, but said nothing about what should happen if there were no Vice-President; and Congress later supplied the deficiency. They assumed the existence of executive departments, and twice referred in the Constitution to the heads *Legislation* of such establishments; yet left Congress to create the departments and to determine what should be their functions and interrelations. The composition of the two houses of Congress was prescribed carefully, but the times, places, and manner of electing both senators and representatives were left to be fixed by the state legislatures, subject to control by Congress itself. In a somewhat belated statute of 1842 on the election of representatives, and another of 1866 on the election of senators, Congress amplified the constitutional law of this subject in much detail. Again, the judicial power of the United States was vested in "one Supreme Court, and in such inferior courts as Congress may from time to time ordain and establish." Aside from the Supreme Court, therefore, the entire national judicial establishment— the names, numbers, grades, and jurisdictions of the courts, together with their procedures—rests upon acts passed from time to time by Congress.

Congress defines commerce and creates agencies like the Interstate Commerce Commission and the Federal Communications Commission to regulate it. The means and methods of governing territories are provided by Congress. And so one could go on. Every time, in fact that Congress enacts a law it, in effect, starts with some express or implied constitutional provision, interprets it, and applies it, perchance in some new area or in some new manner, thereby projecting the Constitution into a new field or extending its meaning in an old one. In doing these things, Congress, of course, does not have a completely free hand; its constitutional interpretations may be challenged, and the courts may overrule them. In the great majority of instances they stand; and legislation thus becomes one of the principal means by which the Constitution grows.

Executive and administrative action

It is not Congress alone that interprets and applies and adds. Within their spheres, the other two great branches of government, executive and judicial, do the same thing. On the executive side, the power starts with the President, who not only is as much entitled to construe the constitutional provisions as is Congress, but is equally entitled to make decisions and perform acts in accordance with his interpretations—subject to similar check from the courts. In the exercise of their powers, many Presidents have taken and maintained positions virtually settling constitutional questions previously considered open, or even giving the Constitution some meaning and application never before attributed to it. Moreover, from the White House this function of constitutional interpretation and adaptation filters down through the various levels of administration. Confronted almost daily with the necessity of making decisions, heads of departments, and even inferiors within their proper spheres, adopt positions, perform acts, or give orders resting, however remotely, upon some interpretation of a constitutional provision, and perhaps stretching the provision's meaning. When such actions escape successful challenge and establish themselves as precedents, the Constitution may be found to have undergone permanent extension, in however limited a particular.

Then there is the significant matter of constitutional expansion at the

hands of the courts. How this comes about must already be apparent. Con-   *Judicial*
gress, or a state legislature, passes a law, or a national or state official per-   *interpre-*
forms an act, which some person or group of persons affected adversely   *tation*
challenges as exceeding proper authority. A case is brought in the courts
and the law or action is attacked as being unconstitutional; whereupon the
judges must decide whether the charge is well founded—in other words,
whether the measure is or is not in conformity with constitutional provision
or reasonable construction. To do this, it is, of course, necessary to determine what the pertinent constitutional clauses mean. This opens wide
opportunity to make them mean something different from, and probably
more than, they previously had been supposed to mean, with the result of
giving the Constitution a new twist or slant. The process operates cumula-
tively. A disputed phrase is so interpreted as to give it new scope and content. This, in turn, furnishes a point of departure for a further extension
when the next similar case comes up. Nearly all of the more important implied powers of Congress are traceable to this source. And these implied
powers have never been projected farther into new areas than during the
past three decades. The most important single reason why the Constitution
has not been amended more frequently is that from an early stage in the
nation's history the Supreme Court has sat (in Woodrow Wilson's words)
as "a kind of continuous constitutional convention," interpreting, developing, and expanding the basic law. One almost may say that every time the
Court hands down one of its weekly batches of decisions, we have a constitution in some respects new.

"Time and habit," remarked Washington, "are at least as necessary to   *Usage*
fix the true character of governments as of other human institutions"; and   *or custom*
so it comes about that still another mode by which our Constitution expands
and develops is usage or custom. This method of change attracts less attention than the others; it does not—at all events at the outset—result in
amendments, laws, or judicial decisions. Superimposed, nevertheless, upon
the instrument of 1787 and its formal amendments, upon the laws that
amplify and the decisions that extend it, is a broad and steadily developing
"unwritten constitution," consisting of usages determining actual governmental practices quite as truly as do the provisions of written law. Plenty
of illustrations will be encountered as we proceed; for the present, it must
suffice merely to call to mind the manner in which the electoral college
functions in choosing the President, the assembling of department heads in
the advisory body known as the Cabinet, the frequent use of "executive
agreements" in lieu of treaties, the caucus and committee systems in Congress, the introduction of all appropriation bills in the House of Representatives, the custom requiring members of the House of Representatives to be
residents of the districts for which they are elected, and substantially all of
the apparatus—caucuses, conventions, committees, platforms, funds—of
political parties.

The general theme need not be elaborated farther. The upshot of all

"The living word and deed of living men"

that has been suggested is that the bare outline of a governmental system contained in the Constitution as it came from the hands of the framers, and as it still can be read in the books, has been amplified and filled in—by amendment, executive action, statute, judicial construction, usage—until it has come to be one of the most elaborate and complicated plans of political organization and procedure known to history. And the process goes on unceasingly. The actual Constitution at any time is what citizens, lawmakers, administrators, and judges think it is. If a time should come when the fundamental law no longer grows and changes, the nation it serves will have vanished.

REFERENCES

C. A. Beard, *An Economic Interpretation of the Constitution of the United States* (new ed., New York, 1935).

M. Borden (ed.), *The Antifederalist Papers* (East Lansing, Mich., 1966).

C. D. Bowen, *Miracle at Philadelphia: The Story of the Constitutional Convention, May to September, 1787* (New York, 1967).

R. E. Brown, *Charles Beard and the Constitution; A Critical Analysis of an Economic Interpretation of the Constitution* (Princeton, N. J., 1956).

J. E. Cooke (ed.), *The Federalist* (Middletown, Conn., 1958).

Documents Illustrative of the Formation of the Union of the American States, 69th Congress, 1st Session, House Doc. #398 (Washington, D. C., 1927). Contains the *Declaration of Independence,* the *Articles of Confederation,* Madison's *Notes,* and many other papers and documents of this period.

J. Elliott (comp.), *Debates in the Several State Conventions on the Adoption of the Federal Constitution* (2nd ed., 5 vols., Washington, D. C., 1854).

M. Farrand (ed.), *The Records of the Federal Convention* (rev. ed., 4 vols., New Haven, 1937).

A. N. Holcombe, *Our More Perfect Union; From Eighteenth-Century Principles to Twentieth-Century Practice* (Cambridge, Mass., 1950).

H. W. Horwill, *The Usages of the American Constitution* (London, 1925).

G. Hunt and J. B. Scott (eds.), *The Debates in the Federal Convention of 1787 Which Framed the Constitution of the United States of America* (New York, 1920).

M. Jensen, *The Articles of Confederation; An Interpretation of the Social and Constitutional History of the American Revolution* (2nd ed., Madison, Wis., 1948).

———, *New Nation; A History of the United States During the Confederation, 1781–1789* (New York, 1952).

A. H. Kelly and W. A. Harbison, *The American Constitution; Its Origins and Development* (New York, 1948).

O. G. Libby, *Geographical Distribution of the Vote of the Thirteen States on the Federal Constitution* (Madison, Wis., 1894).

S. K. Padover, *The World of the Founding Fathers* (New York, 1962).

C. Rossiter, *1787: The Grand Convention* (New York, 1966).

D. G. Smith, *The Convention and the Constitution: The Political Ideas of the Founding Fathers* (New York, 1965).

C. B. Swisher, *American Constitutional Development* (2nd ed., Cambridge, Mass., 1954).

C. Van Doren, *The Great Rehearsal; the Story of the Making and Ratifying of the Constitution of the United States* (New York, 1948).

3

THE FEDERAL SYSTEM

The powers not delegated to the United States by the
Constitution nor prohibited by it to the States, are reserved
to the States respectively, or to the people.—Tenth Amendment

The system estab-lished by the framers

The Constitution established over the American people a new central gov-ernment, strikingly independent of the existing state governments, and endowed it with authority to deal with virtually all those transactions carried on across state lines or beyond the national boundaries. In general, the valid powers of this new agency were to be exercised directly on the people and not through intermediate authorities. The existing governmental institutions in the 13 separate states were left largely undisturbed, except that by express limitation and by fair implication their existing and potential powers were somewhat curtailed. The division of responsibilities between the two levels of authority was achieved by the specific enumeration of the powers of the central government, by the denial of certain powers to the states, and by the reservation of all the unspecified residue to the states and to the people. This arrangement is called a *federal system*. It may be distinguished from a *centralized* or *unitary system,* in which all valid power is entrusted to the central government, and from a *league* or *confederation,* in which the central government is a creature of the regional governments and exercises power only on their sufferance.

American federal system is unique

Some members of the constitutional convention were familiar with other federal systems in ancient Greece and contemporary Switzerland and with the theoretical literature about such systems. The actual assignment of powers, however, was not based on some preconceived formula but rather on the felt needs of the times. The framers were primarily preoccupied with establishing a stronger central government and with giving it as much authority as they believed would be acceptable to informed public opinion. They went no further than absolutely necessary in charting the dividing line between national and state power. As with other aspects of the new charter, they left to future statesmen the resolution of many problems—existent and unforeseen. Much of the political history of our nation has revolved around the problems of national–state powers and responsibilities, and the federal system today is quite unlike that established in 1789.

THE STRUGGLE FOR NATIONAL SUPREMACY

> The Constitution, and the laws of the United States which shall be made in pursuance thereof; and all treaties made, or which shall be made, under the authority of the United States, shall be the supreme law of the land; and the judges in every State shall be bound thereby, anything in the Constitution or laws of any State to the contrary notwithstanding.—Art. VI, Cl. 2.

To many people today the major problem of the federal system is to preserve an important sphere of independent authority for the states and their local units in view of the advancing might of the national authority and its ever deeper penetration into the fabric of American society. To the framers and the statesmen of early America, however, the problem was to protect and preserve the ability of those in command of national power to make national policy effective throughout the nation against the opposition or obstruction of regional interests. Most of the governing in America throughout the nineteenth century and well into the present one was done by the states and local units. During peacetime, national expenditures, national public employment, and the range of national services and controls were considerably narrower than those of the states and their subdivisions. Although regional differences threatened national unity in the controversies over the War of 1812, slavery, and tariff policy, over the years national power became more and more firmly established and now is universally acknowledged to be supreme wherever validly exercised. *The slow growth of national authority*

The achievement of effective national authority throughout the land and across the seas into insular possessions may in great part be attributed to the economic, technological, and social development of the American population from an agricultural, frontier, immigrant, individualist, and isolated people to an interdependent, urban, industrial, mobile, and highly interrelated society. Local authority is largely ineffective in regulating and protecting such a society. It may also be attributed to the establishment, growth, and acceptance of patterns of politics and law and of constitutional arrangements which facilitated the development of modern society, at the same time responding to its pressures. *Growth of industries promotes national authority*

The Constitution itself made a major contribution to the establishment of effective national power through the "supremacy of the law" clause which stands at the head of this section. After much discussion, the framers abandoned a provision which would authorize Congress to disallow state *Judicial review and national supremacy* legislation, and decided in favor of this provision, intended to require state courts to invalidate state and local actions conflicting with declared national policy. To be effective, however, an arrangement for reviewing—overriding, if appropriate—state decisions was clearly required and this was provided by the Congress. In the first judiciary act passed in 1789, authority was conferred upon the Supreme Court of the United States to hear on appeal decisions of state courts in which a state law or official action was upheld although alleged to be in conflict with the Constitution, a national law, or a treaty. Under the vigorous leadership of nationalist John Marshall the court from 1801 began to exercise this review power and thereafter numerous state laws have been rendered unenforceable by judicial determination. The practice by the courts of enforcing the constitutional assignment of powers upon various levels of governments as well as upon the various branches of a particular level is known as *judicial review*. It is a distinctive American contribution to the art and science of constitutional government.

That the arbiter of disputes concerning the legitimate jurisdictions of state and national authority has been the national Supreme Court, an institution organized and staffed by national authority, has helped the national government to attain supremacy. In the words of a writer of an earlier generation, the Supreme Court has throughout our history been "as impartial an umpire in national–state disputes as one of the members of two contending teams could be expected to be." In theory at least, Congress, the President, and the Court acting concurrently can override any attempt to limit national authority in favor of state authority. Among these national agencies over the years have been discovered large areas of unsuspected national power and undoubtedly others will be found in the future.

The President and Congress have aided national power

Standing alone, with no enforcing agents, no national political apparatus, and against the determined opposition not only of many states but of Congress and perhaps even the President, the Supreme Court can be relatively helpless. Some problems have been so deeply divisive and so bitterly disputed that judicial fiat could not resolve them. Congress, and the President, have also made important and lasting contributions to the achievement of national supremacy. When Jefferson captured the Presidency in 1800, the first major challenge to national authority was happily abandoned. While out of power nationally, he and his followers had fashioned and promoted the first state effort (Virginia and Kentucky Resolutions) to veto national policy by state legislative resolution. In this case the target was the Alien and Sedition Acts of 1798, sharply curtailing freedom of speech. The doctrine of state "interposition" was concocted to frustrate national enforcement. These acts expired during Jefferson's Presidency and the state efforts were thus obviated. Several New England states considered resistance to national authority in 1814 at Hartford in a desperate attempt to change the course of national trade policy. Peace with England brought these efforts to an end without further incident. South Carolina mounted a similar offensive in 1832 against national tariff policy, threatening secession if its nullification efforts were ignored. President Jackson firmly resisted and threatened to resort to military measures if necessary to uphold national law. Many and diverse efforts were made in the eighteen-fifties in Massachusetts, Wisconsin, Vermont, and other northern states to frustrate enforcement of the national fugitive slave law but in the major judicial test of their efforts the Supreme Court gave little comfort to state pretensions. It was the Civil War, however, which finally and firmly established the doctrine that this is an indestructible union and that those in possession of national power may and will use it, if challenged, to enforce national policy throughout the land. Upon defeat, the southern states were not only occupied for some years by armies of the national government but were readmitted to the Union only upon terms prescribed in Washington. The passage of the Fourteenth Amendment after this bloody struggle laid the basis for the ultimate extension of national authority into areas never before regarded as the proper concern of the national government, and also endowed the national courts with new powers to review state actions and force them into line with nationally ordained standards.

National-state disputes over labor and civil rights

The Civil War removed most of the remaining barriers to the rapid industrialization and urbanization of the nation. Incident to these developments came new challenges to national power. The national courts struck down several efforts by states to mitigate the disadvantages of rapid industrialization by economic regulation. Several attempts to prevent railroad rate extortion and to safeguard workingmen were disallowed. President Cleveland used national troops to halt the destruction of life and property and to protect the mail service in the Pullman Strike in 1894 against the wishes of the governor of Illinois. In doing so he established an early precedent for the now widely accepted national power to protect national agents and services wherever and whenever the President believes them to be threatened and regardless of the attitude of the local officials involved. Presidents Eisenhower, Kennedy, and Johnson on various occasions in the last few years used troops, federal marshals, and FBI agents to enforce court-ordered school desegregation and to protect Negroes from violence and intimidation in Mississippi, Alabama, and Arkansas.

Opposition to national authority

None of the modern efforts to establish national authority has gone unchallenged, however, nor has any achieved success overnight. For more than 50 years the Supreme Court construed the authority granted by the Fourteenth Amendment to review state actions in the narrowest terms, and the full thrust of its implications has been realized judicially only in the past three or four decades. Many of the large Northern cities were less than wholehearted in enforcing the Volstead Act implementing the Eighteenth Amendment. Southern resistance to racial desegregation in the public schools has called forth the old doctrine of interposition in numerous legislative resolutions. A group of state legislators in 1962 proposed the creation of a new arbiter of national–state power disputes. Dismayed at the nationalizing trend of the decisions of the Supreme Court, they proposed a Court of the Union composed of the chief justices of the highest courts of the 50 states and empowered them on the petition of the legislatures of 5 states to review decisions of the Supreme Court touching on rights reserved to the states or to the people. As yet these efforts have not attracted wide support. The Supreme Court has firmly rejected the interposition doctrine asserting in the words of John Marshall, that it would make the Constitution a "solemn mockery." The Court of the Union proposal has as yet been approved by only a few states.

ADMISSION OF NEW STATES

Original and admitted states

Another important contribution to the achievement of supreme national authority has been the growth of the Union from the original 13 states to the present 50. Whatever prescriptive or traditional rights the original states might claim as against a national authority created with their consent, 37 states owe their admissions to acts of the national government, and 30 of these were administered as territories by national officials before they became states. Furthermore, 4 of the original 13 seceded from the Union and were, in fact, readmitted along with their confederated partners only on terms prescribed by the Congress. Two states (Texas and California) came directly into the Union without prior territorial status and five states (Vermont, Kentucky, Tennessee, Maine, and West Virginia) were formed by separation from other states.

Congressional review of admission requests

The Constitution confers on Congress general power to admit new states subject to two restrictions: (1) No state may be erected within the jurisdiction of any other state except with the consent of the legislature of the latter; (2) No state may be formed by the union of two or more states except with the approval of the legislatures of the states concerned. Congress, traditionally, has authorized the steps for admission of a particular territory and the establishment of a convention to draft a constitution for the new state. It has, also, insisted on reviewing the new constitution before recognizing the new member. Although, legally, a state once admitted becomes the equal of the other states, the admission process has provided national officials with an opportunity to insist upon certain conditions as the price of admission. Ohio, for example, was required in 1802 to agree not to tax for five years public lands within its borders sold by the national government; Nevada, in 1864, to agree never to deny the vote to colored persons; Utah, in 1896, to write into its constitution a prohibition of polygamy; Oklahoma, in 1907, to promise not to move the state capitol from Guthrie before 1913; Arizona, in 1910, to eliminate a provision in its constitution authorizing the recall of judges; Alaska, in 1959, to allow the administration of fish and wildlife regulations to remain under the Secretary of the Interior until he should certify to Congress that the Alaskan legisla-

OUR GROWTH FROM 13 TO 50 STATES

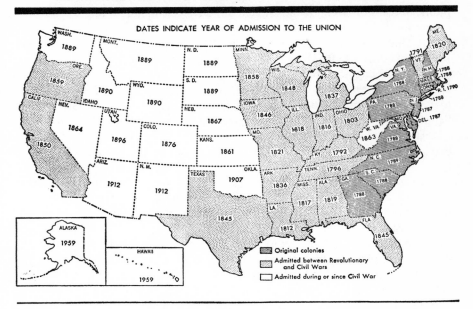

ture had made adequate provision for state administration. In general, only those conditions, usually of a contractual nature, which appear not to compromise the political freedom of the state have been held to be enforceable upon the states after admission.

Admission of Hawaii and Alaska

The newest members of the Union, Hawaii and Alaska, were admitted after submitting constitutions that they had prepared without express congressional authorization and after congressionally required public referenda on the question of admission. The overwhelming public endorsement in the two territories of immediate statehood and the election of congressional delegations set the stage for presidential admission by proclamation: Alaska on January 3, 1959 and Hawaii on August 21, 1959.

NATIONAL REVIEW OF STATE POLITICAL INSTITUTIONS

A third constitutional contribution to national supremacy is the authority now exercised by the national government to review and approve

The
guarantee
of a
republican
form of
govern-
ment
certain state political institutions. The Constitution, for example, obliges the national government to guarantee every state a republican form of government. In fixing terms for the readmission of the southern states after the Civil War, Congress required them to adopt suffrage and other arrangements which the Republican majority professed to regard as essential to a republican form of government. In general, however, neither Congress nor the courts have relied extensively on this provision to support national power. In the single instance prior to the Civil War in which the guaranty clause was invoked, the Dorr Rebellion in Rhode Island from 1841–1842, President Tyler recognized the established government of the state and aided it against a rival government set up by Dorr. According to the Court, the fact that Congress continued to receive the state's elected Representatives and Senators constituted valid and final recognition of the republican form of government of Rhode Island. Furthermore, the Court in this situation declared the question to be primarily a political one to be settled by Congress not a justiciable one to be resolved in a law suit. These views prevailed also when Oregon's popular initiative and referendum was challenged in the courts as direct rather than republican government and when an Ohio law was attacked as an unrepublican delegation of legislative power to an administrative agency.

Judicial
review of
state and
local legis-
lative dis-
tricting
systems
The Fourteenth Amendment and to a lesser extent the Fifteenth Amendment provide the legal basis for the more significant national review of state institutions. Under the provision that no state may deny to any person within its jurisdiction the equal protection of the laws, the modern Supreme Court has held that state efforts to exclude Negroes from participation in the Democratic primary are invalid. It has also invalidated a rearrangement of the municipal boundary lines in Tuskegee, Alabama, designed to exclude most of the Negro population of that city from participating in municipal politics. And, in a most significant reversal of earlier judicial policy, it has recently (1962) asserted that apportionment systems for state legislatures are reviewable by the courts and will be held as denying equal protection if the districts in both houses are not substantially equal in population. The Court has also reviewed districting systems for school boards, city councils, and county boards, although it has not been so clearly insistent on the "one man, one vote" rule in these cases. These decisions claim for the national courts the most sweeping power to overturn long-established state political arrangements many of which have been expressly sanctioned by state constitutions. Critics are now mounting a strong offensive to obtain a constitutional amendment authorizing states to apportion at least one house on a basis other than population.

Review of
discrim-
inatory
administra-
tion of
state
programs
Under the Civil Rights Act of 1964 (Title VI), the national administration is now also endowed with authority to require drastic changes in the practices, policies, and institutional arrangements of the states. "No person —shall be subjected to discrimination under any program or activity receiving federal financial assistance," states the Act. Armed with the power to

cut off grants-in-aid, administrative officials are now reviewing state education, welfare, health, housing, conservation, highway, and other programs receiving aid to determine whether changes are or will be required, and in many instances are demanding and getting cooperation which had been denied to the courts and to the United States' district attorneys.

GROWING PERVASIVENESS OF THE NATIONAL GOVERNMENT

Expanded national activities and powers

The establishment of effective national authority is one aspect of the greatly increased scope of national activities which characterize the modern federal system. The rise of urban industrialism, the extension of American influence throughout the world, and the growth of the huge defense establishment have all paved the way for the tremendous expansion of the national government which is characteristic of twentieth-century America. With one exception these developments have not rested on corresponding changes in the basic constitutional assignments of power. The Fourteenth Amendment supplied the authority for increased national concern with civil rights and racial discrimination. Congress, the President, and the courts have continually reinterpreted national authority and kept these developments firmly anchored to constitutional language.

The doctrine of implied powers

One of the useful tools of constitutional politics favoring the growth of national power was provided early in our history: the doctrine of implied powers. Lively controversies about the limits of national power arose before the new system had been in operation a year. In 1790, Hamilton, as Secretary of the Treasury, proposed the establishment of a national bank. People who considered that centralization had already been carried far enough at once objected that the Constitution, enumerating the powers of Congress, said nothing about a bank; they could show, indeed, that its authors had deliberately refused to give Congress even limited power to create corporations. Hamilton and others who supported his project replied that while the Constitution truly enough did not authorize Congress in so many words to create a bank, the power to do so could easily be deduced from certain grants of authority about which there could be no question—in particular, those relating to currency and other aspects of national finance, supported by the "sweeping clause," which concludes the Constitution's enumeration of the powers of Congress. There the two houses are authorized "to make all laws which shall be necessary and proper for carrying into execution the foregoing powers, and all other powers vested by this Constitution in the government of the United States, or in any department or officer thereof." The Hamiltonian view prevailed and the bank was established by Congress.

Criticism of the doctrine

Led by Jefferson, "strict" constructionists argued that the national government had no powers except those expressly conferred upon it in the Constitution, or, at most those which could be shown to be indispensably invoked in the exercise of these delegated powers. To take a single step beyond the boundaries "specially drawn" around the powers of Congress by the Tenth Amendment, urged the Virginian, "is to take possession of a boundless field of power, no longer susceptible of any definition." Hamilton replied that the national government had all powers which could by any reasonable interpretation be regarded as implied in the letter of the granted powers, and also that it had a right to choose the manner and means of performing its functions, although involving the employment of agencies not necessarily *indispensable* for its purposes.

In the course of time, the question reached the Supreme Court; and in a memorable series of nationalizing decisions between 1809 and 1835, that tribunal—while acknowledging limits beyond which powers could not properly be inferred—lent the Hamiltonian doctrine the full weight of its authority. Classic expression was given the Court's views by Chief Justice Marshall in the case of McCulloch v. Maryland, in 1819, as follows:

This government is acknowledged by all to be one of enumerated powers. The principle that it can exercise only the powers granted to it is now universally admitted. But the question respecting the extent of the powers actually granted is perpetually arising and will probably continue to arise as long as our system shall exist—The powers of the government are limited, and its powers are not to be transcended. But we think the sound construction of the Constitution must allow to the national legislature that discretion with respect to the means by which the powers it confers are to be carried into execution, which will enable that body to perform the high duties assigned to it in a manner most beneficial to the people. Let the end be legitimate, let it be within the scope of the Constitution, and all means which are appropriate, which are plainly adapted to that end, which are not prohibited but consist with the letter and spirit of the Constitution, are constitutional.

The principles here laid down gained general acceptance and are today firmly embedded in our constitutional law. Even the Jeffersonians, after they gained control of the government in 1801, found themselves supporting the annexation of Louisiana in 1803 and the embargo placed on foreign trade in 1807. Time and again Congress has devised programs, created agencies, and established national regulations on the basis of a chain of inference from the most meager phrases of the constitutional text and the courts have followed along usually but not invariably acceding to the congressional will.

The expanding authority of the national government in economic matters The ability of the national government to aid a growing industrial economy by subsidy and service was, as we shall see, never sharply contested, but its authority to minimize some of the worst disadvantages of entrepreneurial aggressiveness and to provide national remedies for economic depressions was confined for many decades by narrow definitions of national power over interstate commerce. Although the national authorities progressively widened the meaning of commerce to embrace the new technologies of transportation (railroads, airplanes, automobiles) and of communication (telephone, telegraph, cable, radio, television) and almost from the beginning had interpreted commerce to mean the movement of people and services as well as goods, until the late nineteen-thirties the courts had insisted that mining and manufacturing regardless of the source of raw materials or the destinations of the finished products were not commerce. Meanwhile mass production, national advertising, and business consolidation had created a national economy in which transportation was but one facet. More than this, certain state efforts to protect workers and consumers were nullified by the national judiciary under a wonderfully ingenious interpretation of the due process clause of the Fourteenth Amendment. National power, thus narrowly defined, to curtail monopoly, forbid child labor, establish minimum wages, and promote collective bargaining affected but a small segment of the industrial system. Confronted with the depression of the thirties, the President and Congress found themselves relatively powerless to curb practices which many felt were unjust and economically repressive. The judicial revolution of 1936–1937 established the principle that the production and distribution of goods and services constituted a more or less completely integrated series of transactions, every one of which depended upon every other, and the national authority over interstate commerce could be effective only if it extended to the entire process of manufacture and sale. In this way, and after several decades of the liveliest agitation, the present vast sweep of national authority over the economy was supported. In consequence, there are today relatively few economic transactions which are not within the reach of congressional power. The area of state action has been progressively contracting as more and more businesses serve regional, national, and international needs. Congress and the courts have left some small freedom to the states to deal with business, transportation, or communication within their boundaries in their own ways under the following circumstances: (1) if the enterprise or activity is wholly and exclusively intrastate and does not substantially affect interstate commerce; (2) if Congress has not seen fit to exercise the power it possesses, provided that the courts find that state regulation in these circumstances either is authorized by the Congress or is not inconsistent with the courts' view of national needs; (3) if a state regulation in the interests of public health and safety imposes only an incidental and insignificant burden on interstate commerce; and (4) if a state regulation is not inconsistent with a national government action and deals with a matter not held to be preempted by national action.

Speaking broadly, this great expansion of national power has now been generally accepted. In fact, Congress has not yet exercised all of the authority that the courts have authorized. Controversy continues, however, as to whether Congress intended to preempt certain subjects and thus to bar all state action on them. Most of the traditional controversy over the "preemption doctrine" centered on the commerce clause and much of it still does, especially in the matter of national–state authority in labor relations. How-

The preemptive authority

ever, the use of the doctrine to strike down a state act regulating subversive activities against the United States has caused much of the recent stir.

A national system of civil rights

The third aspect of increasing national power is the gradual emergence of a system of nationally guaranteed civil rights. For several generations after its adoption the provisions of the Fourteenth Amendment were narrowly construed and added little, if anything, to national power to control state official behavior in this field. Beginning in the twenties, in connection with state curtailment of free speech, the court has progressively expanded the application of the Amendment to include religious practices, censorship, racial discrimination in housing, public facilities and schools, criminal procedure, and systems of legislative apportionment. All of this, followed as it has been by various national legislative and administrative activities, has introduced national authority into areas of social relations and administrative behavior heretofore dominated by states and localities. It has also provoked the strongest criticism and the most energetic efforts to reduce national power of any of the developments of this century.

GRANTS-IN-AID TO THE STATES

National financing of state and local programs

The most powerful engine in this century for reshaping national–state relations has been the "grant-in-aid" system of national financing of state and local activities. Grants by the national government to the states are no novelty: On the contrary, they go back almost to the beginning of our national history. Starting in Ohio in 1802, Congress made a regular practice of bestowing on newly admitted states public land within their boundaries equivalent to one section in every township, to be used for the development of permanent school funds—in fact, two sections after 1848, and even four in the cases of Utah, Arizona, and New Mexico. In the famous Land Grant College (Morrill) act of 1862, Congress set aside still more land for the benefit of the states, specifying that the proceeds should be used by each to endow and maintain one or more colleges devoted primarily, although not exclusively, to instruction in "such branches of learning as are related to agriculture and the mechanic arts." Funds derived from this source help support many of our "land grant" colleges. Not only land but also money (in periods of surplus revenues) was bestowed in earlier times; and not only for education but likewise for roads and canals.

The conditional grant-in-aid system

In the past half-century, a new form of conditional grants has been devised and used widely, and it is this new form that has enlarged national power. Referred to commonly as a "grant-in-aid," its cardinal principle is that Congress will appropriate money for a specified service or activity to be carried out by the states, apportioning the sum for any given purpose among the whole number of states on some fixed basis, but generally permitting a state to share in the subvention only on four conditions: (1) that the state shall spend the national money only for the exact purpose indicated and under whatever conditions may have been laid down; (2) that the state itself, or its subdivisions, shall make concurrent appropriations for the purpose (usually in amounts at least equal to its share of the national grant, but sometimes more, sometimes less, and occasionally none at all); (3) that the state shall maintain a suitable administrative agency—highway commission, extension director, vocational education board, or whatever it may be—with which the national administration can deal in connection with the activity to be carried on; and (4) that in return for the assistance received, the state shall recognize the national government's right (with suitable regard for local conditions) to approve plans and policies, interpose regulations, fix minimum standards, and inspect results. Often, of course, it has been necessary for states to enact new legislation in order to qualify for sharing in a given grant. Usually administrative machinery has been reconstructed so as to open a way for supervision by national officers over activities that previously—if undertaken at all—were entirely in that state's own hands. Ostensibly, no compulsion is exercised. A state may, if it likes, decline to meet the conditions imposed, in which event it simply does not participate in the subsidy. This voluntary aspect of the plan has been of great help to the courts in getting around the constitutional difficulties which some of the legislation dealing with matters far out on the rim of national authority presents. Compliance by the states is, however, less voluntary than appears. For the national funds represent the proceeds of taxes paid by the people of the entire country, and if any state refuses to go into a given arrangement, it thereby cuts itself off from the benefits which its taxpayers are helping to bestow on the states that do participate. Typically, the state has been reluctant to do this; and the same considerations that initially induce a state to accept its share of a grant commonly impel it to live up to the standards and specifications required rather than run the risk of having its subvention withheld. Virtually all existing forms of grants-in-aid are shared in by all of the states.

Beginning in 1887 with cash grants for the maintenance of agricultural experiment stations in the states, the modern grant-in-aid program has steadily reached out to embrace ever larger areas of state and local action. Forestry was added to agricultural research and education as an object of grant-in-aid in 1911, highways in 1916, vocational education in 1917, the National Guard in 1917, health in 1918, social welfare in 1935, low cost housing in 1937, airports and hospitals in 1946, urban renewal in 1949, soil conservation in 1954, libraries in 1956, civil defense in 1958, educational television in 1962, general education and higher education in 1965, antipoverty programs in 1966. From 1895, with the requirement of national audit of state expenditures under the agricultural experiment station programs, the amount and character of national administrative supervision of state agencies has also steadily expanded. Under the social-welfare aid legislation of 1935 even the personnel policies of state agencies spending national funds have come under national review and under the Civil Rights

The spread of nationally aided programs

Act of 1964, their policies with regard to racial discrimination in education, welfare, housing, and other aided public services must be adapted to national requirements. Furthermore, the dependence of the state governments upon income from this source to finance their operations has progressively become greater. In 1967, the national payments ·averaged more than 25 percent of total state receipts from all sources. Finally, the total demands on the national budget made by the grant-in-aid programs have risen from $33 million in 1920 to more than $11.5 billion in 1966. The end of this period of expansion in national financing of state and local functions is not yet in sight. The national government has just begun a program of financing of general public education which is certain to grow.

National-local relations established   The grant-in-aid procedure has, furthermore, reached beyond the states down into the local units of government. Direct fiscal and administrative relations have been established between the national government and cities and counties in such programs as housing, airport construction, urban renewal, youth job opportunity promotion, and mass transportation. For a time during the depression, local relief and public works programs were also supported by national funds. In these programs the state government has been bypassed to link national and local units of government together.

Criticism of mounting national control   The result of this twentieth-century development has been to cast the states and their local units into a new relationship of subordination to the national government. The states are today, for those programs involving national financing, largely administrative subdivisions of the national government. Although they are subdivisions of a novel kind—a good deal of autonomy of method and objective is tolerated—nevertheless they are more dependent upon national money and more susceptible to national control than ever before in our history.

These developments have not been universally approved. The South, however, which has strongly opposed national intervention in race relations has been a major beneficiary of the grant-in-aid system and the attitudes of its leaders, therefore, are ambivalent. Critics of the aid system tend to come from those "overprivileged" states and interests which help to subsidize the "underprivileged." Republican Party leaders have been especially critical of what they call national "give-away" policies. In 1953, when they gained control of the national government, they authorized the creation of a Commission on Intergovernmental Relations to evaluate the system and, it was hoped, recommend its curtailment. However, the report of this Commission delivered in 1955 contained no proposals for drastic changes in the present system but rather accepted the aid system as fundamentally sound and recommended changes of a relatively minor nature. Returning to the attack in 1957, President Eisenhower named a committee of his administrative officers to work with a committee of governors to study what national functions and what revenue sources might wisely be returned to the states. This Joint Federal–State Action Committee proposed that the national government abandon the excise on telephone service and the responsibility for vocational education, disaster relief and other programs. The Congress has not, as yet, implemented any of these suggestions. In 1959, Congress created, in part at Eisenhower's suggestion, a permanent Advisory Commission on Intergovernmental Relations to keep a constant eye on the pattern of grants-in-aid and on national–state relations generally.

Despite these various efforts, the aid system was actually expanded during Eisenhower's Presidency and with his blessing. In fact, no national administration since 1932 has really attempted to abandon any of the aid programs and it is doubtful that Congress would concur if it did. Usually, the aid system has been resorted to only after other expedients have failed and only after a substantial segment of informed opinion has demanded action. In some cases the aid program has served to prevent complete national administration of a service. Critics of national expansiveness are shifting their emphasis to the controls accompanying the aid system and are now advocating block grants to the states, with few strings attached.

THE OUTLOOK FOR THE FEDERAL SYSTEM

There are many who view modern federalism with dismay. Some feel that a finite and certain amount of political power exists and, therefore, that power gains by one level of government must necessarily be at the expense of the other. The states and the nation are rivals in a deadly competition, they argue, and the balance swinging as it has been to the nation will lead to the ultimate destruction of the states. For perhaps 100 years (the eighteen-thirties through the nineteen-thirties) the tenor of court decisions and national political debate served to support this view, and it is still maintained by many self-styled conservatives. Citing the Jeffersonian tradition, they deplore the trend to national authority, talk of keeping government close to the people, despair of managing the giant of the Potomac, and regret the inducements to fiscal irresponsibility of a system in which money raised at one level is spent at another. Others suggest that the various levels of government are partners not rivals. Every major domestic problem, they suggest, requires the cooperative effort of all levels of government. There is enough for each to do. For the states to attempt solutions to what are national difficulties will lead only to frustration and lack of public confidence in self-government. The people are not really as interested in or as aware of the behavior of their local and state officials as they are of what is happening in Washington. This cooperative concept of federalism seems to be supported by the modern Supreme Court and by many congressmen and several Presidents.

*Coopera-
tion vs.
competitive
federalism*

What then is the future of the states? Are they to be completely overborne by the advancing might of the national government? Have they become but provinces in a great centralized colossus of governmental power? In the first place, it must not be overlooked that the states within their

*The
future of
the states*

boundaries are also more pervasive than once they were. They perform more services, employ more staff, spend more money, and have a greater impact on the lives of their citizens than they ever have. They are not dying, but are growing and expanding. All talk of the weakness, helplessness, and moribund character of state governments is at odds with the facts. It is true that the states cannot cope with several of our most pressing problems—economic security, international peace, and military preparedness. Since public interest has centered on these problems much of the time recently, the activities of the states may have been forgotten or ignored by many of us. In the second place, the states, as we shall presently observe in more detail, are vital parts of our system of political parties. Our great national parties are not highly centralized but are more nearly federations of state party organizations. In the states, the parties practice their tactical exercises; leaders are trained in the ways of democratic statecraft; workers energize the electorate into participation in the processes of self-government. The states, furthermore, continue to provide testing grounds for embryonic statesmen. Many congressmen gained their experience of popular lawmaking in state legislatures; the governor's offices have frequently tested candidates for the Presidency; the state courts supply recruits for the national judiciary. The states too are laboratories for experimenting with new ways by which the government can serve and enrich the lives of our people. From their experience, the nation has saved itself numerous failures and heavy additional costs. The states even today assume the heaviest responsibilities for the leadership, the costs, and the day-to-day services in education, law enforcement, rehabilitation of criminals, care of the mentally ill, construction and maintenance of our far-flung system of highways, protection of wildlife, regulation and supervision of the entire election process, and many other areas of public concern. Their greatest failure is their inability to deal constructively with the modern metropolis, but they still have a useful and important life ahead of them.

REFERENCES

W. Anderson, *The Nation and the States: Rivals or Partners?* (Minneapolis, Minn., 1955).

G. F. Break, *Intergovernmental Fiscal Relations in the United States* (Washington, D. C., 1967).

J. Cohen and M. Grodzins, "How Much Economic Sharing in American Federalism?" *Amer. Pol. Sci. Rev.,* Vol. LVII, No. 1 (March, 1963).

The Constitution of the United States of America: Analysis and Interpretation, 88th Congress, 1st Session, Senate Doc. #39 (Washington, D. C., 1964).

D. J. Elazar, *The American Partnership: Intergovernmental Cooperation in the Nineteenth Century United States* (Chicago, 1963).

R. A. Goldwin (ed.), *A Nation of States: Essays on the American Federal System* (Chicago, 1961).

W. B. Graves, *American Intergovernmental Relations* (New York, 1964).

C. G. Haines, *The American Doctrine of Judicial Supremacy* (rev. ed., Berkeley, Calif., 1932).

A. W. MacMahon (ed), *Federalism: Mature and Emergent* (New York, 1955).

R. C. Martin, *The Cities and the Federal System* (New York, 1965).

W. H. Riker, *Federalism—Origin, Operation, Significance* (Boston, 1964).

N. A. Rockefeller, *The Future of Federalism* (Cambridge, Mass., 1962).

J. R. Schmidhauser, *The Supreme Court as Final Arbiter in Federal–State Relations, 1789–1957* (Chapel Hill, N. C., 1958).

M. S. C. Vile, *The Structure of American Federalism* (Oxford, 1962).

K. C. Wheare, *Federal Government* (rev. ed., New York, 1961).

4

CIVIL RIGHTS AND HOW
THEY ARE PROTECTED

We hold these truths to be self-evident, that all men are created equal, that they are endowed by their Creator with certain unalienable Rights, that among these are Life, Liberty, and the Pursuit of Happiness.

That to secure these rights, Governments are instituted among men, deriving their just powers from the consent of the governed.—Declaration of Independence

Two opposing theories of government

Nothing quite so appropriately characterizes the deep ideological gulf separating the leading members of the Atlantic community from the Iron Curtain states or from the totalitarian aggressors of World War II as their various conceptions of the proper relation between the individual and his government. Emphasizing the dignity and worth of the individual, the people of Great Britain, France, the United States, and other Western nations regard government as resting on the consent of the governed and ascribe to even the humblest of citizens a sphere of personal liberty which no state authority, however organized, can impair. Everything that is valuable in this earthly realm, they assert, is created by individual effort and this creativeness requires a large measure of freedom in order to bear fruit. The state they regard as the traditional enemy of individual self-government and hold tightly to the conviction that its power over individuals must be confined by effective constitutional machinery and fair and workable legal procedures. The communists and authoritarians of other shades practice, if they do not subscribe to, the conception that it is enough for the state to serve man. It is neither necessary nor desirable that he possess any right to develop in his own way. The individual has neither right nor destiny apart from that of the group of which he is a member. He must and should conform his behavior and his thoughts to what his rulers have determined group welfare requires. To be an effective instrument of group welfare, the state must not be restricted in any significant way.

Each of the Western democracies has developed its own institutional arrangements to embody these great ideals of freedom. In the United States, we place our faith in the democratic process by which our officials are chosen and in the constitutional recognition of and protection of civil rights. It is, however, necessary to point out that these two facets of the American system are not easily harmonized. The democratic process is predicated on the idea that the scope and direction of governmental effort should be determined by a majority in a process in which all participants are equal to each other. The constitutional system of civil rights, on the other hand, is predicated on the idea that there are some personal liberties which even majorities may not infringe and that a semi-independent and politically irresponsible judiciary is essential to enforce these limitations. It is hard for the American people to conceive of genuine citizen participation in the processes of government without freedom publicly to criticize, explore, and discuss the problems of the day. For the exercise of free speech, they are nevertheless dependent upon a legal rather than an electoral procedure. Another area of conflict between the two notions concerns the rights of property. In the late nineteenth and early twentieth centuries, one of the big unanswered questions of American politics was whether property rights were, like personal rights immune from governmental infringement. A strong and vigorous argument in behalf of property rights issued from those who maintained that the practice of personal freedom depended upon the sanctity of property, but an equally insistent claim came for governmental regulation from those who maintained that personal freedom was enhanced by restrictions on property. In this conflict judicial restraints upon government efforts to regulate property came into disrepute with those who claimed the most progressive democratic ideals.

American ideals not easily reconciled

The rise of the continental dictatorships, both red and black, in the thirties and the spread of communist-dominated states after World War II accompanied by suppression of personal freedom and the use of police-state methods have stimulated in America a renewed appreciation of the importance of civil rights. The rise of subject peoples in Africa, Asia, and the Middle East and the increasingly insistent demands for equality of the racial minorities in America have all contributed to the liveliest agitation on the subject since Reconstruction days. Even now more than a century after the war which gave freedom to the slaves, the Negroes remind us that we have not yet accorded them the full rights of free citizens, which the victors strove to give them. From its position as world leader in promoting the concept of human dignity, this nation has perforce been brought to grips with the question of whether its own practice corresponds to the ideals it professes. Furthermore, along with growing insistence on a better and more broadly conceived application of the traditional *restrictions upon government* in the interest of personal liberty there has developed a mounting demand for *positive governmental exertion* to achieve a more adequate realization of these ideals, especially in the area of segregation of the races.

The mounting pressure for national regulations

As early as 1941 President Franklin D. Roosevelt, in a message to Congress, sought to redefine prevailing concepts, bracketing freedom from want and freedom from fear with the more traditional freedoms of speech and religion as rights to which men everywhere are entitled. From this broad statement of aspirations, attention was directed to a number of concrete conditions and practices widely regarded as calling for remedy. After years of relative indifference, both parties have been including civil rights planks in their national platforms. Early in 1947, President Truman, responding to growing public concern, set up a Committee on Civil Rights, whose report—"To Secure These Rights,"—is rated as one of the great public documents of our time. On the basis of this report, Mr. Truman in 1948 transmitted to Congress a strongly worded message, in which he included a number of proposals calling for governmental action to promote the enjoyment of rights, thus going far beyond the traditional view that governmental action poses the chief threat to such rights. President Eisenhower, too, called upon Congress on several occasions to pass national legislation aimed at breaking down racial barriers to education and to participation in national elections. The two parties adopted increasingly vigorous platform language, the Democratic party against determined southern opposition.

National legislation finally enacted

Finally, in 1957 the first national civil rights legislation since Reconstruction days was passed, followed by a second act in 1960. Then in 1964 after strong urging by President Kennedy and skillful maneuvering by his successor, President Johnson, the sweeping Civil Rights Act of 1964 was enacted by a bipartisan coalition of northern and western Democrats and Republicans. This coalition also passed the Voting Rights Act of 1965 and the strong Civil Rights Act of 1968.

The Civil Rights Acts of 1956, 1960 and 1964

The first acts dealt almost exclusively with Negro suffrage and conferred rather modest powers on the Department of Justice to intercede in behalf of Negroes illegally denied voting privileges. The first act also created a Civil Rights Commission empowered to investigate and appraise discriminatory practices. This Commission, the life of which has been repeatedly extended, provided much of the evidence and leadership for the Acts of 1964, 1965, and 1968. The Act of 1964 added to the power of the Department of Justice and the Office of Education authority to intervene in school desegregation controversies and to aid those seeking effective solutions to racial problems in the schools. It forbade discrimination by private owners or operators of many types of public accommodation (hotels, motels, cafeterias, restaurants, theatres, sports arenas, etc.) where the discrimination is supported by state law or where the goods, travelers, or entertainment move in interstate commerce. An Equal Employment Opportunity Commission was created to enforce prohibitions of discrimination in employment or in union membership and a Community Relations Service was created to assist localities in handling disputes arising from racial problems. Furthermore, discriminatory practices were forbidden in all those state or local programs financed in some measure by national grants-in-aid. While the

Act of 1964 went a long way toward providing a legal remedy for every deprivation of right, it provided no real national sanctions against discrimination in employment, no national regulation in the troubled area of private housing, no guarantee of nondiscriminatory practice in the selection of juries, and no strong protection against violent efforts to halt assertion of rights. Legislation in these areas was finally enacted in 1968 after the assassination of the Negro leader, Martin Luther King, Jr.

Congress has thus responded, although slowly and cautiously, to the mounting agitation. The courts, however, have been in the forefront of the movement to redefine and broaden our civil rights. They have struck down racial segregation wherever supported by any kind of public authority, broadened the definition of free speech, enforced further separation of church and state, and nationalized standards of judicial and executive fairness to those caught in the grip of criminal prosecution. The national executive has desegregated the armed forces and federally supported housing and has sought to eliminate discrimination not only in the national public service but also in firms supplying the government by contract and in national banks. A large number of states and many cities have enacted laws and ordinances outlawing discrimination in employment, places of public accommodation, and housing. In sum, there has been a substantial and continuing response to the claims of minorities and to the new concept of using governmental power to bar private deprivations of rights. *The courts provide leadership*

The Executive also moves

In view of the explosive character of racial tensions and the deep-seated animosities and fears involved, it is perhaps not surprising that civil rights agitation has been heated and, in too many cases, violent. Furthermore, the violence seems to be increasing. Bombings, beatings, and murder have occurred on several occasions in the South. Race riots swept sections of several Northern cities in the summers of 1964, 1965, 1966. Those in Detroit and Newark in 1967 seemed worse than any previously experienced, and in the spring of 1968 in the wake of the assassination of Dr. Martin Luther King, the great Negro leader, new riots swept Washington, D. C., Chicago, Pittsburgh, Baltimore, and other cities. The President's National Advisory Commission on Civil Disorders reporting in early 1968 ascribed the mounting violence to "white racism" and to the widening gap between the expectations of the Negroes and their actual condition. It should be added that many huge rallies, picketings, demonstrations, sit-ins, and many other forms of protest have also been conducted without personal injury or property damage during this long campaign. *Violence sweeps northern cities*

GENERAL CHARACTERISTICS OF THE AMERICAN SYSTEM OF CIVIL RIGHTS

Traditionally, rights to which Americans can lay valid claim have been set forth in bills of rights found in the constitutions of the 50 states

Full enumeration of rights impossible

and in the Constitution of the United States. These have been enlarged or redefined by amendments, statutes, and judicial interpretations and are constantly being reappraised, challenged, and restated in the light of changing conditions. The dynamic character of our system of rights makes it impossible therefore to compile a complete and definitive list. If we turn to the national Constitution, for example, we discover a long and impressive list—chiefly in the first eight amendments, but also in Sections IX and X of Article I—followed, however, by the baffling provision that "the enumeration of certain rights shall not be construed to deny or disparge others retained by the people" (Ninth Amendment). What others? All the state constitutions include lists of rights, but nowhere are these claimed to be exhaustive. In the Slaughterhouse Cases of 1873, the Supreme Court, after considering the matter in some detail, said that interpretation of our system of rights must be "a gradual process of judicial inclusion and exclusion."

Rights are not absolute

Liberty is not license; rights are relative, not absolute. After all, one of the main purposes of government is to prevent the safety and well-being of the many from being jeopardized by the few. Freedom of speech and of the press do not carry with them any right to utter or publish slander or libel or to incite persons to crime or panic; freedom of assembly does not entitle a group to interfere with public order and safety. To be validly claimed, a right must be exercised so as to cause no impairment of the same or any other right possessed by others. The attempt to apply this principle, however, catapults us immediately into all of the major controversies of civil rights. If this principle is carried to extremes, it spells the end of all rights.

Civil rights in wartime

The history of the United States suggests that the emphasis on public order and safety is likely to grow with a concomitant restriction of individual liberty, especially freedom of expression and of association when the nation is engaged in war or feels that war is imminent. Although, legally speaking, constitutional rights are not created or suspended by "national emergency," they are, in practice, sharply curtailed and, typically, with both electoral and judicial consent. Since 1939 this nation has been living through a period of real or supposed emergency, although technically we were at peace from 1953–1964 and from 1945–1950. Concern for the spread of communist influence mounted to such intensity that restrictions piled upon restrictions until as many prohibitions of various kinds of expressions and activities existed as had at any time since 1917. Happily, there has been some relaxation of efforts at "thought control" in the last few years.

The federal system and civil rights

Constitutionally recognized civil rights are not identical throughout the nation. Our federal system not only complicates the pattern of rights but introduces variations into it. There are rights—"the privileges and immunities of citizens of the United States"—that can validly be claimed only by national citizens. There are others which are assigned only to state citizens by state laws and constitutions. There are still others to which all "persons"—natural or artificial (corporation), citizen or alien—are entitled. Some rights may be properly invoked only against the national government;

others, against the states; and still others, against both. Of those which may be claimed against state action, some are based on the prescriptions of the national constitution; others, on the provisions of state constitutions; and still others, on the absence of any express or implied grant of authority to any government.

The variations in state constitutional prescriptions, especially since the Civil War, have been declining in importance. In fact, there has been an unmistakable trend toward centralizing the guarantees of many civil rights in the national government. During the first half-century of our national history the Bill of Rights embodied in the first ten amendments to the Constitution was construed (as plainly had been its intent) as restricting the national government only. The states enjoyed a good deal of latitude for establishing slavery, restricting freedom of religion, speech, and press, tolerating judicial processes now generally discarded, and imposing other restraints forbidden only to the national government. Not only was there a dual system of civil rights, but there was a very wide divergence between rights that were national and those that were state. The Civil War amendments mark the change in this policy—the Thirteenth making it impossible for a state to legalize slavery, and the Fourteenth going much further by forbidding a state (1) to make or enforce any law abridging the privileges or immunities of citizens of the United States, (2) to deprive any person of life, liberty, or property without due process of law, or (3) to deny to any person within its jurisdiction the equal protection of the laws. The broadening of national concern in guaranteeing civil rights which these amendments made possible was, however, realized but slowly. For almost half a century, the Supreme Court construed the Fourteenth Amendment's mandates so narrowly that no great changes resulted. In the nineteen-twenties, however, at a time when state legislatures were attempting restrictions upon freedom of speech, the press, and teaching, the Court began "discovering" the Amendment and declaring its full impact upon the states. In 1925 it affirmed freedom of speech and of the press, protected by the First Amendment from abridgment by Congress, to be "among the fundamental personal rights and liberties protected by the due process clause of the Fourteenth Amendment from impairment by the states." When in later decisions the same view was asserted of religious liberty, freedom of assembly, and freedom of association there arose a single system of rights in these major areas of human freedom uniformly guaranteed throughout the land. There are still numerous variations of state practices in regard to jury trials, grand juries, and other guarantees of procedural fairness. Even in this area, however, the right of an accused person to counsel has been recognized as a nationally protected one, state enforcement officers have been required to obey national standards of "reasonableness" in searches and seizures, and the right of a person to be protected from self-incrimination has been extended to state proceedings.

As we have suggested the rights claimed by and on behalf of Ameri-

Rights national-ized

Public attitude toward rights

cans have not reached final and definitive enumeration. We hear much nowadays of rights to equality of opportunity, to privacy, to vote, to work, to employment security. All of these represent aspirations of various segments of our population that thus far have not achieved legal—as distinguished from political—recognition. The effort to improve the lot of the Negro in America has to some degree shifted the rights struggle from the judicial to the legislative arena and has emphasized that some types of rights must be achieved, if at all, by positive public effort rather than by restraint on governmental agents and activities. This shift is an important one in both theory and practice and its success depends heavily on popular understanding of and commitment to the ideas of human rights. Studies of popular attitudes in America indicate that our politicians, judges, and opinion leaders are far more dedicated to the freedoms protected by bills of rights than are the rank and file of Americans.

SPECIFIC AMERICAN RIGHTS

A. Rights of Personal Liberty

> Neither slavery nor involuntary servitude, except as punishment for crime whereof the party shall have been duly convicted, shall exist within the United States or any place subject to their jurisdiction.—Thirteenth Amendment

1. Right to personal security

"Freedom can exist," said the President's (Truman) Committee on Civil Rights, "only where the citizen is assured that his person is secure against bondage, lawless violence and arbitrary arrest and punishment." No general immunity from personal servitude was legally recognized in the United States until the adoption of the Thirteenth Amendment in 1865. Since that time, slavery in all of its forms has been eliminated. This amendment has been interpreted to mean that a laborer cannot be compelled to work out a debt in his employer's service. National statutes as well as several state constitutions and statutes forbid peonage in this or any other form, and several state constitutions also prohibit imprisonment for debt. Persons may, however, validly be held to the completion of terms of service for which they have contracted (sailors, for example) and may also be conscripted for military, police, jury, or highway laboring duty. These latter are considered appropriate exercises of governmental power and do not, therefore, involve "servitude."

National intervention to protect persons against intimidation

The deprivation of personal liberty by mob violence (lynching) has posed a very different problem of civil rights. For a time after the Civil War, Congress felt that positive action in the form of national statutes was necessary to assure the Negroes of the South the new status which the Civil War amendments sought to give them. In a series of civil rights acts passed between 1866 and 1875, national authority was invoked to prevent intimidation of or violent assault upon American citizens. The Supreme Court and later Congress took the view that the Fourteenth Amendment did not intend to authorize the national government to regulate the behavior of citizens nor to replace local or state law enforcement. The demand for positive national action to guarantee personal security against coercion or violence has been voiced with new vigor in the past three decades. Congress has repeatedly been urged to enact laws against lynching and to strengthen the remnants of the old civil rights acts. The effort to mix the races in the public schools, followed by the vigorous attempts to end discrimination in stores, restaurants, depots, housing, employment, and city buses has led to new lawlessness. Thus far Congress has been unwilling to depart sharply from the traditional paths. In the Civil Rights Act of 1957, the 1866 statute empowering the President to employ troops to enforce or prevent violation of civil rights legislation was repealed. However, in the Act of 1960, the transportation or possession of explosives intended for use in bombing buildings or vehicles and flight across state lines to escape prosecution or to escape giving testimony concerning bombings were made national crimes. Legislation urged by President Johnson in 1966 and 1967, and finally adopted in 1968, provides federal protection for persons attempting to exercise their rights to attend school, to seek employment, to vote, or to use public facilities and accommodations. The executive branch has, in fact, intervened with force on several occasions since 1956 to enforce a national court order or to prevent obstruction to movement of persons engaged in peaceful marches.

> Congress shall make no law respecting an establishment
> of religion, or prohibiting the free exercise thereof. . . .—First
> Amendment

Freedom of religious worship is guaranteed against national legislative impairment by the First Amendment and against state impairment by the prevailing interpretation of the Fourteenth Amendment. It is also guaranteed against state restriction by the constitutions of the states, although not always in identical terms. By these guarantees individuals are, in general, free to cherish such religious convictions as they please, to declare them publicly, to seek converts to them, and to engage in whatever forms of worship they prefer. These guarantees do not, however, confer any exemption from the criminal laws of the land, for example, to practice polygamy or to extract fees from the gullible for occult cures. *2. Right to religious freedom*

Religious beliefs, on occasion, come into conflict with norms of conduct cherished by some members of society as well as with governmentally ordained principles of safety and order. In recent years the vigorously nonconformist sect known as Jehovah's Witnesses has tested the contours of the constitutional guarantees. This sect attracted national attention several years ago when it denounced the practice in some public schools of saluting *Jehovah's Witnesses* the American flag. This, Jehovah's Witnesses said, was idolatry and they refused to allow their children to join in the ceremony. Attempts by local school boards to exclude these children were at first sustained. Later, regulations requiring their expulsion were declared invalid by the Supreme Court. The strident anti-Roman Catholic tenor of their literature and preaching, coupled with their penchant for street corner and house-to-house solicitation, have stimulated a number of communities to attempt to curtail the Witnesses by local ordinances or police regulations. A number of such efforts have been brought to the courts with varying results. On the whole, religious canvassers have been given a rather wide latitude to proselytize without licensure or payment of fees so long as they are careful to keep the streets free and to observe other local regulations governing public meetings in public parks or on public thoroughfares.

Subsidization of parochial schools

The right of religious bodies to establish and maintain their own schools and thus to avoid compulsory public school attendance has long been recognized. In recent years, the related problem of subsidizing religious schools from the public treasury has come increasingly into prominence. In a number of states (Wisconsin, for example) the state constitution forbids subsidy of any kind (books, transportation, buildings, etc.), but in some (New Jersey, for example) the practice is expressly sanctioned by law or constitutional prescription. Several years ago the United States Supreme Court was invited to declare state subsidy of parochial-school pupil transportation a violation of the religious freedom guarantees of the Constitution. In a close and vigorously argued decision, the Court ruled that states could validly subsidize private schooling if they wished to do so. The question of religious freedom was not involved but rather one of public benefit, said the Court majority. More recently (1968), the Court upheld a New York law requiring the public schools to lend textbooks to students in parochial schools. On the other hand, the Court has refused to review state decisions holding subsidization of parochial schools to be contrary to the state constitutions of those states. One of the troublesome issues in the debate on a national grant-in-aid program for public education has been the validity of providing national aid for parochial schools. The program finally adopted in 1965 attempted to sidestep this issue by gearing the aid to "needy" pupils, a method used earlier in the school-lunch aid program. The practice has not as yet been adjudged by the courts.

Religious education in the public schools

Religious education in the public schools, long a sensitive nerve in the anatomy of free public education, has repeatedly been touched in recent years by controversy. The sharpest jar to widely accepted practices came in 1948 when the Supreme Court declared that an Illinois practice of offering religious instruction to willing children by various denominations in the school buildings on time "released" for the purpose by the school authorities was inconsistent with the principle of separation of church and state imbedded in the Constitution. This decision spread consternation among the hundreds of communities then using this or a similar procedure and sent several new cases to the courts to discover if any extant practice could be accepted. The Court, in 1952, set at rest much of the uneasiness created by its 1948 decision by approving a New York City procedure in which denominational religious instruction was provided to those who wanted it on released time outside the public school buildings. "Government may not finance religious groups nor undertake religious instruction nor blend secular and sectarian education nor use secular institutions to force one or some religions on any person," said Justice Douglas for the Court. "It may not make a religious observance compulsory. It may not coerce anyone to attend church, to observe a religious holiday, or to take religious instruction. But it can close its doors or suspend its operations as to those who want to repair to their religious sanctuary for worship or instruction." The Court, in 1962, further held that official prayers, even if denominationally neutral, may not be recited in public schools and, in 1963, that states may not require the reading of selections from the Bible nor the recitation of the Lord's Prayer in the public schools. Led by Senator Dirksen (Ill.) critics of these decisions are pressing for a constitutional amendment authorizing voluntary prayers in the schools.

By way of further definition of allowable state conduct, the Supreme Court in 1961 held that state constitutions and laws may not require office-holders to declare a belief in God as part of the oath of office. "Neither a state nor the Federal Government can constitutionally force a person to profess a belief or disbelief in any religion," said Justice Black. The Court refused, however, in the same year to strike down "blue" laws, restricting the sale of goods and services on Sundays, and they are still found in Pennsylvania and many other states. The Court said that the essential purpose of these laws today is not religious but rather economic and social.

Positive governmental assertion of the value of religious freedom has occurred under trying circumstances in the several wars of this century. The Congress, as an act of grace, has authorized draft boards to call "conscientious objectors," those with bona fide religious scruples against military service, only for noncombatant service or for service in other public programs not operated by the armed services (park improvement, conservation, care of the ill) and thus has excused them from combat. *Conscientious objection in wartime*

Congress shall make no law . . . abridging the freedom
of speech or of the press. . . .—First Amendment

Freedom of speech controversies rarely involve the right to say or to print things that a majority of the people already believe. It is the right to say unpopular, unorthodox, or unconventional things which is really at issue. Further, an untrammeled right to say anything one pleases has never been recognized by any nation. And in the United States from the beginning, speaking and writing have been confined by prevailing standards of decency of language and subject and of slanderousness of intention as well as by *3. Right to speak and write freely* certain imprecise requirements of public peace and safety. Although standards and tastes in these matters have changed from generation to generation, even the most ardent exponents of unfettered communication recognize the wisdom and necessity of some limitation. In our day, as in many prior epochs of our history, the major problems of speech and press arise from the determination of a large number of our people to use the authority and prestige of the government to suppress opinions which they detest and which they believe tend to undermine our scheme of social values, our system of constitutional government, or our national independence. This determination, now as in earlier years, gains added vigor when applied to utterances which betray or seem to betray or can be made to appear to betray an affinity for some foreign state or imported ideology. When, as in the case of England in 1776, France in 1798, Germany in 1917 and 1941, and Russia since 1918, this foreign state is an actual or potential enemy the determination becomes well-nigh irresistible. Under these circumstances, restrictions on freedom of communication have gone and do now go far beyond the suppression of alleged "alien" ideas. They embrace positive injunctions to loyal behavior and speech. Even criticism of the conduct of the government, essential as it is to the conduct of a democratic state, tends to be regarded by some as seditious and disloyal. The modern problem is further complicated by the fact that the opinions and movements which the prevailing restrictions are aimed at suppressing, communism and totalitarianism, are themselves hostile to freedom of expression. Should democratic tolerance be accorded to those who do not believe in it and would not practice it if they had the opportunity?

National legislation restricting speech

The long history of national legislative and executive efforts to restrict speech and publication in the interests of national safety begins with the Alien and Sedition Acts of 1798, which among other things forbade the uttering of defamatory remarks about the President or the Congress or the inciting of the hatred of the people against them. In the Civil War period, the President took the initiative in suppressing pro-southern expressions in the North. Congress passed no general limitations on speech, although it did later ratify some of the executive actions. In World War I, Congress dealt with seditious writing and talking by sweeping restrictions on expressions critical of the government or its wartime policies. In each epoch the courts have, with very few exceptions, sustained these types of laws and their application to individuals.

Clear-and-present-danger doctrine

Out of the post-World War I efforts to curb socialist, communist, and syndicalist movements in the United States by state legislation, the Supreme Court gradually evolved one of its significant doctrines in the field of free speech; the clear-and-present-danger test. As enunciated by Justice Holmes in several dissenting opinions, this theory holds that restrictions on freedom of expression in the interest of public safety can be validly applied only when the statements and the circumstances in which they are uttered involve a clear and present danger of evils which the government has a right to prevent. By 1940, the Court had fully adopted this theory as controlling in such matters, and had, in doing so, considerably broadened its previous theories of the amount of freedom of speech and of the press which would be tolerated.

A new wave of restrictive legislation and executive action began about this time. The first peacetime sedition act since 1798 was passed in 1940 (Alien Registration Act), aimed especially at advocates of the violent overthrow of the government of the United States. This was followed in 1950 by the Internal Security Act designed to force communist-dominated organizations to reveal themselves as such and to place their activities under rigid surveillance. A Communist Control Act in 1954 withdrew from the Communist party or any of its offspring the rights, privileges, and immunities of legal bodies in the United States or in any state. By these and other statutes communists or individuals found to have advocated forceful revolution were denied positions on the public payroll, in the armed services, or in defense plants, were required to disclose their affiliations and were in danger of being jailed. The Supreme Court in 1951 sustained the conviction of eleven top communist leaders under the Act of 1940 and held that the Communist party did advocate the violent overthrow of the government and that Congress had the power to prohibit such advocacy. It also sustained state and national efforts to bar communists or other "subversives" from public employment. Speaking for the Court in the communist case, Chief Justice Vinson said, "an attempt to overthrow the Government by force, even though doomed from the outset because of inadequate numbers or power of the revolutionists, is a sufficient evil for Congress to prevent." The clear-and-present-danger doctrine, he observed, should not be applied or construed to force the government to wait for a violent uprising before it can act.

Contemporary restrictions aimed at communists

After the Korean War ended the furor against subversives gradually abated. Senator McCarthy (Wis.), a prime mover in the agitation, was repudiated by his colleagues. As new cases were brought, it became clear that the court was not going to abandon all legal protections even for communists and much of the ground lost in the early fifties is slowly being regained. Advocacy of violent revolution must be more than just discussion of an abstract right or doctrine. Organizing a conspiracy to overthrow the government must be a present action not one in the past protected by a statute of limitation. A member of the party must be shown to have a specific design or intention to overthrow the government and must be an "active" member. Individuals may not be assailed by state authorities under state law prohibiting overthrow of the national government since the Act of 1940 preempts this field. Although the registration requirements of the Internal Security Act of 1950 are valid as applied to the Communist party, no party official or member can be required to register for the party, since to do so would oblige him to risk self-incrimination under the Act of 1940. Finally, the government may not make it a crime for communists

Liberalization trends in modern decisions

to work in defense plants. With its crucial sections thus emasculated, the Internal Security Act of 1950 became useless, and Congress in 1967 overhauled it. The registration requirements were all removed and the Subversive Activities Control Board was directed instead to hold hearings on cases referred to it by the Justice Department on whether organizations and individuals were communist. Public lists of those found to be members of communist or communist-front organizations were to be prepared by the Board, and persons and organizations might by suit seek to remove their names. Prohibitions against employment of listed persons by the government or by a labor union, and in some cases, by defense plants were continued.

Loyalty oath requirements

Not satisfied with prosecutions for sedition and with denials of certain types of privileges and opportunities to communists or totalitarians, executives and legislatures by law and by the activities of their investigating committees also sought positive declarations of loyalty from civil servants, military men, school teachers, beneficiaries of national grants for research and for collegiate loans and fellowships. Typically, these have taken the form of loyalty-oath requirements and were in the fifties in several cases upheld by the Court. More recently, several (for example, those of the States of Florida, Oklahoma, Washington, Arizona, Maryland, and New Hampshire) were invalidated. Also, an effort by California to require a loyalty affidavit from those who claimed property-tax exemption was declared to be invalid as placing the burden of proof on the taxpayer rather than on the state. An attempt by Congress to demand such oaths from tenants of public, low-rent housing projects was set aside by several state courts and the national administration ceased, in 1956, any effort to enforce the rule. Congress returned to the attack in 1965, however, by requiring a controversial loyalty question to be answered by applicants for Medicare. After upholding in 1952 the application of a New York law aimed at keeping subversives off the faculties and staffs of public schools and colleges, the Court more recently (1967) retreated from that position and overturned the law.

New forms of protest not ruled upon

One final word on the efforts to root out "subversive" influences in American life. There is a great deal of disagreement on what constitutes subversion. Many of the state and national statutes, executive orders, and legislative committee fiats, have been loosely worded and imprecisely aimed. There is some danger that in rooting out the communists we may also be intimidating every type of unconventional opinion. There are far too many in the land ready to stamp out any kind of criticism of our culture on the ground that any criticism of the existing policies or institutions of our society gives aid and comfort to our enemies. The legitimacy of most of the new forms of protest such as obstruction, picketing, howling-down speakers, sit-ins have not been clearly determined. Courts have, on the one hand, dealt severely with prosecution of protestors under vaguely worded disorderly conduct laws and arbitrary collegiate disciplinary actions. However, prosecution for draft-card destruction under the law of 1965 has not been halted. Many new legislative efforts to halt or punish protestors have not yet been construed.

In the age-old conflict between freedom of speech and the press and standards of public decency, courts and public alike have been developing much broader tolerance. Books and magazines today deal with sex in a more uninhibited fashion than would have been tolerated in any other period. Tastes in these, as in so many other matters, change with the years, and the courts are reflecting these changes in numerous cases by staying the arms of local and state censors. Although the Supreme Court has refused to disallow completely censorship of plays and films, it has shifted the burden of proof to the censorial agency in such a way as to weaken, if not destroy, most extant state and local regulations. Local bans of films like "The Miracle," "Pinky" and "The Loners" have been invalidated. A Michigan law was overturned in 1957 on the grounds that it forbade to adults what might be considered corrupting to children. A Los Angeles ordinance making it a crime for a bookseller to have obscene books in his shop was overturned as applied to a storekeeper who claimed he did not know what was in the books in question. *Fanny Hill* has also been protected against attack, and efforts by the Postmaster General to stop the circulation through the mails of magazines dealing with nudism and homosexuality and of *Lady Chatterley's Lover* have been halted. This does not mean that obscenity is now permissible in speech, films, or writing, or that censorship cannot be imposed under proper circumstances but only that broader conceptions of what is censorable and what is obscene are being applied. In one case recently the magazine "Eros" was found to be obscene under national statutes. And more recently a New York law forbidding the sale of "suggestive" printed matter to children was supported by the Court.

Censorship

The ability of the national government to restrain the circulation of undesirable opinions or materials is greatly aided by its operation of the mails. Congress has authorized the postal authorities to exclude from postal privileges indecent, fraudulent, and seditious materials and has conferred rather wide discretion on these authorities in deciding what falls within the prohibition. The licensing of radio and television broadcasting also places the national government in a strategic position from which to exclude by administrative determination similar materials from the air waves. The Federal Communications Commission, although denying censorship, nevertheless, does in fact exercise it indirectly. In wartime, the government has felt obliged to introduce rigid and stern controls on the flow of news concerning the conduct of military operations. Frequently, however, these have gone far beyond the strict requirements of military security. The post-World War II period of international tensions, Korean and Viet Nam police actions, and huge armaments has stimulated the continuation of many types of restriction on free communication to the press and public by executive departments and agencies. The most recent controversy in this field has concerned security regulations issued by President Truman and continued by

Censorship in the national government

Presidents Eisenhower, Kennedy, and Johnson. The newspapers, in particular, have been campaigning nationally against what they regard as a growing and unwarranted suppression of information by government agencies. Scientists too have joined the attack, claiming that important research is being hampered by the secrecy surrounding governmental scientific programs.

> Congress shall make no law . . . abridging the right of
> the people peaceably to assemble, and to petition the gov-
> ernment for a redress of grievances.—First Amendment

4. Right to peaceable assembly and to petition

The right to peaceable assembly is regarded by the Court as equally fundamental with those of free speech, press, and religion, and, therefore, as guaranteed against state encroachment by the Fourteenth Amendment. The right of petition has the same status. It also includes the right to demand positive actions by government as well as a redress of grievances. It does not, however, include a right to have the government take action on the request. For a time (1840–1845), the lower house of Congress refused to receive petitions on the subject of the abolition of slavery. John Quincy Adams, in one of his last great efforts in the House of Representatives, paved the way for the repeal of this rule. Petitions now, as for many years, are regularly delivered by any member of Congress to the clerk for entrance on the records of Congress. Many of these are referred to the appropriate committee. Most are never heard of again. The regulating of public assembly has presented the Court with more difficulties than the preservation of the right of petition. In 1937, the Court struck down a Jersey City ordinance under which the city officials had been prohibiting many types of meetings by leftist organizations. In general, the courts have sustained regulations where the major purpose has been to keep streets and thoroughfares free of obstruction and where licensure is used without discrimination among groups seeking authority to hold meetings in public places.

> A well regulated Militia being necessary to the security
> of a free state, the right of the people to keep and bear Arms
> shall not be infringed.—Second Amendment

5. Right to keep and bear arms

Provisions similar to that above may be found in many of the state constitutions. The arms referred to are those of the soldier; and it is not only the right, but also the duty, of every citizen, if called upon, to bear such arms in the service of his country. Under the police power, the "bearing" of arms intended for private use, however, may be regulated and restricted by both the national government and the state. There are many laws forbidding the carrying of concealed weapons (pistols, revolvers, dirks, bowie-knives, sword-canes, etc.) and the sale, possession, or use of sawed-off shotguns and other weapons not employed for military purposes but habitually used by criminals. Apparently, there are not enough effective laws, however, and the assassinations of President Kennedy in 1963 and Martin Luther King and Senator Kennedy in 1968 have created wide sentiment for stricter controls.

One of the by-products of the developing program to eliminate racial discrimination from most aspects of American life—a program to be described shortly and one which has been conducted under the civil rights banners—has been the unequivocal assertion by the Court of the right of freedom of association as one protected by the due process clauses of the Fifth and Fourteenth Amendments. Several southern states and cities sought to force the National Association for the Advancement of the Colored People (NAACP), a leader in the efforts to halt discrimination, into the open by requiring registration and submission to the authorities of membership lists. In cases from Alabama and later from Little Rock turning on the refusal of the NAACP to comply, the Court held the regulations invalid. "It is beyond debate that freedom to engage in association for the advancement of beliefs and ideas is an inseparable aspect of the liberty assured by the due process clause of the Fourteenth Amendment," stated Justice Harlan for the Court. *6. Right to freedom of association*

Although as yet no general legal recognition has been accorded to privacy as a fundamental but unspecified civil right, the courts have increasingly been urged to recognize such a right. The invalidation in 1965 of a Connecticut statute on the use of and dissemination of information about birth-control devices was largely based on the idea that such a right exists. A family held captive by some desperate convicts newly escaped from a penitentiary attempted to collect damages from the publishers of *Life* magazine, who they said invaded their privacy by reviewing the play, "The Desperate Hours," based on the incident. The plea was set aside by the Court in favor of freedom of the press. *7. Right to privacy*

Racial Discrimination

No state shall . . . deny to any person within its jurisdiction the equal protection of the laws.—Fourteenth Amendment

The most controversial area of civil rights today is racial discrimination. The key constitutional stipulation on this question is the equal-protection clause of the Fourteenth Amendment. Originally intended to protect the emancipated Negroes from discriminatory treatment at the hands of officials of the southern states, it largely failed of this objective until the middle of the present century. After the withdrawal of the troops from the defeated states (1877) a system of race relations was established based upon state-ordained segregation in public schools, public facilities, and places of public accommodation. This pattern developed also in the border states to some extent. When challenged, late in the century, "Jim Crowism" was found by the highest court to be compatible with the Fourteenth Amend- *8. Right to equal protection of the laws* ment, provided the separate facilities were substantially equal. As the Negroes migrated out of the South in larger and larger numbers to the great industrial areas of the North and Midwest, patterns of segregation developed there also, although normally not under the cover of law, but rather on the basis of private decision.

The increasingly vigorous demands of the Negroes for fair and equal treatment and their denunciation of segregated enterprises have finally led to a complete restatement of the equal-protection guarantees and to the outlawing of virtually all governmentally ordained segregation. Through many generations, however, the freed Negro had been segregated and discriminated against by most of American society, North and South, without the constraints of public ordinance. In housing, employment, department stores, theatres, night clubs, sports arenas, hotels and all manner of commercial, industrial, professional, academic, religious, and fraternal enterprises and activities, racial segregation was widely practiced. The negative restraints of the constitutional system of civil rights, are, of course, not aimed at, nor effective in, removing private prejudice. Thus, the opponents of racial discrimination have also sought the support of legislation and executive action to penalize discrimination and to forbid its practice. In this, they have helped redefine our conceptions of civil rights and the duties men owe to one another.

Housing   In the great industrial and commercial cities of the North and Midwest, newly established Negro communities were segregated by various formal and informal devices into ghettos, which were usually slums and overcrowded neighborhoods. One of the favorite devices of the twenties and thirties for enforcing the racial "purity" of certain neighborhoods and thus keeping out Negroes (Jews, Poles, Italians, also, in some cases) was restrictive real estate covenants upheld by state courts at various times in at least 19 states. The first great victory of the modern era for the cause of racial equality and the first effort to reestablish the importance of the equal-protection clause occurred in 1948 when the Supreme Court declared that states could not use the courts to enforce such real estate covenants. Furthermore, said the Court in a later case, state courts may not even entertain suits for damages filed by owner-residents against those who sell in violation of the covenant. With this success the Negro leaders turned their fire on the nationally supported public housing programs which had, until this time, conformed to community practice in the matter of racial segregation. After more than a dozen states (including New York, Illinois, Massachusetts, Michigan, Pennsylvania, Indiana, New Jersey, and Connecticut) and several cities forbade discrimination in publicly supported housing, and after several unsuccessful efforts to get Congress to change the national public-housing laws, President Kennedy in 1962 by executive order forbade racial discrimination in the sale or rental of housing wholly or partially supported by public funds, including housing provided through loans insured or guaranteed by a national agency. In 1963, New York became one of the first states to enact a sweeping prohibition of racial discrimination in all types of private housing except owner-occupied one-or-two family dwellings. A few other states followed and the demand for such legislation spread rapidly. In a statewide referendum in California in connection with the presidential election of 1964, however, such a housing law already on the books was invalidated by a constitutional amendment preventing any legal interference with the right of a person freely to dispose of his own property. This amendment was invalidated two years later by the California Supreme Court. National success finally crowned the efforts of the "open housing" advocates when Congress in 1968, reacting to the murder of Martin Luther King and the pressure of President Johnson, passed the Civil Rights Act of 1968. This act prohibits discrimination in the sale or rental of housing and establishes a schedule for its gradual extension from multi-family dwellings to single-family ones by January 1, 1970.

Employment

Negroes have for years smarted under various open and subtle forms of discrimination in employment and in labor union membership and have felt that they have been denied access to the better-paying part of the labor market. This problem is not a constitutional one, solvable in the judicial forum, but a political one solvable, if at all, in the legislative arena. New York State pioneered in 1945 by enacting a "Fair Employment" law, outlawing discrimination on the basis of race, religion, etc., in hiring and firing or in granting union membership. More than twenty states, including most of the industrial ones, and several cities followed this lead. A few states enacted laws based on consultative rather than compulsive techniques. President Truman strongly urged national legislation on this subject as did the Democratic platform of 1948. Although Congress deliberated without action until 1964, an executive order struck at discrimination in civil service employment, in the armed forces, in the hiring practices of government contractors, and, in 1966, in the employment practices of all banks handling national funds. As part of the sweeping legislation of 1964, a national program to eradicate discrimination in private employment was established. An Equal Employment Opportunity Commission was created, clothed, however, with largely investigatory and educational authority. Local enforcement machinery, where existent, was endorsed and, in some cases, given a preference in handling disputes. Small employers were included only on a gradual basis over a period of five years. By this Act the government of the United States became the avowed enemy of employment practices based on race, color, religion, sex, or national origin.

Education

One of the reasons frequently advanced by the Negro for his relative failure in the job market has been the inadequate quantity and quality of his education under the segregated system of public education practiced in the South, in the border states, and even in northern cities where Negroes are segregated geographically. In the effort to enlarge educational opportunities, these systems were brought under vigorous attack. In a series of cases between 1948 and 1954 several states were ordered to admit Negroes to state-supported collegiate and professional institutions. Finally in 1954, the Supreme Court ordered the abandonment of all segregation in publicly supported educational institutions at all levels everywhere and specifically reversed the traditional doctrine. "Separate educational facilities are inherently unequal," said Chief Justice Warren for the Court. "Segregation (itself) is a denial of equal protection." Recognizing that such a drastic change in the practices and attitudes of many decades invited caution, the Court delayed the execution of its judgment pending further review and invited the states affected to submit recommendations at a later date. Early in 1955 the Court heard arguments on how best to carry out its decision. Florida, North Carolina, Arkansas, Oklahoma, Maryland, and Texas took part in the proceedings, but Virginia, South Carolina, Georgia, Mississippi, and Alabama did not. The Court then ordered (June, 1955) the lower national courts to determine in each case how best to end segregation in the schools. The lower courts were instructed to allow time for the necessary readjustments but to insist on reasonable efforts at compliance. In all cases the burden of proof was placed on the local authorities to show why they could not move faster and that they had a plan to end segregation.

Southern resistance to desegregation in education   Although in several of the border states the integration of races in the public schools has steadily advanced, largely by voluntary methods, since the famous decision, in the deeper South resistance has been widespread, continuous, and determined. For the most part, the conversions have thus far been few and difficult. The congressmen of these states in 1956 signed a resolution pledging themselves to "use all lawful means to bring about a reversal of this decision . . . and to prevent the use of force in its implementation." State legislatures and governors have declared the decision an unwarranted and unconstitutional invasion of their reserved powers and several have invoked the old nullification doctrine of interposition to justify disobedience to the court's orders. Laws and state constitutional amendments have been adopted authorizing the closing of any school ordered to desegregate, the use of public funds to support private schools, the transferral of authority over school affairs from local to state officials. New and ingenious procedures for the assignment of pupils have been devised. Violence has erupted in Little Rock, Arkansas; Clinton, Tennessee; Oxford, Mississippi; Birmingham, Alabama. A very threatening situation also arose in Tuscaloosa. Troops were ordered into active duty at Little Rock, Oxford, and Birmingham, and the National Guards of Arkansas, Mississippi, and Alabama were at various times called into national service to prevent their being used by the governors to obstruct court-ordered integration. The schools of Prince Edward County, Virginia, were closed from 1959 to 1964 to avoid integration and money was paid to private organizations to provide schooling to white children of that county. The Supreme Court, meanwhile, steadfastly adhered to its position. Invited to stay the execution of a desegregation order for Central High School in Little Rock in order to avoid violence, it enjoined Governor Faubus (Ark.) from intervening, denounced state support of segregation "through any arrangement, management, funds, or property" and dismissed the interposition resolutions and assertions as making a mockery of the Constitution.

Throughout the years since the school decision, the executive branch has been relatively powerless to intervene in a positive way to expedite integration. Only when a court order was defied or violence occurred which threatened the lives or safety of national agents or services or when invited by the local officials to help (this occurred only in Clinton, Tenn.) has the executive branch been able to move. As Attorney General, Robert Kennedy did, in 1961, enter the suit involving the Prince Edward County schools on behalf of the government and did participate in the settlement of that controversy in 1964. Efforts to strengthen the enforcement powers of the executive in school desegregation questions were successfully resisted by southern congressmen in the civil rights debates of 1957 and 1960. Finally, by the act of 1964, the Attorney General is authorized to file suit for the desegregation of a public school on the basis of a complaint if he certifies that the complainant is unable to initiate proceedings and that such an action would "materially further" orderly school desegregation. The Office of Education is authorized to offer technical and financial assistance to local school officials planning desegregation or actually achieving it. Most important of all racial discrimination is outlawed in all programs supported financially by the national government. While opposition to racial integration in education still continues in many places in the South, gradually public schools in the urban South (Atlanta, Tuskegee, New Orleans, Birmingham) are being opened to both races. The Office of Education is working steadily against congressional committee criticism and delaying tactics of many kinds to enforce the aid laws of 1964.

Executive support to facilitate desegregation

The racial segregation in living accommodations which has been characteristic of many cities has resulted in de facto segregation in neighborhood public schools in those cities. Encouraged by the effectiveness of their protests, northern Negro leaders are now demanding that northern and midwestern educational officials develop systems of transporting some Negroes out of the Negro neighborhoods to "white" schools and some whites into Negro schools. New York City amidst bitter demonstrations by white parents has made one of the first major efforts to accommodate this new demand. In 1965, Massachusetts passed the first law making racial imbalance illegal in the public school system. Many supporters of racial equality have been chagrined to be reminded by these agitations of the extent of segregation outside the South.

School problems of northern cities

The final area of racial controversy to be considered was segregation of public facilities and places of public accommodation. Like the others, this battle has been waged in the judicial arena when publicly ordained segregation is concerned and in the legislature when the practices of private

Public facilities and places of public accommodation

firms and persons are concerned. In 1946 the Supreme Court held invalid a Virginia Jim Crow law segregating buses to prevent inconvenience to interstate carriers rather than on the grounds of equal protection. In a later case against the Southern Railway turning on its refusal to seat a Negro in the dining car, the Court, in effect, invalidated the laws supporting all forms of discrimination on railroad trains. The Interstate Commerce Commission followed this decision by a sweeping order in 1955 ending segregation in all interstate trains and buses. The next step was a decision in 1956 outlawing an Alabama law and a Montgomery City ordinance requiring segregation on intrastate buses. This decision came in the midst of a boycott of city buses by the Negroes of Montgomery. Ultimately segregation in buses in a number of large southern cities was ended by the bus companies. Using the sit-in system, the Negroes then attacked segregation in restaurants, terminals, and large chain stores. The Court, upon request, outlawed segregation in the terminals as well as in buses and trains. The ICC ordered an end to discrimination in all terminals and in restaurants in terminals in 1961 at the urging of Attorney General Kennedy. The Court also swept away enforced segregation in public parks, playgrounds, golf courses, and public beaches. A provision of the national hospital-aid legislation authorizing aid for segregated facilities was declared invalid in 1964.

In 30 northern, western, and midwestern states, meanwhile, legislation was enacted forbidding discrimination by private persons operating hotels, restaurants, and resorts. Human-rights agencies were established to direct the campaign against discriminatory practices. After years of debate the Congress was finally brought into the struggle against segregation in privately-owned places of public accommodation by the Civil Rights Act of 1965. Under this act discrimination is outlawed in all such places (restaurants, motels, hotels, theaters, stadiums, lunchrooms, cinemas) except owner-occupied units with five or fewer rooms for rent and where the segregation is based upon state laws or official action or where it can be shown that the customers, goods, or entertainers move in interstate commerce. A Community Relations Service, established by the act, handles complaints and seeks voluntary compliance before legal action may be sought by the Attorney General. Locally established agencies are given preference in resolving disputes which might arise.

Despite all these efforts the "rising expectations" of the Negroes are far from satisfied. The gap between the races continues to widen on such matters as education, income, employment, welfare. The war in Viet Nam has delayed or halted programs to rebuild slums and deal with urban and rural poverty started by the Johnson administration. The results are riot-torn cities and the emergence of militant black power advocates, demanding not mixture, but segregation with equal facilities, and pressing their claims through violence. Even at this writing (1968) the King movement led by Rev. Abernathy, marched on Washington to demand action and to camp there to dramatize their plight to the government.

One Man, One Vote

Right to equal represen- tation in legislatures

The equal-protection clause has quite recently been injected into another highly controversial field of American politics: the apportionment of seats in state legislatures. In a series of decisions, the Court has cast aside its traditional position that apportionment systems are not reviewable because of the apparent lack of judicial power to correct legislative error, and has held that such systems for both houses of state legislatures may be reviewed by the national courts under the equal-protection clause and may, if found to depart sharply from equal representation according to population, be invalidated, regardless of state constitutional specifications requiring that attention be given area or governmental unit as well as population in designing districts for one or both houses. Other state political arrangements aimed at maintaining rural or white domination of politics, such as the county-unit systems for counting the vote in statewide elections in Georgia and Maryland and the redrawing of the boundary lines of Tuskegee, Alabama, so as to place most of the Negro population outside the municipal limits, have also been invalidated. The rule has also been applied, less rigidly however, to all forms of local government—school boards, county boards, city councils, and others as well as to representative districts for the national House of Representatives.

B. Right to Fairness on Governmental Procedures

It is an axiom of Anglo-American jurisprudence that a person suspected or accused of illegal behavior is entitled to fair trial, by humane procedures, and with the burden of proof resting on his accusers. This conception sharply differentiates the English-speaking world from that of the modern authoritarians with their secret police, torture-chambers, and stealthy apprehension. The constitutions of the United States and of the several states, in pursuance of our traditional ideas, surround the entire process of criminal justice with restrictions. And while the guilty occasionally escape conviction by hiding behind the ancient guarantees, the innocent usually find refuge in the shelter of these same time-tested rights.

> No person shall be held to answer for a capital or other
> infamous crime, unless on a presentment or indictment of a
> grand jury. . . .—Fifth Amendment

1. Indictment by grand jury

The grand jury is an institution of ancient origin, consisting of 12 to 23 citizens who hear the public prosecutor make accusations of crime and then determine if there is sufficient evidence to require the suspects to be held for trial. It was designed to prevent frivolous or capricious prosecutions by public officials. The procedure, however, is cumbersome and 28 states and the mother country, England, have abandoned it in favor of indictment by "information" of the district attorney. Even the national government authorizes the use of "information" procedure in major but noncapital offenses when the defendant agrees and in minor offenses at the discretion of the prosecution. The Supreme Court has accepted these procedures as within the spirit of the constitutional guarantees. When the grand jury is used, however, it must be constituted so as not to discriminate among races. Furthermore, once called, it cannot be completely controlled by the prosecutor and may call witnesses on its own initiative and thus launch investigations of suspected crime. It operates in secret.

> The privilege of the writ of habeas corpus shall not be suspended, unless when in cases of rebellion or invasion the public safety may require it.—Art. 1, Sec. IX, cl. 2

2. Writ of habeas corpus   The most revered of the great safeguards of personal security is the privilege of the writ of habeas corpus. This writ is a court order, addressed to any officer having custody of a prisoner, directing that the petitioner be brought before the court that the court may inquire if he is being properly detained. President Lincoln's suspension of the privilege in certain areas of the North during the Civil War evoked considerable legal controversy over the question of which branch of the government has this power. The general conclusion from this debate is that the function belongs to Congress but may be exercised by the President if authorized by statute. The state governments are similarly bound by provisions in state constitutions, although some of them have forbidden the suspension of the privilege under any circumstances. The uses of the writ have been steadily expanding over many centuries and the law surrounding its use is still developing. One of its growing uses is to test compliance of state authorities with proper constitutional procedures and it is frequently sought in national courts by those held in custody in the states.

> The trial of all crimes . . . shall be by jury;—Art. III, Sec. II, cl. 3.
>   In all criminal prosecutions the accused shall enjoy the right to a speedy and public trial by an impartial jury of the State and district wherein the crime shall have been committed. . . .—Sixth Amendment

3. Trial by jury   Like indictment by grand jury, trial by jury passed into American usage with the English Common Law. The Constitution provides for it in several places and no state constitution fails to ordain it also. It is, however, by common law that a jury must consist of 12 persons and must arrive at its verdict by unanimous vote. It is also by common law that the right of jury trial does not apply to cases in courts of equity, to cases in contempt of court, and to petty offenses or misdemeanors punishable only by small fines.

Formerly it was supposed that wherever applicable under constitutional provision or common law, jury trial must prevail. The Supreme Court has now held, however, that since the device is intended fundamentally for the accused's protection, he may, if he considers it to his interest to do so, waive the right in national proceedings; and many states allow the same discretion. The Court has now held that the Fourteenth Amendment requires a jury trial in all "serious" criminal cases and even in "serious" criminal contempt cases. The Court, moreover, has ruled that where juries are employed, they must not be made up deliberately to exclude workingmen, Negroes, or any other particular class of persons—although there still are states (Alabama, for example) in which women are debarred. Recently, the Court held that foes of the death penalty may no longer be automatically excluded from the jury in capital cases. State civil procedures that modify the old common law jury requirements have, typically, been upheld by the Court as in compliance with the Fourteenth Amendment.

> **The right of the people to be secure in their persons, houses, papers, and effects against unreasonable searches and seizures shall not be violated.—Fourth Amendment**

Another treasured inheritance from English Common Law is grounded upon the ancient maxim that every man's house is his castle. The language employed in the Fourth Amendment suggests that there are searches and seizures which are *reasonable* and defines them as those conducted on the basis of warrants (1) issued "upon probable cause, supported by oath or affirmation," and (2) "particularly describing the place to be searched and the persons or things to be seized." The Supreme Court has, however, recognized situations in which the police may legitimately make searches and seizures without a warrant. Thus if it is known or thought probable that a person guilty of a felony or breach of the peace has taken refuge in a certain house, officers of the law may go in after him without waiting for written authority. Likewise, if a search is to be made of a boat, automobile, airplane, or other vehicle which could take advantage of delay in order to escape, a warrant is not needed. In general, these rules are also imposed on the states by their constitutions or by the due-process clause of the Fourteenth Amendment as now construed by the Supreme Court. The possibility under our federal system of both state and national jurisdiction over certain offenses has surrounded this ancient right with a number of the most complex questions concerning the use of evidence obtained illegally—by wiretapping, for example—by one enforcement level or the other. The modern Court has been imposing increasingly strict standards on state and national enforcement officials and has forbidden them to use evidence obtained by wiretapping or electronic "bugging" devices except under carefully prescribed circumstances. The Department of Justice has, in consequence, sharply restricted all wiretapping by federal agents except in cases of na-

4. Security in the house

tional security. Widely varying practices by state and local officials in collection of evidence are being subjected to national standards of reasonableness by the courts under the Fourteenth Amendment. State health, fire, and other administration inspectors must have warrants to enter homes or business premises.

> No person—shall be compelled in an criminal case to be
> a witness against himself. . . .—Fifth Amendment

5. Protection against self-incrimination

In the last fifteen years, the frequent invocation of the Fifth Amendment by witnesses in widely publicized congressional hearings investigating subversion has brought into great prominence the ancient guarantees against self-incrimination contained therein. This old English rule, developed largely to prevent persons from being tortured to extract admission of guilt, has come down to us as a well-tested protection against inquisition of almost any type. It may be claimed by witnesses as well as by those accused and be pled as an excuse for not giving evidence even if that evidence only lends support to a charge of crime. Courts have repeatedly lashed out at those who assert that anyone who claims protection of this rule is obviously guilty, and in most courts in the land it is not permissible for the judge or the prosecutor to comment to the jury on the failure of a defendant to testify in his own behalf. The Supreme Court has recently modified an earlier ruling and declared that the privilege may not be infringed by the states under the Fourteenth Amendment. The Court has also held that the registration provision of the Internal Security Act of 1950, the gambling-stamp requirement, and the registration requirement imposed by law for the possession of certain weapons are all violations of the Fifth Amendment. There are a large number of national laws (the most recent is the Immunity Act of 1954, designed to aid investigation by Committees of Congress) and state laws authorizing the granting of immunity from prosecution in order to extract testimony from reluctant witnesses. In general, also, confessions extracted by arresting officers without adequate warning of rights and without legal advice for the defendant can no longer be used in subsequent proceedings.

6. Miscellaneous procedural guarantees

Under the Constitution, in matters involving national offenses and officers of the national government, a person accused of crime is guaranteed a speedy trial by an impartial jury of the district in which the crime was committed. He has a right to confront his accusers, to have counsel in making his defense, to compel the attendance of witnesses in his behalf. He may not be subjected to cruel and unusual punishment or required to pay excessive fines or to offer unreasonable bail. He may not be twice put in jeopardy of life or limb for the same offense. The state constitutions generally contain the same guarantees as against state actions, and the due-process clause of the Fourteenth Amendment assures national protection, as against state deprivation, of many of these rights. Furthermore, the Court has held that juveniles, criminally insane persons, persons on probation, and indicted indigents are all entitled to counsel at state expense if necessary and to most other elements of fair procedure.

The broadest of all guarantees of governmental fairness is the Constitution's requirement that neither the nation (Fifth Amendment) nor the states (Fourteenth Amendment) may deprive any person (individual or corporation) of "life, liberty, or property" without "due process of law," a guarantee which is also contained in all of the state constitutions. Notwithstanding its great significance, the phrase has never been fully and conclusively defined. Broadly equivalent to the "law of the land" as guaranteed in *Magna Charta* and to the "rule of law" upon which English jurists have traditionally placed the utmost stress, it has, like those phrases, been subject to steadily broadening and deepening interpretation. Certainly the constitutions do not fix its bounds, and neither do the courts. Efforts to apply it to the multifold actions and relationships of life have given rise to a stupendous amount of litigation and to an unending stream of judicial decisions.

7. Right to due process of law

As applied to the national government, the due-process clause supplements the more specific guarantees of the other amendments dealing with fair procedure. It imposes on national authorities the duty of providing "persons" with a *fair* trial before a proper court or administrative agency. They must be given proper notice, be allowed to present evidence, and be permitted, ordinarily, an appeal to a court of law to assert their rights. As we have noted above, the modern Court is applying these rules as well as the standards of fair procedure expressly provided in other parts of the Bill of Rights to the states in accordance with the due-process clause in the Fourteenth Amendment.

Due process and fair procedure

Although the due-process guarantee is one of the major constitutional supports of proper governmental procedure, it would claim much less historical interest if this were all it involved. Toward the end of the last century the Supreme Court gave the phrase a new meaning and a new direction which represented a sharp departure from the traditional view. Industrialization and urbanization of the nation were at that time revealing some of their less benevolent aspects, and state governments were attempting by various types of remedial legislation to mitigate the evils of rapid expansion. The Court, repeatedly invited to upset state efforts to regulate the economy, finally yielded to the idea that the due-process clause conferred upon it the power to review legislation to determine if it contemplated an *arbitrary* or *unreasonable* limitation on property rights. The problem was not whether the judicial or administrative procedures used by the state or prescribed by the law were fair, but rather whether the legislation or regulation was itself proper. This use of the constitutional clause is usually referred to as *substantive due process* to distinguish it from the *procedural due process*

Substantive due process

already described. The Court proceeded to invalidate state laws regulating industry, hours of labor, wages, rate-fixing for utilities if not based on proper evaluation of economic factors, and other aspects of the economic relations of individuals and groups. It also discovered new limits on the statutory authority of Congress arising from the Fifth Amendment's due-process clause. In general, the Court seemed to interpret the clause as if it prescribed the economic tenets of Adam Smith and made them the law of the land. In adopting this interpretation of the due-process clause, the Court further found that the word "person" was meant to include corporation. This view allowed it to consider any legislation which might be shown to threaten corporate property. The result of the attitude and theory of the Court was to plunge it into some of the bitterest political controversy of the past half-century and to earn for it the scorn of those determined to bring the economy under public control and the applause of those striving to stave off public regulation. The depression of the nineteen-thirties brought a new appreciation to the vast majority of the nation of the necessity of energetic governmental action in the economic field and, after some political maneuvering by President Roosevelt, it brought a new view to the Supreme Court. From its first reversal of precedent in 1937 when it sustained a state law regulating the wages of women and children, the Court has steadily broadened its view of allowable interference by the government in the economic relations of our society. "We have returned to the original constitutional proposition that courts do not substitute their social and economic beliefs for the judgment of legislative bodies," said Justice Black for the Court in 1963. "We emphatically refuse to go back to the time when Courts used the due process clause to strike down state laws regulatory of business and industrial conditions, because they may be unwise, improvident or out of harmony with a particular school of thought."

REFERENCES

H. J. Abraham, *Freedom and the Court: Civil Rights and Liberties in the United States* (New York, 1967).

A. P. Blaustein and C. C. Ferguson, Jr., *Desegregation and the Law* (New Brunswick, N. J., 1957).

W. J. Brennan, Jr., *The Bill of Rights and the States* (Santa Barbara, Calif., 1961).

I. H. Carmen, *Movies, Censorship and the Law* (Ann Arbor, Mich., 1966).

W. A. Carroll, "The Constitution, the Supreme Court, and Religion," *Amer. Pol. Sci. Rev.,* Vol. LXI, No. 3 (Sept., 1967).

Z. Chafee, *Free Speech in the United States* (Cambridge, Mass., 1941).

E. Cohn (ed.), *The Great Rights* (New York, 1963).

Commission on the Freedom of the Press, *A Free and Responsible Press: A General Report on Mass Communications* (Chicago, 1947).

The Constitution of the United States of America: Analysis and Interpretation, Annotated to June 30, 1964 (88th Cong., 1st Sess., Sen. Doc. #39).

E. S. Corwin, *Total War and the Constitution* (New York, 1947).

T. I. Emerson and D. Haber, *Political and Civil Rights in the United States* (3rd ed., Buffalo, 1967).

M. L. Ernst and A. U. Schwartz, *Privacy: The Right to Be Let Alone* (New York, 1967).

D. Fellman, *The Censorship of Books* (Madison, Wis., 1957).

———, *The Constitutional Right of Association* (Chicago, 1963).

———, *The Defendant's Rights* (New York, 1958).

———, *The Limits of Freedom* (New Brunswick, N. J., 1959).

J. Greenberg, *Race Relations and American Law* (New York, 1960).

E. N. Griswold, *The Fifth Amendment Today* (Cambridge, Mass., 1955).

R. J. Harris, *The Quest for Equality* (Baton Rouge, La., 1960).

H. M. Hyman, *To Try Men's Souls: Loyalty Tests in American History* (Berkeley, Calif., 1960).

A. W. Johnson and F. H. Yost, *Separation of Church and State in the United States* (Minneapolis, 1948).

M. R. Konvitz, *Expanding Liberties: Freedoms Gains in Post-War America* (New York, 1967).

———, *Fundamental Liberties of a Free People* (Ithaca, N. Y., 1957).

J. W. Landynski, *Search and Seizure and the Supreme Court: A Study in Constitutional Interpretation* (Baltimore, 1966).

E. Latham, *The Communist Controversy in Washington: From the New Deal to McCarthy* (Cambridge, Mass., 1966).

Learned Hand, *The Bill of Rights* (Cambridge, Mass., 1958).

R. McKeon, R. K. Merton, W. Gellhorn, *Freedom to Read: Perspective and Program* (New York, 1957).

B. Muse, *Virginia's Massive Resistance* (Bloomington, Ind., 1961).

L. Pfeffer, *Church, State, and Freedom* (Boston, 1953).

R. S. Randall, *Censorship of the Movies* (Madison, Wis., 1968).

To Secure These Rights: Report of the President's Committee on Civil Rights (Washington, D. C., 1947).

M. I. Sovern, *Legal Restraints on Racial Discrimination in Employment* (New York, 1966).

J. Tussman (ed.), *The Supreme Court on Racial Discrimination* (New York, 1963).

U. S. Commission on Civil Rights, *Reports* (Washington, D. C., 1958–1968).

C. Vann Woodward, *The Strange Career of Jim Crow* (New York, 1955).

B The Democratic Process

5

VOTING AND ELECTIONS

Democracy
and the
Constitution Throughout most of the nineteenth century, the American system of government was understood primarily in terms of the constitutional assignment of
powers among the several levels and branches of which it is composed. Since
about 1910 we have come to a more adequate realization of the implications
of the spread of democracy throughout the land. Today, one could, with
compelling reason, begin a description of our polity with the voter and the
elaborate arrangement of interest groups, parties, and communication
procedures by which he seeks to make his will felt in the determination of
public policy. Democracy has modified our constitutional arrangements in
ways and to an extent undreamed of by the founders. Its spread has challenged and will continue to challenge any institutional arrangements which
frustrate majority decision and which safeguard the position of entrenched
minority groups. The majoritarian democrat sees little validity in power
assignments which cannot be modified by popular will. The constitutionalist,
however, sees lawlessness and popular tyranny as the consequence of destroying the nicely calculated prohibitions of our legal tradition. The modern
American polity is, therefore, a complex and dynamic mixture of constitutionalism and democracy and we must now seek an understanding of the
second of these elements.

Government to many of us is some remote *they* who make decisions
which affect us but for which *we* have no direct responsibility. We read about
them in our newspapers, criticize *their* bungling, speculate about *their* mo-
tives and objectives. *We* feel no direct connection with *them*. We like to
think that we believe in something called democracy, a noble conception by
which men, or a large part of them, govern themselves. Only occasionally
do many of us identify our own parts in this great dream. On election day,

for example, thousands of us troop to the polls moved by some deep feeling that what we do on that day will in some way determine the course of national destiny. It is when we come to consider how, in fact, the people govern themselves that we begin to realize the complexities and subtleties of this system of government and also to feel a strong sense of personal identification with it. What then is the basis of our proud boast that here in America the people govern? How do you and I influence the conduct of our national, state, and local governments?

There are at least six ways by which almost every adult citizen may, and many in fact do, participate in this great experiment in popular government: (1) by voting on election day for candidates for the positions of power; (2) by expressing publicly views on the questions of the day; (3) by entreating public officials in behalf of or against a particular program or policy; (4) by joining an organization which expresses to those in power the views of its members on questions of public policy; (5) by contesting a governmental decree before the courts; and, (6) by joining a political party and perhaps working for it and contributing money to it. *How citizens participate in public affairs*

Throughout its short history democracy has meant to its proponents as well as its critics a very high degree of participation by the populace in decision-making. Certainly, most of us have been brought up to believe that an enlightened, interested, and civic-minded citizenry is necessary to successful self-government. There have been disagreements, to be sure, about the legitimacy, as well as the efficacy, of the various methods by which the people do participate in public affairs, but little doubt, that it is the duty of the citizen to pay attention to his government. It is, therefore, with some dismay that we confront the facts now being revealed by survey research techniques that the level of participation in America is after all not very high. From one-fifth to one-third of the adult population are almost completely indifferent to politics; they rarely even vote. About 60 percent vote but participate in no other important way. About 5 to 10 percent are activists who work for or contribute to parties, join interest groups, speak to or attend rallies, and in other ways described above seek to influence public policy. *Participation in America*

It would appear that either our system of civic education is woefully inadequate or that our understanding of the possibilities of the democratic system is incomplete. Students of this subject are energetically reviewing and reappraising the older concepts of what democracy entails. On one proposition at least most of the modern analysts join hands with the philosophers of yesterday and that is that popular elections of those who hold the reins of the state are fundamental to a democratic society. It is appropriate, therefore, to begin our analysis of the American democratic system by a consideration of voting. The other methods of participation or lack of it, we shall consider in subsequent chapters.

THE NATURE AND HISTORY OF SUFFRAGE

. . . the electors [of the House of Representatives] in each
state shall have the qualifications requisite for electors of the
most numerous branch of the state legislature.—Art. I, Sec. II,
cl. 1

Constitu-
tional
basis

Every democratic system defines those who are entitled to vote for the
officers of the government. In every system known to history this definition
has excluded some persons (aliens and children most commonly). It is
obviously of great consequence who makes this definition and on what basis,
since if any great numbers are excluded, especially if any particular class,
race, or religious group is excluded, to that extent the system is not genuinely
based on the great body of citizens. In the United States, this determination
has up to now been made by each of the 50 states. Each state has been left
largely free to determine for itself who might vote for national as well as for
state and local officers. The states are restricted by the Constitution only to
the extent that they may not deny the right to vote to those otherwise
qualified because of their race, color, previous condition of servitude
(Fifteenth Amendment), sex (Nineteenth Amendment), or failure to pay
a tax (Twenty-fourth Amendment), nor may they deny to any person the
equal protection of their laws (Fourteenth Amendment). The national electorate is, therefore, the sum of separate electorates determined by state constitutions and laws.

The
"right"
to vote

It might well be asked at this point, How can any person be denied
the right to vote? Is this not a natural right similar to the right of religious
freedom which cannot validly be withheld? The answer to this in American
constitutional theory and practice is that it is not a natural right of the type
called civil rights. It is a *legal* right that belongs only to those who have been
properly endowed with it. The Constitution does not guarantee to anyone
the right to vote as it does guarantee that freedom of speech may not be
infringed by the Congress or due process of law denied to anyone by the
states. The Constitution may and has been invoked, as we shall see, to
prevent discriminatory state regulation which effectively denied the vote
to certain classes of citizens contrary to its provisions. It does not, however,
confer the voting privilege on anyone.

Expansion
of the
suffrage

The legal theory and practice in determining who may vote may, perhaps, be best understood in the light of the history of the suffrage. When the
Constitution of the United States was adopted it could hardly be said to
have established a system of government as democratic as it is today. Although it recognized the idea of popular participation as the basis of just
government and although, in fact, a larger number of people were authorized

to and did participate in the processes of government than in the major nations of the world at that time, nevertheless, the suffrage was restricted to white, male, property-owners. Since that time, and especially since 1810, one after another of the restrictive qualifications has been abandoned and the suffrage progressively widened to embrace virtually the entire adult population of this country.

The main battle against property qualifications for voting occurred in the older states along the Atlantic seaboard in the period of 1810–1850. The frontier states had no such economic distinctions and virtually all of them entered the Union without property qualifications of any kind. It was partly the political strength and example of the newer states which forced the older ones to extend the vote to the "common" people. Antipathy to Irish-Catholic immigrants induced Connecticut in 1855 and Massachusetts in 1857 to require reading and writing tests designed to disqualify the illiterate foreign-born, but by 1860, the nation had substantially achieved universal, adult, white, male suffrage. *Elimination of property qualifications*

Since 1860, the suffrage has been broadened to include Negroes and women. A few Negroes were authorized to vote in a few states (mainly in New England) before 1860. General enfranchisement of the Negroes came in the northern states, however, only in the Civil War period. In the South, the Negro was enfranchised as a result of the pressure of the radical Republican majority in Congress during the Reconstruction era. The Fourteenth and Fifteenth Amendments were added to the Constitution by the victorious northern forces in an attempt, largely unsuccessful, to guarantee Negro suffrage in the South for all time. In many of the southern states, the Negroes were effectively disfranchised as soon as possible after the Union troops were withdrawn in 1877. In this century, the vote is once again being gradually extended to the southern Negro. *Enfranchisement of the Negro*

Demand for the enfranchisement of women was heard as early as the Jacksonian era. It was pressed rather vigorously in some states during the later stages of the Abolition movement, but the real campaign began in the eighties and nineties and achieved its first successes in Wyoming, Colorado, Idaho, and Utah. By the time the woman-suffrage amendment was placed before the states, women could vote in 11 states. The Nineteenth Amendment forbidding any state to withhold the ballot on account of sex was finally approved in 1920. Victory for the feminists in the struggle for the ballot was part of a larger movement for feminine independence in the home, in industry, and in society. As such, it both celebrated their newly won position and contributed to it. *Enfranchisement of women*

Together with the wide extension of the voting privilege in the last century there were also a few contractions. The addition of the requirement of registration, the development of more rigid residence requirements, and the imposition of literacy tests on some states all have served to reduce the number of persons eligible to participate in any particular election. *Contraction of the suffrage*

THE SUFFRAGE TODAY

General qualifications:

Although the qualifications for voting vary from state to state at the present time, there are some qualifications which are almost universally imposed and others which are employed only in certain states. In the first category are those relating to age, citizenship, and residence.

1. Age

The legal voting age in every state but four is 21. Georgia in 1943 and Kentucky in 1955 lowered the required age to 18. Alaska entered the union with the age fixed at 19 and Hawaii with it fixed at 20. In inaugurating the movement for a lower voting age, the Governor of Georgia (Ellis Arnall) declared that the "fresh viewpoint of youth" was needed in politics and that the young people would benefit from acquiring political experience at an early age. Elsewhere the argument most widely pressed was that if young men and women were old enough for military service they were old enough to vote. In a large number of states the matter was considered at that time and rejected. Interest then subsided until it was revived by President Eisenhower. He proposed in 1954 and again in 1955 that the Congress submit a constitutional amendment to the states authorizing citizens 18 and older to vote. The Congress on both occasions failed to respond. The public opinion polls from 1947 through 1967 showed steadily increased support for lowering the voting age and Congress returned to the question in 1968. President Johnson recommended a constitutional amendment and leading senators sponsored the requisite resolution without success as yet. Meanwhile a number of states have considered the matter and in all but Kentucky it has been rejected.

2. Citizenship

Western states used to bid for settlers by offering voting privileges to aliens who had taken out "first papers." Since 1926, when Arkansas at last fell into line, every state has required citizenship of its voters. A few states require a person to have been a citizen for at least 90 days. For many years the laws of citizenship also varied from state to state but with the passage of the Fourteenth Amendment the confusion ended and since then all persons born in the United States are citizens regardless of the status of their parents. Children born abroad to American parents are allowed to retain their citizenship under national statutes. Citizenship may also be acquired by naturalization on an individual basis by those who are 18 years of age and have lived in this country for five years, if they can read, write, and speak English and have not been associated with criminal or subversive elements.

3. Residence

The typical requirement relating to residence is that the voter shall have lived in the state at least one year, some specified portion of which (frequently three or six months) must have been spent in the county, and some briefer portion (often 30 days) in the district in which one's ballot is to be cast. No one may vote in a given election in more than one place; and this place must be the voter's legal residence, however little of his time he may actually spend there. Such requirements tend to prevent importations of "floaters" at election time, but operate also temporarily to disfranchise honest voters. In view of the mobility of our population, the numbers thus made ineligible probably exceed five million in recent elections.

The payment of taxes as a qualification for voting has at one time or another been a requirement in 19 states. Its major modern use, however, has been in the form of poll taxes required in southern states as part of a system to bar Negroes. After several years of agitation had succeeded in eliminating the tax requirement in all but five states, it was finally outlawed by constitutional amendment in so far as national elections are concerned. The Supreme Court in 1966 outlawed the requirement as far as state and local elections are concerned in the four states then using it. In six states, some kind of property-tax payment is required for those voting on local bond issues or special assessments. *Special qualifications: 1. Payment of taxes*

The imposition of educational or "literacy" qualifications for voting began in Connecticut in 1855 and spread from there to Massachusetts and much later to New York and other New England states. In these states it was aimed at immigrants. The device was borrowed in the eighteen-nineties by several of the southern states to keep Negroes and "poor whites" from voting and was copied by a few western states to exclude Orientals. Nineteen states (including four in New England, four in the West and six in the South) now have this requirement in some form. In a few states the test is confined to ability to read English. In most, however, the ability to write in English is also required—though in some the ability to write one's name is adequate. A few southern states employ an alternative test in the form of demonstrating to an election board (of white members) ability to "understand and give a reasonable interpretation" of a selected passage from the national or state constitution. The test is ordinarily conducted at the time of registration, and in the South at least, wide latitude in administering it is conferred on the local election officials. One of the fairer systems in the country is that adopted by New York in 1921 in which a test of reading and writing designed by experts is administered by the state educational department annually for those who have not successfully completed the sixth grade in public school. Where fairly administered, there is much to be said for this type of qualification, but it has been and is used mainly to keep Negroes from voting. To curb abuses, the Congress, in the Civil Rights Act of 1964 imposed certain standards for its use in national elections: It must be administered in writing and the candidate is entitled to see his corrected paper. Evidence of the successful completion of six grades of elementary schooling constitutes a rebuttable presumption of literacy. Despite these efforts, the tests continued to be administered in a discriminatory way, and on the recommendation of President Johnson, Congress, in the Voting Rights Act of 1965 outlawed the use of such tests in any state or county in which fewer than 50 percent of the voting-age population was registered to or actually voted in the 1964 election. *2. Literacy*

Disquali-
fications

Certain categories of persons are almost universally disqualified from voting: inmates of prisons or asylums; violators of certain election laws, for example, those forbidding bribery; malfeasants in office; vagrants.

THE PROBLEM OF ENFRANCHISING THE SOUTHERN NEGRO

The right of citizens of the United States to vote shall not be denied or abridged by the United States or by any State on account of race, color, or previous condition of servitude. The Congress shall have power to enforce this article by appropriate legislation.—Fifteenth Amendment

The southern states, as we have noted, were compelled to give Negroes the vote if they wished to be restored to partnership in the Union. For more than a decade the armies of the central government occupied the South to insure compliance with these commitments. The results of the northern policies were disastrous from the southern point of view, and the Reconstruction era has always been for them a black page in the nation's history. Gullible freedmen led by northern carpetbaggers depleted their treasuries and mocked their cultural and social traditions. The southern whites resorted to violence and intimidation through the Ku Klux Klan to regain control of their governments and, when the troops were withdrawn (in 1877), firmly and vigorously reestablished white supremacy, partly by these methods. Fearful that national intervention might again be attempted, unhappy over the demoralizing effects of forceful methods, and anxious to legitimatize white dominion, the southern statesmen cast about for "respectable" methods for surmounting the plain requirements of the Fifteenth Amendment. Agrarian discontent in the eighteen-eighties further stimulated certain groups to find methods for weakening the political power of the sharecropper and the small farmer—white or black.

The Mis-
sissippi
plan

In 1890 Mississippi pointed the way for her sister states by writing into her constitution clauses under which, in order to vote, one not only must have lived two years in the state and one year in the election district, but must have paid all taxes assessed against him (including a poll tax of $2), and must be able either to read any section of the state constitution or to give a reasonable interpretation of it when read to him. None of these was aimed at the Negro as such. The lengthy period of residence, however, barred large numbers of Negroes accustomed to drift from plantation to plantation. Even if a colored man succeeded in paying his poll tax on time (and it was artfully required to be paid a year before election time), he was likely to be careless enough to be unable to produce his tax receipt when called for. Few Mississippi Negroes could read, and still fewer could give an interpretation of a craftily selected passage from the state constitution likely to be accepted as "reasonable" by a white official with a strong predisposition against Negro voting. If, too, in replying to searching personal questions a candidate for registration was detected deviating an iota from the truth, he became guilty of perjury, for which he also could be disfranchised. When the Supreme Court scrutinized these provisions in a test case, it was unable to find that they in any manner violated the Fifteenth Amendment. Clauses of similar purport accordingly found their way into the constitutions of most other southern states—all going to show how ingenious men can become when trying to find a way around nationally ordained requirements not supported by local or regional public sentiment.

There was, however, one drawback: While a secondary object of the tests was in some instances to curb the political effects of radical (chiefly Populist) inclinations among poor whites, the restrictions operated to debar too many whites along with Negroes. But for this, also, a remedy was found—in the so-called grandfather clauses adopted at one time or another, as temporary constitutional amendments, in as many as seven different states. The clauses differed in details, but their general purport was to open a way by which any man otherwise qualified could avoid the tax and literacy requirements and become a permanently registered voter if either he or a lineal ancestor had been a voter on January 1, 1867. The significance of this date is that it preceded by two months the first act of Congress prohibiting the disfranchisement of freedmen. No Negro could get on a voters' list under the new provisions, but the poorest and most illiterate white could do so because he was the son or grandson of a voter of 1867. All of the clauses were for a duration of only a few years, or even a few months; and all had served their purpose and expired before the Supreme Court, in 1915, got around, in an Oklahoma case, to pronouncing them discriminatory, contrary to the Fifteenth Amendment, and therefore unconstitutional.

Grandfather clauses

Thus, constitutional and statutory disfranchisement of the Negro south of the Mason and Dixon line was accomplished with one barrier rising behind another in massive array. First of all, there was the poll tax, so obviously designed to trip up the Negro that in many places little or no effort was made to collect the tax at all from whites, and in any event payable only (whether by Negroes or whites) in election years—in effect, therefore, simply a fee for the privilege of voting. If that were surmounted, there was the literacy test, and sometimes an "understanding" test so administered that even instructors in Negro colleges often failed it. Beyond this might lie a "character" test, under which a Negro aspiring to vote must produce "evidence of good character," backed by testimony from as many as ten or a dozen witnesses, and satisfactory to white registration officials disposed to be incredulous. And crowning all this in later days, after the direct primary had come into vogue, was exclusion, by constitutional provision, statute, or party regulation, from participation in the only significant electoral contests in the one-party South: the Democratic primaries.

Negro disfranchisement in the South becomes general

It should be understood that the Negro was not kept from voting solely by these devices. Much evidence exists to show that the Negro had been "persuaded" to stay away from the polls before these laws were enacted. The laws tended to insure that intimidation would be unnecessary in the future. The result of the "persuasion," followed by the laws, however, was that Negro voting in the southern states fell to insignificant proportion. The border states of West Virginia, Kentucky, Tennessee, and Arkansas tended, however, to have larger Negro participation than the states of the Deep South.

New attack on the poll tax

Gradually the suffrage policies of the South became part of the accepted pattern of American politics. The acrimonious attacks of the late nineteenth century abated. In 1912, the Republican party stopped writing in its platform its traditional denunciation of southern practices. In the past three decades, however, the issue has exploded into national politics with almost as much force as before. The two world wars of this century were accompanied by heavy migration of the Negroes into northern industrial centers. Here they have become increasingly articulate participants in party organizations, inspiring sympathetic attention to their demands on behalf of their southern brethren. As a part of a general movement to eradicate racial discrimination in all its forms from the American scene, many groups have also sought to give the vote back to the southern Negro. The first major target of the urban leaders of the North was the poll tax. As recently as 1937, however, the Supreme Court was unable to see that, in the absence of prohibitive national legislation, the tax requirement was invalid. Congress has then been called upon repeatedly since 1942 to outlaw taxpaying qualifications for voting in national primaries and elections. President Truman strongly urged such legislation. Many states voluntarily abandoned the requirement or authorized so many exemptions as to weaken its effect. Finally, in 1962, after most states using it virtually abandoned it, the Congress laid before the states a constitutional amendment outlawing the taxpaying requirement, and the requisite ratifications were procured in 1964.

The attack on the "white primary"

The next attack was on the "white primary" rules of several of the southern states. Efforts to exclude Negroes as such from democratic party primaries had been successfully challenged in the courts in those instances where the exclusion rested on express statutory or constitutional provision. The Supreme Court, however, in 1935 could find nothing wrong with a "white primary" rule uttered by a party convention and not required by a state law. A new assault on the practice before a new court in 1944 brought a reversal of the earlier decision. Primaries form a part of the electoral system, said the Court, and where state law requires primaries this opens the door for a private organization to exclude Negroes. Thus, the exclusion is, in effect, an act of the state and is invalid. Several expedients to evade the consequences of this decision were also invalidated and the southern states then fell back upon the discriminatory administration of their numerous qualifications and applied most of them to primary elections.

With the demise of the "white primary," Negro voting in the South increased sharply but by 1950 probably did not exceed 20 percent of the Negro population of voting age and in some states was below ten percent.

In the mid-fifties, Republican leaders began to join northern, urban democrats in urging electoral reform. President Eisenhower sought legislation authorizing national intervention in behalf of eligible Negro voters. As part of the first civil rights legislation of this century, pushed through Congress against strong southern opposition by a Republican-Democratic coalition, the attorney general was authorized to seek injunctive relief in a national court to prevent threatened intimidation or coercion designed to prevent any person from voting for national officials. The Civil Rights Commission created by the law and authorized to inquire into deprivation of voting privileges held a series of inquiries in several southern cities on voting practices. As a result of the investigations it proposed certain changes in the law including the requirement that registration and voting records should be retained at least five years and that the president should be authorized to appoint a federal registrar to enroll voters in national elections where it can be shown that the state registrars have refused voter registration in a discriminatory way. These became the major issues in the debates in 1959 and 1960.

The Civil Rights Act of 1960 enlarged the powers of the Civil Rights Commission (the life of this Commission had been extended in 1959 for two more years and was extended again in 1961, 1964, and 1967); required that voting records and registration papers in national elections including primaries must be preserved for 22 months; and provided that when the attorney general won a civil suit in a case of deprivation of voting privileges he might then ask the court to make a finding that there was a "pattern or practice" of deprivation in the area. If the court found that such existed, then a Negro in this area could apply to the court for an order declaring him eligible to vote. Voting referees might be appointed by the court to hear requests for registration orders from deprived Negroes.

Under these laws the Department of Justice started numerous suits aimed at discriminatory administration of voting requirements, but the judicial process is a slow one and southern resistance was vigorous and stubborn. In 1961, the Civil Rights Commission issued a new report, *The Right to Vote,* summarizing months of intensive investigation and alleging that in about 100 counties in eight states there were reasonable grounds to believe that large numbers of Negro citizens are denied the vote largely by the discriminatory way in which the requirements are administered by white election officials. President Kennedy called repeatedly and unsuccessfully for more national action. Through 1963 amidst mounting violence, rioting, and determined demonstrations the Congress resisted until, stung by Kennedy's assassination and spurred by one of its own sons, now President, Lyndon Johnson, it finally passed the sweeping Civil Rights Act of 1964. Once again a coalition of Republican and northern–western Democrats

The "white primary" in collapse

The attack on discriminatory administration of voting requirements

Civil Rights Act of 1964

provided the legislative muscle great enough to break the southern filibuster in the Senate and thus make passage possible. The voting rights section was, however, considerably weakened in the process. The new law forbids disqualification from voting in national elections because of minor technical errors of omission or commission in registering or applying to register; makes it illegal to apply different standards to or require different procedures for individuals seeking to vote in the same district. It surrounds the literacy test with certain safeguards already described. After passage, the Negro leaders mounted new offensives to get their followers on the voting rolls and selected Selma, Alabama (in the heart of the "Black Belt"), as a test area for demonstrations against the continued difficulties placed in the way of registration. The National Guard had finally to be called into service to protect them, when during a proposed March to Montgomery, the capital, to petition the governor, they were met with violence. President Johnson then called upon Congress to pass even more sweeping legislation to get the Negro the vote. His proposals submitted in March, 1964, sought federal registrars, suspension of literacy tests, and enhanced authority for the attorney general to intervene in behalf of the Negro, especially in areas or districts where fewer than 50 percent of the persons of voting age are registered and where fewer than 50 percent actually voted in the elections of November, 1964. The Congress approved these recommendations in 1965 and national registrars appointed by the Civil Service Commission were immediately dispatched to the counties and states determined by the Census Bureau to be eligible for them. Included in the new law were not only bans on the literacy tests but also on tests of moral character, of educational achievement, of understanding, and also on requirements that a person be certified by other eligible voters. New voting laws, enacted by affected states to avoid the consequences of the new law, were required to be approved by the Attorney General or the national courts before they could take effect. The Civil Rights Commission, in 1968, reviewing developments under the acts of 1964 and 1965 urged the political parties to require their state party organizations to afford Negroes full and equal participation in all party affairs as a condition for seating of delegates in the conventions of that year.

The Supreme Court, in the meantime, had not been idle. It had outlawed a Louisiana literacy and constitutional-understanding requirement, and had opened the way for the attorney general to proceed against a whole state to enforce the civil rights laws, instead of using the slower district-by-district method heretofore employed. More than 1.3 million Negroes have registered to vote in the 11 southern states since 1965. The new lists now include about 60 percent of the Negro population of voting age. There is much yet to be done, as new forms of harassment are developing; but, although it may take a few years, the southern Negro is going to get the vote.

Voting
Rights
of 196

Negro Voting Registration in the South
1964–1968

STATE	Spring 1968				November 1964	
	WHITE VOTERS REGISTERED	NEGRO VOTERS REGISTERED	% VOTING AGE WHITES REGISTERED	% VOTING AGE NEGROES REGISTERED	NEGROES REGISTERED	% VOTING AGE NEGROES REGISTERED
Alabama	1,212,317	248,432	89.6	51.6	111,000	23.0
Arkansas	616,000	121,000	72.4	62.8	105,000	54.4
Florida	2,131,105	299,033	81.4	63.6	300,000	63.7
Georgia	1,443,730	322,496	80.3	52.6	270,000	44.0
Louisiana	1,200,517	303,148	93.1	58.9	164,700	32.0
Mississippi	589,066	181,233	91.5	59.8	28,500	6.7
North Carolina	1,602,980	277,404	83.0	51.3	258,000	46.8
South Carolina	731,096	190,017	81.7	51.2	144,000	38.8
Tennessee	1,434,000	225,000	80.6	71.7	218,000	69.4
Texas	2,600,000	400,000	53.3	61.6	375,000	57.7
Virginia	1,140,000	243,000	63.4	55.6	200,000	45.7
TOTAL	14,700,811	2,840,763	76.5	57.2	2,174,200	43.3

SOURCE: *Congressional Quarterly Weekly Report*, May 17, 1968, p. 1136.

PARTICIPATION BY THE VOTER

The southern Negro is desperately determined to get the vote. Thousands have and will risk grave injury and death to place their names on the polling lists and cast ballots on election day. And yet millions of their fellow citizens who could vote never do. In the presidential election of 1968, 45 million (38.3 percent) adults of voting age did not vote. In fact, since 1916 the turnout for a presidential contest has never exceeded 65 percent of the potentially eligible adult population and on two occasions (1920 and 1924) was below 50 percent. In mid-term elections for Congress and many state offices, the turnout in the past 50 years has never exceeded half the potential and on three occasions (1922, 1926, and 1942) was smaller than one-third. Local elections and primaries show even smaller rates of participation. Despite the spread of public education and the growing impact of political decisions on the lives of our people, their performance in this regard is much poorer than that of their grandfathers. Several elections in the period 1870–1920 attracted more than 75 percent of the potentially eligible adult population and some more than 80 percent. Most European democracies have much higher ratios of participation.

A part of the problem is legal and institutional. In view of the variations in state requirements and state practice, in every election some number of adult citizens are technically ineligible to participate. Until 1964, for example, residents of the District of Columbia could not vote in national elections and even now are not directly represented in Congress and thus may vote only for the chief executive. Estimates vary, but as of 1968, there were still 1,500,000–2,000,000 adult, southern Negroes as yet not registered for the reasons and by the means already described. The mobility of our population operates to deprive several million adults of their voting privileges because they cannot satisfy residence requirements. Of the 3 million resident aliens, more than half are of voting age but many are not yet able to satisfy residence requirements to become citizens. A large number of adults are on business trips on election day, are in military service, or are bedridden. Procedures for absentee voting are still cumbersome and inconvenient in 15 or 20 states. Of course, adult inmates of prisons are disqualified.

Much effort is currently being expended to eliminate these legal and procedural impediments to greater participation. We have already described the irrepressible determination to give the vote to the southern Negroes. A movement to allow newcomers in the state to vote in presidential elections gained its first victories in 1953–1954 in Wisconsin and Connecticut and has since spread to 13 other states. Seven states also permit former residents who have not acquired residence in their new homes to vote in presidential elections. Absentee voting has increased substantially in the past few elections as procedures have been made more convenient. President Kennedy in 1963 appointed a Commission on Registration and

Voting Participation to suggest further steps to increase turnout. In a report delivered later the same year, the Commission proposed: (1) reducing residence requirements everywhere to six months; (2) easing procedures for absentee voting and broader grounds for permitting it; (3) proclaiming election (national) day a national holiday; (4) eliminating of literacy tests and poll taxes as voting requirements; and (5) numerous other minor changes in state election laws. A judicial challenge to state residence requirements for participation in presidential elections on the grounds that they bore no reasonable relation to the election process was rejected by the Supreme Court.

The major aspect of the problem of nonparticipation, however, is not

POPULAR VOTE FOR PRESIDENTIAL ELECTORS, 1912-1968

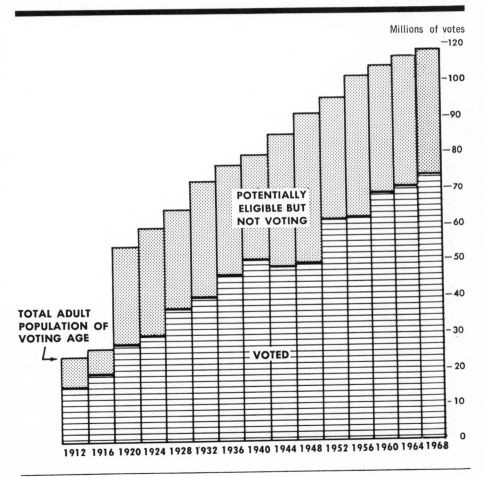

SOURCE: U. S. Bureau of the Census.

Population of Voting Age and Vote Cast for Presidential Electors and Members of U.S. House of Representatives

1920-1968

YEAR	ESTIMATED POPULATION OF VOTING AGE (MILLIONS)	VOTE FOR PRESIDENTIAL ELECTORS		VOTE FOR REPRESENTATIVES	
		NO.	%	NO.	%
1920	60,581	26,748	44.2	25,080	41.4
1922	62,984	–	–	20,409	32.4
1924	65,597	29,086	44.3	26,884	41.0
1926	67,912	–	–	20,435	30.1
1928	70,362	36,812	52.3	33,906	48.2
1930	72,602	–	–	24,777	34.1
1932	75,048	39,732	52.9	37,657	50.2
1934	77,215	–	–	32,256	41.8
1936	79,375	45,643	57.5	42,886	54.0
1938	81,514	–	–	36,236	44.5
1940	83,512	49,891	59.7	46,951	56.2
1942	85,759	–	–	28,074	32.7
1944	89,517	47,969	53.6	45,103	50.4
1946	91,497	–	–	34,398	37.6
1948	94,470	48,691	51.5	45,933	48.6
1950	96,992	–	–	40,342	41.6
1952	99,016	61,551	62.2	57,571	58.1
1954	101,097	–	–	42,589	42.1
1956	103,625	62,027	59.9	58,426	56.4
1958	106,083	–	–	45,818	43.2
1960	107,949	68,839	63.8	64,133	59.4
1962	110,266	–	–	51,264	46.5
1964	113,931	69,007	60.6	65,886	58.7
1966	114,377	–	–	52,902	46.3
1968	120,006	73,212	61.0	66,109	55.1

*Political
indifference* legal and technical but psychological and social. Modern studies of voting behavior indicate that almost one-third of adult America is apathetic to politics. The political dimension of modern life is outside the world of these citizens. They are uninformed and uninterested. They see little connection between political decision-making and the forces that shape their lives. On those rare occasions when some of them can be brought to the polls, their knowledge of candidates is scanty, of issues nil, and their motivations are confused. They identify with no political party and get no effective stimulation from family, school, church, or campaign. The uneducated and undereducated, the unskilled and semiskilled, young people, Negroes, rural-dwellers, and women contribute disproportionately to the ranks of the nonvoters. Some, perhaps, are alienated or cynical, but there is much yet to be learned about personality and electoral behavior. Why is the record of this century so much poorer than that of the last? Was rural and small-town America more civic-minded than metropolitan America? Is it better for democracy to get these people to the polls anyhow, anyway? Until they are adequately prepared may it not do more harm than good to pry them loose from their apathy?

THE CONDUCT OF ELECTIONS

The intentions of the voter are not completely realized unless he can record them in secret, on a ballot which provides him with a choice, in a place which he can get to, under circumstances which are not oppressive, and unless his vote is honestly counted and weighs in the result exactly as much as that of any other qualified voter. The administration of elections is thus an important element in the processes of popular government. More than a century and a half of experience has brought us nearer to the achievement of a fair, convenient, and honest election system but there are still many weaknesses. *Importance of election administration*

As the number of voters increased as a result of the expansion of the suffrage and the growth of population, and especially as people huddled in ever larger numbers in our great cities, the problem of identification of those qualified to vote became increasingly acute. In the small town, where everybody knows everybody, almost any resident could tell who could vote and who could not. In the great cities, however, ruthless political organizations began early in our national history to exploit the anonymity of the city throng by sending their lackeys to vote in one district after another. Some system of identification which would allow only those qualified to participate became necessary. Hence, the rise of systems of registration and of the preparation of voting lists to be used by those directing the election proceedings. Every state but Arkansas and Texas now requires some type of registration in connection with virtually all elections. In general, a voter must appear in person before a registration official some days in advance of the election and establish his qualifications. An earlier preference for *periodic* registration—a system requiring the voter to register annually or at fixed intervals—has gradually given way to the less expensive and more convenient system of *permanent* registration. In the permanent system now used by 45 states (statewide in 37 states and for certain areas in the others) a voter registers but once and his name remains on the list as long as there is no reason for removing it. Typically, if he does not vote in any election for two years his name is stricken from the list. The main problem of the permanent registration system is keeping the lists up to date by adding newcomers and deleting those who have died or moved away. Sluggish and partisan administration of the system opens the door for the "cemetery" and the "vacant house" vote. *Registration*

In order for each voter to be able to get to the polls and to cast his ballot in the same day, it is necessary that cities and counties be divided into polling districts. These districts are called *precincts* and are laid out by city or county officials. Typically, a precinct is designed to contain from 200 to 1,000 voters and is a subdivision of a city ward or a rural township. Each precinct contains a polling place where the voting occurs. In general, school houses, fire stations, or other public buildings are now used for this purpose *Creation of precincts* but in some areas private quarters (stores usually) are rented by the local officials.

Election officials

The next stage in preparing for elections is the designation—largely on a temporary basis—of a large number of election officials to preside over the polls on election day, to count the ballots and to decide disputes. These officials are selected most everywhere on a partisan basis, with the leaders of each party designating their choices for each precinct to the city, county, or state officials charged with the selection. Most state laws require that members of each party serve in each district. The theory that bipartisan selection will prevent fraud in the polling place is only partly supported by the facts.

Casting the ballots

When, on election day, the voter enters the polling place, he takes his turn in identifying himself to the clerks, carries a blank ballot to a screened compartment, or "booth," marks the ballot according to his preferences, folds the ballot, and emerging, deposits it in the ballot-box, and is duly checked off as having voted. Under only one circumstance may his privacy in the voting booth be invaded: if on account of blindness, illiteracy, or other handicap, he asks for assistance, one clerk of each party may, under normal arrangements in most states, enter the booth to give it.

Voting machines

Paper ballots are gradually disappearing and voting machines are coming more and more into use. More than two-thirds of the states now authorize them. Where such machines are employed, the voter identifies himself at the polls in the usual way, but instead of receiving a printed ballot, is directed to the machine, which is enclosed by a curtain. He votes by merely pulling levers—a single master lever (in states providing such) to vote a straight ticket, otherwise individual levers for particular candidates. Automatically recording the votes, and simultaneously adding them up, the voting machine has the great advantages of complete secrecy, economy of time, elimination of defective votes, and full tabulation of results the moment the polls are closed. Aside from hesitancy to adopt new ways, and perhaps in some cases the lukewarmness of politicians toward a device that cannot be easily manipulated, the main obstacle to wider employment of voting machines is the cost of the machines themselves—something like $1,700 apiece, besides transportation and upkeep. A few districts are experimenting with electronic tallying systems. In the elections of 1966, voters in 40 counties or cities registered their preferences on punch cards or ballots marked for computer processing.

Counting and reporting the results

When the polls close, the results are tabulated by the election officials and entered upon an official "return" which is sent to the county or city election board to be consolidated with those from other precincts. In a state-wide or national election these city or county returns are then forwarded to a state canvassing authority. All of this, of course, takes some time and it is usually several days after the election before the official canvass is completed and the results formally recorded. Meanwhile, however, the

FULL VIEW OF A MODERN VOTING MACHINE

totals from each precinct are phoned into the newspapers, the city clerk, the police or the party headquarters where they are totaled, and these unofficial returns are announced hour by hour through the night so that the public is informed how the election is coming out.

The task of the precinct officials is completed when they return to their superiors all of the ballots (used, spoiled, and unused), poll-books,

DETAIL OF A VOTING MACHINE

voters lists, and tally sheets which had been issued to them. When paper ballots are used, all are deposited in a sealed ballot-box where they are kept for a specified period. Dishonest counting, stolen ballot-boxes, stuffed ballot-boxes, and mutilated voting machines appear to be a diminishing characteristic of this phase of election administration. In the past these practices were all too common in virtually every large city.

Disputed elections   The final stage in the process is the issuance of a certificate of election to each person declared elected by the official county (county clerk) or state (secretary of state) canvassing authority. This certificate is prima facie evidence of legal right to hold the office. It is not, however, conclusive.

All state laws make provision for disputed elections. Such cases are commonly settled in the courts except that national, state, and local legislative bodies invariably have the power to settle all such contests involving their own membership. Most states also make some provision for a recount in disputed cases. Many such laws require the candidate making the protest to pay all or part of the costs.

BALLOT FORMS

The Australian ballot in general use

It took about a century for the American voter universally to achieve secrecy in casting his vote. Votes for many decades were cast orally and in public with untold pressures and irregularities surrounding the process. Then, for a time, each party printed its own ballots, frequently on colored paper so that observers could tell how people voted. Since 1888, however, the Australian ballot has been adopted by every state. The essence of the Australian system is that the only ballots allowed to be used at the polls are prepared by responsible public officials at public expense in accordance with forms prescribed by law and can be cast without possibility of detection of the ticket or person for whom one has voted. The ballot is normally in blanket form, that is, bearing on a single sheet the complete list of offices to be filled and of candidates; although when national, state, and city elections are held simultaneously, the names of candidates for presidential elector, and also of candidates for municipal offices, are sometimes printed on separate sheets. Where voting machines are used, these are prepared by public officials in accordance with state laws and are identical for all voters in the same constituency.

Ballot forms

The arrangement of names on the ballot or machine varies from state to state but, in general, tends to conform to one of two plans: the *party-column* ballot, introduced in Indiana in 1889, and now used by 32 states; and the *office-group* ballot, introduced in Massachusetts in 1888, and now used in some form in 18 states. The party-column ballot is designed to facilitate "straight-ticket" voting and the other to emphasize the office rather than the party.

RECALL ELECTIONS

Purpose

Normally, elections are held only when officers' terms are about to expire, or occasionally to fill a vacancy arising from the death or resignation of an incumbent. Elections are sometimes held in reverse, aimed at "recalling" an official in the midst of his term. In the early part of the present century, with a tide of "direct" popular government running strong, many people became enamored of the idea that the voters ought to be in a position to oust an elected official in the midst of his term if they were displeased with him. The idea took hold to such an extent that a dozen states adopted

Democratic Ticket

DEM.	For United States Senator ALEX M. CAMPBELL
DEM.	For Secretary of State CHARLES F. FLEMING
DEM.	For Auditor of State JAMES M. PROPST
DEM.	For Treasurer of State F. SHIRLEY WILCOX

Republican Ticket

REP.	For United States Senator HOMER E. CAPEHART
REP.	For Secretary of State LELAND L. SMITH
REP.	For Auditor of State FRANK T. MILLIS
REP.	For Treasurer of State WILLIAM L. FORTUNE

Prohibition Ticket

PROHI.	For United States Senator LESTER N. ABEL
PROHI.	For Secretary of State J. RALSTON MILLER
PROHI.	For Auditor of State GARNETT JEWELL
PROHI.	For Treasurer of State HORACE N. SMITH

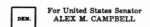

PARTY COLUMN BALLOT FORM

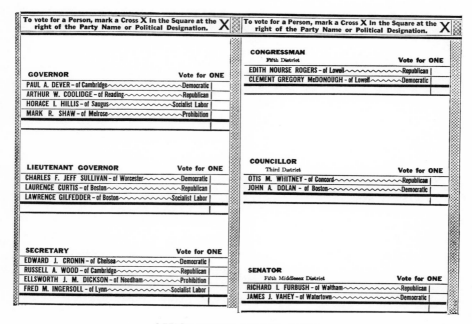

To vote for a Person, mark a Cross X in the Square at the right of the Party Name or Political Designation. X

GOVERNOR — Vote for ONE
PAUL A. DEVER – of Cambridge — Democratic |
ARTHUR W. COOLIDGE – of Reading — Republican |
HORACE I. HILLIS – of Saugus — Socialist Labor |
MARK R. SHAW – of Melrose — Prohibition |

LIEUTENANT GOVERNOR — Vote for ONE
CHARLES F. JEFF SULLIVAN – of Worcester — Democratic |
LAURENCE CURTIS – of Boston — Republican |
LAWRENCE GILFEDDER – of Boston — Socialist Labor |

SECRETARY — Vote for ONE
EDWARD J. CRONIN – of Chelsea — Democratic |
RUSSELL A. WOOD – of Cambridge — Republican |
ELLSWORTH J. M. DICKSON – of Needham — Prohibition |
FRED M. INGERSOLL – of Lynn — Socialist Labor |

To vote for a Person, mark a Cross X in the Square at the right of the Party Name or Political Designation. X

CONGRESSMAN
Fifth District
EDITH NOURSE ROGERS – of Lowell — Republican |
CLEMENT GREGORY McDONOUGH – of Lowell — Democratic |

COUNCILLOR
Third District — Vote for ONE
OTIS M. WHITNEY – of Concord — Republican |
JOHN A. DOLAN – of Boston — Democratic |

SENATOR
Fifth Middlesex District — Vote for ONE
RICHARD I. FURBUSH – of Waltham — Republican |
JAMES J. VAHEY – of Watertown — Democratic |

OFFICE BLOCK BALLOT FORM

110

some form of recall procedure for use against state and local officers (usually elective ones only).

Except for the manner in which it is initiated, a recall election does *Procedure* not differ greatly from any other one. When a movement to oust a given official gets underway, a paper setting forth the charges against him, and known as a "petition," is circulated in a quest for signatures. If the requisite number (usually about 25 percent of the electorate of the area concerned) is obtained, the city clerk or other official with whom it is filed sets a date for a recall election (unless a regular election is about to take place). If the official whose recall is sought chooses not to face the issue, he may simply resign. If, however, he prefers to fight for vindication, his name is placed on the ballot along with the names of any other persons nominated (usually by petition) to succeed him. The voters then render the verdict. If the incumbent polls the largest number of votes, he continues in office. But if one of his opponents outstrips him, the victor forthwith assumes the office and fills out the remainder of the term.

In practice, the recall has proved a very modest addition to our elec- *Results* toral usages. There is, it is true, no way of measuring its moral effect upon officeholders, but one can hardly believe that the comparatively few instances in which the device has been successfully invoked by dissatisfied voters represent all of the situations in which officials deserved to be ousted. A goodly number of local officers, including a mayor of Los Angeles, have been recalled in California—a mayor also in Seattle and one in Detroit. But in only two instances have officials chosen by the voters of an entire state been reached. It is significant that there have been no new state adoptions of the plan in more than 30 years. The terms of most public officers are short enough that dissatisfaction can readily be registered in the regular election.

CRITICISM OF THE ELECTORAL SYSTEM

Although much remains to be done, especially in our larger cities, to *The task* insure a fairer, less expensive, more convenient, and more honest system *of the* for casting and counting the votes, the improvements of the past half-century *electorate* in all these respects have been substantial. The most persistent and thoughtful criticism of our electoral process is that it heaps too large a task on the voter. He is called upon to vote too frequently on too many offices and propositions. Not only is there an election of some kind in many states every year but, if primaries are included, there are two and even three a year. It is not easy for the average citizen to keep up an intelligent interest and to take an active part in so many electoral contests. More serious than this, when he does go to the polls he is confronted with a long ballot filled with scores of names and dozens of offices. He cannot easily be familiar with the duties of so many offices or the qualifications of all of the candidates for them. The length and complexity of the typical ballot may be accounted for: (1) by the fact that in many states national, state, and local elections occur at the same time; (2) by the use of popular referenda in many states which require the voter to express his views on proposed constitutional amendments, municipal charter changes, pieces of legislation or bond issues; (3) by the large number of state and local offices that are filled by election. A great many voters start off well by voting for President, governor, senators, and perhaps members of the House of Representatives but then succumb to "voter's fatigue" and never reach members of the state legislature, the elected state officers, local officers, or referred propositions. The vote on constitutional amendments, for example, is rarely more than 75 percent of the vote for governor or senator. Politicians with a small but solid block of votes to be cast for local officials can frequently determine the outcome of these minor contests. Few voters trooping to the polls to select a President of the United States will be even mildly informed on the candidates for coroner when they reach that office on the ballot.

The short ballot   The movement for reform is commonly called the short-ballot movement. One of the remedies proposed is to hold state and local elections at a different time from national elections. This simplifies the ballot in any given election and also has the merit of focusing attention on state and local issues. This is now being done in a number of states. Another remedy is sharply to reduce the number of elective officers. Among our national officials, only the President and members of Congress are elected. If the same policy were adopted in state, county, and municipal government, the ballot would be much simpler. There is no excuse, say the critics, for electing essentially administrative or judicial officers. Provision should be made for appointing judges, sheriffs, coroners, district attorneys, state treasurers, and all of the other offices of this type, which clutter up the ballot and confuse and irritate the voter. Promoters of these reforms, however, find a deep resentment among many voters against proposals that appear to be taking away the power of the people.

REFERENCES

S. D. Albright, *The American Ballot* (Washington, D. C., 1942).
———, *Ballot Analysis and the Ballot Changes Since 1930* (Chicago, 1940).
D. Anderson and P. E. Davidson, *Ballots and Democratic Class Struggle: A Study in the Background of Political Education* (Palo Alto, Calif., 1943).
E. Burdick and A. J. Brodbeck, *American Voting Behavior* (Glencoe, Ill., 1959).
A. Campbell, P. Converse, W. Miller, and D. Stokes, *The American Voter* (New York, 1960).
Committee on Election Administration, National Municipal League, "A Model Election Administration System," *Nat. Mun. Rev.,* Supp., Vol. XIX, 625–671 (Sept., 1930).
Council of State Governments, *Book of the States,* biennially, articles and tables on election laws, voter qualifications, etc.

J. P. Harris, *Election Administration in the United States* (Washington, D. C.,
  1934).

———, *The Registration of Voters in the United States* (Washington, D. C.,
  1929).

V. O. Key, Jr., *Politics, Parties, and Pressure Groups* (5th ed., New York,
  1963).

———, *Southern Politics in State and Nation* (New York, 1949), Chaps. XXI,
  XXIII–XXXI.

L. W. Milbrath, *Political Participation* (Chicago, 1965).

President's Commission on Registration and Voter Participation, *Report* (Washington, D. C., 1963).

R. Scammon (ed.), *American Votes 3: A Handbook of Contemporary American Election Statistics* (5 Vols., Pittsburgh, Pa., 1962–1964).

C. O. Smith, *A Book of Ballots: Representative Facsimile Ballots of Local, State,
  and National Governments* (Detroit, 1938).

U. S. Bureau of the Census, *Elective Offices of State and County Governments*
  (Washington, D. C., 1946).

U. S. Civil Rights Commission, *Voting* (Final Report, Vol. I, Washington, D. C.,
  1961).

J. L. Walker, "Ballot Forms and Voter Fatigue: An Analysis of the Office
  Block and Party Column Ballots," *Midwest Jour. of Pol. Sci.,* Vol. X,
  No. 4 (Nov., 1966).

6

PUBLIC OPINION AND POLITICAL-INTEREST GROUPS

Voting is
not the
whole of
democracy
The solitary citizen in the privacy of the polling booth, casting his vote for those who will direct his government, is a stirring dramatization of the processes of democracy. In this great drama each player, the humble and the proud, the rich and the poor, the intellectual and the workingman is equal to every other player. It is easy, however, to mistake election day for the whole of government by the people. The people of the Soviet Union also vote and in very large numbers. With them, however, voting is a testimonial to the virtue of their rulers; it is not a process for giving them direction. We believe that a democratic system must offer the voter a choice among competing programs or policies. The victor in the contest must emerge with some sense of what he is to do with his victory. Furthermore, the governors of the nation should, as we believe, be made rather persistently aware of the desires of the governed. We expect our officials to resolve the conflicts in society, and this requires that they know what these conflicts are and who and what is involved.

Group
basis of
politics
Influencing public policy is a far more complex task than selecting persons to hold office. Electing persons committed to the policies that we desire is but one way in which this is done. A great deal more than voting is involved even in making sure that the persons who stand for office are committed to some policies. In this aspect of democratic government the individual, as such, is relatively powerless and ineffectual. By associating himself with others of similar persuasion he mobilizes and articulates his interests and desires and places himself in a position to give direction to the government. The constituent elements of society are not solely atomic individuals or even families but also groups of many kinds. It is through the group that the individual participates in and reacts to society. It is in terms of the group that the individual very largely defines the "public good" or the "general welfare." It is as members of a group that individuals realize their personal or familial ambitions. Group activity is as much a part of the processes of

government as individual behavior. Not all groups, of course, have political implications. A great many of them are formed to advance the interest— religious, economic, social, fraternal, racial—of the individuals who compose them. Advancing the interest of a group, especially the economic interest, commonly involves participation in the political process. The state with its vast power and its traditional prestige is in a position to advance benevolently or to curtail harshly the interest of any segment of society.

Groups which seek to advance the interest of their members in the political arena may be called *political-interest groups* to distinguish them from groups with other objectives. Some authors refer to these groups as *pressure groups,* which is rather a designation of one of their typical methods than a description of their general orientation. It is through such groups, however named, that citizens may influence the policies of government. *Political-interest groups*

One of the outstanding characteristics of the American system of government is the great multiplicity and diversity of political-interest groups which operate within it. The ease of formation, the intensity and scope of activities undertaken, and the political concern of these groups in our society exceeds that of any other in the modern world. This may be attributed in part to the tremendous technological development in the United States in the last century, accompanied as it has been by increasing specialization of function, by increasing interdependence, and by increasing ease of communication over wide distances. The rapidity of technological change has stimulated the formation of groups to soften the hardships associated with such rapid change. To put it another way, groups spring into being as a result of maladjustment in social or economic relations and seek to order anew, relationships which have been shattered by technological change. The labor union, for example, is a response to the factory system, accompanied by the removal of the management from daily face-to-face contact with the laborer. The second factor contributing to the growth and activity of political-interest groups in American society is the tolerance of our laws and customs. Freedom of association is a cherished cornerstone of the American way and is protected against undue governmental restriction. Some observers assert that we are a nation of joiners; the necessity for group identification is a characteristic of the American individual. However this may be, it certainly is demonstrable that our society comprises more political-interest groups than any other today. *Interest groups in American society*

The interests of some groups are very frequently served only at the expense of the interests of others. The clash of such interests is the very essence of political dynamics. From the beginning of our national life the activities of interest groups have been regarded by many as sordid, unpatriotic, and dangerous to social unity and political stability. Sensational exposés of the behind-the-scenes activities of the "interests" in the legislative halls or the administrative offices still shock large segments of the American populace and fill them with a sense of the futility of democratic government and the treachery of their officials. Group interest, in this view, is opposed to *The clash of interests* national, or public, interest. It is unkind but just to point out that the interest groups whose conduct revolts us and whose machinations we distrust are not the groups to which we belong. James Madison, in the most frequently quoted of the Federalist papers (No. 10), revealed his keen understanding of the role of interest groups in society and of the place of the government in respect to them:

> A landed interest, a manufacturing interest, a mercantile interest, a moneyed interest, with many lesser interests, grow up of necessity in civilized nations and divide them into different classes, actuated by different sentiments and views. The regulation of these various and interfering interests forms the principal task of modern legislation, and involves the spirit of party and faction in the necessary and ordinary operations of the government.

In the same essay Madison took some pains to show that the constitutional arrangements of 1787 were designed to prevent any one group from ever getting the upper hand. Whether regarded as signs of illness or of health in the body politic, the activities of interest groups are an essential part of the American scheme of democratic government. It is impossible to understand the behavior of political leaders, legislators, executives, judges, or even the voters themselves except in terms of the groups with which they tend to identify themselves or from which they expect support.

American government and interest groups   One other characteristic feature of our governmental system influences not only the number but the activities of the interest groups of our society. The federal system, the division of power among three branches of government at the various levels, and the two-party system provide an unusually large number of points of access to power and influence. Interest groups thus may aspire to influence by working at a number of entrances, and each of the doors is likely to be well attended by numerous and conflicting groups. No single door leads certainly and inexorably to domination of the state.[1]

POLITICAL-INTEREST GROUPS IN ACTION

Number of groups   How many political-interest groups are active on the American scene no one can say with accuracy. At least 500 maintain permanent headquarters in the national capital but this is only a small portion of those that are politically active at some level of government. The Department of Commerce in 1949 listed 4000 national trade, professional, civic, and other associations. If account is taken of local branches, chapters, affiliated units and independent local groups, there are perhaps 150,000 groups more or less active in politics. The number swells or recedes daily as new groups are

---

[1] For balanced and comprehensive treatments of the role of interest groups in American government consult D. B. Truman, *The Governmental Process* (New York, 1951) and A. F. Bentley, *The Process of Government* (New York, 1908). This section is very largely based upon these two works.

formed and old ones languish. Most of these groups and associations have interests other than political ones and the intensity of their political activity varies widely from one year to the next and among themselves. All of them are at least potential political forces. Even among those that are regularly active politically there is great diversity. Some number only a handful of adherents; others have memberships running into the millions. Some have little money to spend; others have a great deal. Some have more or less elaborate headquarters and secretariat, others engage the attention of one part-time employe. It is possible here to describe only a few of the more important ones.

One of the largest and most aggressive spokesmen for the "business community" is the Chamber of Commerce of the United States. The Chamber is essentially a federation of local Chambers of Commerce and these include firms as well as individuals and typically embrace the merchants, manufacturing establishments, and financial and service institutions in each substantial community. It is thus a cross section of the "business" interests of the country and cannot and does not commit itself to political issues about which the business community is sharply divided. In the national scene it can regularly be found attacking governmental regulation of prices or wages, supporting reductions in the tax rates on profit or investment, advocating rigid economy in government—except in the public works fields where many of its local chapters are strong pleaders for new post offices and river and highway improvements—and assailing any government protection for labor unions. The national headquarters produces and publishes material for the members, for Congress, and for congressional committees, urging its point of view on matters in which it is interested. In *Nation's Business* it presents its views to the public. Its position in national questions is frequently determined by the results of a referendum of its members.

Business groups

Close to the Chamber in size and even more aggressively belligerent in behalf of the interests of industrialists is the National Association of Manufacturers (N.A.M.) organized in the eighteen-nineties. Composed of firms engaged in every type of manufacturing, its chief focus throughout this century has been to counteract the power and influence of organized labor. Since 1933, when it was reorganized, it has been more or less dominated by the large corporations. It can be relied upon to support governmental curbing of labor unions, private enterprise, economy in government, low taxes (on profits, incomes, or manufacturing), and similar views on which industry as a whole is agreed. It maintains friendly, and in some cases paternal, relations with the thousands of trade associations organized in the last three or four decades to promote the interests of particular industries, such as the Cotton Manufacturers Association, Newspaper Publishers Association, Iron and Steel Institute, Automobile Manufacturers Association. In the *N.A.M. News* its staff reports to the members on political developments and policy positions.

The outstanding pleaders for the interests of organized labor are the

Labor
groups

American Federation of Labor and Congress of Industrial Organizations (A.F.L.–C.I.O.) and the railroad brotherhoods. The A.F.L.–C.I.O., like the Chamber of Commerce, is a federation, in this case of unions, and represents a recent merger of the A.F.L. with the C.I.O. Many of the older A.F.L. unions are organized on the craft basis (carpenters, plumbers, etc.) while many of the C.I.O. unions are organized on the industrial basis (auto workers, steel workers, etc.). The federation is importantly concerned with achieving peaceful relations among these unions and with representing the unions' point of view to the public and to the government. Traditionally, the A.F.L. had opposed governmental restriction on the freedom of labor to use its customary methods in dealing with employers. It had also opposed the use of governmental power in regulating many aspects of the economy. It has been gradually modifying its laissez-faire attitude to one more sympathetic to governmental intervention in behalf of workingmen. And now it will usually be found with its new partner supporting minimum wage legislation, unemployment insurance, public housing, and many public welfare programs. The C.I.O. had been more disposed to governmental action from its origin than its parent, the A.F.L. Its representatives could usually be found supporting emergency price controls, wage and hour regulation, social insurance, expanded public educational programs, and many other policies aimed at benefiting the laboring man. The merger of these two great federations late in 1955 produced what has been described as the most formidable interest group in American politics. Since merger, however, one of the largest unions, the Teamsters, has withdrawn amidst charges of corruption and dictatorship in its organization. The railroad brotherhoods are the most conservative of the union organizations. They direct a large share of their political energies to those special programs of government dealing with the railroad industry.

Farm
groups

The most powerful organization representing the farmers' interests is the American Farm Bureau Federation. A product of agrarian discontent in this century, it is a federation of county farm bureaus organized originally around the county extension program of the United States Department of Agriculture. Although its membership blankets the nation, it is especially strong in the Midwest and South and is sometimes described by its critics as an alliance of cotton and corn. Clearly it represents the more successful farmers. The Bureau speaks with a strong, and frequently a compelling, voice on such subjects as price supports, parity, increased agricultural research and extension and against high property taxes, governmental production controls, and trade regulation. The National Grange dates from the agrarian upheavels of the eighteen-seventies and at one time was one of the most belligerent of all farm organizations. Its membership and strength are now largely confined to New England and the Middle Atlantic states and it reflects the conservatism of the farmers of those areas. It is a strong supporter of the family farm against the large commercial farm, an enemy of organized labor, and an eloquent advocate of the spiritual superiority of rural life. The National Farmers Union is the most reform-minded of the great farm groups and represents the marginal farmers of the Plains. Its strength is centered in Oklahoma, Nebraska, Colorado, and the Dakotas. It has been a strong supporter of high, rigid price supports, the cooperative movement and has been consistently friendly to organized labor.

The newest and most militant of the farm organizations is the National Farmers Organization, which has organized a number of strikes for higher prices against processors of farm products.

This is but a small sample of active and influential groups identified with the great sectors of our economy. Every sector has its group or groups. *Other groups* And not only every sector of the economy, almost every sector of our society has a spokesman for its interests. The American Legion and the Veterans of Foreign Wars are constantly pressing the claims of ex-servicemen for bonuses, pensions, rehabilitation grants, hospitalization, and other services and also are active policemen of the purity of our national ideology, laying about them against all critical, "pink," radical, or unorthodox political or economic opinions. The National Association for the Advancement of Colored People battles discriminatory legislation and private prejudice against the Negro; the Navy League sponsors appropriations for expanding the fleet; the Civil Liberties Union patrols the frontiers of the Bill of Rights against judicial, legislative, or executive encroachment; the National Education Association promotes the interests of teachers and administrators of the public schools; the League of Women Voters pushes vigorously for administrative reform and for many other items on its national, state, or local agenda. For every interest—consumer, homemaker, child, patriot, censor, preacher—there can be found some group seeking to protect or advance it.

Effectiveness in advancing the interests of the group in the political arena is generally held to depend in large part on organization. A treasury, *Group organization* a permanent staff, a headquarters, an annual convention, a news organ, these are regarded as minimal needs for group success. Many groups are organized in the most casual way with little money and no staff. The group interests, however, which persist and which command attention and enjoy influence are, typically, highly organized. Commonly, the group is supported by dues or contributions from the members supplemented by gifts from affluent supporters. Several of the groups operate profitable enterprises (publishing, insuring, loaning) as a source of part of their fiscal requirements. Many groups which lay claim to large membership and substantial popular sympathy are entirely supported by a few large contributors whose backing is not apparent. Many of the groups operating in national politics are federations of local or state groups which are active at those levels. These groups are likely to exhibit less cohesion and to have more internal disagreements on policy than the groups with unitary-type organizations. Some groups are directed and controlled by elections and referenda and periodic conventions in which a large part of the membership participates.

Most groups, however, are dominated and directed by a small portion of the total membership. Some are controlled completely by one man. Some groups make no pretense to democratic procedures for determining the group position on public issues. In recent years, however, most groups have claimed to be democratic. Almost every group operates on the basis of a formal constitution approved by the members at some stage in its organization. The permanent staff is likely to be especially influential in most group activities and decisions, regardless of how it may be selected. In some groups the entire staff spend all their time promoting group political interests. In others, with broader scope, this phase of the group interest is assigned to a special bureau, committee, or person.

Methods employed: How do these organized groups go about the business of promoting group interest in the politics of the nation? The best-known method is lobbying before the legislature. This method, as we shall describe later in more detail, takes many forms but may be summarized as presenting the group point of view to individual legislators or before legislative committees. Urging the peculiar claims of one interest group upon public officials is not

1. With the government   confined to the legislative halls. In modern American government, wide discretion to benefit or to harm certain interests is conferred on administrative agencies and individual administrators, and increasingly the spokesmen of interest groups seek out those concerned in the executive branch to make timely representations on behalf of their members. Even the courts are not immune to these representations. A substantial amount of litigation, contesting legislative or administrative decisions, is carried before the judiciary by interest groups rather than by individuals in their own interests. The smaller, less affluent groups are likely to hire skilled pleaders to present their views before the various governmental agencies; the larger groups make this the business of their permanent staffs. Not all of the special pleading before the government is done by or in behalf of interest groups. Some corporations and individuals make representations on behalf of their own interests.

2. With the parties   Interest groups seek to influence the policies and personnel of political parties as well as of the state. Claims on behalf of these groups are frequently urged upon party platform committees at all levels of government and upon individual members of important party committees and conventions. Although many of the groups prefer, and some practice, a kind of neutrality as between parties or among candidates, several of them seek to promote the candidacy of individuals favorably disposed to their claims and to assist one or the other of the major parties to victory. Influence in party circles is sought, and sometimes achieved, in many ways: by contribution to campaign chests, by grants of publicity or office space, by loans of skilled personnel to candidates or parties. Some avowed spokesmen of large interest groups stand for office as candidates in their own right.

3. With the public   In the modern age, interest groups have more and more sought to go beyond the traditional methods of dealing with a few important statesmen or party leaders on a private and personal basis and by propaganda to cultivate a favorable attitude on the part of the great mass of citizens not members of the group. In other words, they have tried to build a broadly based support, a favorable climate of opinion, which legislators and executives will be obliged to respect. Every known medium of communication with the public is used by one or more interest groups: newspaper releases, radio broadcasts, periodicals, television programs, leaflets, brochures, speeches, advertisements. Much of this publicity is so artfully contrived and so skillfully inserted in the stream of daily communication that its source is not apparent and its bias not disclosed. Much of it, of course, bears the imprimatur of the group which has sponsored it.

LIMITATIONS ON INTEREST-GROUP EFFECTIVENESS

Interest-group politics not all of democracy

When exposed for the first time to the activities, especially the successes, of interest groups or their leaders in our governmental system, young citizens are apt to be disillusioned. The idyllic view of the unselfish, responsible citizen majestically casting his ballot in behalf of what is good for the public and not necessarily for himself, and by this process electing statesmen who take the same attitude, is an easy one to puncture. Unfortunately, many citizens never grow in understanding beyond the sophomoric conception that all of the processes of democracy in America can be summarized in the selfish, ruthless, immoral, and deceitful behavior of certain interest groups and their representatives. It is as easy to mistake interest-group operation for the whole of American democracy as it is to mistake voting for the whole of it. What saves us from a polity dominated wholly at each level by the stronger or the wilier interest group or groups at that level?

Conflicting loyalties of group members

In the first place, many citizens, particularly those who are most active politically, identify themselves with a number of interest groups. It is quite possible for a person to be a member of the Retail Grocers' Association, a member of the American Legion, a Republican, a Lutheran, a member of the Parent-Teachers' Association, and a member of the Chamber of Commerce all at the same time. These groups may frequently be found urging mutually contradictory policies upon the government. His Grocers' Association may be attacking a sales tax which his Chamber of Commerce is supporting. His veterans organization may be demanding preference for veterans in teaching positions which his educational association is opposing. His party may require his support of a candidate who is wholly obnoxious to his Legion Post. No group can fairly represent the whole of a citizen's public views. No group can make the politician's job of balancing and reconciling conflicting views unnecessary. When group conflict occurs where overlapping membership is common, the group spokesman cannot command the effective loyalty of the whole membership and cannot, therefore, swing it behind the group program either at the ballot-box or before the officers of the government. The larger the group, the more likely it is that most of its members will have other loyalties which may at any time conflict with loyalty to that group. In any group there is usually only a hard core of members who react to all political issues as members of that group. This hard core is rarely able to persuade the others to follow its lead at election time.

Lack of internal cohesion in groups

In the second place, members of the same group frequently disagree on policies which affect the group. The larger the group, the more unlikely it is that it can reach agreement on anything. The huge federations like the Chamber of Commerce or the A.F.L.–C.I.O. find that the numerical strength which makes them formidable makes them soft. The "business" community is to some extent a myth. Individual men and firms have decided differences on what is good national policy. A high tariff may be a fine thing for the watch-making industry; it may be a bad thing for the automobile industry. What stand can the N.A.M. or the Chamber of Commerce take on the tariff issue and still hold their members' loyalty? Furthermore, there is a tendency for the permanent staff to act as if it were the whole group, to arrogate to itself power to make policies which the group does not in fact support. Balloting has frequently revealed that the members do not act in the way the leaders predict they will. The point is that if the group leaders cannot punish on election day the politicians who have opposed the group interests, they have, to that extent, made it less necessary for the politicians to please them. A politician will, typically, be more responsive to interest-group pressure if he feels that the group can hurt him. Parenthetically, the representation of group interests informs the politician of possible repercussions to policy decisions which he is contemplating. Lobbying, thus, serves the valuable purpose of a barometer of the political weather in the politician's district.

The un- organized interests

Finally, there are a large number of genuine and deeply felt interests in society which are rarely expressed and are almost never organized. There is a great deal of loyalty among our citizens to the traditions of American government as they understand them and to ethical conceptions like the Golden Rule or the Ten Commandments—to the "rules of the game," in a phrase. An organized group interest which flouts any of these traditions is likely to lose the loyalty of many of its members. What is more serious, it is likely to arouse these deep-seated interests on the part of the public, that is, the nonmembers of that group. It is easy to underestimate the force of these unorganized interests in our society simply because they are not organized and ordinarily have no spokesman. When any of these interests are threatened, however, they come vigorously to the surface of the political sea and assail those who endanger them. The best example of the role of the unorganized interest is the attack on corruption in government. There are interest groups that promote their own advantage by coarse methods: bribery, entertainment of officials. When exposed to public view, these methods frequently stimulate the expression of the unorganized interest in honesty in government. When corruption is rife, this interest in preserving honesty in government is likely to become organized and mobilized to "throw the rascals out."

Many politicians and interest-group leaders have found to their sorrow that there is a limit beyond which they cannot go without arousing this slumbering interest in clean and honest government. Loyalty to interests like those in maintaining the separation of powers, respect for the individual, fair play in governmental procedures, and the federal system may seem to be weak and ineffectual compared to the desire for wealth or prestige, but let a group, a party, or an individual attempt or seem to attempt to undermine or destroy them and these interests are quickly manifested. Loyalty to the rules of the game is probably quite as strong, even if latent, as loyalty to an interest group.

PUBLIC OPINION

Party orators and interest-group propagandists ordinarily pose as upholders of the traditions of our society. In seeking popular approval they tend to identify the latent or unorganized interests of the public with party policy or group programs. In so doing they exhibit their belief in the force of these unorganized interests; but more than this, they testify to the widely held assumption that modern government is dependent upon public opinion. The spread of equalitarian ideas, the achievement of literacy among the masses, and the development of elaborate networks of communication have all aided in placing our governors under the strong, if not decisive, influence of public opinion. Even the conduct of foreign affairs, once the preserve of a small, aristocratic clique, is not immune to the tides of mass attitudes.

Every form of government in the modern world seeks mass approval of its policies; fear of public hostility is by no means confined to the democratic states. And yet the democratic system is built upon popular consent and therefore is peculiarly dependent upon public views. Apologists for the democratic ideal—its critics too—have postulated a direct correlation between majority will and public policy. Some see the government in a democratic society, for good or ill, as under the constant and decisive influence of the concerted and more or less spontaneously developed will of the masses. The ballot-box is the most concrete and most important vehicle for the expression of this will but it is not the only one. Individuals are expected to be alert to the tides of affairs and to speak out from time to time on the issues of the day, either alone or in concert with others. In democracies, at least, these views if popular enough are expected to be controlling.

Democracy and public opinion:

1. Myth

New knowledge and bitter experience have combined to challenge the validity, the feasibility, and the wisdom of these cherished postulates. Psychologists probing the subconscious have shown that attitudes and opinions can be and are influenced by nonrational experience and that skillful manipulation of the stimuli can evoke desired response. Thoughtful men everywhere have taken alarm at the brutal and unreasoning aberrations of great masses of supposedly educated people as exhibited in Nazi Germany,

2. Reality

for example. The extent of public ignorance even with the achievement of literacy has shocked others. On many issues in which some are deeply concerned, a vast majority know little, and care little, about the matter in controversy. Opinion which emerges in these cases is actually that of a small minority with high stakes in the outcome. Even the ballot-box speaks in equivocal language. Electoral triumph may depend on "image" carefully contrived rather than on commitment to program or policy.

Testing the assumptions

Heretofore, the problem of empirical verification of hypotheses like those recited above has been formidable. What could be accepted as showing popular attitudes? Are statesmen influenced by the various and frequently contradictory expressions of voter attitude? Is not all of this apparent deference to public will merely a ritual designed to give legitimacy to the actions of the few rulers? Surely, skilled modern sophists can manufacture opinions to specification.

Survey research

The invention of and the continued improvement in the technique of sample-interviewing for testing public attitudes have in the past few decades offered an opportunity to probe the nature and influence of citizen opinion. Many of the best minds in sociology, psychology, and political science are now studying these questions and striving for light in this cave-like world. The validity of modern inquiries is, of course, dependent upon the validity of the sampling technique. Capturing and recording and analyzing the attitudes of a substantial majority of the American people is manifestly impossible. If some small number of (500–5 000) could be taken to represent the whole, then intensive and repeated interviewing of these could reveal many things about opinion that students and statesmen need to know. The polling system may assume that attitudes on public matters are influenced by economic, religious, ethnic, geographical, and similar factors and use these as the basis for constructing a sample of the body politic, or it may select its sample at random on a geographic basis, or it may use other hypotheses.

Predicting elections

The sampling technique achieved wide and impressive popularity when it was used in 1936 to predict the outcome of the presidential election and scored astonishing success, especially when compared with the straw-vote system used for several years by the *Literary Digest* magazine. Until 1948, the preelection polls conducted by the American Institute of Public Opinion, Elmer Roper and others gained increasing prestige and respectability but the forecast in that year of a Dewey victory brought them under a cloud from which their cautious forecasts of 1952 and 1960 and more accurate predictions of 1956, 1964, and 1968 have not completely removed them. Despite the critics, preelection polling is practiced extensively. The parties are using them heavily to plan campaign strategy. Each party and candidate in 1960, 1964, and 1968 expended huge sums on private polling of voter attitudes.

Polling on issues

The sample-interview or polling system is also used widely to measure sentiment on questions of public policy as they arise in the course of events. In fact, some of the leading pollsters assert that polls are valuable, if not essential, additions to the democratic process. They not only tell public officials how the people feel about proposed courses of action—and in a democracy officials should know this—but also reveal areas of ignorance and indifference which should aid those involved in planning programs of civic education. The value of the election poll and of the issue polls is widely debated. Many people feel that predictions cannot be validly made and the effort should be abandoned; others, that the consequences of publishing results are unfortunate—creating band-wagon effects or showing the woefully inadequate state of public understanding.

Whatever the merits of this controversy, the controlled, objective, and increasingly knowledgeable use of the sampling technique by scholars has provided us with much new knowledge about political behavior and public attitude. It has also suggested vast areas of continuing ignorance about the practices and professions of democracy. *Polling and opinion studies*

The picture that is beginning to emerge from numerous inquiries is of a relatively small minority of people who are active politically—running for office, serving party purposes, rallying supporters, speaking out on people or issues—operating within a larger mass characterized by varying degrees of indifference, misunderstanding, and docility. Within the large mass, however, is some vague sort of consensus about the nature and expectations of government. By conviction and expedience the activists tend to operate within the broad limits of this consensus. These activists are probably not so few as to constitute a self-conscious power elite nor so many as to justify the majoritarian hypotheses of some democrats. Clearly, however, the path to citizen influence on government decision is through activism and most citizens do not take it. *Whose opinions matter?*

Among the major influences on the formation of mass opinions are the family, the school, the interest group, the party, and the mass media of communication. Party loyalty, for example, appears to be strongly influenced by family tradition as is a disposition toward political activism. The schools are probably important transmitters of the basic attitudes which comprise the consensus within which the activists work. The interest group encourages and supports its adherents in articulating more precise positions on the direction of public policy. *The formation of opinion*

As sources of information and as sources of influence the mass communications media—newspaper, television, radio, magazines, the cinema—play a critical role in the American democracy. Mass media opinion is likely to be accepted by many as public opinion. When politicians talk about what the public is thinking they frequently base their statements on what the mass media are saying. Although it is true that the press, the radio and the others influence opinions; that many people decide what they think about a particular issue on the basis of what their favorite columnist tells them to think; and that the news of the day can be, and frequently is, written in such a way as to convey approval or reproach, this is still a long way from making their opinion and public opinion synonymous. Media opinion is, in fact, the opin- *The importance of mass media* ion of a relatively small number of individuals (owners, editors, and re-porters) but its power to influence the opinions of those who read it—statesmen or citizens—is great. Many citizens, perhaps a majority, learn what they know about the conduct of public affairs, the character of states-men, and the operations of the government from the newspapers or the television news broadcasts. The primary function of news reporting, accord-ing to journalists, is to inform public opinion. This admittedly is difficult to do without also molding opinion. "Facts" are hard to handle meaningfully and interestingly. Which facts are to be reported? There is not room for all. Which will be read? However informative, factual, and dispassionate the story, if not read it will not inform the public. What significance is to be attached to the "facts"? Reporting happenings without background and statements, without context, is almost meaningless. Some, however, place primary emphasis on the molding and attach only secondary importance to the informing.

Limitation on news-papers as media of communi-cation

On the whole, ours is probably the best-informed citizenry in the world today. Nevertheless, our media are not perfect vehicles of public communi-cation: (1) They have become large-scale enterprises and thus cautious, semi-monopolistic, and dependent upon maintaining a wide reader-interest; (2) they labor under a great shortage of time for reflection and review—they must publish each day; (3) the people who write the news cannot possibly know enough properly to evaluate everything they must report. These attri-butes of the modern metropolitan daily newspaper, the great news telecasts, and the weekly magazines reflect to a large extent the social environment in which they operate. Circulation or listening audience is the key to business success. Getting and keeping readers consists in serving them what they want to read. Mass circulation means mass appeal and this means sensationalism, comics, department store advertising, advice to the lovelorn, sports, and glamor. In spite of their obvious limitations and in view of their vital role in a democratic polity, it is easy to overestimate the influences of newspapers. For 20 years—from 1932 to 1952—the overwhelming majority of Ameri-can newspapers were unsympathetic, if not openly hostile, to the party, and its leaders repeatedly returned to power by a majority of the voters.

Much yet to be learned

About all of this, however, we have much yet to learn. What are the elements of the consensus? How is wide agreement on the rules of humani-tarian democracy produced? How much influence do the various elements of our society exert? How can basic predispositions be modified? What links private and personal attitude to public decision?

REFERENCES

A. F. Bentley, *The Process of Government* (New York, 1908).

G. L. Bird and F. E. Merwin, *The Press and Society* (New York, 1951).

D. Blaisdell (ed.), *Unofficial Government: Pressure Groups and Lobbies* (Phila., 1958).

A. Campbell, P. E. Converse, W. E. Miller, and D. E. Stokes, *The American Voter* (New York, 1960).

————, K. Gurin, W. E. Miller, *The Voter Decides* (Evanston, Ill., 1954).

D. Cater, *The Fourth Branch of Government* (Boston, 1959).

G. Gallup, *A Guide to Public Opinion Polls* (Princeton, N. J., 1944).

————, *Public Opinion in a Democracy* (Princeton, N. J., 1939).

F. C. Irion, *Public Opinion and Propaganda* (New York, 1950).

S. Kelley, Jr., *Professional Public Relations and Political Power* (Baltimore, Md., 1956).

V. O. Key, Jr., *Politics, Parties, and Pressure Groups* (5th ed., New York, 1963), Chaps. II–VI.

————, *Public Opinion and American Democracy* (New York, 1961).

H. McClosky and H. E. Dahlgren, "Primary Group Influence on Party Loyalty," *Amer. Pol. Sci. Rev.*, Vol. LIII, No. 3 (Sept., 1959).

H. R. Mahood, *Pressure Groups in American Politics* (New York, 1967).

J. Monsen and M. W. Cannon, *The Makers of Public Policy; American Power Groups and Their Ideologies* (New York, 1965).

F. Mosteller *et al., The Pre-election Polls of 1948* (New York, 1949).

M. B. Ogle, Jr., *Public Opinion and Political Dynamics* (Boston, 1950).

H. R. Penniman, *Sait's American Parties and Elections* (5th ed., New York, 1952), Chaps. V–VIII.

N. J. Powell, *Anatomy of Public Opinion* (New York, 1951).

The Public Opinion Quarterly. Published at Princeton, N. J., by the National Office of Public Opinion.

C. Schettler, *Public Opinion in American Society* (New York, 1957).

B. Smith, *A Dangerous Freedom* (New York, 1954).

D. B. Truman, *The Governmental Process* (New York, 1951).

H. Zeigler, *Interest Groups in American Society* (Englewood Cliffs, N. J., 1964).

7

POLITICAL PARTIES

Parties are essential to democratic government

None of the procedures by which individual citizens participate in directing the government would be wholly effective without political parties. Unless candidates for office stand for something, voting is likely not to be successful in giving direction to the machine of state. Unless the range of choice is narrowed down, the electorate is likely to be divided among numerous claimants with no single claimant representing more than a small portion of the total. No political-interest group can claim the loyalty of more than a minority of the voters and cannot, therefore, itself dominate and direct public policy. The results would be tragic if it could, for it might push its own claims to the exclusion of those of other groups and so divide our society that rebellion or revolution would ensue. None of the methods for voicing or recording opinions on the questions of the day makes certain that the opinions will be both representative and influential. Although for decades there were grave doubts about the usefulness or the necessity of political parties and even today there are lingering suspicions, it is now generally conceded that strong parties are essential to the practice of democratic government.

THE NATURE OF A POLITICAL PARTY

Nature of a party

In a sense a political party is a kind of political-interest group. It is a group of voters consciously bound together by a shared interest in promoting some kind of public policy and a shared adherence to some sort of traditional values. A party differs rather strikingly, however, from all other political-interest groups or associations in that it seeks to capture the power of the state. It is not content merely to persuade those in power to follow a particular policy. The party offers candidates for office and is willing to assume the responsibility for running the government. Although devoted to some kind of program, its major aim is power and, within certain broad limits, it will shift its program to attain it. The ordinary political-interest group is much more rigidly dedicated to a program of governmental benevolence to its own members than is any party. Strong parties are likely to be much larger than any other type of interest group and to embrace members of many different groups. Of course, parties may be large or small, national or local, highly organized or loosely built. The major parties of American experience, however, have operated on a national scale and have permeated all levels of government.

American parties are loose and amorphous associations. Membership in a party is a vague and elusive matter. How does one join a party? A few minor parties have regular enrollment; the members subscribe to a body of doctrine and, in many instances, pay dues. The major parties, however, have nothing so clear-cut. There is no enrollment, except that arising in several states from preprimary registration of party affiliation. There are no dues, although many efforts have been made to institute regular contributions. There are no rules of behavior for members and no effective sanctions for improper conduct. In common with the large interest groups, there is at the center of each party a hard core of party officials and workers surrounded by a steadfast band of supporters who contribute money and time and influence, if they have it, to promote the success of the party. Close to this core, but not always part of it, are the officeholders whom the party has helped elect. There is the party in Congress and the party in state legislatures and in city and county councils and commissions and the party in the executive branch at all levels. These groups are closely identified with the party hierarchy, may even be part of it, but in view of official positions have responsibilities and loyalties which transcend party status. At any particular time, a segment of the party in office may be at odds with the party hierarchy. Beyond the hierarchy and the officeholders are the office-seekers and others who aspire to influence in the party and in the government. Then there are the myriad hosts of those who regularly support the party at election time, occasionally work for it, usually talk for it in their own circles, and sometimes contribute to its treasury. Beyond this group are a large number of persons who usually support the party but cannot be depended on to do so and who are rather quick to change their loyalties and support another party or other candidates. Finally, there are on election day all of those who vote for the party's candidates. Many of these, however, are not members in any sense save this one and for this short period.

How can a group whose membership is so hard to determine and whose character is so difficult to define be so useful to democratic society? No better agency for mobilizing the electoral power of large numbers of people and channeling it to drive the wheels of government has been found in almost 200 years of experimentation. No other agency assumes for its chief task the formation of a majority so that officials can assume office with the knowledge that they may speak and act for their fellow citizens. No other agency so persistently or so successfully stimulates citizen interest and participation in the processes of self-government. No other agency is quite so

Party member-ship

The use-fulness of parties in American govern-ment

responsive to the feelings of the people. No other agency is in a position effectively to harness the multiple seats of power provided by our federal and tripartite constitutional system and drive them toward an agreed goal. Finally, no other agency has, at the same time that it has promoted political division, also promoted national unity. Only the political party reaches across sectional boundaries, economic distinctions, interest-group competitions, religious differences, and racial antagonisms and softens the conflicts, bridges the gulfs, and helps to cement together a divergent, mobile, and aggressive people.

Parties in author- itarian states   One of the distinguishing characteristics of genuinely democratic government everywhere in the world is the free competition of political parties. The ruling cliques in some authoritarian governments also call themselves parties largely because of their origins in differently organized regimes. In the democratic sense the Communist party in the Soviet Union, for example, is not a political party at all and the system is not a party system. Parties, to correspond to our definition and to function as they do in democratic states, must be free to compete openly for public support and to criticize freely those in charge of the state.

THE DEVELOPMENT OF THE AMERICAN PARTY SYSTEM

The history of party cleavage in America   The disposition of the American electorate to divide into major groups identified with particular governmental conceptions extends back to the very beginnings of our national government. The movement for separation from England sharply divided the people of the colonies, with the Loyalists or Tories opposing the revolutionaries. Achievement of independence was accompanied by a general suppression of Loyalist sentiments. The attempt to replace the Articles of Confederation with a new constitution providing a stronger central government evoked a loose union of its sponsors into Federalists and of its opponents into anti-Federalists. The Federalists drew their chief strength from the commercial, financial, industrial, and plantation interests, their opponents from the small farmers and frontiersmen. These loose coalitions more or less dissolved with the establishment of the new government, only to reappear in slightly different array during the late phases of Washington's presidency. The commercial, financial, and industrial elements of New England and the Middle States retained their party label of Federalist and, led by Hamilton and Adams, sponsored new national programs for the benefit of these sections and interests. Their policies in regard to national debt, a protective tariff, and the role of the national government, however, stimulated Jefferson and Madison to rally the planters along with the small farmers and artisans into a new party—the Jeffersonian Republicans. Jefferson's skill as a party leader, continued expansion of the frontier, quarreling among the opposition leaders, the War of 1812, and other factors too complex for easy summary brought such sweeping victories to this party that by 1816 the Federalist party was driven from the field. Renamed Democrats, the party of rural America held the field unchallenged nationally until 1832. The Jacksonian Democracy of 1828, however, was a coalition different from Jeffersonian Republicanism. Jackson's appeal to the artisans of the city and the farmers of the frontier was much stronger than his appeal to the southern plantation aristocracy. Many of the slave-holders were driven into an alliance with northern manufacturing commerce, and finance in the National Republican or Whig party organized about 1832 and contesting national offices with the Democratic party from 1832 to 1856. The slavery controversy rent the Democratic party still further and created an unbridgeable gulf finally between southern and northern agriculture. The Whig party, too, disintegrated under the fires of abolitionism and secession, its southern wing joining hands with the slave-holding Democrats and its northern industrial wing forming the chief sinews of the new Republican party which emerged in 1860. Lincoln's party successfully united the northern industrial and financial groups with the mid-western free farmers in a coalition for union, against the spread of slavery, and for tariffs. The shades of rebellion hung over the Democracy for decades after the Civil War, but farm depression, rigid credit controls, high tariffs and industrial exploitation drove more and more northern workingmen and farmers to embrace the Democratic standard. Deep distress in American agriculture in the nineteen-twenties, followed by an unparalleled depression in industry in the nineteen-thirties, cemented a powerful new farmer–laborer–southern-plantation coalition which is the basis of the modern Democratic party. The Republican party continues to receive the support of the manufacturing, commercial, and financial interests of the North and Midwest and of the more prosperous farmers of these regions. The Democratic party can thus trace its ancestry back to Jeffersonian Republicans and the Republican party to Hamiltonian Federalists. Each, thus, draws upon traditions and conceptions reaching far back into the past.

This characterization of American major parties as based largely upon economic and sectional interests has only rough validity. There were many cross currents of interests, religious and social, for example, which influenced party affiliation at every epoch of our national history. No party ever enlisted the undivided support of any economic interest or section. Family tradition has proved capable of maintaining party loyalties long after any direct economic attachment is discernible. Regional devotion too has been a strong contributor to party loyalty. The South, for example, still shuns the Republican party as the author of its defeat and the despoiler of its culture. The older a party becomes, the more likely is habit to be a large factor in the devotion of its followers. *Economic and sectional interests not sole determinants of party cleavage*

This capsule history of the American party battle does show, however, that certain great economic and sectional interests have persistently sought political expression through the vehicle of a party. Some of them—industry, for example—have been consistent supporters of a particular party. Most *A two-party system* significant of all, however, the history of American parties reveals the deep attachment of the American voter to one or the other of two major parties. In sharp contrast with continental practitioners of democratic government, English-speaking peoples generally seem to prefer a two-party alignment to a multi-party one. Despite the great diversities of sections, economic groups, and religious loyalties, which in France, Italy, Germany, Belgium, Holland, and the Scandinavian countries have promoted numerous parties contending for power, the American people have tended to coalesce into two great combinations of such interests.

Why we have a two-party system

A number of explanations have been offered for bipartisanship in American politics. On the one hand, some have ventured the belief that the two-party system is more natural than any other. People "naturally" tend either to conservatism or reformism by temperament, upbringing, and disposition. A conservative party and a reform party are, therefore, in keeping with human nature. This explanation is not very satisfying. Human nature is not so simply catalogued; few of us are consistently conservative or consistently reformist throughout all of the phases and facets of our lives. Some find the explanation in American constitutional history. They find that there have usually been but two main attitudes toward our constitutional arrangements: a strict constructionist, states'-rights attitude; and a loose constructionist, nationalist attitude. This explanation fails to reckon with the fact that the party in power in the national government has usually been nationalist while it was in power—whether Democrat, Whig or Republican—while the party out of power nationally has typically been in favor of states' rights. The Republican devotion to states' rights of the last two decades would sound strange to the supporters of Lincoln. Elihu Root felt that the two-party system was the product of longer practical experience of self-government than the continental peoples had enjoyed. Contemporary students believe that the following factors are more important than any thus far mentioned: (1) the single-member district system for electing legislators—plurality election in each district invites, if it does not compel, coalition of interests in order to achieve a decision at the polls; (2) the popular election of the president—this contributes a powerful impetus to unite groups across state, sectional, and economic lines in order to make the voting decisive; (3) once established the system built up its own impediments to any rival scheme.

Minor parties in America

Not all Americans have been content with the two-party division. Dissident elements in the electorate have periodically launched independent or "third-party" movements. One of the first of them was the anti-Masons, appearing in 1826 and spreading over New England, New York, and Pennsylvania. It made a lasting contribution to American politics in the national convention system for nominating presidential candidates. It also formed part of the basis of the opposition to Jackson which later became the Whig party. The equivocation of the major parties on the slavery question stimulated the formation of the Liberty party about 1840, dedicated to abolition, and of the Free Soil party, active in the campaign of 1848 and determined to sustain the Wilmot Proviso. Antipathy to immigrants, especially Irish Catholics, led to the formation of the Native-American or "Know-Nothing" party which flourished in the fifties. The Republican party, itself, began as a third party in 1854–1856. Agrarian discontent on the Plains and in the South after 1870 was largely responsible for the Greenback party of the seventies and the People's or "Populist" party of the nineties. Urban industrial capitalism was the target of the Socialist party organized in the late nineties and of the Communist and Socialist–Labor parties organized after World War I. In this century the National Progressive party of 1912 embodied the presidential aspirations of Theodore Roosevelt; the Progressive party of 1924, those of the elder La Follette; and the Progressive party of 1948, those of Henry Wallace. The La Follette tradition was embraced in

PARTIES IN THE PRESIDENTIAL ELECTION OF 1968

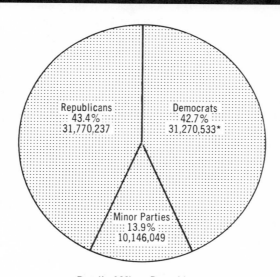

Republicans
43.4%
31,770,237

Democrats
42.7%
31,270,533*

Minor Parties
13.9%
10,146,049

Detail of Minor Party Vote

PARTY	CANDIDATE	TOTAL POPULAR VOTE
American Independent	Wallace	9,906,141
Socialist Labor	Blomen	52,558
Socialist Worker	Halstead	41,300
Peace and Freedom	Cleaver	36,385
New Party	Gregory	47,097
New Party	McCarthy	25,858
Prohibition	Munn	14,519
Other	—	22,161

*Includes over 224,000 votes of the Liberal party in New York and over 194,000 votes of the Alabama Independent Democratic party and the National Democratic party of Alabama.

a new Progressive party in Wisconsin in the years 1934 to 1946. A Farmer–Labor party in Minnesota joined with the Democratic party in 1944 after several years of independent existence. Southern resistance to northern pressure in behalf of the Negro, especially within the Democratic party, has produced States Rights or "Dixiecrat" parties in each election since 1948. New York City continues to be the home of a vigorous labor party, the Liberal party.

Their strength and role

   Some of these parties momentarily attained sufficient strength, especially in pivotal states, to affect the results of a presidential election. One—the Republican—grew into a major party. In only three elections in this century (1912, 1924, and 1968) has the combined vote of all minor parties exceeded 6 percent of the total vote cast, and since 1932 it has exceeded 4 percent only twice (1948 and 1968). The Progressive parties which did so well in 1912 and in 1924 were both short-lived. These minor parties—free to cultivate ideas rather than worry about power—have found their importance mainly in revealing and crystallizing dissenting opinion (usually on economic and social matters). As threats to the rather evenly balanced major parties, third parties have impelled them, whether they liked it or not, to bid for support by taking up issues sponsored by these minority groups. A large proportion, indeed, of leading party issues in the past several decades—the income tax, the regulation of railroads and other corporations, the use of injunctions in labor disputes, woman suffrage, prohibition, farm relief, and others—were "borrowed" from third-party platforms. Except for occasional "one-purpose" parties like the Prohibitionist, minor parties are typically more radical or reactionary than the old-line organizations. The internal heterogeneity and lack of cohesion of our major parties are more than matched by the rigid and doctrinaire character of minor parties.

THE TWO MAJOR PARTIES TODAY

Two parties hard to distinguish

   The two major parties of today are notoriously composite and disunited. In order to capture the loyalty of great numbers of voters scattered throughout the nation, they must stand for many different things and not too rigidly for any one thing. To a foreign observer, especially one accustomed to the doctrinaire parties of Europe, it must seem that the Republican and Democratic parties are identical. James Bryce years ago described them as two bottles carefully labeled but empty. Many observers since his time have been baffled by the excitement engendered in an American political campaign when the contestants seem to be so much alike. This is really not so surprising if one conceives of the campaigns of each as aimed at the so-called moderate vote. Although the line of demarcation between the two parties is blurred, and ideologically there is much overlapping of views, the center of gravity of the two parties is different. They do stand for somewhat different things.

The watershed of modern politics is the Great Depression of the nineteen-thirties and the modern Democratic party was forged in those desperate economic times. It is a coalition of urban workers, urban minority groups, and the southern, white agricultural leadership to which a large number of the less prosperous farmers of the Plains and ranchers and miners of the Mountain States have also given their allegiance. Stated another way, it is a coalition of the dominant white, southern politicians and the highly organized political apparatus of the large cities of the nation. In this coalition, the urban groups have been increasingly influential in presidential politics. This party has carried virtually every large city in the country in every election since 1932 except those of 1952 and 1956. Numerous studies of voter preference show that the party has a strong appeal to laboring men and women and to lower-income groups everywhere. The uneasy partner has been the white South. After a few successes by Hoover, Eisenhower, and Nixon in states like Florida, Tennessee, and Virginia, the Republicans with Goldwater finally carried much of the Deep South in 1964 on the civil rights issue. The victory, however, on these terms cost them the allegiance of the southern Negroes who until that time had no reason to ally with the white Democratic leadership. "Dixiecrat" movements of various kinds had eroded Democratic strength in the elections of 1948 and 1960 and did so again in 1968.

In general the modern Democratic party is the preferred party of a majority of American adults. Repeated surveys in the last several years have indicated that 50–55 percent of American adults think of themselves as Democrats; 32–38 percent, as Republicans; and the rest, as independent or indifferent. The Democratic majority, however, contains a considerable share of those who are least likely to vote and it is hard for the party to deliver its full strength at the polls.

The orientation of the party is indicated further by the kinds of programs it has sponsored. In general, the Democrats have been more willing than the Republicans to control the economy in the interest of the workers; to sponsor programs of public succor for the poor, the underprivileged, the unfortunate; to promote public housing and public power; to favor lower tariffs; and to undertake more extensive international political and military commitments.

The sectional strongholds of the modern Republican party are New England (except Massachusetts and Rhode Island) and the Northern Great Plains (Kansas, Iowa, Nebraska, and the Dakotas). The small towns and the rural areas of the Midwest and Middle Atlantic regions (Wisconsin, Illinois, Indiana, Ohio, Michigan, Pennsylvania, and New York) have also been strongly in the Republican camp for many decades, although the Democrats did attract a large number of Midwestern and Plains farmers in the period 1930–1950. The manufacturing and financial interests have been especially influential in the Party as have upper-income groups everywhere but in the Deep South. Everywhere the party cadres are filled with white, Anglo-Saxon Protestants. In contrast to the Democrats, the Republicans have been less sympathetic to governmental restriction on private industrial management and have tended to emphasize individual initiative and free enterprise as against governmental benevolence and economic security. In international affairs, the Republican party contains a much higher proportion than the Democratic party of those who are critical of international commitments, who favor high tariffs on imports and more vigorous military measures to resist communists.

Composite character of both major parties

It should not be inferred from these thumbnail portraits of the two parties that there are no wealthy Democrats nor poor Republicans, that there are no Republican laborers and no small-town Democrats. There are some of every kind of class, race, religion, and sectional patriot in each party. Each party is furthermore sharply divided within itself. Its unity is assailed by factional contests of the bitterest kind. The conservative southern leaders of the Democratic party are staunch foes of the demands of northern urban leaders for an end to racial discrimination and for stronger governmental protection for labor unions. Agrarian Democrats in the Middle West are likely to find southern preferences for cotton and tobacco do not square easily with their own aspirations in regard to dairy products, corn, and hogs. Eastern Republicans committed to international trade and the support of friendly nations in Europe find themselves vigorously assailed by isolationist Republicans of the Plains and Middle West and by "Asia-firsters" on the West Coast. New England farmers do not easily support the agricultural programs sponsored by the Republican corn farmers of Iowa and Illinois. These intraparty squabbles are often as animated as are the contests between the two parties. Each party does, however, have a center of gravity in particular sections and interests which is different from that of its chief rival. Neither of the central blocs is powerful enough to capture majority support unaided. Each must appeal to other sections and interests to gain victory at the polls. Since it frequently occurs that each of them is appealing to the same group for support, it is not strange that they should sound very much alike at campaign time.

The parties and the states

Although both major parties and most minor parties offer candidates for national office and campaign on national issues over the whole nation, the real strength of the parties is in their state apparatus. The major political parties of America are federally organized in much the same way as the government. In the case of the government, however, the national level is more powerful in relation to the state level than in the case of the parties. Party activity in state and local government resembles that in the national government. Candidates are sponsored for state and local offices; platforms are written dealing with city and state problems; campaigns are conducted for governor, legislator, mayor, councilman, sheriff, district attorney, and all the other offices filled by election. In these contests for local and state power the parties prepare themselves for the national contests. It is here that the skills of the politician are learned and that political leaders are developed. Here the professional politician finds his livelihood in public office and puts himself in position to participate in national campaigns. Here party organization attains its maximum of effectiveness and detail. Each of the major parties has arisen from devastating defeat in national election to contest vigorously the next election with its rival because it still holds place and power in numerous localities and states from which to strike out anew. No party can hope for success nationally unless it is strong in many states and dominant in some. Confronted with imminent defeat nationally, local and state leaders will bend every effort to stay on top in their own states and cities. They have been known even to sabotage their own national ticket if they thought by so doing they could salvage local victory. In 1964, for example, Republican gubernatorial and senatorial candidates in New York, Michigan, Ohio, Illinois, Pennsylvania and some other states did everything possible to avoid outright identification with the party's presidential ticket.

The states are not perfect miniatures of the nation in party matters. *One-party* For decades a goodly number of states have not had genuine two-party com- *states* petition of the national variety. The Deep South has been solidly Democratic since the Civil War, and most of the Plains, New England and, until the nineteen-thirties, the Mid-Atlantic have been predominantly Republican. In these one-party states, factions within the party tend to develop and to offer candidates, contest nominations, and promote controversial policies. These factional competitions resemble bipartisan conflicts, but take many peculiar local forms. The nominating procedure is likely to be the chief battleground in one-party states and the elections less significant. Two-party competition has, however, been increasing in the past few years and there are fewer one-party states today than at any time since 1865.

The cooperative union of national, state, and local politicians in the *Separating* American party pattern has the great value of promoting a similar coopera- *national* tive union of national, state, and local government. It helps to overcome the *politics* *and state* centrifugal tendencies in the federal system. To some, however, the mixture of national issues into state and local campaigns, which necessarily accompanies the federated party organization, is a monstrous evil. Only misgovernment locally results from confusing the voter by injecting national party positions on war, taxes, or international affairs into municipal campaigns, they argue. The stock remedy for this alleged illness is the nonpartisan ballot (one having no party emblems or identifications). And a number of states have adopted such ballots for municipal officials, judges, and state officials. Two states, Minnesota and Nebraska, now select the members of their legislatures in a nonpartisan election. In this nation as a whole, somewhat more than half of all the members of city councils in municipalities with more than 5,000 population are selected in this way. This method has not completely eliminated partisan campaigning but it has certainly reduced it. It has also weakened the influence of city officials in state and national politics. The separation of national, state, and local elections is another way which has been widely adopted for getting at the same problem. This procedure strengthens the state position of a party not in command in Washington and may build one-party dominance. Little is heard any more of "reforms" of this type aimed at weakening the party apparatus. Most students are seeking ways to strengthen the party.

REGULATION OF PARTIES

Parties as voluntary associa- tions

      Political parties are as much a part of the American system of government as the Congress of the United States. They are the most important vehicles for translating individual will into public policy. And yet they developed almost wholly outside the law. The national and most state constitutions are completely silent about them. Even the statutes were relatively indifferent to their existence for 100 years. Congress passed its first laws touching them directly in 1907, and state laws dealing with their machinery and operations are, typically, of more recent origin. Legally speaking, parties are voluntary nonprofit associations with no personality apart from the individuals who compose them. Over the recent decades, however, national and state regulation has invested them with a public status without, however, making them organs of the government.

The develop- ment of public regula- tions: 1. Na- tional

2. State

      Under constitutional authority to regulate national elections including primaries—an authority which in practice would tend to extend also to state and local elections not separately held—Congress might control party machinery and operations. This, however, it has not chosen to do, except with respect to campaign finances. Accordingly, the task is left largely to the states. Congress has, however, closed party competition to the Communist party.

      The old situation in which parties determined their own form of organization, made their own rules, nominated their candidates, and raised their funds with no external controls, was gradually brought to an end in most states by demand that party activities be recognized as matters of public concern and abuses curbed. Regulations (following no single pattern) are now found in nearly every state covering: (1) definition of what constitutes a party with the privilege of a place on the ballot; (2) processes of election, including forms of ballots, use of voting machines, counting of votes, and the like; (3) composition and powers of party committees; (4) manner of making nominations; (5) dates for holding primaries; (6) membership tests for voting in primaries; (7) settlement of disputes in connection with nominations; (8) campaign contributions and expenditures, and other aspects of party finances; (9) corrupt and illegal electoral practices, financial or otherwise; (10) outlawry (in many states) of parties advocating totalitarianism, overthrow of the government by violence, or other "subversive" doctrines or objectives; (11) protection for parties against impostors as candidates in primaries, against misleading and unauthorized use of party names (including adoption of them by separate organizations), and against appropriation of party emblems duly adopted and recorded.

Not infrequently, cases involving party matters get into the courts. In addition to sustaining a great deal of statutory regulation when questioned, the courts have, at various times and places, ruled (1) that a political party has no right to limit the suffrage at a general election or a primary; (2) that it has no authority to add to qualifications for voting specified in state constitutions or statutes; and (3) that it has no authority over eligibility to public office, nor any right to make binding decisions on questions relating thereto.

PARTY ORGANIZATION—STATE AND LOCAL

Every successful party has elaborate organizational machinery to hold its members together, stir them to action, raise funds, carry on propaganda, recruit new members and supporters, and guide the party effort in primaries and elections. This machinery in each of the two major parties enlists more than 150,000 men and women who make a profession or at least a major vocation of their party work. Although there are many local variations, the pattern of party organization is fairly uniform throughout the country. Its characteristic feature is a pyramid of committees ranging upward from the city or county to the national level but with co-operative rather than authoritative relations among the levels. Although in earlier times parties were free to contrive their own organizational arrangements, increasing public control of electoral processes has brought with it public regulation of party machinery. Almost everywhere the structure and mode of election of party committee members is regulated by state law. Typically, they are elected by the voters in connection with a direct primary election on candidates for public office. *Characteristics of party organization*

During the rapid rise of urban, industrial America, the most highly organized party apparatus was in the great cities and the urban machine is still in some sense a model of detailed party organization. Built block by block with workers responsible to a precinct captain or committeeman and he in turn to a ward leader presiding over a ward committee and he to the chairman of the city committee, the party kept in close and year-round contact with a high proportion of its registered affiliates. Fueled by specific rewards—job finding, ticket fixing, poor relief, intercession with police, courts, and city inspectors—the organization was little interested in national issues and greatly interested in assimilation of ethnic minorities into American society. The key piece was likely to be the precinct leader who might occupy a public job (by patronage appointment) the duties of which were such that he could spend most of his time in his precinct and who cultivated his flock with "favors" and "friendship" in return for loyalty to his ticket on election day. At the top of the structure a city or county "boss" dealt with the leaders of other cities and counties in state and national conclaves for determining party candidates and allocating the "spoils." Little was left *The urban machine* to chance in such an organization; voter's canvasses based on lists of registered voters gave the leadership highly accurate knowledge of the ebb and flow of public opinion. The leadership could and did give firm commitments on official attitudes toward utilities, municipal housekeeping services, and vice. This was the politics of "boodle," graft, and spoils but it was also a highly effective mechanism for bringing the immigrant into the American system and for overcoming the frustrations of divided power at the local level. Several developments in the last half century have seriously modified and in some cases destroyed this machinery. The restrictive immigration policy has halted the flow of Europeans into the city. The inauguration of huge programs of poor relief, social security, and public employment offices has eliminated much of the value and need for party benevolence. The outward flow of urbanites into the suburbs has changed the character of the central cities. Radio and television have brought national issues and political personalities into the homes of the voters in ways that overshadow the messages and friendship of the local party worker. A few of the "old-style" organizations like that in Chicago have been able to adapt. The Negroes moving in large numbers into the cities have found the party apparatus useful to accommodate their ambitions. The effectiveness of the organization in getting people registered and then to the polls on election day has made their continuance a matter of great importance to party leadership. Nevertheless, the modern urban party organization is likely to be more issue-oriented, less dependent upon specific rewards, less dominated by ethnic considerations, and less hierarchical than it used to be.

Local party committees   Urban America continues to provide the setting for the most completely organized local party apparatus, with its precinct leaders, ward committees and leaders, and citywide committees. In some cases, there are also intermediate committees organized around state legislative districts. By contrast in rural and small-town America the party apparatus is likely to be most informal and to center around the county courthouse. The most powerful leader is likely to be the chairman of the county committee. This committee is composed typically of township, city, and village representatives. As with the urban ward, legislative district, and city committees, the county committees are importantly concerned in raising money, directing local campaigns, selecting candidates for the various offices at these levels and uniting party support for these candidates, preparing and distributing literature, holding rallies, and performing other party chores.

District organization   Intermediate between the county and the state organization, various types of district committees may usually be found. Congressional and state legislative districts are apt to be formed of several counties and the parties frequently make some effort to create a campaign organization to support their candidates for these posts. A district committee made up of representatives of the county committees in the district is the most common. Rarely are these district organizations effective. They function, if at all, only during a campaign and in many areas have only a shadowy existence.

In earlier days, the supreme party authority in a state was a state convention whose members were elected, in counties or other areas, by the party voters directly or in local conventions. The Supreme Court has recognized a convention as the highest authority of a party. For most practical purposes, however, the state convention has now lost its importance. Supreme party authority on the state level is now centered almost completely in a state central committee and its chairman. State committees vary greatly in size, and their members are chosen in different ways. Occasionally they consist simply of all county chairmen in the state. Usually they are elected directly or indirectly by the voters in counties or other units of representation, with the trend strongly toward direct choice through primaries, and often with men and women elected in equal numbers. Their functions include maintaining effective organization throughout the state, adjusting dissensions, promoting the election of party candidates (in cooperation with the national committee in presidential years, with congressional committees when members of Congress are being chosen, and at all times with county and other local committees), raising funds, occasionally nominating candidates for certain minor offices, sometimes preparing the party platform, and in some states selecting the state delegation to the national nominating convention. Committee membership is often far too large to permit effective collective action, and tasks tend to fall into the hands of a smaller executive committee and especially to such officers as the chairman and treasurer.

The state chairmanship is a post much sought after by politicians and often bitterly fought over by rival party leaders or factions. The state central committee commonly elects the chairman. In doing so, however, it may merely ratify a choice already made by the party nominee for governor or even by a powerful party leader who prefers not to occupy the titular post. In many cases, the United States senator is likely to be influential in selecting the chairman. The party leadership, in any case, is often shared with the governor or a senator. Whether the real leader of his party or a member of the top party team, the chairman, presumably working with the state committee, is the principal director of statewide party campaigns. He usually is influential in making up statewide slates and, in the event of party victory, is importantly involved in dispensing patronage, both state and national.

Throughout our experience of organized political parties the apparatus just described has evoked much criticism. Before the advent of the direct popular election system for filling many party offices, during the time especially when these posts were filled by local caucuses or city, county, or state conventions, the party organization fell rather easily under the domination of a few ruthless and unprincipled leaders who solidified their position by carefully contrived organization and bolstered it by corruption, graft, and spoils. This was notably true in the large cities and the scandals of the Tweed Ring and of Tammany Hall in New York City, of the Penrose and Vare machines in Philadelphia, of the Pendergast machine of Kansas City, of the Kelly–Nash machine in Chicago, and of many others during the past decades

—blackened the reputations of party organizations everywhere. The word *machine,* used to characterize a highly organized and tightly controlled party apparatus, is still an epithet connoting corruption and oligarchy.

"Bossism" "Boss," as the leader of the machine is still called, is also a term of opprobrium. The system of filling party office by election was widely adopted in the period 1900–1915 to make oligarchic or dictatorial control of the party organization more difficult. It was supposed by the reformers that the voters disapproved of machine politics and if given an opportunity would destroy it. The convention and caucus system, it was argued, was much easier to manipulate in the interests of the leaders. State regulation of party organization involving the prescription of party offices and the methods of filling them has not wholly solved the problem or mitigated the criticisms. The fundamental difficulty, if it be one, is that only a small percentage of the electorate are really interested in party organization or in party work. Elections of party officials ordinarily attract a very light vote. Further, it does no good to elect to party office persons who are neither fitted for nor interested in working at the job. The small band of party enthusiasts who do the party's chores and, of course, enjoy the party's rewards are indispensable to strong parties. Since they are a small minority, they can always be criticized as an oligarchy. Even the most dictatorially managed party organization, however, depends in the final analysis on public support. It cannot survive repeated repudiation of its candidates at the polls. The voters in any area have today and have always had it in their power to destroy a "machine" or a "boss." Wherever they continue to exist, and they still do in some places, it is a fair assumption that a majority of those voting approve of what they do.

Development of informal party organization One unintended result of state regulation of party organization has been the development of informal or "voluntary" party organization outside the legally constituted party organization. In Wisconsin, for example, the elected "statutory" party committees are relatively unimportant parts of the party apparatus and real power has shifted to party committees and groups which have grown up outside the law. These groups use the old caucus and convention procedures for selecting officials and candidates just as was done in the last century. "Reform" has brought us full circle.

PARTY ORGANIZATION—NATIONAL

Although much of the strength and vitality of our major political parties is in their state and local organizations, they also are organized nationally to conduct campaigns for the presidency and for members of Congress. In general, however, the national machinery of the parties is a federation of state organizations and lacks the powerful central direction characteristic of some state and many local organizations.

Pursuing the ascending order thus far followed, one finds first among

national agencies two committees of which as a rule the public hears little—   *1. Sena-*
(1) a senatorial campaign committee, composed usually of six or seven   *torial and*
United States senators chosen by the party group in the upper branch and   *congres-*
charged with promoting the election or reelection of the party's senatorial   *sional*
candidates in the biennial contests; and (2) a corresponding congressional   *campaign*
campaign committee consisting in the case of the Republicans of one mem-   *committees*
ber of the House of Representatives from each state having a Republican
delegation, and in that of the Democrats, of one member from each state
having a Democratic delegation, plus also a woman member from each state
insofar as the chairman chooses to designate such. In a presidential contest,
these two committees, typically, place their resources at the disposal of the
national committee (with which, however, they have no organic connection)
and become its close allies. Elections tend to follow the fortunes of the contest for the presidency. In "off years" the committees (which now maintain
permanent working staffs) tend to play an independent role. Relying, of
course, upon the cooperation of national, state, and local committees, they
provide central coordination of the senatorial and congressional campaigns.
In meeting this responsibility they distribute political literature and film
strips, maintain a speakers' bureau, raise and disburse money (giving special
attention to marginal states or districts), offer technical aid on radio and
television appearances, and often intervene to smooth out local factional
differences. Despite much duplication of effort with the national committee,
the congressmen jealously guard the independence of their own campaign
committees.

    Although on the lower levels party conventions have largely been dis-   *2. The*
placed, the supreme organ of the national party is still the national conven-   *national*
tion. It not only nominates candidates for the highest offices and formulates   *convention*
a platform but controls the party organization and "constitution." This con-   *and its*
vention which meets every four years will be discussed in some detail shortly.   *agencies:*
At this point we need only to discuss the two major arms of the convention:
the national committee and the national chairman.

    The national committee of the Democratic party consists of two party   *a. The*
members—a man and a woman—from each state and territory. The Repub-   *national*
lican party, since 1952, has added to these two, the state party chairman   *committee*
from each state which was carried by the party in the preceding presidential
election or in which the governor or a majority of the members of Congress
are Republicans. The two traditional state members of the committee of
each party are formally designated by the conventions on the nominations
of the respective state delegations. In at least 30 states, however, the real
selection is made at primaries or at state conventions and the national delegation simply confirms the local selections. The national committee is most
active during a presidential campaign year. It decides where and when the
nominating convention will be held and makes all the necessary local arrangements. It issues the call to the state party organizations, compiles the
temporary roll of delegates who may attend, and selects the temporary

officers of the convention. Both of the latter decisions are subject to review at the convention. The committee also makes recommendations to the convention for changes in the rules governing the national organization. The convention selects a new national committee, which then bears a heavy responsibility for conducting the national campaign. In between campaign years, the committee is not nearly so active. Its continuing responsibilities for "off year" campaigning and for mobilizing sentiment nationally for the party and its leaders are discharged largely by the permanent staff which each headquarters maintains in Washington, D. C. These staffs supply material for local and state use, recruit speakers, assist in arranging the campaign itinerary of the President, if he is to be active, or of the chief party spokesman—usually the defeated presidential candidate—gather and distribute funds, and generally try to coordinate state party effort throughout the nation.

b. The national chairman   The chairman of the national committee is the active campaign manager of the presidential candidate of the party. He is ordinarily selected by the candidate and formally invested with office by the committee. When the campaign is over, the defeated candidate's manager ordinarily does not stay in the job until a new candidate is selected four years hence. Under these circumstances, the committee picks a chairman to serve until a candidate for president is named. If the campaign is successful, the chairman traditionally steps into the new President's cabinet or onto his personal staff and the President, in consultation with the committee, selects a new chairman. The tasks of the chairman are many and difficult and only the most skillful politicians of long experience are ordinarily selected for this post. In the party, he ranks second only to the President himself as the chief director of its operations.

PARTY FINANCES

To maintain party organization, carry on propagandist and other activities, and wage campaigns requires money, and usually a great deal of it. There have been instances in which use of large sums backfired against a candidate or a party, but no party management ever thinks it has money enough or relaxes its efforts to get more. The first, and often the principal, task of many of the party committees is to raise funds. As a rule, the burden devolves primarily upon the treasurer of the committee concerned, although in states and localities it may be assigned to a director of finance. Such officials commonly leave no stone unturned in their search for the "sinews of war," appeals going not only to people of wealth, but to any and all party adherents. Money is only one factor in winning elections, but it is important enough to tip the scales when two parties or two candidates are rather evenly matched. Some amount of money is essential just to get the candidate's name before the voters.

If they are to remain going concerns, parties must spend money all of the time to support the permanent headquarters and the organizational work which is always going on. Their outlays are highest and attract the most attention in connection with campaigns. It would be interesting if figures could be compiled showing precisely what such outlays are. Few accurate records are kept, however, and it is impossible to discover with exactness what is spent in campaigning in the United States. There are, it is true, certain published figures. Party organizations engaging in national campaigns are required by law not only to stay within a specified maximum, but to make full reports on their financial operations, both intake and outgo. Various states also require reports. However, the regular channel for party expenditure on a campaign—the party's national, state, or local committee—is by no means the only one through which money is spent. All sorts of voluntary, unofficial committees and organizations raise and spend large sums. With possibly three times as much actually spent as reported by the committee, Republican outlays on the presidential (and congressional) campaigns of 1928 to 1936 inclusive reached a high of $14.2 million, and Democratic outlays, of $9.2 million (both in 1936). In 1939, an act (Hatch) was passed limiting a national committee's outlay in any calendar year to $3 million. The committees have, of course, reported spending less than this in each national campaign since that time, but the reported expenditures of auxiliary organizations (citizens groups, labor unions, etc.) and the unreported expenditures of informal, voluntary, and state groups have far exceeded the reported totals. The costs of campaigning since 1940 have increased the same as other costs. Estimates of the total expenditures in the campaign of 1952 vary from a low of $35 million to a high of $140 million. The parties and other participating national groups reported spending $23 million. An exhaustive study by the Senate Subcommittee on Privileges and Elections of the expenditures in 1956, placed the national total at $33 million ($21 million by Republicans, $12 million by Democrats and labor). Reported national expenditures in 1960 were $28 million (Republican, $13 million; Democrats and labor, $15 million). In 1964, the total was $36 million ($19 million Republican and $17 million Democrats and labor) and $9 million more by the Congressional Campaign Committees. In addition, of course, there are heavy state and local outlays, not only in "presidential years," but every year, in connection with the primaries and elections perpetually going on.

Many people contemplate such outlays with apprehension, wondering whether money in politics has not become a menace to our democratic institutions. Rival party organizations or candidates, especially if blessed with less ample resources, habitually take advantage of this popular concern and loudly denounce the "slush funds" of their opponents. It is, however, possible to spend very large sums of money in perfectly legitimate ways. It is true that a good deal of party work is done without pay. Only a small proportion of committee members or other party officials receives any salary

Recent levels of expenditure in presidential campaigns

Why expenditures are so large

or other stipend from the party. The general public pays for much, perhaps without realizing it, when public officials take time off from their regular work to make speeches, collect funds, and otherwise serve their party, especially during campaigns. But even in off years all this is far from enough. There are publicity men, research workers—even clerks and stenographers —to be paid. There is office space (sometimes entire buildings) to be rented, often at high cost in large cities; there are office supplies to be provided; there are heavy demands for postage and travel; telephone and telegraph charges mount up; printing takes its toll, along with many forms of advertising, including banners, buttons, and the like; radio time is essential and both major parties pour money into party periodicals.

Any fair-minded person who will look into the facts will find that in a nationwide political effort it takes only a few items of a perfectly legitimate nature to account for outlays running into the millions. Like other forms of publicity and salesmanship, campaigning has come to be tremendously expensive. One reason is the size of the electorate. A nationwide campaign necessarily involves the expenditure of millions of dollars, in the aggregate, for the rental of headquarters and places for holding political meetings, for printing and distributing campaign literature, for the traveling expenses of speakers and higher party officials, for an army of organizers, canvassers, clerks, copyists, typists, tabulators, and addressers, to say nothing of the towering costs of advertising in newspapers, in magazines, on billboards, and by radio. The largest item in the cost of modern campaigning is broadcasting time and the two parties reported having spent $9 million in 1956, over $14 million in 1960, more than $24 million in 1964, and more than $32 million in 1966 on this item alone from Sept. 1 to Election Day. When all of these entirely proper objects of expenditure are duly listed and footed up, it will not be difficult to understand why, in spite of protracted and searching investigations by special Senate committees in connection with the big outlays in every presidential campaign from 1920 to 1956 inclusive, almost no evidence has come to light justifying suspicion of extensive corruption in the national politics of recent years. This is perhaps the price we pay for stirring interest and getting our citizens to do their civic duty.

Sources of party funds

Whence come the funds with which to meet party outlays on the present generous scale? Speaking broadly, from anybody who can be induced (or coerced) to give. Raising money in humdrum times between elections is a thankless task. Party officers charged with the responsibility do what they can; but naturally—at least in the case of the major parties—nearly all is gathered in at campaign time, and for immediate use. To begin with, candidates are almost invariably expected to dig into their pockets to take care of part of their own campaign expenses. Party members already in public office, whether or not up for reelection, are likewise counted on for contributions, frequently in terms of some fixed percentage of salary received. Especially public officers or employes, national, state, or local, who get their jobs by partisan appointment are expected to contribute to the party. Contributors among the general public during past campaigns are invited to help, and especially associates or friends of candidates. A decade or more ago, widely heralded efforts were made, particularly by the Democrats, to get the general rank and file of party adherents to manifest interest in national campaigns by contributing a dollar apiece or some similar small amount. The most impressive success was achieved in the 1960 campaign but this was still far short of reaching most members and of supplying more than a fraction of the party's campaign resources. A sustaining membership program begun in 1957 by the Democrats has also scored some important successes. The Republicans have never reached the small contributors as effectively as the Democrats.

All of these sources, however, would not carry a major party far toward the vast sums required. By and large, the money for national, and to some extent for state, campaigns comes rather from businessmen, bankers, government contractors, labor unions, and other private citizens who have, or think they have, something at stake in the success or defeat of a given party. These chiefly are the "prospects" on whom the party treasurers and members of finance committees work in their money-raising drives. Corporations are forbidden by law to contribute. This does not stand in the way of gifts by officers, directors, stockholders, acting as individuals. The list, especially of Republican contributors, is filled with the names of the executives of large corporations. Since 1943, labor unions also have been forbidden to contribute to campaign funds, but this has not prevented the A.F.L.–C.I.O. from aiding the campaigns of several Democratic candidates through auxiliary agencies, notably the Committee on Political Education. Although the number of large gifts to either party is small, the bulk of the contributions comes from a comparatively few persons. The six top party committees in 1952 reported 55 percent of their contributions were received from 2407 gifts of $1,000 or more and the figures in 1956, 1960, and 1964 showed about the same thing. Among the efforts to reach the smaller giver, an increasingly popular device is the $50 to $100 plate dinners invented by the Democrats but now used also by the Republicans. This has helped increase the number of givers also and recent estimates place the number of contributors at 8 to 10 million.

Contributions at campaign time

REGULATION OF CONTRIBUTIONS AND EXPENDITURES

The high cost of modern campaigning and the resultant pressure on the party organization to raise huge sums of money raise a number of difficult problems. In the first place, the candidate in modest circumstances who cannot afford a large outlay on his own behalf is either unable to compete or is completely dependent upon the party organization to support him. In the second place, some of the contributions are not wholly disinterested. Some contributors expect personal favors from a successful party or candidate in

The need for regulation

the form of an appointment to office—as ambassador, for example—or of benevolent governmental policies toward the enterprise or group with which they are identified. The political-interest group, for example, is likely to want legislation or administration favorable to the group in return for campaign aid. Concern over the excessive domination of candidates or parties by a few wealthy persons or special interests has induced national and state governments to attempt to regulate political contributions and expenditures by laws known as "corrupt-practices acts."

State regulation   The corrupt-practices legislation of the 50 states varies widely and only a brief summary is possible. Typically, it prohibits such patently corrupt behavior as bribery, treating, intimidation or impersonation of voters, ballot-box stuffing, and tampering with voting machines. It also outlaws many practices not in themselves corrupt and extends to both giving and spending party funds. About two-thirds of the states, for example, forbid contributions by banks and other corporations—although not by the officers or directors as individuals. About one-fourth of the states forbid levies on officeholders. Nearly all the state laws attempt to place a ceiling on expenditures by or on behalf of candidates either as a flat sum or as a percentage of salary of the office sought or as a multiple of the number of voters in the constituency. A few states place a limit on the total expenditures of a state committee. Few of these regulations are effective anywhere. If the law limits the party committee or the candidate, expenditures can be made by unofficial committees or by friends of the candidate. If assessments of officeholders are forbidden, contributions by officeholders rarely are. A more effective part of most state corrupt-practice laws is that requiring publicity of receipts and disbursements. About three-fourths of the states require candidates and parties to file reports of their finances either before or after election or at both times. Publicity after the election is usually not effective, however, and that before the election is incomplete.

National regulation   Congress, on its part, has also attempted to regulate campaign financing in connection with the election of national officers. The congressional efforts have been little more effective than those of the state legislatures. They may be summarized under four heads.

1) *Limitations on the raising of money.* Persons on the national payroll may not be solicited for contributions for political purposes by any officer or employee of the government or by anyone in a government office building. An act of 1907 forbids any national bank or other corporation organized under national law to contribute to any campaign fund whatsoever, and makes it unlawful for any corporation organized under state law to contribute to such a fund in connection with the election of national officials. A clause in the War Labor Disputes (Smith–Connally) Act of 1943 extended these restrictions to labor unions. The Labor–Management Relations (Taft–Hartley) Act of 1947 replaced the expired act of 1943 and prohibited, under severe penalties, contributions *or expenditures* by labor unions or other organizations (equally with banks and corporations) in

connection with national elections and all primaries, caucuses, and conventions held in connection therewith. Finally, under the Political Activities Act (Hatch) of 1939 as amended in 1940 no contributions from relief workers (when such exist) may be received, and no individual, committee, or association may donate more than $5,000 in any calendar year to the campaign of any candidate for a national office, exclusive of any contribution to a state or local committee. No contractor with the national government, further, may make a contribution during the period of negotiation or performance of the contract.

2) *Restrictions on amounts that may be spent.* The Federal Corrupt Practices Act of 1925 limits the expenditures of a candidate for the Senate to $10,000 and of a candidate for the House to $2,500, unless a lower maximum is fixed by law of the candidate's state, in which case that law governs. A candidate has a right, however, to the benefit of an alternative rule under which he may spend up to three cents per vote cast for all candidates for the given office in the last preceding general election, with a maximum of $25,000 for a senatorial candidate and $5,000 for a candidate for the House. One other restriction, found in the amending Political Activities Act of 1940, is that no "political committee" operating nationally may receive or expend more than $3 million in any calendar year.

3) *Limitations on the purposes for which money may be spent.* State laws on this subject are usually quite ample. National restriction does not extend much beyond prohibition of the more obvious types of corrupt practice; indeed, in limiting the amount of expenditure as indicated above, the law expressly exempts outlays of candidates on travel, subsistence, stationery, postage, circulars, telegraph and telephone service, and for "personal" items.

4) *Requirement of publicity.* This takes two main forms. First, every candidate for the Senate or House is required to file with the secretary of the Senate or the clerk of the House, both before and after election, a full report of all contributions received in support of his candidacy and an itemized statement of expenditures. Second, all party committees (and likewise all other committees, organizations, and associations which receive donations or spend money for political purposes in two or more states) must under oath make full periodic reports of their financial operations, and must include the names of all donors of $100 or more (in the case of national organizations, $10 or more).

Some of the reasons why these regulations of campaign finance have not been particularly effective are set forth below.

Weaknesses: 1. Excludes primaries

At the time the Corrupt Practices Act of 1925 was passed, it was widely supposed that Congress could not constitutionally regulate primary elections preceding national elections. Although the Supreme Court now holds the primaries to be subject to congressional regulation, the Congress has never extended the act to include expenditures in primaries. Not infrequently, especially in the South, primary campaign expenditures are larger

2. Excludes personal expense

3. Excludes indirect expenditure

4. Excludes auxiliary organizations

5. Excludes loans

6. Deficits

7. Publicity

8. Enforcement

The problem of improvement

than those in the election campaign. Secondly, a candidate need not report as expenditure any sums paid out for his travel, subsistence, stationery, postage, printing, or personal services. A larger loophole is that there is no restriction or even any reporting required of amounts spent on behalf of candidates by friends or associates or local or state party groups, whether such expenditures are with the knowledge and consent of the candidate or not. The attempt to limit national committee expenditures to $3 million a year has the same weakness. All sorts of new clubs, associations, and informal committees have grown up alongside the national committee as vehicles for additional expenditures, for example, Citizens for Eisenhower, Associated Willkie Clubs of 1940, Citizens for Kennedy–Johnson. The prohibition of labor union or corporation expenditure does not apply to auxiliary organizations which may be supported by union or corporate funds. As for individuals having contributed the legal maximum of $5,000 to a national committee, they are not prevented from making further contributions to auxiliary organizations and to state and local committees.

In their desperate campaign-time search for funds, party authorities not only seek gifts but sometimes contract loans, usually from affluent well-wishers. Whether originally so intended by the lenders, such loans often turn into actual contributions, though at campaign time are unaccounted for as such. Parties sometimes emerge from campaigns with sizable deficits and may raise the money to meet them long after the accounting for the year's expenditures has been made. Publicity requirements of both national and state statutes are very imperfectly met, and accounts are often so poorly kept and reports so carelessly prepared as to be almost unintelligible. In a single recent campaign year, 122 candidates for the House of Representatives completely failed to turn in any reports—and apparently nothing happened. Such looseness and obscurity balk anyone trying to find out what actually goes on and, of course, defeat the purpose of well-meant legislation. Finally—and it is now hardly necessary to add this—the entire system (apart, at least, from the main reports of the two national committees) suffers from inadequate enforcement. In fact, there is no proper and permanent enforcing machinery at all. A candidate alleged to have overspent in his campaign may be haled into court or before a congressional committee by a rival contesting his seat; and after each quadrennial campaign, special congressional committees on campaign expenditures dig through such records as they can lay hold of and issue voluminous reports. By and large, however, it is only occasionally, and often largely by accident, that anything is done really to put teeth into the laws.

The problem of regulating campaign finances is clearly one of great difficulty and complexity. Parties must have money and lots of it. Few people are willing either to give money or to do political work voluntarily. Under the circumstances, it is not surprising that great influence in party affairs and in the government accrues to those who are willing and able to give or to those who although unable to give are willing to work at the chores of democracy. There has been a great deal of genuine improvement over the years in the ethics of political competition. There is little outright bribery, vote buying, and ballot-box stuffing today, and there was a great deal 75 years ago. Party leaders are not quite so anxious to throw money around, callously indifferent to the public reaction, as they used to be. On the other hand, campaigning is more expensive than it used to be. Voters will no longer attend the old-fashioned rallies, which are relatively inexpensive; they want to sit at home and be reached by radio and television.

President Kennedy, in 1961, perhaps sensitive to the charge that his family had spent huge sums to gain him the nomination and election appointed a commission to look at the subject of campaign costs and the ineffectiveness of the national regulations. The commission recommended the repeal of all ceilings on expenditures and the use of more careful and more elaborate reporting and publicity to prevent abuses. President Johnson, after ignoring the matter for a time, strongly urged similar reforms in 1966 and 1967, as well as general tightening of the national laws. The Senate passed the President's bill in modified form in 1967 but the bill died in the House.

In order to reduce the influence of wealth in the democratic process and to equalize party and candidate competition, it has been repeatedly suggested that some or all campaign expenses should be appropriated from the public treasury. In justification it is pleaded that these are necessary costs of our system of government. President Theodore Roosevelt advanced this idea in 1907. In 1910, Colorado undertook an experiment in this direction but the law was declared unconstitutional on the grounds that as drafted it was unfair to minor parties and to new parties. Former Senator Hatch, author of the national legislation in 1939 and 1940, suggested limiting the expenditures of each party in a national campaign to $1 million, with the government giving this amount to each party. In Oregon and North Dakota at present, and in four other states at various times, brochures on the candidates and party platforms have been prepared and distributed for each campaign at state expense. These "publicity" pamphlets are intended to relieve the candidates and parties of some of the costs of getting their names before the voters. Puerto Rico inaugurated in 1957 a system of limited public financing of party activities. The President's Commission on Campaign Costs recommended in 1962 that political contributors receive limited tax benefits. Minnesota in 1955 and California in 1957 have authorized modest recognition for tax purposes of political contributions. Led by Senator Long (La.), the Congress in 1966 authorized the use of personal income tax receipts ($1 per taxpayer) on the approval of the taxpayer to finance presidential campaigns but this was repealed in 1967. President Johnson has supported the idea of a limited income tax credit for political contributions and also of public financing of presidential campaign contributions by direct appropriation from the treasury. In general, the reaction to these schemes for public financing of campaigns has been unfavorable.

Public financing of campaigns

Many people regard this as a private, not a public, problem. A large proportion of the voters are not deeply interested. It would be very difficult to draft a system of public financing which would consider legitimate costs realistically, would be fair to all candidates and parties, and would eliminate competition for additional funds.

SELECTING CANDIDATES FOR PUBLIC OFFICE

Importance of nomination procedure:
1. Facilitates majority rule

Among the many useful purposes in the American system of government served by political parties, none is more fundamental than the designation of candidates to stand for public office. In sifting out the many aspirants for power and place in the vast constituencies of American politics, the parties reduce the alternatives available and thus facilitate majority decision. Without this sifting process the power of the electorate would be scattered among numerous choices, no one of which might command the support of more than a small handful of the voters. Although party efforts do not universally produce majority decisions, they do tend to prevent domination of the electoral process by one or two groups.

2. Has become a part of elections

The grip of the party organizations on the nomination process has been loosened but not shattered by the introduction of direct participation by the voters in the selection of party candidates. The primary election systems have made the nominating of candidates an integral part of the election process. An understanding of nominating procedure is indispensable, therefore, to a proper appreciation of the meaning and nature of the power of the voter in American democracy.

3. Replaces election in one-party areas

In many communities and in several states, where one political party so far overshadows any others that its nominees are virtually assured of election, the nominating procedure is the main point at which real influence can be exerted by the average citizen. In the Democratic South, Republican New England and the Plains, and cities such as Chicago and New York, dominated by entrenched political organizations, the nominating process is frequently more influential in determining the policies of the governments of those areas than is the election.

Nomination by petition

Contemporary nominating procedures are the product of many decades of political experience. They have evolved through successive forms—caucus, convention, primary—each of which has broadened the amount of popular participation over its predecessor but none of which has ever been wholly abandoned. Before we embark, however, on a survey of this development it may be useful to digress a moment and to point out that candidates do not have to be nominated in order to be elected. A qualified person may, legally at least, be elected to almost any office in the nation without ever having been nominated in any formal sense. Aspirants for public office in nearly every state may have their names appear on the ballot on election day by filing a petition supported by some specified number of qualified voters. Such aspirants are not, however, entitled to bear the label of a major political party. They must run as independents or as representatives of a party which cannot or will not participate in the regular nominating process. Moreover, candidates may be selected to office whose names do not appear on the ballot at all. Virtually every ballot (or voting machine) in America makes provision for a voter to "write-in" for any office within his choice the name of an individual whom he wishes to support. Few persons, however, ever attain office either as "independents" or as "write-in" candidates. Occasionally, in small constituencies and for local offices, such candidates are swept into office by their fellow citizens. In the state and the nation, however, election is normally achieved only by those who have been nominated by a party.

"Write-in" candidates

The earliest known nominating procedure in American experience appeared in pre-Revolutionary days in connection with election to city councils or colonial assemblies and came to be called the *caucus*. This method is quite informal and is simply a meeting of party or faction or community leaders in advance of the election at which they agree to support, and to propose that their fellow citizens support, some individual or slate of individuals to the office or offices presently to be filled by election. The caucus sprang up and flourished spontaneously without legal prescription or party rule, and until the Jacksonian era no other nominating procedure was used to any extent. As party organization became more formalized, caucuses also became more formalized and spread upwards to state and national politics much as the hierarchy of party committees reached across city, county, and state lines. Gradually the caucuses at the local (ward, town, city) level began to designate representatives to meet with those from other districts to form county and state bodies which coordinated the selection of party standard bearers for state and congressional offices. As they enlarged their scope they became formalized into county, state, and ultimately national conventions of representatives from local caucuses, and thus the convention system of nominations came into being.

The development of nominating procedures:

Caucus

The predominant mode of designating candidates from 1825 to 1910 was the party convention. Caucuses continued to function as devices for selecting delegates from precincts, wards, or towns to city, county, or state conventions. The national, state, and local conventions became more and more regularized institutions for naming party candidates. Apportionment systems were developed for determining the number of delegates to which each precinct, ward, or election district was entitled. Party rules were adopted, providing for such delegate apportionment and for the methods for selecting delegates. Typically, delegates were chosen from precincts for city or county conventions, from city or county conventions to state conventions and to congressional district conventions, and from state conventions to national conventions. This method, it was asserted, transmitted the wishes of the party voters from the precinct upward to the national conclave by an unbroken chain. The conventions also came to serve many other partisan

Convention

functions. They provided rallying places for energizing the party apparatus and enthusing the party workers. They provided a useful facility for the adoption and promulgation of local, state, and national platforms. They served as testing grounds for party orators and for influential party leaders from other areas of the nation. The convention, although characterized by noise, confusion, and drama, nevertheless provided a means through which party leaders could weigh and balance the qualifications of the candidates. Behind the scenes of the conventions, a few leaders continued as before to meet in caucus and propose slates which the rank-and-file delegates might accept. With this difference, however: A larger and more representative segment of the party members had the opportunity to ratify or veto the leaders' choices.

Criticism of convention

Toward the end of the nineteenth century, the convention fell increasingly into disrepute. The delegate selection procedures, irregular at best, fell periodically under the domination of ruthless leaders who packed local caucuses and frustrated genuine representation of local party sentiment. By the time that attempts to regulate such matters by law became general, the convention system was disappearing. In the state and national conventions, several stages removed from popular participation, opponents of the leaders found it especially difficult to make headway, although frequently they enjoyed wide public support. The continued surge of the democratic ideal, interpreted in this situation as demanding more voter participation, also contributed to the downfall of the convention system.

Direct primary

After 1900, the convention system was gradually discarded as a nominating device. It survives today only for presidential nominations and for statewide offices in a few states (notably Connecticut, Delaware, New York until 1967, and Indiana). In its place the direct primary system for making nominations has been adopted in some form in every state. The essence of the direct primary is the selection of candidates by direct action of the voters themselves. The procedures employed are so similar to those used in the final elections that the primary becomes, in effect, a preliminary intraparty election, and often in earlier days was called *a direct primary election*. Primaries of the different parties are commonly held on the same day, and at the places where the regular elections are held later; they are administered by the regular election officials, with all costs met out of the public treasury; the ballots are like those used in regular elections; and the same corrupt-practice laws and other safeguards apply. Persons seeking nomination to an office may get their names on a primary ballot simply by self-announcement and perhaps payment of a fee; or they may have been picked at some caucus or preprimary convention. The common method, however, is to file a petition signed by some specified proportion of the voters in the area, the proportion being gauged roughly in accordance with the importance of the office, and varying all the way from one-half of one percent to as high as five or even ten percent. Ordinarily a candidate receiving the largest number of votes for a given office is declared the party nominee for that office, even though, with often three or four persons seeking the same nomination, the victor may win by virtue of a plurality. All southern states except Tennessee, however, provide a "run-off" primary when no candidate receives a majority in the first contest. In any event, winners in the respective party primaries automatically get their names on the ballots placed in the voters' hands at the regular elections.

The direct primary presupposes elections on a party basis, and conse-quently is itself partisan. Persons seeking nomination do so as Republicans or Democrats and are so listed on the ballots used. Where, however, non-partisan elections have been introduced (as for legislative members in Min-nesota and Nebraska, and for local offices in many cities and some counties), they usually are preceded by a single nonpartisan primary conducted in all respects like an ordinary party primary, except that the ballots carry no indication of the party affiliations of the persons to be voted for, and that no question as to the voters' own affiliations is raised at the polls. Partisan and nonpartisan primaries, for different offices, may indeed be held at the same time and place, with separate ballots employed for the two. In any event, the two candidates on a nonpartisan ticket polling the highest and next high-est number of votes for each office get their names on the nonpartisan ballot used at the ensuing election, the primary thus becoming "a sort of qualify-ing heat which eliminates the weaker contestants from the final race" and at the same time assuring ultimate election by majority rather than mere plurality. The system tends to decrease the role of party organizations in the election and the dependence of candidates on party labels to win support. *Partisan and non-partisan primaries*

Partisan primaries may be classified as *closed* or *open,* on the basis of the conditions laid down for participating in them. The closed primary is one in which participation is confined to bona fide members of the given party. The intention is to prevent members of the opposition party from helping to select the party's candidate. Two methods of guarding against this "raiding" are employed. One—required by law in 19 of the closed-primary states (including New York, Pennsylvania, and California)—is an advance enrollment of the party affiliations of all voters. This party regis-tration is shown on the voter lists supplied to polling officials on primary election day and enables them to give to each voter only the ballot of the party with which he has claimed affiliation. The other method, employed in most of the remaining closed-primary states, involves a procedure for challenging voters who call at the polls for the ballot of a party with which they are not known to be identified. Such voters may, for example, be asked to state whether they supported that party at the last election, or at all events half of its candidates, or perchance whether it is their expectation to adhere to it in the future. Either of the two procedures can be flouted by persons of easy conscience if there is sufficient motive; the second is particularly weak. By and large, however, a closed primary of a given party is partici-pated in only by more or less habitual adherents of that party. *Closed and open primaries*

A large number of voters, however, have no strong and abiding party allegiance, and nine states frankly accept the fact and maintain open primaries in which there is no attempt to put the voters' party preferences on record. Instead of asking for and being handed a Republican or a Democratic ballot when he presents himself at the polls, a voter is given either a blanket ballot listing the candidates of the respective parties in separate columns (*one* only to be voted) or a sheaf of ballots containing one for each party. In any event, he votes the ticket of his choice, with no one the wiser. Republicans may take a hand in Democratic nominations, and vice versa. Some states ostensibly having the closed form of primary really have the open form in disguise, since the tests which they prescribe notoriously fail to prevent voters from shifting their adherence from one party to the other. Professional politicians and strong partisans generally favor the closed primary on the theory that the primary is really a party affair and should not be open to independents, nonpartisans, or members of some other party. The secrecy of the open primary has a compelling appeal to many voters.

The primary and the platform   The primary is a nominating device and serves none of the other purposes which conventions had come to serve. There is no room in the primary itself, for example, for preparing a party platform for the coming election. In the few states still using the convention system for statewide purposes this is no problem. In the exclusively direct primary states, however, some other provisions must be made for platform preparation. In 14 states, some form of party conference is recognized by law as the platform drafting agency. The Wisconsin system illustrates this procedure. After the primary, the nominees of the party for the state legislature and for the state executive posts and the hold-over party members of the state senate are directed by law to assemble and prepare a platform upon which presumably they will collectively campaign.

Critique of the primary   The direct primary unquestionably gives the rank-and-file voter a larger share in the nominating process than either of its predecessors. It has not, however, eliminated the need for organization to achieve electoral success nor, consequently, the need for some agreement among party leaders on candidates that ought to be offered for the approval of the public. Thus the caucus of party leaders continues to function in many, if not in most, constituencies. With the primary, however, the party voters have to ratify the leaders' choices and minority groups may contest the leaders' slate. Although there is probably less outright vote-buying today than in the heyday of the convention, the cost of getting elected has probably been increased, not decreased, by the primary. With the primary system a candidate has to run twice. Important public office is farther out of the reach of poor candidates unsupported by an organization than ever before. The primary system also tends to weaken party organization and party responsibility. The party apparatus may well find itself obliged to support candidates who are distasteful to it and opposed to its ideology but who have captured the sympathy of the voters. The National Municipal League in its Model Direct

Primary Elections System recommends that the party organization by conference or caucus ought to be allowed to place a slate on the primary ballot. In the home of the statewide primary, Wisconsin, both major parties have gone outside of the legally prescribed party machinery and created unofficial and unregulated party organs (called voluntary committees) to breathe new ideological homogeneity and a sense of party responsibility into their operations. This has taken them back to the convention system; and the Republican party, at least, meeting in unofficial convention endorses candidates for statewide offices and for United States senator to the rank and file of its members. The endorsement carries with it the support of the treasury and of the organization of the extralegal committee. Party organizations by these and other methods are gradually adjusting themselves to the primary system, but it has been a painful and difficult process for many of them. They are still not proof against a strong upsurge of popular feeling sweeping away their most cherished tenets of public policy. In considering the results of the direct primary system, it must also be remembered that state law and practice vary in many details from one state to another. No two systems are identical in every respect. There is, finally, no concerted effort of consequence to abolish the primary and return to any earlier nominating process.

REFERENCES

N. E. Alexander, *Money, Politics, and Public Reporting* (Princeton, N. J., 1960).

T. A. Bailey, *Democrats versus Republicans: The Continuing Clash* (New York, 1968).

W. E. Binkley, *American Political Parties: Their Natural History* (New York, 1943).

H. Bone, *American Politics & the Party System* (3rd ed., New York, 1965).

———, *Party Committees and National Politics* (Seattle, Wash., 1958).

A. Campbell, G. Gurin, and W. E. Miller, *The Voter Decides* (Evanston, Ill., 1954).

Committee on Political Parties, American Political Science Association, *Toward a More Responsible Two-Party System* (New York, 1950).

C. P. Cotter and B. C. Hennessy, *Politics Without Power: The National Party Committees* (New York, 1964).

P. T. David, *The Changing Party Pattern* (Washington, D. C., 1956).

S. J. Eldersveld, *Political Parties: A Behavioral Analysis* (Chicago, 1964).

W. Goodman, *The Two-Party System in the United States* (New York, 1960).

A. Heard, *The Costs of Democracy* (Chapel Hill, N. C., 1960).

W. B. Hesseltine, *The Rise and Fall of Third Parties; From Anti-Masonry to Wallace* (Washington, D. C., 1948).

V. O. Key, Jr., *Politics, Parties, and Pressure Groups* (4th ed., New York, 1958), Chaps. VII–XVIII.

R. E. Lane, *Political Life; Why People Get Involved in Politics* (Glencoe, Ill., 1959).

——— and A. Ranney, *Politics and Voters* (New York, 1963).

A. Leiserson, *Parties and Politics: An Institutional and Behavioral Approach* (New York, 1958).

National Municipal League, *A Model Direct Primary System* (New York, 1951).

R. F. Nichols, *The Invention of the American Political Parties* (New York, 1967).

L. Overacker, *Money in Elections* (New York, 1932).

————, *Presidential Campaign Funds* (Boston, 1946).

President's Commission on Campaign Costs, *Report* (Washington, D. C., 1962).

A. P. Sindler, *Political Parties in the United States* (New York, 1966).

8

NOMINATING AND ELECTING
A PRESIDENT

The democratic process realizes its most significant fruit in the quadrennial selection of the nation's chief magistrate. All of the elements of the process coalesce in this unique and dramatic spectacle. The political parties reach their maximum effectiveness; the nomination process, involving caucuses, conventions, and primaries, captures the interest and enthusiasm of the people as at no other time. Every medium of communication—radio, television, newspapers, magazines, books, pamphlets, leaflets—swamps the public with fact, argument, and exhortation on the affairs of the nation and of those who seek to run it. Political-interest groups strive for places in the sun of each candidate's appreciation. The voters troop out to the polls on election day in larger numbers than on any other occasion. A vast radio and television audience intensely follows the tabulation of the returns. The pageant of an American presidential election is the most remarkable exhibition of popular government anywhere in the world. No other election quite equals it in drama, suspense, oratory, participation in electioneering, carnival atmosphere, ink spilled, or money spent. *The pageant of a presidential election*

It is impossible to fix a precise time at which this great spectacle begins to unfold. In one sense it is going on all the time, for hardly has a new chief executive settled into the White House before some plans are afoot for the next campaign. Late in the year preceding an election year, however, "available" candidates begin to utter declarations or make decisions which convey their willingness to make the run. Organizations then begin to form, "booms" are launched, personal and party groups spar for advantage in the press, in the Congress, in state capitals, city halls, and county courthouses throughout the land. Voter participation in the nominating process begins in March of a presidential year and continues sporadically through April, May, and June. In August the tumultuous national conventions assemble to select their standard bearers. A pause follows while the campaign apparatus of the parties is geared and oiled for the great effort. Then from September *The timetable of a presidential election* until Election Day in early November, the drama moves from scene to scene, mounting in intensity, noise, and enthusiasm. At length the vote is cast, the decision made by 70 million people. It is a stirring demonstration of American democracy in action.

THE CONSTITUTIONAL ELECTORAL SYSTEM

The plan originally adopted

This is not at all the sort of thing that the makers of our Constitution had in view. They did not want the President elected by Congress, because then he would not be sufficiently independent. Neither did they want him elected by the people, because that, they thought, would (in Hamilton's words) invite "tumult and disorder"; besides, the voters, scattered thinly over what already seemed a large country, would not know enough about the qualifications of available men to be able to make wise decisions. The matter troubled the Convention considerably, and 30 different votes on it were taken. At last, however, a plan of indirect popular election was agreed upon under which: (1) each state should have as many "presidential electors" as senators and representatives in Congress; (2) these electors should be chosen in the several states in whatever manner the state legislatures should specify; (3) each elector, at the proper time, should cast a ballot for two persons for the Presidency; and (4) the persons receiving the highest and next highest votes, respectively, should be President and Vice-President. The entire procedure was to be quiet, dignified, and deliberate, with presumably the best qualified men emerging from the sifting. During the struggle over ratification, the plan proved one of the few features of the new Constitution that did not have to be defended. This system produced two Presidents: Washington and Adams. By 1800, it had been modified almost beyond recognition.

Effect of the rise of political parties

In 1788, and again in 1792, every elector wrote the name of Washington on his ballot, with second names scattered. In 1796, with Washington bent on retiring, 13 different persons received electoral votes, John Adams standing first and Jefferson second. In 1800, however, every elector except one, the country over, wrote on his ballot the names of either Jefferson and Burr or Adams and Pinckney. In the meantime two political parties— Federalist and Republican—had organized to capture the Presidency. Each had taken steps in advance of the elections in the states to agree upon particular "candidates" (nominally for the Presidency, but actually for the Presidency and Vice-Presidency), and to put before the voters and legislatures making the choices lists of men who would, if chosen, cast their electoral ballots in all cases for the persons supported by the party to which they belonged. With the party system thus fastening itself upon the country, presidential elections from that time assumed an entirely different aspect from that planned. The way was thus opened for partisan, popular presidential campaigns to develop the "tumultuous" characteristics which the framers would have deplored. The presidential electors became the "row of ciphers," which we know today, with President and Vice-President to all intents and purposes chosen by the people. No better illustration can be found of how the actual working Constitution changes without a hand being laid on the written fundamental law nor of how the spread of democracy has changed the constitutional system.

In the new situation, a tie between the two candidates of a winning party was inevitable unless anticipated beforehand. Jefferson and Burr, in fact, received the highest, and the same number of votes. The Constitution provided that a tie was to be broken by the House of Representatives, voting by states; and in this manner Jefferson finally was elected. The Federalist opposition, however, came near to thwarting the intention of the victors by maneuvering Burr into the highest office; and before the next election came around any repetition of the difficulty was made impossible by an amendment to the Constitution specifying that thereafter electors should in all cases "name in their ballots the person voted for as president, and in distinct ballots the person voted for as vice-president." With the Vice-President thereafter being separately selected, the character of that office underwent a decided change. Thenceforth, the second place on the ticket was awarded largely without regard to the individual's capacity to be President.

The Twelfth Amendment (1804)

MACHINERY FOR NOMINATING CANDIDATES—
THE NATIONAL CONVENTION

The next significant development had to do with a matter for which the framers of the Constitution made no provision, that is, the nomination of candidates. As originally set up, the electoral system did not contemplate "candidates" at all. When, however, political parties arose, their main object forthwith came to be to capture the Presidency. To do this, they must concentrate their support at election time upon a given individual, which, in turn, they could do only if such individual, or candidate, were agreed upon in advance. Thus arose the need for machinery for making the selection in advance of the regular election.

Nominations become a necessity

The first device hit upon was the caucus composed of the (national) senators and representatives of a given party; and it was employed steadily from 1800 to 1824. There were, however, serious objections to it. The caucus acted only by assumed authority; it provided little or no voice for party members in states in which the party was in a minority; and it gave members of the legislative branch an influence in selecting the chief executive which they clearly were not intended to have. The caucus fell from favor when in 1824 it refused to endorse Andrew Jackson. In 1831 both the National Republican (Whig) and anti-Masonic parties turned to popularly chosen nominating conventions, already employed usefully in many state elections. The Democrats fell into line with a convention of their own in

From congressional caucus to national convention

An Early Entrant in the Campaign of 1968

The Nixon Letter

January 31, 1968

To the Citizens of New Hampshire:

I hardly need to remind you of the importance of the New Hampshire Presidential primary—both to the candidates and to the country. This importance stems from more than the fact of its being first. It stems also from the spirit in which New Hampshire's voters approach the election, keenly aware of their special responsibility, of the broad influence of their votes.

In 1968, your responsibility is greater than ever. The nation is in grave difficulties, around the world and here at home. The choices we face are larger than any differences among Republicans or among Democrats, larger than even the differences between the parties. They are beyond politics. Peace and freedom in the world, and peace and progress here at home will depend on the decisions of the next President of the United States.

For these critical years, America needs new leadership.

During fourteen years in Washington, I learned the awesome nature of the great decisions a President faces. During the past eight years I have had a chance to reflect on the lessons of public office, to measure the nation's tasks and its problems from a fresh perspective. I have sought to apply those lessons to the needs of the present, and to the entire sweep of this final third of the 20th Century.

And I believe I have found some answers.

I have decided, therefore, to enter the Republican Presidential primary in New Hampshire.

I will try to meet as many of you as I can—Republicans, Democrats and Independents, those who will vote in March and those who will vote in November. I will invite your comments. I will answer your questions. I will discuss with you my own vision of America's future, and I will ask for yours.

I have visited New Hampshire often—as a candidate, as a public official, and as a private citizen. I appreciate the many courtesies you have paid me. I am deeply grateful for your support in past elections. But in asking your support now, I ask it not on the basis of old friendships. We have entered a new age. And I ask you to join me in helping make this an age of greatness for our people and for our nation.

Sincerely,

s/ Richard Nixon

1832. Many political leaders, including Webster and Calhoun, opposed the new method on the ground that it gave too much power in party matters to the rank and file. Nevertheless, by 1840 the national convention became the generally accepted means of putting both candidates and platforms before the voters; and such it has remained.

Arrangements for conventions: time and place

The national conventions of the two major parties today, and likewise of such minor parties as have built up durable organizations, are held on call of the national party committee. A year or more preceding a presidential election, the committee meets (commonly in Washington in the case of the Republicans and Democrats), decides upon the place and date of the coming convention, and authorizes the party organizations in the states and territories to see that delegates and alternates are chosen in accordance with an apportionment set forth in the call. Except in 1956 and 1960, the Republicans have held their conventions first and the Democrats two weeks or more later. Strong efforts to shorten the campaign by moving the conventions from late June or July to August have been made in recent years with mixed results but both conventions in 1968 were held in August. The national committees are strongly pressured by business interests of many of the large cities to select their cities as convention sites. Eager for the advertising and certain of large sales of food, lodgings, and entertainment to delegates and visitors, the city representatives typically offer substantial contributions to the party treasuries to win approval. The national committees are, however, concerned about more than donations. They must keep an eye on the adequacy of hotel and convention facilities and they seek to gain any partisan advantage they can by selecting cities where the convention enthusiasm may assist the party or a particular candidate. Chicago and Philadelphia have been the most popular convention sites but St. Louis, Cleveland, and Baltimore also ordinarily receive consideration. The West Coast has grown in popularity recently: The Republicans met in San Francisco in 1956 and in 1964 and the Democrats in Los Angeles in 1960. In 1968, the Republicans chose Miami Beach as their site— partly perhaps because of their hopes to pick up the electoral votes of Florida and partly because there would seem to be less opportunity there for racial or anti-war demonstrations. The Democrats found their meeting in Chicago harassed by demonstrations and torn by dissension.

The first national conventions had no regular plan of membership at all but it was soon learned that without a plan partisans from nearby states and cities would swamp the convention. The earliest plan was quite simple: Each state was assigned as many delegates as it was entitled to electoral votes (one for each member of both houses of Congress). In 1852, the Democrats doubled the number assigned to each state, probably to allow more persons to participate in the choice. The Republicans followed the same plan in 1860. Although modified in this century, the electoral vote remains the major determinant of the size of the delegation from each state. *Convention member-ship: 1. Earlier arrangements*

Weaknesses in the traditional system for apportioning delegates were revealed most clearly in the Republican party. The states of the Solid South repeatedly sent to Republican national conventions delegates who really represented no consequential party strength. The Republican delegates from the South were, in practice, representatives of a small group of national officeholders appointed by Republican Presidents. A Republican President could, therefore, and did, usually, control these patronage-delegates and thus was able to wield a powerful influence in the convention. Theodore Roosevelt certainly used these delegates to help bring about Taft's nomination in 1908. When, however, Taft used the same device in 1912 to achieve his own renomination, the party was badly split. Roosevelt, now a strong contender and the clear choice of many rank-and-file Republicans where they had any say in the delegate selection, denounced the system by which Taft controlled the convention and took his followers out of the party into a new Progressive party. This move cost the Republicans the election and *2. Weak-nesses*

3. Re-publican modifica-tion

convinced many of the leaders that something would have to be done about the southern delegations. Beginning with the convention of 1916, the Republicans began paring down the relative strength of the southern delegations with some paring occurring as recently as 1952. The method used by the Republicans has been to make the number of district delegates contingent upon a minimum Republican voting strength and to grant bonus state delegates to Republican states. Strangely enough, the southern states carried by Goldwater in 1964 were the main recipients of bonus delegates for 1968.

4. Present apportionment systems: a. Republican

The system adopted by the Republicans in 1952 and still in use provides:

State Delegates (at large)

1) Four from each state.
2) Two additional for each congressman-at-large (if any).
3) Six additional from each state casting a majority of its votes for the Republican nominee at the last presidential election or electing in the same or the intervening election a Republican senator or governor.
4) Nine from the District of Columbia, three from Puerto Rico, and one from the Virgin Islands.

District Delegates

1) One from each congressional district casting 2000 or more votes last time for the Republican presidential candidate or for the Republican congressional candidate in the intervening election.
2) One additional from each district casting 10,000 votes or more for the Republican candidates for President at the last election or for the Republican candidates for the House of Representatives in the intervening election.

b. Democratic

The Democrats, with party strength more evenly distributed throughout the country, were able to operate without too much friction on the old basis until 1940. In this party, however, the southern Democrats were underrepresented compared to those in New England. In the convention of 1936, when the rule requiring a two-thirds vote for nomination was repealed, the northern supporters of the repeal agreed to reward solidly Democratic states by instituting the system of bonus delegates. The repeal of the two-thirds rule greatly weakened the influence of the South over the Democratic nomination and the bonus system was introduced partially to offset this. The Democrats, also, seem to be under continuing pressure to increase the number of those attending conventions. A modest provision of two bonus state delegates was begun in 1944 and increased to four in 1948, but in 1952 the rules were modified to protect any state from loss as a result of congressional reapportionment. Then in 1956 every state was authorized as many delegates as it had in 1952 plus four more if the state had gone Democratic for President or in the interim for senator or governor. For 1960, a complex plan was devised granting two and one-half delegate votes

How the Republican Apportionment System Works

Delegations from Selected States
1968

STATE	TOTAL DELEGATES	DELEGATES-AT–LARGE	DISTRICT DELEGATES
Alabama	26	10	16
California	86	10	76
Illinois	58	10	48
Mississippi	20	10	10
New York	92	10	82
South Carolina	22	10	12
West Virginia	14	4	10

How the Democratic Apportionment System Works

Delegate Votes from Selected States
1968

STATE	TOTAL VOTES	MAXIMUM NO. DELEGATES
Alabama	32	56
California	174	172
Illinois	118	136
Mississippi	24	44
New York	190	226
South Carolina	28	40
West Virginia	38	48

for each representative and senator and one-half vote for each national committee member but providing that no state might have fewer votes than it had in 1956. And in 1964 and 1968, each state was granted three delegate votes for each senator and representative plus bonus delegates as indicated below:

1) Six from each state.
2) Three for each representative-at-large.
3) Ten additional if the state cast its electoral vote for the Democratic presidential candidate in 1964. These may be distributed among districts.
4) One additional vote for each 100,000 popular votes cast in the state for the Democratic presidential candidate in 1964. These may be distributed among districts.
5) Three for each congressional district.
6) One vote for each of the two state members of the national committee.
7) Five votes each for Guam, Virgin Islands, Canal Zone.
8) Eight votes for Puerto Rico.
9) Twenty-one votes for the District of Columbia.

Strictly speaking, the composition of a national convention is defined in terms of votes, rather than of delegates. In Republican usage, the distinc-

5. *Numbers*

tion has been one without a difference, each delegate having one vote. In Democratic usage, however, many states and territories send delegates in excess of their quota of votes, each delegate in such case casting only a fractional vote. In later days the practice, motivated usually by desire to provide good convention seats for the "boys from home," developed into a serious abuse. On complaint of officials in charge of seating arrangements, the 1940 convention decreed that thereafter no state might send delegates in excess of twice its quota of votes; and delegate attendance fell sharply. In 1952, the convention in violation of its own rules seated oversize delegations from six states, and the total roll was 1642 delegates to cast 1230 votes. In 1960, 3042 delegates were authorized to cast 1521 votes and in 1964, 2944 delegates cast 2316 votes. In 1968, 2989 delegates and 110 national committee members cast 2622 votes. The Republicans in 1968 had 1333 delegates and votes. With one alternate standing ready to fill in for each delegate, the two national conventions are obviously not of "deliberative" size.

SELECTION OF THE DELEGATES

Rise of presidential primaries

Delegates to the national convention were, in the formative years, chosen in a variety of ways—by mass meetings, by caucuses, by district and state conventions, and by party committees. Gradually each party settled upon a fairly standard system. The Democrats, giving great emphasis to the state as the basic unit of representation and expecting the delegations from many of the states to act as units in the proceedings, usually selected their delegations by means of a state convention or a state central committee. The Republicans, much less concerned about state solidarity, preferred to select district delegates in congressional district conventions and statewide delegates in state conventions. When, however, the direct primary began sweeping the country, the application of this procedure to delegate and presidential candidate selection became an important public issue. The first application of the direct primary procedure to the selection of the delegates was made in Wisconsin in 1905. Thereafter the idea spread rapidly and by 1916 more than half of the delegates of the major parties were designated at primary elections by direct vote of the people. In 1912, the Republican convention undertook to withhold seats from delegates chosen in this way on the grounds that the primary procedure was contrary to the party rule requiring convention selection. This position did not prevail against the state laws requiring primary selection.

The spread of presidential preference primaries

The application of the primary method to the designation of presidential candidates proved somewhat more complex and it was not until 1910 that Oregon first provided on the primary ballot an opportunity to the voters to express their preferences among presidential aspirants. The Democratic platform of 1912 urged every state to adopt a *presidential preference primary* and the Progressive platform urged a constitutional amendment which would make it compulsory. President Wilson in his first message to Congress asked for legislation which would allow presidential and vice-presidential candidates to be nominated by direct vote of the people and would thus relegate the conventions to platform-making agencies after the candidates had been selected. The presidential preference primary in this period became linked to the national-convention delegate primary (presidential primary) and shared in its rapid spread over the nation. After 1916, the movement, however, lost momentum and several states which had adopted either or both of the primary procedures abandoned one or the other. The primary in either form has made few gains since that time.

In the conventions held in 1968 fewer than half of the delegates were selected in some form of primary or were committed by some popular vote on presidential aspirants. These delegates came from 17 states and the District of Columbia. The systems by which delegates were elected and preferences expressed may be classified as follows:

1) Direct election of unpledged delegates and no popular vote on aspirants—Illinois (no aspirants entered), West Virginia (no aspirants entered), New York (district delegates only), Alabama (Democratic delegates only).
2) Direct election of unpledged delegates and a separate nonbinding vote on aspirants—Pennsylvania (district delegates only).
3) Direct election of delegates who may be pledged to a particular aspirant and a separate nonbinding vote on aspirants—New Hampshire, New Jersey, Nebraska.
4) Direct election of delegates who may be pledged to a particular aspirant and no separate vote on aspirants—Florida, South Dakota, District of Columbia.
5) Direct election of delegates pledged to a particular aspirant—Ohio, Wisconsin, California.
6) Direct election of delegates who may be pledged to a particular aspirant and a separate binding vote on aspirants—Oregon, Massachusetts (binding for one ballot only).
7) Direct vote on aspirants which is binding on delegates but no vote on delegates—Indiana.

Selection by party organizations

Most of the state delegates to the two conventions in 1968 were selected by party procedures which did not include any type of general, public, primary election. In most of these states, the delegates were selected by district or state conventions or both; in a few states, the delegates were selected by the state party committee. In many of the convention states, popular participation in selecting the delegates to the local or state conventions was widespread. In several, there was little real opportunity for rank-and-file participation. The nonprimary selection procedures differ widely from state to state.

Recent campaigns, especially those of Stassen (1948), Kefauver (1952), Kennedy (1960), McCarthy (1968) have awakened a new interest in the presidential preference primary, stimulated discussion of its value in many parts of the country, and led to several proposals for strengthening and extending it. It is appropriate, therefore, to review the successes and failures of the primary system as applied to delegates and presidential candidates. Despite the apparent lack of enthusiasm by state lawmakers since 1916 for the primary procedure in delegate selection, it is still vigorously defended in the states where it exists. State party leaders tend to prefer the convention method of selection because it is more of a party operation than a public one and thus party leaders are likely to be more influential in determining the result. The advantages of convention selection are perhaps best exhibited in states like New York and Illinois where both methods are used. The convention selection of the statewide delegates in these states makes it possible to provide places in the delegation for important party leaders—the governors, for example—who do not wish to contest such places in a public election. The primary in which delegates are selected and which offers no opportunity to vote on presidential candidates does not, it is argued, attract voter interest to the same degree as the presidential contest.

The real controversy concerns the desirability of giving the voters an opportunity to participate directly in the selection of the presidential nominees of the parties. A secondary controversy concerns the best method for voter participation: the election of delegates pledged to a particular aspirant or a direct vote on the aspirant. The fear of those who strongly oppose direct voter participation is that the voters are in no position to assess the abilities of candidates to unite the party and to make a broad appeal to the nation. Voter sentiment is likely to be divided among many regional candidates, local "favorite sons," and representatives of large interest groups. Only a convention, runs the argument, can reconcile conflicting interests and select a candidate who will unite the party. Experience indicates that such a candidate may not be a willing one and may not, therefore, be in active contention for primary endorsement. Neither of the candidates in 1952 was an active or a willing seeker of public support in every major sector of the nation. Where preference primaries are now used, not all of the candidates compete. In general, candidates enter state contests only when they think they can win and stay out of contests where they might lose. Thus the voters in many primary states are not able to select among all of the aspirants. The preference primary system is best suited to advance the fortunes of avowed candidates and these, say the critics, are not always the ones that the nation needs or wants. On the other hand, the popular preference system opens the door to candidacies which might otherwise be impossible. President Kennedy certainly won his way to the nomination in 1960 in great part because of his successes in the primaries and without the primaries, the campaigns of Senator McCarthy in 1968 or of Kefauver sixteen years earlier could not have been attempted. If the system of pledged delegates is used as a vehicle for voter participation, the convention may find that no candidate has a majority and no delegate can change his vote. The costs in money and energy for a nationwide primary campaign for presidential aspirants is forbidding. The Presidency is already difficult enough without requiring nine or ten months of arduous campaigning to reach it. None of the present primary systems make any provision for the selection of the vice-presidential candidates or for writing a party platform.

The supporters of preference primaries argue that if the primary system is good for all other state and national offices it is good for the Presidency. Popular participation will tend to prevent boss-dominated conventions and will open the presidential contest to the "fresh-air" of public opinion. There is nothing deliberative about the conventions, say the critics. They are too big, too noisy, too expensive, and too tumultuous to do as adequate a job of selection as their supporters pretend. Although variation of procedure from state to state has some advantages, the nation ought to stipulate a minimal procedure which will allow the voters to express their wishes in the matter of candidates in every state.

THE NATIONAL CONVENTION AT WORK

By whatever method selected, the delegates to the two major national conventions are largely professional politicians. Most of them are holders of public office or of party post. Included in the delegations are many of the most prominent state leaders—governors, senators, representatives, mayors, state legislators, and county leaders. The convention meets in a large hall capable of seating more than 15,000 people, with the delegates seated by states on the main floor and the alternates directly behind them. The press is accorded, typically, a very large section to the right and left of the speaker's platform and the galleries accommodate the interested public. Radio and television carry the proceedings to virtually every corner of the nation. The atmosphere of a convention is noisy and hectic. The hall is ordinarily jammed, making it difficult to move about. There is a buzz of conversation in the air except during major speeches and at tense moments in the procedure. Every interval of the official program is filled with music by band, organ, or vocalist. Demonstrations in behalf of various candidates interrupt the proceedings periodically—especially during the nominating speeches— and hired noisemakers and cheer leaders whip the delegates and galleries into frenzied outbursts of movement and noise. The whole proceedings get entirely out of control of the presiding officers at times and sometimes for an hour or more at a stretch. The aisles, rest rooms, snack bars, and lobbies are frequently crowded with caucuses as leaders negotiate and compromise and reconcile conflicting views. There is nothing in the outward show that resembles deliberation. All of the real issues are usually threshed out behind

Surroundings

the scenes, in hotel rooms, restaurants, headquarters suites, and anywhere men can hold private conferences. The convention city also acquires the frantic air of the hall. The hotels housing the delegates and the headquarters of the parties and candidates are seething masses of people. Banners, music, streamers, and noisemakers of all types fill the lobby and corridors with noise and confusion. At the candidates' headquarters, skilled persuaders hand out their wares to public, press, and politicians. Soundtrucks, bands, balloons, and entertainers fill the streets and stimulate flagging emotions. Hundreds of thousands of dollars are poured out in an effort to exhibit the candidates as personifications of the American way and as certain winners in the election contest. Appeals are made to every level of emotion and reason. It is easy to mistake all of this froth for the real decision-making process. The delegates are more or less immune to such frenzied appeals and they sort and weigh chances and choices usually with the calm sagacity of skilled players of the great American game.

Temporary organi- zation   Ordinarily the conventions last four or five days—a few have dragged on for more than a week. On the first day, the meeting is called to order by the chairman of the national committee who, after the prayer and the reading of the official call for the convention, announces to the delegates the temporary convention officers agreed upon by the national committee. This slate of officers is virtually always accepted by the convention. The temporary chairman then takes the rostrum, perhaps after a recess for some oratorical warm-ups, and delivers the *keynote* address to the delegates and to the world. The keynote speech is a cry to close ranks and prepare for battle and for ultimate triumph. The record of the party and of its great leaders past and present warms the delegates to the tasks ahead and the despicable record and potentiality of the opposite party puts the convention in fighting trim. The rules of the previous convention are then adopted temporarily and the convention committees are organized.

The committees   During the next day or two, the convention marks time with oratory and music while the committees do their work. Both national conventions assign certain functions to four great committees. These are (1) credentials; (2) permanent organization; (3) rules and order of business; and (4) platform and resolutions. Each is composed of one delegate from each delegation (named by the delegation) except the fourth which has two delegates (one man and one woman) from each state. Typically, the chairman of the delegation supplies the names to the convention officers. The committees are obliged to report to the convention at the conclusion of their deliberations and the next major order of business is to receive these reports. The committee on rules submits a set of rules governing convention procedure, delegate apportionment and selection, and the composition and powers of the national committee. Typically, these are the same rules as have previously been in effect, but from time to time changes will be proposed. The report is usually approved with little or no debate. The committee on permanent organization submits a slate of officers to direct the convention for the remainder of the sessions. This too is usually accepted, although there have been contests on this question as the managers of rival candidates have sought to place in the chair officers sympathetic to their candidates. The permanent chairman can wield great power in close contests by his rulings on points of order and by his recognition of those who may speak to the convention. The credentials committee prepares a permanent roll of delegates entitled to sit in the convention. For most delegates at most conventions there is no problem of determining who may rightfully participate, but every convention has some contested seats. The Republican convention, especially, has been troubled for several decades by credentials contests in the southern delegations. The party has been small, its organization so fluid, and the selection procedures so informal in the Deep South that contests are almost unavoidable. In 1952, for example, rival delegations appeared from Texas, Louisiana, Mississippi, Georgia, and Florida. The fight over these delegations was the highlight of the convention and the success of the Eisenhower forces in seating their delegates as against those of Senator Taft influenced the result of the convention. The Democrats experienced a new type of challenge in 1964 when a delegation of Negroes from Mississippi challenged the official white delegation on the grounds that it had been improperly elected, since Negroes in large numbers had not been allowed to participate. The committee rejected their challenge but attempted to force a loyalty pledge from the white delegation and admitted two delegates-at-large from the Negro group to the convention. The committee also proposed that in future conventions a bar to discrimination be established. A special Equal Rights Committee sought in 1968 to get state delegations to promise to bar discrimination in selection. There were nevertheless a number of bitter contests and in one case, Georgia, two delegations (Negro and white) were seated, each with one-half the state's votes. Usually, the committee report is approved without debate and without a call of the roll.

When the permanent officers are installed, the permanent chairman *Platform* customarily delivers an address of the "keynote" type but usually a more *adoption* restrained one. The convention is then ready to receive the proposed party platform from the platform committee. Typically, a small drafting committee designated by the national committee from among prospective members of the platform committee has been at work for some days before the convention assembled preparing a draft of a platform. Hearings have been held to allow interest groups to urge their programs and the leading candidates have been solicited for their views. Working day and night in the first few days of the convention the committee will then whip into final shape a platform to be read to the convention. Platform writers are skilled craftsmen of the "glittering generality" and the "emotion-filled symbol," and most controversies within the party are resolved in favor of platitudinous noncommitment. Much labor, however, is poured into the exact platform language on controversial subjects. The convention almost invariably accepts the committee's proposals, although occasionally it has done so only after heated debate as in 1968 in the Democratic convention over Viet Nam. As approved by the convention, the platform of a major party is likely to be about ten pages long and cover a large number of subjects of national policy. On some matters the platform will be relatively clear and specific; on others it will be general and vague. The words *sound, stable, peace, prosperity, reasonable, fair, just,* will be used over and over again. The platform is not so much an outline of proposals as a bid for support. It is invariably overshadowed by the announced views of the presidential candidates and is read in its entirety by very few people. Rightly viewed, it is but one of the less important guides to what this party or its candidates will do if entrusted with power.

Nomination of candidates

At last, by the third or fourth day, the convention arrives at its main objective, the nomination of candidates. The secretary calls the roll of states, beginning with Alabama, and each delegation, in its turn, has an opportunity to place a "favorite son" or other person in nomination. If the delegates of a state which stands near the top of the list choose to do so, they may yield to a delegation which under alphabetical order would not be called until later. This opportunity to get a candidate's name officially before the convention in advance of others, and to touch off a demonstration in his behalf, is believed by some managers to be advantageous. From two or three to upwards of a dozen names may be presented, each in a vigorous eulogistic, and sometimes flamboyant nominating speech followed by briefer seconding speeches by delegates carefully picked to give an impression of widely distributed support. No effort is spared by either the orators or the delegates and spectators favoring a given candidate to whip up enthusiasm for him. At the proper psychological moment, delegates and alternates may break forth with all manner of vocal and mechanical noise, seize flags and standards, and start parading around the hall, and plunge the assemblage into pandemonium from which it can be extricated only when the enthusiasts have reached a state of exhaustion an hour or more later. Rarely are such demonstrations genuinely spontaneous. They are staged according to careful prearrangement and usually fail in their presumed purpose of sweeping the convention off its feet.

Voting on the candidates

When, finally, all of the names have been presented, the convention proceeds to ballot. The roll of states is called again, and each delegation, through its chairman, announces its vote. In both parties, votes as reported may be unanimous for a given candidate or may be divided among two or more. Republican tradition favors full freedom for delegations to divide and to have their vote so recorded, except only as limited by instructions received in presidential primaries. Democratic tradition, however, has been different.

The Democratic "unit rule"

Reflecting the states'-rights antecedents of the party, and yielding the practical advantage of greater power and importance for a state in a convention proceedings, a "unit rule" has been favored under which a state convention may require a delegation to cast its votes in a block for a single candidate. Even if no such requirement is imposed, a delegation may itself, by majority vote, determine how the votes of all of its members shall be recorded. This practice is not imposed by the national convention; state conventions or delegations may invoke it or not as they choose. The national convention will, however, recognize and enforce it when ordained by a proper state party authority. It is usually employed by several states, especially southern ones.

Until thirty years ago, another important difference between Republican and Democratic procedure was that whereas a simple majority of all votes cast was sufficient to nominate in a Republican convention, the Democrats (from as far back as 1836) required two-thirds. This latter rule frequently was responsible for convention deadlocks, and sometimes—as in 1924—prevented the party's strongest candidate from receiving nomination. In 1936, when President Roosevelt was about to be renominated at Philadelphia without opposition and no candidate's chance would be in any way affected, the historic two-thirds requirement was rescinded, with nominations thenceforth to be by simple majority. This change in Democratic practice amounted to a sharp reduction in the influence of the southern wing of the party over the nominations. Under the old "two-thirds rule" the South had exercised a veto over candidate selection. Since the death of President Roosevelt, the power struggle between the northern and southern wings of the party has repeatedly broken out into the open at the national convention. In 1948, a portion of the southern Democrats seceded and founded a "Dixiecrat" party, and in 1952 formal unity was preserved only by the skillful maneuvering of the presiding officers. In 1956 and 1960 rival candidates were offered in several southern states. The South has sought to gain bargaining power by offering a southern candidate and by threatening to bolt. In 1960, unity was preserved by making the leading southern candidate (Senator Lyndon Johnson) the party's vice-presidential nominee. In 1964, the southern favorite was President, and there was thus no opposition to his nomination.

The Democratic "two-thirds rule" abandoned

After the votes of all the states have been recorded and counted, the result is announced. Sometimes—especially when a President is being renominated—a single ballot suffices. But often the votes are so divided among a number of candidates that no one obtains the requisite majority and additional ballots must be taken. These usually follow in quick succession as the leaders try to force a decision. Sometimes, however, a recess is called between ballots to allow the candidates' managers more time to maneuver. Typically, the "favorite sons" drop out early in the balloting and the contest centers around two or three strong candidates. During these hours, the managers work tirelessly dickering with the leaders of delegations, making promises, and bringing outside pressure to bear in an effort to capture a majority. Eventually some one of the contestants (or perchance a "dark horse" agreed upon behind the scenes) emerges a victor. Sometimes the balloting (and bartering) is very prolonged, the record being the nomination of John W. Davis by the Democrats in 1924 on the 103rd ballot, after a deadlock lasting nine days. With a Democratic candidate,

The balloting

however, no longer obliged to muster a two-thirds vote in order to win, there hardly will be another experience so trying.

Nomina-
tion for
the Vice-
Presidency

The nomination for the Presidency having been made, the weary delegates hurry their labors to an anticlimactic conclusion. A candidate for the Vice-Presidency is still to be named; and the same procedure—roll call, nominating and seconding speeches, and balloting—is followed. But the contest usually is not very keen, and a decisive vote is soon reached. As a rule, the grounds on which the nomination is made (sometimes largely by the presidential nominee and always with his assent) leave a good deal to be desired. The prize—such as it is—may be used to placate an important element in the party that has lost in the fight over the presidential nomination or over the platform, or to reward a "favorite son" who has thrown his support to the winning presidential candidate, or to enhance the chances of capturing a pivotal state. It will usually be bestowed also with a view to balancing the ticket: An eastern presidential nominee commonly calls for a western vice-presidential nominee; a dyed-in-the-wool conservative ordinarily must be counterbalanced with a man of known liberal views, or vice versa. Every sort of consideration, indeed, may contribute to the decision except one, the qualifications of the person nominated to become President if anything should happen to the President.

The con-
vention's
closing
acts

One more task, purely formal yet necessary, remains: The party's national committee must be elected, consisting of a man and woman from each state and territory,[1] and charged with carrying on the coming election, looking after party interests during the ensuing four years, and arranging for the next national convention. With all members designated (in theory "nominated") either by state conventions or primaries, by state committees, or by state delegations, election by the national convention, however, is a mere gesture.

Since Franklin D. Roosevelt got his first campaign off to a dramatic start in 1932 by climbing into an airplane at Albany and a few hours later ascending the convention rostrum at Chicago to accept his nomination, old-style notification ceremonies have gradually been dispensed with by both major parties. Successful candidates now signify their acceptance in an address at the convention itself. The convention thus ends on a new call to battle and an eloquent statement of faith by the candidate.

THE PRESIDENTIAL CAMPAIGN

Machinery

Although the conduct of a national campaign involves thousands of party workers, central direction is ordinarily provided by the national committees. Shortly after the conventions, the new committees meet and organize

---

[1] The Republican Committee by rule adopted in 1952 also now includes as ex officio members the state chairman of the party in each state which has a Republican governor or a Republican majority of the states' members in both houses of Congress, or which cast its electoral vote for a Republican President at the last election.

for the great effort ahead. A chairman is selected to manage the campaign, nominally by the committee but actually by the presidential candidate. Headquarters are established or enlarged to house the hundreds of employes added temporarily and, frequently, regional offices are established in key cities. Subcommittees are created to coordinate publicity, fund-raising, speaker activities, and the like. Individuals are assigned to direct all of these processes in collaboration with the committee or under the immediate direction of the chairman. Campaign biographies of the candidate are prepared; "textbooks" are compiled for ready reference by local and state party workers, containing the platform, important speeches, statistics, speech material organized by subject to support the party position on the issues of the campaign, and biographical data on the party candidates; leaflets and brochures of many kinds are prepared, and slogans and mottoes are manufactured for the occasion. Arrangements are also made to coordinate campaigns for state and local offices with the congressional and presidential campaign. Since the limitation on total spending of a national campaign committee was enacted in 1940, more and more use is being made of auxiliary and semi-independent committees to supplement the work of the national committee and to serve as vehicles for the expenditure of funds beyond the ceiling established for any national committee. Auxiliary organizations are used also to reach voters and financial supporters that the regular party organizations do not reach: women, for example, independents, supporters from the opposite party, ethnic groups, professional people, labor, even intellectuals.

The combined costs of all the campaign activities of a single party in *Funds* a national election certainly exceed $20 million and probably exceed $50 million. Raising this money is one of the most trying and most difficult of tasks for the campaign organization, and a great deal of effort must be put into it right down to the closing hours of the campaign. In fact, the fund-raising frequently goes on after the election to pay off deficits piled up during the enthusiasm of the campaign. Experience suggests that both parties rely upon the substantial gifts of a relatively small proportion of their supporters. As has been suggested earlier, attempts to limit expenditures in campaigns have been uniformly unsuccessful as have attempts to limit the amount any person may contribute. A major effort to authorize public funding of part of presidential campaign expenses sponsored by Senator Long (La.) and allowing any income tax payer voluntarily to assign $1 of his tax payment to this purpose was repealed in 1967 after a trial of only one year. President Johnson in 1967 urged national subsidy of campaigns by direct congressional appropriation and Senator Long pushed vigorously but unsuccessfully in 1968 for a bill appropriating to each major party candidate 20¢ per vote cast in the previous election and somewhat more per vote for senatorial and congressional campaigns. A minor party (one receiving 5–20 percent of the total vote) would receive 40¢ for each vote cast for the party candidate.

A considerable portion of the money now spent goes for the purchase

Litera-
ture" and
broadcasts
of radio and television broadcasting time and for the preparation and distribution of party literature. The amount spent for broadcasting has been increasing relatively and absolutely in recent years and there are many indications that television, in particular, will be the major campaign vehicle in the future. The quality and character of the literature and the broadcasts vary widely. Party money is spent on everything from one-minute spot announcements to the televising of a formal oration by the candidate and from windshield stickers to full-length book biographies. More and more, parties are relying upon the cumulative impact of advertising through every medium and less and less upon elaborate, formal, and hortatory speechmaking. They are also relying more and more upon professional advertisers and public relations consultants. The use of television also tends to reduce the relative amount of formal speechmaking. Much of the campaign "literature" reaches the voter only through his favorite newspaper or from his receiving set.

Strategy
and
tactics:
Through the years, professional politicians and seasoned campaigners have developed an elaborate folklore on the art and strategy of campaigning. Little of this has ever been verified scientifically and much of it perhaps never will be. Experts in the matter are usually much more certain after the election is over than while the campaign is in progress. The character of a national campaign, however, can hardly be understood except in terms of those "rules of the game" which the campaigners follow. In most campaigns, in the first place, great stress is placed on the personality of the candidates, and this usually far overshadows the issues of public policy which may be involved. Each side attempts to build a picture in the eyes of the public of a personality which coincides with the supposed inner wishes of the electorate. This picture will, of course, vary with the times. In 1932, the Democrats were anxious to depict their candidate as daring, aggressive, and uninhibited by respect for tradition. More frequently, the candidate is cast in the role of the defender of the best traditions of the American past, as a man who knows the value of his American heritage. The Horatio Alger formula set the style of the "people's choice" for many years: the self-made hero, product of a harsh rural or small-town environment, a boyhood close to the soil and a manhood of successful achievement in competition with the sophisticated city "slickers." It is now wearing thin: Great wealth is no longer a drawback nor is urban upbringing; and foreign travel is desirable. The voters, it is believed, choose more easily and more readily among personalities than among programs. The candidate's personality must also, however, symbolize an approach to the issues of the day: "normalcy," New England shrewdness, engineering efficiency, champion of the forgotten man, eager fighter for honest government, popular military genius, youthful idol of the new generation. The real personality of the candidate is invariably swallowed up by the mythical hero which the publicists have carefully constructed for the campaign.

1. The
candidate

2. The
issues
Much thought and effort is given by the campaigners to the selection of

the issues or themes of the campaign. What in the record should be played up and what ignored? Of the many evidences of dissatisfaction in the electorate, which are the deeper and more decisive? In recent years, the strategists have paid close attention to the results of public-opinion sampling polls in determining what impresses the electorate. In 1952, the Republicans felt that their best issues were the Korean stalemate, communists in government, and corruption. In 1956 and 1960, the Republicans stood on the slogan, "peace and prosperity." In 1956 and 1960, the Democrats cried out against complacency, demanded that the people rise to the challenge of the times. As the campaign of 1964 proceeded, it became increasingly clear that the Democrats' best issues were the public fear of the warlike posture and threats to the welfare state of Senator Goldwater. Disenchantment with the heavy military commitments in Viet Nam and with urban riots proved the central themes of the campaign of 1968.

One of the perennial campaign questions is how to treat the opposition: attack them or ignore them. Franklin Roosevelt was a master of pretending complete indifference to his opponent. Dewey tried this in 1948 and failed with it. Eisenhower generally ignored his opponents as did Johnson and both were successful. Usually the "outs" are forced to more aggressive attacks than the "ins." An incumbent President can frequently ignore his opposition more successfully than they can ignore him. A common device is to appoint a lesser party figure to debate the opposition and to answer their charges, and thus keep the presidential candidates above the debate. A great many politicians believe, however, that you can never catch up with your opponent's charges and, therefore, the best thing to do is to make no attempt to answer but rather to charge him with something else.

3. Offense or defense

The dream of every campaign manager is to make his candidate the center of the campaign. He would rather have a lot of campaign oratory directed against his candidate than to have him ignored. An ideal situation from this point of view was one achieved briefly by Woodrow Wilson in 1912 when Taft and Roosevelt were both attacking him and he was presenting his program to the people. Every candidate was thus discussing Wilson. How to achieve this goal is another question and on this the campaigners differ sharply among themselves. They all agree, however, that the candidate must act and talk as if he were confident of winning. No doubts on this score must ever be allowed to appear in the literature or in the words or actions of the candidate. In recent years the statistical experts in the party headquarters supply the press and public with a great deal of "scientific" data which proves their assertions of victory. Jim Farley's accurate forecast of the 1936 election result—that the Democrats would carry every state except Maine and Vermont—remains up to this time, however, the only occasion in which the "scientific" extravagance of partisan forecasts was sustained by the voters.

4. The strategy of superior place

5. The illusion of victory

The electoral college method of counting the vote for President and Vice-President has considerable influence in campaign planning and execu-

6. Con-
centration
in doubtful
states

tion. Presidential campaign efforts are usually concentrated in "doubtful states" and in states with a consequential electoral vote. President Eisenhower, Vice-President Nixon, and Senator Goldwater, the latter with much success, for example invaded the South. Democratic candidates avoid it because it is usually certain, as they do much of New England and the Great Plains because they are so strongly Republican. President Johnson was one of the few Democrats to invade New England, also successfully. By far the largest effort in money, organization, and candidate speaking appearances is ordinarily made in New York, Indiana, Ohio, Illinois, Michigan, California, New Jersey, Pennsylvania, and Texas.

The
televised
debates
of 1960

     The campaign of 1960 introduced a new dimension into campaigning with four great televised debates between the two candidates. Although extensive use was made of television in the campaigns of 1952 and 1956, all of the programs had been offered under partisan direction on time purchased at great cost for the purpose. The broadcasters, under some fire because of their alleged indifference to concepts of public service, offered to stage these programs free provided Congress would waive the rule of the Federal Communications Commission requiring them to offer equal time to the 14 other minor party candidates for the Presidency. Congress by statute suspended the rule for the campaign of 1960. Representatives of the broadcasters and the candidates then negotiated the terms under which the programs would be presented. Generally, the candidates were allowed a few minutes for set speeches and then were questioned by representatives of the press under carefully controlled time limits for their answers. Each candidate was permitted to comment on the answers of the other. The time thus donated by the broadcasters would have cost the two parties about $2 million if purchased in the traditional way. The best estimates place the audience for one or all of the debates at 115 to 120 million persons, the greatest listening audience ever assembled for any program of any type. Many analysts and opinion surveyors believe that Kennedy's showing was an important factor in his final victory. It can hardly be said that the debates did much to clarify the issues of the campaign. The rigid time limits made thoughtful responses on complex questions, such as farm policy, Quemoy and Matsu, civil rights, etc., impossible. They did project to the voters the personalities of the two candidates and showed their behavior under great stress.

     Assured by all the available polling data of a sweeping victory and with the party treasury in satisfactory condition, President Johnson, in 1964, chose not to share his audience with the Republican challenger. The bill to suspend the equal-time rule was lost in the Senate despite offers of the broadcasters and pressure from the Republicans to repeat the debate. With Johnson's retirement, pressure to renew the debates in 1968 was very strong. A vigorous third party candidate (Gov. Wallace of Alabama), however, complicated the issue, and Nixon would not agree to share the stage with Wallace.

     For all of the planning, thought, money, time, and energy given to a

national campaign, there is a substantial body of evidence suggesting that it   *Value of*
changes very few votes. A vast majority of American voters—perhaps as   *campaign*
many as 80 percent—cast their votes in November exactly as they would
have cast them in June or July before the campaign got under way. If true,
does this mean that campaigns are useless? Not at all, say the politicians.
Elections are always decided by a relatively small percentage of the voters.
Furthermore, one of the tasks of a campaign is to infuse the supporters of a
party with enough enthusiasm to bring them out to the polls on election day.
Apathy is the dread disease of the body politic and especially of the traditional supporters of a party. Only the intense excitement of a campaign will
bring to the polls the 73 million voters who came out in 1968. Furthermore,
the campaign stimulates the party organization, infuses it with a renewed
sense of purpose, tests the merit of its functionaries, and attracts to it new
blood and talent without which it would soon wither and decay. Strong
parties are essential to our system, it is argued, and campaigns make strong
parties.

CASTING AND COUNTING THE ELECTORAL VOTES

What happens after the last local "spellbinder" has descended from   *Presiden-*
the rostrum, the last national "hook-up" has brought the leading candidates'   *tial*
appeals to the voter at his fireside, and the last rosy forecast has been given   *electors*
out by an at least outwardly confident party chairman? Early in the campaign, party conventions, primaries, or committees (as determined by the
legislature) in each state made up the respective "slates" of presidential
electors. Each party designates as many electors as the state is entitled to,
that is, one for each senator and for each representative in Congress. It is
for these men and women that the voters actually cast their ballots on election day, although they may think of themselves as voting for the President
and Vice-President. This is true legally even though the voters may not
know the names of the electors for whom they are voting, and though in a
majority of states their names do not even appear on the ballot. Today, in
every state, the voter casts his ballot for as many electors as his state is
entitled to and the winner of the state contest captures the entire electoral
vote of that state.

A majority of electoral votes is necessary to victory—unless achieved   *"Minority"*
through election by the House. But this does not prevent us from having   *Presidents*
"minority" Presidents, that is Presidents who (strictly speaking, the electors who chose them) received fewer than half of the total popular votes
cast. As a matter of fact, we have had 12 such—two of them at two different
times each. Lincoln, in 1860, obtained more popular votes than did any one
of his competitors, but nevertheless polled half a million less than a majority.
Wilson, in 1912, received 2 million more popular votes than did his nearest
competitor, Theodore Roosevelt, yet only 42 percent of the total. In both

of these cases, the opposition was divided. President Kennedy received 49.7 percent of the popular vote in 1960 and President Nixon only 43.4 percent in 1968. The same thing can happen even if there are only two major tickets in the field. Hayes was elected over Tilden in 1876, although his popular vote was about 300,000 smaller; and Harrison triumphed over Cleveland in 1888, although with 100,000 fewer votes. All that a candidate needs in order to obtain the full electoral vote of a state is a plurality of the popular vote. An opposing candidate may have swept the states which he carried by heavy pluralities and thus gained a large number of popular votes. But, lacking the requisite number of electoral votes, he nevertheless goes down to defeat.

This circumstance accounts for the fact, previously alluded to, that campaign managers are likely to concentrate their efforts in large "doubtful" or "pivotal" states. Party managers are not likely soon to forget that Kennedy captured the electoral vote of Illinois (27) by only 10,000 votes, of New Jersey (16) by only 22,000 votes, and of Texas (24) by only 46,000 votes.

Casting the electoral votes

The theory of the Constitution is that the electors are officers of their respective states, and it was on this account that the states were left free to determine how they should be chosen. The place where each group meets within its state is fixed by the legislature thereof (normally, the state capital); and if the electors receive any remuneration, it must come out of the state treasury. A national statute of 1934, however, requires that they meet in the respective states and cast their ballots on the first Monday after the second Wednesday in December following their election. And the Twelfth Amendment enjoins that the voting be by ballot; that presidential and vice-presidential candidates be voted for separately; that distinct lists be made up showing all persons supported for either office, with the number of votes received by each; and that these lists, signed and sealed in duplicate, be sent to the president of the Senate (nowadays actually to the head of the General Services Administration for transmission to the Senate's presiding officer) at the seat of the national government. As evidence of their power to act, the electors must also transmit their certificates of election bearing the signature of the governor.

The electoral count as now carried out

With rare exceptions, of course, the counting of the electoral votes is a mere formality; the country knows two months in advance precisely what the figures will be. On the day fixed by law—formerly the second Wednesday in February, but now the sixth day of January—the members of the two houses gather in the hall of the House of Representatives, with the president (or president *pro tempore*) of the Senate in the chair, and with four previously designated tellers—a Democrat and a Republican from each house— ready to tabulate and count. The person receiving the largest number of votes for President, provided the number is a majority of the whole number of electors chosen, is declared elected; and similarly in the case of the Vice-Presidency.

In the event that no candidate for President receives a majority, the election is, of course, thrown into the House of Representatives, where each *Provision in case of lack of a majority* state has one vote, bestowed as the majority of the state delegation determines.

Notwithstanding all the constitutional and statutory regulations on the subject, it still is possible for the country to come up to the expiration of a *Some recent safe- guards* presidential term with no President-elect ready to be inaugurated. Not only may the choice itself still be hanging fire, but a person duly elected may have died before the inauguration date, or may have failed to qualify (as, for example, by refusing to serve). Providing belatedly for such contingencies, the Twentieth Amendment, adopted in 1933, specifies (1) that in case of the death of a President-elect, the Vice-President-elect shall become President, and (2) that if at the time for inauguration a President-elect has not been chosen or has failed to qualify, the Vice-President-elect "shall *act as president* until a president shall have qualified."

PROPOSED CHANGES IN ELECTORAL COLLEGE

More than once, the mode of electing the President and Vice-President *Present short- comings* has been pronounced a weak point in our American system of government. Over the years, it is true, improvements have been introduced by the Twelfth and Twentieth Amendments, by statutes like the Electoral Count Act, by state legislation such as that removing the names of electors from the ballot (presidential short ballot), and by party regulations like those now governing the apportionment of delegates to the national conventions. Passing over faults of the nominating process, one finds the plan of election criticized on several grounds. (1) The electoral college no longer serves the sifting purposes for which it was designed, and as a mere recording machine has become useless. (2) The unit system under which a candidate captures all of a state's electoral votes merely by polling a statewide popular plurality is unfair to sections of a state carried by a different party. (3) Occasionally, a candidate wins election with only minority popular backing. (4) The present system exaggerates the electoral importance of the large cities in the pivotal states and, therefore, of disciplined pressure-group blocs. (5) In the absence of state laws so requiring (and these exist only in a few states, such as California and Oregon), there is no ironclad guarantee that electors chosen in the states will vote for the presidential and vice-presidential candidates receiving the largest popular vote in their states. Formerly, this last situation was not a matter of much concern; in over a century and a quarter, only two electors chosen to vote for the candidates of a given party ever ignored their mandate and actually voted for different ones. The confused position of the South in the election of 1948, however—marked by legislation in Virginia empowering a state convention to instruct the state's electors *not* to vote for the regular party nominees, by an unsuccessful attempt in Alabama to compel the state's 11 electors, chosen to support the States' Rights can-

Popular and Electoral Vote for President

1968

STATE	POPULAR VOTE			ELECTORAL VOTE		
	HUMPHREY	NIXON	WALLACE	HUMPHREY	NIXON	WALLACE
Alabama	194,388	146,923	689,009	—	—	10
Alaska	35,411	37,540	10,024	—	3	—
Arizona	170,514	266,721	46,573	—	5	—
Arkansas	184,901	189,062	235,627	—	—	6
California	3,244,318	3,467,644	487,270	—	40	—
Colorado	331,063	409,345	60,813	—	6	—
Connecticut	621,561	556,721	76,650	8	—	—
Delaware	89,194	96,714	28,459	—	3	—
District of Columbia	139,556	31,012	—	3	—	—
Florida	676,794	886,804	624,207	—	14	—
Georgia	334,439	366,611	535,550	—	—	12
Hawaii	141,324	91,425	3,469	4	—	—
Idaho	89,273	165,369	36,541	—	4	—
Illinois	2,039,814	2,174,774	390,958	—	26	—
Indiana	806,659	1,067,885	243,108	—	13	—
Iowa	476,699	619,106	66,422	—	9	—
Kansas	302,996	478,674	88,921	—	7	—
Kentucky	397,541	462,411	193,098	—	9	—
Louisiana	309,615	257,535	530,300	—	—	10
Maine	217,312	169,254	6,370	4	—	—
Maryland	538,310	517,995	178,734	10	—	—
Massachusetts	1,469,218	766,844	87,088	14	—	—
Michigan	1,593,082	1,370,665	331,968	21	—	—
Minnesota	857,738	658,643	68,931	10	—	—
Mississippi	150,644	88,516	415,349	—	—	7
Missouri	791,444	811,932	206,126	—	12	—
Montana	114,117	138,853	20,015	—	4	—
Nebraska	170,784	321,163	44,904	—	5	—
Nevada	60,598	73,188	20,432	—	3	—
New Hampshire	130,589	154,903	11,173	—	4	—
New Jersey	1,264,206	1,325,467	262,187	—	17	—
New Mexico	130,081	169,692	25,737	—	4	—
New York	3,378,470	3,007,938	358,864	43	—	—
North Carolina	464,113	627,192	496,188	—	12	1*
North Dakota	94,769	138,669	14,244	—	4	—
Ohio	1,700,586	1,791,014	467,495	—	26	—
Oklahoma	306,658	449,697	191,731	—	8	—
Oregon	358,865	408,433	49,683	—	6	—
Pennsylvania	2,259,403	2,090,017	387,582	29	—	—
Rhode Island	246,518	122,359	15,678	4	—	—
South Carolina	197,486	254,062	215,430	—	8	—
South Dakota	118,023	149,841	13,400	—	4	—
Tennessee	351,233	472,592	424,792	—	11	—
Texas	1,266,804	1,227,844	584,269	25	—	—
Utah	156,665	238,728	26,906	—	4	—
Vermont	70,255	85,142	5,104	—	3	—
Virginia	442,387	590,315	320,272	—	12	—
Washington	616,037	588,510	76,742	9	—	—
West Virginia	374,091	307,555	72,560	7	—	—
Wisconsin	748,804	809,997	127,835	—	12	—
Wyoming	45,173	70,927	11,105	—	3	—
TOTAL	31,270,533	31,770,237	9,906,141	191	301	46

*The North Carolina elector who voted for Wallace was elected on the Nixon slate.

didates, to switch to Truman and Barkley, and by the persistence of one Tennessee elector in voting contrary to the state popular vote—brought this previously neglected angle of the electoral system sharply to the fore. In the election of 1960, one elector in Oklahoma, elected on the Nixon slate, cast his vote for Byrd, and in Alabama in 1968, four Democratic slates of electors were presented to the voters. President Johnson in 1965 and 1966 urged Congress to support a Constitutional amendment which would eliminate any discretion on the part of electors.

Proposals for betterment have been many. Some of them start from the premise that the people should elect directly, with no intervention of either personal electors or electoral votes, and from this advance to the suggestion either (1) that the country be thrown into a single grand constituency, with the people in the mass electing directly, by plurality or majority, without reference to state lines, most recently supported by Vice-President Humphrey and Senators Morse (Ore.) and Mansfield (Mont.), or (2) that voting continue on a state basis, but with election by popular pluralities in a majority of states. The first suggestion ignores all considerations of state interest and pride, and would increase the need for a uniform national suffrage and election law which could not easily be obtained. The second, opening a way for a number of smaller states to swing an election by means of only a minority (perhaps very small) of the nationwide popular vote, is palpably objectionable. Several plans receiving serious attention presume the retention of ultimate choice by electoral rather than popular votes, the only questions being as to how such votes shall be allotted and whether they shall literally be "cast" by actual persons or be only abstractions mathematically calculated from the popular vote. Three main propositions in this vein have been made. (1) Abolish the electoral college and simply translate statewide popular plurality votes into state quotas of electoral votes, all going in each state (as now) to the plurality candidates. A constitutional amendment of this purport twice narrowly failed to secure the necessary two-thirds vote in the Senate in 1934. This plan would merely write into the Constitution what we already have. To change the system, we have had two principal proposals, differing chiefly in the manner of proportioning electoral votes to popular votes. (2) Continue choosing one elector at large in each state, by plurality, for each senator and for each representative-at-large (if any), but choose all others —as was the common practice in early days—district by district, so as to make possible (and in most cases probable) a division of a state's electoral votes among different candidates. (3) Discard electors, let the people vote directly for President and Vice-President, translate popular votes into electoral votes, and allot a state's electoral quota among the candidates in proportion to the statewide popular votes polled. The national courts have been invited on two recent occasions to overturn the present system and install the district system on the grounds that the equal-protection clause requires it. Suits by citizens of Virginia in 1968 and by Delaware in 1966 were not entertained, however.

Principal proposals

The major arguments raised against the district system of electing presidential electors are: (1) district lines are easy to gerrymander; (2) campaigning might be concentrated in a few marginal districts; (3) minor parties such as the American Independence party of 1968 by concentrating effort in certain districts might swing the election into the House of Representatives. Those raised against the plan of allocating electoral votes in each state on the basis of popular votes are: (1) a "minority" President would still be possible; (2) it would weaken the two party systems by allowing small parties to gain electoral votes and thus prestige. Many persons also say that the present system has served us well and there is no necessity for changing it.

Reform by state action unlikely

Any state might now, if it chose, institute the district plan, or indeed any other plan for proportioning popular to electoral votes—so long as electors were retained. The states already, therefore, have it in their power to deal, at least in piecemeal fashion, with the main problem involved in the whole matter. The same considerations of interest and pride (chiefly the increased political weight accruing from an undivided block of electoral votes) which originally induced one after another of them to give up the earlier district plan may be counted upon to frustrate any attempt within their own boundaries to revive it or anything resembling it.

RESULTS OF THE PRESENT SYSTEM

Thirty-six different men have attained the Presidency—28 by being elected directly to the office and eight by succeeding a deceased chief executive. In exercising their electoral function, what sort of record have the people achieved? How do the Presidents that they have chosen measure up in terms of capacity, vision, diligence, and other qualities of statesmanship?

An uneven record

Many years ago, Lord Bryce included in his classic treatise, *The American Commonwealth,* a chapter entitled "Why Great Men Are Not Chosen President." He did not mean to imply that none such is ever chosen. But looking back over a line of 20 Presidents who had served the nation in its first 100 years, our friendly English critic could not see that the people had shown any consistent disposition to elevate even their strongest men (leaving aside the somewhat elusive quality of "greatness") to the highest office in their power to bestow. Through a century and a half, American Presidents, another foreign observer affirms, have for the most part been mediocre when compared, for example, with British prime ministers during the same period. The judgment seems severe. There have been inferior prime ministers and able Presidents. It is true, however, that many of the ablest American statesmen have never been elevated to the Presidency and have witnessed this high office bestowed on inferior colleagues. Hamilton, Gallatin, Marshall, Clay, Webster, Calhoun, Burton, Sumner, Hay, Blaine, Root, Sherman, and Robert Taft, to select a few giants of the past, although dominant in their parties were passed by in favor, typically, of less influential and, in many cases, of less able men.

It is useless to wonder whether the original plan of the Constitution would have produced better results. The rise of the party system and the spread of democracy doomed the arrangement almost from its inception. It is to the exigencies of party politics that we must look to discover why and how Presidents are selected. The voters in November can pick among two or three candidates, but the party organizations screen the field to narrow the choice. This is not to say that if a big democracy is going to have an elective chief executive at all, there is any better method of choosing him; nor certainly to imply that it would be practicable for choices of such magnitude to be made in any way other than through the instrumentality of parties. It is merely to state a basic fact: that the few persons who ever have a chance under our system to become President get it only when, and because, parties give it to them.

Party responsibility for selection

The considerations and circumstances making a man "available"— the "logical choice"—as a party candidate, and thereby narrowing the field of contenders, are not always such as to guarantee that he will be a strong President. There is, of course, no single formula, or pattern, for presidential timber; the same person might be wholly acceptable to a party under one set of conditions and not at all so under another; everything depends on the character of the times, the prevailing public temper, and many other things. Experience indicates, however, that certain qualities or characteristics are likely to play a major role in making a candidate "available." (1) He should have demonstrated capacity for getting the voters to vote for him, that is, he should have run successfully for an important public office. (2) He should have attained his electoral successes preferably in a "pivotal" or "doubtful" state or section, especially one which the party must almost certainly carry to win the election (this rules out the statesmen of the South, the Plains, and Republican New England). (3) He must be sufficiently regular in his party affiliation to be regarded as reliable on party matters by the leaders. (4) He must be well enough known nationally to have some following outside his own state and yet not be identified with a particular region, cause, or program which is offensive to some other area (this rules out many important congressmen who have been obliged to vote on controversial issues). (5) He must have a group of loyal, devoted, and able supporters who can manage his campaign for him and carry on negotiations with other leaders which he, personally, can never do. (6) He might well have had military experience (12 of our Presidents have had military titles). (7) Until 1960 it was supposed that a Catholic could not get elected. The best route to the Presidency had been from the governor's chair in New York, Ohio, Illinois, or other populous state where party strength is evenly divided between the two major parties. Since about 1950 the senators from these states have been strong candidates. The House has produced few able candidates as has the Cabinet. Luck is also an important factor in President-

Some factors in "availability"

making. Strong candidates, emerging at the same time in the same party have on several occasions battled one another out of the race at the convention and opened the door for a "dark horse" less well known than either— Lowden and Wood in the Republican convention of 1920 paved the way for Harding, and McAdoo and Smith prepared the path for Davis as the Democratic nominee in 1924. These are some of the factors which have kept out of the Presidency many able statesmen. Nevertheless, a system which has produced Washington, Jefferson, Jackson, Polk, Lincoln, Cleveland, Theodore Roosevelt, Wilson, and Franklin Roosevelt cannot be written off as a hopeless failure. It certainly works as well as the participants (the voters) have any right to expect.

One final word is necessary. The office of President, with its awesome responsibilities and its solitary dignity, has accumulated a tradition and a prestige through the years that lift the men who fill it beyond their realized talents. Men try to live up to the marks set by their illustrious predecessors. The ambition of thousands of politicians, although attained by few, its influence raises all to loftier conceptions of the public good.

REFERENCES

H. Agar, *The People's Choice* (Boston, 1933).

L. H. Bean, *Ballot Behavior; A Study of Presidential Elections* (Washington, D. C., 1940).

A. Campbell, P. Converse, W. Miller and D. Stokes, *The American Voter* (New York, 1960).

M. Cunliff, *The American Heritage History of the Presidency* (New York, 1968).

P. David and R. M. Goldman, *Presidential Nominating Patterns* (Washington, D. C., 1955).

———, R. M. Goldman, R. C. Bain, *The Politics of National Party Conventions* (Washington, D. C., 1960).

———, M. Moos, R. M. Goldman, *Presidential Nominating Politics in 1952* (Baltimore, 1954).

J. W. Davis, *Presidential Primaries: Road to the White House* (New York, 1967).

S. Hyman, *The American President* (New York, 1954).

V. O. Key, Jr., *Politics, Parties, and Pressure Groups* (5th ed., New York, 1963), Chaps. XV–XVI.

———, *The Responsible Electorate* (Cambridge, Mass., 1966).

P. F. Lazarsfeld, B. Berelson, and H. Gaudet, *The People's Choice; How the Voter Makes Up His Mind in a Presidential Campaign* (New York, 1945).

S. Lorant, *The Presidency; A Pictorial History of Presidential Elections* (New York, 1952).

N. R. Pierce, *The People's President: The Electoral College in American History and the Direct Vote Alternatives* (New York, 1968).

Official Report of the Proceedings of the Republican National Convention, issued quadrennially; *ibid., Democratic National Convention.*

N. W. Polsby and A. B. Wildavsky, *Presidential Elections: Strategies of American Electoral Politics* (2nd ed., New York, 1968).

K. Porter and D. B. Johnson, *National Party Platform: 1840–1960* (Urbana, Ill., 1961).

President's Commission on Campaign Costs, *Financing Presidential Campaigns* (Washington, D. C., 1962).

E. E. Robinson, *The Presidential Vote, 1896–1932* (Palo Alto, Calif., 1934).

————, *The Presidential Vote, 1936* (Palo Alto, Calif., 1940).

————, *They Voted for Roosevelt; The Presidential Vote, 1932–1944* (Palo Alto, Calif., 1947).

E. N. Roseboom, *A History of Presidential Elections* (New York, 1957).

C. A. H. Thompson and F. N. Shattuck, *The 1956 Presidential Campaign* (Washington, D. C., 1959).

T. H. White, *The Making of the President—1960* (New York, 1961).

————, *The Making of the President—1964* (New York, 1965).

L. Wilmerding, Jr., *The Electoral College* (New Brunswick, N. J., 1958).

II The National Government

A Organization, Powers, and Procedures

9

THE STRUCTURE AND ORGANIZATION OF CONGRESS

Having concluded a survey of the constitutional basis of the American system of government and the democratic processes by which it is operated, we turn now to a consideration of the organizational structure through which legitimate power is exercised by our national government. It is appropriate to begin our discussion with the Congress. Not only is the legislature provided for first in our Constitution, but it may be said to have a certain primacy in any republican form of government. It can claim with some color of truth to be closest to the people and it is the major repository of power to make and declare public policy and to provide the means for its achievement.

THE BICAMERAL PATTERN

> All legislative powers herein granted shall be vested in a Congress of the United States, which shall consist of a Senate and House of Representatives.—Art. 1, Sec. 1

Why two houses were established

With the exception of the Continental and Confederation Congresses and the legislatures briefly established by Vermont and Pennsylvania, the entire political experience of England and of colonial and revolutionary America confirmed the view that a legislature ought to consist of two houses. If a popular assembly were to be provided, a second chamber representing sectional or substantial vested interests ought clearly to review its deliberations. The framers of our Constitution made this decision early in their deliberations and never seriously considered changing it. The compromise by which the federationists were mollified by representing states as such in one house and the nationalists by representing people in the other merely confirmed the wisdom of an arrangement already regarded as indispensable and provided a convenient basis for organizing the two houses upon different principles. In this way, the framers could be assured of some antagonism between the two bodies which would result in mutual restraint as well as accommodation.

General acceptance of the two-house system

The arrangement, although never entirely free of criticism, has become an accepted and approved part of the American scheme. Most of the criticism has come from those who decry the deadlocks, delays, duplications, and diffusion of responsibility which two equal and independent authorities tend to induce. All levels of government at one time or another imitated the national legislature but virtually all cities and one state, Nebraska, have abandoned the bicameral plan and gone over to the one-house legislature, partly as a result of the frustrations alluded to by the critics. Some criticism has come also from those who deplore any organizational arrangements which mitigate or obstruct the clear will of a numerical majority of the electorate as expressed by their representatives. In any event, there are now few serious suggestions to abandon the two-house system in the Congress. A great many competent authorities see it as a positive source of strength to our republic, making possible the acceptance of national authority over an area as vast, as varied, and as populous as that of the United States.

REPRESENTATION IN THE HOUSE—THE DISTRICT SYSTEM

> Representatives . . . shall be apportioned among the several States . . . according to their respective numbers, counting the whole number of persons in each State, excluding Indians not taxed. The actual enumeration shall be made . . . within every term of ten years, in such manner as they shall by law direct the number of representatives shall not exceed one for every thirty thousand, but each State shall have at least one representative.—Art. 1, Sec. 2, cl. 3 as amended by Art. XIV

Reapportionment and increasing the size of the House

Although the Constitution does not expressly require a redistribution of the seats in the House of Representatives to accommodate that body to changes in population revealed by the decennial census, that is clearly what was intended. Until 1920, the Congress never failed to readjust its membership each decade. With the exception of that of 1842, every decennial readjustment up to World War I had been achieved, however, only by substantial increase in the total number of representatives. By the turn of the century, apprehension was gaining that the House was becoming too large for effective deliberation. Given the great mobility of our people, if a limit on the size of the House is to be achieved, some states and, of course, some representatives would have to give up seats. This the state delegations in both houses were understandably reluctant to do. Unable to agree either to in-

CHANGES IN REPRESENTATION IN THE HOUSE OF REPRESENTATIVES UNDER THE REAPPORTIONMENT OF 1961

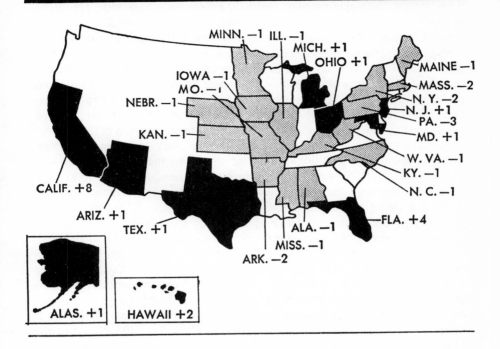

crease the size of the House or to take seats away from some states, the Congress after 1920 did nothing for several years.

Before a census would reveal exactly which states might gain or lose and how much, the Congress in 1929 provided for a "permanent" system of reapportionment which would discourage any further growth in its own membership and would obviate the necessity for any further congressional action on the subject. This act, as amended in 1941, has served as the basis of reapportionment since that time. Under it, (1) the size of the House is fixed at 435; [1] (2) after each census, the Bureau of the Census prepares for the President a table showing the number of inhabitants of each state and the number of representatives to which each state is entitled; (3) the President transmits the information to Congress; and, (4) the proposed distribution becomes effective 15 days after it is sent to Congress unless Congress enacts a different distribution. Up to this time, Congress has allowed the proposed arrangement to take effect without modification. In the reapportionments since 1929, the western coastal states and Florida have consist-

Present method of reapportionment

---

[1] At the time of admission of Hawaii and Alaska, the House was temporarily increased to 437, but reverted to 435 after the decennial reapportionment of 1961.

ently gained seats at the expense largely of New York, Pennsylvania, Illinois, and the Plains states.

The single-member district system

For the first half-century of our national life the method of choosing representatives was determined by state legislatures. Some chose to have them elected by single-member districts, others on a statewide (at large) basis. In the apportionment act of 1842, Congress required every state entitled to more than one representative to divide the state into districts of contiguous territory, each entitled to elect one representative. This language was retained in all subsequent actions by the Congress. The requirement that the districts be composed also of compact areas was added in 1901 and thereafter until 1929. The present act (1929 as amended in 1967), however, omits the requirement that the districts be composed of compact and contiguous territory and authorizes general (at large) election in those states with more than one representative only in the cases of Hawaii and New Mexico which have traditionally elected their two members at large and only until 1970. Bills restoring the compact and contiguous rules have been seriously considered in recent years, but none has thus far passed.

Superiority of the district system

In spite of the modifications mentioned, the single-member district system is predominant in practice and is firmly fixed in the American system of government. No one seriously expects that it will soon be abandoned. Unless some form of voting is used which will guarantee minority representation in connection with the statewide form of representation, the single-member district system is decidedly the better of the two systems. It tends to assure representation to a wider variety of groups and interests, and thus to strengthen the representative character of the lower house. The district system as it now operates, however, is not without its difficulties, and the House of Representatives elected by this system is not a perfect reflection of the national population for which it speaks.

Problems of redistricting

The major problems of the present system spring from the great difficulties—political, emotional, and geographical—of drawing the district boundaries, a job which is assigned to the state legislatures. There are two kinds of impulses that color the views of state legislators on this subject: (1) the hope of partisan advantage from drawing the lines in a particular way; and, (2) the fear, by rural and small-town legislators, of granting to the rapidly growing urban areas the representative strength to which their numbers entitle them. Obviously, it is not possible to have districts which are perfectly equal in population and which also pay some regard to local governmental boundaries. Thus inequality will occur to some extent in the most objective and impersonal efforts to draw the lines. State legislators, typically, have no strong impulse to be either objective or impersonal when drawing the boundary lines of the congressional districts.

Gerrymandering

The practice of drawing district boundary lines with a view to partisan or factional advantage is known as gerrymandering. The method is to spread the known support for your party or faction over as many districts as possible and to concentrate the known support for the other party into as

State Delegations and Districts
House of Representatives

1968

STATE	NO. OF DISTRICTS	LARGEST DISTRICT	SMALLEST DISTRICT	DATE OF APPORTIONMENT
Alabama	8	440,538	383,625	1965
Alaska	1	226,167	—	—
Arizona	3	456,529	405,217	1966
Arkansas	4	453,567	443,892	1965
California	38	446,974	392,973	1967
Colorado	4	493,887	405,889	1964
Connecticut	6	482,135	404,201	1964
Delaware	1	446,292	—	—
Florida	12	448,885	400,061	1967
Georgia	10	455,575	329,738	1964
Hawaii	2	Both at Large		
Idaho	2	364,984	302,207	1965
Illinois	24	451,322	394,481	1965
Indiana	11	428,197	417,158	1968
Iowa	7	442,406	353,156	1961
Kansas	5	453,901	394,109	1965
Kentucky	7	446,689	417,544	1966
Louisiana	8	462,753	370,131	1966
Maine	2	505,465	463,800	1961
Maryland	8	393,210	383,237	1966
Massachusetts	12	432,240	424,523	1967
Michigan	19	417,052	403,263	1964
Minnesota	8	482,872	375,475	1961
Mississippi	5	450,359	420,492	1966
Missouri	10	446,695	420,180	1968
Montana	2	347,701	327,066	1965
Nebraska	3	530,507	404,695	1961
Nevada	1	285,278	—	—
New Hampshire	2	331,818	275,103	1881
New Jersey	15	432,974	374,996	1967
New Mexico	2	500,859	450,164	1968
New York	41	435,880	382,277	1968
North Carolina	11	424,202	407,546	1967
North Dakota	2	333,290	299,156	1960
Ohio	24	457,774	319,968	1964
Oklahoma	6	396,161	380,734	1968
Oregon	4	468,809	404,165	1965
Pennsylvania	27	482,201	359,731	1966
Rhode Island	2	459,706	375,291	1931
South Carolina	6	421,478	375,556	1966
South Dakota	2	351,901	328,613	1965
Tennessee	9	404,968	388,240	1967
Texas	23	450,353	387,794	1967
Utah	2	451,864	438,763	1965
Virginia	10	419,642	377,511	1965
Washington	7	510,552	342,540	1965
West Virginia	5	375,917	368,947	1968
Wisconsin	10	408,677	381,830	1963
Wyoming	1	330,066	—	—

few districts as possible. Few redistricting laws have been passed by state legislatures which do not bear evidence of some manipulation of lines for partisan purposes. Some episodes, however, have been much more flagrant than others.

Effect of urbaniza- tion on redistrict- ing

Virtually every census for the past century has revealed the continuing movement of the American people from farm to city. Every state legislature has, therefore, been repeatedly confronted with the necessity, if districts are to be kept reasonably equal, of increasing the number of seats in the urban areas and, since 1929, of decreasing the number in the rural areas. In most of our state legislatures the rural and small-town areas have been grossly overrepresented in terms of population, and the rural legislators have been reluctant to augment the strength of the urban contingent in Congress. Frequently this cleavage has been aggravated by the fact that one party, usually the Democrats, has been predominant in the large cities and another party in the countryside. This reluctance produced redistricting in which the districts were still quite unequal in size, partial redistricting only, and, in some cases, no redistricting at all. Rural areas, in consequence, have been somewhat overrepresented in the House of Representatives. Rural over-representation also stems from the constitutional requirement that each state have at least one representative.

Various presidential efforts to achieve greater equality of congressional districts have not been successful thus far, nor have those initiated by urban congressmen. Judicial efforts have, however. In 1964 the Supreme Court, reversing a precedent of long standing held that the Constitution requires that districts of representation be as nearly equal in population as practicable. The command that "Representatives be chosen by the people of the several states" means said the Court, "that as nearly as practicable one man's vote is to be worth as much as another's." Since that time 37 states have redistricted, some more than once and some of the remaining state systems are vulnerable to court challenge. In fact more than half the total membership of the House in 1968 was elected on the basis of districting plans getting their first use.

REPRESENTATION IN THE SENATE—STATE EQUALITY

> The Senate of the United States shall be composed of two Senators from each State, elected by the people thereof, for six years; and each Senator shall have one vote.—Art. 1, Sec. 3, cl. 1, as amended by Seventeenth Amendment

Undemo- cratic character of the Senate

The Senate is not troubled by the problems of the district system. Representation in it is not and was never intended to be in any sense related to population. Every state, large or small, populous or not, rich or poor, industrial or agricultural, is entitled to two senators. And it may not be deprived of its equality with the others except with its own consent. The Senate is a federal institution. It is not a democratic one, at least insofar as democratic principles require an equality of representation for people as people. Until the Constitution was amended in 1913 to provide for the popular election of senators, it was not democratic in any respect. The tide of democracy which swept over and modified the American constitutional system during the last century left the federal character of the Senate untouched. To some adherents of the democratic faith, the fact that about 20 percent of the population of the United States can control a majority of the senators remains a conspicuous failure of the American system. The Senate, of course, was not designed by democrats but by constitutionalists intent upon preserving and strengthening the American Union.

THE SELECTION OF MEMBERS OF CONGRESS

Regulated by state law

The manner of electing senators and representatives is largely regulated by state law and thus varies in many details from state to state. Experience in this matter has been little different from that of electing all types of public officers in the United States, and at the present time the predominant mode is nomination by direct primary and election by secret, partisan ballot at the same time as many other public officials are chosen. Congress has exercised its constitutional authority to regulate the election of its members by requiring: (1) the single-member district system for representatives (1842); (2) the secret ballot (1872); (3) the election everywhere to take place on the Tuesday after the first Monday in November of any even-numbered year. The Congress has also enacted regulations governing campaign expenditures in national elections. The qualifications for voting in these congressional elections are established by state law also, but the Supreme Court has held that the right to vote for members of Congress is not conferred by the states but rather is one of the "privileges and immunities" of citizens of the United States protected by the Fourteenth Amendment. Disputed elections of members of Congress are ultimately decided by the House or the Senate.

The adoption of popular election of senators

The most important change in the method of selecting members of Congress was the adoption in 1913 of direct popular election of senators in place of selection by state legislatures, which had been the practice up to that time. Whatever may have been the advantages which characterized legislative selection, toward the end of the last century it fell increasingly into disrepute. Recurring deadlocks left some seats vacant for several years; the preoccupation of state legislators with the selection of senators interfered with the discharge of their state and local responsibilities; concern by the voters for the legislature's selection led to election of state legislators on no other basis except their promised support of a particular candidate. The Senate was widely charged with being filled with the minions of powerful (and at the moment unpopular) interests which browbeat, bribed, and intimidated state legislators into choosing rich men who were not really representative of the state. The swelling enthusiasm for democratic processes instilled in many the conviction that legislative election was undemocratic and ought to be abandoned. The Senate finally, though reluctantly, concurred and the Seventeenth Amendment was added to the Constitution.

Results of popular election

The effects of this change cannot easily be measured. The expectation of its sponsors that money would play a less important role in elections has certainly not been realized. Legitimate expenditures for individuals campaigning over an entire state are probably greatly in excess of what might have been spent to influence a state legislature. Excessive, perhaps illegitimate, expenditures have been made on several occasions. The change in the character or quality of the senators has not been appreciable. Certainly there was no abrupt change in personnel. Contrary to expectation, reelections have been more numerous than under the old system. State legislatures have clearly been made freer to concentrate on the tasks of state government than they were before and deadlocks have become impossible. If under the old system an occasional plutocrat bought his way into the Senate to satisfy purely personal ambition, under the new one the demagogue and the windbag probably get in more readily than before. If, however, our senators today are not demonstrably better than they once were, they are not demonstrably worse as the opponents of popular election predicted. Taft, Douglas, Fulbright, Millikin, Russell, among recent senators, are probably as able and as honest as any that the Senate of the past century can show.

The term of senators is six years and this puts each senator in a much different position than a representative. He is able to devote himself for several years to his senatorial responsibilities without constant anxiety about reelection. He serves through several sessions of Congress and is able to acquire a great deal of understanding and experience before he is obliged to stand before the voters of his state and ask for a vote of confidence. Many senators serve more than one term and periods of service extending to 18 or even 24 years are not uncommon. Continuity of personnel is also obtained by the constitutional arrangement for the election of only one-third of the membership every two years.

Term

The term of representatives is two years. President Johnson in 1966 proposed that the term be made four years in order, he said, to reduce the time spent campaigning and increase the time devoted to legislative affairs. His proposal was not strongly supported in Congress.

QUALIFICATIONS FOR MEMBERSHIP

No person shall be a Representative who shall not have attained to the age of twenty-five years, and been seven years a citizen of the United States and who shall not, when elected, be an inhabitant of that State in which he shall be chosen.—Art. 1, Sec. 2, cl. 2

No person shall be a Senator who shall not have attained to the age of thirty years, and been nine years a citizen of the United States and who shall not, when elected, be an inhabitant of that State for which he shall be chosen.—Art. 1, Sec. 3, cl. 3

Many decades of political experience have resulted in the addition by custom and usage to the bare constitutional requirements. It is virtually a universal requirement that representatives be residents of the district for which they sit as well as of the state in which it is located. In some sections of the country, it is almost indispensable that an individual be a Republican and in others that he be a Democrat, in order to seek election with any hope of success. Every district has by this time a large number of unwritten qualifications which constitute "availability" in a candidate for the national legislature. These are so varied, however, that no safe generalization is possible. Suffice it to say that simple compliance with the age, citizenship, and residence requirements does not "qualify" a person for Congress. *(Qualifications added by usage)*

The two houses of Congress, furthermore, have each chosen to exercise their prerogative of judging the qualifications of those who present themselves for membership by excluding individuals on grounds unrelated to the constitutional specifications. The House in 1900 refused to seat Brigham H. Roberts of Utah on the grounds that he was a polygamist. Victor L. Berger of Wisconsin was excluded in 1919 because he had been judicially convicted of obstructing the war effort. Adam Clayton Powell was excluded in 1967 because of improper handling of committee funds and refusal to cooperate with an investigating committee. In each instance there were members of the House who argued that this procedure was unconstitutional and the proper course was to seat such individuals and then, if they were deemed unfit for membership, expel them. It takes only a majority vote to exclude and a two-thirds vote to expel, and the critics of the three individuals preferred, and successfully persuaded the House to prefer, the easier method. The Senate, on its part, has accepted "questionable" members after some debate on the grounds that the constitutional method is expulsion. Reed Smoot of Utah (1903) and William Langer of North Dakota (1941) were both seated although under attack. On the other hand, in 1928 it refused to seat Frank L. Smith of Illinois and William S. Vare of Pennsylvania on the grounds that they had exceeded by a great deal the legal limit on campaign expenditures in their contests for election. Grave doubts still exist among members of Congress and students as to the propriety and legality of the imposition by the two houses of additional qualifications. Thus far the courts have refused to intervene. *(Qualifications imposed by the two houses)*

CONGRESSIONAL PERSONNEL

The
typical
congress-
man

What kinds of men and women are our lawmakers in Washington? They are not "average" Americans in most respects, but rather well above the average in terms of education, age, and means. A study made of the 90th Congress may be taken as fairly typical of that body in modern times. It revealed that: (1) The average age of our representatives is 51 and of senators 58, well above the average of the population generally; (2) the lawmakers are well rooted in the districts which they represent by birth and long residence; (3) they are affiliated with one or another of the major religious faiths in about the same proportion as the people generally; (4) 88 percent attended college or a professional school or both; (5) many of them had substantial prior political experience in state and local government as legislators, governors, mayors, district attorneys; (6) 12 were women and seven were Negroes; and, (7) a majority are lawyers. In addition to the law, the other professions had some representation as did the world of business and finance. Few members were themselves farmers and two were former labor-union officials.

This summary indicates clearly that our legislators come largely from the upper–middle class economically and socially. The typical legislator is a county-seat lawyer, serving his third or fourth term, comfortable but not rich, a church member, a leader in his community and region, but not well known outside it, a member of one of the fraternal orders, and a person of considerable prior political experience.

THE ROLE OF POLITICAL PARTIES IN THE CONGRESS

Parties
in the
Congress

It is impossible to understand the character and conduct of our national legislature without an appreciation of the powerful influence of political parties in its organization. Sometimes called the "invisible government" of the Congress, the party apparatus, developed outside the Constitution, nevertheless dominates the formal institutions of congressional leadership. All but a small handful of the nation's legislators have come to Congress bearing the label of one or the other of the two great parties. Elected under the sign of the elephant or the donkey, the members profess a certain loyalty to these two great political organizations and to their aims and programs enunciated during the campaign. One of the two parties will normally command the support of a majority of the members of each house and will take possession of the formal positions of authority and leadership; the other, although a minority and therefore not obliged to assume any responsibility for what is done by the Congress, is nevertheless by usage and tradition entitled to certain rights and privileges. Loyalty to these party organizations is a necessary requisite to the achievement of position, influence, and prestige in the legislative process, and this loyalty provides the only consequential bond which unites the party members and fuels the machine of party government.

The font of authority for the agencies of party government is the party caucus or conference. All of the members of each party in each house comprise the party caucuses of the two parties in the House and Senate. Thus all of the Republican members of the House of Representatives comprise the Republican conference of the House. The party conferences always assemble prior to the convening of each new Congress and elect the officers and functionaries of the parties for the Congress and also agree on the party candidates for the major posts to be determined by the legislature. Thus, the House conferences will designate their choices for speaker, clerk, and so on; and the Senate conferences, their choices for president *pro tempore,* secretary, and sergeant. Beyond this, the party conferences rarely meet. They prefer to entrust decisions thereafter to their designated agents. However, when rifts occur which threaten a major breakdown in party loyalty or when the leaders are unable to reconcile differences within the group on major legislative matters, the conferences may and do assemble and try to give new direction to the party apparatus. The practice of determining a party position on legislation by the caucus is a last resort. Leaders seek to avoid it at almost any cost and the members dislike it intensely. For one reason, it is next to impossible to enforce the caucus decision on reluctant members. The Republicans rarely even try. The Democrats, in the House at least, have a caucus rule which purports to bind the members to support a caucus decision reached by a two-thirds vote. The rule admits of certain exceptions, and enforcement has rarely been strict. We see, then, that the party caucuses select both the leaders of the party machinery and, in the case of the majority party, the chief officers of the House and Senate and they also exercise some, but not much, control over legislative programs. In the main, the latter object is achieved by the leaders whom the caucuses entrust with such powers as they command.

The party conference or caucus

One of the major agents to which the caucuses entrust the power and responsibility for the achievement of party goals is the policy committee. This committee was created in 1946 as part of a general reorganization of the Congress and was intended to replace the steering committee which had functioned for many years previously. The Democrats in the Senate, however, continue to use their steering committee for the purpose of assigning their members to standing committees. The Democratic steering committee is elected by the party conference, consists ordinarily of 15 to 17 members and meets only at the beginning of the session or when a death or resignation creates a committee vacancy which the party is entitled to fill. Although the legislation of 1946 creating the policy committees fixed the membership at seven, neither party has hewed to the letter of the law. The Republican Policy Committee now includes 15 senators and the Democratic Policy Committee nine. The members are selected in each case by the party conferences. Each party makes an effort to represent the major regions of the nation and

Agents of the caucus:

Senate Conference Meeting

ANNOUNCEMENT OF DEMOCRATIC CONFERENCE MONDAY, FEBRUARY 15, 1960

Mr. MANSFIELD. Mr. President, I wish to make the announcement to the Senate that there will be a Democratic conference on Monday morning, February 15, at 9:30, at which time we will discuss the President's budget, the joint economic report, and the matter of interest rates. This will serve as a notice to the Democrats that a meeting will be held at that time on that date to cover these particular subjects.

SOURCE: *Congressional Record, Senate,* February 9, 1960, p. 2327.

1. The steering and policy committees

the major factions in the party, although not necessarily in proportion to voting strength in the Senate or to population or party vote in the region. Typically, these committees have been composed of respected and experienced legislators. These two committees meet frequently and, in the case of the majority committee, select bills to be given floor consideration, decide the time when they might be taken up, and in general, formulate positions on some measures which they hope and believe their party colleagues will support. Neither committee has ever really determined policy or formulated a legislative program for the party.

The House of Representatives has never formally created any policy committees. In 1949, the Republicans converted their steering committee, but this was unofficial and no staff and no funds were provided. This committee is composed of 27 members selected by the committee on committees, four ex officio members (the floor leader, whip, conference chairman, and chairman of the congressional campaign committee), and the Republican members of the rules committee. The Democratic Steering Committee, created in 1933 and revitalized in 1962, is composed of 18 members representing a similar number of geographical regions and six ex officio members. Each of the 18 area representatives is selected by the Democratic representatives from that area. The Republicans have used their policy committee with some frequency in the last few years, not really to lay down a policy for the party but to prepare statements on legislative matters and to seek agreement on party positions. The Democrat leadership has not relied on the steering committee to any degree.

2. The floor leaders

The party conferences in each house designate floor leaders to direct the legislative programs of the two parties. In the House of Representatives, the majority leader plans the business of the House, offers the necessary motions and resolutions to keep his party's bills moving through the legislative process, announces the intentions of his group toward future legislative business, speaks frequently in debate on behalf of his party and often on behalf of the national administration. He is, after the speaker, the second in command of his party's legislative campaign. His favorable opinion is

MAJOR PARTY STRENGTH IN CONGRESS, 1932–1968

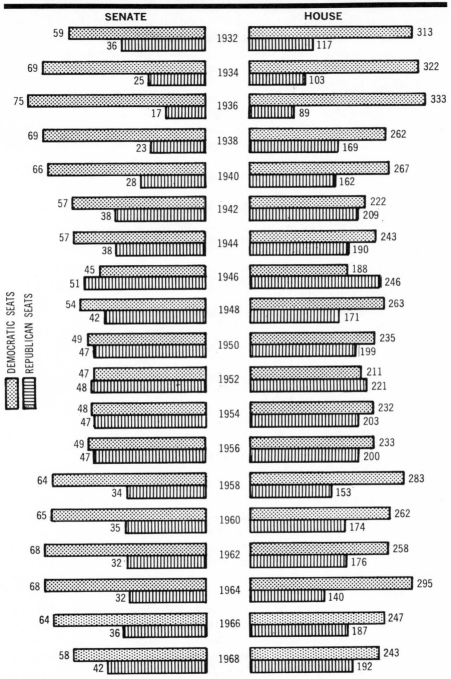

SENATE   **HOUSE**

DEMOCRATIC SEATS

REPUBLICAN SEATS

Year	Senate Dem.	Senate Rep.	House Dem.	House Rep.
1932	59	36	313	117
1934	69	25	322	103
1936	75	17	333	89
1938	69	23	262	169
1940	66	28	267	162
1942	57	38	222	209
1944	57	38	243	190
1946	45	51	188	246
1948	54	42	263	171
1950	49	47	235	199
1952	47	48	211	221
1954	48	47	232	203
1956	49	47	233	200
1958	64	34	283	153
1960	65	35	262	174
1962	68	32	258	176
1964	68	32	295	140
1966	64	36	247	187
1968	58	42	243	192

Divisions of seats based on election results of the respective years. Seats won by minor parties account for the fact that figures do not always total the full membership of the Senate and the House.

almost indispensable to the passage of important legislation. His power and influence over the operations of the lower chamber are exceeded only by that of the speaker, and he may expect to succeed to the speakership upon the death or resignation of the incumbent as long as his party possesses a majority of the House.

The majority floor leader of the Senate occupies a position similar in most respects to his counterpart in the House. His functions and responsibilities are identical but, typically, his personal influence is not as great because of the more individualistic, less regimented nature of the Senate. On

---

Legislative Program for the Week of June 24, 1968

Mr. GERALD FORD. Mr. Speaker, I take this time for the purpose of asking the distinguished majority leader the program for the remainder of this week and the schedule for the next.

Mr. CARL ALBERT. Mr. Speaker, in response to the inquiry of the distinguished minority leader about the program, we have finished the program for this week and will ask to go over upon the announcement of the program for next week.

Monday is District Day, but there are no district bills.
On Monday:
H. R. 3196 to authorize the Secretary of Commerce to make a study to determine the advantages and disadvantages in increased use of the metric system . . . etc.
S 322, land disposals from the National Wildlife Refuge System . . . etc.
For Tuesday and the balance of the week:
The Departments of Labor and Health, Education and Welfare . . . appropriations bill for fiscal year 1969 . . . etc.

SOURCE: *Congressional Record, House*, June 20, 1968, pp. 5320–5321.

THE FLOOR LEADER AT WORK

the other hand, the Senate majority leader has neither a powerful presiding officer nor a powerful rules committee with which he must share some of his power. He does, however, use the policy committee, of which he is a member, a little more often than his counterparts in the House. The Republican party in the Senate assigns different senators to preside over the party conference, to be floor leader, and to head the policy committee. The Democrats expect their floor leader to serve in the other posts also.

The minority leaders of the two houses have nothing like the responsibility of the majority leaders. Their party cannot expect to have a legislative program in any positive sense. As leaders of the opposition, they direct the floor strategy of their followers, attacking, criticizing, delaying the majority's program, or at least those parts of it which they are unwilling to support. In frequent conferences with the majority leaders, they seek to gain appropriate representation in parliamentary institutions and adequate time for the minority to present its views in debate. They also strive, usually successfully, to obtain from the majority leaders commitments as to the ensuing course of legislative business so they can advise their members and plan their tactics. When the party majority shifts in either or both houses, of course, the minority leaders may expect to succeed to the speakership in the House and to the majority floor leadership or presidency *pro tempore* in the Senate.

3. The whips

The floor leaders for each party in each house have been aided, since about 1900, by assistant floor leaders usually called whips. These individuals are selected by the party conferences, typically on the recommendation of the floor leaders. These whips act for the floor leaders when the latter are obliged to be absent from the chambers. The major duty of the whip is to canvass the views of the members of his party on issues before the Congress and to advise the floor leader how many votes he can count on, on any given item of legislative business. Another duty of the whip is to see that the voting strength of his party is fully brought to bear on every significant legislative decision. In the House, the whip ordinarily appoints 15 to 18 assistants to aid him in canvassing opinion and in mustering the members to important roll calls. The secretaries to the policy committees in the Senate perform many of the functions of assistant whips.

4. The committee on committees

One final and very important agent of the caucus is the committee on committees. This group performs the difficult and delicate task of selecting the party membership for each of the standing committees. The House Republican Committee on Committees consists of one representative from each state having Republican representation. Each state Republican delegation selects its own member. Each member of the committee has as many votes as there are Republican representatives from his state. The House Democratic Committee on Committees is the Democratic delegation on the Ways and Means Committee and this is designated by the caucus. The Senate Republican Committee on Committees ordinarily consists of from six to nine senators appointed by the chairman of the Republican conference. The Senate Democratic Steering Committee serves as its committee on committees.

THE SPEAKER OF THE HOUSE OF REPRESENTATIVES

The House of Representatives shall choose their Speaker
and other officers. . . .—Art. 1, Sec. II, cl. 5

From presiding officer to director

Of the formal institutions of leadership provided by the Constitution and by the rules of the two houses, by far the most important is the speaker of the House of Representatives. This office had, had a long history in the English House of Commons before it was transported to the colonial legislatures and from there to the legislatures of the states and of the nation. The powers adhering to the post were never very precisely defined, and almost two centuries of experience have made of the speakership a very different office from its contemporary counterpart in the British Parliament. The speaker is the most powerful single individual in the House of Representatives in determining the legislative product of that body; whereas in England the speaker is simply an impartial presiding officer and has little or no influence on legislation. The power and influence of the speakership in the American system is the product of the rapid expansion of the size of the House, the continuous increase in the complexity of its business and the growth in influence and importance of the informal party government. All of these created a demand for leadership and direction. The speaker, with his party majority behind him and from his strategic post of presiding officer, gradually gathered to himself the powers of direction, some have said of dictation. The major instruments of speaker dominance had been achieved gradually, but by 1910 had collectively constituted a formidable array. In the first place, the speaker appointed the members of all standing committees as well as of all special or select committees of the House. The fate of legislation in the lower house was, and still is, so completely determined by the standing committees that the power to determine the membership of these committees is probably the most important authority in the Congress. Originally the committees had been staffed by vote of the whole house, but the power had slipped gradually into the sole hands of the presiding officer. Secondly, the speaker was chairman of the most powerful of the standing committees, the rules committee. This small committee, consisting at the time of only five men, completely dominated the progress of legislative business on the floor of the House. In the next place, the speaker successfully asserted and exercised the power to refuse to put motions offered by members which he considered dilatory or obstructive. Finally, the rules endowed the speaker with complete control over floor participation of individual members through his right to "recognize" members and their inability to address the House unless recognized.

The attack on the speaker-ship in 1910–1911   The dominion of Speaker Cannon was so complete and his own policies so at variance with that of many of the members even of his own party that a long-simmering revolt against "the system" boiled over in 1910, and a coalition of insurgent Republican with the Democratic minority succeeded in capturing control of the House long enough to deal the speakership a heavy blow. The speaker was removed from membership on the rules committee. In 1911, the power to appoint standing committees was vested in the whole House by the same coalition. These actions deprived the office of two of its most important weapons, and the speaker has never been quite so dominant since.

Powers of the modern speaker   Although weakened by the changes of 1910–1911, the speaker is still the most important and most powerful member of the House. He presides over all sittings of the House, appoints those who take his place when he must be absent, preserves order and decorum, "recognizes" members desiring to speak, signs all acts, resolutions, writs, warrants or subpoenas ordered by the House, interprets and applies the rules, decides points of order (questions of parliamentary procedure raised by members), puts questions to a vote, determines the outcome of most unrecorded voting, appoints all special, select, and conference committees, and assigns bills to the various standing committees. As a member of the House, he may speak in debate and vote on all questions before the House. He is not, however, required to vote except in case of a tie or when the House is voting by ballot.

Among this imposing array of powers and responsibilities the power of recognition may be used to illustrate the role of the speaker in directing the lower house. Under the rules of the House, any member desiring to speak for any purpose must address the chair and be recognized by it. The speaker has the sole authority to accord the necessary recognition. By his refusal to recognize a member seeking the floor, the speaker can influence the course of business. If he knows that a member is seeking the floor to offer motions which might delay or sidetrack business which the speaker wants pushed forward, he refuses to "see" him when he rises. It should not be inferred that the speaker will ignore the minority. Ordinarily, he allots to their adherents a fair share of the debating time, but he is under no obligation to allow them to interfere with the majority program. The speaker is also able to inquire the purpose for which members seek the floor and thus cannot easily be caught off guard by an unanticipated parliamentary maneuver. Debate on legislative measures is customarily controlled by the chairman and senior minority member of the standing committee to which a bill was referred and these men apportion the time for each side. The speaker customarily accepts these arrangements and by rule the two leaders must be allowed the floor. In summary, through the power of recognition the speaker can influence the course of legislative business but is not free to dominate debate. *The power of recognition*

The speaker is now accorded by the rules the powers asserted earlier by Speaker Reed to refuse to put dilatory motions and to count as present all members who, in fact, are present whether they answer to their names or not. Both of these grew out of minority tactics to delay and obstruct majority legislative action. *The power to halt obstruction*

The House of Representatives has come to expect that the speaker will use his enormous power and influence to aid his party. Although the speaker is expected to preside in a judicial manner and to be as fair as the rules permit to the minority, he is an important leader of the majority party and is expected to use his influence in behalf of its legislative program. We have already observed that the speaker, although formally elected by the whole House, is actually the leader of the majority party and is designated for his high office by the members of the party in caucus. In his office, the formal leadership and the informal party leadership are combined. It is because he has his party behind him that he is able to exercise the influence over the proceedings that he does. *Partisanship*

Neither the Constitution nor the rules establish any qualifications for

Qualifica-
tions of
the
speaker

the office of speaker. He does not even have to be a member of the House. Every speaker, however, has been a representative. Furthermore, every speaker, at least for the past half century, has been a member of long service. The average service of the speakers since 1896 has been more than 22 years. Seniority is not rigidly adhered to in the selection, and the speaker has not always or even typically been the member of longest service. He has, however, been one of the most experienced members of the House and, from this fact alone, has stemmed a considerable part of his influence. Like the chairmen of the standing committees, the speaker is likely to come from a "safe" district and, therefore, to emerge from a political environment quite different from that which produces the President.

THE PRESIDING OFFICERS OF THE SENATE

The Senate shall choose their other officers, and also a president *pro tempore* in the absence of the Vice President. . . .—Art. I, Sec. III, cl. 5

The Vice-
President

There is no counterpart in the Senate to the speaker of the House of Representatives. The regular presiding officer of the Senate is the Vice-President of the United States. He is not a leader emerging from the operations of the Senate and, therefore, has not typically enjoyed either the power or the influence of the speaker. He has all of the normal powers of presiding officers, but he is not designated by the majority caucus. He is not a member able to take the floor and argue for his party's program. He does not ordinarily bring to the post many years of continuous service in that body. The rules of the Senate are not designed to enhance the powers of its leaders. A Vice-President is influential in the deliberations of the Senate, and some have been, only if he personally can by his experience and ability command such influence.

The
president
pro
tempore

The president *pro tempore,* with whom the Vice-President shares his presiding functions and who is selected by the Senate itself, comes a little closer to the speaker. Even he, however, is ordinarily overshadowed by the majority floor leader and typically exercises nothing like the speaker's influence. Only since 1890 has the post been a continuing one, and only in part of the period since then has it been an influential one. The reasons for the relative weakness of this post lie in the smaller numerical size of the chamber and the added stature that this gives to each senator. Senators are apt to be exceedingly jealous of their prerogatives. They are not easily led and on many occasions will not be led at all, even by someone of their own choosing. The president *pro tempore* is but one of several leaders of the majority party in the Senate. His is nevertheless an office of considerable power, prestige, and perquisites and it is vigorously sought after. Like the speakership, it is a partisan office and is used to forward the program of the majority party.

THE COMMITTEE SYSTEM OF THE HOUSE AND SENATE

Legislative bodies the world over achieve more careful review of proposed legislation and save the time of the members by referring most matters brought before them to committees for study and report. Nowhere, however, do these committees play such a dominant part in shaping the legislative product as in the American Congress, and especially in the House of Repre-

Development of the committee system

Standing Committees 90th Congress, 1968

HOUSE OF REPRESENTATIVES		SENATE	
Agriculture	35	Aeronautical and Space Sciences	16
Appropriations	51	Agriculture and Forestry	15
Armed Services	40	Appropriations	26
Banking and Currency	33	Armed Services	18
District of Columbia	25	Banking and Currency	14
Education and Labor	33	District of Columbia	8
Foreign Affairs	36	Finance	17
Government Operations	35	Foreign Relations	19
House Administration	25	Government Operations	15
Interior and Insular Affairs	33	Interior and Insular Affairs	17
Interstate and Foreign Commerce	33	Interstate and Foreign Commerce	18
Judiciary	35	Judiciary	16
Merchant Marine and Fisheries	34	Labor and Public Welfare	16
Post Office and Civil Service	26	Post Office and Civil Service	12
Public Works	34	Public Works	16
Rules	15	Rules and Administration	9
Science and Astronautics	31		
Un-American Activities	9		
Veterans Affairs	25		
Ways and Means	25		

sentatives. The development of an elaborate system of standing committees to which are referred every piece of legislative business took several decades, but by the latter part of the last century it had become customary to assign each member of the House and Senate to one or more of the standing committees and to refer all legislation upon introduction to one of them.

In addition to the standing committees, the House still makes use of committees of the whole. It also continues, as does the Senate, to make some use of special and select committees. At present each house, for example, has a select committee on small business. At one time investigations were undertaken very largely by special committees, but since the reorganization of 1946 which sought to make special committees unnecessary this has not been true. The Congress has occasionally created special or select committees which include representatives of both houses. These are called joint committees and may be established by resolution or by statute. Typically, they are entrusted with a mission which it is felt cannot or will not be carried out effectively by the standing committees. Sometimes they are charged with investigations, occasionally with supervising some aspect of

Types of committees

congressional business, such as printing or the Library of Congress. Some statutes, which have sought closer coordination between the legislative branch and the executive branch in a particular field of national affairs, have provided for a joint committee for this purpose, for example, the Joint Committee on Atomic Energy and the Joint Committee on the Economic Report (of the President). Another type of congressional committee is the conference committee, about which more will be said in the next chapter. All of these special, select, joint, or conference committees are appointed by the presiding officers of the two houses. While they may, and do on occasion, achieve great prominence, their influence ordinarily is minor compared with that of the standing committees.

Standing committees:

1. Number and size

The pressure of increasing legislative business and of members for greater recognition and perquisites tends to multiply the number of standing committees, and this multiplication tends to produce overlapping and duplication of committee jurisdictions. Periodically, the Congress has had to reduce the number and clarify the missions of its standing committees. The most substantial effort in this direction was made by the Congressional Reorganization Act of 1946. This act, as later modified, is the basis of the committee system of the present Congress.

2. Assignments per member

In the unreorganized Congress, most members of the two houses served on several committees. In the House, however, only a few members had more than one major assignment. On occasion, therefore, a few members in each house might have influential positions on two or three committees and thus possess unusual personal power. The reduction in committees was accompanied by an attempt, largely successful, to limit each member in the House to but one committee. Senators are generally restricted, under the new scheme, to service on not more than two committees. The result has been a more even distribution of the work load among members of the two houses.

3. Selection of committee members

Although members of Congress are formally elected to the standing committees by vote of the house to which they belong, actually this vote is but a ratification of the selections made in private conference by the committee on committees of each of the two parties in each house. The rivalry for committee posts is intense and the distribution of committee seats is one of the most difficult chores in the Congress. In the House of Representatives especially, the power, influence, and legislative success of each member is largely determined by his committee assignment. Almost his entire participation in the legislative process will stem from his committee work. Therefore, members are all keenly anxious to obtain posts on the more important committees and particularly on those which handle the problems of greatest concern to the districts which they represent. Many years of experience in the troublesome field of committee assignments have induced the two houses to evolve a very rigid but unwritten code to govern the process. Major weight is assigned to length of continuous service. Once assigned to a particular committee a legislator may confidently expect to advance up the ladder of precedence as long as he continues to be elected by the voters. The only major exception to this rule involves members who are willing to sacrifice seniority on minor committees to gain seats on major committees. The job of the selecting agencies thus resolves itself into: (1) determining the number of posts to be filled on each committee; (2) assigning newly elected members to the committees; (3) taking care of as many of those who have already served on each committee as the total party membership on the committee permits; and (4) accommodating as many as feasible of those who are interested in or are obliged to shift from one committee to another.

The number of seats to be assigned to each party on each committee is worked out by the majority party leaders, usually in consultation with the minority leaders. Traditionally, the posts on all but one or two key committees are assigned to each party in proportion to the relative strength of that party in the chamber concerned. Thus, if the Republicans have 55 percent of the representatives they will take 55 percent of the posts on most of the committees of the House and assign 45 percent to the Democrats. The majority party usually insists, however, that it have a disproportionate representation on the committees on rules, ways and means, and appropriations. This is to enable it so to control these committees that a coalition of minority party and insurgents from the majority which might throttle the majority program would be hard to form. Independents and members of third parties fare poorly in committee assignments. If they are taken care of at all, it is usually by the majority party. *Party strength on committees*

The most coveted post on each standing committee is the chairmanship. This post, although formally filled by vote of the House or Senate, goes automatically to the majority member of longest continuous service on that committee. Only a major failure by a member to support his party, in a presidential campaign, for example, or in voting to organize the House of Representatives, is likely to induce the party selection committees to pass over him in designating the chairman. *4. Committee chairmen:* *a. Selection*

The power of the chairmen of the committees is so great that it has allowed them repeatedly to defy their own leaders with impunity and to stifle programs demanded by the White House and by the floor leaders. It is not easy to account for their influence, for it is compounded of many bits of power. The chairman, in the first place, can reward and punish the members of his committee. He appoints the subcommittees and designates those who will participate in the debate for the committee majority. The chairman can usually prevent a meeting of the committee if he doesn't want one and can invariably control the agenda when the committee does meet. He also controls the hiring of most of the staff. Much of his power stems from tradition rather than rule, but it is a tradition that most congressmen support, presumably in anticipation of the day when they will be chairmen and entitled to the privileges of these offices. The chairmen have, of course, attained their relatively great power and influence largely since 1911, when appointment by the speaker was abolished and the method of election instituted under cover of which the seniority system became so firmly entrenched. *b. Power*

The developing power of the committee chairman and the method by which they are selected has given rise to an increasing volume of criticism of the system. There is no demonstrable correlation between seniority and competence, say the critics. There is a demonstrable correlation between seniority and a "safe" constituency. Those districts or states dominated by one party or by one strong interest are likely to return the same congressmen again and again. Those districts where the party battle is intense and the interests divided are likely to change congressmen frequently. Thus, their representatives and senators never achieve seniority. The close districts, say the critics, are the more decisive in national campaigns. The self-determined leaders of Congress may be, and frequently are, the critics allege, out of step with the main currents of public opinion in the nation. Young, able, and ambitious legislators are not given opportunity fully to utilize their talents and grow restive in the grip of seniority. In this way, legislative talent is wasted and discouraged. Of course, if the chairmen were not so powerful, the problem would not be so acute.

The answers to these criticisms put forth by defenders of the existing arrangements are: (1) They have served the nation well, that is, there is no real breakdown of the legislative process; (2) they guarantee that the Congress will be dominated by men of experience; (3) they provide an impersonal and objective standard for determining precedence and one that avoids personalities, bitterness, and manipulation, all of which would destroy the loyalty and cooperation which make legislation possible; and (4) no one, not even the Joint Committee on the Organization of Congress which labored so manfully at the problem of improving the Congress, has yet suggested a better plan that is acceptable to most congressmen.

Each of the standing committees has a commodious office with a secretarial and clerical staff, more or less elaborate files, and occasionally a library. One of the most widely heralded reforms of the Reorganization Act of 1946 was the provision of a professional staff for each of the committees. It was anticipated that each committee might employ, on a nonpartisan basis, from two to four "experts" in one or more of the fields of public policy within the purview of the committee. The persons would be able, it was felt, to collect and interpret data for the committee and to analyze the problems presented for its consideration. While nonpartisanship has not been as conspicuous in the employment of experts as some had hoped, and the change in party domination of the committees has been accompanied by shifts in staff, nevertheless a great deal more continuity and expert assistance has been brought to the aid of committee deliberations than previously.

RULES COMMITTEE OF THE HOUSE

The impressive powers of direction of the speaker and the majority floor leader of the House of Representatives are shared with the Committee on Rules. Although this committee is concerned primarily with legislative

Wholesome Poultry Products Act

Mr. MATSUNGA. Mr. Speaker, by direction of the Committee on Rules, I call up House Resolution 1172 and ask for its immediate consideration:

The Clerk read as follows:
Resolved, That after the adoption of this resolution it shall be in order to move that the House resolve itself into the Committee of the Whole House on the State of the Union for the consideration of the bill (H. R. 16.363) to clarify and otherwise amend the Poultry Products Inspection Act, to provide for cooperation. . . .

After general debate, which shall be confined to the bill and shall continue not to exceed two hours, to be equally divided and controlled by the chairman and ranking member of the Committee on Agriculture, the bill shall be read for amendment under the five minute rule. At the conclusion of the consideration of the bill for amendment, the committee shall rise and report the bill to the House with such amendments as have been adopted, and the previous question shall be considered as ordered on the bill and amendments thereunto to final passage without intervening motion, except one motion to recommit.

SOURCE: *Congressional Record, House,* June 13, 1968, pp. 4937—4938.

A SPECIAL ORDER OF THE RULES COMMITTEE

How the rules committee controls debate in the House

procedure, it has become so influential in determining the way in which the time of the House will be spent that in this way it is able to influence what finally is passed. In the last quarter of the past century the practice of proposing special orders to govern the course of floor debate on a piece of legislation took its present form. This practice constitutes the most important of its present repertoire of privileges and responsibilities. Most of the important bills emanating from the other standing committees must now go to the rules committee for clearance if time is to be found for their consideration. The rules committee, if it approves, may clear the way for floor consideration by bringing in a special order. If adopted by the House, the order, in the form of a resolution, establishes the time for debate and allots a share of it to the majority and one to the minority. Without the aid of a special order, legislation of many types, even though approved by the standing committee which considered it, is likely to languish on the calendar and never be taken up at all. The competition for place on the calendars is so intense, there are so many more bills received than can be debated, that the power to provide for the immediate consideration of a bill regardless of its order on the docket is of great importance. Through this procedure, the committee can demand changes in a bill as a condition for bringing it to debate, can even insist on a whole new bill, and can effectively stop consideration of a bill of which it does not approve. It can also limit floor debate, prevent amendments except those offered by the committee in charge of the bill and can set aside points of order which might be raised. From 1949–1951, as a result of pressure from dissident elements in both parties, the power of the rules committee was weakened by the adoption of a rule which made it possible, though difficult, for a standing committee chairman to bring a bill to the floor despite the opposition of the rules committee. Attempts to reinstate this limitation on the powerful rules committee have been made at the beginning of each Congress since 1951, and finally in 1965 a modified form of the rule was adopted. The power of the Committee in relation to sending a bill to conference was also weakened at this time. Criticism of the committee took a different form in 1961. Led by the speaker (Rayburn), the House voted to increase the size of the committee from 12 to 15 in order to pave the way for the appointment of new members more sympathetic to the programs of the White House.

No
counter-
part in
Senate

The Senate has no counterpart to the rules committee. The time of the Senate is very largely determined by the members themselves; debate is thus freer and more extensive.

CONGRESSMEN AND THE INSTITUTIONS OF LEADERSHIP

The
member
and the
machine

It must be a great shock to a new member of the House of Representatives who comes to Washington, frequently from a position of influence in his small state legislature, to find how insignificant he is in the Congress. He ranks at the bottom of any committee, even a minor one, to which he may be assigned. He is rarely allowed to address the House. In fact, he usually can speak, and even then briefly, only when a bill from his committee is before the House and when he has been assigned a role in the debate by his chairman. On many of the major questions of the day he gains his knowledge, like any ordinary citizen, by reading the newspapers. Only after he has served a few terms is he recognized as a lawmaker by Washington society, administrative agencies, and the nation's press. And only after he has served several terms is he able to assume a position of influence.

Domina-
tion of the
House
by its
leaders

About 30 or 40 men dominate the activities of the House of Representatives, firmly directing the proceedings, controlling the debate, and determining the extent and character of the participation of the other 400 members. This handful of leaders are invariably men of long experience in the processes of the lower house. Ordinarily they command the support of their majority party colleagues. Periodically, however, the leaders, partly because they tend to represent "safe" districts, lose touch with the sentiment of the nation and of many of their fellow representatives. Revolts against the leaders and the institutions of leadership have occurred and these have provoked sharp criticisms of the House "machine" as repressive, ruthless, arbitrary, and essentially undemocratic. No system of leadership comparable to the ministry in parliamentary democracies is provided by the American Constitution. The President, although frequently giving important direction to the Congress especially on large matters of grave import, is outside the legislature and not in a position to provide intimate direction of its processes. Self-developed institutions of leadership have arisen in response to imperative needs, but according to no preconceived plan and largely as the exigencies of party politics have determined. Over the years, as the size of the House has grown and the complexities of legislative problems increased, the power of the leadership has become more and more firmly seated.

At the other end of the Capitol, in the Senate, the situation is quite *The* different. The institutions of leadership, although impressive, sit lightly on *situation* the backs of the senators. The business proceeds at a more leisurely pace, *in the* debate is more spontaneous and also more discursive, and program and *Senate* procedural decisions are based on consensus among a fairly large portion of the members. The traditions and the rules of the Senate are sensitive to the position and perquisites of the individual senator and of the minority. Whereas the House, typically, disposes of a major piece of legislative business in about five or six hours of floor discussion, the Senate will require several days. Every senator who wants to usually can make his contribution to the debate. If the House is widely criticized because of its cursory disposition of significant bills, the Senate is condemned for the opposite. A determined minority can bring the legislative process almost to a complete halt in the upper house. The final product of senatorial deliberations is much more likely than that of the House to bear the stamp of a large number of members representing many different points of view. In weighing the criticisms of the lack of effective organization or leadership in the United States Senate it should be borne in mind that at a typical session of Congress, the Senate will dispose of as much major legislation as the House.

The sharp differences between the two houses in respect to the matters *The differ-* under discussion may be explained by (1) the smaller size of the Senate; *ence ex-* (2) the longer terms of the senators; and, (3) the fact that the senators are *plained* likely to be important party leaders in their home states.

REFERENCES

P. Allyn and J. Greene, *See How They Run: The Making of a Congressman* (Philadelphia, 1964).

Congressional Quarterly, Special Reports, "Congressional Redistricting," Sept. 16, 1966; "Congressional Reform," June 7, 1963 (Washington, D. C.).

Congressional Quarterly Weekly Report (Washington, D. C.).

G. B. Galloway, *Congress at the Crossroads* (New York, 1946).

———, *The Legislative Process in Congress* (New York, 1953).

G. Goodwin, Jr., "The Seniority System in Congress," *Amer. Pol. Sci. Rev.,* Vol. LIII, No. 2 (June, 1959).

B. D. Gross, *The Legislative Struggle* (New York, 1953).

G. H. Haynes, *The Senate of the United States; Its History and Practice* (Boston, 1938).

R. K. Huitt, "Democratic Party Leadership in the Senate," *Amer. Pol. Sci. Rev.,* Vol. LV, No. 2 (June, 1961).

C. O. Jones, *Every Second Year: Congressional Behavior and the Two-Year Term* (Washington, D. C., 1967).

N. MacNeil, *Forge of Democracy—The House of Representatives* (New York, 1963).

D. R. Mayhew, *Party Loyalty Among Congressmen: The Differences Between Democrats and Republicans 1947–1962* (Cambridge, Mass., 1966).

Official Congressional Directory (Washington, D. C.).

F. M. Riddick, *The United States Congress; Organization and Procedure* (Washington, D. C., 1949).

R. B. Ripley, *Party Leaders in the House of Representatives* (Washington, D. C., 1967).

J. A. Robinson, *The House Rules Committee* (New York, 1963).

D. B. Truman, *The Congressional Party* (New York, 1959).

W. S. White, *Citadel: The Story of the U.S. Senate* (New York, 1957).

W. Wilson, *Constitutional Government in the United States* (New York, 1908), Chaps. IV–V.

R. Young, *The American Congress* (New York, 1958).

10

THE LEGISLATIVE PROCESS

Congress at work is engaged in making law and thus legislation is its typical product.

The grist of the legislative process may take at least five different forms: (1) *bills,* which are instruments of general legislation effective when properly passed (passed in the same form by both houses and signed by the President) upon all those individuals to whom applicable and of which there are two major kinds: (*a*) *private* bills for the benefit of a particular person, place, or institution; (*b*) *public* bills dealing with individuals or situations by classes or groups; (2) *joint resolutions,* which resemble bills in almost every respect except that they are commonly used only for the guidance of those charged with administering the laws and contain unusual or subordinate legislation; (3) *concurrent resolutions,* which are not submitted to the President and are not laws, therefore, in the sense that they have no application outside of Congress and which are used to express attitudes, opinions, or intentions that the two houses share; (4) *simple resolutions,* which deal with the affairs of one house only and have no effect beyond the halls of that chamber and which typically express some purpose, policy, or attitude of that house; and, (5) *orders,* which embody the commands or requests of one house typically on procedural matters and which, like simple and concurrent resolutions, are not submitted to the President.

A *bill* is introduced into either house for consideration and when passed by either house becomes an *act.* If both houses enact it and the President signs it, it then becomes a *law* or a *statute.* Some of the bills which the Congress considers are designed to make or declare new law; others, to amend, supplement, clarify, revise, codify, consolidate, or repeal existing provisions of law; and still others not at all to make or modify the law which governs us but to appropriate money, assign duties, or give directions to executive, judicial, or legislative agencies.

Except that there are important differences in the way private bills are handled, essentially the same procedures are used to deal with all of the different forms and types of legislative action. Therefore, an adequate grasp of the legislative activity of a Congress may be obtained by tracing the main steps which a bill takes on its path to the law books.

Constitutional limits to legislative authority

Before we begin the discussion of legislative procedure, we need to remind ourselves that the power of Congress to make laws is not unlimited. Unlike the legislatures of most other democratic states, our national assembly is restricted in its lawmaking function to the subjects especially entrusted to it by the Constitution. Every measure which it can validly enact must be based upon some authorization, express or implied, in the Constitution. Furthermore, the fact that Congress has been invested with authority to legislate on a given subject does not of itself exclude the states from acting on the same subject. Some powers are expressly denied to the states and others by their natures tend to preclude state action, but between these two extremes is a vast field of legislative authority which is or may be occupied both by the nation and the states. While most of the authority conferred upon the Congress by the Constitution may be exercised or not at the discretion of that body, some of the constitutional grants are mandatory. For example, it is the duty of Congress to call a convention to amend the Constitution whenever the legislatures of two-thirds of the states petition it to do so. However, there is probably no legal way that Congress can be compelled to perform an obligatory task if it is unwilling or unable to do so. The courts have repeatedly refused to intervene in such cases on the grounds that they have no means of executing a decision in favor of congressional action.

"Emergency powers"

Many programs in the past three decades aimed at combating the depression or the external enemies of the nation, have been popularly described as stemming from the "emergency powers" of Congress. Legally there are no such powers. The Constitution makes no distinction between "normal" and "emergency" situations in its grant of power to Congress. The Supreme Court has said that "emergency does not create power." Nevertheless, the periods of profound national crisis of our history have repeatedly called forth the exercise of powers not normally exercised, or the exercise of long-used powers in novel ways. Emergencies thus stimulate new congressional activities and conceptions, but legally these, to be valid, must all be traced to the constitutional powers of the Congress.

Importance of the rules of procedure

We need also to note that the entire lawmaking process is controlled by an elaborate and technical system of rules which have been developed over many decades and which are of great importance in determining both the character and the product of legislative activity. It would not be easy to overstate the importance of proper procedure in our national legislature. In the first place, procedural questions can easily and do frequently consume a heavy share of legislative time which is already inadequate to the great responsibilities which rest upon the Congress. Secondly, much of the debate and discussion over matters of considerable import turns on proper procedure. Thirdly, the rights of minorities to speak, to criticize, to propose alternative courses of action, rights which are essential to representative

Union Calendar No. 16

84TH CONGRESS
1ST SESSION

H. R. 1

[Report No. 50]

IN THE HOUSE OF REPRESENTATIVES

JANUARY 5, 1955

Mr. COOPER introduced the following bill; which was referred to the Committee on Ways and Means

FEBRUARY 14, 1955

Reported with amendments, committed to the Committee of the Whole House on the State of the Union, and ordered to be printed

[Omit the part struck through and insert the part printed in italic]

A BILL

To extend the authority of the President to enter into trade agreements under section 350 of the Tariff Act of 1930, as amended, and for other purposes.

84TH CONGRESS
1ST SESSION

H. RES. 170

IN THE HOUSE OF REPRESENTATIVES

MARCH 10, 1955

Mr. PATMAN submitted the following resolution; which was referred to the Committee on Armed Services

RESOLUTION

1   *Resolved,* That the House of Representatives does not
2 favor sale of the facilities as recommended in the report of
3 the Rubber Producing Facilities Disposal Commission.

84TH CONGRESS
1ST SESSION

H. CON. RES. 72

IN THE HOUSE OF REPRESENTATIVES

FEBRUARY 8, 1955

Mr. HOLIFIELD submitted the following concurrent resolution; which was referred to the Committee on Foreign Affairs

CONCURRENT RESOLUTION

Whereas the preservation of democratic institutions everywhere demands united action by the world's leading democracies; and

Whereas the North Atlantic Treaty has already committed its members to "contribute toward the further development of peaceful and friendly international relations by strengthening their free institutions", and to "encourage economic collaboration between any or all of them"; and

---

Calendar No. 8

84TH CONGRESS
1ST SESSION

H. J. RES. 159

IN THE SENATE OF THE UNITED STATES

JANUARY 26, 1955

Ordered to be placed on the calendar

JOINT RESOLUTION

Authorizing the President to employ the Armed Forces of the United States for protecting the security of Formosa, the Pescadores and related positions and territories of that area.

FORMS OF LEGISLATIVE ACTION

219

democracy, find their chief protection in the rules of procedure. Finally, the power of the majority to act, to deal decisively with the problems of the day, is supported and protected by the rules. A perfect balance between the power of the majority to act and the right of the minority to speak is rarely achieved at any time by any set of rules. In the Congress, the rules of the House lean a little heavily to the support of the power of the majority and those of the Senate to the support of the rights of the minority.

INTRODUCTION OF BILLS

How bills are introduced

It is amazingly simple to introduce a bill into Congress. In the House of Representatives, a member inscribes his name on a copy of it and deposits it in a box ("the hopper") on the clerk's desk. In the Senate, a member must first be recognized by the presiding officer, typically during the period when routine business is transacted (the "morning hour"), then announce the introduction of the bill, sometimes with a statement of explanation, and finally send it to the desk of the secretary. Any bill may begin its legislative career in either house except that bills raising revenue are required by the Constitution to begin in the lower house. Once introduced, a bill continues "alive" during the life of the existing Congress or until sooner disposed of. In a subsequent Congress the bill, to be considered, must be reintroduced.

Authorship of bills:

Because bills are introduced by members of the Congress and bear their names, it should not be supposed that these members conceived the ideas set forth in the bills or drafted them in the proper legal terminology.

1. The executive branch

Congress is not to any appreciable extent an originating body. In the first place, a very large and increasing proportion of the major public bills introduced originate in the executive branch. Frequently these "administration" bills are in fully drafted form. The fact that no member of the administration can, as in parliamentary democracies, directly introduce measures has proved no serious obstacle to executive initiative in the American system, since a representative or senator can always be found to sponsor the introduction. Typically, the bill is given for introduction to the appropriate standing committee and introduced through it.

2. Private interests

In the second place, bills originate with persons or organizations entirely outside governmental circles. There are literally thousands of groups and individuals who aspire to change the laws of the land benevolently to their interests or to the objectives of their group. Many of these persons and groups are served by legal counsel or legislative representatives (lobbyists) who cast their desires in the form of a bill or bills and offer them to friendly legislators for introduction. Since introduction is so easy and the legislative sponsor assumes no particular responsibility for the contents of the measure, every year thousands upon thousands of such bills are introduced into Congress. In a large number of cases, one must hasten to add, the congressman and his colleagues have no intention of passing or even of seriously considering measures of this type. Of course, the more powerful interest groups are able, in many cases, to procure consideration of their bills and sometimes even passage. The largest share of these bills of private origin are private bills for the benefit of particular persons, places, or organizations, although the volume of this type has been reduced as a result of the changes in handling certain matters enacted in the Legislative Reorganization Act of 1946. The large numbers of measures introduced, however, clutter up the committee dockets and the calendars of the two houses and contribute mightily to the time and expense of the legislative process.

At the present time about 20,000–25,000 bills and resolutions are introduced into a session of Congress of which perhaps 1000–1500 are enacted in some form.

Drafting bills

Casting legislative ideas into statutory language is a difficult and highly technical undertaking. Few members of Congress or private individuals are able to perform this task without competent advice. Each house provides bill-drafting service for its members through an Office of the Legislative Counsel.

COMMITTEE CONSIDERATION

Referral to a standing committee

Upon introduction, all bills are given a number (for example, H.R. 144 or S. 177), printed, distributed to the members, made available to the interested public, and referred to one of the standing committees. In the case of private bills, the sponsoring senator or representative indicates on the bill the committee to which it should be referred and these instructions are frequently observed in both houses. Public bills are assigned under the direction of the presiding officer in each house, typically by the parliamentarian. In view of the fact that the subject-matter jurisdictions of the several committees still overlap somewhat and the fact that long and complex bills may involve subjects pertinent to several committees, the discretion of the presiding officer is occasionally exercised personally. Rarely is a bill sent to more than one committee or divided among two or more. The membership of either house possesses ultimate authority by majority vote to change the assignment made by the presiding officer and occasionally will direct the withdrawal of a bill from one committee and send it to a different committee. The committee to which a bill is assigned may be sympathetic or it may be hostile, and thus the discretion of the presiding officer and the occasional directions from the chamber sometimes determine the fate of the measure.

Importance of the committees

Both houses have come to expect that the committees will give thorough study to every "deserving" proposal and will then recommend to the parent chamber what should be done. Although there has been a great increase in this century in executive influence in legislative matters, the standing committees are the most important devices by which the legislators stamp their own imprint on legislation. The committees actually go much farther than just to stamp it with their approval or disapproval. They mold or cast the bill into a form which they believe will be acceptable. Certainly, most of the thoughtful and detailed analysis which is given to legislative proposals is given to them by the standing committees. And if the spectator in the gallery, especially of the House of Representatives, is disillusioned by the poorly attended, superficial and perfunctory debate in the chamber, he needs to remind himself that the Congress performs its central legislative duties in the committee rooms. In the Senate, the committee work does not so completely overshadow the general consideration of measures by the entire membership, but even in the upper house it is a rare thing for a committee recommendation to be rejected. The character of the legislative product is determined as much, perhaps more, by what the committees reject as by what they accept or modify. Of the thousands of bills introduced and of the scores, even hundreds, referred to any major committee, only a few are given any serious study. Most bills end their legislative careers in the "inactive" files of a standing committee; the committees are under no obligation to report on every matter referred to them and they never do.

Sources of information:
Upon receiving a measure which is deemed worthy of consideration by the chairman or, in some cases, by a majority of the committee, the committee has then to decide what to do with it. Commonly, at present, such a measure is referred to a subcommittee for study and recommendation, and the whole committee does not hear of it again or participate in the deliberations upon it until the subcommittee reports and recommends a course of action to the whole committee. Whether in fact considered by a subcommittee or by the whole committee, the first requisite for thoughtful analysis is information on the subject covered by the measure. Under the influence of the legal profession, from which a majority of congressmen are drawn, the committees have tended in the past to rely heavily on one or more public hearings to elicit the necessary data. Lawyers are habituated to the idea that justice is best served by public trial in which each of the contestants seeks by every ethical means to present his side in the best light. Out of this combat a skillful judge or attentive jury are supposed to sift the essential facts. Of late, however, the defects in the hearing system for eliciting information have become more and more apparent, and the committees are not using the hearing for this purpose but rather to influence public opinion or executive action or to discover the nature of public attitudes on the measure, especially of those most directly affected. The weaknesses of the hearing system are that all of the needed data is not necessarily made available and that frequently only the proponents of the measure ever appear. The opponents expect the congressmen to protect their interests. Public hearings are still used extensively by the committees and are valuable legislative aids but not solely, or even mainly, to supply necessary information.

1. Public hearing

2. Lobbyists
Much valuable data and opinion are supplied to the committee members by lobbyists, or legislative representatives as they prefer to be called,

representing those who are in favor of or opposed to the particular measure. Some of this is done through carefully prepared statements and exhibits offered during the public hearing on the measure. Much of it, however, is done in private conversations with committee members. It is hard to imagine how committees and congressmen would carry on without the lobbyist. There are many kinds of information about the conduct of particular types of business enterprises or labor unions or professions for which no data comparable to that which they can supply is readily available. A great deal of the data they give Congress is accurate, reliable, and useful. It is also, of course, one-sided. This is not necessarily harmful if the other sides are also supplying data.

A very great part of the information upon which congressional committees base their decisions has always been supplied to them by the executive branch of the government. From the first reports of Alexander Hamilton, as secretary of the treasury, on public credit and on manufacturing to the most recent report of the Defense Department to the Armed Services Committees, the executive branch has made its great store of information and experience available to congressional agencies, usually but not necessarily at the request of a committee. In these days, in which complete legislative programs may be drafted by the executive and sent to Congress, the executive departments are at great pains to see that the committees considering these programs are amply supplied with the data necessary to reach the "proper" conclusion. The interest of the executive in the result of legislative activity has, however, repeatedly aroused the suspicion of many congressmen that they can not rely entirely on the executive departments as their major or especially as their single source of information. Where else, however, might they turn for data on such subjects as national defense? *3. Executive agencies*

Many pieces of legislation reach the Congress as a product of a more or less thorough investigation conducted by the Congress itself through a special or a standing committee, by the Congress and the executive jointly, or by the executive branch alone. Ordinarily these investigations are reported fully and the legislative measures arrive in the committee accompanied by elaborate charts, exhibits, tables, and explanatory material. In these situations, little more data is really required. *4. Investigations*

Through the years many congressmen have felt the need for sources of information of their own, independent of the executive branch, independent of the lobbyists, and not limited by the hearing procedure. It was for this reason that the Legislative Reference Service was established in the Library of Congress in 1914. Its program has slowly developed and in 1946 it achieved statutory recognition and substantial expansion. This Service consists of a professional staff of recognized experts in a large number of fields of legislative interest whose knowledge and research skill and experience are available to supply congressmen and committees with data in which they have expressed an interest. In excess of 51,000 inquiries are now received from Congress and handled annually by the Service. Legislators and com- *5. "Expert" assistants* mittees ask it for everything from a detailed memorandum on the contents of a bill to a chart showing the trend in the production of cotton.

The Legislative Reorganization Act of 1946, which provided the expansion in the Legislative Reference Service, did not stop with that in its effort to supply the need for disinterested data. As we have noted in an earlier chapter, it provided for "expert" assistants for each of the standing committees to aid them in reviewing the proposals submitted for their consideration. This particular action virtually ended a previous committee practice of borrowing "experts" for this purpose from executive agencies. It did not, however, completely solve the problem, since about half of the "experts" seem to be partisans of one degree or another.

Alternative forms of committee action

In private sessions, the committee considers alternative courses of action it may elect to follow. It may approve the bill as it stands and recommend its adoption by the chamber. This is very unusual. It may propose a number of amendments which change portions of the measure before it and then recommend the measure for passage with the amendments added. It may rewrite the bill completely, preserving only the number and title, and present the rewritten measure as a substitute. Finally it may reject the bill. In the latter case, ordinarily the committee takes no further action. But if it approves the bill with or without amendments or in substitution form, it then prepares a report to this effect and seeks an opportunity to acquaint the whole membership with its recommendations. The chairmen of the committees, since 1946, are under obligation to report any approved bills "promptly."

Forcing a bill out of committee

The ease with which a committee can kill a bill simply by not reporting it has been a subject of considerable controversy in the Congress. It is easy to see how, given the method of selecting committee members, a committee decision on some measure might not reflect the desires of a large portion of the membership in either house. One of the changes made in the House in 1910 coincident with the attack on the speaker was the establishment of a procedure by which the House itself might pry a bill out of a hostile committee. This "discharge rule" has gone through various changes since its

---

Motion to Discharge a Committee

August 24, 1965

TO THE CLERK OF THE HOUSE OF REPRESENTATIVES:
    Pursuant to clause 4 of rule XXVII, I, Abraham J. Multer move to discharge the Committee on Rules from the consideration of the resolution (H. Res. 515) entitled "A resolution providing for the consideration of the bill H. R. 4644 to provide an elected Mayor, City Council and nonvoting delegates to the House of Representatives for the District of Columbia..." which was referred to said committee August 11, 1965, in support of which motion the undersigned Members of the House of Representatives affix their signature, to wit....

SOURCE: *Congressional Record, House*, September 3, 1965, p. 22,900.

enactment, but as it now stands a committee may be discharged from further consideration after it has had the bill at least 30 days and by a discharge motion signed by 218 members. This motion for discharge must be on the calendar at least seven days and is in order only on certain days of each month but it is privileged business and must be disposed of. The "seven-day" period is to allow the committee an opportunity to report the bill out on the floor if it cares to do so. The discharge procedure, although it depends primarily on the wishes of a majority of the members, is difficult to operate and is rarely used. Most members of Congress are apparently reluctant to upset the prerogatives of the standing committees and the desires of the leaders.

CONSIDERATION OF BILLS BY THE HOUSE OF REPRESENTATIVES

A House standing committee reports a bill which it has considered favorably by returning it with its report to the clerk of the House. The clerk lists it on one of three "calendars" depending on its nature. Revenue and appropriation bills are placed on the Union Calendar; public bills not involving taxation or expenditure are placed on the House Calendar; private bills are placed on the Private Calendar. Bills are placed on these lists in the order in which they are reported and once on the list remain there throughout the two years of a Congress unless they are taken up and acted upon. The original purpose of these calendars was to regulate the order in which the House would consider the measures which its committees recommended to it. And on certain days as well as at certain times during the daily session the business on one of the calendars is appropriately considered. However, the volume of legislative business has become so great and the calendars consequently so congested that the order is never rigidly adhered to and the House usually adjourns with a lot of unconsidered measures still on the calendars. Revenue and appropriation bills can be taken up at almost any time if the member wishing to get them before the House can gain recognition, but the bills on the House Calendar ordinarily can get before the House only with the aid of a special order from the rules committee. The chairmen of committees wishing to report bills, try to get the rules committee to accept them and intercede on their behalf by special order. It is from this situation that the rules committee derives its important influence on legislation. Conferences and negotiations among the leaders really determine which bills will be taken up and when.

The calendars

An important share of the legislative business of the House of Representatives is conducted by means of the device of committee of the whole. The Union Calendar is made up of bills which are considered by this committee (revenue and appropriation measures) before they are considered, technically speaking, by the House of Representatives. The *committee of the whole* is simply the entire membership of the House sitting as a committee; but as a committee it operates under simpler, less rigid, and less demanding

Committee of the whole

rules than does the House itself. Only 100 members constitute a quorum (the minimum number necessarily present to transact business) in place of the 218 in the House. Debate is governed by a rule which allows only five minutes to each speaker. There can be no time-consuming roll calls, since voting is always oral or by rising or by tellers, and there are no records kept of how any member voted. Certain types of dilatory motions, such as one to refer the matter back to the committee or to postpone consideration of it, are not allowed. At the conclusion of the debate the committee "rises," reports through its chairman back to the House, and then the House acts on the committee's actions. This device is ordinarily in order and enables all fiscal measures to be considered line-by-line for amendment by the entire membership under circumstances which allow maximum participation and critical debate. The House in committee of the whole reveals itself in its best light with many members participating, short and pointed speeches, and quick decisions.

The three readings

It is customary to describe Anglo-American legislative procedure as involving three formal readings for each legislative proposition. This is an accurate description only in a very loose sense. The first reading occurs upon introduction and is not a "reading" at all. The title is simply entered in the records. When the bill emerges from the standing committee it is given its second reading, either in committee of the whole or in the House itself. This may be and occasionally is an actual reading of the bill line-by-line with opportunity for discussion and for amendments to be offered. If, however, the bill is being considered under a "closed" special order of the Committee on Rules, it may not be amended from the floor. Ordinarily these "closed" orders are used for complex tax bills. The conclusion of this stage of legislative consideration is a vote on the question "Shall the bill be engrossed (i.e., reprinted as amended) and read a third time?" If the vote is favorable, the bill is then brought before the House again and is given its third reading. This reading is by title only, no further amendments are in order, and the debate, if any, is only on the whole bill as it stands. The conclusion of this phase is a vote on final passage. If the vote is favorable, the bill is signed by the speaker and sent to the Senate or, if it has already been passed by the Senate, to the President. This formal order of procedure here outlined may, of course, be rudely set aside by unanimous consent, by special order of the rules committee, or by suspension of the rules.

Limits on debate in the House

The chief contrast between the procedure in the House of Representatives and that in the Senate is the limitation upon debate in the House. Normally debate occurs in the House only during the second reading and even this debate is sharply curtailed. Over the years the House has evolved a number of devices which restrict debate, and the most important of these are (a) special orders of the rules committee which fix the total time for consideration of the bill and allot it between the proponents and opponents; and (b) the previous-question rule which since 1811 has authorized a motion for the previous question to be made at any time during debate (except in committee of the whole) and which if adopted requires the House to vote immediately on whatever is pending. The motion itself is not debatable and may not be laid on the table. Debate in committee of the whole is limited by the five-minute rule and in the House it is limited by the rule that no member may speak longer than one hour. Typically, the time of debate is fixed in advance by the leaders and either by special order or by "gentleman's agreement" an equal amount of time is given to each side. The chairman of the standing committee reporting the bill ordinarily controls the time of the majority and designates the members of his committee who will speak for the proponents. The ranking minority member opposing the bill usually controls the time of the opponents. Tables placed about half-way up the aisle on either side of the chamber are used by the two teams to assemble their papers and documents for the debate. If any time remains after the two teams have made their respective contributions, members of the House who are not members of the committee may participate. This is unusual. The effect of all of these rules and customs is to make dilatory and obstructive tactics by the minority very difficult. About the only dilatory devices which are readily available are "quorum calls," roll-call votes, and demands that the clerk (in committee of the whole) actually read every word of a long bill.

CONSIDERATION OF BILLS BY THE SENATE

After a bill is passed by the House, it is certified by the clerk and delivered to the Senate. There it begins a journey which is quite similar to that it has already traversed in the lower house and to that traveled by a bill which originates in the Senate. There are, however, some striking differences in the procedures of the two houses when the bill emerges from the standing committee. The Senate uses only two calendars: the Calendar of Business on which all bills and resolutions are placed in the order in which they are reported; and the Executive Calendar on which nominations and treaties are placed. The Senate no longer uses committee of the whole except for the consideration of treaties. Furthermore, the Senate has few special devices for moving bills off the calendar onto the floor. There is, in the Senate, no powerful rules committee to step in with a special order bringing a bill before the chamber. The calendar listings are followed fairly closely, therefore, except that by unanimous consent measures may be taken out of order. The most notable difference in the two houses, however, is the relative freedom of debate in the Senate. By custom, supported in part by rule, debate in the Senate is virtually unlimited. There is no time limit on speeches; there has been no "previous question" procedure since 1806. There is no requirement that the speaker must talk on the question. As long as any member has anything to say on the matter before the chamber, whether pertinent or not, debate cannot easily be halted.

Differences between House and Senate procedure

The great freedom of the individual senator to participate in the discussion on the floor of the chamber has provided minorities with one of their most potent weapons: the filibuster. When legislative time is precious, for example, when adjournment is near or when appropriation authority is expiring and money bills must be voted, a handful of members can get the floor and by spelling one another (yielding the floor to each other) can halt legislative business until their terms are met. There is no rule like that in the House requiring the senators to speak to the question and these talkathons sometimes range over the whole field of human endeavor. Prior to the adoption of the "Lame Duck" Amendment (20th) in 1933, the Senate was most vulnerable to this tactic in the closing days of the short session. The Senate had to adjourn by March 4, for its life would then expire. The absence of a binding adjournment date since that time has strengthened the procedure against filibustering but has not made it impervious. There have been at least 11 significant filibusters in the Senate since 1933. This surrender of command of the Senate to a few senators at critical times in various sessions has provoked sharp criticism of the Senate rules. This is government by minority, charge the critics, and sometimes a small minority at that. Surely the majority should be allowed to act after a decent amount of debate. The major, although not exclusive, use of the filibuster in the past decade has been by southern senators to defeat various types of proposed legislation aimed at discriminatory practices against Negroes.

The device most widely considered as a remedy for this alleged defect in senatorial procedure is some form of closure rule. In 1917, as a result of a successful filibuster against President Wilson's proposed legislation for arming America's merchant vessels against German submarines, Wilson induced the Senate to adopt the current rule which can be used to limit debate. This rule (XXII) authorizes 16 senators to submit a motion for closing debate on any matter pending before the Senate and, after two calendar days, this motion must be put by the presiding officer and a vote taken on the question: "Is it the sense of the Senate that the debate shall be brought to a close?" If two-thirds of the senators present vote for closing the debate, each senator is thereafter entitled to speak one hour and then the debate ends. This is obviously a very mild form of closure. It had been invoked successfully only four times and had been tried at all only 19 times prior to 1949. Amendments to the rule in 1949, while eliminating many dilatory motions (for example, to approve the Senate journal), nevertheless made the closure motion itself debatable and thus subject to filibuster. From 1949 to 1959 the rules required the approval of two-thirds of the total membership rather than two-thirds of those voting. Closure motions have been offered on 24 occasions from 1950 to 1969; four have been successful. For the first time in history, closure was successfully invoked to force the way for the passage of the Civil Rights Act of 1964 and then twice, thereafter: in 1965 to aid passage of the Voting Rights Act and in 1968 to aid passage of the Civil Rights Act of 1968.

These successes have abated somewhat the mounting criticism of the *Present* Senate rules, especially as they were used to frustrate action in the field of *contro-* racial discrimination. Nevertheless, most sessions of the Senate open with *versy* *over the* some efforts to change the rules. Thus far, the Senate has been unwilling *rules* seriously to modify its rules on the subject of freedom of debate. On the contrary, many of the Senate leaders contend that despite the time consumed by filibuster the Senate does as well as the House in getting through its legislative agenda—in five recent Congresses, for example, it passed more bills and resolutions than the House—and that the frequently used device of "unanimous consent," by which the members agree in advance to limit speeches and vote at a certain time, serves every desirable need of the Senate. Finally, the protagonists argue that opposition to filibustering by some senators is largely insincere, since they do not hesitate to use the device when their own interests are threatened.

CONFERENCE COMMITTEES

A bill which passes both branches of Congress in identical form is sent *Resolving* to the President for signature. The Senate may, however, amend a House *conflicts* *between* bill, the House may amend a Senate bill, and each of these actions occurs *the two* frequently. Unless one house will recede from its position and concur with *houses* the changes made by the other, a deadlock occurs which somehow must be broken. The device by which disagreements between the two houses on specific pieces of legislation are reconciled is the committee of conference, appointed for each legislative measure in dispute. So frequent are these disagreements, especially on major legislative proposals, that the conference committee is a standard fixture of the American legislative process. One-third to one-half of all the public bills, including virtually all of the important ones, have in recent years been referred to conference committees at the appropriate stage of their legislative careers.

The rejection by one house of the views of the other house on certain *The con-* items in a bill or resolution under consideration is almost invariably accom- *ference* *committee* panied by a request for conference. The request having been agreed to—and *at work* it is never refused—the presiding officer of each house names from three to nine members of his house to meet with those named by the other to attempt to reconcile the differences. By custom, the presiding officers name the chairman and ranking minority member of the standing committee which considered the bill, plus others from each side who have figured prominently in the debate and who, typically, are also members of the same standing committee. The views of the majority of the chamber are always represented by a majority of the "managers" named to represent that house in the conference. The minority view, however, is always accorded some representation. The two sets of managers then meet and discuss the points at issue, seeking by compromise to arrive at something acceptable to both houses.

Agreement must be reached under the rules by a majority of each group voting separately, so that the fact that one house occasionally names more managers than the other is of no consequence. Sometimes the task of reconciliation is easy and is performed in a few hours; sometimes it is difficult and requires days, weeks, even months. If no agreement can be reached, the bill fails or a new committee may be named to try again. Generally, agreement is reached and the proposals of the committee are accepted by both houses. It must be added that the rules and the customs of the two houses confer upon these conference committees an unexpected amount of power to determine the final form of legislation. The reports of conference committees are highly privileged in both houses and thus have the right of way over most other forms of legislative traffic. The reports of the committees must be accepted or rejected as a whole. They may not be further amended. Each house has got to take the dose compounded by the conference or go without any medicine. The deliberations of the conference committees are secret and unrecorded. They ordinarily hold no hearings and listen to no outside testimony. Finally, the bill—or those parts of the bill in dispute—which emerges from the deliberations of the committee may not resemble the view of either house and may, in fact, contain matters never before considered exactly in that form by either house. The conference committee is also an arena of continuous struggle between the two houses for legislative supremacy. The customary assumption that the Senate is predominant in conferences is not borne out by studies of these committees.

THE PROBLEM OF LOBBYING

The increase in interest-group activities

Interest groups and their legislative representatives have become an established feature of the American political landscape. Providing a different kind of representation for the citizens, supplying the legislature with much necessary data, initiating countless proposals for public consideration, these groups undoubtedly render a unique service to, and provide a significant voice for, the participants in democratic government. Their activities on the national scene are not, however, an unmixed blessing. Their information tends to be one-sided; their objective is usually economic gain; their methods are occasionally devious; and their influence disproportionate to their numbers. Statesmen and students alike have been troubled by the problems of special-interest representation in the legislative process as the scope and scale of their operations has multiplied. Today more than 400 national organizations maintain more than 1000 paid agents in the national capital and spend uncounted millions of dollars to influence the course of legislation and the public attitudes which lie behind the legislation. In spite of numerous attempts to make the lobbyist a respected and indispensable adjunct to democratic lawmaking, the name is still an epithet and connotes some kind of wrongdoing. About three-fourths of the states have enacted laws designed to curb lobbying activities and to disclose its objectives. None of these efforts has been wholly successful and few of them have achieved anything substantial. In Washington, the matter has received intermittent attention over several decades, but the House of Representatives has typically stifled efforts at regulation initiated by the Senate. The two houses did finally compel utility lobbyists to register in 1925 and agents of foreign interests in 1928, and in 1926 compelled agents of shipping interests to record the objects of their activities. Not until 1946, in connection with the general reorganization of the Congress, were the two houses able to agree on a procedure for dealing with lobbying.

The system finally adopted by the Congress is based very largely on the practice of several of the states. The fundamental premise of the Regulation of Lobbying Act is that undesirable behavior by interest groups and their agents can best be controlled by publicity rather than by prohibition. Lobbyists are required to register with the clerk of the House and the secretary of the Senate and to disclose in their registration the association or individual by whom employed and how much paid. Quarterly thereafter, each registered lobbyist is required to file a statement of receipts and expenditures, including the purposes for which the sums were expended. Tabulations of these reports are published in the *Congressional Record* to apprise all interested persons of the facts. Furthermore, the law requires any organization which solicits or receives contributions to support its legislative activities to give annual public accounting of these contributions and the expenditures made from them. Failure to comply with the law may result in fine, imprisonment, or suspension of the privilege of lobbying. *The Regulation of Lobbying Act of 1946*

In practice, the registering and reporting provisions of this law have supplied the public with more significant information about the extent and scope of lobbying than has ever before been available. The enforcement of the law has, however, been embarrassed from the beginning by the uncertainties and obscurities in the law itself. In an effort to exclude organizations who lobby rarely or only incidentally to the regular and major purposes of the organization, the law covers only those whose "principal purpose" is to influence legislation. Many of the most energetic and extensive national organizations operating in Washington claim that the law does not apply to them because lobbying is not their principal purpose. Further, the Supreme Court has held that the law applies only to direct dealings with members of Congress and does not require reports on funds expended on propaganda directed at the voters. The law, of course, does not in fact regulate lobbying and certainly has not and was not intended to curb it. It merely brings certain types of information about lobbying out into the open where the public can, if it wishes, scrutinize it. *Results*

THE LEGISLATIVE INVESTIGATION

As an important, some would say indispensable, adjunct of its responsibilities for the conduct of the national administration and for the development of legislation the Congress relies extensively on the legislative investigation. The investigative procedure has been widely used for the development of data and the revelation of opinion on national problems for the purpose of propounding a legislative solution. Its major use, in the past decade at least, has been to bring to light the conduct of public employees and administrative agencies. The investigation has become one of the major ways by which the committees of Congress hold the administration accountable to the Congress and to the public for its conduct of affairs. In time, energy, expense, and publicity, the investigating activities of recent Congresses, for example, rivaled their legislative activities. Investigations of administrative behavior have been conducted by both the regular standing committees and by special committees designated for the purpose. The Legislative Reorganization Act of 1946 contemplated the use of regular standing committees, and since its enactment, special committees have been used sparingly. Several notable inquiries have been directed by joint committees of the two houses and, in a few cases, members of the executive branch and representatives of the public have been invited to serve with the legislators.

The use of the investigative procedure

Of the more than 800 investigations conducted in our national history, several have been outstanding in bringing to light and correcting egregious misconduct within the administration. Both the Teapot Dome oil reserve scandal of the Harding era and the income tax administration scandal of the Truman regime, to select two of this century, have been aired by this method. In the broader uses of the investigative power to inform legislative policy, there have also been many of lofty purposes and far-reaching accomplishments: the studies of immigration, lobbying, munitions manufacturing, stock exchange operations, conservation, monopoly in industry, the organization of Congress, and the organization of the executive branch of the government are examples from this century which come readily to mind. The investigative function, however, has not uniformly achieved its maximum potentiality. Although many, perhaps most, have been well intentioned and seriously pursued, some have had only personal or partisan malice as their stimulus and campaign ammunition or personal aggrandizement as their object. As the Congress has relied more heavily upon investigation in an attempt to redress the balance of power lost to the executive branch during this century, the difficulties and criticisms have increased.

Problems arising from use of investigative function:

In the first place, the field of inquiry has extended in recent years to the political sentiments and loyalties of numerous individuals and groups in American society, including teachers, preachers, writers, movie stars, labor union executives, and others. One standing committee of the Congress—the House Un-American Activities Committee—has no other major function. In many cases, these inquiries have borne no apparent relevance to contemplated legislation or to administrative indiscretion. They have had as their apparent major purpose the enlightenment of the public, and as a subsidiary purpose the discrediting of certain opinions and of those who hold them. Many persons have argued that the scope of congressional investigation is, or ought to be, confined to the legislative and administrative responsibilities of that body and that committees have no right to invade personal privacy except under the impetus of grave policy-making enterprises. The courts have increasingly been urged by reluctant witnesses to declare some limits on the scope of these inquiries and on the procedures by which they have been conducted. It is now generally conceded that the powers of investigation are not unlimited. The Supreme Court summarized the matter thus in a recent case:

> The power of the Congress to conduct investigations is inherent in the legislative power. That power is broad. It encompasses inquiries concerning the administration of existing laws as well as proposed or possibly needed statutes. It includes surveys of defects in our social, economic, or political system for the purpose of enabling the Congress to remedy them. . . . But broad as is this power of inquiry, it is not unlimited. There is no general authority to expose the private affairs of individuals without justification in terms of the functions of the Congress.

In the same case the Court condemned the mission assigned by the rules of the House of Representatives to the Committee on Un-American Activities as ambiguous. "No one could reasonably deduce from the charter the kind of investigation the committee was directed to make," said the Court. After a change in personnel, however, the Court in later cases agreed that the investigation of communist activities was a legitimate and authorized purpose of the Committee and that if the questionee is explicitly told the relevance of the questions he is being asked to the communist activity under investigation and the questions are relevant to such an inquest, then the investigation is legitimate and witnesses may not properly refuse to answer. The Court continues, however, to scrutinize the conduct of the Committee with great care. The Court has also suggested that serious questions of free speech might be raised by investigations into propaganda activities under the guise of inquiring into lobbying.

Secondly, the congressional investigating process during the early fifties took place amidst an inordinate amount of publicity. Newsreel and television cameras and radio microphones, not to mention crowded spectator areas, became the standard environment for many of the hearings. The opportunity that this provided for political adventure by those who direct the inquiries stimulated competition among legislators for strategic posts from which to launch personal campaigns and created concern for the abuse of the hearing process to serve these personal ambitions. Criticism of the practice of making spectacles of these inquiries had mounted to the point that Speaker Rayburn early in 1952 and as long as he was speaker, ruled that meetings of the committees of the House of Representatives could not be broadcast, televised, tape-recorded, or photographed by moving picture cameras unless

1. Scope of the inquiries

2. Televising of committee hearings

and until the rules of the House were changed specifically to authorize these practices. In the interim his successor, Speaker Martin, allowed each committee to decide the matter for itself. Speaker McCormack has followed the Rayburn rule.

3. Fair procedures for witnesses

The third problem that has arisen in connection with inquiries and the publicity surrounding them concerns the status and rights of persons who appear before the committees. Traditionally, congressional committees have admitted many kinds of testimony under a variety of conditions. They have not been bound, nor have they wished to be bound, by the rules of the judicial branch in these matters. Many legislators have felt that judicial procedures which include elaborate rules on accreditation of witnesses, admissibility of evidence, and rights of the accused are too restrictive for the type of information which committees hope to elicit. Concern for a "fair" trial and for the position of the "accused" is out of place in legislative halls, they would argue. We are not trying anyone; we can invoke no criminal penalties against anyone, save to compel testimony or to initiate proceedings against perjury. The labeling of individuals as subversive, the identification of them with unpopular and unorthodox opinions, or the recounting of their youthful indiscretions, argue those who are concerned for the witnesses, is or may be more damaging to them individually and socially than conviction of a crime. Their reputations can be placed under a cloud and their employment prospects seriously curtailed. Under these circumstances, say the critics, a more judicial attitude ought to be introduced and rules of procedures adopted which will prevent hearsay evidence, which will allow a person to confront and question those who assail him, and which will provide an opportunity for those who are attacked to appear and answer the attack. Several committees (really subcommittees conducting inquiries) have actually modified their rules to take account of these criticisms. The House of Representatives early in 1955 amended its rules to provide more uniform procedures for its investigating committees, to abolish one-man hearings, and to afford greater protection for individuals called to testify. The Rules Committee of the House since 1955 has also been reviewing projected investigations.

4. Compulsion of testimony from private citizens

The fourth problem relates to the extraction of testimony from unwilling witnesses. Persons from whom information is sought are not always disposed to cooperate. Gradually, however, the Congress, with the support of the judiciary, has gathered authority to employ compulsion. Any duly constituted committee now has power to subpoena witnesses and administer oaths, to require the production of books, papers, correspondence, contracts, or other records deemed relevant, and to invoke judicial aid, if necessary, to obtain them. Persons refusing to answer questions properly put to them or refusing to produce records or papers may be cited by either house for "contempt of Congress." During the period 1947–1952, for example, 155 persons were cited for contempt, 100 of them witnesses before the House Un-American Activities Committee. Testimony before congressional committees may lead to prosecution by the Department of Justice for perjury as well as for contempt. The celebrated case of Alger Hiss, former official of the Department of State, convicted of perjury arising out of testimony before the House Un-American Activities Committee, is an example of this type of action.

With more and more frequency, witnesses before congressional committees have been claiming the protection of the Fifth Amendment and refusing to respond to questions which, if answered, they plead, might tend to incriminate them. So frequently has this plea been raised that Congress in 1954 enacted a law granting to its committees the authority to grant immunity from prosecution to a reluctant witness to compel him to testify. This law requires, however, the notification of the attorney general and the approval of a District Court and also stipulates that such grant must be requested by a two-thirds vote of the full committee membership.

Thus far our discussion has centered about the problem of obtaining information from a balky or uncooperative private individual. A' very different kind of problem arises out of the various attempts by committees of Congress to obtain papers and documents or testimony from the executive agencies or officials of the government. On the one hand, there is no doubt about the constitutional right of Congress to inform itself on the conduct of the executive branch. On the other hand, Presidents, beginning with Washington, have regarded themselves as entitled to refuse to open their personal files for congressional inspection and even to throw the cloak of immunity around any department or agency if they believed that the public interest would be served by so doing. Thus far, at least, the President has successfully asserted the powers claimed. The legal rights of the two branches have never been fully adjudicated. The Congress has in every case stopped short of citing for contempt any official who has refused on executive order to honor a subpoena. The net legislative result of a prolonged inquiry in 1958 into government secrecy by a House Special Subcommittee on Government Information was the amendment of an ancient statute conferring power on department heads to control the custody, use, and preservation of records. The amendment simply declared that the act of 1789 could not be cited as authorization for withholding information.

5. Compulsion of testimony from public officials:

THE NONLEGISLATIVE FUNCTIONS OF CONGRESS

Enacting laws, while perhaps the most important, is not the sole function of the Congress of the United States. The several nonlegislative functions reveal the extent to which the framers of our Constitution departed from any rigid theory of separation of powers but rather linked the various organs of government together in such a way that they cannot easily be fit into the categories of power recognized in theoretical political science.

1. Constituent

We have in earlier chapters referred to the essential role of Congress in amending the Constitution and to the part it plays in electing the President and Vice-President. We shall in a later chapter discuss the executive func-

2. Electoral

3. Execu-tive

tions of treaty-making and appointments which the Senate shares with the President. It is appropriate here, however, to enlarge upon the judicial function of removal of civil officers.

4. Judicial:

In order to furnish the legislative branch with a shield to protect itself and the people against treasonable and criminal officials who might by some mischance make their way into the highest offices of the nation, the framers

a. Im-peachment

endowed the representatives with the historic power of impeachment and the senators with the power to try those thus accused. The House of Commons had for some centuries exercised the power of impeachment and, while it had fallen into disuse during the Tudor period, it had been revived under the Stuarts and was a potent weapon in the Parliament's struggle with the Crown. Under the Constitution, the President, Vice-President, and all civil officers of the United States are made subject to impeachment and removal. The grounds upon which such action may validly be taken are restricted, however, to grave criminal offenses. This is not a procedure to be invoked because of political disagreements, incompetence, or unethical conduct. Any member or group of members of the House of Representatives may prefer charges against an official. These are referred either to the Judiciary Committee or to a special investigating committee. The committee reports its findings to the House; and, if the majority votes to impeach, "articles of impeachment" setting forth the grounds for removal are drafted. Managers are appointed to represent the house in presenting the case against the official in the Senate.

b. Trial

The Senate has no choice, once the procedure has gone this far, but to hear the case. A day is appointed for the hearing, the accused is furnished with the "articles" upon which he is to be tried, and when the appointed time arrives the Senate converts itself into a court to determine the fate of the accused. The chief justice of the United States presides over the trial of a President. For all other officials the regular presiding officer of the Senate directs the proceedings. The accused is allowed counsel, and testimony, his as well as that of witnesses for or against him, may be heard. At the close of the case, the Senate votes secretly on the charges. A two-thirds vote is necessary for conviction. Anything short of this is acquittal. The penalty is removal from office, to which may be added disqualification forever in the future from holding "any office of honor, trust, or profit under the United States." Once removed from office, the individual may be tried and convicted in an ordinary court if he has committed an indictable offense.

Whatever may have been the experience of our English ancestors, the impeachment and removal powers of Congress have not proved very formidable in dealing with the executive branch. Only 12 officers, most of these judges, have been impeached in our national history and only four of these convicted. President Johnson, however, escaped removal by a single vote. The difficulty with the impeachment process is that it is designed only for grave offenses, and few of our national officials, happily, have been flagrant offenders against the laws of the land.

Of all of the nonlegislative functions of the Congress none is more burdensome nor more time-consuming than the function of representing individuals and groups before the government at Washington and informing them about its operations. Every day brings to each congressman scores of letters, dozens of phone calls and telegrams, and several callers from the home district or state. Many, perhaps most, congressmen spend more working time running errands for their constituents, explaining the meaning of governmental requirements or policies to them, and adjusting conflicting interests between constituents and administrative agencies than they do in discharging their legislative responsibilities. As our government has grown larger, more complex, and more pervasive, this part of a congressman's job has become more demanding. Many lawmakers complain bitterly that they are unable to grapple intelligently with the great and forbidding questions of our times because they have to give so much of their energy to this "errand boy" work.

5. Representing constituents before the executive branch

The demands upon a member of Congress for special and benevolent intercession with the executive agencies are numerous indeed. In a small portion of the cases they are highly improper. Although most are routine requests for information or pleas of unnecessary hardship, some are for undeserved privileges or favors. Few congressmen are in a position to weigh fairly the merits of the petitioner's claims and equitable administrative behavior is not well served by the sporadic and irresponsible intervention of legislators. Every administrative agency of any size has to maintain a sizable staff just to process congressional inquiries. Congressmen, furthermore, are in a position to punish by deprivation of funds administrative indifference or resistance to their importunings. On the credit side it may be observed that congressmen act on these matters as humanizers of the vast impersonal machinery of government. If some of them ask for favors that are undeserved, all of them do much to obtain favorable acceptance of administrative activities by explaining to their people the need for the rules or regulations under which they are fretting. The representative duties of congressmen also have a healthy influence on administrative behavior, bringing to the attention of top executives callous, arbitrary, or capricious decisions by their subordinates and revealing the sources and character of popular discontent with their agencies. The legislative activities of the Congress are strengthened by the revelations of defects in existing programs which come in a congressman's mail. The typical congressman feels that he can neglect this function only if he is willing to give up his chances of reelection.

REFERENCES

D. Acheson, *A Citizen Looks at Congress* (New York, 1957).

S. K. Bailey, *Congress Makes a Law; The Story Behind the Employment Act of 1946* (New York, 1949).

———, *The New Congress* (New York, 1966).

A. Barth, *Government by Investigation* (New York, 1955).

D. Berman, *In Congress Assembled: The Legislative Process in the National Government* (New York, 1964).

G. S. Blair, *American Legislatures: Structure and Process* (New York, 1967).

D. C. Blaisdell, *Government Under Pressure,* Pub. Affairs Pamphlets, No. 67 (New York, 1942).

J. M. Burns, *Congress on Trial; The Legislative Process and the Administrative State* (New York, 1949), Chaps. IV–V.

S. Chase, *Democracy Under Pressure; Special Interest vs. the Public Welfare* (New York, 1945).

Committee on Congress, American Political Science Association, *The Reorganization of Congress* (Washington, D. C., 1945).

Congressional Quarterly Weekly Report (Washington, D. C.). Published since 1945 by Congressional Quarterly Inc. presenting very comprehensive and trustworthy information on all aspects of the session.

Congressional Record. Published daily during sessions by the Government Printing Office at Washington, D. C. (obtainable through members of Congress or by subscription through the Superintendent of Documents).

"Economic Power and Political Pressure," Temporary National Economic Committee Monograph No. 26 (Washington, D. C., 1941).

L. A. Froman, Jr., *The Congressional Process: Strategies, Rules and Procedures* (Boston, 1967).

B. D. Gross, *The Legislative Struggle* (New York, 1953).

G. H. Haynes, *The Senate of the United States; Its History and Practice* (2 vols., Boston, 1938).

A. Holtzman, *Interest Groups and Lobbying* (New York, 1966).

E. Kefauver and J. Levin, *A Twentieth-Century Congress* (New York, 1947).

N. MacNeil, *Forge of Democracy—The House of Representatives* (New York, 1963).

F. M. Riddick, *The United States Congress; Organization and Procedure* (Washington, D. C., 1949), Chaps. IX–XI.

A. M. Scott and M. A. Hunt, *Congress and Lobbies: Image and Reality* (Chapel Hill, N. C., 1964).

G. Y. Steiner, *The Congressional Conference Committee* (Urbana, Ill., 1951).

N. C. Thomas and K. A. Lamb, *Congress: Politics and Practice* (New York, 1964).

H. Walker, *The Legislative Process* (New York, 1948), Chaps. X, XII–XVII.

W. Wilson, *Congressional Government* (Boston, 1885), Chaps. II–IV.

R. Young, *The American Congress* (New York, 1958).

B. Zeller, "The Federal Regulation of Lobbying Act," *Amer. Polit. Sci. Rev.,* Vol. XLII, 239–271 (April, 1948).

11

THE PRESIDENT AND CONGRESS

The most striking difference between the government of the United States and those of most other democratic nations in the world today is the relation between the executive and the legislature. In the parliamentary democracies (Britain, France, Canada, Italy, Sweden, etc.) the executive is inseparably yoked to the legislature. Prolonged disagreement or conflict between the two is impossible. The ministry or cabinet is drawn entirely or very largely from the legislature and remains in possession of the effective executive authority only so long as it commands the confidence of that body. Substantial disagreement results either in a new ministry or a new legislature. The parliamentary system is intentionally designed to guarantee harmony of the two central agencies of democratic government and to fix responsibility for the conduct of the government clearly and firmly upon the majority party or coalition of parties. The American presidential system, on the other hand, with its independently elected executive serving a fixed term and without power to dissolve the legislature, deliberately creates a gulf between the two branches, disperses responsibility for the conduct of national affairs and invites, if it does not encourage, mutual antagonism and the need for accommodation. The American system suffers under these disadvantages in their most acute form when, as on numerous occasions in our history, the Congress has come under the domination of a party or a faction espousing a program quite at variance with that of the President or his party. The parliamentary system, on the other hand, leads to the decline of importance of the parliament as it tends to become a creature of the ministry or to the frequent change of ministers wherever party coalition is required to form a majority. It also suffers from a weak and unstable executive if no party is able to capture a clear majority. France and Germany have both felt it desirable to strengthen their elected presidents and make them independent of transient parliamentary majorities.

    The framers of the American Constitution would have made little sense out of the arguments of the twentieth century on the proper legislative role of the President. Familiar with the colonial and state experience of guberna-

Presidential and parliamentary democracies compared

Development of American Presidency:

torial–legislative dealings, frightened by the excesses of the legislatures, and versed in the theories of Locke and Montesquieu, these statesmen contrived a chief magistracy which they hoped would be above the factionalism of

1. The view of the framers

representatives and equipped to deal firmly with their ambitions. The modern form of cabinet responsibility to the parliament had not yet clearly emerged even in the British constitution. Parties in their modern form were unknown, and factional politics, the eighteenth-century equivalent of modern party politics, was reprehended. It was not executive domination or direction of the legislature that the framers anticipated, but legislative domination of the executive.

2. Washington to Jackson

For a few years after the establishment of the national government it seemed as if the relations between executive and Congress would evolve in about the same way as in England, where the modern cabinet system was taking shape. Alexander Hamilton, from his post as secretary of the treasury, strove skillfully to make himself first minister, Washington a sort of constitutional monarch, and the Congress a reviewing body for policies and measures formulated by the cabinet. This development was halted by the emergence of organized political parties. Hamilton's opponents rallied around Jefferson and Madison and, operating from the Congress, asserted the independence of the legislative branch and eventually wrested control even of the executive away from the Hamilton group. Jefferson as President maintained the appearance of legislative autonomy, although achieving executive direction in fact by intrigue and manipulation of his partisans in the Congress. When the Presidency came into less skillful hands, presidential initiative in legislation subsided. Congressional dominance of policy formulation was strengthened also by the assumption by the legislature of practical control over the selection of the chief executive.

3. Jackson to Kennedy

The development of the modern Presidency begins with the Jacksonian era in which legislative control of presidential nominations was swept away and out of which emerged the modern nominating convention. This action removed the last obstacle to genuinely popular selection of our chief magistrate. The Jeffersonians and Federalists had already stultified the electoral college system by their organization of broadly national political parties. The election of the President by popular and partisan processes paved the way for his emergence as a "tribune of the people" and encouraged him to assert his position as representative of the whole people against the sectional and local representatives of the Congress. Almost a century, however, was required to realize the contemporary presidential position. The pull toward presidential leadership in the field of legislation, although erratic in force, has been persistent in direction. Chief executives learned that they and they alone were held accountable for the redemption of campaign pledges and for the realization in public policy of the programs to which they and their party had committed themselves. The fulfillment of these responsibilities demanded that the chief executive attempt to influence the Congress. Although Congress had meanwhile developed its own institutions of leadership, none of these sufficed to overcome its sectional and centrifugal tendencies. None of its institutional arrangements, further, achieved real coordination of the two houses. Furthermore, its preference for seniority as the major determinant of leadership tended to increase the likelihood that its leaders could not rightly interpret the will of the nation. As Woodrow Wilson wrote in 1908:

> The nation as a whole has chosen him [the president], and is conscious that it has no other political spokesman. His is the only national voice in affairs. Let him once win the admiration and confidence of the country, and no other single force can withstand him, no combination of forces will easily overpower him. His position takes the imagination of the country. He is the representative of no constituency, but of the whole people. When he speaks in his true character, he speaks for no special interest. If he rightly interprets the national thought and boldly insists upon it, he is irresistible, and the country never feels the zest of action so much as when its president is of such insight and caliber. Its instinct is for unified action, and it craves a single leader.

Wilson's views remind us that the White House has also been occupied in this century by Theodore and Franklin Roosevelt, both of whom interpreted their responsibilities as did Wilson. All three of these men left an indelible impression on the office of President of the United States. To theirs must be joined the names of Abraham Lincoln and Grover Cleveland who, in their own ways and in an earlier age, added to the groundwork laid down by Andrew Jackson. Today, national policy as expressed in legislation is a joint product of President and Congress. The chief executive has become also chief legislator. His is now the principal initiative for all major legislation.

The historical tendencies which produced the legislative position of the modern President have not been universally admired. Plenty of people now and in the past have not liked what was happening. The charge of dictator has been hurled at every one of the Presidents who sought to direct the legislative process. And it certainly must be admitted that, whatever view the framers may have taken of the ultimate position of the President, there is little in the Constitution that foreshadows his contemporary role. Experience confirms also the view that much of what has been said about the President's legislative position depends, in fact, on the personality and ability of the individual who occupies the office. Presidents have achieved influence over the legislative process when they were able as well as willing to do so. Presidents have varied also in the vigor with which they have sought congressional support. Several Presidents since Jackson have been content to defer to the Congress. There is a partisan complexion to this debate. Since the Civil War, the Republican party seems to have preferred for the highest office men who were likely to respect the prerogatives and autonomy of the Congress. The Democrats have tended to support avowed protagonists of the view that it is the duty of the President by every fair means to influence, if not to direct, the legislative process.

Criticism of the modern Presidency

Executive–
legislative
relations
not finally
fixed:
It seems clear that the relations between the President and Congress have not achieved their final form. The balance between the two is shifting and unstable and subject to the accidents of personality. The trend toward executive leadership in legislation has been persistent and unmistakable, but it has been achieved largely outside the formal constitutional arrangements and at the expense of traditional conceptions of separation of powers and checks and balances. American constitutional democracy has yet to work out an agreeable method for achieving proper coordination between these two great branches of our government.

CONSTITUTIONAL BASIS OF THE PRESIDENT'S LEGISLATIVE ROLE

He shall from time to time give to the Congress information of the state of the Union, and recommend to their consideration such measures as he shall judge necessary and expedient; he may on extraordinary occasions, convene both houses, or either of them, and in case of disagreement between them, with respect to the time of adjournment, he may adjourn them to such time as he shall think proper. . . .
—Art. II, Sec. 3

The Congress and the President, although constitutionally separated, are not completely isolated one from the other. Despite the general injunction that "all legislative powers" are vested in the Congress, the President is expressly assigned several important powers and responsibilities in connection with the formulation and enactment of legislation.

1. Control
over
sessions of
Congress
The Constitution confers a modest and relatively inconsequential power on the President to control the sessions of the national legislature. The power to adjourn sessions in case of disagreement has never been exercised and the power to call either or both houses into "extraordinary" or "special" session is rapidly falling into disuse. The Twentieth Amendment obviated the need for such sessions by changing the congressional calendar so that the Congress would be in session ready to receive the program and to act upon the appointments of a newly elected chief executive. Almost the only present need for a special session would be a serious domestic or international crisis requiring immediate legislative action and arising in the fall or early winter after mid-summer adjournment of a regular session.

2. Mes-
sages
to the
Congress:
The constitutional directive to the President to inform the Congress on the state of the nation and to recommend measures for its consideration is a duty rather than a power, but it has proved over the years to be of some consequence in influencing legislative behavior. The time, place, and manner of fulfilling this responsibility is, of course, discretionary with each President.

It long ago became customary, however, for the President to transmit at the   *a. "State*
opening of each session of Congress a comprehensive statement of his views   *of the*
on all matters requiring legislative attention and on the kind of legislation   *Union"*
which it ought to enact to meet each situation. Washington and John Adams   *message*
appeared personally before joint sessions of the two houses to deliver their
important messages. This practice, abandoned by Jefferson and his successors, was revived by Woodrow Wilson, and since Franklin Roosevelt has
become standard procedure. The increasing utilization of radio and television broadcasting in our political life has enhanced the importance of
these annual addresses. Today the State of the Union message of the President is an address to the people of America and of the world as well as to
the Congress of the United States. It is a solemn occasion of state, and
modern Presidents have grasped the advantages that the spectacle offers for
dramatizing their aims and policies. This appeal to the people is, in fact, a
procedure of increasing usefulness and importance in gaining congressional
sympathy and support for the President's recommendations. The changing
tone of the messages reflects these developments: As presented about 1900,
the messages were collections of proposals from the various departments
strung together with conjunctions; today they are carefully written to emphasize one or more themes and are likely to contain fewer but more significant suggestions.

In recent times the State of the Union message is followed in quick   *b. Other*
succession by the President's annual budget message—required by the   *messages*
Budget and Accounting Act of 1921—and by the economic report of the
President—required by the Full Employment Act of 1946. Both of these
messages, probably because of the statistical character of their contents, are
invariably delivered in writing rather than in person. In such cases, the
messages are actually read (usually in a monotone) to the houses by their
clerks and consequently do not capture national attention in anything like
the degree that those delivered in person do. In addition to these, every
modern President has sent numerous special messages to Congress at various
times in any session. Ordinarily, these deal each with some special subject
and are designed and timed to push some item on the President's legislative
agenda a little nearer final passage. Sometimes these messages accompany
reports embodying extensive investigations or studies by or on behalf of
the executive branch. On unusual occasions the President will deliver a
special message in person. This is especially true if the subject is of overwhelming importance or if the need for immediate congressional action is
imperative. President Eisenhower, for example, delivered in person in 1957
his message on the troubled situation in the Near East even before his annual
message.

The effect of the messages of the President upon national legislation is
hard to measure. Congress is under no legal obligation to follow the President's lead. It is free to act or not to act and, if it acts, to act in accord with

or directly opposite to the President's stated wishes. The objective of the President himself is not always immediate legislative action in the form suggested. He may be using the message to stimulate public interest without desiring immediate action. He may, in fact, be willing to accept a more moderate form of action than he has outlined. He may be warning a foreign nation of possible American reaction to its prospective behavior. He may be interpreting or summarizing American views for the benefit of the rest of the world or of some important part of it. Whether the President succeeds in any or all of his stated or intended purposes depends on a number of factors unrelated to the messages. The constitutional duty to inform the Congress of his views has become an opportunity to convince both Congress and the people of his wise leadership, but we must continue our analysis of the relations between President and Congress if we are to discover how or why he succeeds or fails in getting the Congress to adopt his suggestions.

a. Proposal of legislative measures
The Constitution directs the President to recommend specific measures for the consideration of the Congress. This might be construed as an invitation to the President to assume leadership of the legislative process. Not all of our chief magistrates have so regarded it, however, and the pattern of executive leadership established by Washington through Hamilton and by Jefferson was followed only by Jackson, Polk, Lincoln, and Cleveland in the last century and not completely even by them. In this century, however, Theodore Roosevelt, Woodrow Wilson, Franklin Roosevelt, Harry Truman, John Kennedy, and Lyndon Johnson have all aspired energetically to enhance the influence of the Presidency. A large proportion of the major bills which crowd the calendars of a modern Congress originate in the executive branch. More and more commonly, messages are accompanied by or are shortly followed by bills designed exactly to achieve the President's desires. Although the Congress freely edits, amends, and modifies these measures, nevertheless at final passage many of them still carry numerous marks of their origin. It may be pleaded that this has been, thus far, a century of crises calling forth unusual presidential energies and that when more "normal" times return presidential initiative will subside. However this may be, our chief executives now believe that they are expected to devote their major energies to devising the laws which Congress ought to pass and then trying to get Congress to pass them. When the time for a public reckoning occurs, every modern President has been anxious to exhibit an impressive record of legislative achievement.

b. Direction in the field of finance
Among the many areas of congressional concern, the national finances bring the President and Congress into the most intimate and mutually dependent relations. The Congress has never developed an effective agency of its own for attaining cooperation between the two houses or for formulating fiscal policy for the government as a whole. It has come, therefore, to depend almost entirely upon the initiative of the President in this field, typified by the annual budget message.

THE VETO POWER

Largely as a reaction against the unrestrained concentration of power in the legislatures of the revolutionary state governments, the authors of our Constitution endowed the President with one of his most impressive legislative powers: the power to veto bills and resolutions of the Congress. Although the President must proceed indirectly by suggestion and innuendo to obtain the approval of the Congress for what he wants, he is equipped to

Presidential Veto

TO THE SENATE OF THE UNITED STATES:

I return herewith, without my approval, S 327, to provide assistance to the states of California, Oregon, Washington, Nevada and Idaho for the reconstruction of areas damaged by recent floods and high waters.

This bill authorizes additional funds and other special assistance to aid in the reconstruction and repair of damage caused in the Pacific Northwest by the devastating floods of last winter. I am in complete sympathy with the purpose of this legislation. However, in spite of the bill's general desirability, section 5 seriously violates the spirit of the division of powers between the Legislative and Executive Branches. Despite my strong support for the substantive relief, I must withhold approval until this unwise and objectionable provision is deleted.

The provision is contained in that part of section 5(a) stipulating that:

"The President, acting through the Office of Emergency Planning, is authorized to perform all or any part of the recommended work determined to be in the public interest and to reimburse any common carrier for any of such recommended work performed by such carrier, but no appropriation shall be made for any such work which has not been approved before June 30, 1966, by resolution adopted by the Committees on Public Works of the Senate and House of Representatives, respectively."

The Attorney General advises me that this provision is clearly a "coming into agreement" with a Congressional committee requirement. This device requires an Executive official to obtain the approval of a committee or other unit of Congress before taking an Executive action. It is not only an undesirable and improper encroachment by the Congress and its committees into the area of Executive responsibilities -- it also leads to inefficient administration. The Executive Branch is given, by the Constitution, the responsibility to implement all laws -- a specific and exclusive responsibility which cannot properly be shared with a committee of Congress.

The proper separation of power and division of responsibilities between Congress and the Executive Branch is a matter of continuing concern to me. I must oppose the tendency to use any device to involve Congressional committees in the administration of programs and the implementation of laws. I have spoken out against this before. Less than a year ago, in a signing statement on the Water Resources Research Act of 1964, I requested deletion of a provision much the same as the one in S 327.

Although I am unable to approve S 327 in its present form for the reasons stated, I am anxious that the relief to the states involved be made available as quickly as possible. Accordingly, I will approve S 327 immediately when the Congress has eliminated the provision in section 5 which infringes upon the responsibilities of the Executive Branch. I see no reason why this cannot be accomplished in a few days and have directed the Executive Branch to cooperate fully with the Congress to this end.

LYNDON B. JOHNSON.

SOURCE: *Congressional Record, Senate,* June 7, 1965, pp. 12669-12670.

deal firmly and forthrightly with what he does not want. Despite the broad language of the constitutional grant, embracing as it does even resolutions and orders, the Congress through the years has carved out a small sphere of legislative authority free from presidential oversight by the use of the concurrent resolution described in the previous chapter. At the same time, the Congress has probably surrendered more than it needed to by its own dilatory and complex procedures which expose a large share of its measures (those passed in the last few days of a session) to the absolute veto provided in cases where adjournment prevents reconsideration by the Congress of a vetoed measure.

How the
veto works   When confronted by a bill or joint resolution, the President may constitutionally take any of four courses of action. (1) He may sign it, and it then becomes a law. (2) He may hold it for the prescribed time (ten days) and, if Congress is still sitting, it will become law without his signature. This is an unusual course for a President to adopt and it rarely occurs. But occasions have arisen when a President was unable or unwilling to make up his mind about a measure in the period. Some Presidents have also used this procedure when they disliked certain measures but felt that a veto would be useless or unwise politically. (3) If Congress should adjourn during the ten-day period, the President may by inaction veto the measure. This "pocket veto" is absolute; it cannot be overridden by the Congress. Furthermore, it does not require the President to make any explanation of his disapproval. Although some Presidents, notably Franklin Roosevelt, have offered explanations of their decisions to the public or to the Congress, most Presidents have welcomed the opportunity offered by the pocket-veto procedure quietly to kill a measure without explanations which may be embarrassing politically. Many bills are halted on their path to the statute books by this procedure, as a result, especially, of the habit of Congress of passing a disproportionate number of its enactments during the closing days of the session. (4) The President may veto the bill outright and return it to the proper house of Congress with his statement of reasons for disapproval. Such a course of action requires the Congress to reconsider its position on the measure in question and, if the required support of two-thirds of the members of each house can be mustered behind the measure, it may be repassed and become law without presidential signature.

The use
of the
veto
power: Hamilton in *The Federalist* predicted that the veto would be employed cautiously and infrequently and that most Presidents would use it too little rather than too much. He proved a good prophet for the period prior to 1865. Since that time the veto has been used with increasing frequency and vigor. The turbulent era of Reconstruction, accompanied as it was by bitter

1. Fre-
quency   dissension between the President and Congress, witnessed the first really vigorous exercise of the veto power, if one excepts the administration of Andrew Jackson.

2. Scope   More important than the increase in mere numbers of vetoes has been the change in presidential attitude on the scope of the veto power. Until

Jackson, the veto power was used not to express presidential disapproval of the merit or wisdom of an enactment, but to question the constitutionality of it or to halt it because of technical errors. Jackson, however, employed the veto to stifle measures which he felt were unwise, even though he conceded they were constitutional and were properly drawn. Since 1865 our Presidents have tended to follow Jackson rather than Washington, Jefferson, Polk, and the others. It is now generally conceded that the veto is properly used to express disapproval of any kind and to any degree of policy or legality, of technicality or of procedure, on major issues and on minor ones. President Eisenhower vetoed the Natural Gas Act of 1956, for example, because he did not like the lobbying activities accompanying its passage, although he approved of the substance of the bill. The result has been to make the President a more potent factor in legislation than he was during the greater part of the past century.

This should not be taken to mean that in recent decades the veto has been employed loosely and without adequate grounds. On the contrary, it is typically employed reluctantly and only after considerable reflection. It means that Presidents have come to rely more certainly on their own views of the needs and aspirations of the people. Furthermore, the output of the

3. *In-fluence*

The Use of the Veto 1789–1967

PRESIDENT	TOTAL VETOES	REGULAR	POCKET	VETOES OVERRIDDEN
Washington	2	2	0	0
Madison	7	5	2	0
Monroe	1	1	0	0
Jackson	12	5	7	0
Tyler	10	6	4	1
Polk	3	2	1	0
Pierce	9	9	0	5
Buchanan	7	4	3	0
Lincoln	6	2	4	0
Johnson, A.	28	21	7	15
Grant	92	44	48	4
Hayes	13	12	1	1
Arthur	12	4	8	1
Cleveland	414	304	110	2
Harrison, B.	44	19	25	1
Cleveland	170	42	128	5
McKinley	42	6	36	0
Roosevelt, T.	82	42	40	1
Taft	39	30	9	1
Wilson	44	33	11	6
Harding	6	5	1	0
Coolidge	50	20	30	4
Hoover	37	21	16	3
Roosevelt, F.	631	371	260	9
Truman	250	180	70	12
Eisenhower	201	83	118	3
Kennedy	25	14	11	0
Johnson, L.	26	17	9	0

Congress has increased markedly in the past several decades and thus more bills and resolutions come under presidential scrutiny. Many presidential vetoes have been widely popular and few Presidents have suffered serious election reverses because of them. Furthermore, relatively few presidential vetoes have been overturned by the Congress. In practice, therefore, the direct, messaged veto tends to become very nearly an absolute veto.

Reform of the veto power

Periods of acute tension between the President and Congress have produced criticism of the presidential veto. Some have proposed that the veto power be weakened by requiring only a simple majority to repass a vetoed measure and others have proposed strengthening the power by requiring the support of two-thirds of the entire membership, rather than of those present, to repass a measure over presidential objection. Neither of these suggestions is currently receiving any serious attention. The most serious contemporary criticism of the veto power is that it does not extend to items or parts of bills, especially appropriation bills, but embraces only the whole

The item veto

measures. Most states have equipped their governors with item-veto power in reviewing appropriation measures in an effort to achieve more responsibility and sobriety in the spending of public funds. Their experience has commended this reform to many observers of and participants in the national scene. As matters stand, the President has no effective veto power over appropriations. Confronted with one of the major annual appropriation bills passed by the Congress, the President must accept it or risk exposing one whole program of public services to extinction for lack of funds. Since he has to have appropriation authority to conduct the government or any part of it, he ordinarily must accept whatever Congress sends to him. His discretion is reduced further by the fact that such bills ordinarily reach him quite late in the session, sometimes after Congress has adjourned, and thus there is no opportunity to repass a necessary appropriation, even one more nearly in line with the President's desires. Congress is, therefore, free to add sums to the appropriations suggested by the President without on many occasions adding to the national tax program to meet the obligation thus incurred. In addition, the argument runs, Congress has repeatedly added sections to appropriation bills which dealt with other aspects of public policy or administration and which it knew the President would disapprove if presented to him in any other way. These "riders" have been condemned by almost every President as an attempt to evade the constitutional system of checks and balances.

Opposition to the item veto

The reasons offered by the opponents for their refusal to accede to presidential requests have been (1) that such a grant would add greatly to the President's legislative power, allowing him, for example, to discriminate among the appropriations to favor his friends and punish his enemies, and that the balance of power has already been tipped too far in the presidential direction; (2) that experience in some states indicates that the effect of such a veto might well be to increase rather than to decrease legislative irresponsibility, that is, legislators would fall into the easy habit of pleasing everyone by voting extravagant sums, knowing that the executive would veto them, and thus transferring to him the onus for so doing; (3) that, in view of the fact that the President already has the power to recommend the budget, if he could veto congressional additions to his suggested program, then Congress would be completely powerless in the field of national finance.

One of the difficulties in the debate over the presidential item veto is the continuing disagreement among statesmen and scholars alike as to the best way to accomplish this reform. Some, including the two Presidents who recommend it, have held that an item veto could be conferred by the Congress by writing the pertinent language into each appropriation bill. Others, including several senators, have held that a constitutional amendment is the only valid way to achieve the change. President Eisenhower in 1955 selected a novel way of handling the "rider" problem. He announced in signing a major appropriation bill that the department needed the funds but that he intended to ignore certain provisions of the bill which he held to be unconstitutional. President Johnson followed the same procedure in signing certain public works appropriation bills in 1964 and 1965. A final observation on the item-veto debate: It seems quite unlikely that the Congress would enact the appropriations in their present form if the President's veto power were extended to items. The proponents of an appropriation which might draw presidential censure would certainly be sagacious enough to combine it with an item that the President could not or would not veto.

EXTRACONSTITUTIONAL DEVICES TO ACHIEVE PRESIDENTIAL INFLUENCE IN LEGISLATION

The role of the President as a lawmaker is by no means confined to the powers and duties specifically mentioned in the Constitution. If one is to gain a real appreciation of the power and influence of the American Presidency, it is necessary to consider the numerous practices devised by energetic Presidents outside the Constitution and now accepted parts of the repertoire of our chief magistrate.

Influence may be exerted not only by using the veto power but by threatening to use it. If a President allows congressional leaders to believe that he will veto a particular measure if it is presented to him in the form contemplated, he may be able to achieve changes before final passage and thus influence the final form of the measure. By indicating that he will veto a given measure in any form, he may be able to prevent its passage and even its introduction. Theodore Roosevelt, in many respects the father of the modern Presidency, was the first President who admitted using this technique extensively and also the first to proclaim its use publicly. Since Roosevelt, the threat to veto has become a familiar tool of presidential intervention. No chief executive in modern times has employed it as extensively as Harry Truman. It is necessary to add that on several occasions, notably in the

1. Threat of veto

Truman era, the threat only succeeded in stiffening the resolution of the Congress to proceed on its intended course regardless of presidential hostility.

2. Use of patronage

Every President has at his disposal a very large number of favors which he may dispense to legislators and their friends and supporters. The discriminating distribution of these favors is perhaps the chief behind-the-scenes source of presidential influence in Congress. These favors range from administrative benevolence toward certain interests in the home district of the congressman to the appointment to national office of persons recommended by members of Congress. The distribution of public offices in this way is ordinarily referred to as patronage, although in the broad sense the word may be used to embrace any type of favor granted for political or partisan advantage. Although the extension of the civil service merit system of appointment to the national public service has gradually reduced the number of positions which any President may fill by partisan methods, there are still several thousand posts which change occupants with each change in the political character of the national administration. Virtually all of these positions require senatorial confirmation and it is this procedure which encourages congressmen to urge the claims of their friends to posts in their own states or districts. By withholding such appointments from fellow partisans in Congress, the President is in a strong position to bargain for their support of his legislative policies. These matters are rarely handled by overt threats or definite bargains, but members of Congress are not indifferent to the advantages which accompany the position of supporters of presidential policies. We have the word of a former President (Taft) that the control over legislation arising from the President's appointing power is great. This particular extraconstitutional device is obviously most effective in the first months of a term of a new President. Once most of the posts are filled by a new administration the President's bargaining power is reduced. The fact that Presidents have typically experienced a declining influence on the Congress as their term has progressed partially reflects this. Presidents have customarily striven to get as much of their program as possible out of the first Congress that they deal with and before all of the job plums have been distributed. Jobs for friends, however, are only one kind of presidential favor which can ease the political life of a legislator. In fact they appear to be among the lesser rewards available to a "cooperative" Congressman. Public installations, defense contracts, special national facilities are more important benefits bestowed by the modern executive. As we have noted, constituent pressure brings every member of Congress into daily communication with agencies of the executive branch. The presidential blessing opens the doors of powerful administrators to congressional importuning much more readily than might otherwise be the case. At any rate, a legislator who incurs outright executive hostility is likely to find many obstacles in the way of serving his and his constituents' interests the way he would like to serve them. A congressman, on his own, has relatively few favors to bestow.

Still another source of presidential influence is personal conference.

While it is true that in our system the President does not appear on the floor of either house of Congress or participate in the debate, this does not prevent him from achieving the same objective privately in consultation with members of the Congress. Every modern President's visiting list has contained the names of numerous legislators, and he has felt bound to spend a fair portion of his working hours persuading, cajoling, threatening, and pleading with legislators for support. From early in his first administration, Franklin Roosevelt made systematic use of a weekly conference with the leaders of his party in the Congress. This practice has been continued by his successors. At these meetings the President receives reports on the status of legislative business and of his measures in particular and indicates his wishes concerning the matters pending before the Congress. Presidents also call into conference the influential members of a committee which is considering one of their measures and by whatever arts of persuasion they can command try to get the committee to act favorably on their requests. It is not at all unusual for members of Congress during the course of debate to indicate that they have recently discussed the pending issue with the President and to indicate to their colleagues what the executive's views are. And these views, so reported, are likely to be influential.

3. Personal conference and persuasion

The President does not have to carry the immense burden of dealing with Congress and congressmen alone. He has under his direction what is sometimes called "the most powerful lobby in Washington." A large share of the work of persuading and of explaining administration policies and programs is, in fact, carried on by his subordinates in the executive departments and agencies. Virtually every one of these great organizations maintains close and continuing relations with the Congress. The secretaries, bureau chiefs, and other top administrators spend much time appearing before committees, conferring with party leaders, and interpreting their programs to individual members of the legislature. Each of the great departments and many of the independent agencies have a staff of officials who do little else than coordinate departmental or agency relations with the Congress. The President himself ordinarily assigns one of his own administrative assistants to keeping track of his dealings with the Congress, and in the Bureau of the Budget another group of officers undertakes to review all bills emanating from the executive branch and to screen out those not consistent with current presidential policy. All of this activity is clearly indispensable to the effective operation of our national government but it is also widely criticized as an abuse of administrative discretion, especially when views are urged upon the Congress that the Congress or the critic is reluctant to adopt.

4. The "presidential lobby"

None of the devices thus far described is quite so useful to the President as energetic and articulate public support. Members of Congress are most sensitive to the views of their constituents, and if the President is strong with the voters he is likely to be successful with the Congress. Realizing this, Presidents court public approval in every way they can. Some, of course, are much more adept at it than others. All have unequaled opportunities for

5. Cultivation of popular support

publicity. We have noted how the messages and addresses to Congress are more and more commonly directed beyond the Congress to the people who support it. To these may be added the many addresses that Presidents are called upon to give on occasions of state and to various influential groups throughout the nation, the consultations which are held with influential leaders of opinion, letters addressed to private individuals but intended for public consumption, "fireside chats" on the radio, and carefully prepared television programs. All of these are and can be used to build and maintain a public opinion that Congress dare not ignore. The attention lavished on the President by newsmen is, perhaps, unequalled elsewhere in the world. His every movement and utterance is reported. A crowd of reporters follows him wherever he goes and no aspect of his personal life escapes attention. Much of this is not by his design but the result is that his personality more fully dominates the news on public affairs than in any other nation in the world and his ability to use this publicity for constructive ends is unmatched by Congress.

The presidential press conference   "The White House," said Theodore Roosevelt, "is a bully pulpit." The "gospel" as there expounded is carried to the nation today largely by means of the press, the radio, and television. Special mention is, therefore, appropriate of the use of these media by the President to achieve the support he needs. The presidential press conference is one of the most effective contemporary devices of presidential politics. The practice of meeting regularly with the representatives of the press and submitting to their direct questioning was initiated by Woodrow Wilson. He abandoned it for the prepared release when the United States entered World War I. President Harding revived it but proved unequal to the task of handling direct questions skillfully and required the advance submission to all questions in writing. This practice reduced the publicity value of the conference but it was continued by Coolidge and Hoover. Franklin Roosevelt cast the press conference in its modern guise. He had a shrewd sense of publicity and achieved the maximum in public sympathy and understanding through his semiweekly conferences. Presidents Truman, Eisenhower, Kennedy, and Johnson have attempted to continue the Roosevelt practice but each of them has met the press less regularly and less frequently. With recent Presidents, the conference has become more wide-ranging in coverage. None has liked to close off a line of questioning by saying "no comment." Eisenhower, further, opened his conference to news and television cameramen. President Kennedy has followed most of the Eisenhower practices. President Johnson tried several different formats but seemed most satisfied with "quickie" conferences called without much notice and held before the reporters who happened to be around. Franklin Roosevelt also pioneered in using the radio to reach the American people, largely through his famous "fireside chats," and proved one of the most skillful of modern practitioners of radio broadcasting. Truman and Eisenhower have attempted to follow the Roosevelt pattern but neither has been as effective. Presidents Eisenhower, Kennedy, and Johnson have sought public support by televised addresses.

THE PRESIDENT AS PARTY LEADER

The relations of the President with the Congress and the effective employment by him of the constitutional and customary forms and techniques described are colored and influenced by the fact that the President is the leader of his party. The emergence of the President as a party leader has been one of the major contributing factors to the contemporary legislative role of the chief executive. Chosen as a party candidate to head a government operated under a party system, the President surrounds himself with advisers of his own party, consults chiefly with the leaders of his party in Congress, unites to his the interests of his fellow partisans in the legislature through patronage, and depends primarily on the loyalty and support of the members of his party in Congress for the realization of his legislative program. The President represents his party throughout the nation as his colleagues in Congress cannot. The country looks to him, much more than to the Congress, to fulfill the pledges made by his party. Under these circumstances, he is bound to claim, ordinarily successfully, direction of the party's national machinery. He selects, while still a candidate, the chairman of the national committee and frequently reviews the appointments of other dignitaries in the party apparatus. He suggests and sometimes even dictates planks in the national platform on which he expects to campaign. He is consulted and his views may be decisive on all important questions of national party policy.

Presidency strengthened by role of President as party leader

As leader of his party, the President derives an additional lever to pry his program out of the Congress. He succeeds to a very great extralegal power to reward and to punish individual legislators of his party. He can exert great influence in such party decisions as the distribution of campaign funds among the states and representative-districts, the issues that will be played up in the campaign, the local and state leaders who will be aided and encouraged. As the chief campaigner of his party, the President can take the stump or not in aid of his congressional colleagues. Modern Presidents usually do. He can endorse the congressman to the voters of his district or withhold his approval. All of these courses of action are likely to influence the election prospects of a member of the legislature. A few Presidents, notably Franklin Roosevelt, have even gone so far as to campaign openly against hostile legislators of their own party. However, many professional politicians believe that a President dare not go this far. He is more likely to hurt himself than his opponent, for the voters tend to resent the intrusion of outsiders into local campaigns. In any event, this procedure has rarely accomplished the desired object. In sum, most congressmen are keenly aware of the great advantages to be gained politically from supporting presidential measures.

Influence on Congress from party leadership

It should be apparent from this discussion that the President's relations with the Congress, including his influence on legislation, depend upon the party situation in the Congress. Confronted with a Congress dominated by the opposite party, few of the techniques of partisan leadership are likely to

Party complexion of the Congress influences presidential success

prove effective in winning congressional support. In these circumstances, and they have been all too frequent, the President's role as party leader is rather an embarrassment than an aid to his legislative aspirations. The Presidency is the best prize of the American party struggle and the congressional leaders of the rival party are always strongly tempted to resist presidential advice in order that by discrediting his influence they can capture his office. The most favorable situation for presidential influence is for the White House to be newly occupied after an impressive election triumph which includes a strong majority in both houses of Congress. Midterm congressional elections have normally diminished presidential influence. Commonly, the President's party loses ground in these elections and even when his party retains control, its legislative members do not feel quite so keenly the ties with a chief executive who has not been in the campaign himself. Furthermore, as we have noted, the job patronage will be all dispensed. The lowest point in the ebb and flow of presidential leadership is when it becomes clear that the President will not seek reelection. Both party and congressional leaders then seek identification with a new leader.

CONTROL OVER THE PRESIDENT BY CONGRESS

*Constitu-
tional
controls*
        The continuing gain in the influence of the President upon the Congress and the impressive array of constitutional and customary devices for making this influence effective should not be interpreted to mean that, as between the two branches, influence flows only in one direction. Congress in its turn is capable of bringing powerful influences to bear upon the President. Few of the powers of the President can be exercised without money, and for every dollar of executive branch expenditure, the President must depend on the Congress. If the President shares the legislative power of the Congress, the Congress as we have seen, shares the executive and administrative power of the President. He and his deputies are ordinarily obliged to make an accounting of their stewardship in connection with the annual review of appropriation requests and his departments and agencies are periodically brought under critical scrutiny by the investigating arms of the Congress. The organization of the executive departments and commissions, the powers entrusted to them, and the procedures used by them are all dictated in more or less detail by congressional enactments. Except in the field of foreign affairs, the President must rely upon Congress for virtually every major change in public service, program, or policy. Even in the field of foreign affairs, the President must get senatorial approval of his treaties, congressional assent to war, and congressional approval of any financial support required for any international understanding. Finally, in extreme circumstances, the President can be impeached and removed from office by the Congress.
        Congress is not powerless either in those day-to-day dealings between the two branches which have developed outside the formal constitutional

specifications. If senatorial confirmation of his appointments gives the President an opportunity to reward his congressional supporters, it also results in congressional selection of the incumbents in many executive branch posts. If the position of party leader endows the President with substantial influence upon the electoral success of his party members in Congress, it also requires him, more often than not, to accept and even to support members of his party whom he may find personally obnoxious and who may very well be working to accomplish the defeat of his most cherished ambitions. If he can cultivate popular support by the press, radio, and television, congressional committees have shown themselves quite adept at capturing national attention with these devices, commonly when they are investigating the national administration. Furthermore, Congress is so organized that even if the President achieves great influence over the rank-and-file of his party, a few hostile leaders can still defy him with impunity and effectively frustrate legislative action. *Extra-constitutional controls*

In sum, directing our national government is jointly the responsibility of the President and the Congress. Neither is in a position completely to dominate the other. The realization of public opinion in national action requires genuine cooperation between the two.

PROPOSALS FOR IMPROVING LEGISLATIVE–EXECUTIVE RELATIONS

The boldest way of seeking greater harmony and unity between Congress and the President would be to abandon our historic principle of separation of powers and frankly go over to the British parliamentary system. The President would then become a titular chief executive with only formal and ceremonial functions like the British king. The actual executive would be a cabinet drawn from the majority party in Congress and directing both legislation and administration. Congress would then serve a fixed term only if the cabinet so decreed, for the executive would have to be able to dissolve the legislature in case of disagreement and call for a new election. The Senate would have to be radically reconstructed and demoted to a subordinate and largely suspensive role. One needs only to recite the major changes involved in copying the British system to reveal how visionary and impractical any such proposal it. Not only are the American people wholly unprepared for anything so drastic, but the size and complexity of our society and the sectional character of our political parties make it unlikely that the system would really serve our needs. *Adoption of the parliamentary system*

Most of the admirers of the parliamentary solution to the problem of legislative–executive relations have sought rather to modify the American presidential system by grafting on to it some of the features of cabinet government that might be most readily assimilated. Perhaps the mildest suggestion is that the heads of executive departments be extended the privilege of the floor in both houses of Congress for the purpose of giving information, *Floor privileges for Cabinet members* answering questions, and engaging in debate but not voting. This would allow, it is argued, the administration to defend itself directly and before the entire membership and would obviate the back-door procedures which are now used to accomplish the same end. The position of the administration and the reasons therefore could be stated openly and forthrightly and need not be relayed second-hand to the Congress. Much of the current investigating activity of congressional committees might be obviated if the legislators could ask questions directly of the department heads. It is hard to see, however, how a cabinet member could say anything that had not been cleared with the President beforehand and, therefore, there would be little spontaneity of discussion.

A Cabinet of congressional members

Presidents Taft and Wilson favored a plan under which, when selecting department heads, the chief executive should take most or all of them from among senators and representatives, the persons chosen retaining their seats and positions in the Congress. This would bring the two branches much closer together than the more modest proposal of giving the cabinet floor privileges. It would still, of course, leave the President outside of the legislature and free as now to accept or reject the advice of his counselors. A constitutional difficulty to this proposal is the specification that civil officers of the United States are ineligible to membership in Congress. This is probably not, however, an insurmountable barrier. Another difficulty in this suggestion would arise when the President and Congress are of opposite parties.

Presidential powers of dissolution

One school of thought holds that the real key to harmony in the cabinet system is the power of dissolution of the legislature possessed by the ministry. Believing that the most critical juncture of presidential–congressional relations is when the Congress rejects all or most of the President's program, these analysts recommend that the President be empowered to call a new congressional election. The people would then decide the controversy by their votes. The logic of this view is that if the voters returned a Congress still opposed to the President's policies, the President should resign. Some writers and statesmen have recommended that if a midterm election goes against his party and his program, the President ought to resign in any event. It is hard to see how the dissolution power could be integrated to the staggered terms of the senators. Another suggestion is that all members of Congress be elected for the same term and at the same time as the President. This would virtually guarantee that the same party would dominate both branches at any given time.

A legislative–executive council

Several students of the problem suggest that the wisest course is to disturb the existing institutional arrangements as little as possible but regularize and formalize the relations between the leaders of the Congress and the President and his advisers. One proposal along this line would organize the chairmen of a reduced number of standing committees into a legislative council or cabinet to meet frequently with the President to coordinate legislative programs. Another proposal would organize a council of eleven members of each house and three members named by the President to screen all proposed legislation and to consult directly with the President. The combination of legislative council of committee chairmen and President's cabinet into a grand council for formulating public policy is yet another suggestion. The joint committee on the organization of Congress suggested four policy committees, one for each party in each house, which would formulate the legislative programs of the respective houses and parties. The two majority party policy committees would meet regularly with the President. The failure of the House of Representatives formally to create the contemplated committees and the great difference between how these committees in the Senate actually work and how they were expected to work has not made these reforms fruitful.

One school of thought feels that the role of the executive branch as the major initiator of legislation ought to be recognized and accepted. Change the rules of the two houses, these men argue, and assure clear priority to administration measures. In fact, when the President has a working majority of his party in both houses, something very like this happens anyway. When he does not, no amount of priority could probably get his program accepted. *Priority for administration measures*

Although the prospects for immediate adoption of any of these proposals are not bright, the very existence of so many suggestions reveals a widespread notion that further improvement of our constitutional arrangements is both possible and necessary. The root of the problem is now widely held to be the difference in constituencies between the leaders of Congress and the President and his entourage. Most of the reform proposals are not aimed at changing this. Meanwhile, the incumbents of the Presidency have been attempting to establish on an informal basis the type of consultation and cooperation in executive–legislative relations which will more nearly achieve the desired goals.

REFERENCES

W. E. Binkley, *President and Congress* (New York, 1947).

J. Burnham, *Congress and the American Tradition* (Chicago, 1959).

D. Cater, *The Fourth Branch of Government* (Boston, 1959).

E. S. Corwin, *The President: Office and Powers; History and Analysis of Practice and Opinion* (4th ed., New York, 1957), Chap. VII.

A. de Grazia, *Republic in Crisis: Congress Against the Executive Force* (New York, 1965).

R. Egger and J. P. Harris, *The President and Congress* (New York, 1963).

H. Finer, *The Presidency: Crisis and Regeneration* (Chicago, 1960).

A. N. Holcombe, *Our More Perfect Union; From Eighteenth-Century Principles to Twentieth-Century Practice* (Cambridge, Mass., 1950), Chap. VIII.

S. Hyman, *The American President* (New York, 1954).

C. Jackson, *Presidential Vetoes, 1792–1945* (Athens, Ga., 1966).

L. W. Koenig, *Congress and the President* (Chicago, 1965).

H. J. Laski, *The American Presidency* (New York, 1940), Chap. III.

C. P. Patterson, *Presidential Government in the United States; The Unwritten Constitution* (Chapel Hill, N. C., 1947), Chaps. VI–VII, X.

R. S. Rankin (ed.), *The Presidency in Transition* (Gainesville, Fla., 1949).

C. Rossiter, *The American Presidency* (New York, 1956).

W. E. Travis (ed.), *Congress and the President* (New York, 1966).

R. Young, *This Is Congress* (New York, 1943), Chap. II.

12

THE PRESIDENCY

The executive power shall be vested in a President of
the United States of America. He shall hold his office during
a term of four years. . . .—Art. II, Sec. 1

The President of the United States of America is, without question, the most *The*
powerful elected executive in the world. He is at once the chief formulator *President,*
of public policy as embodied in legislation, leader of a major political party *the most*
boasting thousands of functionaries and millions of adherents, chief archi- *powerful*
tect of American foreign policy and spokesman for this nation before the *executive*
world, director of one of the most gigantic administrative machines ever *in the*
created, numbering over 3,000,000 civilian employees organized into 65 *world*
separate jurisdictions and expending more than $120 billion annually, com-
mander-in-chief of more than 3,400,000 men in uniform equipped with the
latest weapons of offense and defense, and ceremonial head of the government of the United States. And his power and responsibility are increasing.
It may seem ironic that a nation so mistrustful of officialdom and so certain
of the corrosive effects of political power should construct such an office.
However, the President falls heir to these powers by the peaceful suffrages
of his countrymen and he holds them for but a short time.

Given the great apprehension of American revolutionary leaders of *The Con-*
executive power, it is difficult to believe that the modern Presidency is a *stitution,*
deliberate creation of the founding fathers. The major decision of the Con- *a poor*
stitution-makers was that we should have a single executive. The remaining *guide to*
characteristics of the office are largely the product of practical political ex- *present*
perience. Like the British cabinet system, it is not to the sagacity of a few *office*
solons but to the pragmatic adjustments to time and circumstance by ordinary statesmen that we owe the institution of the American chief executive.
To no part of our American system is the Constitution so poor a guide.
Custom and usage have wrought the office far more than constitutional
prescription. The development of the presidential office has, nevertheless,
remained firmly anchored to the provisions of the Constitution.

The consti-
tutional
convention
and the
Presidency

The principal designer of the constitutional President was James Wilson, who argued skillfully and frequently for a single executive, independent of the legislature. No problem bothered the framers quite so much as the executive; they repeatedly postponed action when firm decisions were impossible and reversed decisions already made. Not until the closing days of the convention did the Presidency finally take its ultimate form, and only after a majority vote had been recorded and rescinded for legislative election and after the proponents of a plural executive, or at least of an executive council to assist the President and share his powers, were beaten down for the last time. In fact, so preoccupied were the framers with these two questions and with the question of eligibility for reelection that the powers and duties of the executive office were inadequately debated and summarily handled. What is meant by "executive power"? Why were some "executive powers" listed in Article II and others omitted? What should be the role of the "officers in each of the executive departments"? The debates in the constitutional convention throw little light on the framers' intentions. Only experience has yielded answers to these questions.

THE OFFICE OF PRESIDENT

The third-
term
problem
resolved

The decision of the constitutional convention for a four-year term with no limitation on the number of terms any individual might serve, in preference to a single seven-year term, turned out to be largely unacceptable to many of our nation's leaders. The first President was willing to serve only two terms, although he probably could have been reelected. The third President, Jefferson, declined to serve more than eight years as a matter of principle. He steadily opposed indefinite reeligibility of the chief executive. Madison and Monroe both bowed out after eight years and Jackson, who undoubtedly could have been reelected, vigorously supported Jefferson's precedent. Thus an "anti-third-term tradition" was established which lasted until Franklin Roosevelt successfully sought a third term in 1940 and then a fourth term in 1944. Roosevelt's departure from tradition called down upon his head a great storm of criticism and abuse and encouraged his opponents staunchly to reassert the tradition. Soon after his death and following a Republican victory in the congressional elections of 1946, an amendment to the Constitution limiting presidential tenure was laid before the states. Aided by growing antipathy toward President Truman, then serving his second term, the forces pushing the amendment finally achieved ratification by the thirty-sixth state (Nevada) early in 1951. The Twenty-second Amendment makes it hereafter impossible for any person to serve as President of the United States for more than two terms.

Presiden-
tial
qualifi-
cations

At the time that an individual assumes the office of President, he must, according to the Constitution, be at least 35 years of age, have lived in the United States 14 years, and be a "natural born" citizen of this country. In accordance with the Twelfth Amendment, the Vice-President must also have these three qualifications. Here again, the constitutional specifications are practically of small importance in determining presidential eligibility. All of those qualities which make up what we have described earlier as "availability" in a potential candidate are the decisive determinants.

Although Benjamin Franklin argued eloquently on the corrupting allure of wealth and against any presidential emoluments, the President has been paid a generous salary from the beginning of our national life. The Constitution expressly protects him from congressional attack or embrace through his pocketbook—a favorite colonial device for dealing with recalcitrant British governors—by providing that his salary may be neither increased nor diminished during his term of office. He is also forbidden to receive any other emolument from the United States or from any state. This has not, however, prevented his being supplied with an executive mansion, a suite of offices, a secretariat, a yacht, an airplane, a private Pullman Car, a fleet of automobiles, and special entertainment and expense funds. George Washington's salary was fixed by the first Congress at $25,000. Today the salary is $100,000.

Salary and allowances

THE POWERS AND DUTIES OF THE PRESIDENT—A GENERAL VIEW

Exactly what powers the Constitution confers or the framers intended to confer upon the President is anything but clear. Controversy has buzzed around this subject throughout our national life and the clamor has by no means abated. Demonstrably, the framers wanted firmness and vigor in the executive without autocratic domination. These are qualities imparted to an office by an individual, however; not to the individual by the office. To make the executive the servant and not the master of the subjects has ever been the goal of constitution-builders, and the history of tyranny testifies to the almost insuperable difficulties in the road of such endeavors. Perhaps the framers were content to allow time and experience to decide the major contours of executive authority in the American system. Perhaps this would have happened in any event, no matter in what language they had finally depicted the presidential power. They did, however, fall below the high standard of lucidity and consistency which characterizes most of our Constitution when they came to describe this high office. On the one hand, *all* executive power (not the power *herein granted* as in Article I) is conferred upon the President; and on the other, specific powers of an executive character—to appoint officers of the United States, to be commander-in-chief, to grant pardons, to make treaties, to take care that the laws be faithfully executed—are also conferred. Furthermore, the Congress is endowed with the power to make "all laws which shall be necessary and proper for carrying into *execution*" the powers granted to it. Does the Constitution mean that the President has some executive powers in addition to those specifically

Constitution not clear on executive powers

mentioned? Does it mean that the President must look to Congress to provide not only the means but the authority to act when, for example, rebellion, industrial violence, depression, national catastrophe, or war threatens the stability of our institutions and the happiness and security of our people?

Two concep-tions of executive power:

1. Broad view

If we allow for variations in detail, two broad and competing conceptions of presidential power emerge from the debates engendered by circumstance, personalities, and constitutional obscurity. Hamilton, Madison (before he became President), Jefferson (while he was President), Jackson, Polk, Lincoln, Cleveland, Theodore Roosevelt, Wilson, Franklin Roosevelt, Truman, Kennedy, and Johnson have supported the view that presidential power is broader than the specific items enumerated, that it is not completely dependent upon express congressional authorization, and that, although it should be carefully confined normally, the existence of a critical or emergency situation justifies the most vigorous and independent exercise of all of the force and authority that the chief magistrate can command. In this view, the Congress, the courts, and the people of the time have generally concurred. Theodore Roosevelt best expressed this view when he labeled the President "the steward of the people" and insisted that it was not only his right but his duty to do anything that the national welfare required unless it was expressly prohibited by the Constitution or the laws.

2. Limited view

President Taft, in *Our Chief Magistrate and His Powers,* sums up the opposite view:

> The true view of the executive function is, as I conceive it, that the president can exercise no power which cannot be reasonably and fairly traced to some specific grant of power or justly implied or included within such express grant as necessary and proper to its exercise. Such specific grant must be either in the constitution or in an act of Congress passed in pursuance thereof. There is no undefined residuum of power which he can exercise because it seems to him to be in the public interest.

To this view, many of our chief executives, for example, Buchanan, Grant, Harding, and Coolidge, the Congress and occasionally the courts have also intermittently subscribed.

Precedents for the broad view of presidential power

The exponents of the broad, rather than the limited, view of presidential authority largely molded the office of the Presidency as it stands today. They established most of the significant precedents. They defined the functions. They inspired their successors. They also stimulated the vigorous assertion of the opposite view and invited reaction and retreat when they thrust too far beyond the ground already occupied. The landmarks in the evolution of presidential power are Washington's proclamation of neutrality in the Franco–British war; Jefferson's decision to acquire the Louisiana territory, although he believed there was no constitutional authority for such an acquisition; Jackson's resolute annihilation of the Bank of the United States despite its strong congressional support, and his strong determination to prevent the secession of South Carolina; Lincoln's assumption of virtually plenary power to deal with the southern "rebellion" with or without congressional authorization, in consequence of which and without express grant of Congress he raised armies of volunteers, appropriated money from the Treasury, suspended the execution of the writ of habeas corpus, issued the Emancipation Proclamation, and restored states occupied by the Union armies (many of his actions were, to be sure, later validated by the Congress); Grover Cleveland's determination to repress industrial disorder with national troops in the Pullman strike despite the opposition of the governor of the state concerned; Theodore Roosevelt's dramatic intervention in the coal strike of 1902 and his assertion of the "stewardship" conception of the presidential office; Wilson's successful assertion of the President's complete responsibility for direction of American participation in World War I, although he acted on the basis of congressional assignment of power; the Supreme Court's decision in the Myers case supporting the view that the President's removal power is unrestricted; congressional delegation to Franklin Roosevelt of great powers to deal with economic depression and to direct the American effort in World War II; Truman's assignment of American forces to battle in Korea under the United Nations without express congressional authorization; the movement of national troops into Little Rock by Eisenhower and into Oxford and Tuscaloosa by Kennedy against the wishes of the governors of the states concerned; the imposition of a naval blockade of Cuba by Kennedy to force the removal of Soviet missiles; the sharp escalation of the conflict in Viet Nam by Johnson and the commitment of more than 500,000 American soldiers to the struggle without a declaration of war and in the face of considerable public and congressional criticism.

The Congress and the courts have provided most of the precedents for the more limited view of presidential power. The Senate by resolution denounced Andrew Jackson's actions against the Bank of the United States as unconstitutional—a resolution which it later expunged. Lincoln's "dictatorship" was bitterly assailed from Capitol Hill and so were the actions of the Roosevelts and Wilson without, however, any official action. Andrew Johnson's attempt to assert Lincoln's powers without Lincoln's skill brought him within one vote of removal from office. The Supreme Court has declared against presidential assumption of power on several occasions. The most recent occasion for Court declaration on this weighty subject represents a rebuff to presidential claims. President Truman in 1952, in an effort to halt a threatened steel strike which he claimed would jeopardize our national defense effort, ordered the Secretary of Commerce to seize the steel factories and to operate them. The President based his order on his power as commander-in-chief of the armed forces and the "executive power" of the President, admitting that no congressional authority for such an action could be found. When the steel companies sought to prevent the seizing of their properties, the Court held that in the absence of congressional authorization and in view of the fact that Congress had clearly intended not to grant such

Precedents for the limited-power concepts

Steel seizure case

authority, the constitutional provisions governing executive power and power as commander-in-chief conferred no such power on the President. The law-making power, said the Court, is entrusted to the Congress alone in "both good and bad times."

If the President's authority and responsibility have increased strikingly in the history of our political system, to the incumbent they usually fall far short of allowing him to achieve his goals by command. President Truman once observed that what the power of the President amounts to is the ability to persuade people to do things they ought to do without persuasion.

The powers of the President depend, in practice, upon the skill, imagi-nation, energy, outlook, and resources of those who occupy this high office and upon their understanding of the techniques by which in our democratic system they may achieve the policies to which they are dedicated. Ordering things done is frequently a last resort and is not certainly decisive. The development of the office as outlined has meant that we expect more of our chief executives and that they are also acting on a greater stage before a larger audience than ever before. It is helpful in considering the scope of presidential activity if we look next at the various constitutional assignments of responsibility.

POWER AND RESPONSIBILITY TO ENFORCE THE LAWS

> . . . he shall take care that the laws be faithfully ex-
> ecuted, . . .—Art. II, Sec. 3

Law-enforce-ment power

The presidential oath of office obligates him to protect and defend the Constitution and the Constitution itself solemnly enjoins him to enforce all national laws (by implication this includes treaties and ordinances). A great many of the laws of Congress expressly confer upon the President or upon his subordinates in the executive branch specific powers of enforcement. Some laws confer powers which may be exercised at his discretion or at the discretion of his subordinates. The sum of these constitutional and statu-tory grants is the enforcement power of the Presidency at any given time.

Presiden-tial assist-ance in law en-forcement

For discharging this lofty responsibility the President has virtually the entire facilities of the executive branch, including the thousands of officials and employes working in the numerous agencies of which it is constituted. One particular agency, the Department of Justice, is charged with the gen-eral responsibility for law enforcement, notably of those criminal laws the enforcement of which is not specifically assigned by the Congress to some other national agency. As an alternative to the use of troops, agents of the Department have also been used to halt violence. Attorney General Kennedy ordered a large number of U.S. marshals into Birmingham, Alabama in 1961 to "assist" local law enforcement officers in preventing attacks on the bus loads of Freedom Riders then touring the South in the interests of desegregation. The governor (Patterson) of the state did not request this assistance and the congressional delegation vigorously protested the procedure.

The President has also under his command the armed forces of the *Suppres-* nation and even those of the states if and when called into national service. *sion of* The President's power to employ military force in the enforcement of na- *disorder* tional laws has steadily increased through the years as a result of congressional action and of presidential initiative. It now seems clear that such power is not wholly dependent on congressional authorization nor, in cases of internal disorder, on the invitation of the governor or legislature of any of the states. If the President can validly assert that the disorder threatens the performance of any national function, the safety of national property, or the flow of interstate commerce, he can intervene with force to restore order whether the governor or the state legislature wants him to do so or not. Supporting this view, the Supreme Court said, "The entire strength of the nation may be used to enforce in any part of the land the full and free exercise of all national powers and the security of all rights entrusted to its care." The use of troops in Little Rock in 1957, in Oxford in 1962, their prospective use in Birmingham and Tuscaloosa in 1963, in Selma in 1965, in Detroit in 1967, and in the capital in 1968 are recent actions illustrating the scope of presidential authority. In the first case, a reluctant President felt compelled to intervene with force when the governor of Arkansas (Faubus) called out the state militia to prevent compliance with a national court order to desegregate Central High School in accordance with a plan for admitting Negroes carefully worked out by the local school authorities. The President asserted that "the powers of a state governor may not be used to defeat a valid order" of a national court. In the second, the governor of Mississippi (Barnett) attempted to obstruct the admission of a Negro to the University of Mississippi. Even while rioting was in progress, President Kennedy pled for obedience but made it clear that his obligation was to implement the orders of the courts with whatever means were necessary. In Birmingham, the Governor of Alabama (Wallace) expressly requested that the situation be left to the local authorities. No rioting surrounded the effort to enforce the court-ordered admission of Negroes to the University of Alabama at Tuscaloosa but Governor Wallace before he capitulated attempted personally to obstruct their entrance. In Selma, Alabama, President Johnson federalized the national guard to protect the voting-rights marchers. In Detroit, the governor called for help to deal with the devastating race riots of 1967.

As awesome as the President's responsibility for law enforcement may *Limitations* be and as broad as some Presidents and courts have found his power to be, *on en-* in practice there are numerous restraints, legal and political, upon his ability *forcement* to fulfill such responsibilities or to exercise such powers. Whatever reservoir *power* of enforcement power may be found from time to time to exist in the constitutional mandates unsupported by specific statutory authorization, normally the President must look to Congress to prescribe his exact authority to enforce any given law, for the procedures by which such enforcement is to be achieved, and for the penalties which may be invoked against transgressors. Whether or not he is dependent upon Congress for the power, he is certainly dependent upon it for the personnel and supplies, that is, the money, to do the job. The President is also dependent upon the quality of the national public service, most members of which he did not hire and, in practice, cannot fire. His appointment and his removal powers are circumscribed in many ways, as we shall observe in the next section of this chapter. The lieutenants upon whom the President must largely depend for the enforcement of any law are not, in every case, bound to him and to him alone by an unbroken chain either of authority or of communication. The President inherits not only most of the people upon whom he must depend, but the organization of these people into bureaus and departments with all the institutional traditions that these organizations have accumulated through the years. Most Presidents have found that they are supporting these institutions and the men who occupy them much more often than these are supporting the President.

Executive rule-making power and its limits

The power of enforcement necessarily entails large powers of discretion. In applying general laws to particular circumstances it is essential that enforcement agencies decide what the law means in these varying circumstances. From this necessity has flowed an increasingly broad stream of presidential direction in the form of executive orders, ordinances, rules, and regulations which are in plain fact laws made by the executive. Congress has repeatedly, especially in the last half-century, established national policy in very broad terms and assigned to the executive the power to achieve these broadly stated objectives by uttering detailed rules and regulations. This discretionary power, essential as it is to effective law enforcement, is limited by congressional power to recall the delegation or to spell out the details, contrary to presidential policy. On the other hand, the presidential directives frequently come under the scrutiny of the courts. And when called upon in law enforcement, the courts have the final say as to what the law is.

Law enforcement and public opinion

The effectiveness of law enforcement depends in the final analysis on the attitude of the public toward the law in question. The many futile attempts to enforce the Volstead Act of 1919 (the law designed to give effect to the Prohibition Amendment) illustrate the great difficulties in the path of presidential fulfillment of his constitutional duties in the face of a hostile or lethargic public opinion. Furthermore, a great and growing number of national policies set forth by Congress and President cannot really be achieved by enforcement in the sense of seeking out and punishing violators. They can be achieved only by methods which are essentially educational and non-coercive. The needy aged, for example, cannot be properly cared for by a program based mainly upon uncovering those wrongfully receiving public support. The "enforcement" responsibilities of the President in these types of programs can be fulfilled only with adequate public understanding and support.

POWER TO APPOINT AND REMOVE PUBLIC OFFICERS

> . . . he shall nominate, and by and with the advice and con-
> sent of the Senate, shall appoint ambassadors, other public
> ministers and consuls, judges of the Supreme Court, and all
> other officers of the United States, whose appointments are not
> herein otherwise provided for, and which shall be estab-
> lished by law; but the Congress may by law vest the appoint-
> ment of such inferior officers, as they think proper, in the
> president alone, in the courts of law, or in the heads of depart-
> ments.—Art. II, Sec. 2, cl. 2

That the President is solely responsible in law and in the polling booth for the conduct of the far-flung national administrative machinery is a truism of American law and politics. His ability actually to direct the administration is dependent upon a variety of personal, political, and legal conditions. Not the least of these is the scope of his power, legally and practically, to hire and fire the individuals who compose the national civil service and the cadre of national officers who guide them. The Constitution clearly circumscribes the President's appointing authority of individuals in the executive branch in several ways. Except for members of the diplomatic service and judges of the Supreme Court, the officers to which presidential appointment may extend must be created by the Congress. The authority to create an office carries with it the power to establish the duties of the office and the qualifications of any individual who may occupy it. Congress has, in practice, set forth such qualifications of many kinds, geographical, political, personal, and professional. Congress, furthermore, may vest the appointment of "inferior" officers—and, by and large, the Congress has decided which are "inferior" officers—in department heads as well as in the President. In fact, the Congress has assigned the appointment of more than 85 percent of the 3 million civilian employees of the executive branch to department and agency heads and has limited the freedom of the department heads by the requirements of the merit system. The direct appointing power of the President now extends to about 25,000 national officials. However, any particular incoming President may be able to fill only about 6000, but these include virtually all of the top-ranking posts in the official hierarchy—secretaries, assistant secretaries, some bureau chiefs, commissioners, agency directors. The President's hand does, therefore, reach those who appoint the others and who give them their orders and assign them their duties. Many students of the American system, it is necessary to add, feel that the President's appointing power is still too extensive and that if he were confined to appointing only two or three hundred of the major executives this would be ample for the purpose of achieving the kind of directional authority which he ought to have. Presidents

Scope of the President's appointing power

for years past have complained bitterly about the unconscionable burden of appointments cast upon them. This was especially the case before the extension of the merit system throughout the civil service.

Senate
participa-
tion in
appoint-
ments

One of the most important limitations of presidential authority is the prescription that the Senate must be consulted on his selections. Except in those few cases (there are about 375 such posts) where Congress has vested the power in the President alone (for example, the officers of his own immediate staff), all presidential nominations must be confirmed by majority vote of the Senate before appointment may be made. In practice, the Senate has tended to divide presidential appointments into two classes with respect to the character of its participation. It has been customary for the Senate to approve, almost as a matter of course, the President's choices for the highest positions in the executive branch. It has come to be recognized that the heads of the great departments and agencies are the principal advisers of the President—the departmental heads compose his Cabinet—and that he bears direct responsibility for all of their acts and relies upon them to direct the agencies in keeping with his policies. He should, therefore, have the widest range of freedom in selecting them. Although there has been serious opposition on several occasions to the President's choices, only nine nominees for Cabinet posts have ever been rejected. The President's designees for subordinate executive posts, for Supreme Court judgeships, and for diplomatic posts are contested somewhat more frequently, but even these are normally not seriously challenged.

Recess
appoint-
ments

In skirmishes with the Senate over executive posts, the President is fortified by his power to make recess appointments without senatorial approval. A few Presidents have used this procedure to keep men in office of whom the Senate disapproved. Of course, the Senate is more likely to be sympathetic to presidential wishes when his party is in the majority.

"Sen-
atorial
courtesy"

There is another class of presidential appointment, however, about which the Senate is not nearly so deferential. Several thousands of the posts filled by presidential appointment are not major executive posts at all and are positions in the field service (regional offices outside Washington, D. C.). These include collectors of customs, certain positions in government corporations, U.S. district attorneys and marshals, and judges and court functionaries of the lower federal courts. The appointment process for these positions is normally dominated by partisan considerations and the sum of these posts constitutes the job patronage of any given administration. Senatorial confirmation operates in this category of presidential appointment to enforce upon the President the nominees of his fellow partisans in Congress. For those posts located in states where at least one of the senators is of the same party as the President, that senator's approval of the appointment is almost mandatory. The Senate has a deeply rooted tradition that it will rally to the support of any senator in the circumstances described and reject any nominee not acceptable to him. This tradition is called "senatorial courtesy" and is typically invoked by a senator declaring that the nominee is personally obnoxious to him. For posts which are located in congressional districts, the members of the House of Representatives of the President's party expect to be consulted and this practice too may be enforced upon the President by the senators. In states not represented by a senator of the President's party, the President is obliged for party reasons and by tradition to rely on suggestions from the state party leaders, typically the national committeeman. In sum, the President has not much real freedom in making appointments to the vast majority of posts which he is entitled by law to fill. The actual selections are made by party supporters in the House and Senate and by party leaders in the state where the jobs are located. We have already described how, by the skillful use of this patronage, the President may gain support for his legislative program from the Congress and thus compensate in a sense for the restrictions upon his appointing power.

The ability of the President to get the vast national administrative service to march to his tune is strongly influenced by the scope of his power to dismiss those who disobey his orders, impair the efficiency of the service, resist his program, or neglect their responsibilities. Obviously the constitutional impeachment process is not designed for this purpose. Since the Constitution is otherwise silent on the dismissal of government officers, does the President have this power or does the Senate share responsibility for dismissal as it does for appointment? Can the Congress by law prescribe the procedure for firing employes and officers of the national government? This problem arose early in the life of the Constitution and while many of the framers were still alive. Madison persuaded his fellow statesmen of the time that the removal power, insofar as officials in the executive branch are concerned, was part of the executive power and of the power to enforce the laws which the Constitution entrusted to the President alone. On another occasion, however, Madison did say that Congress might create certain types of offices—not wholly executive in character—for which some different removal procedure might be established. Until 1867, the Madison doctrine of presidential removal authority was generally accepted in law and practice. In that year, however, and as an incident to the acrimonious contest between Congress and President Johnson, the Congress passed over his veto a Tenure of Office Act which provided that the President could not remove without the concurrence of the Senate any official whose appointment the Senate had confirmed. This measure was partially repealed in 1869 and wholly expunged in 1887, but another act passed in 1876 established the same principle for postmaster appointments. Several decades later, President Wilson, probably deliberately, violated the Postmaster Act and called the constitutionality of the limitations into question. The postmaster (Myers)—later his estate—carried the matter to court and in 1926 the Supreme Court, through the mouth of Chief Justice (former President) Taft, declared in favor of the Madison doctrine that the removal power belonged to the President and could not validly be restricted by the Congress in the manner described.

The President's removal power

The Myers Case

The case of the independent commission

The decision of the Court in the Myers case, because of its sweeping assertion of presidential power, caused immediate concern for the tenure of officials appointed to commissions, such as the Interstate Commerce Commission, which Congress had endeavored to exempt from direct presidential domination. This aspect of the problem was brought to the court for judgment about a decade later when, in 1933, President Roosevelt dismissed William S. Humphrey, a Republican member of the Federal Trade Commission, whose policies did not agree with those of the President. In doing so, the President made no pretense about adhering to the statutory requirements concerning the tenure of members of the "independent commission." In this case, the Court went back and picked up the other part of the Madison doctrine and held that Congress had the power to establish agencies in the executive branch which were not exactly executive in function and that it could clothe these with a certain immunity from presidential direction. The independent regulatory commissions are of this type, said the Court, and Congress was acting within its power when it specified the terms ("inefficiency, neglect of duty, or malfeasance in office") upon which commissioners may be removed. In a later case the court said that even if Congress does not expressly provide for removal, if the nature of the agency is such that it was clearly intended to be exempt from presidential direction, the President may not remove an incumbent.

Removal of inferior officers

The power of the Congress to prescribe dismissal procedures for the "inferior" officers has long been recognized. Since 1883, Congress has gradually extended the protections of merit system tenure to these offices, and thus for all practical purposes the President's power to dismiss merit system employees is sharply restricted. In the absence of legislative provision, however, the President may remove "inferior" officers at his discretion.

Congressional removal power

Congress has frequently and by a variety of methods attempted to remove or to force the President to remove officers of the executive establishment, and these efforts suggest that the President's authority in removal must be viewed also from a different vantage point: the role of Congress in removals. In 1924, the Senate by resolution called upon President Coolidge to request the resignation of his secretary of the navy in consequence of his relation to the naval oil reserve scandal. The President strongly repelled the notion that this was any of the Senate's concern and took no official recognition of the request. By statutory provision, one officer of the government, the Comptroller General of the United States, may be removed from office before the end of his term only by joint resolution of the two houses of Congress. The rationale of this law, as set forth in an act of 1945, is that this officer is peculiarly a subordinate of the legislature. The easiest and least debatable procedure available to the Congress for ousting administrative officers is to abolish their positions. In 1952, for example, the Truman Wage Stabilization Board was abolished because of congressional disapproval of its findings in the steel-labor controversy and a new board with similar functions created. Another method tried by the Congress is to specify qualifications for positions which the incumbents do not possess. The Congress has also tried, unsuccessfully, to deny salaries to particular administrators of whom it disapproves. Finally, the Senate has sought, also unsuccessfully, to recall confirmations of appointments of officials.

POWER AS COMMANDER-IN-CHIEF OF THE ARMED FORCES

The President shall be commander-in-chief of the Army and the Navy of the United States and of the militia of the several States, when called into the actual service of the United States.—Art. II, Sec. 2, cl. 1

Effect of military responsibilities on the office of President

Among the many factors which have contributed to the aggrandizement of the office of President, none is more important than his military and diplomatic responsibilities. The three Presidents—Lincoln, Wilson, Franklin D. Roosevelt—who piloted this nation through its major wars extended the scope of presidential authority beyond any other holders of the office. In this century especially, wars both hot and cold have centered responsibility for the peace and safety of the nation more firmly in the Presidency than has been true in any other era save that of the Civil War. The security of this nation depends in great measure upon the maintenance of a firm military posture of readiness and upon the skillful operation of our diplomacy abroad. In both of these areas of governmental activity, the President is uniquely in the focal position. The country looks to him rather than to Congress or courts to save the day.

"War powers" of the President

The constitutional basis for the President's military authority is the assignment to him of the position of commander-in-chief of the forces. If to this be added his constitutional responsibility for law enforcement, we have virtually the entire legal framework upon which has been erected the towering structure of what Lincoln called the "war powers" of the President. Until Lincoln's day, it was quite generally assumed that the duty of commander-in-chief vested the President with purely military powers, such as to deploy the armed forces, to order their internal management, and to appoint and dismiss their officers. Lincoln regarded his constitutional duties as including far more than this. He was obliged, he said, to save the nation and to suppress insurrection and as commander-in-chief he must do whatever was required to serve those ends. Lincoln did ask the Congress subsequently to ratify most of his acts, which the Congress did. However, he acted upon the view that the initiative and responsibility were his and that as commander-in-chief he was peculiarly responsible for preserving public order and combating insurrection. The Presidents charged with the conduct of two world wars and the two "police actions" in Korea and Viet Nam have assumed that Lincoln's view of presidential power to deal with rebellion is also applicable when the country is fighting a foreign enemy. Franklin D. Roosevelt, for example, in a message to Congress in 1942 dealing with the Emergency Price Control Act, invited the Congress to take action to stabilize wages and prices but, he said, "in the event that the Congress should fail to act, and act adequately, I shall accept the responsibility and I will act." "The President," he went on to say, "has the powers, under the Constitution and under congressional acts, to take measures necessary to avert a disaster which would interfere with the winning of the war."

The Cold War and presidential authority

The Cold War of the present era has stimulated the application of the Lincolnian doctrines to hostile situations where no war has been formally declared, as in Korea. Our obligations under the United Nations charter can, of course, be cited as adequate legal grounds for assignment of American troops to Korea without express congressional approval. The deployment of American troops as "technical assistants" to the French–native forces in Indo-China and later to Thailand and the substantial commitment of troops into the battle of Viet Nam were presidential decisions unsupported by United Nations resolution or specific congressional enactment. The Steel Seizure case alluded to above represents a setback for the most sweeping assertion of the authority of the commander-in-chief, but the power of the commander to deploy American troops anywhere in the world (Berlin, for example, where President Kennedy strengthened our troop deployments in 1961) is still widely accepted. President Eisenhower, however, usually tried to associate Congress with any major decision to commit American forces abroad as in the Formosa crises of 1955 and 1958 and the Mid-East crisis of 1957. In the Cuban crisis of late 1962, President Kennedy imposed the naval blockade to halt arms shipments to the island and to force the removal of missiles and jet bombers largely on his own authority. Congress had, however, with little or no presidential urging, earlier passed a resolution authorizing the use of the military, if necessary to prevent Castro influence from spreading in this hemisphere or from threatening American security. Kennedy asked for and got authority from the Congress to order units of the Ready Reserve into active duty. Johnson has repeatedly cited the authorizations of the Tonkin Gulf resolution of 1965 to support his forceful intervention in Viet Nam. Military intervention in Santo Domingo in 1965 was also taken on presidential initiative. In summary, the extent of the power of a President when acting as commander-in-chief is mainly undefined, but that it is considerable no one now doubts.

THE PARDONING POWER OF THE PRESIDENT

> . . . and he shall have power to grant reprieves and pardons
> for offenses against the United States, except in cases of
> impeachment.—Art. II, Sec. 2, cl. 1

Scope of the pardoning power

The power to exempt individuals from the punishment ordained for the offenses of which they have been convicted is one which has been associated with the chief executive in Anglo-American law for many centuries. The framers of our Constitution simply borrowed the practice from England. It should be noted that the President's power extends only to individuals convicted of national crimes and that it may not be used to veto congressional convictions resulting from impeachment. The pardoning power has come to embrace the power to diminish the punishment, for example, by commutation of sentence, or to delay its application by reprieve, as well as to cancel it entirely. Although the Supreme Court at one time said that the effect of a full pardon is to make the offender, in the eye of the law, "as innocent as if he had never committed the offense," the power is now regarded as not quite so sweeping, and judicial cognizance may be taken of a conviction even though the individual was pardoned.

INSTITUTIONS OF PRESIDENTIAL LEADERSHIP—THE CABINET

Need for presidential assistance

The sum total of the powers and responsibilities of the President of the United States, when added to the aspirations of those who occupy the position, is a crushing burden of work and care. It is almost too big a job for any mortal being. Two of the last eight Presidents (Harding and Franklin D. Roosevelt) have succumbed under the tremendous strain while still in office, a third (Kennedy) was felled by an assassin, and a fourth (Wilson) was stricken with paralysis and emerged from the Presidency broken in body and spirit. The life of a fifth (Coolidge) was undoubtedly shortened by his presidential anxieties. Twice during his service, a sixth (Eisenhower) was felled by serious heart attacks. Strange as it may be that men willingly seek such an office, it is stranger still that they are able to bear up under the stresses and worries of it and to perform in it as well as they have done.

It should be obvious to any thoughtful student that the President cannot do all the things he is supposed to do or carry all the weight of affairs he is required to carry without help. However solitary and self-contained the office of President may seem to be in law and in the eyes of the throng, the President, himself, is quite dependent upon his assistants, high and low, for the effective discharge of his responsibilities. It is not too much to say that the quality of presidential assistance and the organizational arrangements through which it is brought to the aid of presidential decision are major determinants of presidential success. More than this, they make it possible for one human being somehow to fill the Presidency.

Origin of the Cabinet

Among the institutional arrangements for presidential assistance none is more interesting or less helpful than the Cabinet. The office of President was designed by the fathers of the American Constitution with great misgiving that any man could be found to whom could safely be entrusted such power and responsibility. Many proposals were made to share presidential burdens with a council of some kind. None of these proposals was ever adopted. The Cabinet, as we know it, grew up outside the Constitution and unknown to the law. President Washington looked first to the Senate to share some of his burdens and to offer him timely advice and then to the Supreme Court. He was rebuffed by each of them in turn. And, finally, when the House of Representatives discouraged the appearance of his departmental heads in the midst of its deliberations, he was forced to turn in upon the resources of the executive branch. Washington came to rely entirely on his own subordinates, the heads of the four executive departments, for advice and assistance and thus the Cabinet was born. Hamilton's effort to model the institution into an agency of collective responsibility somewhat like the later British model was unsuccessful. Throughout the decades the Cabinet has remained a purely advisory body.

The Cabinet is what the President makes it

As the years have passed, the traditions and customs of the Cabinet have become more and more settled. These settled traditions, however, concern the membership, the relative rank of the members and the formalities of meeting. Few decisive traditions have been established regarding the purpose of the Cabinet, the subjects of its deliberations, or the regard which must be given to its decisions. Cabinets have been and are now whatever the President chooses to make of them. Some Presidents, Pierce, Buchanan, and Harding, for example, consulted their Cabinets at every turn and ordinarily acted upon their recommendations. Eisenhower relied on his Cabinet a good deal more than his immediate predecessors and during his illnesses it came very close to being an agency of collective responsibility. Others have ignored their Cabinets. Jackson, preferring to lean upon personal friends and political aides, discontinued Cabinet meetings altogether. Lincoln is reported to have polled his Cabinet on a critical issue of the day and finding all opposed to his own opinion, nevertheless decided in favor of his own proposal. Wilson, Franklin D. Roosevelt, and Kennedy leaned lightly on their Cabinets; they rarely submitted any major policy questions to the meetings. The following passage from the most recent and most comprehensive study ever made of the operation of the executive branch states rather exactly the modern position—or lack of it—of the Cabinet: [1]

> The members of the cabinet are the primary advisers to the president. He is free to select them, to decide the subjects on which he wishes advice, and to follow their advice or not as he sees fit. The cabinet as a body, however, is not an effective council of advisers to the president and it does not have a collective responsibility for administration policies. That responsibility rests upon the president. The cabinet members, being chosen to direct great specialized operating departments, are not all fitted to advise him on every subject.

Meetings

Cabinet meetings are ordinarily held once a week in a special room in the White House expressly designed for the purpose. The President and the heads of the twelve executive departments sit around a large oval table,

[1] *Report to the Congress by the Commission on Organization of the Executive Branch of the Government,* "General Management of the Executive Branch" (Washington, D. C., 1949), pp. 17–18. One cannot repress the notion that this passage was written by the chairman of the commission, former President Herbert Hoover.

the President in the middle and the others flanking him in order of rank. The Vice-President is commonly in attendance, as on many occasions are heads of some of the large agencies which do not have departmental status. Proceedings are informal; there are no rules of debate; no minutes are kept; and, rarely are any votes taken. Under President Eisenhower, however, a regular agenda was prepared in advance for the meetings, a secretary to the Cabinet was established, and decisions taken were noted and efforts made to see that they were properly implemented. President Kennedy, although he retained a special assistant to serve as Cabinet coordinator, relied on his Cabinet very little. Meetings were irregular and infrequent. Johnson brought his Cabinet together somewhat oftener. Traditionally, the matters discussed were those introduced by the President and very commonly included party and campaign problems as well as problems of a legislative, executive, or administrative character. These discussions, at best, bring out useful information and opinions, clarify the issues, and promote morale among the top executives of the administration. Almost never do they culminate in decisions on policy by mere show of hands.

It might well be asked why the Cabinet has developed the way it has. *Influences on Cabinet appointments* Surely a President could only strengthen his position and lighten his cares by sharing some of his responsibility with the Cabinet, by leaning on them for advice and guidance, and by utilizing more fully the very considerable administrative and political talents which every Cabinet contains. Furthermore, the senatorial power of confirmation provides no great barrier to Cabinet unity and loyalty. The Senate has, as we have noted, accorded unusual freedom to the President to make his own selections. The answer to the question appears to be that, although the Senate has left the President largely free to make his own appointments, the political traditions of the nation have not left him free to gather around him a group of advisors upon whom he can certainly depend for loyal support. When a modern President comes to choose his Cabinet he is obliged to take account of many factors other than personal loyalty and dependability. Most Presidents have felt that the Cabinet must be an instrument of party harmony and that, therefore, the various factions and regions which are influential in party councils must be represented in it. The men and groups over whom the President climbed on his way to the nomination have got to be placated in the interests of presenting a united front to the people and a strong claim upon the party's followers in Congress. In some instances, the managers of the successful candidate have even promised cabinet appointments to some men in order to win their support in the party convention. Only on rare occasions have Presidents stepped outside their parties to name men of slight political influence or men identified with the other party.

Cabinet not fitted to share presidential burdens Each President has tried to make his Cabinet as broadly representative as he can, with someone from the West (usually to head the Department of the Interior); someone from the South; someone from the group he is trying to detach from the other party (Eisenhower's appointment of Martin

Durkin, the Democrat leader of the A.F.L. union, for example); someone from labor, from agriculture, and from industry. The aspirations of almost every major group in the body politic are recognized in some way by the Cabinet selections. Under these circumstances, a President is surrounding himself with men and women whose loyalty to him and enthusiasm for his program is not always wholehearted. Secretary Chase, in Lincoln's Cabinet, spent much of his time trying to unseat Lincoln and capture the Presidency for himself. Bryan was never really sympathetic to Wilson's pro-Allied foreign policy. Hoover rose to the Presidency from a Cabinet post under circumstances which did not endear him to Coolidge. Thus, we see that when a President calls his Cabinet together for the first time he will discover as he looks around the table, men whom he did not know at all until a few days or weeks ago, men whom he has every reason to distrust, men with whom he will never be able to agree on any matter of fundamental policy. Only here and there will a familiar face of a true friend and well-wisher appear. It is for these reasons that many Presidents have preferred to seek advice elsewhere and to confine Cabinet discussions to questions of party policy or to anecdotes and trivia.

Cabinet qualifications   It should not be supposed from what has been said that Presidents are utterly indifferent to the competence, administrative or technical, of the individuals appointed to Cabinet position. The attorney general is always a lawyer; the secretary of the treasury is frequently a financier; the secretary of agriculture is a member of some agricultural organization. Perhaps an increasing proportion of individuals are selected for their special knowledge and experience of the matters with which their departments deal. In the main, however, these qualifications are secondary in importance to the ones already discussed.

THE EXECUTIVE OFFICE OF THE PRESIDENT

The most effective institutional arrangement for lightening the President's load and helping him to get through his daily chores is a product of the last three decades. It is the staff assistance provided through the Executive Office of the President. This institution is a product of the first of the two great studies of this generation of the operation of the executive branch of the national government: the Report of the President's Committee on Administrative Management (1937).

The creation of the Executive Office of the President   Until well into this century, the President relied almost entirely on the departments for bringing to him timely reports, carefully conceived recommendations, answers to the questions propounded by his visitors, his correspondents, and his legislative colleagues, and estimations of the future. His own staff included only a private secretary to handle his visiting list, his mail, and his directions, some assistants to help in processing the mail, and an executive clerk to direct the various employes of the White House. Through personal contacts, Cabinet meetings, and directives, the President tried desperately to coordinate and give direction to the movements of the growing complex of agencies which comprise the executive branch. This responsibility added to his other cares impelled him to labor far beyond the powers of most persons. The first major device for equipping the President to take a broad, superdepartmental view of his responsibilities was the Bureau of the Budget, created in 1921. Although placed at first in the Treasury Department, this Bureau nevertheless became a tool of presidential direction and its director the major financial advisor to the President. In 1928, the number of secretaries to the President was increased to three and the work of his office compartmentalized into correspondence, reception of visitors, economic research, legislative matters, and press relations. His purely ceremonial military aides were replaced at this time by distinguished officers able to advise the President on grave military questions. The tremendous expansion of governmental services and staff incident to combatting the depression engulfed the President in a new flood of papers, people, and programs demanding his personal attention. "The President needs help," said the Committee on Administrative Management in 1937. The President should have at his command a staff of assistants who can be his eyes and ears and bring to him the data necessary to inform his judgment. This staff, said the Committee, should consist of men "in whom the President has personal confidence and whose character and attitude is such that they would not attempt to exercise power on their own account." Furthermore, the Bureau of the Budget should be brought directly into the presidential entourage.

Pursuant to these recommendations and to the Reorganization Act of 1939, the modern Executive Office of the President was created by Executive Order in 1939. Under the roof of the Executive Office was established the White House office, embracing the personal secretaries and newly created assistants to the President and their staffs. Under President Johnson, the White House office consisted of approximately 300 employes, the most important of whom were a press secretary; a correspondence secretary; an appointment (calendar) secretary; a special legal counsel; military aides from the three armed services; a personal physician; an executive clerk; special assistants dealing with legislative relations, speech writing, Cold War planning, science and research, national defense, and other subjects. President Eisenhower had a chief-of-staff directing the activities of all of the others in the office but President Kennedy abandoned this practice. President Truman made a practice of holding daily conferences with his chief lieutenants in the White House office at which time the day's duties were reviewed. The President gave directions to each man and received from each advice on the upcoming matters of the day. President Eisenhower relied heavily on his chief-of-staff to coordinate all of his aides of the White House staff. These men, in each administration, have been the Presidents' own selections and have had a compelling influence on what and who are brought to the attention of the "boss." All except the most influential men

Components of the Executive Office:

1. The White House office

in national life who set out to capture the President's ear end up by seeing one of his assistants.

2. Bureau of the Budget

The Bureau of the Budget was transferred from the Treasury Department to the Executive Office by executive order and its functions expanded to embrace not only fiscal policy but general administrative management in the executive branch. Its function of screening all departmental and agency proposals for legislation was broadened and strengthened at the same time. The present Bureau, with its 1000 employes, is the key planning agency for the nation's finances, and because of its proximity to the chief executive himself is able to exercise a profound influence on all departmental programs and policies, as these must be supported by adequate financing.

3. Council of Economic Advisers

The Employment Act of 1946 added a new unit to the President's office when it created the three-man Council of Economic Advisers. This agency was and is charged with keeping its fingers on the pulse of the American economy, advising the President on the state of the nation's economic health, and preparing periodic reports for him to submit to the Congress on the subject.

4. National Security Council

As an outgrowth of the struggle for unified direction of the defense forces and of the strategy of the nation, two important cabinet committees were created and practically, although not formally, made a part of the executive establishment. The National Security Council and the National Security Resources Board, established in 1947, were designed to improve the ability of the President to coordinate military and diplomatic policies and military mobilization policies and industrial and resources programs. The staff of the National Security Council is part of the Executive Office of the President.

5. National Aeronautics and Space Council

Controversy over the proper direction and the assignment of the responsibilities for American efforts in space precipitated by the Russian Sputnik led to the creation in 1958 of the National Aeronautics and Space Council in the Executive Office. Like the National Security Council, this is essentially a Cabinet committee headed by the Vice-President and charged with coordinating the space program.

6. Office of Emergency Planning

The chairman and staff of the National Security Resources Board were, in 1953, consolidated with the director of defense mobilization into the Office of Defense Mobilization. In 1958, it became the office of Civil and Defense Mobilization and in 1961, the Office of Emergency Planning. The present office now serves as the principal planning agency for all matters relating to current and future efforts to prepare the American economy for war, for rehabilitation in case of attack, and to deal with disasters of an emergency character.

7. Office of Science and Technology

The rapid growth of the research efforts of the national government contributed to the formation in 1962 of the Office of Science and Technology in the Executive Office of the President. The Director is the science advisor to the President and coordinates scientific programs with the welfare and defense needs of the nation.

To administer the war on poverty proposed by President Johnson and approved by Congress in 1964, an Office of Economic Opportunity was created in the Executive Office. The director is responsible for developing plans for the youth training, job corps, community action programs, business aids and other devices contemplated by the law for eliminating poverty in America.

8. Office of Economic Opportunity

The new Executive Office has seemed so exactly to fit the needs of the times that it has grown steadily in importance and utility in the past three decades. Surrounding the President, as it does, with a "palace guard" of devoted servants and multiplying by several fold his ability to breast the waves of reports, orders, problems, and advice rising from the bureaus, offices, and agencies of the vast administrative sea, it provides the most effective support to the President of the United States. This was perhaps most clearly revealed by the way the office functioned during Eisenhower's illness. The Presidency has thus become not a man but an institution. Its occupant reads a very small portion of all the written matter he receives; he writes an insignificant number of the papers he signs; he prepares almost none of the messages and speeches he delivers; he sees a fraction of those who would consult with him. Only thus can a mere man today "execute the office of President."

Executive Office grows in usefulness

Despite the impressive successes of the Executive Office, few statesmen or students are wholly satisfied that the presidency is still within human capacity and that the American genius for organization has yet solved the problems of coordinating the efforts of the huge executive establishment. Each year brings a new spate of proposals for improvement. Ex-President Hoover believed we need a second vice-president, appointed by the President and responsible to him, to whom might be delegated a large part of the routine chores. Governor Rockefeller (New York) has proposed a deputy president. Ex-President Eisenhower, father of the chief-of-staff system in the White House, is believed to favor a first-secretary above the Cabinet and below the President. Ex-President Truman and a subcommittee of the Senate, headed by Senator Jackson (Wash.), opposed these solutions. A study undertaken for the Jackson group suggests the need for a national research organization to undertake long-range studies of foreign and military policies and a planning staff in the Executive Office to evaluate programs and policies for the President.

Continued efforts to aid the President

THE VICE-PRESIDENCY AND PRESIDENTIAL SUCCESSION

The Vice-President of the United States has no constitutional function except to preside over the Senate and to assume the office of President in the case of the death, resignation, removal, or disability of the incumbent. As presiding officer of the Senate he is not a member of that body, has no vote except when a tie occurs, and participates in the deliberations only infor-

Office of Vice-President

mally, if at all. As heir-apparent to the Presidency, he is an executive officer of the government potentially rather than actually. Since 1836, the only occasions upon which the Vice-President has succeeded to the office of President have been the result of death of the President. Eight Presidents have died in office and a like number of Vice-Presidents have assumed the Presidency. No President has resigned; none has been removed. No President has been incapacitated to such an extent and for so long a period as to lead to the assumption of his duties by the Vice-President. Such a transfer was, however, seriously discussed when Garfield lay dying for two months, stricken by an assassin's bullet, when Wilson suffered a paralytic stroke which held him in bed for weeks, and when Eisenhower had a heart attack in the fall of 1955 and a mild "stroke" in the fall of 1957. Eisenhower's illness, in part, precipitated a considerable effort to find a statutory or constitutional remedy for the present situation in which the President alone is really the sole judge of his own disability. President Eisenhower in 1958 and President Kennedy in 1961 entered into agreements with their respective Vice-Presidents by the terms of which the Vice-President was to become acting president in case of presidential disability until the disability was ended. If the President were unable to communicate then the Vice-President might make the determination of disability himself after "appropriate consultation." Finally after Kennedy's assassination dramatized the matter further, Congress proposed and the states ultimately approved a new system—incorporated in the Twenty-fifth Amendment—under which the Vice-President and a majority of the Cabinet or other body designated by Congress may declare a President disabled and with the support of a two-thirds vote of both houses of Congress the Vice-President may continue to act as President in face of the incumbent's efforts to regain command.

The role of the Vice-President   The rise of the party system, the passage of the Twelfth Amendment providing separate voting for President and Vice-President, and the rarity with which Presidents have dropped the reins of power have combined to reduce the office of Vice-President to comparative insignificance. The result is that candidates for this office are not selected with the same care as presidential candidates. Many worthy and experienced statesmen have, in fact, refused to be considered for the nomination. The candidates are in practice selected by the presidential candidate himself to balance the ticket, that is, to appeal to regions and interests with whom the presidential candidate is not identified. The Vice-President has, in consequence, proved hard to fit into the chain of command or the framework of responsibility in the executive branch. Although it would appear reasonable that the Vice-President be kept informed of the policies and plans of the administration, Calvin Coolidge was the first Vice-President regularly to attend Cabinet meetings. This custom has by now become fairly well established. The Cabinet meeting, however, is not the most effective institutional device for keeping the Vice-President informed. A succession of Vice-Presidents, Garner, Truman, Barkley, Nixon, Johnson, and Humphrey selected from the Senate, have uncovered new uses of the office. These men proved valuable intermediaries between the President and the Congress. Nixon, Johnson, and Humphrey have also played active roles in foreign affairs and served the President as special emissaries abroad on several occasions. When, on November 22, 1963, President Kennedy was cruelly felled by an assassin's bullet, the country was indeed fortunate that the Vice-President, Lyndon B. Johnson, could bring to his accession to the Presidency long and highly responsible service on Capitol Hill, and a knowledge of the inner workings of the administration unmatched by any previous Vice-President. Perhaps the Vice-President is at last coming to share some of the burdens of the President. Certainly the fact that two of the leading candidates for President in 1968 were former Vice-President Nixon and Vice-President Humphrey may also elevate the post in political significance.

There is no assurance at any given moment that there will be a Vice-President to assume the presidential duties. Vice-Presidents may also die, resign, be removed, or become incapacitated. The Constitution authorizes Congress to provide for this contingency by "declaring what officer shall then act as president." Congress has provided three different plans of presidential succession over the years involving the Cabinet members and the speaker of the House and president *pro tempore* of the Senate. With the adoption of the Twenty-fifth amendment which authorizes the President to appoint a Vice-President with the approval of a majority of both houses of Congress when that office becomes vacant, it is unlikely that the congressional succession plans will be of any consequence in the future.

Arrangements for presidential succession

REFERENCES

J. Bell, *The Splendid Misery: The Story of the Presidency and Power Politics at Close Range* (New York, 1960).

W. E. Binkley, *The Man in the White House; His Powers and Duties* (Baltimore, 1959).

———, *President and Congress* (New York, 1947).

E. S. Corwin, *The President: Office and Powers; History and Analysis of Practice and Opinion* (4th ed., New York, 1957), Chaps. II, III–IV.

D. C. Coyle, *Ordeal of the Presidency* (Washington, D. C., 1960).

R. F. Fenno, Jr., *The President's Cabinet* (Cambridge, Mass., 1959).

J. P. Harris, *The Advice and Consent of the Senate* (Berkeley, Calif., 1953).

L. L. Henry, *Presidential Transitions* (Washington, D. C., 1960).

E. J. Hughes, *The Ordeal of Power: A Political Memoir of the Eisenhower Years* (New York, 1963).

W. Johnson, *1600 Pennsylvania Avenue; Presidents and the People 1929–1959* (Boston, 1960).

J. E. Kallenbach, *The American Chief Executive: the Presidency and the Governorship* (New York, 1965).

L. W. Koenig, *The Chief Executive* (Rev. ed., New York, 1968).

H. J. Laski, *The American Presidency* (New York, 1940), Chaps. I, II, IV.

E. R. May (ed.), *The Ultimate Decision: The President as Commander-in-Chief* (New York, 1960).

G. F. Milton, *The Use of Presidential Power, 1789–1943* (Boston, 1944).

R. E. Neustadt, *Presidential Power: The Politics of Leadership* (New York, 1960).

C. Rossiter, *The American Presidency* (New York, 1956).

G. A. Schumbert, Jr., *The Presidency in the Courts* (Minneapolis, 1957).

T. C. Sorensen, "The Olive Branch or the Arrows: Decison-making in the White House," Speranza Lectures delivered at Columbia University, 1963, Reprinted in *Congressional Record, 1963,* 10,708–10,716.

R. G. Tugwell, *The Enlargement of the Presidency* (New York, 1960).

E. G. Williams, *The Rise of the Vice-Presidency* (Washington, D. C., 1956).

13

THE ORGANIZATION AND PROCEDURES OF THE EXECUTIVE BRANCH

THE NATURE AND IMPORTANCE OF ADMINISTRATION

Just as the characteristic activity of the Congress is legislation, that of the executive branch is administration. Governmental administration is the attempt to realize in practice the policies established by Congress and the President. The spirit of the American system of government is that public policies will be determined by elected representatives of the people, although it may be necessary to employ nonpolitical technicians to carry them out. However, the line which separates policy determination from policy execution is neither precise nor stable. Many laws and executive orders leave a great deal of discretion to the technicians; many technicians are able to exert powerful influence upon the formulation of the laws and orders. The chief of the national administration faces both ways—in collaboration with Congress he is policy determiner, and in collaboration with the executive agencies he is policy executer. The Congress on its part does not confine its attention to policy alone; it is constantly involved in administration. Thus, in practice, there is a large twilight zone between the two spheres of governmental activity in which administration and legislation are inseparably intertwined. That policy in our system of government should be determined by politically responsible officials who must account to the voters for their conduct represents, therefore, both an aspiration which must be earnestly sought and an achievement which has largely been realized.

Administration and the American system

The importance of administration in the vitality of the American system of government has only recently thrust itself upon the awareness of the American people. As a people we have tended to assume that legislation is the prime corrective of all ills of the body politic. We have a greater penchant for passing laws about things than almost any other people on earth. Only

Importance of administration

in the past half-century have we been gradually brought to the realization that passing wise laws, as difficult as that is, is easier than having them economically and effectively administered. Many of us still do not appreciate that the laws are no better than their administration. What is more, there are many problems, foreign and domestic, that cannot be solved by laws, and some type of administrative procedure is the only method available to the government to deal with them. During much of the nineteenth century, administration was regarded as the legitimate booty of political party struggles and its aim to sustain the victors in their triumph. Almost any citizen of mature age and average mentality could administer virtually any program decided upon by the policy determiners, it was thought. Woodrow Wilson pioneered in directing the attention of the American people and their leaders to the importance of good administration. Interest gradually increased, and since about 1920 administration at all levels of government has become the subject of extensive research, writing, and experimentation. The result of this interest has been increased understanding, and this, in turn, has produced a remarkable improvement in the administration of governments of all kinds.

As rapidly as administrative reform has followed administrative reform in the past decades, it is doubtful if improvement has kept pace with the problem. Like the swelling mushroom of an atomic explosion which soon dwarfs all other features of the horizon, national administration has burgeoned into a swelling cloud of money and employes by comparison with which Congress and the courts are but specks on the national landscape. None of the changes through the years in the government of the United States is quite so startling or quite so consequential as the tremendous growth of the executive branch. In point of cost, volume of activities, and numbers of people employed, the "big government" of which so much is heard these days is really "big administration." Can an enterprise of this magnitude be managed by ordinary human beings? Can it effectively deliver the services and solve the problems which are expected of it? Can it somehow be paid

Improvement in administration has not kept pace with the problem

Growth of the National Government

DATE	NO. CIVILIAN EMPLOYES	ADMINISTRATIVE BUDGET EXPENDITURES
1790	350	$4,269,027
1801	2,100	9,394,582
1816	6,327	30,586,691
1831	19,800	15,247,651
1861	49,200	66,546,645
1881	107,000	260,712,888
1901	256,000	524,616,825
1921	562,252	5,115,927,690
1941	1,370,110	12,710,629,824
1951	2,879,000	44,632,822,000
1961	2,441,000	78,900,000,000
1967	2,646,618	125,718,000,000

for without exhausting the resources and the economic health of the nation? Can its technical skills and organizational energies be harnessed to the cart of constitutional democracy? Can the people's representatives really hold the reins? These are the more important of the problems raised by the growth of this young giant.

THE STRUCTURE OF THE EXECUTIVE BRANCH

One of the determinants of whether the vast array of officials and employes who comprise the executive branch can, in fact, be brought under the directing will of the President and his aides and under the general supervision of the Congress is the way in which they are organized to perform the tasks assigned to them. The need for organization is, of course, a product of the size and complexity of the operation, and the importance of proper organization tends to increase directly with growth. Direction of the modern executive branch of the national government would be unthinkable unless the individuals who comprise it were grouped into units on the basis of some rational pattern. Skillful administrative organization aims at assigning duties to groups of employes in such a way that each group has a clear and consistent mission and that the group commander can be held responsible for the performance of that mission. It seeks to bring all units into due subordination through an unbroken chain of command to the chief executive. It strives to relate the size of the unit and the resources at its command to the size of the task assigned to it. Failure to observe any one of these precepts of good organization may well frustrate the intention of President or Congress. However, faithful adherence to these precepts will not of itself produce good management, for an organization can be no better than the people who serve in it.

Importance of proper organization

The traditional organizational unit of the executive branch is a single-headed department to which has been assigned a more or less homogeneous group of programs aimed at a major section of national governmental responsibility. The directing head is commonly called secretary and is, typically, a member of the President's Cabinet. This organizational pattern was established by the Confederation Congress and its continuance was assumed by the framers of the Constitution. Prior to 1870, the Congress showed little disposition to assign new executive functions to any other type of agency; each new or enlarged responsibility was customarily assigned to one of the existing departments. This attitude has been modified in the years since 1870, but there is still a strong tendency to find a home for any newly established operation in one of the departments. Those charged with administering programs in nondepartmental agencies rather persistently strive for departmental status. There is an aura of permanence and maturity about the department form of organization which makes it the model in an ideal as well as in a historical sense of executive branch organization.

The department

Charac-
teristics of
depart-
mental
organiza-
tion:
1. Political
direction
The 15 departments (12 of Cabinet rank) of the contemporary executive branch exhibit numerous variations in structure and operation. There are, however, enough common characteristics to allow useful generalizations. In the first place, the top management of all of the departments consists largely of partisan politicians, appointed for political reasons ordinarily from the ranks of the President's party. This politically oriented management staff includes the secretary, the under-secretary, the assistant secretaries, the legal counsel, the director of public relations, some of the bureau, office, or division chiefs, and the more important aides of each. Experience has convinced most Presidents and members of Congress that the enforcement of responsibility to the voters upon the permanent staffs of the departments requires not only a politically responsible secretary but a cadre of political assistants commanding all of the main channels to him of information and authority.

2. Cen-
tralization
of author-
ity in the
depart-
ment head
On the whole, authority and responsibility for departmental management are concentrated in the office of the department head. Each department head is subject to the general direction of the President and holds most of his power subject to that direction. Within his domain, however, he is a miniature President. The authority of the department head typically includes (1) the power to appoint subordinate officials and employes, virtually all of them in accordance with the practices of the civil service merit system; (2) the power to remove subordinates appointed by himself, again subject to the tenure provisions of the merit system; (3) the power to issue binding rules and regulations for the conduct of departmental business and, in many instances, for the purpose of supplementing legislation administered by the department; (4) the power to decide appeals from the decisions of departmental subordinates not only on departmental matters, but, in many instances, in matters affecting private citizens; (5) the power to issue formal or informal orders to all of the component units of the department governing the work performed by each. Together with this authority is complete responsibility to the President, the Congress, and the public for the conduct of the department. The department head is expected to represent the views and interests of the institution he directs before the President, the Cabinet, and the Congress. He is also expected to represent to the department the policies and desires of the President. He is expected finally to support the President and his party on all occasions.

3. Hier-
archical
arrange-
ment of
subordi-
nate
organiza-
tional
units
The component organizational units of each department are, typically, arranged in hierarchical pattern by virtue of which the authority of the department executive permeates throughout the organization in a more or less unbroken chain of command. There is no standard nomenclature for designating the major organizational units in a department, but the most frequent title is bureau. To each bureau is assigned a more or less homogeneous group of department functions and services. The head of each bureau ranks next below the top-management staff already described. A substantial and increasing proportion of these bureau executives are career civil servants protected

by the merit system. The bureaus, in their turn, are subdivided into divisions, branches, and sections, proceeding down the ladder of administrative authority.

The organization of the typical executive department, including the names, numbers, and functions of the bureaus is largely determined by statute. Department executives are not free to arrange the pieces to suit their own estimate of departmental needs. Many of the bureaus, in fact, had legal status and traditions long before the departments of which they now are parts were established. *4. Congressional control of departmental organization*

Outside the 15 executive departments are a number of single-headed organizations directly under the President called agencies or administrations. They possess every characteristic of departments save one: The head is not traditionally a member of the President's Cabinet. In recent years, however, the major agency heads have in fact attended Cabinet sessions. The precedent for this type of executive agency was set with the establishment by the first Congress of the postmaster general's office in 1789. And from time to time since that date Congress has elected to house a new function in an agency of this kind because it has not wished to increase the size of the Cabinet or because it has hoped that the function would not become a permanent one or because it has felt that it was not sufficiently important to justify departmental status. Contemporary examples of this type of agency are the Veterans Administration and the General Services Administration. *Other single-headed agencies*

The third type of executive agency, the "independent" regulatory commission, is a product of the last 80 years and is an incident to the increasing governmental intervention in the economy which has characterized that period. The prototype of this new form of organization is the Interstate Commerce Commission created in 1887. The typical commission is a plural body of from five to 11 members appointed by the President for overlapping terms of from five to nine years. Typically, no more than a majority may be members of one party and the members are not subject to the unrestrained removal power of the President. Subordinate to the commission itself is a staff of career civil servants who assist it in the performance of its duties. The commission is, therefore, the executive head of the agency directing by order and by regulation the work of numerous subordinates. It is also a rule-making agency, just as are many of the department heads. However, a large portion of its rules, much larger than those of the typical department, are binding upon that part of the public which comes under its regulatory authority. Finally, the commission is an appellate tribunal, hearing and determining a large number of cases arising from the decisions of referees or trial-examiners who are, at least nominally, its subordinates. These cases involve, typically, the application of commission-made rules to private firms. To such an agency, typically, has been entrusted the regulation of some private enterprise sector of the national economy which Congress has determined to bring under detailed government scrutiny. The power to regulate has ordinarily been entrusted to these commissions in the broadest possible terms *The "independent" regulatory commission* and has extended, for many private economic institutions, to the prices charged the consumer and to the profits of the owners. Because of the singular power over these economic institutions entrusted to commissions, Congress deliberately sought to protect them from the kind of partisan political direction which the single-headed department or agency is designed to facilitate. The combination of legislative (rule-making), executive, and judicial powers which the commissions possess also suggested that the powers should be exercised in a relatively nonpartisan environment. The procedures which Congress has directed to be used to accomplish the desired regulation, furthermore, tend to make these commissions more directly responsible to the courts than to either the President or to the Congress. The location of these agencies in the executive branch, however, has meant in practice that they have not wholly escaped the influence of presidential direction. It should also be observed that neither their powers nor procedures are unique—they can be found also in departments. In other words, the Congress has not adhered to a consistent pattern in assigning responsibilities among the various types of executive branch organizations. There are always many factors, personal as well as political, which color any legislative decision as to the proper agency to entrust with any particular function.

Nonregulatory commission   The executive branch also houses a number of boards and commissions which have no consequential regulatory responsibilities. There are numerous reasons, in addition to those discussed, for using multi-membered agency directorates to preside over national programs or services. In some cases, it is highly desirable to ensure representation of various sections, economic interests, or social groups in the composition of the directing body. This is particularly true where the functions are largely advisory, as in the case of the Tariff Commission. It is also true where the functions are investigative, as in the Commission on Organization of the Executive Branch of the Government. Another compelling reason for the use of boards is the desire to avoid one-man responsibility and to insure that decisions will be taken only after various views have been canvassed. The most important nonregulatory commission at present is the Atomic Energy Commission and the principal purpose in creating this type of agency to develop atomic and thermonuclear weapons and power generators was to place this program on a nonpartisan footing as far as possible.

Corporation: 1. Development   The two world wars of this century, the expansion of American national interests in foreign countries, and the depression of the nineteen-thirties stimulated governmental programs essentially similar to those which had been or were being performed by privately owned business concerns. In order to provide a "business-like" atmosphere for the administration of these programs and to provide somewhat greater flexibility in their fiscal administration than the traditional government bureau possessed, the corporate form of organization was established in the executive branch. Although a corporation was first used by the Congress in 1791 to provide a United States Bank, the modern government corporation is a product of the twentieth century.

There are now more than 80 of these corporations in existence and their combined assets are somewhat more than $30 billion. Most government corporations are, at least nominally, attached to one of the departments or agencies. The extent of the control over their activities which the department head derives from this attachment is uncertain and ill defined. A few of the corporations, notably the Tennessee Valley Authority, are independent establishments in name and in fact. Many of these corporations were created by presidential directive rather than congressional enactment, and all of them enjoyed for a time a great measure of real autonomy over the spending of the earnings arising from the sale of their services. All of them are, however, arms of the government. It owns them, supplies most of their capital, defines their functions, and regulates their procedures. Like business corporations, virtually all of the government corporations have boards of directors and under them general managers.

Growing criticism of these agencies for their alleged independence of congressional and even of presidential direction led the Congress in 1945 to bring them under more systematic scrutiny. The Government Corporation Control Act of 1945 provides that only Congress may create them in the future, subjects their finances to scrutiny by the Bureau of the Budget and the General Accounting Office, and requires them to administer their personnel more nearly in accordance with civil service merit system procedures. *2. Control*

THE CONTINUING NEED FOR REORGANIZATION

The proper and effective organization of the executive branch is not something that can be achieved with finality. The public, through the Congress and the President, constantly demands new services or expansions in older ones. Emphasis shifts from one function to another as changes occur in domestic or international conditions. Presidents, department heads, commissioners, and bureau chiefs change and each subtly molds his organization to suit his own interests, ambitions, and conceptions. Like any other institution built of human hopes and fears, the organization of the executive branch is a dynamic, not a static thing. It will be different tomorrow than it is today. The consequence of these factors is that the organization of the executive branch is in constant need of attention if the purposes of the government are to be realized and its principles observed.

As our nation became increasingly aware of the importance of administration, criticism began to be heard from journalists, administrators, students, and congressmen and their constituents that the organization of the executive branch was not adequate to its tasks. Congress, which dictates the structure of the executive branch, could be brought to act but slowly, despite the prodding of Presidents Taft, Wilson, and Hoover. It became clear that only the President had both the will and the information to achieve effective organization of the executive branch and to keep the organization in tune with *Growing criticism of executive organization* changing circumstances. President Franklin D. Roosevelt was the first modern President entrusted by Congress with organizational authority over his own domain. This was in 1933 and few changes were made by executive order before the power expired in 1934. Then in 1936, after dozens of new agencies had been created to combat depression and promote human welfare and the executive branch was more topsy-turvy than ever, and after the

Committee on Administrative Management

President had been firmly established in his second term by a tremendous popular plurality, he named a Committee on Administrative Management to survey the organization of his branch of the government. The report of his Committee, a landmark of its kind in the annals of government, led the Congress to assign to the President the power to achieve a reorganization of the executive branch. The power was, however, granted only for two years and several agencies of the executive were exempted from its provision. The most important achievement under this act was the reconstruction of the President's own office described in the previous chapter. New grants of authority, largely confined to war agencies, were voted in 1941 and 1945 but durable achievements were few.

Hoover Commission

The triumph of the Republican party in the congressional election of 1946 ushered in a new era of administrative reform under the auspices of a party bent upon cutting the executive branch down to more "manageable" size. The Congress this time took the initiative and created and generously financed a Commission on Organization of the Executive Branch of the Government. This body, headed by ex-President Hoover, prepared and submitted to the Congress and to the President in 1949 the most comprehensive analysis and report on the subject in our history. It would be impossible even to summarize the 288 separate recommendations made by the Commission. Like its predecessors, this group insisted that authority to reorganize the executive branch must be vested in the President, and Hoover took the stand to support the broadest possible grant of such power to President Truman.

Reorganization Act of 1949

With this impressive support the Congress in 1949 voted the most sweeping reorganizing power ever granted to a President. No agencies were exempted from the President's authority as had been the case in all previous acts. However, the Congress insisted that the power must be limited as to time and provided for the expiration of such power on April 1, 1953. Congress also insisted that it must retain a veto on all presidential proposals as it had done in previous acts. In most previous acts, a presidential proposal could be killed by a concurrent resolution of disapproval passed by both houses within a specified time limit. In the act of 1949, a presidential plan could be nullified by a resolution of disapproval passed by a majority of the membership of either house within 60 days of its submission. President Truman during his term of office submitted plans to Congress and took other actions

The second Hoover Commission

within his power to achieve about half of the Commission's recommendations. President Eisenhower continued the effort. The reorganization authority under the Act of 1949 was extended repeatedly and for his entire service. A second Hoover Commission was established in 1953 and in a new series of reports in 1955 charted new paths for the future. A new department, Health, Education and Welfare, was created. President Kennedy also was granted reorganization power by extension of the Act of 1949 until 1963. He achieved a few successes, although most of his efforts to reorganize the independent commissions were thwarted by Congress. His effort to create a new department of urban affairs was also halted by Congress and in fact, the power to create a new department by executive order has been expressly denied to the President by Congress. Reorganizing authority as thus modified was granted to President Johnson by extension of the Act of 1949 until 1968. He achieved several changes, one of the most important of which was, in 1965, to abolish patronage in the Bureau of Customs.

The task of adjusting the organization of the executive branch is never completed. Although Congress has up to now insisted on placing time limits on the power of the President in this matter, it may well become by regular extension a normal attribute of presidential authority.

THE GROWTH OF MANAGEMENT SERVICES

Another consequence of the tremendous growth in the size of the executive branch has been the growth of those parts that facilitate management and provide services for the rest of the organization. Students and administrators customarily distinguish among the functions of an organization those that have directly to do with the purpose of the organization—called *line* functions—from those that serve purely internal needs—called variously *staff, overhead, auxiliary, housekeeping,* or *management service* functions. The men who work in the local post office sorting and delivering the mail, the soldiers in a combat division, the social workers calling upon the disabled, all of these are engaged in line functions. Those who keep the accounts of the Post Office Department, or administer the personnel procurement program, or handle the publicity of the department are engaged in management services. Some entire agencies and many bureaus are, in the modern executive branch, engaged in management service rather than line functions, and every agency has a substantial portion of its employes engaged in such functions. *[The difference between line functions and management services]*

Specialization of function and the development of techniques for each specialty are widely regarded as important keys to American industrial efficiency. Carried over into public administration, this conception has contributed to the growth of the managerial services. Fiscal administration, purchasing, personnel administration, legal advisement, public relations direction, space allocation, statistical analysis, procedures analysis, program planning, operations analysis, among others, are now considered the proper domain of technicians especially skilled in these functions and are separately and centrally organized in many of the large organizational units of the executive branch. The top-executive staff of each department, agency, or ad- *[Specialization and the growth of management services]* ministration, and of many bureaus and divisions includes these specialties and provides them to the rest of the organization.

The control exercised through the service functions

Although most of the expert practitioners of these managerial service functions profess the conception that these functions and processes are subservient to the line responsibilities of the organization, in practice these management assistants frequently influence and occasionally dominate the agency. These service functions are almost universally practiced quite near the seat of authority, whereas the line functions are often largely discharged at some field station or office miles from headquarters. Although it is undoubtedly true that the effective management of the executive branch would be impossible without central controls over the standard procedures for accounting, personnel transactions, and supply procurement, the growth of these functions in size, importance, and influence has created new difficulties in communicating the aspirations of the Congress and the President for effective public service throughout a large and far-flung organization. This growth has also reduced the proportion of the tax dollar which goes directly into alleviating distress, defending the nation, protecting the lives and property of our citizens, and husbanding our natural resources.

The public demand for internal controls over administration

It is but just to add at this point that the American people are themselves partly responsible for the controls exercised by the administrators of management services. Through Congress and the President, they have insisted that line administrators should not be allowed to hire and fire freely but should be required to observe the rules of the civil service merit system. They have also sought to achieve a higher standard of honesty of public officials by requiring that certain procedures (public bidding, for example) be observed whenever supplies or equipment are purchased by government agencies. They have insisted that the most rigorous audit be made of fiscal transactions and that unrelenting vigilance be exercised by corps of accountants on the expenditure of public funds. All of these requirements and many others enacted into law by Congress or imposed by executive order have contributed to the growth in numbers and influence of those officials who administer these laws and orders in the executive branch. Nowhere in our system of government is the public distrust of officialdom so patent and its consequences so clear. A large portion of the executive branch is expected to spend a good deal of time and money checking up on the rest of the branch.

ADMINISTRATIVE PROCEDURES

The procedures used by the executive branch to accomplish its objectives are as varied as the trees of the forest. They do not as readily lend themselves to classification and explication as those used by the courts or by the Congress. The success of any public program may well depend, however, on the procedure used to achieve it.

It is convenient as well as instructive to regard executive-branch methods from the vantage point of the amount of coercive authority or sanction associated with them. Throughout history, government has been closely identified, in the eyes of the governed, with coercive power. Traditionally, the method of public executives is arrest and the vehicle the police. The enforcement of law everywhere has had as its ultimate sanction fine, imprisonment, corporal punishment, death, or banishment. The detection and prosecution of law violators remains to this day one of the primary methods of executive government. Many governments, however, and particularly modern democratic ones, have tended to lay increasing stress on the prevention of antisocial behavior rather than the punishment of those found guilty of it. This objective requires far more complex and subtle methods of administration than does the traditional method of arrest. Furthermore, in the American system of government the state and local authorities, rather than the national executive, deal with most offenders against the traditional criminal laws. The Treasury Department's Secret Service and Coast Guard, the F.B.I., and the military police in the armed services, are almost the only real police forces in the national executive establishment. The Department of Justice through the district attorney in each judicial district is the chief prosecutor of offenders against national laws brought in by the various police officers of the executive branch.

1. Detection and prosecution of law violators

The offices of the courts are used extensively by the executive branch in civil litigation as well as criminal prosecution. The sanctions associated with litigation are impressive and include the assessment of costs, damages, and the expenses of the litigation itself. They are not so drastic, however, as those associated with criminal prosecution. Litigation is used by the government to collect money owed it by taxpayers or by contractors or for purchases of its services. It has also been relied upon heavily, although with indifferent success, to curb the development of monopoly in industrial organization and to enforce administratively determined orders upon business or labor organizations. Most administrators avoid litigation because of the expense of and the time consumed in judicial processes.

2. Litigation

A third coercive method widely used by the modern executive branch is adjudication. This is essentially a judicial procedure developed within the executive branch in order to achieve specialization of interest and greater flexibility than the regular court procedures provide. The independent regulatory commissions are the major, although not the exclusive, practitioners of adjudication. Typically, the process consists of advocates for the regulatory authority on the one hand and defenders of the regulatee on the other presenting their diverse views on the proper rates or services of the enterprises in question before a plural body which adjudges the case and issues appropriate orders. Most of the decisions thus reached by executive branch adjudicators are reviewable by the national courts. The process is similar but not identical to administrative legislation which is also practiced by these same agencies and consists in supplementing broad statutory policies by

3. Adjudication

specific rules binding upon the regulated enterprises. Adjudication is applying these rules to specific individual situations.

4. Inspection and licensure

Inspection accompanied in many instances by licensure is a fourth coercive method used extensively by the national executive. This is a genteel police method which frequently has as its purpose the achievement of proper conduct by the inspectee rather than his punishment for improper behavior. Government inspectors are used extensively to achieve proper working conditions in factories subject to national regulation, safety on board ship and in interstate transportation, safe and sanitary meat and food products moving in interstate commerce, safety in mines, and numerous other public purposes. The requirement of a license for the operation of or practice of some profession, vocation, or business enterprise adds the convenient sanction that, without criminal proceedings, the license may be revoked for violation of the laws governing the matter. In virtually all situations where licensure and inspection are used, the government has determined a minimum standard of conduct, cleanliness, health, or safety which it seeks to achieve throughout the nation. The inspectors attempt to make certain that the standard is observed.

5. Education

The change in the functions of the executive branch associated with the industrialization of the nation and with the attempt to insure a fairer distribution of the products of the national economy have accentuated those executive activities which are not coercive and which do not rely in the last analysis on the power of the government to punish transgressors. A high standard of public health, for example, can be achieved only if individuals voluntarily change their habits and customs. The improvement of agricultural production in which the government has played such a conspicuous role has been achieved largely without coercion of any kind. Education and exhortation rather than compulsion are coming more and more to be major methods of the national administration. They constitute its chief procedures as it seeks positively to improve the environment both physical and social for the welfare of its citizens. Education as here used is a broad term involving every type of persuasion from publishing brochures to operating demonstration farms and includes official exhortation; visitation by expert consultants, such as public health nurses, county agricultural agents, or social workers; operation of experimental laboratories; development of voluntary codes of business or advertising practice; organization of scientific conferences, and thousands of other similar activities not excluding the instruction of young people in classrooms. The teacher must thus be placed beside the policeman as the great executive agent of modern American government. Not only are educational procedures the major reliance of agencies like the Department of Agriculture and the Public Health Service, they are also more and more widely used to supplement, if not to replace, the methods of prosecution, litigation, adjudication, and inspection. The railroads of the United States are directed almost as much by informal nonlitigious conferences between railroad operators and I.C.C. agents as by the formal procedures for which that commission is so well known. It is fair to add that the educational methods seem to work best when accompanied by the power ultimately to invoke sanctions against those who do not respond to persuasion.

The executive branch of the government is not only engaged in transmitting information and urging individuals to better practice; it is also heavily engaged in discovering information. Research has become a large concern of the national administration. The conquest of disease, the improvement of our military striking power, the expansion of agricultural productivity are but a few of the continuing objects of research by scientists under the direction of the national executive. The national government is today the leading research institution in our country. *6. Research*

War is the ultimate compulsive method for conducting the foreign relations of any nation. Eschewing this, it must rely on the noncoercive method of negotiation to serve its interests beyond its shores. The practice of diplomacy accompanied the rise of the national state and has been a traditional function of states for several centuries. The method of negotiation, while practiced extensively by the Department of State, is by no means confined to it. The Departments of Defense, Commerce, and Agriculture, for example, are extensively involved in our foreign relations. The processes of negotiation, which are essentially the dealing across the table of equals, are also used in internal matters, for example, to achieve peaceful settlement of labor disputes, to purchase land for public use, and to determine state–national responsibilities in connection with grant-in-aid programs. *7. Negotiation*

This brief catalogue by no means exhausts the repertoire of executive agencies in attempting to realize public policies. It does, however, point up the fact that the executive is not only an enforcement agent and that new government functions require new methods for their successful administration.

PERSONNEL ADMINISTRATION

The quality of administration of the national government depends, in the last analysis, on the quality of the officers and employees of the executive departments and agencies. Effective organization, appropriate procedures, and suitable authority are secondary to the ability of the individuals who comprise this vast institution. The survival of the American system of government may well depend upon its ability to attract and to hold the ablest members of our society. No system of administrative audits, no amount of congressional investigation, no inspirational leadership from the President could quite compensate for mediocre, unimaginative, or time-serving public employes. Certainly a decisive determinant of the responsiveness of the executive department to the principles of the American system of constitutional democracy is the character and ability of the men and women who comprise it. *Importance of proper personnel selection*

For a generation or more after the national government was organized, the selection of public employes was largely based on character and fitness. *Civil service reform*

The rise of political parties, the limited resources of many of their functionaries, and the exigencies of campaigning soon fastened the spoils system of partisan selection upon the national administration. Throughout most of the past century, it was the predominant mode of selection. Every change in the Presidency was accompanied by a wholesale replacement of public officers and employes. Despite the stubborn defense of its supporters and the strong arguments which could be mustered in its behalf, the system nevertheless fell into increasing disrepute after 1865. It was widely associated with the politics of graft and favoritism. Public-spirited reformers, organized in The National Civil Service Reform League, pressed their attacks with increasing vigor. Finally, when the nation had been stirred by the assassination of President Garfield by a disappointed place hunter, the modern merit system of selection was established.

Establishment of the merit system   The Civil Service Act of 1883 provided that admission to certain positions would henceforth be solely on the basis of open, competitive examinations of a practical character testing the abilities of the applicant for the position sought. A bipartisan Civil Service Commission was established to

COMPETITIVE CIVIL SERVICE JOBS IN THE NATIONAL GOVERNMENT

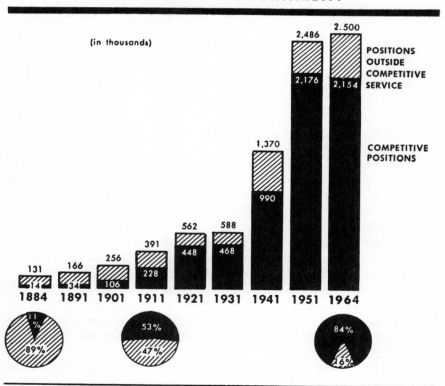

SOURCE: U. S. Civil Service Commission.

administer the examinations and to police the service against wrongful removal, partisan selection, or unauthorized campaign solicitation from or electioneering by employes covered by the law. As enacted, the law extended only to 14,000 positions or about one-tenth of the total executive branch. In the years since 1883, the provisions of the act have been extended by statute and executive order to virtually the entire branch. Today (1968) all but 350,000 out of 2,500,000 are filled under its provisions. Of those outside the competitive system, however, a great majority are in the Foreign Service, the F.B.I., the Central Intelligence Agency, and other agencies with very high standards of merit selection. Not many more than 20,000 posts may be filled by partisan procedures.

The primary object of the Civil Service Act of 1883 and the later amendments, executive orders, and new statutes extending its provisions throughout the executive branch has been to promote appointment on the basis of tested capacity and to assure those thus appointed reasonable security during proper performance of their duties.

The opportunity for appointment has, however, always been limited by law in ways not necessarily related to merit. Applicants must be citizens; there must be some apportionment of appointees among the states; veterans are given preferences of various kinds; and there must be no taint of subversive activities or associations on the part of prospective employes. Furthermore, heavy, although not exclusive, reliance is placed on tests of various kinds designed to measure knowledge of the duties of the position to be filled. Experience has indicated that tests of general rather than special knowledge are likely to be more effective in bringing able and well-educated young people into the government. *Appointment under the merit system*

Although every employe is liable to disciplinary actions at the hands of some superior authority, every effort has been made to protect merit system employes from partisan or capricious dismissal. Until 1939, dismissal could not be based on political opinions but Cold War emergencies have produced "loyalty" requirements aimed at eliminating from the service those of "subversive" or "tainted" associations. Merit employes are also forbidden to take active part in political campaigning or in the management of party affairs. *Protection of employes from partisan influences*

THE ENFORCEMENT OF RESPONSIBILITY

The American system of government is built upon an abiding hatred for bureaucracy and a deep-seated distrust of officialdom. It is not surprising, therefore, that the growth of the national executive has been viewed with concern in many quarters. Is it possible, the critics ask, for such an army of public officials with such a large share of the national income at their disposal to submit to direction from the voters and their representatives? Will they not rather seek to dominate the Congress by favors and the public by propaganda? How can the executive agencies, manned as they are largely by persons with permanent tenure, be made responsible to the elected officials and responsive to public opinion?

Presidential direction

The principal safeguard against the rise of an irresponsible bureaucracy built into the executive branch itself is the position of the President. The elected Presidency is essentially a political office responsible to the voters and vested by the Constitution with the executive power. By custom of long standing, presidential direction of the executive agencies is supported by a cadre of his political lieutenants at the helm of each agency and in command of the major channels of authority and communication. The top management of each agency changes office with each change in the national administration and thus, fresh from an election triumph, can be said to enjoy the confidence of the public. Only the independent commissions are insulated against this kind of direction. The authority of the political managers of the executive branch is weakened in practice by their inexperience and by their lack of technical competence. They must perforce rely upon the experienced technicians of their agencies for guidance. Traditionally, this guidance is supplied fully and freely regardless of the political views held by either individual. For this too is part of the American tradition, that the professional civil servant will serve any master placed over him by vote of the people.

Congressional oversight

The second great safeguard against government by technicians is the constitutional and customary powers of the Congress. Money may not be spent by executive agencies except on the basis of congressional appropriation. Each year the administration must pray Congress to grant the funds necessary for its programs and each year must, in consequence, account to the Congress for its conduct. This great power of Congress is weakened in practice by the enormous complexity of the financial structure of the national government and, in consequence, by the fact that few congressmen are familiar with more than a small portion of the total appropriations. It is nevertheless quite an impressive power in molding executive agency policy. The Congress prescribes not only the programs and policies which the administration will pursue but also the organizational structure and the procedures for pursuing them. The practices of Congress in exercising this power have tended to weaken presidential direction of his own branch and tend to diffuse responsibility for performance. They nevertheless represent a real brake upon agency expansion and agency indifference to public desires. The Senate, as we have seen, participates in the appointment of numerous offices in the executive branch. Through the power of investigation the Congress may review the conduct of any executive agency in which it is interested. No legislative process is held in such great fear by the executive branch as the investigating one. None has been so abused by the Congress nor been so effectual in cleaning out a corrupt or incompetent agency.

Judicial review

There is an impressive body of opinion in the United States, held mainly by members of the legal profession, that the principal safeguard against the rise of an irresponsible bureaucracy is the power of the national courts to review the acts and decisions of officials of the executive branch.

Under the American system of jurisprudence most of the actions, threatened or accomplished, of administrators are reviewable by ordinary courts of law. This review customarily extends to the validity of the law on which the action is based as well as to the action itself. This type of control over administrative behavior is designed to assure conformity to constitutional prescriptions regarding personal and property rights and regarding the allocation of governmental powers between the nation and the states and among the several branches of the government. Judicial review is a device for assuring not responsiveness to democratic processes but obedience to the Constitution. It is intended to make men subservient to laws, not necessarily to other men who happen to enjoy public confidence.

The practice of judicial review of administrative decisions is much less clear-cut than the principle. Congress has from time to time endowed administrative agencies, notably the independent regulatory commissions, with powers of a judicial character (referred to by the lawyers as *quasi-judicial*). It has also attempted to limit the power of the courts to review certain types of administrative actions. It has conferred lawmaking power on many agencies confined only by the most general standards.

REFERENCES

American Assembly, *The Federal Government Service: Its Character, Prestige, and Problems* (New York, 1954).

P. Appleby, *Big Democracy* (New York, 1945).

————, *Policy and Administration* (Univ. of Alabama, 1949).

M. H. Bernstein, *The Job of the Federal Executive* (Washington, D. C., 1958).

J. C. Charlesworth, *Governmental Administration* (New York, 1951).

J. J. Corsun and R. S. Paul, *Men Near the Top: Filling Key Positions in the Federal Service* (Baltimore, 1966).

Commission on Organization of the Executive Branch of the Government, *Reports to Congress* and *Task Force Reports* (Washington, D. C., 1955), published separately.

P. T. David and R. Pollock, *Executives for Government: Central Issues of Federal Personnel Administration* (Washington, D. C., 1957).

B. M. Gross, *The Managing of Organizations* (New York, 1964).

J. D. Millett, *Government and Public Administration; the Quest for Responsible Performance* (New York, 1959).

————, *Management in the Public Service* (New York, 1954).

J. M. Pfiffner and R. V. Presthus, *Public Administration* (4th ed., New York, 1960).

N. J. Powell, *Personnel Administration in Government* (New York, 1958).

President's Committee on Administrative Management, *Report of the Committee, with studies of Administrative Management in the Federal Government* (Washington, D. C., 1937).

O. G. Stahl, *Public Personnel Administration* (New York, 1962).

P. P. Van Riper, *History of the United States Civil Service* (White Plains, N. Y., 1958).

L. D. White, *The Federalist; A Study in Administrative History* (New York, 1948).

———, *The Jacksonians; A Study in Administrative History* (New York, 1955).

———, *The Jeffersonians; A Study in Administrative History* (New York, 1951).

———, *The Republican Era, 1869–1901; A Study in Administrative History* (New York, 1958).

P. Woll, *American Bureaucracy* (New York, 1963).

14

THE NATIONAL JUDICIARY

The judicial power of the United States shall be vested in one Supreme Court and in such inferior courts as the Congress may from time to time ordain and establish.—Art. III, Sec. 1

The crowning defect of the Articles of Confederation, declared Alexander Hamilton in *The Federalist,* was "the want of a judicial power"; and in planning a "more perfect union" the framers of the Constitution asserted in the preamble their purpose to "establish justice" and went on in Article III to place full judicial power alongside of executive and legislative power as one of the three main pillars of the national authority. In so doing they prepared the way for the establishment of a system of national courts, separate from the state courts, and deriving its existence and jurisdiction solely from the Constitution. When to these provisions the framers added (Art. VI) that this Constitution and the laws and treaties made under it were to be the "supreme law" of the land, binding judges in state courts, regardless of the provisions of state laws or constitutions, they laid the foundation for a national court system superior to all other courts and obliged to interpret and apply the supreme law in a uniform manner throughout the nation.

A separate national system of courts

SCOPE OF THE NATIONAL JUDICIAL POWER

Judicial power has been defined as the power to decide "cases" and "controversies" in conformity with law and by the methods established by the law. The important words in this definition are *cases* and *controversies*. Unlike the President and the Congress, courts do not initiate actions; they dispose of matters brought before them on the initiative of outsiders. They are powerless to influence the conduct of government except as they rule for or against the executive branch when it is one of the parties to a contest

Nature of judicial power

or as they construe the laws and orders uttered by the other branches as an incident to determining the relative merits of the claims of the litigants. In a system of government based upon a written constitution, however, the ultimate power to declare what the constitution means in any given situation is a very important power indeed whether it is exercised incidentally to the discharge of some other function or not.

The nature of the judicial function was determined early in our national history when the Supreme Court decided that it could not give legal advice either to the President or to Congress. Its only function was to decide lawsuits properly brought before it. In deciding lawsuits, the courts must say what the law is that must be applied to any controversy before them and this obligation requires that they interpret statutes, treaties, executive orders, constitutions, and judicial precedents. The other branches of the government are constitutionally obliged to defer to the views of the courts. Under our system, a court is entitled to have its decisions reviewed and perhaps reversed only by a *higher court.* Judicial power has also come to embrace the authority to support valid findings of administrative agencies with orders which can be ignored only at the peril of fine or imprisonment for "contempt of court." The national courts have, however, acquiesced in allowing what they regard as questions of "fact" to be determined in some situations by agencies of the executive branch and questions which are "political" to be determined with finality by either or both of the other two coordinate branches of the government.

Marginal judicial activities

It would be quite wrong to suppose on the basis of what has been said that national judges have no other function save presiding over legal contests. Our national courts have become increasingly the managers of important business enterprises through their power in bankruptcy proceedings, for example, to appoint receivers responsible to them for the management of assets pending the outcome of litigation. Many judges thus find themselves engaged in the operation of railroads, mines, and factories and obliged to deal with all the problems of these enterprises which harass business executives. The rehabilitation and correction programs of the Federal Bureau of Prisons involve the judges in the affairs of prisoners sometimes for many years after trial and conviction. The national judges, like their counterparts in the states, marry and naturalize individuals as well as perform many other functions which are called judicial but are not necessarily litigious.

Basis of national jurisdiction:

It should be clear at this stage of our study that the national government created by the Constitution has only enumerated powers. This is true of the national courts as well as of the legislature. Jurisdiction, the power to hear and to determine, is conferred upon the courts only over certain kinds of cases and controversies. The state courts have jurisdiction over all

1. Nature of the controversy

others and even over some that the national courts may try. The national judicial authority is extended by the Constitution to certain classes of cases on the basis of the subject matter of the controversy and to other classes on the basis of the status of the parties concerned. The first class includes (1) all cases in law and equity arising under the Constitution, laws, and treaties of the United States, and (2) all cases of admiralty and maritime jurisdiction. Whenever in any law suit a legal right is asserted which is based upon some provision of the Constitution, national laws, or treaties, the case may be tried in the courts of the United States. Admiralty and maritime jurisdiction has to do with offenses committed on shipboard and with contracts which must be executed on the high seas or on navigable waters of the United States. Prize cases are also included in the scope of national judicial power.

2. Status of the parties

The category of cases assigned to the courts of the United States because of the status of the parties includes (1) all cases affecting ambassadors and other public ministers and consuls; (2) controversies to which the United States is a party; (3) controversies between two or more states; (4) controversies between citizens of different states; and (5) controversies between a state, or the citizens thereof, and foreign states, citizens, or subjects where the state is the party plaintiff.

Congressional power over jurisdiction

The assignment of certain classes of cases to the courts of the United States by the Constitution does not of itself confer power over all of these matters. Rather the Constitution specifies the limits beyond which power may not be conferred, and Congress may or may not endow the courts with all of the power within the constitutional limits. Congress thus possesses the authority to limit the jurisdiction of the courts. Congress originally conferred only a portion of the jurisdiction. Throughout most of the last century Congress gradually added to the jurisdiction until it had conferred all that the Constitution contemplated. In this century the jurisdiction has been somewhat contracted. In several types of cases, for example, Congress has prescribed that the amount in controversy must exceed a certain sum before the litigants may use the national courts.

Jurisdiction shared with state courts

Much of the jurisdiction which has been conferred by the Congress is shared with state courts. The national courts, in other words, do not have exclusive authority over it. In general, only in cases in which the United States or a state is a party (unless the action is between a state and one of its own citizens), or which involve the representatives of foreign governments, a crime against the United States, or admiralty, maritime, patent, copyright, or bankruptcy laws, do the courts of the United States have complete and exclusive jurisdiction. In virtually all other types of cases to which the judicial power extends, the plaintiff may begin his case in either a state or a national court.

KINDS OF CASES TRIED

The types of actions brought in the courts of the United States fall into the two broad categories, civil and criminal, into which are classified the actions brought in the state courts as well. With a few unusual exceptions, the same courts and judges handle both types of cases.

The criminal actions brought in the national courts represent a small

1. Crim-
inal
actions
in the
courts
of the
United
States

proportion of the total number of criminal prosecutions in this country. The vast majority of all criminal offenses are state offenses and the offenders are brought to the bar by state and local enforcement officers and are tried by state judges. The only concern of the national courts with these cases is to enforce upon state courts the guarantee of a fair trial which has been construed to be required by the Fourteenth Amendment. Authority to try criminal actions in the first instance is lodged in the courts of the United States only for offenses against the United States or against the laws of the United States as defined by Congress and the Constitution. The Constitution mentions only piracy, counterfeiting, treason, violation of international law, and offenses in the territories and dependencies of the United States. Congress, however, typically prescribes penalties for violation of the laws it enacts and thus the United States Code includes, among others, such crimes as mail fraud, smuggling, sabotage, and election fraud, which are clearly incidental to its powers to establish post offices, regulate imports, wage war, and regulate national elections.

2. Civil
actions

The most numerous category of actions tried in the national courts are civil actions, usually between two private parties but frequently with the United States government as one of the parties. Civil actions ordinarily arise out of civil wrongs, called torts, and breaches of contract. Torts include such wrongful actions as trespass, property damage, negligence, libel, and assault.

a. At law

In settling civil disputes the national courts apply state law as well as national law. Cases which get into the national courts because of the diversity of the citizenship of the parties, for example, may involve only the application of state law. This state law may be either statutory (enacted by a state or local legislative body) or common law (the system of judge-made law brought to America from England and modified here by the decisions of American judges and by legislation).

b. In
equity

The national courts also have equity jurisdiction, the power to interpret and apply the law of equity to appropriate civil actions. Equity is a branch of Anglo-American jurisprudence which developed side by side with the common law and as a supplement to it, designed to provide substantial justice in a large number of situations to which the strict application of the forms of action and procedures of the common law would result in unnecessary hardship. The typical redress, for example, available under common and statutory law is money damages and it is granted only after the wrongful action has transpired and the injured party can show his "wounds." Equity jurisdiction provides legal remedies for many situations in which money damages are not appropriate or come too late to be helpful. Thus the court of equity may issue orders (writs of injunction) which forbid certain actions which would cause immeasurable or irreparable damage if committed. The court of equity may issue decrees of "specific performance" requiring a party to a contract to live up to his bargain, for example, by delivering the race horse he promised when the other party is willing to pay the money and thus a damage award would be useless. To the ordinary citizen the distinction between law and equity is of no major consequence; both are administered in the same courtroom by the same judge, sometimes on the same day. Lawyers, however, frequently prefer equity to civil law procedures because there is no jury in equity and because the procedures are less hedged about by technical formalities.

We have noted that the national courts administer statutory law, the common law, and the law of equity. They also administer international law —the law among nations based upon treaties, agreements, and other types of international understandings—and admiralty law—the law of the high seas and navigable waters of the United States based upon the technical rules of an admiralty code developed over many centuries by English and American legislatures, courts, and administrative agencies.

c. In international law

d. In admiralty law

The procedure used by the national courts in trying all of these different types of cases is largely devised by the courts themselves. The constitution, as we have seen, prescribes a number of requirements for criminal actions designed to protect individuals from unfair or unwarranted prosecution and conviction. The Congress has from time to time regulated the procedure by statute and many of the present rules are incorporated in the United States Code. The power to make rules governing civil procedure in the courts of the United States has repeatedly, however, been delegated to the Supreme Court, and in 1940 a similar power over criminal procedure was delegated to this body. In formulating its rules, the Court relies heavily on advisory committees representing both bench and bar.

Legal procedure for trying cases

STRUCTURE OF THE NATIONAL JUDICIAL SYSTEM

The national judiciary comprises three levels of tribunals. All of these have been established by Congress and none except the Supreme Court is specifically mentioned in the Constitution.

The lowest level of courts is the district or trial courts. The 50 states are divided into 88 districts for the purpose of providing a trial court within easy reach of litigants. Each state embraces at least one district. There is also a district court for the District of Columbia and one for Puerto Rico. Each of these courts is manned by from one to 24 judges, depending mainly on the volume of litigation but also, of course, on the pleasure of Congress. Whatever the number of judges, each holds court separately, except for certain unusual occasions, and the chief justice of the United States may (since 1922) transfer judges temporarily from one district to another to assist in relieving accumulated backlogs of cases. Virtually every judge is aided by a law clerk in reviewing the legal problems presented for his consideration and the staff of the court also, typically, includes clerks who preside over the records and calendars; reporters who take the proceedings; criers; and other functionaries. Attached to each district is a district attorney who, under the direction of the Department of Justice, conducts criminal

1. District courts

prosecutions, a marshal who executes the orders and serves the papers of the court, a number of referees in bankruptcy and commissioners who hold preliminary hearings in criminal cases.

Jurisdic-
tion
The volume of business brought to the district courts is large; approximately 100,000 cases are handled yearly. All offenses against the laws of the United States are tried there. These criminal cases are given priority by the courts and the dockets are normally up-to-date. All civil actions arising under the Constitution, laws, or treaties of the United States ("federal questions") may originate in the district courts as may all cases based upon the "diversity of citizenship" of the parties, but in both types of cases the amount in controversy must exceed $10,000 for the national courts to have jurisdiction. The original jurisdiction of the district courts extends also to a variety of civil actions regardless of the amount involved, for example, cases in admiralty, bankruptcy proceedings, patents, copyrights, postal laws, and nationally protected civil rights. Despite the addition of a large number of new judges the disposition of civil actions in the district courts is seriously delayed. For some time these courts have been about a year behind in their dockets. Most cases begun in the district court also end there. But appeals may be taken from their decisions to the courts of appeals and in a few cases, for example, where the district court has held an act of Congress unconstitutional, directly to the Supreme Court. The district courts, themselves, have no appellate jurisdiction. Cases appealed from the decisions of state high courts go directly to the Supreme Court; they do not start all over again at the bottom of the national hierarchy.

2. Courts
of appeal
The intermediate courts of appeals which today handle the great bulk of appellate work in the national judicial system did not achieve their present status until 1911. For most of the past century, circuit courts shared original jurisdiction with the district courts and handled some appeals. Originally one justice of the Supreme Court was assigned to each circuit into which the nation was divided, and together with the district judges held circuit court. The rapidly mounting dockets of the Supreme Court gradually made this duty of the judges more and more impractical and the confusion of having two courts of original jurisdiction led the Congress finally in 1891 to create nine circuit courts of appeals. These new courts divided the appellate work with the Supreme Court. In 1911 the circuit courts were at long last abolished, leaving the district courts virtually all of the original jurisdiction of the national judiciary. Since 1948, the intermediate courts created in 1891 have been designated simply "courts of appeals." The nation is now divided into eleven judicial circuits, including one for the District of Columbia, with a court of appeals in each. Each court is composed of from three to nine judges and at least two are required to consider any case.

Functions
With every form of original hearing excluded, the work of the courts of appeals consists in hearing appeals from the decisions of the district courts within the respective circuits and of enforcing the determinations of na-

tional regulating agencies such as the Federal Trade Commission and the National Labor Relations Board. Appeals are carried to these courts from the district courts as a matter of right and the judges have little or no discretion in the matter. In keeping with the long-term trend of relieving the Supreme Court of much of the burden of appellate work, the decisions of the courts of appeals are final in the vast majority of the cases brought to them. Review of the decisions of courts of appeals by the Supreme Court is largely at the discretion of the latter and occurs in few cases. Only in cases in which the appeals court holds a state statute contrary to the Constitution, laws, or treaties of the United States does appeal lie to the Supreme Court as a matter of right. In all others appeal is at the pleasure of the Supreme Court.

At the top of the system stands our most august tribunal, the Supreme Court of the United States. In its infancy this tribunal showed little or no promise of becoming the powerful institution it now is. President Washington found it difficult to keep the six judgeships filled with able men. Under Chief Justice Marshall (1801–1835), however, the power and prestige of the Court grew by giant strides. His great decisions establishing judicial review and enlarging the authority of the central government over the states provided the basis of the centralizing tendencies which have characterized our system ever since. Under his guiding hand the Court not only served notice on the states of its determination to strike down every local obstruction to the achievement of union but informed the other two branches of the national government of its intention to hold them to their proper functions. Through many periods of weakness as well as strength, the Court has developed into our most independent agency of power, the one most removed from popular influence.

3. The Supreme Court

a. Development

Originally, the Court was composed of a chief justice and five associate justices. The total number, as fixed by Congress, has since been as high as ten, although for about a century now it has been nine. All who have served at least ten years may retire on full salary at age 70. Although receiving slightly more pay, the chief justice has no more legal weight or influence in deciding cases than any of his associates. He presides over the sessions of the Court, assigns to his associates the task of writing the Court's opinions, and writes many of them himself. He appoints members to serve on committees which revise the rules of procedure and has many administrative duties in connection with the whole judicial system.

b. Membership

Regular and public terms, or sessions, of the Court are held annually in the new Supreme Court building adjacent to the Capitol, beginning on the first Monday in October and ending at the close of the following May or June. Six justices must be present at the argument of a case, and any decision must be concurred in by a majority of those hearing the matter— in other words, by at least four justices. If a majority cannot be obtained for a decision, a rehearing may be ordered, but an evenly divided court on a

c. Sessions and quorum

question of reversing a lower court has the effect of upholding the earlier decision. During a typical term of court, about 2 500 cases are considered and about 100 written opinions issued.

d. How the Court works

Americans commonly think of their government as built on plain republican principles and as lacking the pomp and circumstance of European institutions. A view of the Supreme Court in operation will quickly dispel this myth. Ensconced in its Greek temple, the Court marches daily to its task at 10:00 A.M., announced to the standing audience by cries of acclaim. Seated in high-backed chairs at an enormous elevated "bench," behind them marble columns and red velour drapes, the black-robed justices hear the polite and honorific diction of learned pleaders. These counselors, dressed in morning clothes, supplement their elaborately printed briefs with oral arguments from a central lectern well below the level of the seated dignitaries. Occasionally the worshipful attention of the ten score of spectators is aroused as a justice addresses a question or two to the earnest pleader. A century ago the chamber of the Court rang with the orotund and interminable rhetoric of Webster and Calhoun, who argued and pleaded with the Court not for hours but for days. The press of business, however, has compelled counsel to put more in the brief and less in the delivery, and oral argument is now limited to one hour. Arguments are heard on a series of cases and then the Court recesses for research and reflection. Currently, conferences of the justices are held on Fridays and it is at these meetings that the Court arrives at its decisions. When a point of view is finally agreed to by the requisite majority, the chief justice if he agrees with the majority designates some member of this group to write the opinion of the Court. After review by others, the opinion is read at an ensuing Monday sitting of the Court and becomes a part of the documentary history of the American system of government.

e. Concurring and dissenting opinions

The opinion of the Court ordinarily sets forth the line of reasoning by which the justices arrived at the conclusion. One or more members of the majority may have arrived at the same decision by a different line of argument and may be impelled to present a "concurring" opinion which supports the decision but offers different grounds. The minority, if any, has the privilege of presenting its views to the public in one or more "dissenting" opinions. Occasionally these have stimulated more concern than the majority opinion and, in some cases, the Court has swung around to accepting as decisive the arguments of the dissenters. All of the opinions are a part of the record and are published by the government in a series of volumes called *United States Reports,* prepared under the supervision of a Court reporter.

f. Jurisdiction

Cases come before the Supreme Court in one of three ways: (1) by original suit; (2) by appeal from the decision of a lower court; and (3) by certiorari or discretionary review of a lower court decision. The three are of very unequal importance. By far the largest share of cases get before the Court by certiorari. The original jurisdiction of the Supreme Court is set forth in the Constitution and includes cases affecting the representatives of foreign governments and cases in which a state is a party. Its jurisdiction is exclusive, however, only in controversies between two or more states and in actions against representatives of foreign states. It also has original but not exclusive jurisdiction in actions brought by ministers of foreign states, in controversies between the United States and a state, and in actions by a state against aliens or against citizens of another state. This jurisdiction may be regulated and has been by Congress as to its exclusive character but it may not be validly enlarged except by constitutional amendment. The only part of this original jurisdiction which has proved significant is that involving suits by one state against another.

The right of appeal to the Supreme Court is sharply limited and extends only to those few categories of cases already mentioned which have been decided by the highest state courts, the courts of appeals, and the district courts of the United States. Even in these cases the right of appeal is not absolute, for the Court may dismiss an appeal if the question involved is "insubstantial." With increasing frequency the Court has been doing just that. Most cases are brought to the Court by certiorari procedure. The history of this aspect of the judicial system has been one of progressive expansion of the Court's certiorari or discretionary jurisdiction and contraction of its "obligatory" jurisdiction. The rules of the Supreme Court indicate that review of lower court decisions by certiorari procedures is to be granted only when there are special or important reasons for it. Some of the circumstances which induce the Court to review are (1) that the case involves an important principle of constitutional or statutory construction; (2) that the case involves a conflict of interpretation of law among the courts of appeals; (3) that a state high court has decided a "federal question" of substance not before determined by the Supreme Court and probably contrary to the tenor of Supreme Court decisions. In general, the Supreme Court is thus relatively free to select from among all of the cases urged upon it only those cases upon which it wishes to pronounce. Typically, it now rejects from 70 to 85 percent of all requests for review by certiorari, frequently without any explanation of its reasons. Despite assertion of the judges that denial of certiorari means only that fewer than four judges thought the case ought to be heard, many members of bar, bench, and public interpret denial as support of the lower court's decision. Thus even the negative aspects of the work of the Court may have far-reaching implications. The figures already cited indicate that even with its crowded docket the Court decides a small proportion of the total number of cases which enter the courts of the United States or which might arise from the high courts of the states.

Certiorari procedure

JUDICIAL INDEPENDENCE AND ITS LIMITATIONS

While deliberately interlocking the executive and legislative branches of the government by numerous checks and balances, the Constitution's

Compensation and tenure

framers designed the judicial branch to enjoy a high degree of independence. It is most unlikely that our national courts could have successfully asserted the power to review the actions of the other branches had they not occupied a position from which they were hard to control. The constitutional corner-stones of judicial freedom are (1) that all national judges "hold their offices during good behavior," and (2) that their compensation may "not be diminished during their continuance in office." The latter provision, intended to protect them from a hostile Congress, has always been observed to the letter. The life tenure provisions has normally been observed also.

Courts gain independence also from the fact that the Congress has always had a large complement of lawyers among its members. Lawyers by training are accustomed to defer to the pronouncements of judges. Our people, too, have approved the freedom accorded our courts as is demon-strated by the strong disposition of the voters to return judges to office again and again when, as in the states, they have the opportunity of electing them. The successful assertion of the power authoritatively to construe the Constitution, and thus to prescribe the limits on the powers of the other branches of government, has provided the courts with a potent weapon to resist any aggressive thrusts in their direction by Congress or the President. At the same time, no valid power is lodged in any other branch to construe or limit the power of the courts. None of its decisions can be appealed; none of its members can be easily intimidated by threats of removal. The late Chief Justice Stone once remarked that the only check on the Supreme Court is the judges' own "sense of self-restraint."

Limita-tions:

1. Im-peachment

The courts are not, however, perfectly free. There are some important limitations on the actual and potential power of the national judiciary. In the first place, it is possible to remove a judge from office. He may be im-peached for and convicted of "treason, bribery, or other high crimes and misdemeanors." In other words, a national judge is subject to the same procedure as other national civil officers. Although the constitutional im-peachment procedure is largely unworkable except for the most flagrant cases of official wrongdoing nevertheless it has been used against judges more than against any other officials. In all, nine members of the judiciary have been impeached and four convicted.

2. Con-gressional control over the structure of the courts

In the second place, Congress has relatively large powers to create courts, determine the number of judges, fix their salaries, and establish the range of their jurisdictions. This means that Congress can abolish courts (ex-cept the Supreme Court), reduce the number of judges, and curtail the num-ber and kinds of cases they may hear. In practice, Congress has influenced or attempted to influence the decision of the Supreme Court by increas-ing the number of judges on that bench in order that enough "right-minded" new ones might be appointed to alter the anticipated decision. It has also deprived the Supreme Court of its appellate jurisdiction in a given class of cases because it anticipated a "bad" decision on an issue it regarded as vital. Both of these things occurred during the Civil War–Reconstruction period and, of course, are not typical of the relations between the two branches. They are illustrative, however, of what an aroused Congress, presumably supported by public opinion, can do. The creation in 1801 of a large number of new judgeships and then the appointment of partisan Federalists to them in order to ensure continuing control over at least one branch of the government by a party which had been repudiated at the polls, and the subsequent abolition of most of these posts by the Jeffersonians, is an illustration from our earlier history of congressional and executive attempts to influence the judiciary for partisan purposes. Most of the recent changes in the structure of the court system have been relatively free of this type of motivation. The attempt by President Roosevelt and his followers in Congress in 1937 to achieve a more "sympathetic" Supreme Court by legislative reconstruction was defeated by the Congress. The remarkable change in the outlook of the Supreme Court which accompanied the controversy has, however, usually been regarded as a victory for the President in the real war despite the loss of the battle in the Congress.

The major influence of the political and responsive branches of the government over the judiciary stems from the method of selection of judges. The Constitution provides that national judges are to be appointed by the President, by and with the advice and consent of the Senate. From the first development of factions in our government, Presidents have been strongly motivated to select men of their own faction or party to serve on the national bench. Many of our chief executives have also been deeply concerned not only with the political affiliation of their nominees but with their constitutional philosophies. It should be clear to the student of our institutions that the Constitution does not always speak for itself in clear and unmistakable language and even our wisest statesmen have differed about what it means. Presidents appear to desire that their appointees to the bench agree with them on fundamentals. There have, of course, been exceptions and Presidents have on occasion, willingly or unwillingly, elevated to judgeships illustrious men of the opposite party or of contrary constitutional views. These are exceptions, however, not the rule. It is interesting to note that prior judicial experience has rarely been considered an essential qualification for appointment.

3. Partisan considerations in appointments

There are two important considerations which mitigate the effectiveness of presidential influence over the judiciary. Once appointed, as many Presidents have learned to their chagrin, the judge obtains life tenure and thus safe from presidential ire, may change his mind about some of the issues. Secondly, few Presidents get an opportunity to appoint as many as a majority of the members of the Supreme Court. Furthermore, the Senate has got to be considered in the appointment process. The dominant party in the Senate is probably as interested as is the President in naming "right-thinking" judges to the bench. It occasionally happens that the President and the Senate do not agree. The President has to select an individual who will also be acceptable to the leaders of the Senate. In the lower courts of

the United States, the President is narrowly confined in his appointing prerogatives by the practice of "senatorial courtesy." National judgeships are
now customarily regarded as patronage for the senator or other state party
leader in whose state the court is located. Under these conditions, new appointments to the lower and intermediate courts of the United States are
invariably made from loyal supporters of the party in control in Washington.
It goes without saying that the fitness of the individual for judicial office will
not always be weighed as carefully as it might be. It is curious to note that
despite the political and even partisan influences on the selection of judges,
our courts are still widely supposed to be free of the taint of partisanship.

*4. Enforce-
ment of
court
processes*
We have already explained that the courts must rely on others to
bring them the business that they get. The executive branch, for example,
brings all criminal cases and a large number of civil actions. More important, however, is the fact that the courts have no substantial enforcing
agency even for their own decisions. They must rely on the executive branch
to back up their orders if the recipients are unwilling to respect the commands of the United States marshals who serve the courts' papers. An
uncooperative President has been able on a few occasions to frustrate the
authority of the Court by refusing to be diligent in enforcing its decisions.
The most famous example of this was the refusal of President Jackson to
enforce against a recalcitrant officialdom of the State of Georgia (1831–
1832) a decision of the Supreme Court abrogating an attempt by the state
to ignore its treaty obligations to the Cherokee Indians. A good illustration
from modern times of the great difficulties in the way of enforcing a controversial decision is the effort to achieve desegregation of races in public
schools discussed earlier in this volume. The prestige and independence
of the judiciary may thus be compromised by executive inaction or indifference and by congressional or local opposition.

THE SUPREME COURT AND JUDICIAL REVIEW

In deciding cases and controversies, all courts are obliged to consider
whether the legal claims at issue are based upon laws which are consistent
with relevant constitutional provisions. It thus becomes the most important
and distinctive function of the Supreme Court of the United States to pass
finally on the constitutional validity of state laws, state constitutions, laws
of Congress, and executive actions. In performing this function it stands as
the guardian of the boundaries which separate the legitimate powers of the
three branches of the national government as well as those which separate
the powers of the national government as a whole from those of the states
and of the people. The origin of this function of judicial review and its importance in strengthening the national government in relation to the state
have already been discussed. We have noted that the Constitution itself does
not expressly confer this power on the Court and there have always been

those who regarded its exercise as sheer usurpation. But from John Marshall's day to this it has become a settled part of the American system of government and most statesmen throughout our history have regarded it as not only a desirable but a necessary concomitant of a written constitution and a scheme of limited government with divided powers. Our people have also largely accepted it and even have acclaimed it. It is one of the unique contributions of the people of the United States to the art of constitutional self-government.

Since the jurisdiction of the Supreme Court has come to be largely discretionary, the great majority of cases which the Court now hears involve the constitutionality of some action by some branch of the national or a state government. The review of state action stands upon a somewhat different basis, insofar as its effect upon our constitutional system is concerned, than the review of national actions. In earlier days this was the form which judicial review customarily took, and long lists of state laws and even some state constitutional provisions have been struck down by the Supreme Court as contrary to the Constitution of the United States. It is hard to imagine how any major principle of government could be uniformly applied throughout the United States unless some national agency performed this function. Furthermore, the fact that the Supreme Court is a national agency has meant that the states-rights doctrine has never received consistent support from it. Finally, in exercising a review of state action, the Court has been able to thwart encroachment by the state legislatures and executives on the national authority. This was one of the major problems of the first half-century of our national life. *Judicial review of state action*

The review by the Supreme Court of congressional and presidential actions is of a different magnitude. In these cases, the Court is dealing with allegedly coordinate branches of government. Its determination to hold these as well as the states to their proper spheres of power may, and occasionally has, brought it into conflict with those who claim the right resulting from election to give effect to popular demands. The other branches, it may be added, can assert also the duty to interpret the Constitution themselves. The other two branches are equipped by the Constitution, as we have already seen, to influence considerably the character and methods of the Court. For these and other reasons, the Supreme Court has been much more reluctant to declare congressional statutes and presidential actions contrary to the Constitution than it has state actions. Until 1865, the Supreme Court declared only two acts of Congress unconstitutional; since that time it has upset several dozen more, but still a small number compared to the number of state laws it has overturned. *Review of national laws and acts*

Perhaps a more vivid conception of how judicial review operates can be gained by some concrete illustrations. In 1897, the legislature of New York passed a law limiting employment in bakeries to 60 hours a week and ten hours a day, presumably on the theory that baking was a kind of industry in which longer employment was unhealthful and the products might *How judicial review operates* be thus made more dangerous to the consumer. After several years, an employer, Lochner, was accused of and indicted for violating this law. He was convicted of the offense in the state trial court and his conviction was upheld by the highest state court, despite the pleas of his attorneys that the law in question violated the Constitution of the United States. He appealed his case to the Supreme Court of the United States on the basis of this plea and as a matter of right since the state court had found the law valid. Five of the nine justices of the Supreme Court held that this law deprived bakery employes of their freedom (to contract their labor as they pleased) guaranteed against state deprivation without "due process of law" by the Fourteenth Amendment. Four justices held that the state law was valid and that the due-process clause contained no such guarantees as the majority inferred. Thus, Lochner was relieved of any penalty; the Court declared, in effect, that it would not punish anyone brought before it for violation of this particular New York law, and the law thus became unenforceable. This was done on the basis of five justices finding something in the Constitution that the other four could not find.

In 1943, the Congress adopted as a provision in an appropriation act that no funds available under any act of Congress should be used to pay the salaries of three individuals named unless before November 15, 1943, the President should procure senatorial confirmation of their appointments. The three named men had been the subject of attack by the House Committee on Un-American Activities and had been accused of subversive activities against the United States. They were serving as "recess" appointees and the effect of the language of the act was to force their removal from office. The three men instituted action in the United States Court of Claims to recover salary they alleged was due them because of wrongful dismissal. The court ruled in their favor and the case was certified to the Supreme Court. A majority of the Court held that the section of the appropriation act in question constituted a bill of attainder, which they defined as a legislative act which inflicts punishment without trial, and therefore violated the constitutional prohibition of such bills (Art. I Sec. 9). Two justices held that the men were entitled to back salary but that the congressional action was not a bill of attainder, since it did not adjudge the men guilty of any offense. In this decision, the three men won back pay and the Court, in effect, said to Congress, you cannot remove officials whom you dislike from national office by this procedure.

Effect of a decision invalidating a law   It will be noted in these examples that the Court did not veto or annul either the New York statute or the act of Congress. It declared, rather, that in situations like those which confronted it, it would not enforce the laws against persons who rightfully sought its protection. State and national authorities make their own inferences from these decisions as to how the Court might regard similar laws or actions. Furthermore, the Court's action may come many years after the law was originally passed. The legal doctrine in the matter of validity is that every law is presumed to be constitutional until otherwise declared by a court in a proper case and that the burden of proof is on those who question its constitutionality.

It should not be surprising to the observer of our political institutions that on numerous occasions the decisions of the Supreme Court have been unpopular and have attracted wide criticism. Abraham Lincoln campaigned for United States senator and, in part, for President on his assertion that a Supreme Court decision (Dred Scott's case) was unwise, illogical, politically motivated, and ought to be overturned. Critics of the Court have frequently asserted that the judges are deliberately frustrating popular will on the basis of their own personal and partisan views, that the judges are ignoring underlying technological, economic, and social changes in our society which have changed the meaning and importance of legal or political conceptions, and that despite the presumption of validity a majority of one on the Court can and does overturn laws which their colleagues believe to be reasonable. The judges themselves habitually disclaim any disposition to do anything but apply impersonal and objective legal principles to the problems presented to them. Thus Mr. Justice Roberts said:

Attacks on and defense of judicial review

> It is sometimes said that the Court assumes a power to overrule or control the action of the people's representatives. This is a misconception. The Constitution is the supreme law of the land ordained and established by the people. All legislation must conform to the principles it lays down. When an act of Congress is appropriately challenged in the courts as not conforming to the constitutional mandate, the judicial branch of the government has only one duty—to lay the articles of the Constitution which is involved beside the statute which is challenged and to decide whether the latter squares with the former. All the Court does, or can do, is to announce its considered judgment upon the question. . . . This Court neither approves nor condemns any legislative policy. Its difficult and delicate task is to ascertain and declare whether the legislation is in accordance with, or in contravention of, the provisions of the Constitution, and having done that its duty ends.

Few students of the activities of the national judiciary accept the Justice's statement as a wholly satisfactory explanation or defense. If the matter were so simple, they argue, few cases would ever be brought. The Constitution is ambiguous in many places and the judges necessarily bring to the task of clarfying the unclear a great many preconceptions as to the "real" nature of our political system. A large number of the constitutional controversies concern matters on which the Constitution is silent and toward which the framers could have had no intention since they could not possibly have foreseen the problem. In order to perceive an intention where none exists, it is necessary for the viewer to bring a great deal of mental and emotional equipment to the task. Many members of the Court itself have never subscribed to the Roberts' theory. Justice Holmes, in the Lochner case already described, said:

This case is decided upon an *economic* theory which a large part of the country does not entertain. If it were a question of whether I agreed with that theory, I should desire to study it further and long before making up my mind. But I do not conceive that to be my duty, because I strongly believe that my agreement or disagreement has nothing to do with the right of the majority to embody their opinion in law. . . . The Fourteenth Amendment does not enact Mr. Herbert Spencer's Social Statics. . . . A constitution is not intended to embody a particular economic theory, whether of paternalism . . . or of *laissez faire*.

The modern Supreme Court is not too sympathetic with the Roberts' doctrine; many of its more recent decisions contain references to social and economic facts and opinions which are quite outside the more traditional concern for precedents and legal authorities. Times change and so do justices. The Court is not infallible and its views of constitutional questions may be and have been altered. But that it is a maker of law and not merely a discoverer of it, and that it exercises a profound influence upon public policy few would now dispute. However this may be, it has retained its hold upon the loyalty of the American people as a whole. They believe that it ought to exercise the powers that it does exercise and they, and their elected deputies, defer to its opinions and respect its detachment. Its critics of yesteryear, when it was smashing attempts to regulate business, are its friends of today when it is striking sledgehammer blows against all forms of discrimination in defense of its conception of the civil liberties of the American people.

SPECIAL AND LEGISLATIVE COURTS

"Constitutional" and "legislative" courts

The courts of the United States thus far described are the principal repositories of the judicial power conferred by the Constitution. They have been established by Congress under Article III of the Constitution and are the closest approximation which the national government has to courts of general jurisdiction. In establishing them Congress has been controlled by the provisions of the Constitution relating to judicial tenure and compensation. Congress has, however, created a number of other courts, some incidentally to certain of its enumerated powers. These are special courts and most of them are referred to as "legislative" courts by virtue of the relative freedom of Congress in creating them to prescribe terms of office for the judges and to endow them with nonjudicial functions.

Court of Claims

At least two of these special courts have, however, been specifically designated as constitutional courts by the Congress. The Court of Claims was created in 1855 under the power to appropriate money to pay the debts of the United States. It was authorized to hear and adjudicate claims of private persons against the government and to report its findings to Congress or to the department concerned. Since 1887 it has also heard suits against the United States for breaches of contract and since 1946 (Federal Tort Claims Act) suits for injuries caused by negligent or wrongful behavior of a government employee. In order to clarify the confused status of this court, the Congress in 1953 declared it to be a court established under Article III of the Constitution. The Court of Customs and Patent Appeals—created in 1910 under the power to regulate commerce and to regulate patents and authorized to decide questions arising under the customs, patent, and trademark laws largely through the review of decisions of the Customs Court, the Patent Office, and the Tariff Commission—was declared a constitutional court in 1958. The Customs Court, created in 1926 out of the Board of United States General Appraisers under the power to regulate commerce, and authorized to review decisions of customs collectors and appraisals of imported merchandise was designated a constitutional court in 1956. *[Court of Customs and Patent Appeals]* *[Customs Court]*

The "legislative" courts now include (1) the Court of Military Appeals, created in 1950 under the power to make rules for the government of the armed forces and authorized to review decisions of courts-martial; and (2) territorial courts, created on various occasions under the power to administer the territories of the United States and including district courts in Guam, Puerto Rico, the Virgin Islands, the Canal Zone, and the District of Columbia. All of these territorial district courts except that in Puerto Rico have, in addition to regular national jurisdiction, jurisdiction over all those matters which in the states belong to state courts. *[Court of Military Appeals]* *[Territorial courts]*

All of these legislative courts, except those in the territories, may be accurately labeled also as administrative courts dealing as they do with questions between private persons and government agencies. In this sense they are an exception to the general rule of Anglo-American jurisprudence that cases arising out of the administration of laws shall be adjudicated by the regular courts. *[Administrative courts]*

REFERENCES

H. J. Abraham, *Courts and Judges: An Introduction to the Judicial Process* (New York, 1959).

———, *The Judicial Process* (New York, 1962).

———, *The Judiciary: the Supreme Court in the Governmental Process* (New York, 1965).

C. L. Black, Jr., *The People and the Court: Judicial Review in a Democracy* (New York, 1960).

C. Bunn, *A Brief Survey of the Jurisdiction and Practice of the Courts of the United States* (St. Paul, Minn., 1949).

R. K. Carr, *The Supreme Court and Judicial Review* (New York, 1942).

J. E. Clayton, *The Making of Justice: The Supreme Court in Action* (New York, 1964).

H. G. Fins, *Federal Jurisdiction and Procedure* (Indianapolis, Ind., 1960).

P. T. Freund, *On Understanding the Supreme Court* (Boston, 1949).

C. G. Haines, *The American Doctrine of Judicial Supremacy* (2nd ed., Berkeley, Calif., 1932).

R. J. Harris, *The Judicial Power of the United States* (Baton Rouge, La., 1940).

J. W. Hurst, *The Growth of American Law; The Lawmakers* (Boston, 1950), Chaps. IV, VI–VII.

R. H. Jackson, *The Supreme Court in the American System of Government* (Cambridge, Mass., 1955).

R. G. McCloskey, *The American Supreme Court* (Chicago, 1961).

A. T. Mason, *The Supreme Court from Taft to Warren* (Baton Rouge, La., 1958).

A. T. Mason and W. M. Beaney, *The Supreme Court in a Free Society* (New York, 1960).

L. Mayers, *The American Legal System: The Administration of Justice in the United States by Judicial, Administrative, Military and Arbitral Tribunals* (New York, 1958).

W. F. Murphy, *Congress and the Courts: A Case Study of the American Political Process* (Chicago, 1962).

J. W. Peltason, *Federal Courts in the Political Process* (New York, 1955).

C. H. Pritchett, *Congress v. The Supreme Court, 1957–1960* (Minneapolis, 1961).

———, *The Roosevelt Court; A Study in Judicial Politics and Values, 1937–1947* (New York, 1948).

E. V. Rostow, *The Sovereign Prerogative: the Supreme Court and the Quest for Law* (New Haven, 1962).

J. R. Schmidhauser, *The Supreme Court as Final Arbiter in Federal–State Relations* (Chapel Hill, N. C., 1958).

G. A. Schubert, *Constitutional Politics: The Political Behavior of Supreme Court Justices and the Constitutional Policies that They Make* (New York, 1960).

B. Schwartz, *The Supreme Court: Constitutional Revolution in Retrospect* (New York, 1957).

A. F. Westin, *The Anatomy of a Constitutional Law Case* (New York, 1958).

B Functions and Services

15

GOVERNMENT AND THE NATIONAL ECONOMY

The purpose of government in the American ideology is to serve the people over whom it presides. The state is not an end in itself with a purpose and a destiny distinct from that of the persons who comprise it, as many European thinkers have held and rulers have practiced. The American believes the state is an agency for fostering the safety and welfare of individuals and has no other object. It is fitting, therefore, that we now turn from how the government is organized to what it does. In its programs we find the justification for its existence and a basis for determining its effectiveness.

Among the vast array of national programs, past and present, none has commanded more widespread interest nor more persistent attention than maintaining a high level of economic well-being among our people.

Government and the maintenance of prosperity

There has never been a time when the government was indifferent to the health of the economy. Policies or programs appropriate to one stage of our economic development have not necessarily been useful or acceptable at other stages but once begun are hard to stop. Opinions have differed widely through the years on how best to achieve economic health and the great interests of our society have each sought governmental aid and have urged mutually contradictory programs upon those in power. The result is that the government has never followed a wholly consistent theory of political economy and does not do so today. It is, nevertheless, possible to discern major changes in economic policies over the years and to appreciate that the scope of governmental concern today as well as the tools of public economic activity and the general tone of opinion on the proper role of government are all different than they were in the past.

THE DEVELOPMENT OF NATIONAL RESPONSIBILITY

The Constitution itself and the policies of the first administration under it were intended to and did improve the position of the business and finan-

Economic policies of the past

cial community. Impediments to interstate trade were eliminated, a sound monetary system established, the national credit placed on a secure basis, and manufacturing encouraged. In fact, so favorable to these interests were the earliest national economic policies that they stimulated the organization of the agricultural interests and the expression through Jefferson's party of policies more popular among farmers: easier access to the public domain, purchase of Louisiana, exploration of the West. Jacksonianism brought new policies: annihilation of the Bank of the United States, freer access to public employment, greater protection to the frontiersman, continued additions to the national domain. The business community responded through the Whigs and pressed for higher protective tariffs and better arteries of transportation (canals, turnpikes, river and harbor improvements). The Civil War paved the way for the establishment of policies—promotion of the railroads, provision of free land, maintenance of high tariffs on manufactured goods— for the rapid industrialization and urbanization of the nation. The rise of the factory system and of huge corporate combinations to control the supply or processing of commodities over the whole nation produced the highly interdependent economy of the present century. It also stimulated reaction and the articulation of demands for government regulation and for intervention to protect working people, farmers and small businessmen from the consequences. Gradually, the government swept its mighty arm over certain sectors of the economy, fixing conditions of competition, regulating prices and profits and services and placing floors below which standards for working conditions might not sink. Nevertheless, in the first quarter of this century the prevailing tone of public discussion of the political economy was that governmental intervention was untypical, limited in aim, and in many situations of dubious effectiveness.

Change in policy in the thirties
    Complacency about the American system of predominantly private enterprise and limited governmental responsibility was shattered by the Great Depression of the thirties. As factories closed, unemployment mounted from 5 to 10 to 13 million and paralysis spread through the system with untold suffering and waste of precious human resources. The New Deal determined to halt the downward spiral, to start the wheels turning again, and to relieve want tried numerous experiments. What was not adequately achieved by public works and poor relief was finally achieved by World War II; prosperity with full employment. During the war it became necessary for the government to take almost complete control of the economy— regulating access to and rationing raw materials, fixing prices, allocating consumer goods, dominating transportation, and promoting increased agricultural production. At its end, many contemplated the return to the situation of 1939 or of 1929 with deep misgivings. It was widely believed that a deep industrial depression would follow disarmament, demobilization and the shift to consumer goods production and even more serious dislocation in agriculture would result as European and Asiatic fields were put back into cultivation. So deeply had the bitter experience of the thirties etched its

message on American society that few, indeed, were the voices raised for a return to laissez-faire: Most statesmen were convinced that the government must keep its hand on the economic pulse of the nation ready to administer stimulating medicine whenever it appeared to flag or falter.

The controversies of the modern era, in consequence, have been about what the government ought to do not whether it might do anything. Every modern President has proposed measures aimed at preserving and improving our economic well-being. The differences have been about means and about the nature of the illness. Furthermore, the rising commitments to friendly and developing nations abroad, the maintenance and enhancement of a vast defense establishment, and the attempts to conquer outer space have all added new dimensions to the public economy. The continued revolution in technology on the farms and in the factory has flooded the nation with more and more goods turned out in most cases with fewer and fewer workers. Continued deficit financing of public expenditures, rapidly rising military costs in Viet Nam, sharp depletion of gold reserves have also generated serious economic dislocations. Thus unemployment, wasted resources, heavy inflationary pressures, and surplus commodities continue to plague a nation which otherwise has enjoyed unrivalled prosperity over almost the whole of the postwar epoch. *Controversies today over how, not whether!*

The contemporary commitment of the government of the United States to preserving economic well-being is contained in the Employment Act of 1946 in the following language: *Government responsibility fully endorsed*

The Congress hereby declares that it is the continuing policy and responsibility of the Federal Government to use all practicable means consistent with the needs and obligations and other essential considerations of national policy with the assistance and cooperation of industry, agriculture, labor, and state and local governments, to coordinate and utilize all its plans, functions, and resources for the purpose of creating and maintaining, in a manner calculated to foster and promote free competitive enterprise and the general welfare, conditions under which there will be afforded useful employment, for those able, willing, and seeking to work, and to promote maximum employment, production, and purchasing power.

This awkward and tortuous passage was the product of months of controversy and numerous compromises. It represents what a majority of the Congress at that time were willing to agree upon as the duty of the national government. It is the upshot of an effort begun under President Roosevelt, through the National Resources Planning Board to encourage the government to undertake a substantial program of economic planning, public works, and social security designed to guarantee full employment. The act in which it is found was, in fact, developed and introduced by a Senate committee which had been studying the problems of economic adjustment in the postwar period. Certain members became convinced that only a determined *Signs of economic ill health* effort at public economic planning backed by a willingness to use the vast resources of the national treasury would enable us to avoid a disastrous postwar depression. The significance of the act is that it created the Council of Economic Advisors in the executive office of the President and thus provided the Chief Executive for the first time with the means of appraising the state of the economy and required him to report annually on his findings together with remedial proposals if he found them necessary. The act also shows that despite the growing feeling that more governmental control of economic decision-making was both desirable and inevitable, the preservation of a competitive, free enterprise system was earnestly sought. Furthermore, the act highlighted what had been its original aim: the achievement of full employment, as the major goal of a healthy economy.

Postwar experience emphasized the danger to economic health of inflation and reminded our people of the bitter experience of other nations, notably Germany in the twenties, with this problem. The removal of governmental controls over the civilian economy and the pressure of pent-up consumer demand sent commodity prices into a sharp upward spiral followed by pressure on wages and salaries and then frequently, when these were allayed, by new rises in the price level. Those with fixed incomes were

CONSUMER PRICE INDEX FOR CITY WAGE EARNERS, 1929–1968

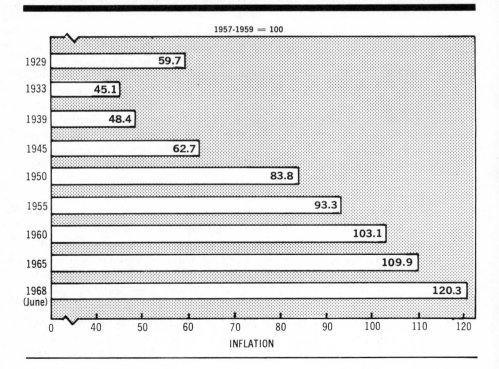

1957-1959 = 100

Year	Index
1929	59.7
1933	45.1
1939	48.4
1945	62.7
1950	83.8
1955	93.3
1960	103.1
1965	109.9
1968 (June)	120.3

INFLATION

caught in this squeeze as well as those dependent upon a stable monetary and credit system. Many public policies especially of the fifties were intended to halt pressure on prices or wages and to hold the cost of living as steady as possible. Rapidly rising expenditures in Viet Nam, not backed by new revenues until mid-1968, and continuing balance of payments deficits brought new inflationary pressures during the Johnson Presidency.

Rising prices and wages combined with heavy American grants and loans to allied and developing nations, and substantial private investments abroad contributed to a relative fall in our trade balance and soon stimulated a heavy outflow of gold reserves. These developments of the late fifties and sixties added a new dimension to the definition of economic health—

U.S. GOLD STOCK, 1949–1967

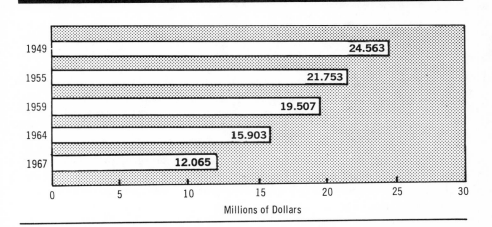

preservation of the soundness of the dollar in the international market. A new set of policies were fashioned to cope with this new threat including restrictions on tourists' imports, increased income taxation, and tighter credit controls. The dollar was so seriously threatened in 1968 that a new international scheme to stop the gold drain was conceived by the Western powers.

The general expansion of the economy from 1946 to the present (1968) has been interrupted four times by recession: 1947–1948—11 months; 1953–1954—13 months; 1957–1958—nine months; and 1960–1961—nine months. Each of these has been accompanied by falling industrial production and rising unemployment. After each recession until 1965, the unemployment rate never quite returned to what it had been. It rose from 3 percent in 1951 to 4 percent in 1955 to 5 percent in 1959 and to nearly 7 percent in 1961. It finally fell below 4 percent again only in 1965 and has remained below since. In each case the cushions against

Labor Force and Unemployment

Selected Years, 1929–1967

(Thousands)

YEAR	TOTAL LABOR FORCE INCL. ARMED FORCES	UNEMPLOYMENT	% CIVILIAN LABOR FORCE
1929	49,440	1,550	3.2
1933	51,840	12,830	24.9
1939	55,600	9,480	17.2
1945	65,300	1,040	1.9
1950	64,749	3,351	5.3
1955	68,896	2,904	4.4
1958	71,284	4,681	6.8
1961	74,175	4,806	6.7
1964	76,567	3,466	4.7
1967	75,391	3,628	3.8

SOURCE: *Economic Report of the President*, February, 1968.

FULL EMPLOYMENT?

disaster built-in, in the thirties—unemployment insurance, for example—helped to prevent more suffering but did not completely allay concern. Again and again the national policy-makers have sought to reduce the rate of unemployment by special programs aimed at depressed areas and under-trained laboring forces.

Modern economic analysis has concentrated much of the attention of students, statesmen, and leaders of the various sectors of the economy on the total goods and services produced by the economic system, called the gross national product (GNP). Many analysts regard the rate of growth of this product as a major indicator of the health of the national economy. International rivalry between the United States and the Soviet bloc and

Gross National Product

Selected Years, 1929–1967

(Billions of Dollars)

YEAR	AT CURRENT PRICES	AT 1968 PRICES
1929	$103.1	$203.6
1933	55.6	141.5
1939	90.5	209.4
1945	211.9	355.2
1949	256.5	324.1
1955	398.6	438.0
1959	483.7	475.9
1964	632.0	581.1
1967	785.1	669.2

SOURCE: *Economic Report of the President*, February, 1968.

ECONOMIC GROWTH

between the United States and the friendly industrial nations of Europe has also stimulated comparison between the growth rates of the various systems and countries with which we are in competition. For many of the postwar years our growth rates of 2 to 3 percent were compared unfavorably with the much higher rates of France and West Germany, for example. The Kennedy–Johnson administration witnessed commendable improvement in growth, and since 1961, the realized rates of growth have been above 4 percent per year. Economic growth is essential if standards of living are to be improved and if the labor market is to absorb the millions of new addi-

Economic Indicators

Weekly Comparisons

	JULY 5 LATEST WEEK	JUNE 29 PRIOR WEEK	1967
Commodity index	93.8	94.0	96.8
*Currency in circulation	$48,114,000	$47,644,000	$45,256,000
*Coml, indl, agric loans	$71,088,000	$71,267,000	$65,935,000
Steel production (tons)	2,697,000	2,785,000	2,143,000
Motor vehicle production	174,900	141,385	131,006
Daily oil production (bbls)	9,249,000	8,586,000	8,917,610
Freight car loadings	443,377	539,144	405,594
*Elec Pwr output, kw-hr	24,485,000	26,114,000	21,766,000
Business failures	134	145	158

Statistics for commercial-agricultural loans, carloadings, steel, oil, electric power and business failures are for the preceding week and latest available. *000 omitted.

Monthly Comparisons

	†JUNE	PRIOR MONTH	1967
Employed	77,273,000	75,931,000	75,391,000
Unemployed	3,614,000	2,303,000	3,628,000

	†MAY	PRIOR MONTH	1967
Industrial production	163.7	162.5	155.6
*Personal income	$674,000,000	$669,800,000	$618,200,000
*Money supply	$186,100,000	$184,400,000	$174,400,000
Consumers' Price Index	120.3	119.9	115.6
*Construction contracts	$6,170,471	$4,877,920	$5,269,683
*Manufrs. inventories	$84,254,000	$83,956,000	$80,341,000
*Exports	$2,719,700	$2,888,500	$2,546,900
*Imports	$2,751,900	$2,640,500	$2,139,900

†Figures shown are subject to revision by source. *000 omitted.

Commodity index, based on 1957–59 = 100, and the consumers' price index, based on 1957–59 = 100, are compiled by the Bureau of Labor Statistics. Industrial production is Federal Reserve Board's adjusted index of 1957–59 = 100. Imports and exports as well as employment are compiled by the Bureau of Census of the Department of Commerce. Money supply is total currency outside banks and demand deposits adjusted as reported by Federal Reserve Board. Business failures compiled by Dun & Bradstreet, Inc. Construction contracts are compiled by the F. W. Dodge Corporation.

SOURCE: *The New York Times*, July 14, 1968.

THE PULSE OF THE ECONOMY
Issued Weekly by the Council of Economic Advisors

tions each year. Economic growth and full employment are thus closely related.

TOOLS FOR GOVERNMENTAL ECONOMIC ACTIVITY

The major domestic concern of the President and the Congress is to promote prosperity and to guard against economic maladjustment. The Council of Economic Advisors issues weekly, monthly, quarterly, and yearly bulletins on the condition of the national economy and estimates of its prospects. What medicine do the national leaders keep on hand for new or recurring ailments?

Impact of budget decisions

In the first place, the national budget has such a sweeping impact on the whole economy that the decisions taken annually by the President and Congress about it are increasingly taken in the light of their economic consequences. The national government is the largest single employer; one person of 14 in the employed labor force is either a civilian or military employe of the government. It is also the largest single purchaser of goods and services. The annual total outlay of more than $156 billion is in itself a major determiner of economic activity. Within the total, the amount allocated to defense contracts, space technology, and atomic energy developments are all of critical importance to those regions, industries, and workers engaged. A sharp cut-back, for example, in our defense program would send shock waves through the entire economy. Heavy annual subsidies to farmers to maintain commodity prices also have a strong bearing upon the rural economy. Then there are the questions of tax and debt policy. Deficit spending is inflationary to some degree. The government must borrow to pay its bills and the borrowing creates the possibility of creating more currency unrelated to other changes in commodity production or consumption. Many leaders, especially of the business and financial community, regard a balanced national budget as the major determinant of economic health. The amount taken by the government in taxes is in itself of major importance and the Kennedy–Johnson administrations fought for and achieved a major cut in national taxes in 1964–1965 unrelated to a cut in expenditures and presumably for the purpose of stimulating a flagging consumer demand. The immediate spurt in production incident to the cut makes it almost certain that cuts in taxes will be considered, in fact strongly urged, the minute the economy falters again. President Johnson, on the other hand, pled for in 1967 and 1968 and finally achieved in 1968 a 10 percent increase in income tax liabilities (individual and corporate) to combat inflation and maintain dollar stability. He was obliged to agree to cut-backs of proposed budget allocations for 1968–1969 of $6 billion to win the tax rise from a reluctant Congress. These decisions on tax levels, spending levels, debt incurrence and the governmental programs to be expanded or contracted are all made today with at least one eye on their anticipated economic consequences.

In addition to the recurring decisions on the national budget, the authorities in Washington have another set of medicines to counteract a downswing in the business cycle. The vast program of unemployment insurance established in 1935 and described in more detail in a later chapter provides a first buffer. It makes possible the continuance of wage payments, although at a lower level, to workers laid off by falling demand. These payments help support a higher level of consumer purchasing than would otherwise be possible but, of course, are of relatively short duration. In the recessions of 1957–1958 and 1960–1961, Congress authorized a temporary extension of the number of weeks for which benefits would be paid. In the areas hardest hit by rising unemployment the available funds were exhausted fairly rapidly but clearly many workers were helped by the added weekly payments. To replenish the reserves against future demands, the payroll taxes which support the system were temporarily increased in 1962 and 1963. *Unemployment Insurance*

The favorite remedy of many for rising unemployment, dating from New Deal days, is to increase public works expenditures in order to compensate for falling private investment, and to increase demands for capital goods and to increase the supply of available jobs. Widely practiced in the nineteen-thirties the pump-priming system is likely to be one of the first things suggested when economic trouble appears. In each postwar recession, Congress and the President have stepped up the works program already planned and authorized; speeded up government spending for supplies and equipment; increased the authorization for various kinds of domestic public construction. There has been also much pressure on agencies to have available standby programs of construction—the blueprints for which can be hauled out and dusted off on very short notice. In 1962, President Kennedy requested and Congress approved—on a reduced basis—a Public Works Acceleration Act which gave the President authority to allocate funds for job-creating public works to communities and areas with heavy unemployment. The act also gave the President standby authority for more projects if he found them to be necessary. The Johnson Public Works and Economic Development Act of 1965 broadened the Kennedy measure, provided loans as well as grants, and promoted regional planning for economic development. It also extended to other areas of the country the aid provided earlier to the 11-state area of Appalachia. To be effective, the public works must be financed by deficit spending. If taxes are raised to pay for the construction, then there is no net gain in economic activity. New Deal experience suggests a number of problems with the public works remedy. In the first place, the amount of governmental activity must be quite large. It was a $100 billion annual expenditure for waging war that finally brought full employment, not the $2 to $4 billion annually of the thirties. With governmental expenditures already massive, small increments will hardly be felt. The public works programs, furthermore, are not easily put together nor accomplished rapidly. There is not extant a huge drawer of *Public works expenditures* plans that can be opened, let out for bids, and work started rapidly enough to halt or reverse a downward swing in the economy. There are, of course, many who still urge that a balanced budget is more desirable in encouraging expanded private investment in capital replacement or expansion than the inflationary consequences of government deficits. Those who are eager to incur deficits to halt recession find a great deal of resistance in good times to achieving surpluses in order to reduce the deficit.

Money and credit controls The Federal Reserve Board has been endowed for many years with power to influence the supply of money, the interest rates, and the supply of credit. There is some sentiment that these tools are or can be especially useful in countering recession as well as inflation. In general, the monetary policies of the board were geared in the late forties to helping the Treasury finance the public debt by fixing government bond prices and keeping interest rates low. During the mid-fifties, after an agreement with the Treasury in 1951 gave the board more flexibility, interest rates were raised and the board generally followed tight-money policies. The main object of these policies was, however, to counter inflation rather than to stimulate economic growth. Faced with recession, however, the board has, for example in 1961, authorized banks to loan more money by reducing the reserve requirements and has encouraged borrowing by reducing interest rates. Usually, these policies have been followed by raising the rates once recovery seems apparent but in 1962 the board eased requirements again. Late in 1965, the Board sharply raised the interest rates to halt rapid credit expansion and followed this by other raises in 1967 and 1968 aimed at inflation and the promotion of dollar stability until the rates are now as high as they have been since the twenties. The difficulties with the monetary and credit policies as methods to combat recession are that (1) the board is not directly controlled by and, therefore, not completely amenable to influence by the President or the Congress; (2) changes in monetary arrangements, interest rates, etc., have to be judged also in the light of their international consequences and for a number of years recently the loss of gold reserves has been sufficiently serious to justify separate consideration; (3) exclusive reliance on monetary controls was badly discredited in the early thirties when the traditional monetary remedies for recession failed to work; (4) expansion in the private sector of the economy is influenced by many factors of which the price of hiring credit and its ready availability is only one.

Wage and price controls Another tool of the executive in dealing with the economy is the effort to keep wage and price increases within the "guidelines" published regularly by the Council of Economic Advisors. These are based on gains in productivity and are used to curb increases which will require price increases and thus lead to inflation. The conflict of Kennedy with the steel industry was based on these "guidelines" and he did get a price roll-back. Johnson's use of them further in 1967 and 1968 was less determined and generally less successful.

Because of the incredible complexity of the economy and the numer-

UNEMPLOYMENT PICTURE—THE HARD-PRESSED AREAS IN THE U.S.

The shaded areas are those with chronic unemployment designated as redevelopment areas under national legislation.
The circles indicate communities with unemployment rates above 6 percent for over a year.

(as of 1962)

SOURCE: *The New York Times*, April 1, 1962. © 1962 by The New York Times Company. Reprinted by permission.

Aid to depressed areas

ous factors involved, there are many who are skeptical of the generalized treatments of the type described. Certain sectors of the economy suffer from continuous malnutrition, they argue. While generalized medication may be useful, perhaps indispensable, we should deal directly and specifically with the diseased parts. In surveying the postwar national economy, it is apparent that certain groups, regions, and industries have been chronically depressed: cotton-textile manufacturing, staple-crop farming, coal mining and processing, railroading. These activities and the regions, cities and workers dependent upon them have been especially affected. The first legislative accomplishment of the Kennedy administration was the passage of an Area Development Act aimed at areas of high chronic unemployment. The Congress had on two previous occasions fashioned similar legislation only to have it vetoed by President Eisenhower. The Act of 1961 provided cheap credit for industrial-facilities development, technical assistance, and cash grants for public facilities to areas qualifying as depressed. The Department of Commerce has been responsible for working with local communities in developing projects looking toward economic rehabilitation. President Johnson in 1964 and 1965 recommended and Congress supported the continuation and enlargement of this program.

Aid to Appalachia

A special form of aid for depressed areas was proposed by President Johnson and approved in 1965 by Congress: aid to Appalachia. The eastern mountain range running from Pennsylvania to Alabama has been an area of chronic unemployment for several years. Its economy has been particularly

APPALACHIA
1965

influenced by the subsidence of coal mining. Based in part upon a program urged by the governors of the states of the region, the Act of 1965 (extended through 1969 in late 1967) provides a varied program of aid including special funds for road-building, vocational schools, reclamation of mining areas, and for the development of timber and water resources. An Appalachian Regional Commission is established to coordinate projects and to develop an economic program for the 360 counties of the area. As noted above, many of the programs for this region were generalized for the nation as a whole in later enactments.

There is yet another way of looking at the problem of a healthy economy and that is to pay attention to those who are not successful. Some sink to the bottom or begin there and never rise for lack of opportunity or for crippling illness or some other reason; and while it is important to support industrial expansion, consumer demands, chronically depressed areas and

Aid to under- privileged people

Poverty in the United States

Families with Incomes of Less Than $3,000 a Year at 1966 Prices
Selected Years, 1947–1966

YEAR	NO. OF FAMILIES (MILLIONS)	MEDIAN INCOME 1963 PRICES	NO. OF POOR FAMILIES (MILLIONS)	%
1947	37.2	$4,401	10.8	28.9
1950	39.9	4,479	11.5	28.9
1955	42.8	5,377	9.8	22.8
1959	45.1	6,041	8.9	19.7
1961	46.3	6,243	9.0	19.4
1963	47.4	6,637	8.3	17.5
1966	48.9	7,436	7.0	14.3

SOURCE: Department of Commerce, Bureau of the Census.

farmers, it is necessary to improve our human resources. In this spirit, President Johnson in 1964 launched an all-out war on poverty and the Congress responded with the important Economic Opportunity Act of that year giving to the government still another group of procedures for improving the American economy.

The programs launched in 1964 and 1965 and continued in 1967 in somewhat modified form through 1968, aimed first at youth—school dropouts—whose economic future is particularly bleak. These may enlist in a Job Corps and receive special training in conservation camps and vocational training centers. Each of the 45,000 potential recruits receives basic education and special vocational training in a new environment. On-the-job training programs are also established in the home communities to support young men and women who wish to resume their education and special help is provided for needy college students. Communities are also encouraged by the act to develop active programs aimed at the poor in the community and financial aid and technical assistance is provided by the national government. Volunteers are invited to aid in helping the poor (VISTA) through special training, welfare, and counselling services. Training in new skills is made available for adults on relief. Governors of the various states are made parties of the community action programs for each project must be referred to the chief executive for his comments. Special programs aimed at rural areas, migrant workers, and small business are also authorized. Central national direction of the attack on poverty was given to the Office of Economic Opportunity in the Executive Office of the President.

In summary, the available tools for maintaining and improving the American economy are numerous, wide-ranging, and based upon several not wholly consistent theories as to the proper and effective role of the national government. A modern President is expected to look to our prosperity and to take timely action to prevent another economic catastrophe.

Closely related to the general economic policies and practices described are numerous special programs aimed at various sectors of the economy and at particular problems of social justice as well as of affluence. We must now, therefore, turn our attention to a more detailed consideration of the relations of government and business, labor, and agriculture, if we are to gain a full appreciation of the involvement of national officials in economic decisions.

REFERENCES

S. K. Bailey, *Congress Makes a Law: The Story Behind the Employment Act of 1946* (New York, 1950).

A. R. Barach, *U.S.A. and Its Economic Future* (New York, 1964).

Congressional Quarterly Service, *Congress and the Nation, 1945–1964* (Washington, 1965), Chaps. 4 and 8.

Economic Report of the President (Washington, D. C., Annually).

S. E. Harris, *The Economics of the Political Parties* (New York, 1962).

C. B. Hoover, *The Economy, Liberty, and the State* (New York, 1959).

E. Janeway, *The Economics of Crisis: War, Politics, and the Dollar* (New York, 1968).

G. McConnell, *Steel and the Presidency, 1962* (New York, 1963).

H. P. Miller, *Rich Man, Poor Man* (New York, 1964).

National Commission on Technology, Automation, and Economic Progress, *Technology and the American Economy* (Washington, D. C., 1966).

E. S. Redford and C. B. Hagan, *American Government and the Economy* (New York, 1965), Parts I and VII.

G. Soule, *Men, Wages, and Employment in the Modern U. S. Economy* (New York, 1954).

16

GOVERNMENT AND BUSINESS

From the earliest days, there has been a great deal of sentiment in this country that the way to maintain a sturdy economy is to aid business in part by direct assistance but largely by maintaining a climate of opinion and practice favorable to investments and profits. The business interests have, furthermore, on many occasions been powerful enough and persuasive enough that Presidents and Congresses have responded favorably to their urgings. In fact, most of the time during the first century-and-a-half of our history the government's only policies toward business enterprise were to encourage and assist it. However, the rise of the factory system with its cruel use of labor power and of monopolistic corporations with the annihilation of competitors and the growing dependence of the staple farmer on transportation all combined to invite counter pressures from farmers, laboring men, and small businesses. Ultimately, the government was pressed to halt abuses, to regulate certain business activities and forbid others and then to protect laboring men from the worst aspects of the factory system. Its modern relations with the business community are, therefore, a mixture of benevolence and regulation.

A general view of government– business relations

So complex have the relations between government and business become that it is impossible today to characterize them by any simple rubric like *laissez faire or* socialism. Intermingled throughout our economy are (1) private ownership and private operation, illustrated by the railroads and most other utilities, most banking, oil production, steel and textile manufacturing, and most life and fire insurance; (2) public ownership and public operation, illustrated by the postal service and by a long list of government corporations like the Commodity Credit Corporation, the Inland Waterways Corporation, and the Tennessee Valley Authority; (3) private ownership and government operation, as seen in the federal reserve system; and (4) public ownership and private operation, less common but illustrated by publicly built and owned munitions plants operated by private companies during World War II. While public ownership and operation have been on the increase sufficiently to cause many people to worry over a trend toward socialism, there is far more private and far less public economic enterprise than in any other major country. In particular, the American system contrasts with not only (*a*) the totalitarian U.S.S.R. with its collectivization of virtually all industry and business, but even with (*b*) democratic Great Britain, which under a socialist Labour government from 1945–1951 has seen the coal, transportation, gas and electric, and other top industries "nationalized," and with (*c*) equally democratic Scandinavian countries with their mixed, "middle-way," economies in which the governments have a controlling interest in most major economic enterprises. Finally, our penchant for private ownership and management has stimulated our heavy reliance upon governmental regulation of privately owned and operated business organizations and procedures. Broadly, public ownership and operation is the European way, private ownership and operation, with public regulation, the American way.

The unity of business interests

In reviewing governmental policies and programs aiding and controlling business, we must bear in mind also that the business community exerts a powerful influence on the government. There is no way of knowing precisely how many people in this country are now engaged in business. The number has been estimated at between 8 and 10 million, depending upon what is considered "business." But in any case the gamut runs all the way from the independent corner grocery to the industrial or financial colossus like the Du Pont Company or General Motors counting its assets in billions of dollars. At first glance, there is little unity in the picture. Small business contends with big business; independent dealers fight the chains; railroads do battle with bus and air lines; high-cost producers seek political protection against low-cost producers; some manufacturers want protective tariffs, importers want none; New England textile interests combat newer interests of the kind in the South; competition is bitter within industries and between industries; scores of trade associations do whatever they can to get favors and advantages for their own industries, localities, or regions.

There is, nevertheless, more solidarity than appears. Business interests, large and small, have, as is often said, a "businessman's point of view"; large over-all organizations like the National Association of Manufacturers and the United States Chamber of Commerce encourage and express this point of view, consolidating sentiment and speaking for the business community as a whole. Although often rivals, textile interests, iron and steel interests, transportation interests—each with its own trade association, or perhaps several such—have common ground and may work together for common purposes. At many points, big business pulls little business along with it; interlocking directorates and financial relationships blur the pattern of dispersion and harmonize conflicting interests and objectives. Big bankers influence lesser ones, and they, still lesser ones within their radius of contact. So, too, with corporations and industries of other sorts—influence radiating downwards, indeed, through all levels, and certainly not excluding the millions of people who, having investments in General Motors or the

Penn Central Railroad or any one of hundreds of other enterprises, large or small, instinctively incline toward the viewpoints of those bearing responsibility for operating the business. Notwithstanding incessant internal clashes of interest and policy, therefore, the American business world on a great many issues presents a common front of immense prestige and potentiality.

Furthermore, this common front is utilized powerfully for political ends. Back of it stand millions of voters. While we hear less of the business vote than of the labor or farm vote, no one can fail to perceive that at every presidential and congressional election it is thrown heavily to some particular party—normally the Republican party—and presidential candidate. But it is not alone through nominations and elections that business seeks to mold and guide national policy. There are also broad avenues for influence upon the President by advice and persuasion, upon department heads in their work of planning and administration, upon the great regulatory commissions, and upon Congress in connection with legislation. Here we enter, of course, the labyrinth of interest-group activities, including lobbying; and the fact already has been stressed that among the scores of groups and interests assiduously endeavoring to influence senators and representatives to support or oppose given tax, tariff, currency, labor, farm, and other proposals, a prominent place must always be given business organizations and groups. Furthermore, one of the major lessons which business has learned in the past generation is the folly of ignoring or defying public sentiment—the wisdom, indeed, of cultivating such sentiment in every possible way. And millions are spent annually to create a public attitude sympathetic to the aspirations of the business community.

Business in politics

NATIONAL ASSISTANCE TO BUSINESS

Almost everything the national government does affects business, most of the time benevolently. The maintenance of friendly intercourse abroad fosters trade across national frontiers, the defense of the nation not only preserves the plants and facilities of the business world against destruction or capture but also provides an immense market for the sale of privately manufactured armaments of all types. The preservation of law and order guarantees ownership against theft and depredation and facilitates the free movement of goods and services over a vast continental area. Assistance to the aged, the infirm, the sick, the veteran, and many others insures a market for many types of consumer goods; and granting of economic and military aid to friendly foreign powers in recent years has assured a market abroad for many types of American commodities. There are, however, many forms of assistance aimed particularly or exclusively at the business community or at segments of it. These programs are summarized and illustrated in the following paragraphs.

Throughout the country's history, business has profited immensely

1. Sub-
sidies

from subsidies from the national treasury; and some branches of it still do so. Most conspicuous among beneficiaries has been the railway industry, on which more than $1.25 billion, chiefly in public lands, has been bestowed. But transportation by air, sea, and highway have also been and are now being subsidized: contracts with air carriers for transporting mail are frankly drawn to subsidize a young industry, and airport facilities are extensively supported by national, state, and local expenditures; the trucking industry has been subsidized by immense national, as well as state and local, expenditures on highways which are its roadbed; the newspaper, magazine, book publishing, and direct-mail advertising industries are sustained by mail service charges which are admittedly below cost and the differential must be made up by appropriations from tax funds. One of the special recipients of treasury largesse has been the American shipping industry. The efforts of the government to stimulate trading in American vessels have included tonnage tax advantages and subsidies to private operators by lucrative mail contracts, by government construction of vessels which are then leased to private operators, by payment of the difference in cost of operation between American-owned and foreign-owned vessels. The list of subsidies might be extended for several paragraphs. All told the business community has been the direct beneficiary of billions of dollars of national expenditure and a substantial share of the national budget currently is allocated for this purpose. Contrary to some of the pronouncements of its associations, the business community has never opposed public subsidies as such. What it opposes are subsidies to other sectors of the national economy.

2. Tariff
protection

The most important concealed subsidy received by business throughout our history has been that arising from protective tariffs. A *protective tariff* is a duty on imports fixed high enough to offset any price advantage which foreign goods might enjoy in competition with home-produced articles. Every tariff act from 1789 to 1930 had as one of its purposes, and often the main one, to give American products (chiefly manufactures, until eventually agricultural products were added) a competitive advantage over foreign products in our markets. The peak of such favoritism was reached under the Tariff (Hawley–Smoot) Act of 1930. The pros and cons of this policy have been argued warmly for 175 years. Producers of raw materials such as cotton have usually opposed tariffs on manufactured goods. Manufacturers have usually argued the benefits to be derived from fostering the development of home industry and the advantages accruing to American labor by being protected against lower European or Asiatic wage scales. The point is that business has at all stages been the beneficiary of what amounts to a tax, in the form of higher prices, on the country's consumers. Since 1934 the nation has gradually retreated from the extreme protectionist position of 1930. More and more business interests feel able to survive foreign competition and are especially anxious to enlarge their export markets, expecting that tariff reduction at home will stimulate reciprocity abroad. There has been a change also since 1934 in the procedure by which tariffs are fixed. Dissatisfaction with congressional tariff-making increased steadily in this century. General tariff bills had by 1910 become such labyrinths of facts and figures that even the most conscientious legislator could inform himself on only a small portion of the duties. The influences of special interests in promoting high rates on particular goods were enormous. Fluctuations in economic conditions at home and abroad made any set of rates soon out of date.

The first reform efforts accompanied a desire to reduce tariffs generally and led to the creation in 1916 of the United States Tariff Commission. This agency, directed by six members appointed on a bipartisan basis, was charged with continuous review of the tariffs in relation to costs of manufacture at home and abroad and with keeping both the President and Congress fully informed. Originally the Commission had no authority even to make recommendations except in very general terms but in 1922 it was charged with the duty of investigating differences in the cost of production between any protected domestic commodity and its foreign counterpart and required to recommend to the President specific increases or decreases in tariff rates based upon its studies. The President, in turn, was authorized to change rates by as much as 50 percent up or down.

Flexible tariff introduced

The amount of tariff revision accomplished by this procedure was more than offset by the new high rates of the Tariff Act of 1930. A new Democratic administration, determined to stimulate international trade and to improve the tariff procedure, persuaded Congress in 1934 to inaugurate a broad new tariff program. The Reciprocal Trade Agreement Act of 1934 empowered the President to bargain with foreign countries for mutually advantageous tariff concessions and to lower the tariffs by as much as 50 percent without further congressional approval in so doing. The President's power was to expire after three years. Succeeding Congresses renewed the grant of power to the President up to June, 1970. In the last few extensions, the role of the Tariff Commission has been enhanced so that the President must await their studies before concluding agreements and they are directed to lay before him and before Congress any evidence of injury to domestic interests from the extant duties. The Trade Agreements Extensions Act of 1958 provided further that Congress might by a two-thirds vote veto any presidential tariff orders in those instances where the President has rejected the advice of the Tariff Commission. The extension, of 1962, extended his authority to 1967 and that of 1968 to 1970. The Act of 1962 broadened considerably the President's powers, especially to increase the free list in collaboration with the European Economic Community. It also, however, removed Poland and Yugoslavia from the benefits of the most-favored-nation principle and lowered the vote needed for congressional veto of certain orders to a simple majority. Under this act, the celebrated Kennedy Round of multilateral negotiations among more than 40 nations (under the aegis of the organization springing from the General Agreement on Tariffs and Trade [GATT]) entered into by executive agreement in

U.S. TARIFF HISTORY, 1821–1966

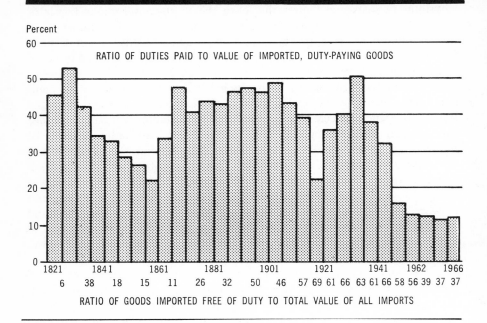

Percent

RATIO OF DUTIES PAID TO VALUE OF IMPORTED, DUTY-PAYING GOODS

1821	1841	1861	1881	1901	1921	1941	1962	1966
6	38 18	15 11	26 32	50 46	57 69 61 66	63 61 66 58 56 39	37	37

RATIO OF GOODS IMPORTED FREE OF DUTY TO TOTAL VALUE OF ALL IMPORTS

SOURCE: *Statistical Abstract of the United States, 1967.*

1948 was finally completed in Geneva in June, 1967. President Johnson hailed the results as unprecedented and asked for new authority to seek lower barriers to international trade. He got extension of existing power for two years.

The result of the reciprocal agreements program to date has been a very substantial reduction in tariff levels. Average duties are now about 12 percent as compared to 53 percent in the early nineteen-thirties. Agreements are now in effect with more than 45 countries. Tariff-making has to a considerable degree been removed from legislative arena to the administrative one, although Congress can and has revised some of the base rates of the Tariff Act of 1930. Each recent extension of the President's power to make agreements has been contested and "protectionist" influence is still significant but not paramount in the Congress. In the last year or so, the trade program has been complicated by heavy outflow of gold due to foreign aid and investment abroad. Fear of exclusion from the European Common Market also stimulated wider business support for liberal trade policies embodied in the Kennedy Round results under the 1962 Act. The program commands wide "administration" and commercial and industrial support. It is an important item of our contemporary foreign policy and will not be easily cast aside. However, little progress has been made in dealing with nontariff trade barriers such as quotas and discriminatory taxes. Most of the lowering of tariffs has been for manufactured goods and for trade among industrial nations. The developing countries are clamoring for special trade privileges for their raw material exports.

Until World War I, business commonly depended for credit upon banks and other private financial institutions. A War Finance Corporation was then set up, however, to make government loans mainly to industries requiring them for increased war production. While that agency eventually disappeared, its place was taken during the depression by the Reconstruction Finance Corporation (R.F.C.), charged with rescuing embarrassed railroads, banks, trust companies, insurance companies, and other businesses, both large and small. During World War II the government again expanded its loan functions to stimulate the manufacture of war goods. By 1950 the national government had developed into the country's largest banker, with its lending operations extending to agriculture, housing, foreign trade as well as to business of almost every variety. In 1951 and 1952 the R.F.C. was sharply criticized in Congress. Investigation by a Senate committee revealed both partisan and personal favoritism in its operations. When the Eisenhower Administration took office pledged to reduce governmental business operations, the R.F.C. was one of its prime targets and the agency was liquidated by act of Congress. The same Congress, however, created a new Small Business Administration (SBA) and authorized it not only to assist small businesses to obtain government contracts but also to loan money to such businesses for plant expansion, modernization of equipment, and similar purposes. More recently, loans for plant expansion in "depressed" areas have been made available under the Area Redevelopment Administration. In 1968 more than $20 billion of loans were outstanding on the government's books for housing, rural electrification, farm purchase and improvement, commodity support, export–import loans, and business development. Furthermore $21.7 billion more in private loans were insured or guaranteed by the national government.

3. Lending operations

One of the great defects of the Articles of Confederation from the point of view of the business community was the freedom it allowed to debtor-controlled state legislatures to multiply the amount of money in circulation by various kinds of "cheap money" expedients. The authors of the Constitution were virtually unanimous on the need for a sound and uniform system of "hard" currency. Congress was endowed with specific authority to "coin money [and] regulate the value thereof" and the states were forbidden to "coin money, emit bills of credit, or make anything but gold and silver coin legal tender in the payment of debts." From that day to this, one of the important functions of the national government in serving business has been to provide a monetary system which will facilitate domestic and foreign commerce and will remain fairly stable as a storehouse of economic values. Although occasionally the Congress has fallen under the

4. Provision of a monetary mechanism

influence of debtor—usually agricultural—interests and has sought to "ease" the plight of the "downtrodden" by multiplying the amount of currency in circulation, in general, national management of the currency has been dominated by "sound" money policies. However, the sharp drop in gold reserves accompanying the continued imbalance in international payments led Congress in 1965 to remove the requirement that the Federal Reserve Board maintain a 25 percent gold-certificate reserve against its bank notes and in 1968 Congress removed the remaining requirement of a 25 percent gold reserve against notes in circulation. Thus there is no longer any relation between our gold holdings and currency.

5. Provision of uniform standards of weights and measures
    One of the most useful services performed by the national government in support of nationwide markets for manufactured goods, foodstuffs, and fibers is the establishment of uniform standards of weights and measures. The authority given Congress to "fix the standard of weights and measures" is so broad that it can be, and has been, exercised in connection with all manner of measurements—length, weight, volume, temperature, strength, quality, and others. One of the great landmarks in this field and one of the numerous benefactions to this nation by the Adams family is the report in 1821 by John Quincy Adams on a system of uniform measures. To aid in determining such standards, the Bureau of Standards is maintained in the Department of Commerce. Along with the familiar units taken over from old English usage—the pound, yard, gallon, bushel, and so on (with their derivatives)—the metric system employed in Continental countries, and having conspicuous advantages, has been given official status, even though as yet but little actual use is made of it outside of scientific circles. As developed to the present time, the function of the national government is merely to fix standards, keep models in the Bureau of Standards, and furnish models or copies to the states, leaving it to state and local governments, in the interest of honesty and regularity, to require compliance with the appropriate standards in business and other transactions. Congress might not only *fix* standards, but set up machinery for enforcing them nationally. This, however, it has never done.

6. Scientific research and the provision of useful data
    The business community is under a heavy and growing obligation to the national government for the collection and dissemination of useful data on trade, markets, foreign exchange, labor supply, cost of living, consumer income, investment opportunities and thousands of other subjects reflecting in great detail the condition of the economy of the nation and of the world. Monthly periodicals like the *Survey of Current Business* and *Economic Indicators* keep business supplied with timely information on the state of the economy. An elaborate network of observation posts and reporting installations supplies daily and weekly data on the weather. Less extensive but no less elaborate data is also developed on minerals, water, and other resources. The government is, however, not solely a statistical collecting agency; it is also pushing the frontiers of scientific knowledge. Through such agencies as the Bureau of Standards, the Atomic Energy Commission, the

National Science Foundation, the National Aeronautics and Space Administration, and the Department of Defense, new data, much of it of great practical utility to industry, is being discovered and made available. If one includes the research program in agriculture and that in public health, it is not too much to say that the national government has become the greatest research institution in modern America.

From its inception the national government has sought to promote the progress of science and the useful arts "by securing to authors and inventors" the exclusive right to their respective writings and discoveries. The exclusive right conferred is by way of exception to the common-law rule against monopolies, the purpose being, of course, to reward talent and encourage creative effort. Slightly over 100 years ago, a commissioner of patents soberly recommended to Congress that his office be abolished because "everything had been invented." How far wrong he was is indicated by the fact that from 50,000 to 70,000 patents are granted every year. In fact the 3 millionth patent was awarded, amidst much publicity, in September of 1961.

7. Protection of copyrights and patents

The credit structure upon which so much of modern business enterprise depends is protected and strengthened by the provision of uniform procedures for discharging unpaid obligations through bankruptcy. Under the Constitution, bankruptcy is one of the matters over which the national and state governments have concurrent legislative power. For more than 100 years (except for three brief intervals) it was left entirely to state control. In 1898, however, Congress passed a general bankruptcy act; and thereupon former state laws on the subject either were repealed or fell into a condition of suspended animation. It still is permissible for a state to legislate on bankruptcy. The national law, however, takes precedence and this law is so comprehensive that little need for state action survives.

8. Provision of uniform bankruptcy procedures

NATIONAL REGULATION OF BUSINESS—PRINCIPLES

The Congress shall have power to . . . regulate Commerce with foreign nations, and among the several States, and with the Indian tribes.—Art. 1, Sec. 8, cl. 3

The power of Congress to promote business interests by subsidies, loans, and services is sufficiently broad to encompass almost any conceivable program of this type. Few limitations of consequence have ever been discovered or enunciated by the courts to the spending power of the national government. So long as Congress declares with some reason that the object of the expenditure lies within the broad conception of public welfare, the courts appear willing to accept its power to make outlays. The power of Congress, however, to regulate business activities, that is, to penalize certain types of conduct and forbid others and to place limits upon the freedom

The power to regulate

of decision of the owners, stands on a very different constitutional footing. It is subject to a number of constitutional restraints. The most important of these are (1) that the regulatory authority of the Congress is largely confined to interstate and foreign commerce, and (2) that the power must be exercised so as not to deprive any entrepreneur, partner, or corporation of "due process of law."

All of the economic activities which are embraced in the concept of "business" are not historically included in the word *commerce* and all of those which are included are not interstate or international in character. The limitations on the power of Congress to regulate business, which are based upon the protection of property in the due-process clause of the Fifth Amendment, have already been discussed in an earlier chapter.

Expansion of the meaning of "commerce"

The history of the constitutional meaning of interstate commerce is one of progressive expansion by statute and judicial interpretation so as to embrace not only the great technological changes in the fields of transportation and communication but also to embrace more and more forms of business activity. The regulation of all forms of interstate transportation and communication has been validly entrusted to the Congress for many decades. Only after a long controversy and in the midst of economic depression and political attack did the Court come around to the opinion that, nearly all manufacturing and other production being, under present-day conditions, carried on with a view to the interstate or national, or even the international, market, the commerce clause may properly be construed to permit Congress to regulate as commerce any business transactions or operations resulting in or otherwise associated with interstate or foreign commerce, however indirectly. From this seminal concept, it was but a step to holding, more specifically, that all manufacturing, mining, lumbering, and other productive enterprises in which raw materials or finished products, or both, are carried in interstate commerce are inseparable from such commerce, and are, therefore, within the scope of congressional regulative power. It was on this basis that many of the regulating statutes of the New Deal were ultimately sustained.

Present scope of congressional power

Under the prevailing theories of the power of Congress over interstate and foreign commerce, therefore, only the most parochial of business activities are exempted from national authority. Such business transactions must begin and end within the confines of a single state and must have no demonstrable effect upon or relevance to transactions which go beyond the state borders. This does not mean, however, that the states are wholly denied the power to regulate business activities which come within the scope of national power. They may be authorized by Congress or by the courts to exercise regulatory authority if not inconsistent with national policies or with judicially determined national needs. The states, therefore, continue to regulate many types of business transactions and institutions, even some which have interstate aspects. For the most part, however, their regulations must be consistent with national statutes or regulations or with judicial decisions on the scope of national power.

The power to regulate, it must be added, includes also the power to prohibit. Embargoes on foreign commerce, for example, have been imposed several times in our history (for example, in 1794, in 1812, and in 1917–1918) suspending trade completely with some countries or in some commodities. Congress has prohibited the transportation across state lines of lottery tickets, stolen goods, prostitutes, "filled" milk, liquor if being taken into "dry" states, and prison-made goods if in violation of state laws. *Regulation includes prohibition*

Regulatory authority over foreign commerce is broader than over interstate. The exclusive and virtually unrestricted jurisdiction of the national government over our relations abroad applies to commerce no less than to everything else and, this adds materially to the regulative power conferred in the commerce clause—in addition to opening up methods of dealing with commerce otherwise than by congressional act, for example, by treaty. Authority to regulate foreign commerce, furthermore, extends to every act of transportation or communication cutting across our national boundaries, no matter how deep into the country may be the point of beginning or ending. *Authority over foreign commerce broader than over interstate commerce*

Despite the broad sweep of authority now believed to reside in the Congress to regulate business, it has not seen fit to bring the entire business community under detailed scrutiny of the national administration. The amount and character of national regulation vary widely from one type of business activity to another and from one epoch of time to another. In World War II, for example, the national government regulated businesses of all types in more minute detail than it had before or than it has since. In general, the regulatory power has been exercised more completely in those fields of business where monopolistic conditions—actual or potential—have threatened a weakening of the supposed regulatory effect of competition in free market. The Congress has also sought to safeguard the position of employes against exploitation by powerful corporate combinations. This type of restraint upon business we shall consider in the chapter on labor. *Exercise of power to regulate*

REGULATION OF BUSINESS—TRANSPORTATION

A discussion of the practices of business regulation must necessarily begin with the railroads, for these were the first major objects of concern. In the long struggle to bring the owners and managers of these great instrumentalities of commerce under the control of the government there was established a pattern of regulatory theory and procedure which has been closely followed when other forms of business activities have been brought under public control.

It is hardly too much to say that the United States, as a nation of continental dimensions, has been made by transportation. Certainly growth in territory, population, wealth, and power not only has paralleled the sequence of horse and rider, stage coach, steamboat, railroad, automobile, and airplane but would not have been possible without it. By and large, *Transportation development:*

transportation development has been one of the great achievements of our boasted free private enterprise. At the same time, it never could have taken place without a great deal of government aid.

1. Railroads: Federal regulation becomes necessary

Until long after the Civil War—and after most of the great expansion in the West and Southwest had taken place—regulation of railroad financing, operations, and procedures was left almost entirely to the states. As roads extended their networks through many states, and vast countrywide systems were built up, the situation got out of hand. By the later seventies and the eighties, railroad management and operation had become "big business," with formidable financial and other economic powers involved, with intense rivalries engendering ruthless policies, and with fabulous profits at stake. The railroad magnates took full advantage of the lack of effective competition. More than this, they used their great power by rebates and preferential rates to force monopoly into other segments of the business community. Abuses calling for remedy were many and glaring. The states attempted at first to correct matters insofar as they could. But their spheres were restricted; railroad magnates and lobbyists often dominated their legislatures; regulations by only one or a few states were ineffective; the Courts denied state authority over fares in interstate commerce. This placed the matter squarely in the hands of the Congress.

The Interstate Commerce Act (1887) and its expansion

The upshot of all this experience and of continued popular dissatisfaction and protest among western farmers and eastern small businessmen, was the passage by Congress in 1887 of an Act to Regulate Commerce, forbidding excessive charges, discriminations, and other unfair practices, and creating a special agency—the Interstate Commerce Commission—to administer and enforce the principles and rules laid down. Under it and the laws and decisions supplementing it is now regulated all interstate transportation of persons and commodities carried on by railroads, by common carriers by water (both inland and coastal), by express companies, by sleeping-car and other private-car companies, by freight forwarders, by motor-bus companies, and by pipelines except those for the transportation of gas and water. Bridges, ferries, car-floats, and lighters, and indeed terminal and other facilities of whatsoever character when used in the interstate transportation of persons or goods are also regulated. Until 1934, the act applied also to instrumentalities and facilities used for the transmission of intelligence by means of electricity, such as telegraph, telephone, cable, and wireless systems.

Restrictions imposed

Upon railroads—and, so far as applicable, upon all other instrumentalities of public service subject to the basic law—are imposed numerous restrictions each prompted by some earlier abuse. Thus, (1) rates for the transportation of persons and freight must be just and reasonable, and calculated to yield merely a "fair return" on the value of the property employed; (2) charging a higher rate for a short haul than for a long one over the same line in the same direction is forbidden, except when authorized in special instances by the Interstate Commerce Commission; (3) rebating directly or indirectly, and undue discrimination or preference among persons, corporations, or localities are prohibited; (4) free transportation may be granted only to narrowly restricted classes of persons; (5) railroads are forbidden, except in a few special cases, to operate, own, or control, or to have any interest in, any competing carrier by water; (6) except under strict supervision of the Commission, competing lines may not combine, merge their receipts, and apportion resulting profits; (7) carriers may not transport commodities (except timber and its products) in which they have a direct property interest; and (8) they may issue long-term securities, purchase or build additional lines, or abandon old lines, only with the Commission's consent.

In addition, numerous positive duties are prescribed. For example, (1) printed schedules of rates must be kept open for public inspection, and changes in them may be made only with consent of the Interstate Commerce Commission; (2) full and complete annual reports must be made to the Commission, covering such matters, and arranged in such form, as the Commission may require; (3) all accounts must be kept according to a uniform system authorized by the Commission; (4) in case of injury to any of its employes while on duty, a carrier must grant pecuniary compensation, unless the accident was caused by willful act or negligence of the injured party; (5) the standard or basic work day for railway employes engaged in the operation of trains is eight hours, and carriers must conform their wage schedules to it and grant overtime pay; (6) all trains engaged in interstate commerce must be equipped with automatic safety appliances; and (7) all railway companies so engaged must maintain compulsory retirement and pension systems for their superannuated employes.

Duties prescribed

The Interstate Commerce Commission (I.C.C.)—charged with enforcing the regulations outlined above and many lesser ones as well—consists of 11 persons appointed by the President and confirmed by the Senate for seven-year terms, and has a staff of some 1900 clerks, attorneys, examiners, statisticians, investigators, and technical experts, organized in 3 divisions embracing 9 distinct bureaus and offices. The commissioners themselves work almost entirely in panels or divisions of three members each; and a decision of a panel has the same force and effect as a decision of the Commission itself—subject to the entire Commission granting a rehearing. Any person, corporation, municipality, or other private or public group may lodge with the Commission a complaint concerning any alleged infraction of the interstate commerce laws. The Commission, acting ordinarily through one of its panels, must institute an inquiry. If preliminary investigation discloses that the complaint may be well founded, a hearing follows, of a sort not unlike those to be observed in a court of justice: plaintiff and defendant are represented by attorneys; books, papers, and other materials (which the Commission has full power to order produced) are placed in evidence; witnesses are examined; and at the end the Commission, that is, in most instances the appropriate panel, embodies its

The Interstate Commerce Commission

conclusion or finding in an order enforceable in the courts, although also with right of appeal to those courts by the party affected adversely. Orders may relate to rates, quality or conditions of service, or any one of literally scores of other things falling within the scope of the laws; and disobedience renders the offender liable to prosecution.

Control over rates

Under the original law, the Commission did not have power to make or revise rates, either on its own initiative or on complaint of shippers that existing rates were unreasonable. Ultimately, however—although only after a vigorous campaign of popular education, and in the face of persistent opposition from the carriers—the necessity of conferring extensive rate-making power was brought home to the public. Under the transportation acts of 1906 and 1920, the Commission (as agent of Congress for the purpose) is authorized, on complaint and after hearing, not only to fix "just and reasonable" rates, regulations, and practices, but also to prescribe definite maximum or minimum charges. The Commission finds itself in consequence of this heavy responsibility, perpetually under crossfire from shippers and other interests clamoring for lower charges, and, on the other hand, carriers insisting that rising operating costs or other factors call for rate increases. On the ground that to compel even property "affected with a public interest" to be used without suitable compensation would amount to confiscation, the Court has declared that rates should be such as to insure a "fair return" on the "value" of the property involved. But upon what constitutes "fair return," especially as to how "value" is to be determined, there can be, and is, a great variety of opinion. The matter is too involved to be discussed here, but it may be observed that, whereas until later years the Supreme Court was inclined to support valuation based (for example, in the case of a railroad) on what it would cost currently to reproduce the road and its facilities, less an allowance for depreciation, the present tendency is rather to favor valuation in terms of the more stable and manageable criterion of the amount of money actually put into constructing and developing the road from its beginning, again of course with a deduction for depreciation.

The pattern of regulation

The pattern of government regulation which emerges from the efforts to control the railroads is (1) that the regulating agency be an independent commission removed by legislative intent from the direct oversight of the President and exercising its powers in a more or less judicial atmosphere; (2) that the regulatory authority be granted by Congress in the broadest terms—"just and reasonable rates"—with the agency authorized to specify in particular how the authority will be discharged; (3) that the actions of the agency will be carefully scrutinized by the courts on appeal and that such court scrutiny will emphasize the protection of property rights against administrative impairment; (4) that competition will be encouraged as a "natural" regulator until it is demonstrably obvious—as it has been since 1920 in the case of the railroads—that the effort to inject competition is either impractical or unwise; (5) that, although the original grant of regulatory power may extend only to certain aspects of the business under consideration, the power is likely to be broadened subsequently to bring under scrutiny more and more facets of the enterprise.

After more than 80 years of railroad regulation by the procedures and under the policies outlined, a few observations are in order. In consequence of vast and rapid technological change, more and more goods are now being moved by highway and air and more and more people are traveling by private motor car. The once proud and truculent railroad industry is sick unto death. Whatever monopoly it once could claim has nearly vanished. Its great stations are falling into disrepair and its small stations disappearing. Each of its chief competitors receives subsidy and benevolent supervision. The continuance of commuter service in our large cities prob- *Results of regulation*

Rise and Decline of the American Railroad System

DATE	NO. OF LOCOMOTIVES	NO. OF FREIGHT CARS	NO. OF MILES OF TRACK
1880	17,949	539,255	115,647
1890	31,812	1,061,952	208,152
1900	37,663	1,365,531	258,784
1910	60,019	2,148,478	351,767
1920	68,942	2,388,424	406,580
1930	60,189	2,322,267	429,883
1940	44,333	1,684,171	405,975
1950	42,951	1,745,778	396,380
1960	31,178	1,690,396	381,745
1966	30,124	1,524,000	370,104

SOURCE: *Statistical Abstract of the United States, 1968.*

ably depends on subsidies and tax advantages and in Washington pleas for financial help are advanced in every Congress. The detailed, case-by-case method of insuring fair rates and reasonable service under a bipartisan and judicial commission seems peculiarly ill-adapted to the problems of the day. How by these procedures can the relative claims of highway, air, and rail be fairly weighed? Faced by organized labor's demand for higher wages how can higher rates be promised? How relevant is the case law on "fair return" to either of these questions? How can terminals, yards, switching and sorting facilities be consolidated and moved to cheaper land to save taxes, labor costs, and transit time? There are no easy answers to these questions. The commission system, however, has not conclusively demonstrated that it can accommodate itself readily to a fast changing world. For virtually all other forms of transport government policy is directed by the Department of Transportation created in 1966 and directed to coordinate highway, air, and water transport and government efforts in relation to them. Except, of course, rate-fixing and service regulations continue to be imposed by independent regulatory commissions patterned after the I.C.C. *Department of Transportation created*

Historically, the regulation of interstate transportation has, until this

2. Water transportation

century, been largely a matter of regulating railroads. A good deal of such commerce, however, has always been water-borne—in vessels plying the coastal waters of the country or its rivers and lakes. For most of our history, national attention to this type of commerce took the form almost entirely of expenditure for the improvement of rivers and harbors. Over the years billions of dollars have been spent for this purpose, sometimes legitimately and wisely, but often only on the basis of congressional log-rolling. River and harbor bills have traditionally been a favorite source of congressional "pork." Only when the railroads began to complain that they suffered unfairly from the competition of unregulated water traffic did the Congress attempt to bring such traffic under conrol. In the Transportation Act of 1940, Congress prescribed a system of regulation of rates, services, and management of water shipping under the purview of the I.C.C. The Act of 1940, however, made numerous exemptions and perhaps 90 percent of the tonnage of domestic carriers is unregulated.

Shipping engaged in foreign commerce and commerce between the continental United States and the island territories is regulated by a Federal Maritime Commission. The Board also works in close association with the Maritime Administration in the department of Commerce which administers the various programs of governmental subsidy and assistance to the shipping industry engaged in foreign trade. The Johnson effort in 1966 to transfer this function to the new Department of Transportation was defeated. The government is still searching for a viable maritime policy. The U.S. merchant fleet has declined to fewer than 1000 vessels and carries less than 8 percent of the nation's foreign commerce.

3. Motor transportation

Meanwhile, however, the jurisdiction of the I.C.C. had been enormously extended in another direction. The automobile had been introduced, and trucks and buses had come into use. For a good while, distances covered were usually limited and no regulation was deemed necessary beyond state or local provisions concerning licensing and safety. As truck and bus business developed, however, on something approaching its present huge scale, serious difficulties and abuses arose—cut-throat competition between companies and especially between them and the regulated railroads, underpayment of employes, laxity about accident insurance, dubious financing. Although remedial measures were instituted by some states, it became apparent that the business had so largely assumed an interstate character that, as the Interstate Commerce Commission long urged, the problem was fundamentally one for the national government. In 1935, therefore, Congress passed a Motor Carrier Act, bringing all interstate truck and bus lines within the pale of national law and making the I.C.C. the regulating authority. If it intends to operate across state boundaries, a truck or bus company must initially secure a certificate of convenience and necessity from the Commission. Thereupon, its financing, rates, accounts, records, hours of labor, safety appliances, and general level of service become subject to that body's supervision substantially as in the case of railroads.

It might be supposed that regulations thus applied to trucks and buses would make possible a coordinated policy for land transport within the I.C.C. However, wholly outside the purview of the Commission is the huge highway program of the national government, laying at public expense the roadbed for the automotive industry and providing a key determinant of

The Changing Pattern of U.S. Passenger Traffic
1946-1965

TYPE	PASSENGER MILES (BILLIONS)			
	1946	% TOTAL	1965	% TOTAL
Railroad	66.3	18.7	17.6	1.8
Bus	26.9	7.6	23.3	2.5
Waterway	2.3	.6	3.1	.3
Airplane	5.9	1.7	58.1	6.2
Private Auto	253.6	71.4	838.1	89.2

SOURCE: *Statistical Abstract of the United States, 1967.*

costs. Furthermore, a large portion of highway hauling is unregulated, except for safety and labor protection rules, since trucks wholly owned by shippers are exempted. The I.C.C. estimates that its controls reach fewer than 20 percent of the motor carriers.

Shortly after World War I (which imparted a considerable impetus to aviation), a standing interstate conference having as its object the promotion of uniformity in state legislation brought forward a uniform state law for aeronautics; and numerous states adopted it. As time went on, however, much, if not most, flying became interstate; and in 1926 Congress passed the first act regulating air traffic. A Federal Aviation Act of 1958 established the present regulatory and promotional system dividing these duties between a Federal Aviation Agency and a Civil Aeronautics Board. The former concerns itself principally with mapping, lighting, and marking interstate airways, providing regular and emergency landing fields, licensing planes and pilots, devising and administering safety programs, and fostering aviation research. The latter is concerned principally with the regulatory functions of controlling rates and services for the interstate transportation of passengers, mail, and goods, reviewing accident findings and promulgating rules on safety, issuing certificates to airlines, suspending or revoking licenses, and generally controlling the economics of air transport. In 1967, the Department of Transportation absorbed the Federal Aviation Agency and the safety responsibilities of the Board. In a domain in which strict uniformity of rules and practices is peculiarly desirable, the states have in most instances risen to the need by incorporating all national regulations into their own aviation codes. As in the cases of rail, water, and road transportation, the government has participated heavily by expenditures for facilities and by mail subsidies. For a good while the

4. Aviation

facilities program (airport construction and flight control) was well ahead of the traffic but by the late sixties congestion in the nation's major airports has become a serious problem and major new financing perhaps supported by user taxes is being seriously considered.

5. Pipelines

For a good while, crude oil and various petroleum products have been transported from the great southwestern oil fields to the North and East not only by rail and water but also by pipeline. World War II saw a considerable expansion of this form of interstate commerce. By its nature, natural gas definitely requires this method of transportation; and one of the most extraordinary developments in the transportation field since the

THE CHANGING PATTERN OF U.S. FREIGHT TRAFFIC

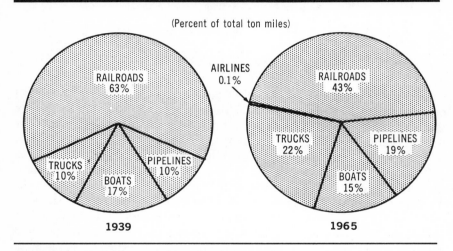

(Percent of total ton miles)

SOURCE: *Statistical Abstract of the United States,* 1967.

recent war has been the multiplication and extension of transmission lines linking gas-producing areas from Kansas to Louisiana with principal cities and many smaller ones throughout more than half of the country. Under appropriate conditions, rates and services are now regulated, with the Interstate Commerce Commission functioning in the case of petroleum and the Federal Power Commission in that of gas.

REGULATION OF BUSINESS—COMMUNICATION

As illustrated by motor and air transport and indeed, by the steamship and the railroad, science and technology are responsible for many new modes of transportation, progressively expanding the instrumentalities of "commerce" and augmenting the task of regulation. In the field of communications, even more revolutionary developments have occurred in the techniques of producing and distributing newspapers, the methods of handling the mails, and especially the harnessing of electrical energy. In most European countries, facilities for electrical communication—telegraph, telephone, radio and television—are government-owned and operated, directly or through auxiliary corporations. Apart from some limited ownership and operation of facilities for its own use by the national government, all of these instrumentalities in the United States, on the other hand, have been developed and, speaking broadly, are owned and operated privately. Since all more important ones necessarily are interstate, and in some instances international, substantially all fall within the range of congressional control over commerce.

When first developed, intrastate wire communications were regulated, rather ineffectively, by the states, and interstate communications not at all. And this continued to be the situation even after Congress, in 1910, gave the Interstate Commerce Commission jurisdiction over telegraph, telephone, and cable companies operating in interstate and foreign commerce. Preoccupied with railway problems, the Commission paid but little attention to its new task. Partly on this account, and partly because of unsatisfactory experience with the first machinery set up for regulating radio, Congress in 1934 concentrated all responsibility for both wire and wireless communications in a new independent regulatory body, the present Federal Communications Commission (F.C.C.), consisting of seven members appointed by the President and confirmed by the Senate for seven-year terms. Here again the impetus to effective national regulation was the existence in practice of monopolistic conditions. It is neither wise nor practical to have competing telephone or cable systems. The American Telephone and Telegraph Company (actually confined to telephone service save for providing the wire circuits for Western Union), now covers the entire country with its facilities. Since the merger of the Postal Telegraph Company with the Western Union Company in 1943, there are no telegraph competitors of any importance. Therefore, virtually all telegraph and all long-distance telephone services are now under national regulation, as of course, for obvious reasons, are all cable lines. Submarine cables may be licensed only by the President, who also is responsible for seeing that reasonable rates and services are maintained. The F.C.C. controls the actual transmission of messages. The telegraph and telephone lines are "common carriers"; their services must be adequate; their rates must be just and reasonable, authorized by the Commission, publicly advertised, and changed only with notice given the Commission and public; no discriminations may be practiced; new lines may be constructed and existing ones extended only with the Commission's consent; and full reports must be rendered, with access by the Commission to all records and accounts.

The basic problem of the telegraph industry is the same as that of

1. Telegraph, telephone, and cable

the railroads. It is in decline and its functions largely shifted to long distance telephone, teletype machinery, and air mail. In the telephone industry, a different set of problems plague the regulators. The powers of the F.C.C. do not extend to certain major subsidiaries of the Bell and A. T. and T. systems such as Western Electric from which virtually all equipment is purchased. Most of the rates and services of the system are controlled by state rather than national regulatory commissions under various procedures and formulas.

2. Radio and tele- vision
Radio broadcasting had its actual beginning in 1920, and seven years later Congress belatedly recognized a need for regulation. Nature imposed the monopoly here by making it impossible for listeners to hear two broadcasts on the same wavelength. The first act assigned the function to a Federal Radio Commission of five members, and charged it with licensing stations, assigning wavelengths, and exercising other supervision. The arrangement did not work well, and in 1934 the Commission was abolished and its functions vested in the new Federal Communications Commission. Radio and now television broadcasting—on the theory that air waves may cross state boundaries—has been from the beginning under *exclusive* national control; and, subject to the ultimate authority of Congress, all power over it is in the F.C.C. The number of channels being limited by nature, the first and largest problem is that of choosing among large numbers of applicants for the privilege of operating a station those persons (citizens only) who shall be given licenses, and deciding what frequencies they shall be assigned. The criterion required by law is "public interest, convenience, and necessity," which, as in the other regulatory laws, leaves almost complete discretion to the Commission.

Unlike regulation of transportation systems, the regulation of broadcasting has never involved control of rates or profits. Broadcasting companies are not "common carriers" in the eyes of the law and are, therefore, not required to offer services to customers on a carefully regulated basis. Although the major control exercised over them by the F.C.C. stems from the assignment of wavelengths and frequencies, it is by no means confined to this and includes the practices of the broadcasters in what is put out over the air.

From the beginning the task of the F.C.C. has been extremely difficult. What standards should be considered in designating those few among many applicants who are to receive the privilege of operating a lucrative enterprise? Among the distinct interests—those of the manufacturers of receiving sets, those of the operators of broadcasting stations, those of the great networks (three in television and seven in radio), those of the advertisers and their clients, those of the receiving public—which are to be favored and to what extent? Are there other uses of broadcasting facilities than commercial ones—education, for example—that ought to be encouraged and facilitated? Is competition desirable between broadcasters or between broadcasting and other media of communication or is it better to regulate a few large concerns than many small ones? In the interests of decency, political competition, civic education and community morality what control, if any, should be exercised over program content?

In determining policies for the assignment of broadcast channels, the Commission seems to have been guided by (1) priority—that is, those already in the business because of their huge investment in facilities are likely to be preferred to newcomers; (2) technical adequacy—that is, the quality of the equipment and the engineering personnel such as to justify licensing; (3) financial responsibility—that is, is there adequate proof of strong backing by the users of time and by the owners of the company; (4) public service—that is, is the program content merely propaganda or are the listeners assured of reasonably well rounded programs aimed at popular taste. All of these, however, especially the last one, are difficult to measure and judgments about them differ widely. From the beginning the Commission has been expressly forbidden to exercise censorship but it certainly must interest itself in the character and quality of the programs being offered. Required from the start also, to provide equal time to all candidates for office, it has found it difficult to encourage the use of broadcasting for civic educational purposes. The waiver of this requirement in the presidential campaign of 1960 remains as yet an exception to the requirement rather than a permanent modification of it.

In view of all the uncertainties of the situation, the deep and abiding differences of view about proper public policy, and the great value of the privilege which the Commission can confer, it is not surprising that the F.C.C. has been caught up in controversy almost from its inception and has suffered through several periods of obloquy. In the most recent of these—1958–1960—the Commission was investigated by a committee of the House, many questionable practices were revealed and one commissioner was forced out of office. A scandal in network broadcasting also came to light during this period. Quiz shows of various kinds were shown to be rigged and record companies were shown to have encouraged the promotion of their records by various broadcasters through gifts of cash and other items of value.

COMSAT

The Soviet–American thrusts into outer space of the sixties provided the technology for a new dimension in international communication: the orbiting of T.V. and telephone relay stations. In 1962, Congress in the Communication Satellite Act authorized the creation of a private corporation with considerable public participation and control to establish a satellite system and in 1964 we joined with ten other countries in the formation of an International Tele-communications Satellite Consortium for the purpose of international cooperation in the orbiting and control of such satellites. Fifty-eight nations are now members of this consortium. The executive branch is in 1968 reviewing the problems arising from the efforts to unite our now predominantly privately owned system which reaches beyond our shores with those (predominantly publicly owned) of other nations.

REGULATION OF BUSINESS—POWER GENERATION

*Public
power
and
regulation*

Although as we shall recount in the chapter on Conservation, the major modern thrust of national power policy is for publicly owned generators and transmissions systems, since earlier in the century the national government has also regulated privately owned power facilities. In order to control the manning of our river systems for hydroelectric power generation purposes, the Congress in 1920 created the Federal Power Commission to license such projects and to control the rates for interstate electricity distribution. Originally a Cabinet committee, the Commission became a fully independent entity of five members, like the others already described, in 1930. Its jurisdiction presently extends not only to hydroelectric power projects but also to the interstate sale of electricity, however generated. Most generation and distribution of electric power continues, however, to be regulated closely by state public utility commissions and the national influence on the costs of electricity is derived more from its public power projects than from F.P.C. regulation. The Commission has important but limited duties and responsibilities in connection with nationally owned hydro-power facilities. It also, under the National Gas Act of 1938 and subsequent Supreme Court decisions regulates the rates of natural gas distributed by pipelines across state lines.

The Atomic Energy Commission has since 1946 also been concerned with the promotion and control of nuclear reactors used for electric power generation whether by private or public agencies.

REGULATION OF BUSINESS COMBINATIONS

*Corpora-
tions,
trusts, and
holding
companies*

Business in this country attained its present immense proportions mainly through the growth of corporations and the pyramiding of such corporations, in turn, into combinations of still greater size and power. Public, or "government," corporations obtain their charters from Congress. Private corporations may do so likewise, but usually get them rather from a state (Delaware being a favorite because of the easy terms permitted), with legal rights ostensibly restricted to the state of incorporation, but in practice extended to other states as well by simple formalities of registration. Their owners are the people who hold shares of stock; capital is obtained also from those who lend them money, receiving certificates of indebtedness in the form of bonds. The officers and directors who operate them are largely immune from personal responsibility, with the organizations, as such, also sustaining only limited liability at law. Sixty or seventy years ago, corporations began forming associations or alliances aimed at combinations based upon agreements fixing prices, dividing sales territory, limiting production, and sharing profits. Presently there appeared also *trusts,* in which stocks of a group of corporate units were gathered largely or wholly into the hands of a single company acting as trustee, with of course control over all of the affiliates. In time, too, arose *holding companies,* with assets consisting solely of stocks of operating companies whose affairs they controlled, and developed particularly in the field of gas, electric, and other public utilities. And on such a scale did these various developments take place that by 1933 our 100 largest industrial units (corporations, trusts, holding companies, and other combinations), with assets aggregating almost $100 billion conrolled not only nearly half of the country's industrial wealth, but one-fifth of the entire national wealth.

From such concentration of economic power, evils long ago began to flow—overcapitalization, "watered" stock, and the like, but chiefly monopoly, with its attendant strangulation of smaller competitive enterprises, its complete domination of an economic function or group of functions, its independent and irresponsible control over services and prices. Manifestly, in certain fields monopoly is hardly to be avoided. Speaking generally, it is not practicable for two or three gas or electric companies to operate in the same city; and in such cases public regulation has been widely introduced. From England, however, America inherited a deep-seated antipathy to monopoly in general, and the common law as brought across the Atlantic (and still basic to our legal system) made unlawful any monopolistic powers and practices unreasonably obstructing trade—in other words, interfering with the freedom of competing businesses, large and small, to organize and operate on equal terms. And this free scope for individual initiative and enterprise, leaving the way open for failure and disaster, but also for opportunity and achievement, and insuring the consuming public the benefits of quality and price flowing from a competitive quest for markets and profits, has always been highly prized by the American people. By the same token, the protection of this conception—in other words, the curbing of monopolistic abuses—has been, and remains a major public concern.

The problem of monopoly

For upwards of 100 years, in part because of the limited definition given to commerce by courts and Congress, the states were left to deal with monopolistic and other practices interfering with the free flow of trade. The correctives they brought to bear rested either upon the old common-law principle that all combinations operating to restrain trade *unreasonably* were illegal, or upon statutes defining or modifying that principle's applications. In the era of big business, state regulation proved almost wholly ineffectual.

State regulation proves inadequate

In 1890, therefore, Congress, taking a novel view of its commerce power risked judicial disapproval by passing a vigorous measure—the Sherman Antitrust Act—aimed at protecting trade and commerce "against unlawful restraints, and monopolies," and to that end declaring in sweeping terms, every contract, combination, or conspiracy in restraint of trade

National control introduced —the Sherman Act (1890)

or commerce among the several states or with foreign nations to be illegal, and providing heavy penalties for violations. Congress, however, left enforcement to the Department of Justice, with no special machinery and hardly any funds provided; busy with other things that Department showed little zeal for action. When it did finally bring action against the Sugar Trust in 1895, a Supreme Court decision severely narrowed the scope of the law by ruling that although the defendant produced all but 2 percent of the sugar used in the United States, its business was primarily *manufacturing* rather than *commerce,* and therefore subject to regulation only by the states. For another decade virtually nothing happened—with most of the really huge industrial trusts of later days meanwhile getting their start.

The "rule of reason"

"Trust-busting" was one of President Theodore Roosevelt's prime interests, and successful prosecution in 1904 of a prominent holding company charged with monopoly in the railway field (the Northern Securities Co.) gave him fresh impetus. Notwithstanding government victories in other cases, however, the Supreme Court in 1911 again weakened the law by setting up a distinction between combinations which, in the Court's opinion, involved only a "reasonable," and those which amounted to an "unreasonable," restraint of interstate or foreign trade.

Further legislation required

Experience of this sort suggested that if the law applied only to "unreasonable" combinations, some means should be provided by which well-intentioned combinations might know whether they would be regarded by the government as "reasonable," and therefore lawful, without first being subjected to a criminal prosecution to determine the matter. Demand arose, too, for clarification as to the kinds of arrangements that the government would look upon as unreasonable restraints of trade, and as to the corporate practices that it would regard as constituting unfair competitive methods. The outcome was (1) the passage, in 1914, of the Clayton Antitrust Act to reinforce and supplement the Sherman Act of 1890, and (2) the simultaneous creation of the Federal Trade Commission as an agency to cooperate with the Department of Justice in the enforcement of antitrust laws, new and old, and especially to curb unfair competitive practices in the conduct of business.

The Clayton Antitrust Act (1914)

Earnestly sponsored by President Wilson as a "new law" to meet "conditions that menace our civilization," though opposed with equal vigor by business interests, the Clayton Act (1) forbade price-cutting to drive out competitors, granting rebates, making false assertions about competitors, limiting the freedom of purchasers to deal in the products of competing manufacturers, and a long list of other abuses, discriminations, and restraints of trade; (2) forbade corporations to acquire stock in competing concerns, if the effect would be to lessen competition, and outlawed interlocking directorates in the case of larger banks, industrial corporations, and common carriers; (3) made officers of corporations personally liable for violations of the act; and (4) made it easier for injured parties in cases arising under either this act or the original antitrust law to prosecute their suits.

The object of the new legislation of 1914 was to close the gaps in the Sherman Act, and President Wilson hailed it as supplying "clear and sufficient law to check and destroy the noxious growth [of monopoly] in its infancy." Notoriously, however, it proved less effective than had been hoped. Congress failed to provide adequate funds for properly staffing the antitrust division of the Department of Justice, leaving it possible to prosecute only the most flagrant cases in a few large industries. In interpreting "unfair methods of competition," the courts grew increasingly tolerant. To a deadweight of opposition from large business interests was added honest doubts of disinterested persons, including some officials, as to whether the entire program was practicable, or even desirable, and especially as to whether corrective regulation of trusts and other combinations was not preferable to attempts to break them up completely. Efforts, too, to make directors personally liable for the acts of corporations almost completely broke down. During World War I, the entire program was, to all intents and purposes, suspended; through ensuing Republican administrations, the legislation was seldom invoked. When the National Recovery Act of 1933 was placed on the statute books in an effort to rescue the country from a great depression those laws were expressly waived for as long as the emergency legislation should remain in force. This period of suspension proved, however, of only two years' duration, and thereupon the laws came back into at least nominal operation. Presently, too, as the New Deal administration shifted its economic ground some new vigor was placed behind their enforcement. Thurman W. Arnold, was placed in charge of the antitrust division of the Department of Justice and forthwith became the most assiduous "trust-buster" that the country had known, instituting in five years 44 percent of all proceedings started under the antitrust laws between 1890 and his retirement in 1943. There was, however, some shift from the old idea of "trust-busting" as an object in itself to that of defending a free market in the necessities of modern life. With this broader social end in view, prosecutions were directed primarily against private groups that had established themselves in strategic positions of control—against "bottle-necks of business" that blocked the distribution of products anywhere along the line from the raw-material stage to purchase by the ultimate consumer.

With the outbreak of World War II the antimonopoly campaign was slowed down. The government sought more benevolent relations with the larger corporations in order to encourage armament production. President Roosevelt announced in 1942 that, while every effort would be made to protect the public interest, with no violation of law escaping ultimate punishment, prosecutions would be postponed whenever it could be shown that they would tend to interfere with production of materials for war use. In

A quarter-century of irregular enforcement

The situation during World War II

the same year, indeed, Congress expressly exempted from prosecution at any time any acts or omissions "deemed in the public interest" and approved by the chairman of the War Production Board after consultation with the attorney general.

More recent developments

After the war President Truman showed concern, and indeed during the campaign of 1948 made a great deal of political capital out of attacks on "big business," special interests, trusts, and Wall Street. After the election, moreover, Administration forces launched a twofold program, on the one hand a vigorous drive for antitrust law enforcement, and on the other a more cooperative approach aimed at clarifying for business the many ambiguities of existing law and drawing sharper lines between what the government considered legal and what illegal combinations and practices. The period from 1948–1952 was another period of vigorous enforcement. In 1950 the Clayton Act was amended (Anti-Merger Act of 1950) to prohibit not only the acquisition of stock of a competing corporation but also of its assets where competition was lessened by such action. Suits were started or activated against some of the largest enterprises in the nation: the "Big Four" meat packers (Swift, Armour, Wilson, and Cudahy), DuPont, American Telephone and Telegraph, the A & P grocery chain, Aluminum Company of America, the leading motion picture distributors, the three large farm machinery manufacturers (International Harvester, Deere, and Case), and many others. The Supreme Court, meanwhile, enunciated interpretations more friendly to the antimonopolists. It reversed an earlier position and held that size alone could be objectionable. It also held that the power to raise prices or to exclude competition is an abuse whether these things have been done or not.

The Eisenhower administration from 1952–1960 abated, somewhat, the aggressiveness of the campaign against monopoly. Attorney General Brownell announced his policy as primarily one of promoting competition rather than attacking bigness and stated that criminal prosecution would rarely be used. A large number of new suits were, nevertheless, started and numerous pending cases were terminated by agreement. The major emphasis seemed to be to halt mergers rather than attack existing combinations. The Kennedy administration emphasized price-fixing conspiracies as the object of its major antitrust prosecutions and has successfully attacked that in the electrical-equipment industry. Suits against the major steel companies and several major drug firms were started in 1963.

The results of the activities of the past two decades are mixed. The Aluminum Company was ordered to divest itself of its Canadian properties. The A & P Company was fined $175,000 and ordered to divest itself of a subsidiary wholesale operation, the Atlantic Commission Company. It successfully resisted efforts to break it up into seven retail divisions. The DuPont case, dismissed by the district court after months of argument, was carried to the Supreme Court by the government and the company was ordered to divest itself of its stock in the General Motors Corp. This position it reaffirmed vigorously after the government again appealed a district court order calling only for limited divestiture. The case against A. T. and T. was settled by consent decree before adjudication was complete and while the company was ordered to license a large number of its patents free to all applicants and others for a reasonable charge, it was not required to divest itself of Western Electric, its chief supplier of telephone equipment. I.B.M. agreed by a similar procedure to offer for sale as well as rental its tabulating and computing machines and to license a number of its patents free or on a "reasonable" royalty basis. A proposed merger of Youngstown Sheet and Tube Company with the Bethlehem Steel Company was halted by injunction requested by the government in 1958. Perhaps the most damaging attacks were those against the largest manufacturers in the electrical industry including Westinghouse Electric Corp. and General Electric Company. Charged in late 1960 with a price-fixing conspiracy on heavy electrical equipment, the major defendants pleaded guilty and several officials were actually sent to jail. Acquisition of the Rome Cable Company by Aluminum Corporation of America was nullified by the Supreme Court in 1964 and a proposed merger of a leading manufacturer of metal containers with one of glass containers was vetoed on the grounds that the competition to be preserved is for the whole market.

Over a 79-year stretch, frontal attack on monopoly through the Department of Justice has yielded mixed and not highly impressive results. A limited number of large concerns, for example, the Standard Oil Company and the American Tobacco Company, have been broken up; others have been brought to book and penalized; many minor punishments have been inflicted along the way. Large obstacles, however, remain, and by their nature can never be wholly overcome. Among them is the dependence of the laws for vigorous enforcement upon the economic predispositions, and personal inclinations of successive Presidents, attorneys general, and other high officials concerned. A second impediment is recurring uncertainties, despite all the legislation and court decisions, as to what, in many situations, actually constitutes "unfair competition," "unreasonable" restraint of trade, and the like. A third is the sometimes wavering support given by the courts. And the most obstructive of all is divided opinion, with resultant hesitation, springing from the circumstance that large-scale production and merchandising, requiring large-scale organization, make for economies, and therefore often for more and cheaper goods and services for the consuming public. Big business it is argued is performing economic miracles for our society and now is acting more and more from a sense of social responsibility. It is also argued that bigness in industry is offset and held in check by bigness in labor organizations and bigness in government. There is, furthermore, some evidence that the era of concentration of corporate power may be passing. There has been a rapid increase in the number of firms during the postwar years and the huge corporations are not expanding as rapidly as the smaller ones. On the other hand, there

A continuing dilemma

have been many mergers in the postwar period. A number of our larger industries are dominated by three or four huge firms rather than one and operate under what has been called administered rather than competitive prices. They compete on many levels, but not in pricing.

POLICING BUSINESS PRACTICES AND PROTECTING CONSUMER INTERESTS

1. Func-
tions

The Sherman Act, as we have observed, depends for enforcement almost entirely upon the antitrust division of the Department of Justice. The Clayton and Federal Trade Commission Acts of 1914 directed at dishonest and unfair, as well as monopolistic, business practices provided a new independent establishment in the form of the Federal Trade Commission, consisting of five members appointed by the President and confirmed by the Senate for seven-year terms with not more than three drawn from any one party. No clear jurisdictional line between the two enforcing agencies was established at first; both were intended to curb the formation of trusts and the growth of monopolies. The entire development of the Federal Trade Commission, however, has been rather in the direction of defining fair and prosecuting unfair trade practices of whatever business organizations and establishments happened to exist at any given time. In other words the Commission has sought to maintain "fair" competition rather than to attack monopolies. It has also sought to police business practices in the interest of the consumer. In pursuance of these purposes it enforces not only the Acts of 1914 as amended but also (1) the Anti-Discrimination (Robinson-Patman) Act of 1938, designed to clarify price-discrimination provisions of the Clayton Act, and aimed at preventing sellers from arbitrarily giving advantages to some buyers as against others through disguises such as advertising allowances and brokerage fees; (2) a Truth-in-Advertising (Wheeler-Lea) Act of 1938, applying especially to the food, drug, and cosmetics businesses; (3) a Wool Products Labeling Act of 1940, which seeks to protect producers, manufacturers, and consumers against the presence of unrevealed substitutes and mixtures in wool products; (4) the Export Trade (Webb-Pomerene) Act of 1918, amending the Clayton Act by permitting exporters to form and operate associations more or less in the nature of cartels (which otherwise would be illegal), so long as approved by the Commission as not "substantially" lessening competition in the domestic market; (5) the Fur Products Labeling Act of 1951 which seeks to protect consumers and manufacturers against misleading labeling of furs and fur products; (6) the Flammable Fabrics Act of 1953 as amended in 1967 to protect consumers against unlabeled and highly flammable products like wearing apparel, draperies, bedding, upholstery, and office furnishings; (7) the Textile Fiber Products Identification Act of 1958 which seeks to protect consumers against mislabeling of various yarns and cloths; (8) the Fair Packaging and Labeling Act of 1966 aimed at protecting the consumer against misleading labels and packing devices; and (9) the Child Protection Act of 1966 to prevent sale of toys made of harmful materials.

In pursuance of its many duties, the Commission (1) enforces the laws against unfair competitive practices on the part of corporate and other businesses participating in interstate commerce (except banks, common carriers, broadcasting companies, and other enterprises regulated through different channels); (2) works out lists of unfair practices and holds conferences in which representatives of industry are encouraged to agree to avoid such practices (although the line between lawful and unlawful agreements is not always easy to fix); (3) issues "cease-and-desist" orders when violations of law are discovered and the violators are not disposed to desist of their own accord; (4) requires corporations to submit reports covering aspects of their business on which the Commission desires information; (5) advises with corporations on organizational and other matters with a view to helping them avoid running afoul of the law; (6) guards against unlawful acquisitions of stock by corporations and against prohibited interlocking directorates; (7) investigates trade conditions and practices in and with foreign countries where combinations or practices may affect the foreign commerce of the United States; and (8) recommends to Congress new legislation calculated to uphold the principle of fair competition in the interest of both business itself and the public.

2. Activities

In enforcing the laws against unfair and fraudulent practices, the Commission may act in response to a complaint received, or by direction of the President or of Congress, or at the suggestion or request of the attorney general. As a rule, however, action starts with a complaint lodged by some individual, group, firm, or corporation having a grievance against a specified business concern because of some practice which it is alleged to be pursuing. Hundreds of such complaints are filed every year. If, upon preliminary investigation, the Commission finds a complaint groundless or trivial, or relating to something over which the Commission has no jurisdiction, or not affecting the public interest (mere private controversies have no status under the law), nothing happens. If, however, the protest is believed to have merit, the offender is called upon to explain—often with the result that all parties consent amicably to a "stipulation," or agreement, that the practice complained of shall be abandoned. If, finally, the concern under attack is not prepared to yield so readily, and if after hearings the Commission finds it clearly in the wrong, a "cease-and-desist" order will command the offender to discontinue the objectionable practice or practices within 60 days. If there is failure to comply, the Commission may ask the appropriate court of appeals to affirm its order, which, if done, subjects the offender, in case of continued disobedience, to action for contempt of court.

3. Procedures

The Commission has a mixed record of achievement. Some of its difficulties grow out of the obscurities of the law. It has not always had adequate financial support from Congress; its members have been shifted rapidly, and often have been selected primarily on political grounds. Although supposed, too, to be final judge of the facts in a case, it frequently has found the courts insisting upon making their own inquiries, and many times has seen its cease-and-desist orders overthrown. Further, the "cease-and-desist" system, dependent as it is upon protracted litigation for its enforcement, is greatly weakened by long delays between issuance and final determination. The process was speeded somewhat by an Act of 1958 aimed at expediting court consideration. President Kennedy in 1961 urged additional legislation aimed at the same problem. While it has played an insignificant part in curbing monopoly by preventing misleading advertising, deception, fraud, and misrepresentation, and by otherwise policing the business world, the Commission has done much to raise the standards of

The
rapid
develop-
ment of
consumer
protection
activity

American business. On the other hand, the growing interest in the protection of the American consumer has risen rapidly in both Congress and the executive branch. President Johnson delivered special messages on consumer problems in 1966, 1967, and 1968 and appointed a special advisor on consumer problems in his own office. The problem has largely outgrown the capabilities of the Federal Trade Commission. The Departments of Commerce, Agriculture, and Health, Education and Welfare are all deeply involved: Commerce helps fix standards under the various labeling acts referred to above, Agriculture is primarily responsible for control of meat processing and packaging under laws dating back to 1907 and greatly strengthened in 1967, also for food and fibre processing: HEW administers the pure food and drug laws and also took the lead in the attack on cigarette smoking of the 1960's. A new Truth-in-Lending Act passed in 1968 requires all lenders and consumer creditors to provide their customers with full, honest, and comparable information on the cost of the credit that they are buying. Responsibility for enforcement of this act falls mainly on the Department of Justice.

REGULATION OF FINANCIAL INSTITUTIONS

Because of its responsibility for the monetary system and because the credit structure of the economy is so intimately tied to the system of banking, the national government has long evinced great interest and exercised special authority in this field. Under the leadership of the Federalists and over the strenuous objections of the Jeffersonians, the government first chartered a Bank of the United States to serve as the principal fiscal agent of the government and as the main regulator of private financial institutions. The Supreme Court in the celebrated case of McCulloch v. Maryland (1819) triumphantly affirmed the Federalist position and a government bank served the nation until 1836. When Andrew Jackson finally strangled this "monster," as he called it, the control of banking devolved entirely on the states. The chaotic situation which resulted with "wild cat" banks, unsupported currency, special charters, and many other abuses was not brought under control until 1863. The necessities of Civil War finance stimulated the Congress to find a better method of controlling currency and also of marketing its bonds. The result was a system of national banks and a confiscatory tax on state bank notes.

Under the national banking system, privately owned banking firms could be chartered as national banks with the right to issue paper money and with the obligation to accept national regulation of their fiscal practices including audit of their accounts. State banks continued to exist, as they do today, but most of the large firms became and have remained national banks and are closely supervised by the comptroller of the currency in the Treasury Department. *a. National banks*

Originally, national banks were entirely separate establishments, with no more means of coming to one another's relief in time of stress than railroads or merchandising enterprises. From the ups and downs of business during recurring cycles of prosperity and depression flowed embarrassments and failures which often might have been mitigated. To remedy this situation by linking up all national banks in an integrated series and imparting greater elasticity to their operations, Congress in 1913 created an independent establishment known as the federal reserve system which ever since has been a principal feature of our national banking arrangements. *b. The federal reserve system:*

First of all, the country is divided into 12 federal reserve districts, in each of which is located a federal reserve bank, usually in the district's principal city. In each case, all or nearly all stock is subscribed by the member banks within the district, and control is vested in a board of nine directors, three named by the general management of the reserve system in Washington, six by the member banks. The general management referred to consists of a board of governors (the Federal Reserve Board) of seven members appointed for 14-year terms by the President and confirmed by the Senate, with due regard for both geographical distribution and representation of financial, agricultural, industrial, and commercial interests. This board, endowed with broad supervisory and regulatory powers, bears full responsibility for formulating monetary policies and exercising general direction of the system. All national banks must belong to and hold stock in the federal reserve bank of their district; state banks may do so if they meet the requirements and find membership to their advantage—as most of them do. *1) Organization*

The federal reserve banks—often referred to as "bankers' banks"—do not carry on a general banking business with individuals and corporations, but instead perform services, directly at least, only for the national government and for the member banks of their respective districts. Services to the government are many and various. Proceeds of revenue collections are deposited with them, and in general they have custody of government *2) Workings* funds which in earlier days were left idle in subtreasuries; they make transfers of such funds according to instructions; and they serve as fiscal agents in selling securities and paying government checks and coupons. For member banks, they act as clearing houses for the handling of checks and other financial instruments, serve as depositories for surplus funds, and, more important, provide rediscounting facilities enabling the needs of customers to be met and a greater volume of business to be done.

What happens in this latter connection can be explained briefly. A national or state bank loans money to individuals and corporations, taking the borrowers' notes—"discounting" them, as the phrase goes. If demand is heavy, the bank may reach a point where it has no money at its disposal; and in the old days that would end matters—the bank would simply have to refuse further applicants. Nowadays, however, what a bank in this situation almost invariably does is to transmit at least a substantial part of its accumulated "commercial paper" (which may include mortgages and various forms of collateral) to the federal reserve bank to which it belongs and get it "rediscounted," that is, borrow money on it just as the original borrower did; and with this money it can make new loans and of course earn new profits. But that is not all. On the basis of the commercial paper thus pouring in with also backing of gold certificates based on the government's stock of gold, the reserve bank can issue paper money with which to perform its rediscounting operations (the national banks themselves no longer can do this). In this way arise the federal reserve notes which constitute by far the largest part of the paper currency circulating in the country today.

3) Stabilization of the credit structure

One of the ways in which the Federal Reserve Board seeks to stabilize the credit structure of the country and control cyclical tendencies to alternating prosperity and depression is by expanding or contracting the credit facilities of commercial banks by lowering or raising the rediscount rate. A lower rate will give the commercial banks easier access to funds and encourage them to help business by lending at moderate interest rates, a higher rate of course having the opposite effect. Stabilization is sought also through the open-market buying and selling of commercial paper and of government bonds and other securities by the reserve banks—large purchases of commercial paper naturally having the effect of supplying member banks with more free funds and, in the case of government bonds, strengthening the market and keeping up prices—both of which may prove desirable in depression-time. The Board also determines the reserves required by banks against their deposits and by raising or lowering these amounts can influence the interest rate and the amount of credit available.

c. The banking crisis of 1933 and some remedial measures

As set up under the legislation of 1913, the federal reserve system served useful purposes and indeed seemed to have solved our major banking problems. Certainly it helped greatly to carry the country through the expansion and later contraction of its economy incident to World War I. In the "roaring twenties," with their gross overextension of credit, however, it failed to furnish a sufficient brake. After the stock-market crash of 1929, our banks proved unable to weather the storm in any such fashion as did those of Great Britain, Canada, and some other countries. The experience was harrowing, and it is small wonder that a good deal of remedial banking legislation of permanent character (too complicated and technical to be reviewed here) was enacted in the next two years. Speculative temptations to which large numbers of banks had succumbed in the past were at least partially removed by requiring that thenceforth banking establishments should not engage in both commercial, that is, general, banking and "investment" banking. If they insisted upon continuing the latter, they had to give up the former. In the hope that if depositors could be assured that their money would be safe in banks, they would be willing to leave it there, thus averting bank "runs" and resulting bank closings, a plan of governmental guaranty of bank deposits was introduced. Deposits in all banks included within the federal reserve system, nationally authorized trust companies, and all nonmember state banks applying and meeting certain specifications—in all, some 13,400 institutions—are now insured through a Federal Deposit Insurance Corporation with a maximum protection of $15,000 on each separate deposit. The insurance, of course, is purchased by the participants by premiums paid on their deposits.

In the recessions of 1957–1958 and 1960–1961 the federal reserve system played an important and much debated role. Under the Eisenhower administration, the Board on several occasions acted to tighten credit in order to halt inflation and was vigorously urged to ease it to combat the fall-off in business activities and the spread of unemployment in 1958 and in 1960. The Board, on occasion under Truman and later, came into conflict with the Treasury Department over the question of the influence of its decisions on the interest rate and marketability of government bonds. Widespread disagreement still exists over the proper role of the Board and the proper policies for combatting inflation or recession. Its recent efforts (1965–1968) have been to counter inflation and seek greater dollar stability by raising interest rates and generally tightening credit.

The stock-market crash of 1929 which signaled the beginning of the "great" depression led not only to an overhauling of the government's system of controlling banking. It stimulated national concern with abuses in the management of stock exchanges and in the sale of stocks and bonds. State action having been tried for a generation in the form of "blue sky laws" regulating securities vendors was found inadequate to the task of protecting the interest of the millions of shareholders. Congress under the spur of President Roosevelt assumed regulatory authority in this field with the passage of a Securities Act in 1933 and a Securities Exchange Act in 1934. *2. Securities*

The primary purpose of these two interlocked pieces of legislation is to protect investors against every sort of fraudulent practice in the issuing and handling of securities offered for sale in interstate commerce. To this *The Securities Act of 1933* end, the act requires all issues of stocks, bonds, or other securities (with certain exceptions indicated below), if to be offered in interstate commerce or by mail, to be registered with (originally the Federal Trade Commission) the Securities and Exchange Commission (S.E.C.) set up in 1934. Every such registration must be accompanied by a registration statement containing full financial and other information, and also by the prospectus intended to be used in soliciting purchases by the public, and containing all information which an investor ought to have when making a decision. Selling or offering to sell to the public in interstate commerce or through the mails any security not properly registered with the Commission is made a penal offense. Not only so, but heavy civil liability is laid upon any corporation, including its directors and principal financial officers, for any untrue or only partly true declaration of a material fact in a registration statement or prospectus. It is not the business of the Commission, any more than that of a state securities commissioner, to pass upon the inherent value of securities issued or upon the outlook for prosperity of the corporation issuing them. No action by the Commission is to be construed as a recommendation of any security to potential purchasers. The agency's only function, up to this point, is to see that complete information concerning a security is made available to the public, that this information is accurate, and that no fraud is practiced in connection with sales.

3. The Securities Exchange Act of 1934

To aid in promoting this general end, the Securities and Exchange Act of 1934 went an important step further. A large proportion—doubtless the major part—of the securities registered with the Commission are bought and sold on stock exchanges found in 20 or more of our principal cities, the largest and best known being that in New York. Formerly, however, transactions in securities in these markets were subject to little regulation beyond the few restrictions which the exchanges themselves saw fit to impose upon their members. These provided little protection for the investing public. All manner of unsavory and dishonest practices grew up— "wash sales," matched orders, "rigging the market," "jiggles," pools, and other manipulations—by which prices were pushed up or forced down for the benefit of insiders, while innocent investors were fleeced. Speculation "on margin," too—that is, paying only a certain percentage in cash for what is bought—reached scandalous proportions, notably in the frenzied market operations shortly preceding the crash of 1929, and threatened to precipitate the entire national credit structure into chaos.

To remedy this situation, the transactions of all exchanges engaged in interstate commerce (as every one is) are declared to be "affected with a national public interest" which makes it necessary to provide for their regulation and control "in order to protect interstate commerce, the national credit, the national taxing power, to make more effective the national banking system and the federal reserve system, and to insure the maintenance of fair and honest markets in such transactions." Annual and other reports are required to be filed with the exchanges and the Commission by all corporations or companies having securities listed, and any deviations from material fact constitute grounds for suspending or withdrawing a given security from trading. Various provisions outlaw objectionable practices of the past, and, all in all, the measure seeks to make the exchanges fair and open marketplaces for investors rather than mere rendezvous for conspiring speculators. One will not be so naive as to suppose that all stock-market operations have since been, or will in future be, beyond reproach.

A major review of the effectiveness of these regulations of the security market was finally completed by a special study group for the S.E.C. in 1963, and numerous changes in the basic laws were enacted in 1964. Most of the changes plugged loopholes in extant procedures, and expanded the scope of S.E.C. authority to various persons, securities and fiscal institutions not then covered by the laws, and improved the "self-regulating" practices of the exchange managements.

REFERENCES

W. Adams and H. M. Gray, *Monopoly in America* (New York, 1955).

American Assembly, *United States Monetary Policy* (New York, 1962).

M. Anshen and F. Wormuth, *Private Enterprise and Public Policy* (New York, 1954).

R. A. Bauer, I. de S. Pool, L. A. Dexter, *American Business and Public Policy: The Politics of Foreign Trade* (New York, 1963).

A. A. Berle, Jr., *The American Economic Republic* (New York, 1963).

————, *The Twentieth Century Capitalist Revolution* (New York, 1954).

M. H. Bernstein, *Regulating Business by Independent Commission* (Princeton, N. J., 1955).

T. C. Blaisdell, Jr., *Economic Power and Political Pressures,* Temporary Nat. Econ. Committee, Monograph No. 26 (Wash., D. C., 1941).

Commission on Money and Credit, *Money and Credit: Their Influence on Jobs, Prices, and Growth,* Committee on Economic Development (New York, 1961).

J. B. Dirlam and A. E. Kahn, *Fair Competition: The Law and the Economics of Antitrust Policy* (Cornell, 1954).

M. Fainsod, L. Gordon, and J. L. Palamountain, Jr., *Government and the American Economy* (3rd ed., New York, 1959), Chaps. I–V, IX–XX, XXI, XXIV, XXVI.

J. K. Galbraith, *American Capitalism: the Concept of Countervailing Power* (New York, 1952).

E. W. Kintner, *An Anti-Trust Primer* (New York, 1967).

H. Koontz and R. Gable, *Public Control of Economic Enterprise* (New York, 1956).

W. Letwin, *Law and Economic Policy in America: the Evolution of the Sherman Anti-Trust Act* (New York, 1965).

E. S. Mason, *Economic Concentration and the Monopoly Problem* (Cambridge, Mass., 1957).

V. A. Mund, *Government and Business* (New York, 1950), Chaps. VI–XX.

L. D. Musolf, *Government and the Economy* (Chicago, 1965).

E. S. Redford and C. B. Hagan, *American Government and the Economy* (Chicago, 1965).

G. W. Stocking and M. W. Watkins, *Monopoly and Free Enterprise* (New York, 1952).

H. B. Thorelli, *The Federal Antitrust Policy* (Baltimore, 1956).

R. E. Westmeyer, *Economics of Transportation* (New York, 1952).

S. N. Whitney, *Antitrust Policies: American Experience in Twenty Industries* (New York, 1958).

C. Wilcox, *Public Policies Toward Business* (Chicago, 1955).

17

GOVERNMENT AND LABOR

The development of a labor interest in our society is a product of the Industrial Revolution in which small handicraft industries were replaced by large mass-production factories and in which management was separated from daily contacts with employes. In the early years of our history, the laboring men did not participate in political processes. Voting and office-holding were reserved for property owners. The democratization of the suffrage paved the way for labor interests to be represented. Before the rapid industrialization of the nation after the Civil War, however, the laboring multitudes seemed to accept the idea that cheap land and low taxes were the most useful public policies to serve their needs. Only after the victorious northern Republicans swung the full weight of the national government behind the rapid development of industry did the industrial worker emerge as a strong claimant for governmental protection. The emergence of labor as a powerful interest in modern politics, furthermore, has followed closely upon the organization of this interest in the economic sphere through unionization. At first, labor sought to achieve better conditions, higher pay, and shorter hours by purely economic procedures. Only as governmental power and prestige were repeatedly thrown into the struggle on the side of employers did labor come to appreciate that political power was also essential to its ambitions.

Labor in the national scene

Even before 1800 mechanics and artisans in a few of the larger cities began drawing together in unions. As industry expanded and workers multiplied, consciousness of a weak bargaining position without organization, combined with growing desire for improvement of labor conditions in other respects, led to unionization on a steadily increasing scale. Employers did not like what was going on; public opinion was skeptical; and in pursuance of old common-law doctrine, the courts long looked askance at unions as constituting, or threatening, criminal conspiracy. In spite of numerous obstacles, the movement began to take root and after about 1870 went steadily forward. In time local unions began drawing together in regional, or even nationwide, federations. In 1881, a Federation of Organ-

The development of unions

UNION MEMBERSHIP, 1869–1966

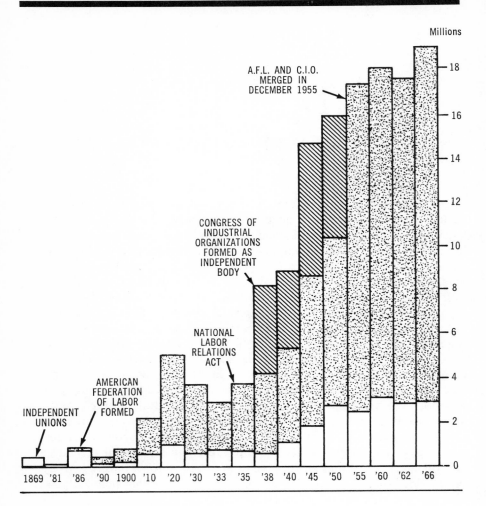

SOURCE: U.S. Department of Labor

ized Trades and Labor Unions became the common voice of organized labor. In 1886, the present name of American Federation of Labor (A.F.L.) was adopted and for another half-century this organization held the field almost alone. In 1935, however, a militant rival, the Congress (until 1938 Committee) of Industrial Organizations (C.I.O.) was created by the secession of several unions from the parent body. Outside of these over the years grew the powerful Railroad Brotherhoods and numerous minor independent organizations. In 1955, the C.I.O. and A.F.L. unions were reunited into one grand federation. The Teamsters Union, one of the largest in America, was expelled by the Executive Council in 1957 for corrupt management, and the auto workers in 1968 forced their own ouster. Both are now independent unions.

Throughout the period 1880–1932, the growth of labor unions was stubbornly and bitterly, sometimes violently, contested by the business interests. "Freedom of contract" and "criminal conspiracy" doctrines were asserted by business and enunciated by courts to justify fine and imprisonment for the leaders of strikes and boycotts, labor's principal weapons in the economic sphere. The Sherman Antitrust Law of 1890, designed as we have observed to halt the consolidation of corporate power, was applied with devastating effect to certain labor union activities. Congressional sympathy for the aims of organized labor, expressed in the Clayton Act's apparent exemption of labor from the antitrust laws, was overcome by judicial hostility and virtually all of the alleged protection was repealed by judicial interpretation. The courts, furthermore, fell increasingly into the habit of granting injunctive relief to business concerns harassed by labor disputes, actual or threatened, and in so doing prohibited the use of many of labor's most effective economic weapons. In spite of this hostility the A.F.L. slowly grew in numbers and influence, but by 1932 it still counted only 3 million members and had little real strength in most of the large industries (steel, textiles, automobiles, rubber). It is only since 1932 that organized labor has deployed upon the national scene as one of the great economic interests of modern America. With a drastic change in governmental attitude from a suspicious pseudo-neutrality to benevolent protection, labor unions have flourished as never before. Their membership has steadily advanced until they now speak for about 25 percent of all persons gainfully employed in the United States and for 30 percent of industrial, transportation, and service employes.

Hostility of business and the courts

Throughout most of its history, organized labor in America has eschewed any attempt to build its own political party. Several nineteenth-century efforts to do so, beginning with the Working Men's party of 1828, were not conspicuously successful. Marxism, around which so many European labor parties were built, has never strongly appealed to the American laborer. Labor's political doctrine was largely supplied by Samuel Gompers, leader of the A.F.L. He preached abstention from independent party organization and participation in the American two-party system by supporting friendly candidates in either party and by appealing to both parties for favorable platform declarations and for benevolent legislation. Labor's main weapons, he felt, were economic, not political. Theoretically, the Gompers policy is still supported, but both of the large federations of unions have swung more and more heavily toward active intervention in political campaigns. Through generously financed subsidiaries like the C.I.O. Political Action Committee and Labor's League for Political Education of the A.F.L., and now the Committee on Political Education of the A.F.L.–C.I.O., labor

Labor in politics

has sought to sway the electorate in behalf, usually, of Democratic candidates. In New York City a powerful independent labor party has been organized by local trade unions and their party (the Liberal party) has held the balance of power in several municipal and state elections. Labor is in politics to stay and its influence, especially in the Democratic party, has been growing steadily in the large industrial cities of the North and Midwest.

NATIONAL PROTECTION OF LABORERS

State regulation   As industrialization rapidly spread throughout the nation in the latter half of the nineteenth century, laboring men increasingly demanded protection from unhealthy and dangerous working conditions, from competition on the job market from children and immigrants, from long hours and low pay, and from many other abuses of mechanized manufacturing and corporate management. Much of their effort was directed to state legislatures in the belief that the national government had no power to regulate the conditions of mining and manufacturing. State action, and there was a great deal of sympathetic legislation in the period of 1880–1932, was always embarrassed by the fear that any particular state would place its own industry at a competitive disadvantage with that of other states if it imposed costly standards of safety, health, and welfare. Despite this difficulty, labor won important gains from state after state in the fields of industrial safety, child labor, improved factory conditions. In fact, much of the legislation protecting labor interests at present on the law books is still state law, and the states continue to play an important role in regulating industry benevolently toward working men and women.

Early efforts at national protection   Although national regulation of industry in behalf of workers is largely a product of the New Deal period, the national government had never been completely indifferent to labor interests. As far back as 1840, the government adopted the policy of setting a standard for private employers in its treatment of its own employes. The movement to restrict immigration, especially of contract laborers, which began in 1882, was largely motivated by a desire to protect the job security of American workers. Unlike workers in industry, those engaged in transportation early looked to the national government for protection and after prolonged agitation an Hours of Service Act in 1907 limited to 16 the hours of consecutive employment of train crews. In 1916, and at the behest of the by now strongly organized railway brotherhoods, the Congress passed an 8-hour-day law for all trainmen. Coincident with state action to protect workers against industrial accidents, the Congress in 1908 passed an Employers' Liability Act for the protection of workers in interstate commerce. This act drastically amended the old common-law rules of "contributory negligence" and "assumption of the risks of employment," which up to this time had substantially allowed employers to escape liability for the injury or death of workmen while performing their duties. The Seaman's (La Follette) Act of 1915 surrounded employment in the merchant marine with guarantees of proper conditions, hours, food, and wages. In 1920, the benefits of the Employer's Liability Act were extended to sailors. Several major efforts of this era, however, proved abortive as the Supreme Court struck down laws aimed at child labor and at fixing conditions for female employment. So rapidly did national interest in the plight of the workingman unfold in this century that by 1913 the Congress was persuaded to establish a separate Department of Labor of Cabinet rank by breaking up the Department of Commerce and Labor created in 1903. This new agency was designed "to foster, promote, and develop" the welfare of wage earners in the United States, to improve their working conditions, and to advance their opportunities for profitable employment. It should be added, however, that the methods selected by Congress for the achievement of these goals were largely educational and noncoercive.

As the nation entered the depression, the national government had already thrown its protective mantle around certain laboring groups (railroad workers and sailors) but was still largely restrained from interceding for the great mass of laborers by narrow judicial construction of its commerce and taxing powers. Impressed with the plea that the descending spiral of economic activity could only be reversed by placing more purchasing power in the hands of consumers (labor), the New Deal early addressed itself to improving the wages and working conditions of the great mass of industrial wage earners. The first major effort in this direction was embodied in the *The National Recovery Administration* National Recovery Act of 1933 which, among many other specifications, provided that codes of fair competition be drawn for similar industries by joint labor-industry-government teams and that these codes should set minimum wage levels, fix maximum hours, eliminate child labor, and spread available employment. These codes would then be enforced upon the industries concerned by the national government. In 1935, however, the entire procedure was called into question by litigation and the Supreme Court invalidated the core of the Recovery Act, mainly on the grounds that the code procedure constituted an invalid delegation of legislative power to an administrative agency.

Operating within the prevailing conception of constitutional power, *Establishment of labor standards for public contractors* Congress next sought to establish standards of employment for all those firms supplying the government by contract. The Public Contracts Labor (Walsh-Healey) Act of 1936 prescribed the payment of prevailing minimum wages, limited hours of employment to 40 per week, outlawed child and convict labor, and prescribed minimum standards of health and safety for the employes of all businesses holding government supply contracts in excess of $10,000. These prescriptions were made a part of every appropriate government supply contract.

Incidental to the attempt of President Roosevelt to reconstitute the Supreme Court, a series of decisions issued in 1936 and 1937 indicated the

Court had revised its views on the extent of national power to protect industrial wage earners and that it no longer found any constitutional barriers to national legislation regulating manufacturing and mining benevolently toward labor. With its sweeping triumph at the polls in 1936, the Roosevelt administration promptly moved to occupy the new ground opened to it; in 1938 in a Fair Labor Standards Act a large portion of workingmen were placed under the protection of the United States government.

As amended through 1968, the Fair Labor Standards Act now extends to about 37 million wage earners of both sexes "engaged in interstate commerce, or in the production of goods for interstate commerce," or those in almost any style of enterprise including retail stores where the gross sales exceed $500,000 per year, the benefits of minimum standards of employment. A minimum wage of $1.60 an hour is established (originally 25 cents) for all covered employes, except those newly brought under the Act in 1966 who will reach the present minimum by 1971, and a maximum work week of 40 hours (originally 44 hours). For all hours worked in excess of the maximum, overtime at the rate of one and one half times the base pay is required, except that by collective-bargaining agreements in certain industries the work week may be extended. The employment of children under 16 is forbidden in manufacturing, mining, transportation, hazardous agricultural employment, and commerce, and under 18 in occupations declared by the Bureau of Labor Standards in the Department of Labor to be "particularly hazardous . . . or detrimental to their health and well being." In other occupations and businesses covered by the law, children of 14 or 15 may be employed in periods not interfering with their schooling and under beneficent working conditions. In 1963, the Act was further amended to require equal pay for equal work regardless of the sex of the worker, and in 1966 to prevent discrimination because of age. Challenged before the courts soon after its passage, this bold effort to provide a nationwide floor below which the conditions of employment in industry might not sink was sustained unanimously by the Supreme Court.

NATIONAL PROTECTION OF LABOR UNIONS

Throughout the period of developing governmental concern with the plight of labor, there has always been an impressive argument made by some that elaborate legislative and administrative efforts to protect labor from exploitation are both unnecessary and unwise. Let the government, it is argued, encourage the unionization of employes or at least do nothing judicially or otherwise to discourage such unionization and the unions will take care of wages, hours, and working conditions. It was not, however, until the depression of the thirties that this point of view won wide, although never universal, acceptance. As the national economy rapidly plummeted, the arguments of the labor leaders and their friends gained increasing support. Here again was an opportunity to sustain consumer purchasing power and to spread employment by the actions of unions.

The first target of the labor unionists was their ancient enemy, the injunction. The broadening concept of corporate property rights which characterized the decisions of the national bench from 1875 to 1936 and which embraced as property such nebulous values as "good will" and "going-concern value" suggested to able members of the bar a device for thwarting the spread of unions. Strikes, picketing, and boycotts, the central weapons of the labor movement, could normally be shown to a sympathetic court as threatening irreparable damages to corporate property thus broadly defined. The writ of injunction, an old common-law process issued by courts of equity on proper plea and in circumstances in which only one side is normally heard, was designed, they said, exactly to ward off such damages. From about 1890 onward courts fell into the habit of granting injunctions against union leaders and members, ordering them to continue work or to refrain from actions which might threaten property loss. Violation of such an order placed a unionist in contempt of court and subjected him to summary (without jury trial) punishment. In the decade of the twenties these injunctions became more and more sweeping in their prohibition of all the traditional methods of union agitation. The Anti-Injunction (Norris-La-Guardia) Act of 1932 represents the first successful national effort to foster trade unionism in the United States and marks the turning point in the attitude of the government. This act surrounded the injunction procedure in the national courts with so many safeguards to protect labor union interests that the injunction became largely useless as a device by which employers could break existing unions or thwart their organizational efforts. This act also declared the "yellow-dog" [1] contract as contrary to public policy and unenforceable in national courts.

Anti-Injunction Act of 1932

The New Deal's National Recovery Act of 1933 carried governmental benevolence to unions one step further. Bent upon leaving no stone unturned and no theory of depression-beating untried, the act not only provided for the labor standards already mentioned but required in famous Section 7(a) each industrial code to include a provision recognizing the right of employees "to organize and bargain collectively through representatives of their own choosing." It also provided for the codes to carry a prohibition against forcing membership in a company union or forcing anyone to agree not to join a union as a condition of his employment. Thus the company-dominated unions of the twenties were outlawed. A National Labor Relations Board was set up within the N.R.A. to administer these provisions of the law and to conduct employe elections where the question of representation in collective-bargaining arguments was at issue.

The N.R.A. and labor unions

Congress and the President moved swiftly to salvage the policy of labor union protection from the wreckage of the Supreme Court's decision

---

[1] A "yellow-dog" contract is one in which a prospective employe binds himself as a condition of his employment never to join a labor organization.

The
National
Labor
Relations
Act of
1935
condemning the N.R.A. The National Labor Relations (Wagner) Act of 1935 represents the fruit of this effort. This act proclaims as the policy of the national government the fostering of collective bargaining between employes and employers through unions and surrounds the process with safeguards for unionization which substantially deprive the employer of several of his traditional weapons. Using the Federal Trade Commission Act as its guide, the act specifies a number of "unfair labor practices" and prohibits them to employers. Company-dominated unions are outlawed; employers are forbidden to coerce or restrain employes in the exercise of their rights to become members of a union and to bargain through such organization; employers may not hire or fire employes in such a way as to discriminate against union members or officers; employers are required to bargain with the proper representatives of their employes. A National Labor Relations Board (originally of three but now of five members) was established independently of any existing agency and authorized to enforce the new law upon employers engaged in industries "affecting" commerce. Through a network of regional offices the Board was empowered to discharge its responsibilities by (1) ascertaining by election procedures or otherwise who are the bona fide representatives of the employes in covered industries or plants; and (2) determining on complaint of an employe or his representative, if an employer is engaging in an "unfair practice." Should the Board, after proper hearing, find an employer to be violating the law, it may issue a "cease-and-desist" order against him which may be enforced by a proper national court.

This legislation, with its strong deterrents to employer interference in the unionization of his employees, has ever since been regarded as the Magna Charta of the labor union movement. It represents the greatest gain in governmental benevolence ever achieved by organized labor. And, by staying the hands of management, it contributed in no small way to the tremendous increase in union membership which followed upon its enactment. When attacked in the courts, they sustained the administration's argument that the national power to regulate interstate "commerce" embraced the power to regulate the labor relations of concerns whose raw materials or finished products were shipped across state lines even though the firms were not themselves directly engaged in commerce. More than any other decision of this period, this pronouncement celebrated the change in the Court's attitude toward national power to regulate business.

From its inception, the National Labor Relations Act has been the target of a large segment of the business community. The theory of this act, the business interests argue, is that employers and employers alone are to blame for the plight of the working mass and for spreading industrial unrest. Only employers can commit unfair labor practices. Unions can coerce employees into becoming members without penalty under the law. Special safeguards are provided for "closed-shop" agreements (agreements which require an employe to belong to the union in order to be employed) and all forms of company unions are proscribed. Labor has responded that employers still have ample legal sanctions for dealing with unlawful behavior by union leaders and agents. Nothing in this law authorizes unions to commit violence or modifies existing limitations on picketing or boycotting. During World War II the controversy over national policy toward unions abated. It broke out with renewed vigor in the postwar era, however, and led finally to a new policy of governmental regulation of unions as well as of management.

THE PROMOTION OF INDUSTRIAL PEACE; REGULATION OF UNIONS

Much as some groups have argued in behalf of a governmental policy of hands-off economic questions like the relations of labor and management, and much as the government has in the past few decades sought to relieve itself of some of the burden of regulating industry by strengthening the hands of the unions, the government has never been able wholly to turn its back upon the combats between labor and management. As unions have grown in size and power, their controversies with the great corporate combinations have threatened not only local and sporadic violence as of old but also national economic paralysis. The strike or collective work stoppage is the oldest and strongest bargaining device the unions have, and when they are able to shut down the entire steel industry or coal industry or railroad system the national economy must grind slowly to a complete halt. There has developed, in other words, a public interest different from that of either labor or management in a particular industry which demands that this paralysis never be allowed to creep through the whole of society. The government's interest in promoting industrial peace has grown steadily as unions and corporations have grown and is, perhaps, at the present time its paramount interest in the field of labor relations. In times of war or of war-emergency there has been no question of the transcendent necessity for maintaining full production, but even in "peace" the government must prevent economic collapse. *The public interest and industrial peace*

Prior to the Anti-Injunction Act of 1932, the national policy toward labor disputes was that labor was largely to blame for them and that its leaders must be closely restrained whenever serious property damage or obstruction to the free flow of commerce was threatened. In prosecuting the leaders of the Pullman strike of 1894, the Cleveland administration invoked the national power to prevent interference with the mail to justify its actions in moving into Illinois against the wishes of Governor Altgeld of Illinois. Subsequently, as was mentioned earlier, the Sherman Antitrust Act was invoked time and again to punish the participants in strikes and boycotts and to reestablish peaceful relations in various industries. The injunctions granted by national courts were also widely used to stop strikes and thus to terminate industrial unrest. From all of this it is plain that there has never *National power to deal with disputes* been a serious question of the power of the national government to intervene in many types of labor disputes and that its intervention until well into this century was largely repressive and punitive, especially in regard to labor. A very large share of the responsibility for fostering industrial peace was, nevertheless, left to the states so long as the disputes were largely local in their scope and effect.

Mediation procedures established for rail-roads

The shortcomings of these wholly negative procedures for dealing with labor disputes were first clearly realized by the national government in the field of transportation. In this field also the power of the government to experiment with other procedures was unquestioned. Starting with legislation dating from as early as 1888 and culminating in the Railway Labor Act of 1926 (strengthened in 1934), a scheme for handling disputes in that field has been developed based upon a gradation of three mediatory or fact-finding agencies. This system has worked poorly in the past decade as the unions have vigorously resisted efforts to reduce required crews. The President has had to lend his prestige to settlements and Congress in 1963 and again in 1967 had to provide virtually for compulsory arbitration.

National mediation in disputes of all types

When the Department of Labor was separately organized in 1913, Congress authorized it to act as a mediator in labor disputes. Through a Conciliation Service thereafter established, agents of the government offered their good offices in thousands of controversies and, without any coercive authority of any kind, nevertheless contributed to the peaceful adjustment of a large number of them. The Service proved unable, however, to cope effectively with the great strikes of the post-World War II era. Its location in the Department of Labor lent some slight color to the charge of its critics that it was biased in favor of labor. In 1947, amidst the general reorienting of governmental policy toward unions and industrial peace, the mediation functions were withdrawn from the Department of Labor and independently organized as the Federal Mediation and Conciliation Service. This service, through its regional offices, continues to promote peaceful settlement of labor disputes by lending to the parties its trained conciliators. In a typical year it will be involved in 18–20 thousand disputes and is likely to contribute to the settlement of a very high percentage of them.

World War II and industrial peace

As governmental policy toward labor and labor unions was sharply changed in the thirties, great reliance came to be placed on first the N.R.A. and then the National Labor Relations Board for heading off industrial conflict. Under the theory that most violence and intransigence in labor disputes was employer directed rather than union stimulated, it was supposed that the protection of the bargaining rights of workers would contribute to industrial peace. The entrance of the United States in World War II brought a new dimension to the government's interest in industrial peace and a new urgency for finding more compelling procedures for dealing with strikes and strike threats in coal and steel and other "essential" industries. A determined Congress in 1943 passed over a presidential veto a War Labor Disputes (Smith–Connally) Act which imposed strong deterrents to work stoppages.

The President was empowered to take possession of and operate any plant, mine, or facility in which a labor disturbance threatened the production of materials needed for the war effort. As long as governmental operation continued, any interference in production by strike, lockout, slowdown, or any other tactic was illegal. Coincident with the expiration of this act (at the end of World War II) a new rash of strikes swept the country and stimulated bitter debate over the proper method of dealing with them. In the absence of effective legal sanction, the President personally intervened on many occasions to bring the stoppage to a halt by the power of public opinion and his own prestige. In those parts of the economy still under wartime price controls, wage settlement boards and committees threw their energies into peaceful amelioration of the swelling tide of unrest as unions sought desperately to keep wages up to the rising spiral of inflationary prices.

Changing attitudes toward unions The election in 1946 brought to Washington a group of legislators determined to remake the whole governmental policy and machinery for dealing with labor disputes and with labor–management relations. By this time a large segment of articulate opinion was convinced that the major fault for the dreaded paralysis of industrywide strikes lay with the unions. Swollen by increased employment and governmental benevolence, it was argued, they had become too powerful and their leaders too arrogant. The public interest in resisting inflation and in stopping the hardships of prolonged strikes in key industries demanded that these new giants of economic power be brought under governmental control. Such was the setting for the passage of the Labor–Management Relations (Taft–Hartley) Act of 1947.

The Labor–Management Act of 1947: In form, the Labor–Management Act of 1947 is an amendment to the National Labor Relations Act of 1935 and thus preserves for labor all of the basic guarantees of the earlier law. The general principle of unionized labor is accepted as axiomatic. At the same time, the right of every worker to "refrain from . . . concerted activities," that is, to identify himself with no union, if he so prefers, is expressly recognized and protected. Every union *1. Rights and duties of unions* desiring to be in a position to avail itself of the services of the Labor Relations Board in defense of its bargaining and other interests is required to keep on file with that agency full information on its membership, officers, finances, rules and regulations.

2. Closed and union shops When the act was passed, 30 percent of all organized employes (notably in the printing industry and the building trades) worked in closed shops, that is, in establishments in which one must be a union member even to be hired; and more than that proportion were under "union shop" rules requiring every worker in an establishment to become a union member, if not already such, within 30 days after taking employment. Under the Act of 1947, the closed shop is completely banned, and "union shop" may be maintained only if a majority of all workers in a plant eligible to vote on the question so demand, and only under other restrictions aimed at protecting employer interests. If state law forbids "union shops," it will be controlling.

The basic rights and procedures of collective bargaining guaranteed

*3. Col-
lective
bargaining*

in the legislation of 1935 are reaffirmed, with full freedom for both employers and employes to choose the agents who will represent them at the
bargaining table. But whereas previously only employers were compelled to
bargain, employes now are equally forbidden to refuse to do so; and whereas
formerly employers might not, in the course of bargaining or otherwise,
make even noncoercive statements to their employes or others without risk
of having what they said adduced as evidence of unfair practice, now they
may do this with impunity.

*4. Unfair
practices*

The new law adds to the unfair practices of employers several unfair
practices sometimes engaged in by unions. Employes, for example, may
not be coerced to join unions; members in a union shop may not be required
to pay excessive initiation fees or dues; employers may not, under the
practice popularly known as "featherbedding," be required to pay for services not rendered, for example, to pay a textile worker for operating a single
machine when he could just as well operate four or five, or, in the case of a
radio station using records, to hire "live" musicians. Secondary boycotts
(in which one party refuses to deal with another unless the other will, in
turn, refuse to deal with a third) and jurisdictional strikes (arising, for
instance, out of conflicts between A.F.L. and C.I.O. unions, or between
any such and independent unions) are forbidden. For all of the practices
named, unions are made liable to suit.

*5. Labor
disputes*

The act attempts to strengthen the traditional governmental procedures
for dealing with strikes. In general, the right to strike when other measures
fail is fully recognized. However, certain kinds of strikes, for example,
jurisdictional strikes and strikes against the national government (for which
the penalty is instant dismissal) are absolutely prohibited; and for situations
threatening strikes in themselves legitimate, procedures are ordained in connection with the new Federal Mediation and Conciliation Service designed
to give the parties a chance to "cool off" and mediation an opportunity to
achieve its purpose before overt action occurs. A special procedure is established for dealing with industrywide strikes or those threatening a serious
economic breakdown. The President, when he finds such a strike or lockout
threatens national health or safety, may appoint a board of inquiry to examine the causes. On receipt of a report from this board, the executive may
request an injunction to stop this strike or lockout. If the proper court finds
such a dispute is industrywide and if continued will threaten national health
or safety, it may issue the injunction regardless of the provisions of the
earlier act limiting such orders. The parties are then required to continue
to seek agreement with the aid of the conciliation service and the Inquiry
Board for at least 60 days. Then the inquiry board's final report is made
public and a secret ballot of the employes must be taken by the Labor
Relations Board in 15 days to see if they will accept the board's terms. At
the end of this process the injunction is lifted, and if no settlement has yet
been reached the strike may proceed.

*6. Political
provisions*

There also are provisions of political import. Benefit of National Labor
Board procedures, for example, hearing and deciding complaints against

employers, cannot be claimed by any union having any officer who refuses to declare under oath that he is not a member of the Communist party and that he does not favor the forceful or unconstitutional overthrow of the government. The Federal Corrupt Practices Act of 1925 is amended to bracket labor unions with corporations by forbidding them to make any contributions or incur any expenditures from union funds in connection with any election to any national political office.

Finally, the National Labor Relations Board is increased from three to five members, and its activities confined largely to adjudication. This was done to meet the criticism that formerly the Board was at the same time "investigator, prosecutor, judge, and jury." All work of investigation and prosecution is devolved upon a new official, the *general counsel,* appointed by the President and confirmed by the Senate for four years, and with full supervision over 20 regional offices and their field staffs. *7. Administrative arrangements*

This act thus clearly marks a new phase in governmental policy toward labor and toward disputes. Labor unions are regulated nationally for the first time and peace is to be achieved by adjudicatory determination of the rights and grievances of both parties. Crippling strikes may be halted for a time by injunction and executive intervention in disputes is supported by law.

More than two decades have now elapsed since the government sharply changed its policy toward labor unions and sought to promote industrial peace by a different approach. Has the new policy been successful? There is little agreement on this question. Labor for years yielded little in its demand for outright repeal of the new policy, and business has steadfastly supported the act. In the campaigns of 1948, 1952, and 1956 the Democratic presidential candidates pledged their party to repeal while the Republican candidates, especially General Eisenhower, pledged only to seek modifications. Congress has sternly refused to modify the law in any important respects. Recent candidates have not made much of this issue. President Johnson promised to seek repeal of the section (14 B) recognizing state laws forbidding the union shop. He failed, however, to move Congress. Experience thus far under the new law indicates that its effects were not wholly anticipated by either side. The unions have not grown appreciably in membership since 1947 despite an increase in the labor force. Many factors may account for this, for the experience has not been different in earlier boom periods. Industrial peace has certainly not been completely achieved. Relatively few of the disputes since 1946 have been crippling. The inquiry board and injunction procedure have been used about 30 times. The most successful uses were those halting longshoremen's strikes in 1953, 1956, and 1961. Several strikes in coal and other industries were not halted. The steel strikes of 1952 and 1959 presented the most severe challenges to the Act. President Truman refused to use the procedure in 1952 and referred the issue to the Federal Wage Stabilization Board set up during the Korean emergency. When this failed to bring settlement he attempted unsuccessfully to take over the steel plants. In the prolonged strike of 1959, the injunctive procedure was challenged by the union on the grounds that there was no *Experience under the new policy*

Work Stoppages
1946-1967

YEAR	NUMBER	WORKERS INVOLVED	MAN-DAYS IDLE
1946	4,985	4,600,000	116,000,000
1947	3,693	2,170,000	34,600,000
1948	3,419	1,960,000	34,100,000
1949	3,606	3,030,000	50,500,000
1950	4,843	2,410,000	38,800,000
1951	4,737	2,220,000	22,900,000
1952	5,117	3,540,000	59,100,000
1953	5,091	2,400,000	28,300,000
1954	3,468	1,530,000	22,600,000
1955	4,320	2,650,000	28,200,000
1956	3,825	1,900,000	33,100,000
1957	3,673	1,390,000	16,500,000
1958	3,694	2,060,000	23,900,000
1959	3,708	1,880,000	69,000,000
1960	3,333	1,320,000	19,100,000
1961	3,367	1,450,000	16,300,000
1962	3,640	1,230,000	18,600,000
1963	3,362	941,000	16,100,000
1964	3,655	1,640,000	22,900,000
1965	3,963	1,550,000	23,300,000
1966	4,405	1,960,000	25,400,000
1967	4,595	2,870,000	42,100,000

real emergency and that the courts were being made part of the executive branch contrary to constitutional theory. Although the Supreme Court upheld the use of the injunction as proper, the strike was not settled by the inquiry board or by injunction but rather by the mediation of the Secretary of Labor (Mitchell) strongly supported behind the scenes by the Vice President (Nixon). The effort to outlaw the closed shop and to place the union shop under more rigid control has had mixed results. More plants now have some form of union security agreements than before but the unions have been less able to discipline their own members, since expulsion from the union no longer carries with it loss of the job. However, state "right-to-work" laws which place even more severe restrictions on union shops have been spreading (19 states now have them in some form).

Controversy over the wisdom and effectiveness of the Act of 1947 is presently overshadowed by issues of public policy raised by the revelations of corruption, racketeering, association of union officials with "crime rings," and other union abuses by the investigations in 1957–1958 of a Senate Select Committee headed by Senator McClellan (Arkansas). These investigations, directed by the late Robert Kennedy and dealing largely with the Teamsters' Union, brought the union movement and its leaders once again under a cloud of public suspicion and paved the way for greater and more detailed national regulation of unions. The upshot of this new controversy was the passage of the Labor–Management Reporting and Disclosure Act of 1959.

The Labor-Management Reporting Act of 1959

This act seeks in the first place to protect the rights of individual members of labor organizations by guaranteeing them (1) equal rights and privileges to participate in elections and meetings; (2) freedom of speech and assembly to discuss the conduct of union officers; (3) secret balloting in the determination of dues, fees, or other assessments; (4) the right to take legal action against officers; and (5) protection against arbitrary or improper suspension, expulsion, or other disciplinary action. Labor unions are, further, required to adopt constitutions and bylaws and file with the Secretary of Labor copies of these together with other detailed information on such matters as the rules governing admission, dues, audits of funds, selection of officers, and strike votes. They are also required to file annually complete financial reports. The non-Communist affidavit requirement of the Act of 1947 is repealed but members of the party or ex-members are barred from holding union offices. Officers are required to disclose to the Secretary financial transactions of their own with employers. Employers are required to report certain payments to union officials or to union members or to personnel consultants. Private personnel consultants are required to report any agreements involving union matters which they may undertake in behalf of employers. Trusteeship agreements by which one labor union controls or influences another are also regulated. The selection of union officers is carefully regulated and maximum terms are prescribed as well as secret ballots and some effort is made to keep the nominating procedure open and competitive. The fiduciary responsibility of union officers managing labor funds is spelled out in more detail with various safeguards provided, and convicted criminals are disqualified from holding union positions. The act also tightens the prohibitions against secondary boycotts of the Act of 1947 and adds to its unfair labor practices, picketing aimed at forcing recognition of a union not supported by the employes. Finally, the confused controversy over the relative extent of the jurisdiction of the N.L.R.B. and of state labor boards is partly resolved by authorizing the N.L.R.B. to refuse to accept jurisdiction in many types of "small" cases.

REFERENCES

S. K. Bailey, *Congress Makes a Law; The Story Behind the Employment Act of 1946* (New York, 1950).

D. O. Bowman, *Public Control of Labor Relations; A Study of the National Labor Relations Board* (New York, 1942).

M. Fainsod, L. Gordon, and J. C. Palamountain, Jr., *Government and the American Economy* (3rd ed., New York, 1959), Chap. VII.

F. A. Hartley, Jr., *Our New National Labor Policy* (New York, 1948).

J. H. Leek, *Government and Labor in the United States* (New York, 1952).

W. H. Leiserson, *American Trade Union Democracy* (New York, 1959).

S. Lens, *The Crisis of American Labor* (New York, 1959).

A. K. McAdams, *Power and Politics in Labor Legislation* (New York, 1964).

H. A. Millis and E. C. Brown, *From the Wagner Act to Taft–Hartley; A Study of National Labor Policy and Labor Relations* (Chicago, 1950).

H. R. Northrup and A. F. Bloom, *Government and Labor* (Homewood, Illinois, 1963).

G. W. Taylor, *Government Regulation of Industrial Relations* (New York, 1948).

D. H. Wollett, *Labor Relations and Federal Law* (Seattle, Wash., 1949).

18
GOVERNMENT AND AGRICULTURE

Agriculture the favored interest The seal of the United States Department of Agriculture declares, "Agriculture is the foundation of manufacturing and commerce." This motto expresses a view, widely held in the life of the American nation, that agriculture is the backbone of our society. Cities, industry, and commerce may all be swallowed up in the maw of war or pestilence and life would still be possible; if the soil or those skilled in making it yield its bounty were to be destroyed, all life would disappear. Furthermore, in this view, rural life is demonstrably superior to urban life on every significant count: it is healthier, better for raising the young, and spiritually stronger. It produces a self-reliant, independent, vigorous, and healthy people. Trade and manufacturing produce the urban swarm, dependent, frail, neurotic, materialistic, and fearful. These convictions are properly described as agricultural fundamentalism and have played an important part in shaping the policy of the government toward agriculture. That these views have not been decisive on all occasions of national controversy is due, in part, to the fact that they have been sharply contested by another view which holds that agriculture, like every other economic interest, should find its proper place in the national economy through competition. If the calculus of the market place decrees that manufacturing should rise and farming decline, so be it. Agricultural fundamentalism, however, has been sufficiently impressive in the national scene that the government has usually been disposed to grant to the agricultural interest whatever that interest was agreed upon. The rural interest has been bolstered also by the fact that our political institutions have not been geared perfectly to represent majority opinion. Having once been a majority, the rural interest has clung to institutional arrangements which give it political strength disproportionate to its numerical strength in the population. Because of this and because of the appeal of the fundamentalists' creed, it would not be unfair to say that agriculture has been treated benevolently by the government more consistently than any of the other great economic interests. Despite the faith of the fundamentalists and the bounty of a sympathetic government, the place of agriculture in American life has slowly but certainly declined. This decline and the conflict of ideologies about it provide the setting for most of the modern controversies surrounding the determination of national agricultural policy.

The position of agriculture in modern America has been determined largely by the tremendous revolution in agricultural technology which has been occurring since about 1850. This revolution, although obscured from the view of the city-dweller by the blinding light of the Industrial Revolution, has been just as sweeping in its impact. The continuing application of scientific methods and power-driven machinery have been pushing the output per farmer and per acre to unimagined heights. In 1830, for example, it took about three farm families to produce enough food and fiber beyond their own needs to feed and clothe one city family. In 1967, one farm family could feed and clothe more than 40 persons. The improvement in productivity has been striking in just the last two decades. Wheat yields were about 17 bushels per acre in 1945 and 26 bushels in 1965; corn yields were 32.7 bushels per acre in 1945 and 61 bushels in 1964. Stated another way, the revolution in agriculture has meant that a constantly increasing share of agricultural produce is for sale rather than subsistence—more than 90 percent in 1968. Agriculture has become a great "business" venture and is no longer simply a way of life. The most prosperous 1200 farms produced $1.4 billion of crops and livestock in 1960. Even so, 78 percent of the farms in 1960 produced little more than subsistence for their owners or operators. The income of many of these farmers was greater from working in nearby cities than from their farms. The tremendous outpouring of agricultural products thus comes from not more than one-fourth of the farm population. In fact, the most productive 10 percent of the farms produce more than half of the agricultural output measured in terms of dollars.

The revolution in agriculture

Fewer and fewer farmers are producing more and more crops, and whereas in 1860 the United States was 80 percent rural, today fewer than 6 percent of our people are actually on farms. The farm population has been declining relative to the city population since 1790 but it has been declining absolutely since 1916. The farm population of 15.6 million in 1960 is about the same as it was in 1864 and by 1966 it had fallen to 11.5 million. The number of farms reached an alltime high of 6.8 million in 1935; by 1967 there were only 3.1 million. The farmer's share of the national income has also been falling: it was less than 5 percent in 1967. It is well known, further, that even the present reduced farm population can, with the aid of modern technology, produce much more of many crops than the nation has been able to consume or to export. The American farmer has turned Malthus right around: in the United States, the food supply is pressing on the (farm) population.

The decline of the farm population

The faith of the fundamentalists, sorely tested by these developments, is being challenged further by the persistence and spread of rural blight. The argument for the superiority of rural ways could, in the past, be bolstered by reference to the statistics of infant mortality, disease, death, crime,

Rural blight

PRODUCTIVITY IN AGRICULTURE
(PER MAN-HOUR)

1830 HAND METHODS

1896 EARLY MACHINES

 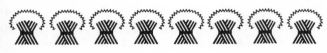

1950 MODERN MACHINES   Each symbol represents 40 lbs. of wheat produced   PICTOGRAPH CORPORATION

and other symptoms of social ills. In all of these respects and with minimal governmental efforts, the rural areas were superior to the urban ones. In each year that passes, however, the city has gained. In infant deaths and in many diseases, the urban areas are now ahead of the rural ones, as they are in amount of education and average income. The rural birth rate, especially among the poorest people remains high, however. There are some cities, in fact, that are superior in every respect to the rural areas. Underlying these developments is not only aggressive urban governmental attack on the problem but also subsidence in the rural economy. More than one-fifth of all acreage now tilled is so eroded and its fertility so depleted that it ought not to be cultivated any longer. One-crop agriculture produces

Rural poverty

surpluses and eats up the soil. Among that half of the farm population which produces little above subsistence, living standards, real income, and per capita wealth are all quite low. In fact, much of the most desperate poverty in the United States is on the farm and rural slums rival the worst that our large cities can produce. There are 1.5 million small farmers who earn less than $5,000 per year and the plight of the 1.7 million agricultural laborers is even more desperate. If the national government were to withdraw its benevolent hand and capacious pocketbook from agriculture, it seems clear that the misery, disease, crime, and suffering in rural America would compare with the worst that our great cities have ever produced.

The farmers in politics

The farm interest, like that of business and of labor, relies heavily today on its great associations to press its claims before Congress, the executive branch, party committees, and state governments. The strongest of these, described in an earlier chapter, are well financed, competently led, and frequently effective. Unlike the business interest, the farmers are not so solidly dedicated to one party. They are influential in both parties and are more inclined to shift loyalty from one party to the other if harassed by economic distress or assuaged by promises of benevolence. The farm vote appeared to be influential, for example, in the victory of Truman in 1948, after having aided the Republicans to gain control of Congress in 1946. The farmers, furthermore, unlike business and labor, have historically provided the basis for several strong third parties: Republican, Greenback, Populist, and Non-Partisan League, for example. Farmer-supported minor parties have captured control at various times of several state governments. No labor party has ever achieved as much success. Economic distress in agriculture has produced as much home-grown radicalism in both economics and politics as has distress in any other segment of the economy. This has been articulated through party platforms and campaigns as frequently as for any other interest.

Any discussion of the farm interest in American politics is predicated *Unity of* to some degree on a myth. Like the business interest, the farm interest is *farm* nothing like as homogeneous as it is frequently made to appear. Cash crop *interests?* farming is frequently at odds with subsistence farming. Truck crop farming is not as dependent on world economic conditions as export crop farming. Southern cotton agriculture is usually at loggerheads with midwestern dairy

The Declining Position of American Agriculture

YEAR	FARM POPULATION (MILLIONS)	% TOTAL U.S. POP.	NO. FARMS (MILLIONS)	AVERAGE SIZE OF FARMS (ACRES)
1935	32,161	25.3	6,814	155
1945	24,420	17.5	5,967	191
1950	23,048	15.3	5,648	213
1954	19,019	11.8	4,798	251
1959	16,592	9.4	4,105	288
1960	16,635	8.7	3,956	298
1967	10,807	5.4	3,146	360

SOURCE: *Statistical Abstract of the United States, 1967.*

farming. Tenant farmers oppose absentee landlord farmers. Small operators battle large operators. On few questions of public policy is the farming population agreed. Few there are, in fact, who speak for the migratory laborer or for the depressed third. Most farmers accept the tenets of agricultural fundamentalism, but beyond this there is little agreement. Even the fundamentalists are likely to export their children to the urban-industrial areas of America.

THE IMPROVEMENT OF AGRICULTURAL PRODUCTION

Although by nature and tradition the most highly individualistic form of enterprise, agriculture long ago turned to government for encouragement and assistance. And from the earliest days, local governments have provided roads for the movement of farm products to market, have supported land title registration and surveys to insure the rights of ownership, have financed fairs and exhibitions to encourage better breeding of plants and animals, and in numerous other ways have aided the farmer in his struggle against nature. The states too have responded to the farmers' claims by providing programs of research and education designed to supplement local efforts. The farmers turned to the national government with some reluctance and only after they became convinced that state and local efforts were not adequate to their needs. Out of its power to spend money, to regulate commerce, to provide post roads, the Congress has found constitutional authority to support an everwidening array of programs for the benefit of American agriculture.

The distri-bution of the public domain

Among the oldest and perhaps the most persistently pursued program through the years has been the improvement of production. Until about 1890, one of the major methods used by the national government to achieve greater output of food and fiber was its program for the distribution of the huge public domain. More and more land was thus brought under cultivation and the priceless heritage of the American people was distributed among those who undertook to cultivate it. Until the Civil War the policy for the distribution of land was determined by statesmen with one eye on the treasury, but the Republican party pledged itself to give away the national domain as quickly and as cheaply as possible. By 1890, the last usable land had been placed under cultivation and the frontier was gone.

Provision of scientific research

A more enduring method of national assistance to agricultural production has been the provision of scientific research. The first appropriation for agriculture was made by the Congress in 1839 in the amount of $1000 for seed collection and distribution and for agricultural investigations. The first full-time employe devoting himself to agricultural problems was a chemist. When the Department of Agriculture was created in 1862 as a separate agency under a commissioner, one of the major functions assigned to it was the collection of information about agriculture by the conduct of "practical and scientific experiments." From these modest beginnings the research program of the Department of Agriculture has grown by mighty leaps until it is the most comprehensive of its kind in the world and the Department one of the greatest research establishments. From it each year flow hundreds of bulletins describing the results of the experiments and investigations. Chemists, engineers, economists, bacteriologists, geneticists, management experts, nutritionists, horticulturists, and scores of other experts labor daily at the task of showing the American farmer how to wrest larger yields, larger profits, greater leisure, and higher standards of living from nature. This research is carried on not only in the departmental laboratories and at the great 12,000 acre Agricultural Research Center at Beltsville, Maryland, but also in hundreds of state and territorial experiment stations and state college laboratories. Beginning in 1887, the agricultural experiment station program has been supported by national grants to state agricultural colleges. The states and territories, on their parts, appropriate matching and supplementary funds to the colleges and stations, altogether more than doubling the total annual investment in agricultural research. This comprehensive attack on farm problems has throughout the years contributed importantly to the revolution in agricultural technology which has done so much to shape the modern American economy.

Complementing the great program of discovering new knowledge beneficial to agriculture has been a powerful national effort to improve agricultural education. Scientific farming requires scientific farmers and these require institutions dedicated to instruction in agricultural arts and science. It is not coincidence that the same Congress which created the first Department of Agriculture also created the first national-state program of agricultural colleges. The Land Grant College (Morrill) Act of 1862 granted millions of acres of the public domain to the states for the support of state colleges of agriculture, engineering, and home economics. Out of this program grew the great state universities and agricultural colleges of modern America. Since 1890, national money grants have replaced the land grants, and state appropriations have grown to exceed many times over the national gifts. Through the national grants, of course, the national government exercises a continuing influence over the programs of the agricultural colleges. *Improvement of agricultural education*

The colleges, however, can work directly with only a small portion of the agricultural population. A new program designed to carry the knowledge and skills of the colleges and the experiment stations to the farmers' backyards was inaugurated in 1914. The Cooperative Agricultural Extension (Smith–Kerr) Act of that year provided the basis for the modern extension service. Through county agricultural agents supported by national, state, and county governments, the accumulating knowledge about agriculture is today carried into the farmyard and there adapted to the needs of the individual farmer. The Extension Service unites the levels of government in a unique way to produce an itinerant encyclopedia of farm science at the beck of virtually every farmer in the land. With this triumvirate of college, experiment station, and extension agent under the mild, generous, and beneficent hand of the national department, the American farmer is the recipient of more solicitous concern, expert advice, and improving instruction than any other sizable group in the population. *The development of Agricultural Extension Service*

IMPROVING THE ECONOMIC POSITION OF THE FARMER

Unlike factories, farms cannot close down when the supply of agricultural products produces a glut on the market. The only recourse to a farmer in a period of falling farm prices is to try to increase his output. This is especially true of highly specialized, one-crop, staple agriculture. The great technological advance in agriculture, stimulated partly by the determined *The problem of surpluses* efforts of government scientists to improve productivity, has helped to produce in this century a new and unusual farm problem—surpluses. Two world wars added new urgency to the expansion of agricultural production as European cultivation was halted by the guns of opposing armies. The restoration of European production, the exhaustion of foreign purchasing power, and the growing restrictions on international trade combined in the postwar eras to reduce the export market for American staples and to leave the greatly expanded output of American farms without markets to absorb the yield.

Early aids to marketing

The farmer's interest in improving the marketing and distribution of his crops is, of course, not new. The long battle of the midwestern, southern, and plains farmers in the 1870's and 1880's against the railroads and the grain elevators represented a determined effort to improve distribution and to gain for the farmers a larger share of the ultimate price to the consumer of their products. Until the New Deal era, however, the demands of agriculture for governmental aid in distribution were largely met by: (1) inaugurating an elaborate system of collecting and disseminating timely data on crop prospects and market prices; (2) establishing and maintaining by state cooperation uniform grades and standards for commodities shipped to out-of-state markets; (3) regulating bonded warehouses, stockyards, commission merchants, brokers, and commodity exchanges in the interests of fair play for the producers. All of these programs, directed for the most part by the Consumer and Marketing Service of the Department, have been strengthened with the years and are still key activities of the national department. However, they all fell short of striking decisively at the heart of the farmers' problem after World War I.

The first Agricultural Adjustment Act

The Roosevelt administration faced in 1933 a deep and disastrous drop in industrial activity. It faced a situation in agriculture which had been aggravating since 1922 and which was bankrupting the great agricultural regions of the nation. Borrowing the ideas of the farm bloc of the 20's the New Deal struck boldly at the heart of the problem. In the Agricultural Adjustment Act of 1933 it sought to increase farm income by raising farm prices and to raise farm prices by curtailing production and subsidizing the farmer for the curtailment. The price level on farm products sought was one which would restore the purchasing power of farm products obtaining in the relatively favorable period of 1909–1914. To achieve this "parity" the act aimed to reduce production to the extent necessary to bring agricultural prices up to the relative level of industrial prices. For this curtailment, the farmer was to be paid out of the proceeds of a tax levied on "processors" of the commodities for which curtailment was directed. This tax would, of course, be passed on to the consumer in the form of higher prices. Originally the act extended to only seven commodities: wheat, cotton, corn, rice, tobacco, hogs, and milk. Later, beef, dairy cattle, peanuts, barley, flax, sorghum, sugar beets, sugar cane, and potatoes were added. The Secretary of Agriculture was charged with administering the program through voluntary agreements with farmers to reduce acreage, plow under a portion of crops already planted, kill surplus animals, and by other means to produce less in consideration of a cash subsidy. Within one year, 40 million acres were withdrawn from cultivation and farm income, including the subsidy, had increased 39 percent. The Secretary was also given broad power to eliminate "unfair" trade practices in the marketing and distribution of all kinds of agricultural commodities. In 1936, this much-debated effort to improve the relative position of American agriculture was swept away by the Supreme Court. The Court held the processing taxes which financed the subsidy program to be unconstitutional. These are not taxes in a real sense, said the Court, but levies upon one group of people for the benefit of another. The field of agricultural production, further said the Court, is reserved to the states and may not be the object of national regulation thinly disguised as taxation. Actually the plan had cost almost twice as much as the tax had yielded.

The objectives of the farm policy of the New Deal were partly aided by the devastation of drouth, dust storms, and floods in 1934. While helping to keep production down, these disasters also spread new distress among the farmers of the plains, driving them in large numbers from their homes and onto the highways as itinerant farm laborers. The catastrophes also convinced the nation's leaders that they had some obligation to preserve the nation's resources. The combination of ideas and events suggested to the Congress a way out of the predicament created by the Court decision. In the Soil Conservation and Domestic Allotment Act of 1936, production control was made incidental to soil conservation. Restoration of 1910–1914 farmer purchasing power was now sought by benefit payments to farmers for soil conservation practices which also reduced production of basic commodities. By shifting land from soil-depleting crops (corn, tobacco, wheat, cotton, etc.) to soil-building crops (clover, alfalfa, pasture grasses, etc.), the farmers were stimulated to reduce surpluses of staple crops and save the soil at the same time. No special tax was levied this time: the whole program was financed out of general receipts.

Production-control tied to soil conservation

The curtailment in production under the new program was still not adequate and, when 1937 and 1938 proved exceptionally good crop years, the old vicious spiral of commodity surpluses and sharply declining prices set in again. Accordingly, in the latter year, Congress passed a new Agricultural Adjustment Act, scrupulously avoiding processing taxes and any other devices likely to encounter judicial disapproval, but nevertheless contemplating, like the ill-fated measure of 1933, control of agricultural production. Without abandoning the conservation tie-up of 1936, the new law sought to achieve the desired control by supplementary arrangements briefly as follows: (1) if in any year the production of wheat, corn, cotton, rice, or tobacco threatened to create a surplus that would break the price, the Department of Agriculture should take a referendum among the producers of a given crop on the desirability of imposing limitations for the

The second Agricultural Adjustment Act (1938)

next crop year; (2) if two-thirds voted favorably, the Department, operating through state committees, should allot to each producing county for that year, on the basis of the average acreage seeded during the preceding ten years, the number of acres that might be planted to the given crop; (3) within each county, and with the cooperation of democratically elected local farmer committees, an allotment should be made, in turn, to each producing farmer (again on a basis of past average production) of a maximum acreage from which he might market his product without restriction; (4) a farmer suffering a reduction in income under his allotment should be compensated by a governmental subsidy; (5) on the other hand, he might raise more acres of the crop if he wished, but if marketing products from excess acreage during a period of surplus, he should be subject to fine; (6) on surplus crops so produced, he might, nevertheless, receive loans from the Commodity Credit Corporation in the Department of Agriculture in amounts calculated according to "parity" prices; (7) such surplus crops should be stored under government seal in elevators or warehouses until a time of scarcity, when the farmer might sell them at the parity price and repay his loans—such sales operating to prevent the market price from ever rising far above parity; and (8) when the price of a given stored commodity should fall below parity, the producer should be entitled to receive from the government payments sufficient to make up the deficiency. In short, surplus crops were to be stored in years of superabundance, without the farmer being left short of cash, and then would be available to be thrown on the market in years of shortage from drouth or other cause.

To this system of an "ever-normal granary"—keeping part of the supply out of the market so that what remains will bring a "just" price—were added arrangements for crop insurance, starting tentatively with wheat in 1938 and later extended to cotton and flax. The idea of the insurance program was to protect producers against losses from depleted yields caused by drouth, flood, hail, insect infestation, and plant diseases. Insurance costs (i.e., premiums) were made payable by the insured to the government either in cash or in surplus wheat (or other products), the latter becoming an additional reserve of the ever-normal granary. The revamped farm program was sustained as constitutional by a now reconstructed Supreme Court and it has formed the basis of all subsequent legislation in this field.

The new program found constitutional

As the nations of the world in 1939 gave up diplomacy for the battlefield, the main agricultural problem of the United States shifted once again to need for expanded production. In 1942, the Department of Agriculture announced its goal as "the largest production in the history of American agriculture." The farmers, with bitter memories of the twenties still alive, were, however, reluctant to expand their production facilities without governmental assurance of protection against the inevitable drop in exports at the close of the war. A sympathetic Congress promised (the Stabilization Act of 1942) that the government would support prices of the staple agri-

Agriculture in World War II

cultural products (cotton, corn, wheat, rice, tobacco, and peanuts) at not less than 90 percent of "parity" for the two years after the emergency ended. A benevolent government also made every effort to raise farm income during the difficult periods of wage and price controls and rationing. The result was that American agriculture entered the postwar period in what was probably the strongest financial position it had ever known.

President Truman declared the war emergency at an end in December, 1946. The postwar recession in the national economy and especially the precipitous decline in markets for agricultural products predicted by most of those charged with plotting national policy did not occur immediately. Pent-up consumer demand in the United States and the Marshall plan of aid to shattered economies abroad sustained a lively demand. And when price and wage controls were abandoned by a government bent on returning to "normalcy," agricultural prices led a headstrong upsurge in prices which in a few short years drove the American cost of living to dizzy heights. As the time approached in 1948 for the expiration of the price-support guarantees, a Republican Congress began to hammer out a new farm program in the light of the intoxicating farm prosperity of the forties. Farm groups, however, fearful that the bubble would collapse, leaving them with high production costs and expanded facilities, continued to demand governmental price supports. A bitter wrangle, lasting until the hour of adjournment, developed between the supporters of rigid price supports for the staples at 90 percent of parity and the supporters of a more flexible support program (60–90 percent) by which production might gradually be readjusted to consumption. In the end, the Agriculture (Hope-Aiken) Act of 1948 provided for a temporary continuance of rigid, 90 percent, supports until 1950 and then a "long-term" program of flexible supports. The old 1910–1914 base period for determining parity with industrial prices was abandoned—as it had been in fact during the emergency—and was replaced with a new formula using prices of the war and postwar periods. Since this meant a decline in a few staple prices (wheat, notably), the act provided a transitional period in which the new lower level of prices would gradually be achieved. The support program, although intended for the staples, was authorized for many other crops at the discretion of the secretary of agriculture if trouble developed in marketing those commodities at "fair" prices.

Postwar price-support program

The repudiation of the Republican record in the election of 1948 was taken by many Democrats as an authorization to abandon the "flexible" features of the Act of 1948. The Agricultural Act of 1949 was largely a victory for the high, rigid, price-support program as against the flexible program. Although provision was made for adjusting support for most types of agricultural products to the market situation, the basic staples which had been the center of the difficulty through the years were virtually assured of a high level of support. The parity formula was once again revised to take account of the high postwar wages of farm labor and the war-

The Agricultural Act of 1949

time subsidy payments to farmers designed to hold consumer prices down.

The Eisenhower administration confronted a changed situation in agriculture. The world markets had fallen away as after World War I, and even the Korean episode and the high level of industrial activity which it stimulated could not bridge the growing gap between production and consumption. The government warehouses, elevators, bins, cribs, and refrigerators were bursting with the protected commodities bought up by the Commodity Credit Corporation in keeping with the high level price-support mandate of the Act of 1949. The supported prices made it difficult for American crops to compete for part of the world market.

The Agricultural Act of 1954

The new administration finally unveiled its new farm program in 1954 after a panel of farm representatives had reviewed the matter for several months. The result was a new Agricultural Act which conformed in broad outlines to the recommendations of President Eisenhower and his secretary of agriculture, Benson. This act: (1) directed the Commodity Credit Corporation to "set aside" from its inventories large quantities of wheat, cotton, cottonseed oil, butter, milk solids, and cheese which, subject to Presidential direction, might be donated for disaster relief, school lunches, or research purposes, bartered with foreign nations, transferred to the national stockpile of strategic materials, or sold on the market at not less than 105 percent of the parity prices of the commodities; (2) provided for the "basic" or staple commodities a system of flexible price supports at 82½ to 90 percent of parity prices and for dairy products at 75 to 90 percent of parity prices; (3) directed the Veterans Administration and the Defense Department to accept supplies of milk, butter, and cheese from the Commodity Corporation from its stocks; (4) expanded the national program for eliminating brucellosis from dairy cattle; (5) tightened the provisions aimed at preventing expansion of staple production into new areas; (6) established agricultural attachés to be located in diplomatic missions abroad for the purpose of promoting the marketing of American agricultural products.

The "soil bank"

To this program was added in 1956 on the recommendation of the President a "soil bank" arrangement aimed at reducing by voluntary and compensated effort the acreage planted to the protected crops—mainly, corn, wheat, cotton, and rice. Farmers could retire acres from cultivation putting them into pasture, trees, or grasses and receive payments for the loss of production involved. Under this program 28 million acres were retired from cultivation from 1956 to 1960.

The Kennedy Program

Meanwhile the Democrats recaptured control of the Congress in 1954 and held it through Eisenhower's second term. Efforts to restore rigid price support programs were turned back in 1956 and in 1958 by Presidential veto. The proposals of the Kennedy administration in 1961 and 1962 looked to much greater flexibility in the whole program to adjust acreage and marketing controls to the current situation in any of the protected staples. Strict acreage controls combined with moderately high price supports were preferred to the low price support program of the previous administration. In general, Kennedy was urban oriented and anxious to hold down farm subsidies. Congress responded by expanding the secretary of agriculture's marketing-order authority but refused to delegate major power for acreage and price control. A patched up law, passed late in 1962, was satisfactory to no one, and in 1963, for the first time in 30 years, a production control referendum among wheat farmers was defeated. President Johnson attempted throughout his service to shift the emphasis from price supports to general improvement in rural life, linking his efforts to maintain farm income with his general attack on poverty. The Food and Agriculture Act of 1965, one of the high points of the domestic program achievements, recognized that stabilizing the market supply of the staple crops was a continuing, not a temporary problem. It continued a moderately flexible price support program until 1969, combined with production control through acreage allotments. A program of relatively long-term removal of land from staple crop production was begun on a small scale and surplus commodities were diverted to the needy at home through a food-stamp plan and the needy abroad through the food-for-peace program. In 1968, Johnson recommended the creation of a stockpile for feed grains through a national Feed Bank to contain some of the surplus production.

The Johnson Program

The heart of the modern effort to sustain a relatively high level of farm prosperity is the purchase by the government of the excess yields of farm products. The chief instrument for its accomplishment is the Commodity Credit Corporation in the Department of Agriculture. This Corporation is governed, under the general supervision of the secretary, by a board of directors of six members appointed by the President with the consent of the Senate. It is authorized to borrow $14.5 billion to carry out its missions. The Corporation's typical method of operation is to loan to eligible farmers the full value of their harvest at the supported price with the harvest as security. If the farmer cannot dispose of his crop on more favorable terms, he simply allows the Corporation to possess the crop. Commodities are also purchased in the open market at the support price. During World War II, the Corporation gradually disposed of its holdings, usually at a profit, but the modern era of falling exports and rising production has forced the Corporation to take on more and more commodities. Its inventories had grown through the postwar high support years to $7.4 billion in June of 1961. Its storage costs alone exceeded $1 billion in the late 50's. Through disposal overseas under food-for-peace programs and at home through better adjustment of output to consumption the assessed wealth of commodities was reduced by 1967 to under $1 billion. Until 1951, the farm price subsidy cost about $350 million a year but in the decade of 1952–1961 it has cost about $2.2 billion a year and in 1968 is running about $1 billion yearly.

The Commodity Credit Corporation

Every effort by the experts of the Department of Agriculture to promote the diversification of agriculture in the great staple producing areas, to improve marketing practices, to find new uses for the staple crops, to reduce acreage devoted to price supported commodities, to dispose of surpluses to needy children, and to barter surpluses abroad has thus far fallen short of bringing production into line with demand. The supporters of a "flexible" price program believe it offers the only feasible hope for gradually adjusting production to effective consumption. Those favoring "rigid" supports cite the distress of the twenties, the pledges of the government during World War II, and the importance of the great staple producing areas in the nation as justification for heavy and continuing annual subsidies to the producers. The subsidy, however, appears to be more than adequate for the highly mechanized, heavily capitalized large farm units but not sufficient for the poorest third of the farmers. These continue to abandon agriculture and seek urban job opportunities. In the cities, they are helping to swell the ranks of the unemployed. There is not on the horizon a politically acceptable program looking toward the return of a free market for agricultural production. In an imperfect world, it is, of course, better to be troubled by glut than by famine.

IMPROVEMENT OF RURAL LIFE

Throughout the years and especially since 1933, the national government has supplemented its concern for production and distribution with programs aimed at improving the human, or social, aspects of farming. Impelled to do this by rural backwardness and distress brought sharply to view by the depression of the thirties, and by the continued exodus from farm to city, the Department of Agriculture, with a good deal of backing from Congress, now regards as part of its task the systematic promotion of better living conditions on the farm and in rural communities. Only a few outstanding services of this nature can, however, be mentioned here.

1. Relief for farm tenants

Agricultural credit institutions have been developed to aid in farm purchase, farm-home construction, and purchase of farm equipment. These are designed primarily to benefit farmers who own, or have an ownership interest in, the land they cultivate. There is another large agricultural element that cannot avail itself of these agencies, for the reason that those belonging to it own no land and little, if any, other property that might serve as security for loans. These less fortunate people—commonly excluded also from wage and hour provisions, unemployment insurance, and workmen's compensation—are the tenant farmers, sharecroppers, and farm laborers, who from 1880 until fairly recently steadily increased in proportion to the number of farm owners, and now comprise at least one-third of the total number tilling the soil. They (or many of them) are the people who give rise to rural "blight"; and the areas where large numbers of them live, notably the southern and southwestern states, form our "rural slums." Following a penetrating and fairly startling report in 1937 on the conditions and outlook of these submerged groups, submitted by a committee on farm tenancy appointed by President Franklin D. Roosevelt, Congress in the same year passed the Farm Tenant (Bankhead-Jones) Act, under which the government, operating through state and local machinery terminating in county committees of farmers, offers 40-year loans (at 5 percent and up to $12,000) to farm tenants, farm laborers, and sharecroppers (with preference for veterans) to enable them to acquire homes and lands of their own; and likewise "rehabilitation loans" (at 5 percent and to a maximum of $5,000) for the purchase of livestock, seed, fertilizers, and farm equipment, for refinancing indebtedness, and for family subsistence, including medical care. Mortgages on loans for similar purposes made by private lenders also are insured. Loans (made through offices commonly located in county-seat towns) are not confined to the categories of persons mentioned, but are extended also to better situated "family type" farmers who for some reason cannot get the credit they need elsewhere, at all events on favorable terms.

2. Rural electrification

Until two decades ago, the United States lagged behind several other countries in bringing electrical energy within the reach of rural populations, and even today, with 400 farm uses for electricity known, some 2.5 percent of the nation's more than 3 million farms still are without electric light and power. In 1936, however (when only 10 percent of farms were electrified), Congress passed a Rural Electrification (Norris-Rayburn) Act launching a long-term program under which large progress has been made toward providing farms with cheap light and power, relieving the drudgery of the farmer and his wife, and adding to the farm's income-producing equipment. Management of the undertaking is vested in a Rural Electrification Administration (R.E.A.), since 1939 a unit within the Department of Agriculture. Such management consists principally in making long-term, self-liquidating, 2 percent loans up to 100 percent of cost (1) to associations (usually farmer cooperatives organized for the purpose), corporations, or local-government bodies, to enable them to build transmission lines and buy generators for furnishing electrical energy to people in rural areas for whom central-station services are not available, and (2) to individuals or firms engaged in wiring farm buildings and installing electrical and plumbing appliances and equipment—no loans being extended directly to consumers. Private utility companies also have, of course, been expanding their services in rural areas—sometimes, it is charged, deliberately to discourage government-financed undertakings from being started. Fifty-seven percent of all farms electrified since 1936, however, get their power through systems developed by R.E.A.

3. Rural telephone service

The government's task of rural electrification is expected to start tapering off and to be completed in a few years. In 1949, however, Congress decided to move also into the field of rural communications and passed an act authorizing the R.E.A. to begin making 2 percent loans to independent telephone companies (of which there are 5762 in the country), farm cooperatives, and nonprofit mutual associations to establish and extend telephone services for the 60 percent of the nation's farms still without such conveniences. Critics of the plan objected that it would inflict unfair competition upon private companies, that the telephone might become obsolete, leaving the government with a useless investment, and that the undertaking might prove an entering wedge for government control of all communications and for curtailment of freedom of speech. But such arguments did not prevail and by mid-1968 the R.E.A. had loaned $1.5 billion for telephone service extensions.

4. General program for rural relief   All of these programs, however, have fallen short of bringing major relief to the desperately poor who live on farms and in rural areas. President Johnson has included the rural poor in his attack on poverty and has sought by such programs as that in Appalachia to improve health, education, and highway services in the poorest areas. The Food Stamp plan and School Lunch program have been expanded somewhat in the late sixties, but are still not reaching many of the poor who need them most. Congressional agricultural leadership as well as that of the major farm associations have not interested themselves in the problems. A Presidential commission on rural poverty reported in late 1967 that the urban riots had part of their roots in rural poverty. The rural poor have not been aided by agricultural programs; these aid the better farms. They have been missed by much of the welfare programs based on state and local contributions and they have not shared the general improvement in educational opportunities. The Department of Agriculture in 1968 was stung to rejoinder by a T.V. series on hunger which indicated that a large number of the Department's clients were starving.

REFERENCES

G. Baker, *The County Agent* (Chicago, 1939).

M. R. Benedict, *Farm Policies of the United States, 1790–1950,* Twentieth Century Fund (New York, 1953).

D. C. Blaisdell, *Government and Agriculture; The Growth of Federal Farm Aid* (New York, 1940).

R. M. Christensen, *The Brannan Plan: Farm Policies and Politics* (Ann Arbor, Mich., 1959).

W. H. Clark, *Farms and Farmers; The Story of American Agriculture* (Boston, 1945).

Congressional Quarterly Service, *U.S. Agricultural Policy in the Postwar Years: 1945–1963* (Washington, D. C., 1963).

M. Fainsod, L. Gordon, and J. Palamountain, *Government and the American Economy* (3rd ed., New York, 1959), Chap. VI.

J. M. Gaus and L. O. Wolcott, *Public Administration and the Department of Agriculture* (Chicago, 1940).

T. S. Harding, *Two Blades of Grass; A History of Scientific Development in the United States Department of Agriculture* (Norman, Okla., 1947).

D. E. Hathaway, *Government and Agriculture; Economic Policy in a Democratic Society* (New York, 1963).

E. Higbee, *Farms and Farmers in an Urban Age* (New York, 1963).

W. McCune, *The Farm Bloc* (Garden City, N. Y., 1943).

F. M. Muller, *Public Rural Electrification* (Washington, D. C., 1944).

19

CONSERVING THE NATION'S RESOURCES

Early in the twentieth century, in schools and churches, parlors and meeting halls across the country, a new song was being sung, "America, the Beautiful." Reaffirming love for and faith in a land by its people, it soon became the national hymn. A beautifully rich and varied land had been conquered and molded together. Devoted forebears, republican institutions, science, and technology had brought this land and its people near to another Eden—"a brotherhood of man from sea to shining sea."

Even as the words and music were being written, however, there were *Early* some, like Lincoln Steffens (*The Shame of the Cities*), who said that the *conserva-* "alabaster cities" did not "gleam, undimmed by human tears." And there *tion efforts* were others, less critical, but not less emphatic, who warned that the resources of this fabulous land were being shamefully and carelessly wasted and destroyed. Such was John Muir, the naturalist, whose writings and crusade to preserve the beauty of the High Sierras were instrumental in the establishment in 1890 of one of our first national parks, Yosemite. Outstanding was President Theodore Roosevelt, under whose impetus and leadership the *protection* of the country's resources became a concern of national policy. Deploring the rapidity with which forest wealth was disappearing at the hands of lumber companies and other private exploiters, he and later Presidents set aside generous portions of the public domain as national forests. However, it was not until the Great Depression had sharpened public vision that actual ugliness was seen in the countryside. Suddenly, as it seemed, rural slums were evident. The Dust Bowl, the area in the southern Great Plains affected periodically by severe wind erosion, was an affront. In those years, *rehabilitation* of the land became *an instrument of national recovery*. As a Department of the Interior report put it, conservation meant "the management and wise use of natural assets to prevent their depletion and at the same time produce wealth." Still, conservation, even in this emphasis, was hardly a vital concern in its own right. Today, the pressure of an alarmingly growing population and the needs of the underdeveloped areas of the world have necessitated looking at land and water with new eyes. When we look at ours, what do we see? In answering, we indict ourselves.

The need today

The conviction is growing that we have not conquered a continental span. We have plundered it. Despite the early warnings, our forests are still being slashed and depleted; soil is being washed and blown away; and to the old bad practices of land use, we have added new ones. Bays and estuaries, rivers and lakes are brown with silt and rank with wastes. Our cities are choked with traffic, smog, and blight. True, we have an agricultural production that is the envy of the world. We have great conservation projects like the T.V.A. We have reforested. We have made former desert land bloom with crops. Yet we still have wasted soil, exhausted rivers, drouth, flood, polluted air. Are good husbandry and technology not enough?

The new conserva- tion

The relatively new science of ecology is supplying answers and a new approach for conservation thinking. This study of the interrelationships between and among animals and plants and the environment teaches that we can never *control* nature. Ecological interrelationships are so complex that no part of the environment can be altered without damaging the whole. We can never accumulate enough knowledge to preserve the delicate balance that nature strives for and maintains. Exploitation will, therefore, always be self-defeating. So say the ecologists. Since we have to use and *develop* resources, it is the manner in which this is done that needs reformulation to acknowledge an ecological responsibility. This is not an easy task for policy makers, administrators, and technicians. To the natural environment has been added the artificial one of cities; to natural resources have been added artificial resources—all the products of industry as well as the dams, highways, high tension lines, conduits, culverts, and pipelines that serve the artificial environment. The very existence of the man-made environment has adversely affected the natural one even to complete destruction in places. Its waste products are one of the major factors degrading environmental quality. Man's works are so ubiquitous, in fact, that some doubt exists that there is any "natural course" left. A course must be found, however, for "violent biological or psychological reactions in humans cannot be discounted if environmental conditions are allowed to become increasingly hostile."

Change is so rapid today and there are so many, often conflicting, demands on the environment that traditional methods for making choices are almost valueless. More than ever we need the land-man ethic first propounded by the great conservation teacher, Aldo Leopold. He pleaded for an extension of the social conscience from man to the land—for an ecological conscience, for the fault has not been in our technological progress

EFFECT OF POPULATION INCREASE

MORE PEOPLE CROWD OUR NATION

1st U.S. CENSUS 1790   1965   2000

OUR NATION'S WATER WILL BE USED AT A STEADILY INCREASING RATE

ON PRODUCTS USING MINERALS   **AND ENERGY**

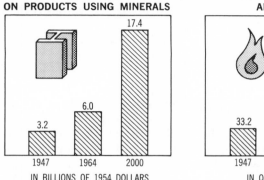

IN BILLIONS OF 1954 DOLLARS
(Metals and Nonmetals Only)

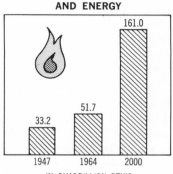

IN QUADRILLION BTU'S

---

but in the lag of social values and political institutions. In the words of Secretary Udall of the Department of the Interior:

Our resource problems today are measured by the fly-way of a bird, the length of a river, the half-life of an element, the path of the wind, the scope of the oceans, the shape of our cities. The years ahead will require both public and private conservation statesmanship of the highest order.

Like so many of our public enterprises, the work of conservation is complicated by our federal system. Natural areas do not follow state and county lines. Nature knows only habitats and life zones, river basins and watersheds, arid and humid regions. Nor is the environment in any one area conveniently divided into resource management units. The techniques for fitting conservation programs into governmental jurisdictions and agency functions are as varied as in other areas, but even more necessary. If they were placed on a continuum, at one extreme would be the mere encouragement of comprehensive environmental planning. At the other extreme would be vast regional programs like the T.V.A. In between would be

Conservation and the federal system

every degree of national, state, and local cooperation from regional conferences through interstate compacts to joint administrations. Subsidies, grants, technical assistance, research results, and education filter down, while needs and problems percolate up. In the process, hardly any part of the government is unaffected. Most states have conservation commissions and large cities have planning and other bodies with environmental responsibilities. On the national level the departments of Agriculture and Interior carry the bulk of conservation work. The Department of the Interior calls itself "The Department of Natural Resources" for the trend has been to transfer these responsibilities to it. Agencies with no conservation responsibilities per se, such as highway agencies, are being put under a public obligation to take into account the effects of their programs on the environment. Only the military has been exempt, and even this is changing.

WATER RESOURCES

Political aspects of a water program

The difficulties in formulating and actuating resource policies are nowhere better exemplified than in the case of water. Recognized by technicians and politicians alike as the number one problem in conservation, water has been the most wasted and abused of all our resources. In building reservoirs and other physical facilities to manage water for beneficial uses, spectacular progress has been made, especially during the sixties. But where new or more effective social techniques are needed, the pace of progress has been barely discernible. The recent "drouth" in the northeast is a case in point. All the while restrictions on water use were in effect in New York City, the Hudson River flowed on so foul it could not be used. We have taken water for granted and thereby made it cheap. Our industrializing and urbanizing society is making water more valuable everywhere, especially water of suitable and good quality, but what costs will be acceptable? Not only money costs, but the intangible ones involved in social choices? Growing demand coupled with competition among uses and user groups is the most important postwar development in water management. As a nation, we have never had to limit the *use* of water. Even in the Southwest, the traditional approach to possible shortages has been to allocate amounts among users. Most programs assume that given enough data, money, time, and goodwill *all* users can be satisfied. Such is the premise of the present Pacific Southwest Water Plan of the Bureau of Reclamation. To secure the support of California and the Northwest to the Central Arizona Project, which allocation controversies stalled for two decades, it relies heavily on scientific advances to find *new* sources, such as salt water or brackish water, that would be economically feasible to develop. These problems will not be confined in the future to the arid regions for urban expansion like a leitmotif runs through all aspects of water conservation.

WATER USE IN THE UNITED STATES, 1900-1980, BY PRINCIPAL CATEGORIES OF WATER USE

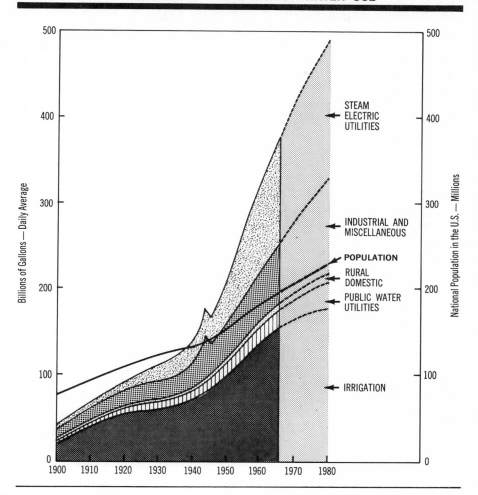

SOURCE: U.S. Department of Commerce, BDSA, Water and Sewerage Division.

The national government has ample authority to regulate and improve navigable streams for navigation, flood control, irrigation, pollution abatement, and power. In conjunction with these, it may develop recreation and fish and wildlife habitats. There are more than 50 federal agencies dealing with water resources. Most projects are so vast only the national government has the resources to undertake them. Many have such far-reaching effects that only in a national forum can these be assessed. The region most logical for water resource development is the

National authority and role

river basin. Rivers, commonly thought of as dividing lines because they so often form boundaries, are in reality unifying agents. Their watersheds, to right and left, are generally alike physically, homogeneous socially and economically, and in need of the same power and other services. This has been recognized since the days of Theodore Roosevelt but we have only one fully integrated water resource system, the Tennessee Valley Authority. The trauma of instituting that gigantic enterprise has affected national water resource policy ever since. Despite the recommendations of three study commissions (Hoover, Paley, Cooke) and the avowed policy of Congress, national programs have suffered most from lack of comprehensive planning.

Water resource planning

Attempts to provide for overall planning by river basin areas have characterized the present decade. A critical water situation, second generation problems stemming from past mistakes, and increasing complexities and costs of the solutions proposed are providing a climate of opinion favorable to methods that reduce waste. In 1961, a Senate Select Committee on Water Resources recommended that comprehensive plans be prepared for all (22) major river basins by 1970. To meet this goal, federal agencies have been planning more comprehensively. State and local representatives have been asked to participate in more stages of the process. The Model Program being prepared for the Potomac and the aforementioned Pacific Southwest Water Plan are examples of both these trends. In 1965, a stimulus to comprehensive planning was provided by the Water Resources Planning Act. The Water Resources Council, composed of the secretaries of the Interior; Agriculture; Transportation; Army; Health; Education; and Welfare; and the Chairman of the Federal Power Commission, was given the responsibility to further the coordination of federal programs and promote river basin planning. Actual planning, however, is to be done by federal-state river basin commissions, four of which have been established and are operating in the Pacific Northwest, Great Lakes, New England, and Souris-Red-Rainy basin regions. States are encouraged with matching grants to do their own planning, provided it is comprehensive and coordinated with federal recreation programs. The Council is to maintain a continuing assessment of water requirements in each region, but it does not have authority to study interbasin transfers of water. Another National Water Commission to assess *alternative* programs (a difficult task for any interagency group such as the Council), explore the effect of federal water programs on regional development, and develop long-range federal policy on water and related land resources, was authorized in 1968. Though this is an area in which interstate compacts might be expected to be useful, they have not been particularly popular. One federal-interstate compact, established in 1961, is in operation under the Delaware River Basin Commission. It has comprehensive water resource conservation, development, use, and antipollution functions, and the planning responsibilities to go with them. It is noteworthy that it operates in the east where federal water projects have not been as extensive as in the west. The Water Resources Council is encouraging the formulation of similar compacts for the Potomac, Susquehanna, and Hudson basins.

The most important factor in water demand is the industrial one. *Supply and* From 1960 to 2000, increases in population of 17 percent per decade are expected *demand* while 46 percent increases per decade in the amount of water withdrawn for industrial purposes have been projected. New processes in mining necessary to extract "hard-to-get-at" minerals use more water. The largest manufacturing uses—aluminum, copper, iron, steel, and chemicals—are also withdrawing increasing amounts of water for cooling, sorting, moving. Water is a cheap "processor." These requirements are expected to be six times the 1960 use by the year 2000. The largest industry, electric power production, is both the nation's largest water user and a "conditioner" of water needs "all down the line." Automation increases industrial water requirements; farm modernization increases rural water use; automatic appliances increase domestic water use. (In fact, electrification has wiped out the difference in water use between urban and rural homes.) Recirculation of used water has already halved potential manufacturing needs and this trend is expected to continue but this will not decrease the amount of water *consumed*. Consumption occurs when water is lost by evaporation during use or is incorporated into a product and thereby not returned to the source to be used again. A 66 percent increase for each decade has been forecast for industrial *consumption* of water. First, new products, such as plastics and synthetics, have been tending to incorporate more water. The chemical industry, of which these are a part, is also one of the fastest growing segments of the economy. Second, as water using processes become more common, more industrial water is lost by evaporation. Third, increased recycling within the same process will also raise consumption, for a point can be reached when the used water becomes completely useless.

Until the day when water can be wrung from the clouds or the salt squeezed from the sea, the water available for use comes from rainfall and snow-melt and is contained in streams, lakes, and underground. Of this, yearly stream flow is the supply that is measured and equated to demand. Neither lakes nor underground stores can be used long-term to *increase* the supply potentially available in streams. Movements of water underground from streams and lakes to the water table (the zone of saturated rock) and back again eventually balance out. Where underground stores have been depleted beyond replacement, serious problems have occurred —water shortages, land subsidence, and, near the sea, saltwater encroachment into fresh supplies. Fundamentally, though, the most important limitation on supply comes from the natural variability of stream flows from year to year, season to season, even month to month. If flows were not artificially modified by storage in reservoirs and regulated release therefrom, a *dependable* supply would be the *minimum* yearly flow. A maximum water yield of 50–54 percent of the total annual flow can be sustained throughout the year by reservoir regulation. Nationwide, this would amount to some 600 BGD (billion gallons daily). Since half this should be retained in streams at all times as a minimum for navigation and other in-channel uses (hydroelectric power, recreation, fish habitat), the allowable level of depletion would be the other half or 25 percent of total flow. Depletion of streams by consumption of water was 6 percent of total annual flow in 1950 and is expected to be 17 percent by 1980 and 21–23 percent by 2000. Implicit in these figures are certain debatable assumptions—that the amount allocated to the in-channel uses will also satisfy all withdrawal uses (*i.e.,* those that return the used water), and that water can be endlessly treated and reused without loss of quality. Even assuming these *and* national transportation of water—a not unlikely accomplishment—either streams will be seriously depleted or demands will have to be scaled down or both. In any event, since gross withdrawals of water are expected to be 74–81 percent of total annual flow by 2000, the necessity to recirculate water and use and reuse it most efficiently will become absolute, even if new sources are found.

New sources of water

The National Science Foundation is the agency working on weather modification, as a means of providing more water, but the conversion of salt and brackish water to fresh is nearer realization. The Office of Saline Water (OSW), Department of Interior, has been doing basic research and demonstrations. It operates five prototype plants, each using a different conversion process. The concepts for which the plants were designed have now been demonstrated and the office is turning to testing facilities and "modules," which simulate the action of complete units. Pioneering in plant design, basic research, evaluating applicabilities of processes to different situations, and improving them are its basic purposes. Worldwide concern about the need for additional fresh water supplies makes the work of this agency internationally important.

Water pollution

The absolute necessity for recycling and reuse of water has given treatment to improve quality the highest priority rating. Traditional criteria of water quality have been based on bacterial content and traditional methods of treatment have been based on bacteriological methods of decomposition. Aquatic life purified and streams and lakes diluted the remaining wastes. Today many new contaminants are either not biodegradable—rusts, salts, acids, detergents, oil—or they use up or interfere with the action of the dissolved oxygen necessary for decomposition and for aquatic life. The natural capacity of streams to dilute wastes has been seriously overtaxed and in lakes, where water runs slower, it has been lost. Bays and estuaries are so foul not even the tides can cleanse them. The major sources of industrial pollution are in mining and in wood pulp, rubber, fibers, and steel processing. Many come from new processes but most have been with us for a long time. One of the most troublesome, acid mine drainage, comes also from abandoned, worked-out sites. Municipal sewage effluent is, however, the worst offender. There were over 5000 obsolete or inadequate systems and unsewered communities (often in growing exurbia) in 1965. Combined storm and sanitary sewerage systems also increase pollution when large storm runoffs dump untreated sewage in someone else's water supply. It has been generally conceded to be too costly to separate all these. Fertilizers used on agricultural land and sewage effluent supply streams with too many nutrients—a process called eutrophication that is also polluting. It induces growth of nuisance vegetation and the putrid masses of algae common near too many inland and bay beaches. Agricultural processes also supply streams with concentrated amounts of pesticides that kill fish.

The large scale of the pollution problem and its interstate ramifications have made it necessary for the federal government first to enter the field (in the fifties), then to constantly expand its role. Federal programs center around quality surveillance (monitoring by the U.S. Public Health Service and the Geological Survey by automatic devices continually feeding data into computers), research grants, and enforcement of federal antipollution laws. These latter, administered by the Federal Water Pollution Control Administration (FWPCA) of the Department of the Interior, were strengthened in 1965 by the Water Quality Act. Under it, enforceable standards on water quality, applying to all interstate and coastal waters, have been prepared by all 50 states (since they have the *primary* responsibility for enforcement) and submitted for approval. Thirty-six have been approved since June, 1968. For giving technical assistance in their preparation and for assessing the resulting standards, the FWPCA divided the nation into 20 basin regions. Consideration of the uses to which each state desired to put its water was implicit in the setting of standards. After approval, these will be a basis for preventive action lacking in the past and will also let conscientious users know what is expected of them. Incentives and means for compliance with the antipollution laws are provided by research contracts and grants. The Clean Waters Restoration Act of 1966 liberalized this program considerably. Grants are given to and contracts made with institutions and industries for research and demonstrations of improved and new methods of treatment, such as chemical disintegration. Industries are interested for they prefer to use treated fresh water rather than reclaimed brackish water or sewage effluent. States, interstate agencies, municipalities, and metropolitan districts may receive grants for planning and construction of water supply, sewage collection and treatment facilities, and for demonstrations on controlling discharge of inadequately treated waste waters from storm sewers and combined systems. More money was made available for construction of large plants. Maximum grants (55 percent of toal cost) are obtainable if the state has enforceable standards for intrastate waters and contributes a certain share of the cost and if the proposed plant is part of a comprehensive metropolitan plan. River basin planning was advanced by provision for grants to any state, interstate, or international agency that would be capable of developing an effective pollution abatement water quality control plan for a basin. These plans do not have to be approved but must be consistent with the quality standards in existence. For the five years beginning in fiscal 1967, almost $4 billion dollars were authorized for grants and contracts. Besides the FWPCA, grants are administered by the Farmers Home Administration (Agriculture), Economic Development Administration (Commerce), Land and Facilities Development Administration (Housing and Urban Development), and the Appalachian Regional Commission. Bills to liberalize the program even further are being considered. The present programs largely overlook lake pollution and acid mine drainage. Estuarial pollution and misuse have hardly been tackled at all.

WATER PROJECTS

Multi-purpose reservoirs

Having enough water of good quality is one aspect of water use and conservation. Having it at the right time and place and as a steady, dependable supply is another. Since the variability of stream flow is the greatest natural obstacle to full use of this resource, the dam that stores water for later use or diversion has become the keystone of federal water policy. Because stream flows are more variable in the (arid) west than in the (humid) east (200-fold difference between maximum and minimum flows as compared to tenfold), most water projects are in the western states, where they are also an excellent means for regional economic development (as T.V.A. has shown). Beginning in 1928 with Hoover Dam, large dams have been depended on to accomplish this. These make possible the greatest use of a river's power potential, create larger lakes for water sports, and permit more uses. The latter is very important. Wise use of renewable resources today means putting each one to as many uses as possible. Authorizations to build additional capacities into reservoirs now include storage for flood control, irrigation, recreation, municipal and industrial supply, power, and stream flow regulations to improve navigation and upgrade quality. Reservoirs may also be built large enough for anticipated needs. Though fish and wildlife conservation is an "equal project purpose," it is debatable whether inundation furthers or obstructs it. It is possible, however, that the day of big-dam building is drawing to a close. The best sites are gone and competition from other land uses for the remaining sites is growing. Two of the three large dams proposed lately have been stopped because they would have adversely affected the Grand Canyon of the Colorado.

Limitations to reservoir use are hydrological as well as social. First, it is not possible to put all water to use everywhere all the time. Some water will go by unused, especially when conserving practices are followed. Second, as successive reservoirs are built on a stream to increase water yield, the costs per unit volume of water controlled increases. At economic limit, an appreciable amount of water will go by unused in the wetter years. The more reservoirs there are on a stream, the more surface evaporation until more water is lost than is gained. Reservoirs become less efficient with age. Mineral content increases and they silt up. Fifty years may thus be the effective life span of a dam. Another one is usually built to replace it or to stretch its usefulness. These limitations, however, only affect *increasing* water yield. Regulation may be for another purpose, even for reducing yield. Man-made additions to wetlands for waterfowl production would have this result. So would ground water recharge. As the uses to which reservoirs are put multiply, so do policy-making and management problems. More competing uses are introduced. Some of the new ones cannot be as successfully compromised as the old ones have been. Recreation users are offended by the unsightly shore lines that result from fluctuating water levels, often caused by accommodating essentially incompatible water requirements. For example, flood control is best accomplished by an empty reservoir, municipal and industrial needs by a full one. For these reasons, most reservoirs are managed for a dominant use, others being incidental. The major purposes we will now examine in detail.

Though billions of dollars have been spent on flood control in the last *Flood control* thirty years, costly damages continue to mount and hardly a year passes without a devastating flood occurring someplace. Though some of the cost is attributable to inflation and though damages *averted* by the actions of all levels of government have been estimated to be just as high, doubts of past flood control measures have been growing. Actually flood control is a misnomer to describe the prevention of damage and the storage of flood waters for later use. The latter has been covered. How can damage best be prevented? There are two means that have been used and some that are new.

Since the 1936 Flood Control Act, the national government has accepted flood prevention and disaster relief as national responsibilities though states have not been absolved from their primary obligations to protect their citizens. The Corps of Engineers-Civil of the Department of the Army, long charged with planning and constructing public works on navigable waters, has been the major proponent of the high, deep draw-down dam as the basic construction for flood prevention. They operate and maintain some 180 reservoirs and dams which they have constructed for this purpose. They also build locks, dikes, levees, floodwalls, and canals, most of which are operated and maintained by local agencies. A neglected area of flood prevention has been urban storm runoff. Cities, in general, contribute to floods. The impervious layer of roofs and asphalt interferes with natural seepage into the ground. Storm runoff flows from them down gutters, into culverts and sewers, and eventually into a river with all the characteristics of a natural flood—concentrated flow, loaded with silt. Urban storm runoff has been estimated to carry six times the amount of silt as rural runoff, plus other assorted debris. In addition, channel improvements that protect one city may cause cumulative damage downstream.

Land treatment is the second major means for preventing flood dam-

Watershed protection

age and lately is receiving more attention and support from conservationists. The Soil Conservation Service of the Department of Agriculture is responsible for a balanced land *and* water conservation program. Their projects include construction of networks of small head waters, detention basins and reservoirs for flood control and/or irrigation. Their constructions are small to separate their jurisdictional field from that of the Reclamation Bureau. They also promote watershed protection by technical advice and loans to farmers for on-the-farm water conserving practices. Land management practices that prevent soil losses from sheet and gully water-caused erosion and vegetative cover that increases seepage possibilities and reduces storm runoff are stressed. The Conservation Needs Inventory (1961) claimed over 50 percent of the mainland area of the United States could use such project action, most of it in the east. Holding more water on the land can also be furthered by any program that preserves wetlands. Marshes and bogs are nature's sponges. Many of them, drained for farming, proved unsuited for dry-land crops and are now being restored.

Flood-plain management

Catastrophic floods, however, occur *after* the ground has been thoroughly saturated. River channels naturally broaden and establish flood plains. If these could be left free from development, damages would be obviated. A realization of these factors is causing a gradual shift in policy from prevention to adaptation to floods. Prohibiting new building on flood plains or curtailing it by zoning have both been proposed. Another approach involves an acceptance of risk. Federal guarantee of flood plain insurance coverage has been suggested.

Irrigation

Beginning in 1902, the Bureau of Reclamation of the Department of the Interior has been charged with conserving and distributing the limited water resources of the 17 states from the Rocky Mountains to the Pacific coast. The first objective was to transform dry lands into permanently producing ones. Today's agricultural needs in the west, however, are for supplemental water on lands already producing. Nationwide, from 40–50 percent of land already being irrigated needs additional water. Though fears have been voiced that irrigation could aggravate agricultural surplus problems, the results in improved local economies usually override this objection. (New authorizations have prohibited use of reclamation water on crops in surplus elsewhere for the first ten years.) As dietary habits change from a reliance on cereals to the consumption of more proteins, fruits, and vegetables, irrigation becomes more necessary. Additional water increases production of the latter two even in humid areas, as any gardener knows. The importance of federal irrigation projects is probably best illustrated by the Central Valley project in California and the Colorado-Big Thompson Project. The first brings water from the mountains to an area where ground water was seriously depleted by wells but where fertility is high and the climate enviable. It has made possible the continued production of high-value fruits and vegetables for nationwide winter consumption. The second project diverts water from the wet side of the Continental Divide through a 14-mile tunnel to the dry side. It has brought agricultural stability for the first time to northwestern Colorado.

With 397 dams and dikes and 40,000 miles of canals and lateral ditches, the Reclamation Bureau has water-conserving problems, as do others who provide water for irrigation. Irrigation is a highly consumptive use—80–90 percent depending on the efficiency of the system. Conveyance losses caused by seepage and water-consuming weeds and surface evaporation are high. Silt and weeds plug canals and further reduce the amount of water that can be moved. Since 1964 Reclamation Bureau projects have been authorized singly and reauthorized biennially presumably so that Congress can keep track of their financial soundness and efficiency.

Though the overwhelming percentage of these systems are locally *Municipal* owned by cities or metropolitan districts or by the industries concerned, *and* the Bureau of Reclamation has moved into this field strongly. In the last *industrial* 15 years, the number of its projects serving nonagricultural purposes has *water* doubled and the amount of water controlled for them has increased tenfold. *supplies* This represents 75 percent of all the water controlled by reclamation works. Over 13 million urban dwellers are using this water. The largest project (with this for a main purpose) serves 11 cities in the Texas Panhandle.

The great river systems of the United States have afforded almost un- *Hydro-* limited opportunities for harnessing and utilizing waterpower to generate *electric* electricity to drive the wheels of industry and bring convenience and com- *power* fort to homes and businesses. From one conservation standpoint, the use of water as a prime mover is superior to using irreplaceable coal, oil, and gas. This use is almost completely nonconsuming and nonpolluting. (Recycling uses some as mentioned above.) From another conservation standpoint, however, hydroelectric power is losing popularity. Competing land uses (as mentioned above) are becoming more important. These are being helped by the economics of the power industry. Steam driven generators produced 66.7 percent of the country's electricity in 1940 and 81 percent in 1965. Large steam plants are today more efficient than all but the lowest cost hydroelectric plants. The national government has, however, a stupendous investment in hydroelectric plants—almost $8 billion by 1965. Its extensive development of multipurpose dams and reservoirs has made it feasible to extract power from these projects at favorable cost rates so long as major installation costs are charged to other uses of the project.

Despite opposition from eastern industry, coal producers and unions, *National* and private power interests, the national government has steadily increased *develop-* the amount of public electric power generated on government projects. *ment of* While opponents have bitterly opposed using their tax payments to increase *power* competition in the South and West, the advocates of publicly supplied *projects* power cite the discouragement of monopoly and the need to encourage regional development in support of their position. In recent years, the dependence of municipal utilities and rural cooperatives on federal projects (where they receive preference treatment) for low cost power has often made it necessary to expand federal programs to meet their increasing needs. One of the most bitterly fought federal power generating projects of the last decade concerned these customers. The issue at stake was the use of by-product steam from the Hanford reactor of the Atomic Energy Commission to generate electricity. When federal project use was defeated in Congress, 16 local public municipal utilities built a conversion and generating plant. Their group, the Washington Public Power Supply System, contracted with the A.E.C. for the steam and with the Bonneville Power Administration to market the resulting electricity. One half of the production is to be sold to public utilities and one half to private ones under an agreement with Bonneville Power Administration (BPA) signed by 76 utilities.

Though federal government projects supplied only 13 percent of the total electrical capacity of the nation in 1965, half of the electricity consumed in the Northwest was federally supplied and in the Tennessee valley area, the T.V.A. is the primary source of supply. The installed capacity of the Bonneville Power Administration in the Northwest is 7.3 million kilowatts and that of the Tennessee Valley Authority is 18.1 million kilowatts (only three million of which comes from hydro installations at its large dams and reservoirs). In addition to these two large areas of publicly supplied electricity, the Army Engineers–Civil and the Bureau of Reclamation operate power plants throughout the south and west. (Proposals for developing public power in New England have been repeatedly defeated.) The Engineers have 55 multi-purpose projects, the power features of which have an installed capacity of 11.7 million kilowatts. Except for a small fraction this power is marketed by the Department of the Interior through the Southwestern Power Administration operating in Arkansas, Louisiana, and parts of Kansas, Oklahoma, and Texas; the Southeastern Power Administration in ten southeastern states; the Bonneville Power Administration in the Columbia basin; and the Bureau of Reclamation in the Colorado and Missouri basins. The Bureau also markets electricity from over a hundred of its own projects in these areas and in the Central Valley of California (but not from its projects in the Northwest where the Bonneville operates). The newest public power installation serves Anchorage, Alaska. The Alaska Power Administration can supply 30,000 kilowatts and is planning to expand. According to the Federal Power Commission, Alaska has the largest undeveloped power potential.

Public power and technological change

Though large steam plants are the most efficient, only the Tennessee Valley Authority has moved into this field. Steam driven generators supplied 79 percent of its total service in 1967. It is also building larger and larger plants. Its first nuclear fuel-using installation will have unit capacities of over a million kilowatts. Integration of systems locally in grids and pools and regionally by extra-high voltage transmission lines enables utilities to realize large plant economies over long distances. Small plants fear they will be left stranded on a high cost plateau. Local public utilities are particularly vulnerable. The Federal marketing agencies—Bonneville and the

PACIFIC NORTHWEST—SOUTHWEST INTERTIE

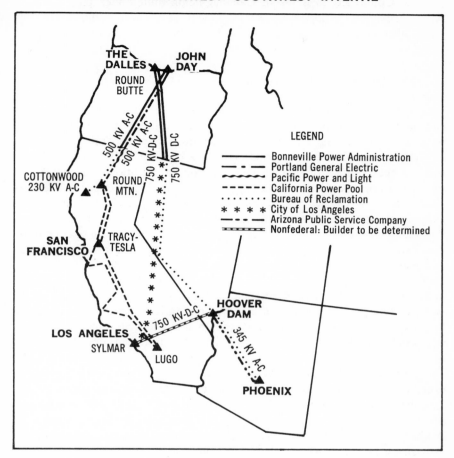

Southwestern Power Administration and the T.V.A.—have, therefore, been authorized to build substations, grids, and transmission lines mainly to serve them. Southwestern's sales, for instance, are 46 percent to REA cooperatives who would be in severe straits if they had to buy power in the open market in order to expand. The most exciting development in this field is the Intertie. Consisting of four main extra-high voltage long distance lines and connectors from the John Day and Dalles dams on the Columbia to Hoover Dam and the city of Los Angeles, this network will bring low-cost power from the Northwest to a high-cost area in the Southwest and by exchanging power between the two areas, whose power needs are complementary, it will actually increase capacities in each system. The Bonneville Power Administration is building the world's longest line and this nation's first direct current line for the beginning of the endeavor. The whole network will be another joint undertaking of private and public utilities. Connected to dams in Canada, being built under the Columbia River Treaty, it is hoped eventually it will be an international network 1800 miles long from northern British Columbia to the Mexican border.

TENNESSEE VALLEY AUTHORITY

1. Purpose   Conservation as practiced in this country has drawn heavily on science and technology, as we have seen, but politically its planning and management have left much to be desired. Resources are separately treated in artificial geographic areas, sometimes only because of historic accident, other times because of jealous guardianship of traditional "rights." The integrated approach has been used only once. In 1933, under the leadership of Senator George W. Norris of Nebraska and with the enthusiastic support of President Franklin D. Roosevelt, Congress passed the Tennessee Valley Authority Act. This region suffered from eroded soils, burned and cutover timber, and floods. It had a low-income agrarian population that was leaving the area to find employment where it did not then exist. Over this potentially rich and productive area of almost 41,000 square miles (four-fifths the size of England), embracing portions of seven states and having a present population of 7 million, agriculture and industry were to be reconstructed, forests restored, soil erosion checked, mineral resources developed, cheap power and chemical fertilizers produced, flood waters put to use, and the inhabitants assured the benefits of a "more abundant life." To carry out the plan, the Tennessee Valley Authority was created as a government corporation under a board of three directors appointed by the President with the consent of the Senate and operating with funds supplied by Congress, supplemented by the proceeds of bonds which the Authority might issue in certain amounts and by sales of power. As envisaged by President Roosevelt and by the T.V.A. itself, the project was a significant undertaking in democratic management and in the relatively new art of regional planning. It was hoped the project would blaze the way for enterprises of similar nature and scope in other suitable sections of the country, but the hope was unrealized. Authorities proposed for the Missouri and Columbia basins were resoundingly defeated. The Pick-Sloan plan eventually adopted for the Missouri basin in the 1944 Flood Control Act was not a plan so much as a mere listing of projects and even this was abandoned in 1964.

2. Activities and achievements   From its inception, T.V.A. was characteristically a multiple-purpose enterprise. It carries out directly enterprises like building dams, but, in the case of activities like soil conservation, it rather provides funds and centralizes planning, with administration decentralized, so that the area's people themselves and their governments may bear an active share in what is done. Although by no means overlooking other objectives, the Authority

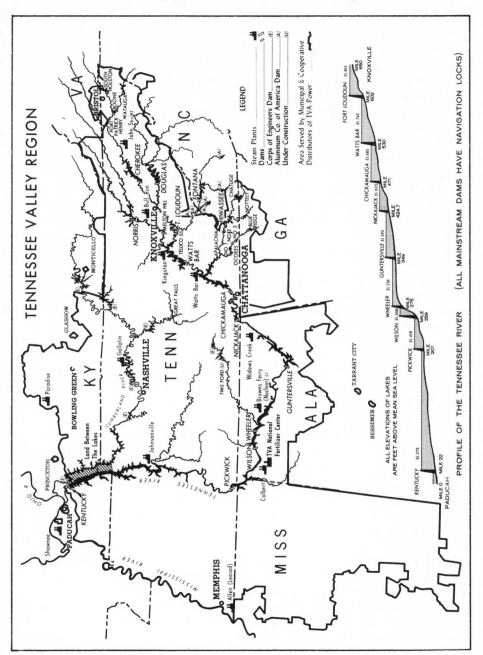

SOURCE: *T.V.A. Annual Report*, 1967.

during its early years focused its efforts mainly upon taming the unruly Tennessee River, thereby promoting navigability, reducing flood hazards, and, in particular, providing great quantities of electric power. Since then, it has turned its attention to managing the water control system and keeping it up-to-date. The Tennessee is tamed. Tributary area development is a field it is now entering in cooperation with the Economic Development Administration (through the districts in the area organized to receive its aids) and the Appalachian Regional Commission.

Today, the T.V.A. can point to significant achievements. Over a million acres have been reforested, muddy waters have become clear lakes, the population has increased, and total employment has grown faster than the national trend. The region is changing. In 1967 manufacturing accounted for 32 percent of total employment—a fourfold increase over 1933. The T.V.A. brought the area an abundant supply of water and power but it is only holding the line on quality. Pollution of the air and water is becoming the same problem here that it is in other industrializing areas. It is modernizing its own installations to prevent waste products from escaping into the environment and is encouraging industries and localities to do likewise, but the existence of the problem points up the conclusion that, though it is a huge enterprise, the T.V.A. is not the only one in the region and probably not the most influential. Fears that the Authority would usurp the private sector and disrupt local democracy seem odd in this context.

LAND AND LAND USE

Public land:

1. National role

Historically, in the United States, different forms of conservation have been developed separately. For water resources, the difficulties this has caused in duplication of effort and confused attack on problems is being rectified by coordinated planning for river basin areas, by a few integrated programs, and by experiments in joint federal-state-local projects. No such unifying efforts have characterized land use and conservation. The reasons are not hard to find. Private ownership is dominant and not until the last 30 or 40 years has the national government had either the authority or the inclination to concern itself with any land other than what it owned. In land resource this is still its basic concern though its ownership responsibilities have changed with the times. Beginning with the soil conservation and agricultural programs of the thirties, however, programs that affect land use have multiplied. As these effects are recognized in more and more areas—urban redevelopment, highway construction, park use, to name a few—regional land use planning becomes more necessary. In an increasing number of instances, local action on this is a condition for receiving federal aid. Federal agencies are also involved in regional land use planning to protect investments of public money and effort on public land.

Of the total 2.2 billion acres contained in the United States today, upwards of 80 percent has at one time or another been "public land," land nationally owned. Of this, more than a billion acres have been sold or given away, leaving a present national holding of somewhat over 700 million acres or more than one-third of the total national area, mostly in Alaska. Of lands disposed of, vast quantities were in earlier times granted to the states for sale in aid of education and internal improvements; later on, much was bestowed upon transcontinental railroads; a great deal was allotted to soldiers and sailors; large tracts were sold to speculating land companies; and under terms of the Homestead Act of 1862—offering 160 acres to anyone who would pay a registration fee of $10 and perform a limited amount of work on his holding during a period of five years— millions upon millions of acres were parcelled out among pioneering home-seekers. Prodigality and fraud often went hand in hand; yet vast areas passed into the possession of thrifty populations and helped make the country what it is today. With the new idea of conserving, early in the century, the government grew less lavish. Restrictions were imposed on free entry (not a great burden, however, since the good arable land was gone). More important for the future was the withdrawal from entry and reservation of vast tracts of land for the creation of national parks and forests. The remaining land, which is technically known as the *public domain,* lay idle, unwanted, and disregarded for decades. Comprising over 450 million acres, administered by the Bureau of Land Management, today this public domain contains some of the most sought after real estate in the country. Land hungry suburbanites, businessmen and industrialists, resort promoters, and ski-tow operators eye it. And so do the conservation groups. Open spaces for urban millions, "room to roam," abounding in game and usable resources, it is regarded as a treasure storehouse for the future.

Embarking in the sixties on a program of active and intensive management to restore the public land to full use, the BLM was without guidelines. Laws for entry and use were obsolete. Mineral rights were sometimes reserved—an awkward impasse should a miner lay claim to and proceed to dig a suburbanite's lawn. Ownership patterns were often discontinuous. In consequence, the land was eroded, misused, trespassed. To make it a model of land management, new authority was needed. In 1964, Congress responded by passing three acts which were the first directives the BLM had ever had—the Land Law Review Commission Act, the Public Land Sale Act, and the Classification and Multiple Use Act. According to the first act, by 1970 the Commission's recommendations concerning changes in law and regulations that would realize the maximum public benefit from the land are to be finished. Under the second act, local government participation in planning the orderly development and zoning of land slated for urban or industrial expansion is required. By the third act, the BLM is to be finished

2. History

3. Use

by 1970 with a classification as to their values for disposal or retention of all public domain lands. Land needed for state and local government purposes and for urban residential, commercial, and industrial sites would have a high disposal value. Land best fitted for the present uses would have a high retention value. These uses are: wildlife refuge, watershed protection, recreation, wilderness preservation, future urban and industrial needs, and resource use for timber, mineral and oil extraction, and range. Concerning resource use, federal lands (including forests) are the resource base for only about seven percent of the gross national product, hardly a significant factor in the national economy. However, locally it can be dominant. In Alaska, Nevada, Utah, Oregon, and Idaho there is more federal than private land. Many of the values that benefit the general public are intangible while the impact of federal action locally can be economically assessed. Conflicts of purpose can sometimes be mitigated by the multiple-use principle of resource management.

Soil con-
servation:

1. General

The greatest need for land conservation, however, is on private rural land—to encourage its best use and to build up and protect the precious top soils on which our food and timber production depend. Over 30 years ago it was recognized by agricultural experts that this soil was being depleted in almost every area where land was ploughed and in great regions of the West and Southwest with startling rapidity. Yellowed rivulets and turbid major streams alike, after every rain, testified mutely—as did also clouds of powdery dust borne eastward across the country by air currents in periods of drouth—to the irrecoverable wealth that was being lost; fields once productive grew barren and useless; farm after farm went to ruin.

The vehicle selected by the Congress in 1935 to achieve soil conservation on farms was the specially created Soil Conservation district rather than the traditional Agricultural Extension system. Every state and major territory has now enacted laws under which soil-conservation districts (often coinciding with counties) may be set up for carrying out the program under direction of a state soil-conservation committee and of locally elected farmer committees. By 1963 a total of 2952 such districts, embracing 98 percent of all the farms and ranches in the country, had been organized. Individual landowners within any district have a right to help and guidance from field offices of the Conservation Service, or from county agents, in planning "layouts" (contouring, strip-cropping, terracing, crop rotation, farm drainage, and the like) adapted to the particular needs and productive capacities of their farms or ranches. The Service undertakes to send technicians to advise and work directly with any one in need of them. A farmer may participate in the plan or not as he chooses; there is no compulsion, either national or state. The acreage in districts doubled after the war, an increase attributed to the popularity of this work with large business operators. The program has been technically based, and this would appeal to them. Its main drawback has been its farm-by-farm approach. A Resource Conservation and Development Act (1964) authorized the Service to extend planning assistance to multi-county projects, over 20 of which have been started. For the Great Plains region with its cyclically recurring drouths and for Appalachia with its depressed economy, complete land conservation plans are prepared with the participating districts.

Protecting soil from erosion by wind and water, the primary objective of land conservation, is a continuing endeavor based on good land treatment practices. What is grown on the land is also a basic concern. Some crops are soil depleting; some land is more subject to erosion. The Soil Bank, begun in 1956, retired some 28 million acres of overworked, staple-producing croplands as part of the crop adjustment program. Its conservation aspects were, however, incidental. In the first years of its operation, the land was mostly left idle. Later, income producing cover crops that would hold the soil were encouraged but these were determined a priori. Today's programs are based on determinations of land capability and suitability for carrying its burden of use. Land is not necessarily retired from crop use but converted to the best use or uses aimed at the highest economic return. In 1958, the Soil and Water Conservation Needs Inventory found over 100 million acres of poor land being cultivated to the detriment of the owner and the land while almost 300 million acres of land well suited for crops were in uses that could be served as well by less potentially arable land. Under the Cropland Conversion and Adjustment Programs, individual producers and, in some instances private organizations, may receive various forms of financial, material, or service assistance to divert land from unneeded crops to approved soil and water conserving uses and under the Agricultural Conservation Program to carry out approved conservation practices. The approved uses and practices typically include, in addition to the traditional ones, creation of wildlife habitats, farm ponds (to conserve water), and recreation facilities. Under the Crop Adjustment Program in certain areas, bonuses are provided if public access is permitted for hunting, fishing, trapping, bird-watching, etc.; CAP funds can also be transferred to any other governmental agency—federal, state, or local—that may acquire cropland and wish help in developing it for wildlife, recreation, pollution abatement, or preservation of open spaces and natural beauty. Over a million acres of cropland are retired from production each year but not always as scientifically as these programs would indicate. Ownership changes with little regard for land capabilities. Over half the acreage lost to crops has, however, been going to urban uses. There is still available for cultivation, should the need arise, as much land as is now plowed. It lies mostly in the southeastern and Gulf Coast states and is indicative of the broader economic and social problems of that area.

2. Cropland

Though the amount of land devoted to crops has been steadily decreasing, that used for cattle has been just as steadily increasing and the need for pasture and range is growing, for with prosperity, more people eat more meat. Forage from the national forests and grasslands and from the public domain supplements and stabilizes the range economy of the

3. Pasture and range

West in many important ways. The first attempt by Congress to regulate grazing on public domain was in 1934 with the Taylor Grazing Act, which brought order to the overgrazed and eroded public range by setting up grazing districts (55 now). This land is the responsibility of the Bureau of Land Management but the districts are powerful in establishing policy. The National Grasslands were established in 1960. They comprise 3.8 million acres within the National Forest System, made up of submarginal land purchased during the thirties under the resettlement program. Ranchers pay fees for permits and allotments to use this land for grazing. The Forest Service cooperates with them (as does the BLM on a smaller scale) in making range analyses and management plans to restore and sustain the productivity of range land. For their share in improvement projects, ranchers can take advantage of the agricultural credit and conservation programs delineated in previous sections. Important, too, is the fact that they can pool their resources because range ownership patterns—public and private—are so mixed. The Conservation Needs Inventory reported that three-fourths of the pasture and range land in the country needed conservation treatment.

Forests   As a positive program deliberately adopted, conservation in this country had its beginning 50 or 60 years ago in an effort to preserve and extend the nation's forests. Theodore Roosevelt not only perceived the immense value to the people of forests yielding lumber, stabilizing the distribution of moisture, preventing soil waste, fostering wildlife, and furnishing recreational facilities, but deplored the rapidity with which forest wealth was disappearing at the hands of lumber companies and other private exploiters. Under legislation dating from 1891, he and later presidents set aside generous portions of the public domain as national forests. Envisaging a forest program for the entire country, Congress in 1911 provided for extensive purchases for forest purposes on the watersheds of navigable streams, wherever situated. Purchases of other submarginal areas were later authorized. As a result, the United States has today, under custody of a Forest Service in the Department of Agriculture, a total of 152 national forests, situated in 39 states and Puerto Rico, and with an aggregate area (182 million acres) considerably exceeding that of the state of Texas. Many states, too, have set apart forests or created parks of their own. Not far from one-third of the country's total wooded territory benefits from direct national or state protection. To be sure, the public forest areas are not simply walled off as reserves for the future. Accordingly, in the national forests (and usually in state forests as well), timber is cut and marketed by private companies, under government supervision. The federal government holds more commercial forest than the forestry industry does—21.1 percent of the total forested area as compared to 12.8 percent (1958 figures).

Nearly the entire expanse is open to campers and other recreation-seekers, under regulations permitting no damage to the wooded growth. Recreational visits quadrupled in the 1950–1960 decade. The first consideration, however, is the preservation of the forests as *forests;* and to that

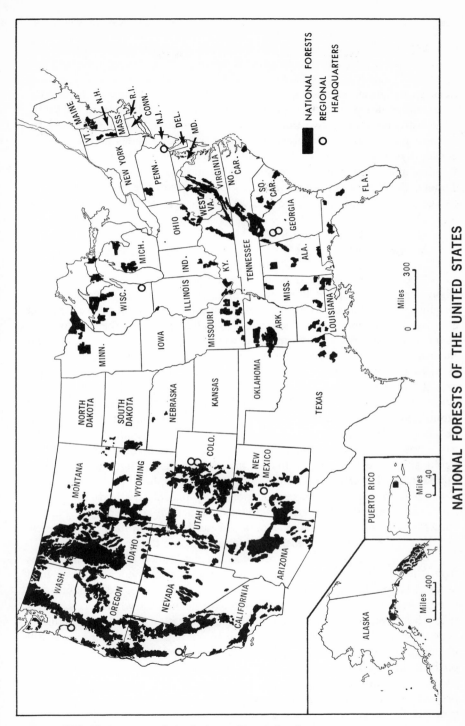

NATIONAL FORESTS OF THE UNITED STATES

NATIONAL FORESTS
REGIONAL HEADQUARTERS

Miles
0   300

PUERTO RICO
Miles
0   40

ALASKA
Miles
0   400

SOURCE: U.S. Department of Agriculture, Forest Service.

end they are given all possible protection against fire, insects, disease, soil erosion, flood, and damage from indiscriminate grazing, as well as from destructive cutting. In areas that require it, systematic planting of young trees is carried on, whether as reforestation of lands that have been denuded or as afforestation of lands not previously wooded but likely to be useful only if made so. Over two-thirds of the forest resources of the country remain in private hands, 86 percent in small woodlots. States and nation are constantly encouraging sustained yield management of these precious resources and collaborate to protect these forests from fire and disease. Though the record is here poor by comparison with the protected land (a category, however, in which most forest industry land falls), it is improving.

MINERALS—PETROLEUM

Resources   Top soil, when lost, can be replaced only very slowly and precariously; when minerals disappear, they are irreplaceable—except in geological time. Originally, the United States was richly endowed with mineral wealth; and compared with many other countries, it still is so. Nevertheless, for 100 years there have been heavy use and wastage. A machine civilization and mechanized warfare have taken terrific toll of supplies once lightly viewed as virtually inexhaustible. On the present scale of consumption, including export, we are told we still have enough coal for several hundred years. With oil and gas already cutting sharply into demand and civilian uses of atomic energy in the offing, not all of the underground stocks may ever be needed. We still have long-range supplies of low-grade iron ores, oil, gas, phosphate, and molybdenum, but consumption of the "heavy metals" (gold, silver, mercury, tin, antimony, nickel, platinum, palladium, tantalum) far exceeds domestic production and known supplies. The conservation concern is to find new sources, economically feasible methods for mining previously inaccessible deposits, better techniques for recovering all mineral values inherent in the available ores, means for full utilization, and new and/or synthetic fuels and metals or substitutes for them.

Regulation —oil   Only 2 percent of the oil produced in the United States today comes from the public domain. Although the amount produced on state-owned lands is larger, the great bulk of the annual output is yielded by lands that have passed into private ownership—which means that whatever is undertaken by government in the interest of conservation must, by and large, *proceed by public regulation* rather than by management of a resource still in public possession. Until within the last 30 years, not much was accomplished, and wastefulness ran riot. Under the "law of capture," any landowner in an oil-producing area was at liberty to drill as many wells on his property as he liked, tapping pools under it and drawing off oil from underneath neighboring properties as well.

Beginning with Oklahoma in 1915, some states sought to curb extravagance by regulation but the results were not happy. Only after discovery of the rich eastern Texas fields in 1930–1931, augmenting output and shattering prices, were two lines of action started which in time led to the restrictive system that we now have—(1) interstate agreement and (2) national control through the commerce power.

A code for the oil industry, with the secretary of the interior as administrator, was put into operation under the National Industrial Recovery Act. Tested in the courts, this arrangement collapsed. The damage, nevertheless, was not irreparable. To begin with, the states returned with fresh vigor to the policy of cooperative regulation; and, with authorization from Congress granted in advance, a group of them entered into a compact prorating volume of production and of allowable interstate or foreign shipments. By 1963, 30 states (producing 90 percent of the country's oil) were adhering to it. The "Hot Oil" (Connally) Act of 1935 directly forbids interstate and foreign commerce in petroleum in violation of state regulation.

The task of identifying, locating, investigating, and mapping mineral *Research* resources falls principally to the Geological Survey in the Interior Department. Prolonged researches of this agency have resulted in detailed classification and descriptions of all surface resources and are going further and further into the earth's crust, the ocean's floor, and even onto the moon via satellites. A *National Atlas of the United States of America,* now being prepared by them, will be a valuable tool for all land and resource conservation. The same Department's Bureau of Mines engages in research and pilot projects that look for better recovery and use of by-products and less wasteful extraction methods. The office of Coal Research seeks more uses for coal to protect the liquid fuels and other resources in shorter supply. New fuels and energy sources are also being tapped. Nuclear fuels are slowly replacing coal for production of electricity and research is going forward on the direct use of solar heat and energy.

Of growing concern are the pollution problems posed by mining and the ultimate disposal of the finished product. Strip or surface mining is a land destroyer. Only a third of the land so damaged is being reclaimed. Surface scars in toto will cover an area as large as New Jersey in a few years. Land damage from metallurgic processes in situ are even more difficult to deal with. They need decades to heal. Federal agencies, like the T.V.A. insist on land reclamation from their lessees. Congress recognized the problem in the 1965 Appalachian Regional Development Act which called for a report on the effects of strip mining on streams, fish and wildlife habitat, and urban development. Proposals to extract oil equivalents from tar sands and oily shales on the public domain have been opposed for the same reason as has atomic blasting to get at deep deposits. Progress, though, is being made on experiments in both these fields. With urban complexes encroaching on the once-remote areas where blasting and quarrying have been carried on, these operations assume more importance. Recovery of scrap metals is also an urban problem. The Solid

Waste Disposal Act of 1965 gave an impetus to federal research and assistance in this field. As much iron lies in municipal dumps as is currently being mined commercially. If it could be recovered, land now used for dumps or land-fill could instead be recovered for productive use. Techniques for separating usable metals from the discarded automobile carcasses littering the countryside are also moving forward. But so far no one has found a second use for the indestructible and ubiquitous aluminum beer can.

PARKS, RECREATION, AND WILDLIFE

*The
National
Park
System*

Not all of this nation's precious resources are so closely identified with material well-being as are soil, timber, water power, and minerals. Conservation to many of our people embraces also the preservation of scenic beauty, of spectacular natural phenomena, of scientific and historic spots, of areas which may remind us of the land before the white man came. The opportunity to enjoy and understand these things should also be passed on to our children's children. Beginning with the establishment of Yellowstone in 1872, the national park system has grown to 27.5 million acres located in 44 states and two territories. This acreage, administered since 1916 by the National Park Service, a more or less independent unit of Interior, administers 34 national parks and 226 other areas of national significance. More than 100 million visitors are enjoying these places each year and each year brings, on the average, a 9 percent increase in attendance. The first mandate of the Park Service is to preserve natural areas unimpaired. Multiple use, therefore, has never been a park service policy. Grazing, hunting, mining, logging, and summer houses have generally been disallowed and facilities for *mass* recreation have been resisted. Crowding, however, poses the same kinds of threats to natural environments. The second mandate of the Service, to provide for use and enjoyment of the parks, seems lately to be in conflict with the first, for now the parks are crowded every summer. But crowding per se is not an inevitable accompaniment to use. Accordingly, park land is being classified as to the intensity of use each part can sustain. This will lead to zoning if present policies continue. Cooperation with the Forest Service and private developers is also being sought to spread visitor accommodations and services throughout the surrounding countrysides. Acquiring new areas is, however, the paramount way to provide for the growing numbers of recreation seekers and vacationers. The trend is to locate new units of the system nearer to urban dwellers than the older parks and monuments. Examples of the newer areas are: National Seashores, Lakeshores, Recreation Areas, Parkways, and Scenic Rivers and Trails. With these burgeoning, it is believed the system of large, remote parks, each exhibiting unique natural phenomena, will be completed during the seventies.

Wilderness

With pressures on federal land agencies mounting to open more areas to development, it was feared the last remnants of the land the pioneers

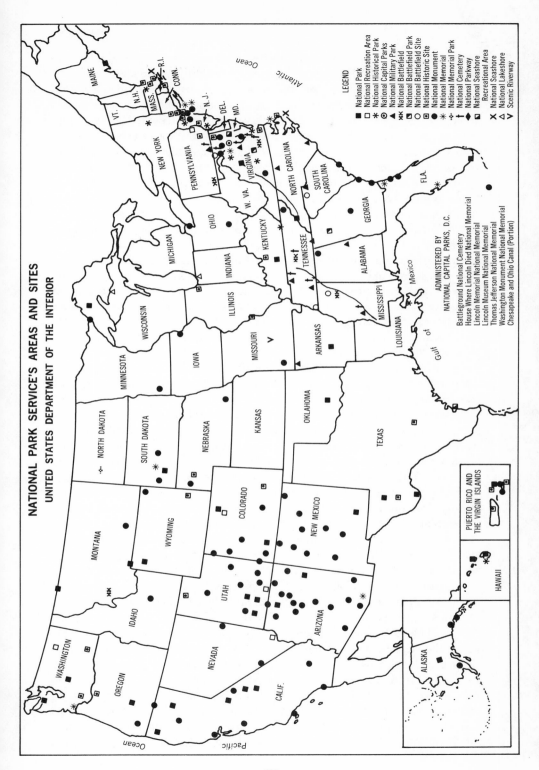

NATIONAL PARK SERVICE'S AREAS AND SITES
UNITED STATES DEPARTMENT OF THE INTERIOR

LEGEND

- ■ National Park
- □ National Recreation Area
- ✱ National Historical Park
- ◉ National Capital Parks
- ▲ National Military Park
- ▲ National Battlefield
- ▲ National Battlefield Park
- ▲ National Battlefield Site
- ○ National Historic Site
- ● National Monument
- ● National Memorial
- ✱ National Memorial Park
- ✝ National Cemetery
- ◆ National Parkway
- ▣ National Seashore
- ▣ Recreational Area
- ✕ National Seashore
- △ National Lakeshore
- ✓ Scenic Riverway

ADMINISTERED BY
NATIONAL CAPITAL PARKS, D.C.

Battleground National Cemetery
House Where Lincoln Died National Memorial
Lincoln Memorial National Memorial
Lincoln Museum National Memorial
Thomas Jefferson National Memorial
Washington Monument National Memorial
Chesapeake and Ohio Canal (Portion)

425

saw would be lost and the last refuge of quiet and solitude gone before we even knew what we were losing. Congress, therefore, in 1964 set aside over 9 million acres of roadless, primitive national forest land, and put it into a National Wilderness Preservation System. Since this only represented about 20 percent of the de facto wilderness then in federal land holdings, procedures were established for inclusion of other large tracts. Each one is to be studied individually for its wilderness qualities, recommendations on boundaries made, and field hearings conducted. Final establishment is by Act of Congress. Four areas have thus been given formal wilderness status to date—San Rafael and San Gabriel wildernesses on national forest land in California and Paysayterr and Glacier Peak wildernesses in the state of Washington. It is hoped this will better protect them from man-made improvements. The areas under study are "managed" as wilderness now and agency jurisdiction will not be changed. Machines are prohibited in wilderness areas and only appropriate, nondamaging uses such as hiking are allowed. Campers either back-pack or go in by boat and animal. Buffer zones are usual at the boundaries. Present incompatible uses may continue but mineral prospecting and developing may be done and claims patented only until 1973 on national forest land. Probably the most fruitful aspect of the wilderness procedure is the unprecedented opportunity for public review of official land conservation policies afforded by the field hearings. These may be laying the groundwork for effective regional planning of park and recreation potentials.

Outdoor recreation   Outdoor recreation is becoming so important that facilities for it are provided at all federal water projects and by all federal land agencies. Recreation also is encouraged as an agricultural land use and is an important part of economic opportunity, area development, and model cities programs. The President's Council on Recreation and Natural Beauty, assisted by a Citizens' Advisory Committee, provides a focus for all this activity, but the agency with more specific coordinating responsibilities is the Bureau of Outdoor Recreation. It coordinates recreation planning, development, and land acquisition within the Department of the Interior. It also assists states and their local subdivisions in developing recreation opportunities by technical advice (which is also available to private efforts) and grants-in-aid. The Bureau is to prepare and keep up-to-date a national recreation plan and an inventory of recreation needs. The most urgent need can be simply stated—land, especially in the East and near metropolitan centers. This is expensive. There is no public domain here, the bank from which the western national parks and forests have been drawn. Land near cities is valuable; uses are long established in the East. But everywhere, east and west, there is need for more state and county parks. Entrance fees, user excise taxes, fishing and hunting licenses have not been producing enough revenue for the purchase of recreation land and legislators, national and state, have too often been niggardly in dispensing general tax revenues for this purpose. This state of affairs has partly been rectified by the Land

and Water Conservation Fund created in 1964 and expanded in 1968. This fund is now guaranteed $200 million annually until 1973 for acquisition and development of recreation land and water areas. Revenues from entrance fees, motorboat fuel taxes, and sale of surplus federal property are first put into the fund; then general tax revenues applied; if these are not adequate, revenues from outer continental shelf oil and gas leases can be used. Sixty percent of the fund is available to the states on matching bases if a state submits and has approved a comprehensive state recreation plan. All 50 states are now thus eligible for grants. These may be passed on to local units. The major beneficiaries of the federal share are the park, forest, and wildlife services.

It is appropriate to end this chapter with a discussion of wildlife for the ecological approach can be here summarized and its significance understood. Fish and wildlife preservation and management for wise use would be futile, in fact impossible, without the application of ecological principles. Game managers know this. Though, except for fish, wildlife resources are no longer a major source of food, their value has not declined. On the contrary, an awareness is growing that wildlife has intrinsic value. Hunters are being joined in the field by just plain watchers who, with cameras and binoculars, trek from the crowded cities to see, observe, and sometimes envy. But over and beyond this, we are realizing that wild populations serve as sensitive indicators of the condition of the outdoor environment. They can and do give warnings of air pollutants and water contaminants that we would do well to heed in time—for our own self-interest, at least. *Fish and wildlife*

The responsibilities of the federal government in fish and wildlife conservation involve commercial fisheries and products that move in interstate commerce but we are here concerned with those activities that are linked to recreation. These are under the jurisdiction of the Bureau of Sport Fisheries and Wildlife in the Department of the Interior. This Bureau conducts research on wildlife management and enhancement, assists states financially and with technical advice, and helps other federal land and water agencies on project wildlife features. The wildlife service maintains 317 wildlife refuges. Some are big game ranges; others exhibit unique habitats such as the island breeding rocks (rookeries) of colonial nesting birds; but the vast majority are for migrating waterfowl (250 primarily for ducks and geese). Navigating birds have been protected by treaty since 1918. Species threatened with extinction have been officially protected since 1966 when the Endangered Species Preservation Act was passed. Doubtless, though, many species benefit from the refuges just because they are there. Traditionally, state game laws have been enforced on federal land but stricter regulations are often necessary. Sometimes these are worked out cooperatively; other times dissatisfactions rankle; always pressures are present for more harvest. However, game and fish management is today much more than open and closed seasons, creel and bag limits. Habitat restoration is a primary concern and activity.

   As agriculture and concrete march across the land, living space for
wild creatures is broken up and finally lost altogether, area by area. Native
species retreat and their populations dwindle. Forty entire species have
been lost, half of them since 1900. Another 78 are on the "critical list."
Pesticides are taking another toll. It is feared the bald eagle, the national
emblem, will fall victim to their cumulative effects. In this matter of habitat
there is no isolated piece. We share the perils of environmental pollution
but we also share the benefits of restoration. When the wildlife service
develops refuge uplands for grouse cover, soil is also conserved and when
they restore wetlands for mallards, water is prevented from running off in
useless floods. There is still much to be done to create a quality environment for the human species, for the loss of wild habitat is fundamentally a
symptom of a larger degradation. The price of quality is constant vigilance.

REFERENCES

Advisory Board on Wildlife Management, *Reports to the Secretary of the In-
    terior:*
    I. *A Problem in the National Parks , Wildlife.*
    II. *Federal Policies in Predator Control.*
    III. *Policy Recommendations on Wildlife Refuge System,* 1968.
D. L. Allen, *Our Wildlife Legacy* (New York, 1954).
Bureau of Mines, *Mineral Facts and Problems, Bulletin 630* (Washington, D. C.,
    1965).
A. H. Carhart, *The National Forests* (New York, 1959).
R. Carson, *Silent Spring* (Boston, 1962).
G. R. Clapp, *The T.V.A.: An Approach to the Development of a Region* (Chi-
    cago, 1955).
M. Clawson and B. Held, *The Federal Lands: Their Use and Management*
    (Baltimore, 1955).
————, *The Federal Lands Since 1956* (Baltimore, 1966).
F. Darling and N. D. Eichorn, *Man and Nature in the National Parks* (Wash-
    ington, D. C., 1967).
Department of the Interior, *Yearbooks* (Washington, D. C.) :
    Quest for Quality, 1965.
    Population Challenge, 1966.
    Third Wave, 1967.
    Man: an Endangered Species, 1968.
P. Farb, *Ecology* (New York, 1963).
P. O. Foss, *Politics and Grass* (Seattle, 1960).
R. Highsmith, Jr., J. Jensen, and R. D. Rudd, *Conservation in the United States*
    (2nd ed., New York, 1968).
W. G. Hoyt and W. M. Langbein, *Floods* (Princeton, N. J., 1955).
J. Ise, *Our National Park Policy: A Critical History* (Baltimore, 1961).
H. Kaufman, *The Forest Ranger* (Baltimore, 1960).
A. Leopold, *A Sand County Almanac* (New York, 1966).
B. Lyons, *Tomorrow's Birthright: A Political and Economic Interpretation of
    Our Natural Resources* (New York, 1955).

A. Maass, *Muddy Waters; The Army Engineers and the Nation's Rivers* (Cambridge, Mass., 1951).

C. McKinley, *Uncle Sam in the Pacific Northwest* (New York, 1952).

R. J. Morgan, *Governing Soil Conservation: Thirty Years of the New Decentralization* (Baltimore, 1966).

Outdoor Recreation Resources Review Commission, *Report: Outdoor Recreation for America* (Washington, D. C., 1962).

President's Materials Policy Commission, *Report: Resources for Freedom* (Washington, D. C., 1952).

President's Science Advisory Committee, *Report: Restoring the Quality of Our Environment* (Washington, D. C., 1965).

Report of the President's Water Resources Policy Commission (Washington, D. C., 1950–1951), 3 vols.

R. and L. Rienow, *Moment in the Sun* (New York, 1967).

J. Savine and J. L. Kammerer, *Urban Growth and the Water Regimen,* Geological Survey Water-Supply Paper, 1951-A (Washington, D. C., 1961).

Senate Select National Water Resource Committee, *Report,* S Rept. 29 (Washington, D. C.).

J. R. Stewart, *Not so Rich as You Think* (Boston, 1968).

S. L. Udall, *The Quiet Crisis* (New York, 1963).

Yearbook of Agriculture, *Outdoors USA* (Washington, D. C., 1967).

20

PROMOTING PUBLIC HEALTH AND WELFARE

GOVERNMENT AND WELFARE

The welfare function

An ideal society would be one in which every individual had enough to eat and wear, adequate shelter, protection for health and safety, a chance for a good education, and an opportunity to earn a living by moderate toil, with safeguards against worry and want in old age. Such a society never existed, and some people would say that in the troubled world in which we live there is no use dreaming of one. Doubtless the United States has come nearest to realizing something of the kind, but not even our rich resources and technical competence have availed to prevent much poverty, misfortune, and insecurity. It has been necessary from earliest days for the more fortunate to help the disadvantaged through private agencies and through government on all levels. The promotion of public well-being has been a primary responsibility of government for generations. In a sense, everything that government does is intended to advance the people's well-being. Public activities contributing to health, safety, morals, rehabilitation, recreation, poor relief, and social insurance are aimed at that objective most directly. These are the important elements in modern public welfare programs.

Local and state welfare activities

The earliest welfare activity on record (using the term in the specialized sense in which it will be employed here) was care of the poor. In England, this responsibility, insofar as not discharged by relatives or other private benefactors, early fell to the church parish. Even before the American colonies were founded, however, parliamentary legislation authorized taxation for this purpose, and the colonies inherited the concept of poor relief as a public, tax-supported function. In New England and some of the middle colonies, the town became the relief agency; farther south, the parish—soon replaced, however, by the county. To this day, towns and counties throughout the country raise and spend much revenue for this purpose. More than 100 years ago, the states also entered the field—

establishing hospitals and asylums for special classes of unfortunates such as the feebleminded, the insane, hardened criminals, and the blind; setting up boards and other authorities to administer such institutions; organizing departments of welfare; and in some cases supervising local services. In times of stress, programs of public succor sometimes proved pitifully inadequate. On the other hand, deficiencies were met to some extent by the private charities for which our people have traditionally had a commendable record. Early in the present century, states began helping their local governments extend financial aid to persons outside of institutions, chiefly the aged, the blind, and needy mothers. Meanwhile, too, states and localities were contributing to welfare in the broader sense by developing health services, introducing safety requirements in transportation and industry, building up educational systems, providing highways, fostering agriculture, protecting natural resources, regulating working conditions for women and children, fixing hours and minimum wages in industry, enacting workmen's compensation laws, encouraging good housing, and in many other ways.

From early days, the national government likewise had a good deal to do with welfare in the broader meaning of the term. In the case of the states, broad constitutional authority flowed from reserved powers; in that of the national government, such authority was ample also, not only because specific powers like that of regulating interstate and foreign commerce could be drawn upon, but especially because of the blanket grant of power to raise money "to provide for the . . . general welfare of the United States." And through the years—particularly after 1900—national welfare activities took such forms as: (1) humanizing the conditions attending immigration; (2) curbing the transmission of diseases and the distribution of impure food and drugs; (3) maintaining hospitals for certain classes of the ill and injured; (4) conducting research on problems of health and creating a public health service to cooperate with and assist state health services; (5) imposing safety regulations on railroads, air and water carriers, and mines; (6) taxing out of existence injurious forms of manufacturing, for example, making matches from white phosphorus; (7) curbing and controlling traffic in narcotics; (8) prohibiting the circulation of immoral matter through the mails and the interstate transportation of persons for immoral purposes; (9) matching state contributions for support of vocational rehabilitation; (10) promoting the well-being of Indians on reservations; (11) caring for veterans; and other services too numerous to mention. Until the Great Depression, however, the national government largely left to the states the task of caring for the poor, the sick, and the unfortunate. In 1912, a Children's Bureau was established in the then existing Department of Commerce and Labor, to encourage the states to enact remedial legislation on child labor. In 1918, small grants to the states were initiated for combating venereal diseases, and in 1920 for encouraging vocational rehabilitation. In 1921 a Maternity (Sheppard-Towner) Act gave the states limited funds for five years for promoting the well-being of mothers and infants. Although

The national government and welfare

judicially sustained when challenged, this measure was allowed to lapse at the end of its period. Not until after 1930 was anything further added to the record.

FROM RELIEF TO SOCIAL SECURITY, 1929–1935

The shock of depression

During the lush decade of the twenties, local and state welfare services expanded only slightly and along traditional lines. National programs remained as before. The nation, thus, entered the depression firmly attached to a system of public care for the unfortunate which emphasized local responsibility and which was supported mainly by local taxes. In its main contours the American system of poor relief had been designed in Elizabethan England. The swelling tide of unemployment spreading want, fear, and despair over the face of the land soon engulfed the private charities and the town, parish, and county poorhouses and dole systems. The states attempted to bolster the local units with grants and loans and work programs but they too were soon swamped by falling income and inadequate machinery. Still unemployment mounted, to 10, then to 12 millions, and private charity, local units, and state governments looked to the national government for help.

The first national efforts took the form of loans by the Reconstruction Finance Corporation to state and local governments for public works construction to give employment and for direct cash relief. These units soon exhausted their credit as the "natural" recovery hoped for by the Hoover administration failed to materialize. And to the ensuing Roosevelt administration it fell to attack the problem with fresh determination and a new philosophy. The policy of the new regime was to put vast new resources at the disposal of the states and local units and also to act directly, on many different fronts, to create employment and provide relief. Most of the major steps taken have been touched upon at various points in preceding chapters of this book, and need not be reviewed here. Suffice it to say that billions of dollars were appropriated, piling up a national debt considered extraordinary until dwarfed by that incurred during the later years of defense effort and war. Through a Federal Emergency Relief Administration, a Public Works Administration, a Civil Works Administration, a Works Progress Administration, and other huge agencies that came and went, vast programs of employment and relief were carried forward by direct action of national agencies and through grants to states, counties, and cities.

The Social Security Act (1935)

Down to 1934–1935, thought and effort were centered largely upon breaking the back of the depression. Huge outlays for relief, employment on public works, and vast loans and gifts to states and localities, however, could not go on forever, even though the conditions currently requiring them easily might recur. Moreover, there ought to be ways not only of cushioning the impact of "hard times" when encountered, but of giving large

POPULATION CHANGES BY AGE GROUP, 1940–1960

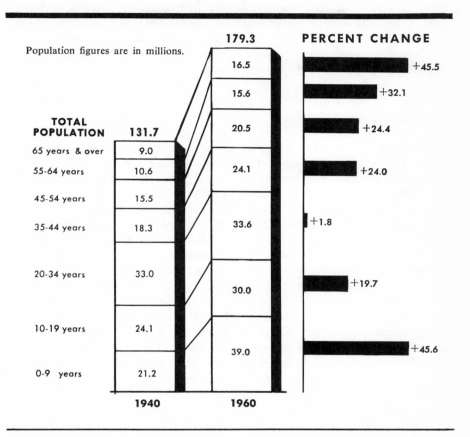

Population figures are in millions.

179.3

PERCENT CHANGE

		1940	1960	Percent Change
	TOTAL POPULATION	131.7	179.3	
65 years & over		9.0	16.5	+45.5
55-64 years		10.6	15.6	+32.1
45-54 years		15.5	20.5	+24.4
35-44 years		18.3	24.1	+24.0
			33.6	+1.8
20-34 years		33.0	30.0	+19.7
10-19 years		24.1	39.0	+45.6
0-9 years		21.2		

1940   **1960**

masses of people a new sense of security against hazards of both bad times and good. The interest of those having to do with making national policy now turned, therefore, to devising ways by which the states, with the help of insurance systems and relatively modest grants-in-aid, could be brought back into the center of the welfare picture. National spending on employment-making public works and on other forms of relief went on to some extent until after the economic situation was sharply reversed by the defense and war effort starting in 1940. In 1935, however, and after careful studies of the social insurance systems in Europe, and of the question of a permanent program for this country, Congress, by heavy majorities, passed an omnibus Social Security Act representing the first concerted nationwide attack involving all levels of government on the problem of economic security for wage earners and their families. Conceding that the measure as enacted did not provide complete protection against "the hazards and vicissitudes of life," President Roosevelt, at all stages a vigorous sponsor, nevertheless characterized it as "the most useful and fundamental single piece of legislation ever enacted in the interest of the American wage earner." As now operating after several expansions of coverage, the program furnishes impressive testimony to the accepted responsibility of government on all levels for assuring all people in all parts of the country a reasonable degree of economic and social well-being.

SOCIAL INSURANCE

1. Unem-
ployment
compen-
sation:

Towering above all else in the general scheme provided by the Act of 1935 are two plans of social *insurance:* (1) unemployment; and (2) old age and survivors. These two insurance programs represent efforts to provide long-term solutions to the central problems of social security.

a. The
national–
state
basis

Loss of their jobs by millions of workers during the Great Depression sharply emphasized the hazards of layoff and dismissal confronting industrial workers. A major objective of the legislation of 1935 was to encourage the states to soften the impact of such disasters by providing benefit payments from which employees, usually with meager reserves, could, when laid off or dismissed, keep themselves and their families going for at least a limited period without turning to public relief. Virtually every state already had workmen's compensation laws under which employers were required to carry insurance to enable them to pay benefits to employes kept from work by industrial accidents or occupational disease. This had become an accepted part of the cost of production and was passed on to the consumer in the price of goods produced. To this was now added benefits for employees kept from work, not by accident or illness, but by lack of employment. The cost was to be part of the legitimate expense of doing business and passed on to consumers. Like the President's Committee on Economic Security, whose recommendations were largely followed, Congress weighed the desirability of a straight national system of unemployment insurance, uniformly compulsory and nationally administered. Fearing, however, that such a scheme would be held unconstitutional, and considering it desirable not to dictate any one of the many different forms that such insurance might take, the two houses agreed upon a plan offering the states substantial inducements (including subsidies to cover costs of administration) to devise and set up unemployment compensation systems of their own. If any state failed to do so, the minimum system prescribed in the law would be applied to the industries of that state by the national government. With this type of sanction, every state promptly established its own program. Speaking strictly, therefore, under existing law there is no national system of unemployment compensation, but only a variety of state systems operating under national standards and with national supervision.

The heart of the plan is the arrangement for financing the insurance from payroll taxes paid by employers. In the first place, the national government levies a 3.1 percent tax upon the payrolls of all employers of as many as four persons during at least 20 weeks of a calendar year. The taxable payrolls are so computed, however, as not to include anything paid to any employee in excess of $3000 a year. In the second place, each state levies its own payroll tax, for support of its own unemployment compensation system, set up and operated under its own law. The state tax may apply only to those liable to the national tax or it may be, and in many states is, applied to more employers. In the third place, when an employer pays his national tax, he is allowed an offset for the amount he is paying his state; in other words, he actually pays the national government a payroll tax of 0.4 percent. A state therefore can tax an employer at the rate of 2.7 percent without imposing any additional burden, because anything up to that amount will be deducted when the national tax is paid. In all states except one, 2.7 percent is the maximum rate of state tax. However, most states have established systems of "merit" or "experience" rating by which employers with good records for steady employment may reduce their state tax liability without increasing their national taxes. The average rate of tax is, therefore, appreciably less than 2.7 percent of covered payrolls (2.1 percent in 1966). Should any state elect to remain out of the system, its employers still would be liable for the national tax, the proceeds of which in such a case would be retained in full by the national government and used nationally. All funds collected by the states go into an unemployment trust fund in the national treasury (held, however, in separate state accounts), and are invested in national bonds, subject, of course, to requisition by the states as needed for benefit payments. During the recessions of 1958 and 1960–1961 unemployment rose rapidly and thousands of covered employees exhausted their benefits while still out of work. Congress on both occasions provided for a temporary extension of payments to these persons for an additional 13 weeks. In the first instance (1958), 17 states that had exhausted their own reserves were authorized to borrow from the national reserve to make the payments. By 1961, none of these had paid back anything and the second effort was also financed by advances out of the reserve. The national payroll tax was raised from .3 to .4 percent in 1960 and then to .8 percent for one year (1962) and to .65 percent for one year (1963) to replenish the national reserve.

b. Financial arrangements

To participate, a state must meet certain requirements. It must, of course, set up an unemployment compensation system, levy the necessary tax, and provide for administration through a regular industrial commission, a special unemployment commission, or some other suitable agency. It must arrange to have all benefits paid through public employment offices or other approved agencies. It must agree that funds withdrawn from its treasury account in Washington shall be used solely for payment of benefits. There are also restrictions upon its liberty to withhold benefits under special cir-

c. State patterns

cumstances arising from industrial disputes. Apart from these restrictions, a state is free to adopt any particular type or scheme of compensation preferred, to determine the categories of unemployment to be covered, and to fix the scale of benefits to be paid. Under these conditions—with every state and the District of Columbia participating—there are many differences from state to state. The tendency over the years has been for the various state systems to become more and more similar. Nine states started by taxing employes as well as employers, but now only New Jersey, Alabama, and Alaska do this. Nearly all states follow the national act in excluding from coverage self-employed persons, agricultural workers, domestic employes, and employes of nonprofit agencies and institutions. Almost half of the states, however, cover smaller firms than the national act.

Altogether 45 million workers are now covered by the system out of a labor force of 78 million. The only major changes in coverage since 1935 have been: (1) the extension of coverage to employes of the national government in 1954; (2) extension to smaller firms beginning in 1956; (3) removal of railway employes in 1938 and provision for them by a separate system; (4) addition of maritime workers in 1946; and (5) inauguration of a special coverage for exservicemen in 1958. President Kennedy sought unsuccessfully in 1961 and in 1963 to extend the coverage to small firms and nonprofit organizations. President Johnson sought similar but broader inclusions in 1966; his program was turned back by vigorous lobbying by business groups.

Inflation in the postwar era has markedly reduced the real value of the benefit payments despite the fact that most states have been increasing their maximum weekly rates. The most recent tabulations (1966) show the average weekly payments for the entire United States is $40. Benefits are paid during any one year for not more than 26 weeks in most states. Eligibility for benefits is computed according to somewhat varying wage-credit formulae in which length of employment and taxable wages received are principal factors. Many students of the subject consider that the maximum weekly payment ought in no case to be less than $45 nor the maximum period less than 26 weeks. Both Kennedy and Johnson proposed (1963 and 1966) to raise the benefits and also to raise the amount of taxed wages and generally to overhaul the system in many particulars. The system is designed only for short-run or seasonal unemployment. It is not, it must be remembered, geared to take care of prolonged economic depression. It should also be clearly understood that this system is designed to take care of those who are ready, willing, and able to work. It is not for the disabled, the sick, the infirm, or the aged. To receive benefits, a worker is obliged to register at the nearest public employment office, operated by the state in conjunction with the unemployment insurance program, and he must accept "suitable" employment if offered to him.

The other insurance plan provided by the Social Security Act of 1935 was designed especially for the aged. The problems of the nation's senior citizens were brought into sharp focus by the depression. Layoffs had been especially heavy among workers over 50. The mechanization of industrial production and the introduction of assembly-line techniques had made it difficult for the older workers to keep up with their younger rivals. The great improvements in this century in private and public health had produced a rapid increase in the percentage of our population over 60. The urban family unit, unlike the rural family, was not equipped by living space or income to take care of its overaged dependents. The result: a disproportionate share of those in distress were in the older age group. Public works programs, the preferred method of the Roosevelt administration, did not greatly aid those who were past their prime and thus unable to do heavy labor. Everywhere in the nation the older citizens were demanding special attention—many of them through the Townsend movement for old-age pensions.

In essence, the system established in 1935 is a nationwide contributory retirement system under which annuities or pensions, graduated in amount on the basis of earnings and duration of employment, are payable at age 65 from a fund built up from money paid in equally by employers and employees. The national government was intended to make no financial contribution beyond meeting the costs of administration. It does bear undivided responsibility for operating the system and plays the combined roles of collector, bookkeeper, and manager. The states and their subdivisions have no part in the undertaking. On the employe's side, the plan is one for compulsory savings—in other words, for spreading wages over his adult lifetime rather than over merely his wage-earning years, so that after retirement he may have a resource on which to draw for a living. And on the theory that the employer (not to mention the taxpaying public) has a stake in fostering employe frugality and in keeping his employes from eventually going on relief, he is required to give his workers, in effect, a premium for their industry, and in so doing to help make the plan workable, as a scheme of "cooperative thrift," by sharing in creating and maintaining the fund. Under the system, 20 million retired workers already are drawing benefits, while other millions still on the job are building up potential rights to future old-age income.

At the outset, old-age insurance applied to substantially the same workers as unemployment compensation, with approximately the same groups, for example, agricultural workers and domestic employes, excluded. Whereas, however, the coverage of unemployment insurance never has been expanded on any large scale, that of old-age insurance has been greatly broadened. In 1939, 1.5 million workers not previously reached were brought in, the name was changed to "old age and survivors" insurance, and coverage was further widened to include protection not only for the worker but for his family, through provision for monthly benefits for aged wives and young children of retired workers, and for widows, orphans, and aged parents of workers dying before retirement. After prolonged agitation, an amending act of 1950 brought under the system, in addition, 4.7 million self-employed nonfarm workers, 1.45 million employes of state and local governments, a million household servants, 750 thousand regularly employed farm workers, and certain smaller groups—an aggregate of some 10 million. In 1954, another 10 million workers were potentially added to the system, including public employes in all jurisdictions desiring it, farm laborers, and members of many professions. In 1956 a system of disability insurance was made available for covered workers and in 1965 insurance for medical costs for all those drawing retirement payments was instituted. More than 90 percent of the country's entire labor force is now covered by the system.

c. Benefits   The result of the old-age-insurance system as now operated is a minimum guaranteed retirement income, albeit a modest one, for virtually every employed person when he reaches age 65 (in some cases 62) or for his widow and family if he dies before that time. Beneficiaries are also now able to earn modest incomes. The worker's dependents are also protected against his disability and now, at long last, against the terrible drain on their meager resources of the rising costs of the medical and hospital care which he is likely to need in his declining years. The national old-age security system is now also integrated or supplemented by a growing number of privately financed pensions and retirement systems. More than 25 million persons are now covered by these programs in addition to old-age insurance.

d. Financing   Contributions made by employes and employers alike started at 1 percent each of the wages received or paid in 1937, and under the original law would, by stages, have reached a maximum of 3 percent each in 1949. Because, however, huge reserves were necessarily built up in anticipation of future claims, Congress, from year to year, and usually over Presidential objection, "froze" the tax at 1 percent. Beginning in 1950, however, the levy was allowed to rise to meet the costs of increased benefits, lower retirement ages, and greater allowances for widows and dependents. The original schedule has been repeatedly modified not only to finance higher monthly benefits but also for life, disability, and health insurance. The levy on each in 1968 was 4.4 percent and is scheduled to rise ultimately to 5.9 percent. In addition, persons 65 and over may voluntarily enroll in a medical insurance program at a cost of $4.00 per month. In the beginning the tax was paid on the first $3000 of annual wages; it is now paid on the first $7800.

e. Results   Accompanying the tax increases in the postwar years has been a general increase in benefits paid out by the system. Under the original act, average monthly payments of $20–$25 were typical, with lower payments to surviving widows and higher payments to families with children. Increases granted at various times have raised the average monthly benefits to $90–$100 for a retired worker and $70–$75 for his wife. Each rise in the benefit schedule has also been accompanied by rises in the allowable earnings of retired beneficiaries. The reserve created against future claims had by 1967 reached the staggering total of over $25 billion. In recent years, however, the annual outgo in payments about equals the annual income in taxes.

There has been a good deal of controversy, first and last, about whether this system is actuarially sound and solvent. The long delay by Congress in raising the tax rates as originally planned gave a great deal of support to those who argued that ultimately deficit financing by congressional appropriation would be required. A special review of the program in the light of the changes of the 1950's, conducted in 1958 by an Advisory Council for the board of trustees of the OASI trust fund, pronounced the present system reasonably sound, but the changes in coverage since and the addition of health and medical insurance have reopened the argument. The impact of the medical care program will not be fully realized until we have a few years of experience under it.

PUBLIC ASSISTANCE

The two insurance systems established in 1935 were designed to make long-range provision for the aged and the temporarily unemployed. Neither scheme was intended to relieve immediate distress. The Social Security Act of 1935, therefore, provided a program of immediate and continuing assistance to certain needy individuals. In examining the types and conditions of persons who needed help at that time and would be likely to need it in the foreseeable future, the Congress selected certain categories of such persons for whose welfare the national government ought to assume continuing responsibility. The sponsors of the *categorical assistance* program expected that responsibility for virtually all other classes of unfortunates would, henceforth, fall wholly on the states and local communities.

Categorical assistance:

The first group for whom the act established a continuing program of succor were the needy aged. Obviously no insurance program would help those at or near retirement age at the time, and, as we have noted, thousands and thousands of such persons were destitute in the mid-thirties. The pattern selected for aiding those needy aged was one which had been tested in some of the states. A few states had experimented with old-age pensions as early as 1923 and 25 states had some kind of system in operation in 1935. In most cases, however, the state systems were inadequate as to both coverage and benefits. Using the familiar grant-in-aid technique, the Act of 1935 created a joint national-state program of old-age assistance. National money was appropriated to any state which qualified by meeting the minimum national standards. These standards were: (1) that aid be paid on the basis of need; (2) that aid be extended beginning at age 65; (3) that the program cover the entire state; (4) that a single state agency administer the state's part of the program; (5) that the state pay a portion of the costs

1. Old age assistance

of the assistance; and, (6) that all personnel—state or local—engaged in administering the program be selected on a merit basis. To states with approved programs, the national government agreed to pay 50 percent of all administrative costs and, originally, about 50 percent of the assistance grants up to $50 per month for any single beneficiary. Most states quickly enacted laws qualifying them for participation and today every state, Puerto Rico, Guam, the Virgin Islands, and the District of Columbia participate in the old-age-assistance program. There are, of course, many variations in practice from state to state. Since the amount of actual benefit depends upon need and need is determined in each case by state or local public welfare workers, standards of assistance show wide regional variations. Eligibility for aid is also based upon varying requirements as to residence, responsibility of relatives, and citizenship. Under new amendments passed in 1962, ablebodied recipients may be required to work on community projects for part of their grants. The states' programs vary also in the amounts they are willing to put into the program. Many states, for example, have higher maximum monthly grants than the national formula entails. The average monthly payments, in fact, vary from $10 to $90. Modifications in the formula for national grants have been made in the ensuing years in the direction of increasing the national contribution. In 1960, a program of medical assistance was inaugurated for those who were indigent, including those who were indigent primarily in terms of their ability to pay for their own medical care. It was hoped by some that this might solve the problem of medical care for the aged. This hope proved groundless, but the program continues to provide help for those who cannot be helped under the old-age-insurance system. At present, the national government pays 60 percent of the total cost of old-age assistance. During 1967 approximately 2.3 million persons (almost 10 percent of all men and women over 65 in the United States) received an average of $68 a month.

It might well be asked at this point why the old-age-insurance system has not after thirty years eliminated the need for old-age assistance. In the first place, the insurance program did not until 1950 include several million workers. As the coverage has been extended (in 1950, 1954, and 1958), the need for old-age assistance has been declining. In 1951, the number reached by the insurance system finally exceeded the number receiving assistance; more than 15 million received insurance payments and 2 million, old-age-assistance checks. Some persons, particularly some farm laborers, are still not included in the insurance program. Secondly, the benefits paid under the insurance program are in some instances not adequate to maintain a decent level of subsistence and must be supplemented by grants of assistance. Thirdly, the continued rise in longevity accompanied by major increases in medical care costs made it necessary at least until 1967 to use assistance grants for medical purposes. It should be noted that there are more than 5.3 million aged with incomes below the poverty level.

The concern of the national administration for the aged, however, does not end with insurance and relief. President Johnson, in particular, has sought to remove discrimination against older workers in the job market. He has successfully urged preferred claim to certain housing facilities and has sought to stimulate the development of community recreation facilities, the provision of tax advantages, and the establishment of special educational programs for the aged.

The second category of needy persons selected by the Congress in 1935 for a continuing national-state program of assistance was the blind. In general, the standards required for state participation were the same as for the aged, except that payments were to be made beginning at age 16 or 18 to persons whose deficiencies of eyesight incapacitated them for normal work. All of the states and territories participating in old-age assistance now also participate in assistance to the blind. In 1968, 83 thousand persons (less than one-third of the blind population) received an average grant of $88 per month, of which the national government paid 45 percent.

2. Aid to the blind

Many dependent children are cared for (in a fashion) in privately or publicly supported asylums, orphans' homes, and foster homes. With a view, however, to salvaging the advantages of home care wherever possible, numerous states, even before 1935, enacted laws providing pensions or other forms of aid for needy mothers having children in their charge. The Social Security Act undertook to generalize this type of beneficence by instituting grants-in-aid for its support. State-operated systems vary, but in virtually all instances assistance is available only in behalf of children under 16 years of age (18 if in school) only if financial need is shown, and only if living with a parent or relative, although some provision is now made for children in foster homes. All states now receive subsidies for the purpose. In recent years, this assistance program has aroused more concern and criticism than any of the others. On the one hand, while the number of people on the other rolls has been declining in the midst of the prosperity of these days, the number of needy children has risen—about 3.5 million are now receiving support payments together with more than 1 million of their mothers. Many of these children are illegitimate, many inhabit the ghettoes of the cities and the slums of rural America. On the other hand, the levels of support are quite low, making it difficult for the children to escape the poverty of their birth. The protests of the poor, especially of the Negro poor, have aroused the fear of some and the sympathy of others. Congress in 1967, revising the original concepts (aimed at keeping mothers at home to look after their needy young) insisted that those able to do so should be pressured to seek employment and that day-care centers be developed to care for the young. Some states shut off help for those whose mothers lived with able-bodied men—an effort halted by the Supreme Court in 1968 as contrary to the Social Security Act; other states in an attempt to bring the rolls down have disqualified those who have not established sufficient residence—the Court has also been asked to halt this. Congress also demanded in 1967 that after June 1, 1968, the

3. Aid to dependent children

rolls not be increased relative to the population. President Johnson in 1968 appointed an Advisory Commission to review the whole problem.

4. Aid to the totally and permanently disabled
A fourth category of needy beneficiary of national grant was added to the original three by the amendments of 1950: the totally and permanently disabled. National grants were, thereafter, made available to acceptable state programs which made provision for grants to persons 18 or over who were totally and permanently incapacitated and who were not mentally ill or tubercular. In 1968, 635 thousand persons received grants averaging $88 per month of which the national government paid about 55 percent.

Under the categorical aids program the national government has undertaken a continuing indefinite commitment to pay a share of the costs of providing assistance to all persons found to be eligible by state and local agencies. In this respect, the assistance aids differ from all other types of grant-in-aid programs operated by the national government. With need and eligibility determined locally or by the state and with national, state, and, in some cases, local contributions to the total costs, a pattern of assistance has been worked out which unites all of the levels of government.

CHILD HEALTH AND WELFARE SERVICES

For a few years in the early 20's, the nation had aided state programs for improving maternity care and child welfare. The Social Security Act reestablished a child health and welfare service program. Under it grants-in-aid are now made to the states and some territories for general support of appropriate state activities. The grants are made in proportion to demonstrated need and on condition that standards are met and matching funds appropriated by the state.

1. Maternal and child health services
To share in maternal and child health grants, a state must not only have a health department but within such department a maternal and child health division with a physician in charge. The function of the division must be principally to help county health departments develop and operate health services for children from birth through school age and for mothers before and after childbirth. With emphasis on prevention rather than treatment, prenatal clinics are held, child health conferences organized, schoolchildren given medical and dental examinations, immunization precautions taken against communicable child diseases, and nutritional information imparted. In both quantity and quality, national-state-county services of these kinds vary greatly from state to state, and even from community to community. That they have more than proved their worth is indicated by a decline of mothers' deaths in connection with childbirth from 58 to 3.5 per 10,000 during the first 30 years of the system's operation, and of infant deaths, on the same numerical basis, from 560 to 229. However, at least 10 other nations have lower infant mortality rates than does the U.S.

Grants are also made, as provided by the law, to "extend and improve

[especially in rural areas and in areas suffering from severe economic dis-
tress] . . . services for locating crippled children, and for providing medical, surgical, corrective, and other services and care, and facilities for
diagnosis, hospitalization, and after care, for children who are crippled
or who are suffering from conditions which lead to crippling." In 1967,
more than 450 thousand crippled children were registered in the various
states, many of them receiving help. Every state except Arizona participates in the program, but in few areas are the funds sufficient to finance
an adequate state-wide service for all those suffering physical handicaps.

Dependent children may stand in need of help beyond that of a financial nature; and many not classified as dependent require assistance also.
They may suffer from neglect, abuse, physical or mental deficiency, the
stigma of illegitimacy, or tendencies to delinquency. The national government's yearly grant in their behalf is designed to assist state child welfare
departments in supervising and aiding local services in arranging for foster-
home or institutional care, protecting against mistreatment, conducting
clinics, encouraging neighborhood activities tending to curb juvenile delinquency, assisting schools and courts in handling children's cases, and
other such activities.

In connection with his general attack on poverty begun in 1964, President Johnson secured congressional approval for a program of preschool
training for children of the ghetto and the rural slum. Designated Operation Head Start, the program brought educational-readiness preparation to
several hundred thousand deprived children. It sought to bridge the gap
between home and school and although President Johnson's proposals were
not entirely supported by Congress, he continued in 1967 and 1968 to
push for greater educational and health services for deprived children.

GENERAL PUBLIC HEALTH SERVICES

The Social Security Act of 1935, a landmark in the development of a
coordinated national program for the care of the needy and the handicapped, also marked the beginning of a growing national-state public
health program. Public health grants to the states, abandoned in the twenties, after a brief history, were reestablished on a broader scale than ever
before. The earlier grants for venereal disease control (1918–1925) and
child and maternal hygiene (1922–1929) had been swept away by econ-
omy-minded statesmen. When the nation turned its attention to the enduring causes of widespread suffering, it found that illness was a major contributor to loss of job, family breakdown, and individual destitution.
Concern for the health of our citizens was not wholly a new responsibility
of the national government. A United States Public Health Service of
trained scientists and physicians had been in operation in the Treasury
Department almost since the founding of the nation. Founded for the care

of ailing sailors by the Congress in 1798, a Marine Hospital Service had slowly acquired new functions—controlling epidemics, aiding states in the development and enforcement of quarantine regulations at ports of entry, investigating the causes, methods of transmission, and cures of communicable diseases, regulating the interstate sale of biologics, loaning trained medical scientists to the armed services and to other agencies—and by 1912 it had become the modern Public Health Service. To this Service the Act of 1935 assigned responsibility for directing a new grant-in-aid program to assist states in improving their general public health services, including vital statistics gathering, communicable disease control, public nurse services, and many others. The original appropriation for these purposes of $2.5 million has now grown to more than $40 million.

Venereal disease program

The thirties brought a new frankness to discussions of sex problems in American society and thus opened the way to a concerted drive on one of the nation's greatest health problems: venereal diseases. Led by Surgeon General Parran, a campaign against these dread scourges was launched. In 1938, Congress enacted the Venereal Disease Control Act which revived the grant-in-aid procedure of 1918 and made national funds available for approved state programs of education, treatment, and case-finding. Aided by the discovery of penicillin and other antibiotics during and after World War II, the national-state programs have helped markedly to reduce the incidence of venereal diseases. From a peak annual appropriation to the states of $3 million, the national program had dropped to $700 thousand but with recent rises in the disease rate, has now climbed again to $4.8 million.

Modern program

Considerable success in the battle against venereal disease marked one of the last major episodes in the attack upon communicable disease that had begun with Pasteur's great discoveries in the late nineteenth century. To be sure, much suffering and death were and are caused by tuberculosis, and a new aid program to assist states in case-finding and treatment was inaugurated in the Public Health Service Act of 1944. Also poliomyelitis (now fortunately controlled by Salk and Sabine vaccines), rheumatic fever, measles (now also nearing controllability by new vaccines), and others continue to cause incapacitation. The mortality tables of the sixties reveal, however, that cancer and heart and circulatory diseases are now the chief causes of death. The modern killers and disablers do not respond to the techniques developed to combat the contagious diseases. The emphasis in public health work has, therefore, been gradually shifting to: (1) research to discover causes and cures; (2) education on proper living; and (3) early diagnosis.

1. Grants to the states

Among the great disabling diseases of modern America, none produces as much distress as mental illness. About half of all the hospital beds in the United States today are occupied by mentally ill patients. During World War II, 12 percent of all the men 18–37 examined for induction into

THE TEN LEADING CAUSES OF DEATH IN THE U.S.
1900 AND 1965

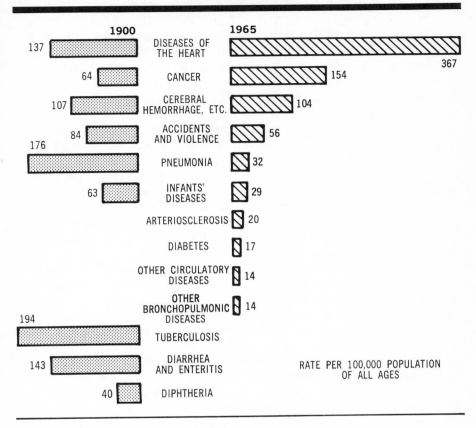

1900   **1965**

137 — DISEASES OF THE HEART — 367

64 — CANCER — 154

107 — CEREBRAL HEMORRHAGE, ETC. — 104

84 — ACCIDENTS AND VIOLENCE — 56
176

PNEUMONIA — 32

63 — INFANTS' DISEASES — 29

ARTERIOSCLEROSIS — 20

DIABETES — 17

OTHER CIRCULATORY DISEASES — 14

OTHER BRONCHOPULMONIC DISEASES — 14

194 — TUBERCULOSIS

143 — DIARRHEA AND ENTERITIS

40 — DIPHTHERIA

RATE PER 100,000 POPULATION OF ALL AGES

SOURCE: *Statistical Abstract of the United States, 1967.*

armed services were rejected because of mental and personality disorders. The Metropolitan Life Insurance Company has estimated that one out of every twenty persons born in this country will at some time have to be hospitalized for mental disorders. Responsibility for the care of the mentally ill has traditionally belonged to the states. The National Mental Health Act of 1946 marks the beginning of a national program in this field. Under this act grants are now made to state mental health agencies for community programs. Grants to the states for cancer control were instituted in 1947 and for heart disease programs in 1948. Grants are also made to the states for reducing pollution of air and water as more and more emphasis is now being placed on environmental sanitation in the promotion of public health. The Clean Air Act of 1963 and the Air Quality Act of 1967 are two of the landmarks in the new development as are the creation since 1965 of several water resource study centers.

2. Research

The major effort of the United States Public Health Service in the fields of chronic illness and death-causing disorders is research. The older National Institute (now Institutes) of Health has been greatly expanded and now includes a Cancer Institute dating from 1937, a Mental Health Institute created by the Act of 1946, a Heart Institute, a Dental Institute, and a Microbiology Institute created in 1948, an Institute for Arthritis and Metabolic Diseases, and one for Neurological Diseases and Blindness created in 1950, one for Allergy and Infectious Diseases in 1955, one for General Medical Science and another for Child Health and Human Development in 1962. These institutes carry on their programs in a Clinical Center created in 1953 and in other facilities of the Service at Bethesda, Maryland. Grants are made to medical schools, universities, laboratories, and public and private hospitals for research projects. Fellowships for work in the national facilities are awarded and conferences of scientists and doctors are sponsored. More than $1 billion annually is now poured into this stupendous effort.

Grants for hospital construction

One of the key problems in the postwar era in improving the health of the American people has been the shortage of hospital and clinical facilities. With a larger and larger portion of available beds occupied by sufferers from protracted and chronic illness, and with construction and operating costs climbing beyond the capacities of local private organizations, the national government moved in to give the states a lift. The Hospital Survey and Construction Act of 1946 inaugurated a new grant-in-aid program by which national funds—originally $75 million a year—are now made available to states to pay a portion of the construction costs for public and private hospitals, public health centers, and other health facilities. An additional $60 million annually to subsidize construction of nursing homes, diagnostic and treatment centers, and rehabilitation centers was made available beginning in 1955, and the total appropriation now exceeds $250 million annually. Grants for medical schools and for facilities for training nurses and technicians begun in 1963 were greatly expanded in 1965.

The continuing controversy over finding some way to help unfortunate people meet the rising costs of modern medical care have been, at long last, resolved, at least for the aged, by the passage of the Medicare (insurance) and Medicaid (aid for medically indigent) programs already described. There is nevertheless much yet to be done for those not yet receiving old-age payments.

The efforts to reduce smoking

One of the most contentious areas of public health activity in recent years has been the efforts of the Public Health Service to establish the relationship between smoking and lung cancer. After some years of agitation based on statistical studies showing a high correlation between heavy smoking and the incidence of lung cancer, emphysema, chronic bronchitis, and arteriosclerotic heart disease, a report prepared by an advising committee to the Service and issued in 1964 concluded that smoking was unquestionably injurious to health and that heavy cigarette smokers had much higher death rates from heart and lung diseases than nonsmokers. The Federal Trade Commission then announced it would require a health warning on cigarette packages and in all cigarette advertising. Congress, by legislation in 1965, required the warning on cigarette packages but suspended for four years the effective date of the FTC requirement of a warning in all cigarette advertising.

PUBLIC HOUSING

The acute housing shortage experienced by the country during and after World War II and the pleas from the ghettoes in the fifties and sixties, focused attention upon a problem really as old as our present industrial society. Rural housing often is far from what it should be. But when our population dwelt almost entirely on farms or in villages and small towns, most people had reasonably good homes, even though frequently with primitive equipment; and there was not much for public authorities to do about the matter. With the rise of great industrial centers, however, the situation changed, and decidedly for the worse. Rising land values produced building congestion; detached houses gave way to drab tenements; high rents forced families into pitifully inadequate quarters; immigrant workers congregated in teeming ghettos, Little Italy's and the like. The slum—dreary, crowded, and dangerous alike to health and morals—became a blot upon an otherwise fair social economy. Aside from some control over fire hazards and structural safety, the first serious attention given to housing by public authorities was directed to ameliorating the condition of low-income groups in slum areas. *Beginnings of a major problem*

Even in the third quarter of the nineteenth century, a few cities bestirred themselves to some extent about the matter, enacting local codes prescribing building regulations and sanitary standards. The effects, nevertheless, were slight, and in time people concerned turned with more hope to the legislatures of the states. From this source in certain of the more highly industrialized sections did indeed come measures fixing standards with beneficial results. At best, however, the laws merely imposed regulations on private owners of existing housing or upon private construction, without directly bringing new and better housing into existence. New York, it is true, went farther by enacting measures calculated to encourage private enterprise to undertake a good grade of building for people of low incomes, and by setting up a state housing board charged with planning and promoting slum clearance in the crowded districts of the metropolis and with supervising the construction of model tenements. But for a long time no other state emulated the example thus set. Principal ways in which states *Slow development of local and state action* and localities eventually contributed to housing betterment included municipal building codes and zoning regulations, rent regulation, loans for home construction and repair, tax exemptions for newly constructed dwellings, and redevelopment corporations for undertaking slum clearance and new building. But in nearly all states these ameliorations came late and slowly.

The national government enters the field   Aside from some provision for the housing of war workers during World War I, the national government kept almost completely out of the field until the Depression of the thirties. From that time, however, it has been continuously involved, in many different ways, and through the medium of legislation and administrative machinery so complicated and so frequently changed as to bewilder almost anyone except a professional student of the subject. The first form of national effort, undertaken at a time when large numbers of people were losing their homes through mortgage foreclosures, was aimed not particularly at increasing or improving housing but at enabling hard-pressed homeowners to avoid being dispossessed. The method consisted in setting up (in 1932) a series of home loan banks (under a Federal Home Loan Bank Administration) to provide credit for local institutions engaged in home-financing and in addition a Home Owners' Loan Corporation (in 1933) to make direct long-term mortgage loans out of national funds and at low interest rates to distressed homeowners who for one reason or another could not borrow through other channels. Almost simultaneously, however, encouragement of new low-cost building and of renovation of run-down residential properties was undertaken through a Federal Housing Administration, authorized not only to insure lending institutions against possible losses on loans made for the purposes indicated, but itself to make loans to these institutions to be employed in promoting low-rent dwellings. To this point, the objectives had been primarily to enable people to save their homes and to stimulate employment in home building and modernization. Growing concern with the social values of good housing, however, to say nothing of the financial saving in terms of fire hazards, disease, delinquency, and crime, was reflected in a United States Housing (Wagner-Steagall) Act of 1937, setting up in the Federal Works Agency a United States Housing Authority charged with making long-term loans (up to 80 percent of the costs involved) to state or local housing authorities for the construction of low-rent housing and for slum-clearance. The national agency was not to engage directly in the work of construction or demolition, but merely to make construction loans and annual operating grants; municipal or other local authorities directly concerned were to plan projects, furnish such additional funds as might be needed, and execute the different enterprises. Within four years after the legislation was enacted, all but nine of the states qualified for aid by setting up the requisite authorities, sometimes with jurisdiction confined to one or two cities, but often extending to all cities and towns and even to rural areas.

The plan outlined had only limited opportunity for operation before the national defense effort launched in 1940, together with the ensuing war, gave the housing problem a new slant and emphasis. With the rapid expansion of shipyards and of plants for manufacturing airplanes, explosives, and other war materials, the building of new plants for such purposes, and the construction of military camps and training quarters, hundreds of thousands of workers and their families flocked to localities not equipped to house them; and, partly in order to meet this situation, partly because of scarcity of labor and materials, and partly because Congress virtually cut off supporting appropriations, the general program of civilian construction and slum clearance came almost to a stop. Indeed, under legislation of 1940 national housing activities were substantially restricted to such as had to do with taking care of the armed forces and of war-plant workers; and between 1940 and 1945, nearly 1.5 million war-housing units were constructed or reconstructed, about half of the number publicly and about half privately. *Housing and World War II*

Almost complete cessation of civilian building for five or six years (on top of heavily reduced building during the preceding Depression decade), an unexpected increase of population in the meantime, return from overseas of millions of servicemen looking for homes, and continued deterioration of a great deal of housing long obsolescent—these and other factors produced a severe shortage for several years after World War II. In the steady advance of our people toward material well-being, housing had lagged: working hours had been reduced by a third to a half; food consumption had increased; education and recreation had progressed; social security had been initiated; even the average span of life had been lengthened. But millions in the low-income groups still lived in slums (both urban and rural), and other millions in homes more or less substandard. Only about one-half of the nation's families owned the places in which they dwelt. *The postwar problem*

After the war, the record of achievement had its bright spots, yet hardly was one to stir enthusiasm. The program under the United States Housing Act of 1937 came back into practical operation and by 1950 some 192,000 new dwelling units in 268 localities had been provided under it. In a limited way, the program was extended to rural areas.

What the situation seemed to require was a coherent long-term program under which the government would not merely *loan* but also *spend*, and with some liberality; and as early as 1945, a measure of this purport known as the National Housing (Taft-Ellender-Wagner) Bill made its appearance in Congress and passed the Senate. For almost four years, however, the project, bitterly fought by real estate and building lobbies, languished in the House of Representatives, and only in the early summer of 1949 was it found possible, after bitter contention in the two houses, to get an act of the kind, amending and extending the legislation of 1937, on the statute book. Under the new law—aimed particularly at urban and *The National Housing Act of 1949* rural slum clearance and redevelopment—a total of 810,000 new housing units (separate houses or small apartments, but only for low-income families) was aimed at over a period of six years. All projects were to be developed, owned, and operated by local housing authorities (usually municipal) established under state statutes. While the national government was to expedite construction by loans in individual instances where needed (a total of $1 billion was made available for the purpose), local authorities were expected usually to provide for costs by sales of nationally supported, tax-free bonds to private investors. To supplement contributions by local governments, the national government was to subsidize the system to a maximum of $100 million a year for five years to help make up the difference between the economic rent (based on annual operating costs and debt service) and the rent families of the low-income group could afford to pay, estimated at not over $30 a month.

Developments in public housing since 1950

The fighting in Korea (1950–1953) and the renewed emphasis it induced on national defense resulted in redirecting national housing interest into housing for defense plants and military installations. The Defense Housing and Community Facilities and Services Act of 1951 reflects this shift in emphasis in the public housing program. The Eisenhower administration, although pledged to reduce national programs competing with private enterprise, revealed deep sympathy for the public housing program. In a message to the Congress early in 1954, the President called for a broadening of the objectives of the national public housing program to include urban redevelopment as well as slum clearance. In this way cities might salvage declining neighborhoods and stop others from deterioration and not have to await the appearance of the slum for national help. He also asked the Congress to extend the low-rent public housing program of the Act of 1949, although at a reduced rate of 35,000 new units per year for the next four years. The Housing Act of 1954 substantially met the President's request except that it limited the commitment on public housing units to one year. The President again in 1955 asked for a broader program of public housing and finally wrested authority for 45,000 more units from a reluctant Congress.

Returning to the attack in 1956, the President got congressional approval for 35,000 more units for 1956 and an equal number for 1957. No units were authorized in 1958. In 1959, the Congress twice passed housing bills providing for a renewed and expanded low-cost housing construction program but the President vetoed each. Authorization for 37,000 new units was finally approved. The Housing Act of 1959 also launched a new loan program aimed at promoting private construction of facilities specially designed for elderly persons and expanded somewhat the loans and grants for urban renewal programs. Metropolitan regional planning through state or regional agencies was also promoted by grants-in-aid. President Kennedy, shortly after his inauguration, called for a much expanded housing and community rebuilding program and Congress responded with a Housing Act of 1961 that: (1) removed the statutory prohibitions on the yet un-built 100,000 low-cost housing units contemplated by the original act of 1949; (2) expanded the loans available for college housing, housing for the elderly, and farm housing; (3) increased the monies available for grants for urban planning and for urban renewal projects; (4) authorized new loans to improve urban transportation facilities and utilities; and (5) authorized new grants for community purchase and development of open adjacent areas for recreational or conservation purposes. In an effort to strengthen and dramatize his program of aid to the cities, Kennedy also proposed the creation of a new department of urban affairs to include the various housing agencies. Congress vetoed his effort to do so under reorganization power and refused to create the department by statute.

In 1965, President Johnson returned to these themes and gave them vigorous and effective support. A new Housing and Urban Development Act inaugurated rent subsidies for needy families to help pay for housing when suitable accommodations could not be obtained for 25 percent of their income. The program was confined to housing provided in public or government-insured housing. The new act also: (1) expanded the FHA program of low-interest home financing for low and modest income families and for veterans; (2) authorized local public housing agencies to lease units in private housing for occupancy by needy families; (3) expanded the urban renewal programs to embrace areas closely related to those previously eligible for renewal; (4) extended the low-rent public housing programs until 1969 at a level of 60,000 new units per year; (5) expanded loans for college housing; (6) authorized grants to local units for various types of public facilities including water works, sewer systems, health and recreation centers; (7) inaugurated grants to local units for acquisition of open areas and for urban beautification. Johnson also proposed the creation of a department of housing and urban development and the Congress endorsed his request. *Congress approves rent subsidies and new department*

Not satisfied with these efforts and anxious to get private capital and private enterprise more deeply involved in housing, slum clearance, and urban renewal, Johnson made major legislative efforts in 1966, 1967, and 1968. For the most part, Congress responded giving the President almost everything he requested. The rent supplement program was expanded; various devices for involving private enterprise by subsidizing interest rates on long-term financing were enacted; private developers were encouraged to enter the public building field by authorizing public agencies to buy or lease projects designed for low-income persons; programs for interest subsidy of rental payments for people of incomes above the level that might qualify them for the existing type of public housing were started; special programs for housing the aged were stimulated. In 1966 at the President's request, the Congress enacted the Demonstration Cities Act, aimed at comprehensive planned renewal for cities of all sizes. This program sought to unite all related nationally financed urban-slum programs in a concerted attack on blight. Expansion of the effort was sought successfully by the President in 1968. Urban riots, protests, arson, and pillage in the slum areas of our large cities in the late sixties indicated that all of these efforts were still far short of solving the problems.

THE NATIONAL GOVERNMENT AND EDUCATION

Aid to vocational education

The mounting controversy in the last two decades over national aid to public education has in some minds obscured the fact that the national government was already deeply involved by subsidy and direct expenditures in the field of public education. In earlier chapters we have described the programs of national assistance for agricultural education at the college level and through the Extension Service. A new program (National Defense Education Act) of aid to university students and staff was begun in 1958, renewed in 1961, and greatly expanded in 1964. In 1917, a broad program of national grants to the states for vocational education, largely at the high school level, was inaugurated. Expanded greatly in the past four decades, this program now provides national funds for and national supervision over training for young men and women in skilled trades, distributive occupations, industrial techniques, home economics, practical nursing, and agriculture. Funds are also granted for preparing teachers in these subjects to staff the vocational schools. Many states have been stimulated by the national grants (some had them before the national grants began) to establish a system of vocational schools under the supervision of a state agency and to appropriate funds for the purpose of providing such education. Related programs of vocational training to help workers displaced by automation were established beginning in 1962 with the Manpower Development and Training Act. To this program of education aids was added, beginning in 1920, and greatly expanded in 1954, aids for vocational rehabilitation for training the physically handicapped for useful employment.

Temporary grants during depression and war

During the depression numerous grants, loans, and direct national expenditures were made for school construction, remodeling, and equipment. Thousands of local school districts benefited from these temporary measures. Beginning in World War II and continuing to the present, substantial grants have been made for school construction in areas heavily burdened by military or defense facilities and for the establishment of child-care centers, nursery schools, and other educational facilities. Grants were also made to aid school districts obliged suddenly to make provision for large numbers of children whose parents were stationed at military installations. A huge subsidy to education has been made by the national government by means of the veterans' aid program inaugurated in the G.I. Bill of 1944 and continued in modified form for veterans of Korea and Viet Nam.

Through continuing grants for school lunches for needy children and for aid to school districts affected by national installations, the national government has made and continues to make important contributions to public primary and secondary education in the United States. All of this did not, however, set at rest the urgent demand for national grants for general public education aimed at helping localities deal with the great flood of school-going children and at placing a floor below which, regardless of local revenues, educational programs may not fall. President Eisenhower early in 1955 asked Congress to inaugurate a new program of national assistance to local school districts for building construction to help them meet these needs. He suggested: (1) that the national government buy local bonds for construction at a low interest rate; (2) that the states be aided in creating state school building authorities with power to borrow national funds and build schools that could be leased to local districts that have already exhausted their borrowing power; (3) that grants be made for construction to school units that are unable to finance needed construction. These recommendations he renewed on several subsequent occasions. President Kennedy entered this field to battle on behalf of school aids early in 1961 and continued his efforts until his death. He proposed aids to help pay teachers' salaries as well as for construction of facilities. He has also proposed both grants and loans for college and university facilities. As with all previous efforts, the Kennedy program foundered on the two great shoals of educational legislation: (1) the religious issue— Catholics generally oppose general aid programs if parochial schools are not somehow taken care of and many doubt if constitutionally the government can aid religious education; (2) the racial issue—many northern congressmen feel that aid must not be given to segregated schools and most southern members will not support aid on this basis.

It remained for President Johnson to find a path through the legisla- tive maze. He did so in 1965, in which year the first general aid program to primary-secondary education was established. The Johnson proposal tied school aids to help for the needy in order to avoid some of the constitutional and emotional problems of race and religion. The national grants are to be given to states on the basis of a formula which includes the amount spent per child in the state school program and the number of children from families with incomes under $2000 in each school district. The aids are to be given by the state to the school districts and may be spent as the districts wish, subject to approval by state and national authorities. Grants are also made available for the purchase of library materials and textbooks for children in public and private schools and may not include religious literature. Additional grants are also made to the state for: (1) community-wide educational services not provided by individual schools; and (2) strengthening and improving state departments of education. Altogether more than $1 billion annually is authorized under the Act of 1965. In two years the program brought aid to 9 million disadvantaged youngsters in 18,000 school districts. Congress in 1967 extended the authority to 1970 and added funding for several types of special programs for preschool children, for research and evaluation. The President, signing the amending law of 1967, said that the Acts of 1965 and 1967 were the "greatest victories of his life."

REFERENCES

C. Abrams, *The Future of Housing* (New York, 1946).

Advisory Council on Public Welfare, *Having the Power, We Have the Duty*, Report to Secretary of HEW (Washington, D. C., 1966).

H. D. Babbidge, Jr., and R. M. Rosenzweig, *The Federal Interest in Higher Education* (New York, 1963).

E. M. Burns, *The American Social Security System* (Boston, 1949).

M. L. Colean *et al.*, *American Housing; Problems and Prospects* (New York, 1944).

Committee on Economic Security, *Social Security in America* (Washington, D. C., 1937).

Council of State Governments, *Unemployment Compensation in the Postwar Period* (Chicago, 1944).

R. M. Elman, *The Poorhouse State: The American Way of Life on Public Assistance* (New York, 1967).

M. Fainsod, L. Gordon, and J. C. Palamountain, Jr., *Government and the American Economy* (3rd ed., New York, 1959), Chap. xxv.

D. Gagliardo, *American Social Insurance* (New York, 1949).

M. E. Gettleman and D. Mermelstein (eds.), *The Great Society Reader: the Failure of American Liberalism* (New York, 1968).

J. R. Louis, *Cities in a Race with Time: Progress and Poverty in America's Renewing Cities* (New York, 1967).

M. B. Schnapper [comp.], *Public Housing in America* (New York, 1939).

K. de Schweinitz, *People and Process in Social Security* (Washington, D. C., 1948).

G. Y. Steiner, *Social Insecurity: the Politics of Welfare* (Chicago, 1966).

E. E. Witte, *The Development of the Social Security Act* (Madison, Wis., 1962).

21

CONDUCTING FOREIGN AFFAIRS

Despite the triumphs of science and the demands of salvation, the world is not one but many. The number of centers of decision-making in the world is increasing not decreasing. Talk of one world, a bipolar world, or a tripolar world is, like it or not, more and more at odds with the tide of events. Two-thirds of the way through the twentieth century the world remains divided into more autonomous political communities than ever, each zealously striving to secure what its leaders believe the community interest requires. We, like others, seek to preserve our territorial and political independence, to sell our products beyond our shores, to buy what we want or need from others, to enforce respect for our nationals when outside our boundaries, to obtain adherence to agreed rules of international intercourse as well as to specific commitments mutually undertaken, to resist threats to our interests or interference in our way of life, and, on the whole, to settle international disputes peacefully. These aims necessarily and inevitably involve us in regular and continuing dealings with virtually all the other nations on the globe and these dealings collectively constitute our foreign affairs. The management of these affairs is assigned exclusively by the Constitution and by decades of tradition and practice to the national government and is one of its major responsibilities. *A divided world*

If the earlier generations of American statesmen were to revisit the scenes of their earthly endeavors nothing might surprise them quite so much as the prominence now given to the conduct of foreign affairs. For generations, the American people had worked out their various purposes largely indifferent to the aspirations of the peoples of the rest of the world. They were determined not to allow the quarrels, the dynastic rivalries, the military demonstrations or the ills, suffering, or triumphs of others to entice their notice away from the main show of building a free and prosperous nation out of a wilderness. Separated by broad oceans from nations powerful enough to menace their independence, selected by immigration from among those most dissatisfied with the societies of the "old world," confident of the virtues of a political system built upon freedom, the Ameri- *The continental tradition* can people felt they had little to fear and nothing to learn from Europe or Asia. Their outlook was continental but extended to those parts of the Western Hemisphere which because of propinquity might, if dominated by powerful European nations, threaten their coasts, water systems, or trade routes. Occasionally, their idealism and wealth might be enlisted on behalf of feeding or Christianizing the Chinese, the Armenians, or some other hapless people. Statesmen seeking nondivisive appeals for public support frequently lectured the "power hungry" or "cynical" statesmen of Europe on their bad behavior and discussed international affairs in highly moralistic tones. Mainly, however, America had few important ties beyond the seas and wanted none. Its diplomats were more observers than participants. "Why," in the language of Washington's Farewell Address, "by interweaving our destiny with that of any part of Europe, entangle our peace and prosperity in the toils of European ambition, rivalship, interest, honor, or caprice?"

The revolution in our foreign outlook

Things are quite different today. The United States is tied to nearly half of the world by military alliance, its troops, planes, and ships of war are stationed thousands of miles from home, its treasure is exported in billions to bolster the defenses and the economies of friendly or potentially friendly nations. Its sons are even now dying by thousands in battles of containment in which neither conquest of the enemy nor occupation of his country is sought. Its influence is exerted in virtually every international controversy. Its newspapers and airwaves are filled as never before with reports of activities in Asia, Africa, the Middle East, Europe. Its legislative halls resound to the clash of oratory on the conduct of affairs in Saigon, Seoul, Hue, Cambodia, Bangkok, Bonn, Aqaba—places the average American never even heard of until yesterday. The utterances of our leaders are heard and considered with sympathy, fear, or distaste, but never indifference, by those of every nation on earth. The earth has shrunk. The technology of transportation and communication has annihilated space. Our distant neighbors of yesterday are next door today. The strong controls over much of the world exercised by Western Europe have dissolved. Ties of subservience—colony to imperial power, yellow and black people to white, East to West, peasant to landlord, farmer to trader, Moslem to Christian—are fraying. A new world is aborning. Communism is on the march. Nationalism and higher living standards beckon the peoples of Africa, Asia, Latin America, and the Middle East. Amidst these revolutionary movements stands the United States, facilitating some, trying to stem the communist advance, seeking to preserve the culture of the West and to lead what we like to call the "free world." Since the forceful resolution of international disputes may lead to the complete destruction of those involved, failure in the conduct of foreign affairs can well mean the end of all of us.

The importance of contemporary international relations heightens the struggle within—as well as without—America to determine the policies and procedures according to which these relations will be conducted. Our extramural involvements are to a large degree the product of domestic politics. Virtually every interest and aspiration articulated by parties, interest groups, and organs of opinion has implications abroad and the struggle to influence national policy is every bit as intense in the foreign as in the domestic area. America is not omnipotent, however, and even the agreed goals of domestic politics must face the interests and strength of other nations. Unless we are prepared to fight to impose our will in every controversy, we must settle for what can be gained by negotiation. Ordinarily, this means giving due consideration to the differing needs and interests of other nations, great and small. Dean Rusk, the Secretary of State, puts it thus: "We are the center of the world only to ourselves." These non-American interests can, of course, not be strongly represented in our politics, and even consensus policies of our foreign relations are not always within either our means or our abilities. Supportable policies, nevertheless, are usually firmly anchored to rather widely accepted national interests.

The close relation of foreign policy to domestic politics

FORMULATING AND CONTROLLING FOREIGN POLICY: THE ROLE OF THE PRESIDENT

Every action taken by the government in dealing with other nations presumably reflects a policy. The sum of these actions at any given time is our foreign policy or policies. These policies normally are intended to realize certain objectives and may be based upon certain principles cherished by the American people. Disturbed by the shifts and turns characterizing our dealings with other nations over the years, critics have charged that our conduct is not based upon consistent principles but merely zigzags from position to position as the rough winds of international politics toss the ship of state about. For several generations our continental outlook, physical isolation, and avoidance of long-term commitments seemed to manifest a negative attitude on matters of great concern to other nations. Even these aims, however, reflect some kind of policy and, in fact, we have sought and stated various objectives in our foreign dealings over the years and have frequently asserted aspirations toward particular nations and situations. As our involvement in world affairs has broadened and deepened in recent years, we have encountered dozens of situations about which we have been obliged to have policies and objectives. It scarcely needs emphasizing, therefore, that the ability to decide what our policy will be is of transcendent importance in modern America.

Do we have a foreign policy?

Under the American system, the determination of these policies is not the exclusive function of any single branch of the national government. All three have important responsibilities and influence. Beyond these, the apparatus of the political parties, interest groups, and associations of many types, media of communication, opinion leaders, corporate managers, spe-

The President is chief architect of foreign policy

cial pleaders, all play significant roles and struggle to gain advantage in influencing our foreign affairs. The supreme architect of modern American policy is, however, undoubtedly the President. His preeminent role is a consequence of the machinery by which our foreign dealings are carried on, of the constitutional assignment of powers and responsibilities, of the need for prompt decision, of the technology of modern combat and of modern communication, and of the cumbersome deliberativeness of the judicial and legislative processes.

He controls daily intercourse with other nations   Basic to everything else is the maintenance of the day-to-day intercourse with foreign governments and for this the President—typically through the facilities of the Department of State—is the official channel. He appoints, subject to senatorial confirmation, all ambassadors, ministers, consuls, and other foreign-service officers stationed abroad and may remove them or change their assignments. Indeed, he may even employ "special," "secret" or "personal" agents to represent him personally, bypassing the formal channels of diplomacy, the Secretary of State, the foreign service, and the Senate. The modern foreign service is, however, so large, far-flung, regimented, and elaborately organized that it no longer receives much personal direction from the White House and little enough from the secretary of state. American missions abroad are largely staffed by the career officers of the foreign service, and the President and the secretary normally follow the recommendations of the service in making appointments and promotions. The White House continues to interest itself in the selection of the top representatives abroad—ambassadors and ministers—in part, at least, because many of them are likely to be chosen from the ranks of the President's partisans. While normally relying entirely on the State Department, the President may and has taken matters into his own hands and conducted foreign dealings from the White House. He may even go abroad to lead in the negotiations of important settlements as did Woodrow Wilson at the end of World War I, Roosevelt and Truman during and after World War II, and Eisenhower, Kennedy, and Johnson in recent years on occasions too numerous to record.

The normal work of the American representatives, obtaining information, declaring policies and attitudes, pressing claims, offering settlements, replying to inquiries, advising and assisting American nationals, participating in conferences, speaking of American life and hopes—is all ultimately under presidential directions, however little of it he may normally

Congress may not communicate formally with foreign states   be able to take an interest in. Congress, on its part, may not address any foreign power nor receive any communication from one, and any private citizen or corporation is forbidden "directly or indirectly . . . to carry on verbal or written correspondence with any foreign government or its officers or agents designated to influence the measures of conduct of (this) government in relation to any disputes or controversies with the United States."

Out of the steady stream of communications to and from Washington, however, arise the issues, demands and controversies which may require immediate attention at the highest level. Thus when some new situation anywhere in the world presents itself, it is the President—usually through his secretary of state—who has the first opportunity to say what, if anything, the United States will do about it. By the stand first taken the nation may be committed to goals or policies which become very difficult thereafter to change. Not only is the President or his principal deputy in position quickly to hear of new developments and promptly to decide how to deal with them, he is also in daily receipt of a quantity and quality of information which makes his participation far more effective than that of most others who might wish to be involved. The foreign service is a great fact-gathering agency and to the extent possible, these facts are arranged, sorted, classified, and categorized in aid of the decision-making process. Information independently available to Congress, the Courts, interest groups, and opinion leaders is by contrast uncertain, spotty, and irregular.

The President, furthermore, on his own responsibility receives all foreign ambassadors and ministers with power also to break off dealings with them and, in effect, send them home. Thus, he can exercise considerable influence over the representations made in Washington by other governments. He cannot, of course, prevent them from discussing their problems with congressmen, judges, opposition leaders, journalists, association executives, or other frequenters of the nation's capital. The constitutionally authorized powers of appointment of American representatives abroad and of reception of foreign representatives in Washington place the President in position to determine the attitudes of our government toward newly risen states or to newly established regimes in existing states. Recognition may *The form* take the form of welcoming into the family of nations a state that has lately *of* asserted its independence as President Monroe after 1817 recognized a *recognition* number of Latin American republics which had cast off the Spanish yoke and as modern Presidents have done for the dozens of new states of Africa, the Middle East, and South and South East Asia. The far-reaching conse- *Impor-* quence of some acts of recognition may be illustrated by the recognition of *tance of* Texas in 1837 leading to trouble with Mexico, of Cuba in 1897 leading *power of* to the crisis with Spain in 1898, of Panama in 1903 leading to the con- *recognition* struction of the canal. Recognition may also take the form of instituting official relations with a new political regime that has taken over in a given country. In 1928, for example, President Coolidge recognized the new Kuomintang government of China by concluding a treaty with it, and in 1933 President Roosevelt concluded an agreement with an invited emissary of the Soviet Union opening official relations with this mighty state some 16 years after the Communists had taken over its government. In the modern era, recognition has usually been accorded new regimes as soon as their actual hold on the state apparatus has become clear. The Castro regime in Cuba, for example, was recognized only six days after the flight of the dictator, Batista, leader of the displaced government. The *And of non-* President may also withhold recognition. Wilson contributed to the down- *recognition* fall of the Huerta government in Mexico in 1916 by refusing to have any dealings with it. Hoover and Franklin Roosevelt steadfastly refused to recognize the Japanese-created state of Manchukuo, established on Chinese soil in 1932 and in disregard of our stated policy of maintaining the territorial integrity of China. Truman, for a time, withheld recognition of the "friendly" regimes in Bulgaria, Yugoslavia, and Rumania established and supported by the Soviet Union in defiance of decisions at Yalta to hold free elections in those states. None of the Presidents since World War II have recognized the incorporation into the Soviet Union of the Baltic states (Estonia, Latvia, Lithuania) in 1940 nor has any recognized the East German People's Republic created with support from the Soviets out of their zone of military occupation of Germany. For twenty years our Presidents have also refused to recognize the communist government of mainland China, although we have participated with them in the Geneva Conference on French Indochina in 1954 and have maintained diplomatic contact with their representatives in Poland. Nonrecognition is not necessarily synonymous with the complete severance of diplomatic relations. Relations may be broken off in wartime or during periods of acute international tension. For example, during the Arab–Israeli war of 1967, the Arab states broke off relations with the United States; presumably they will be renewed in due course.

President's power as Commander-in-Chief strengthens his hand in foreign policy

The President's influence in foreign affairs is greatly strengthened by his powers and responsibilities as Commander-in-Chief of the nation's armed forces. We shall enlarge on this theme in the next chapter. Suffice it to say here that diplomacy must frequently be supported by the potential or actual use of force. To be credible, the force must be available for timely deployment in the right place and the President's unquestioned authority to order the forces about the world allows him to support his aims, back up his threats, and exert pressure in delicate situations. He can also, of course, place the nation in a situation in which war is inevitable. Only the President could have provided planes for the government of the Congo, military advisors to Thailand, warships to patrol the Formosa straits or the eastern Mediterranean, or weapons to India and Pakistan. In every case these forces influenced the course of events in these areas. No contestant in the internal struggle for influence over our foreign policies can match these resources.

Economic power is also considerable

Although subject to considerable congressional influence arising from the required statutory authorizations, the foreign aid, technical-assistance, and reciprocal-trade–agreements programs place in the hands of the modern President economic resources of considerable potency. His ability, within the limits of the legislation, to offer a grant here, a trade concession there, and a loan the other place and, of course, to withhold these, places him in an enviable position to influence the conduct of national leaders elsewhere, to throw his weight about internationally, in other words.

The President is also constitutionally authorized to make treaties with other nations, provided that the Senate concurs by a two-thirds vote. The nature and extent of the President's authority thus formally to commit the nation to some course of action has been contested for years but few would deny that he now has a paramount role. An early question as to whether the Senate should participate formally in the negotiations leading up to the treaty was resolved during Washington's time in favor of complete presidential control of the negotiating processes with the Senate receiving the completed instrument for its ratification or perhaps disapproval. The consent of the Senate, in actuality, is simply to a final act of ratification to be performed by the President. Either branch of Congress, singly or jointly, may advise or request that a treaty be negotiated and the President, on his part, may consult with influential senators during the course of negotiations. If the President chooses, however, he can begin them without the agreement or knowledge of either house of Congress. Even if the Senate agrees to ratification, the President can—but rarely does—decide not to proceed farther and can nullify the whole enterprise. Furthermore, the President may without consulting Congress validly determine whether any specific treaty provisions have lapsed.

President's power to make commitments by:

1. Treaty

Once duly ratified by the governments concerned and proclaimed by the President, a treaty becomes, from the international point of view, a contract between the United States and the nation (or nations) constituting the other party, and from the domestic point of view, an extension of the law of the land, supreme and enforceable like any other portion of the law. Both national and state courts must give it full effect. Of course, not all treaties are, or are intended to be, permanent. Some expressly provide for their own expiration; some are terminated by war; some are replaced by new agreements; some are abrogated by being "denounced" by one or more of the parties. When it is desired in this country to dispense with a treaty, or some portion thereof, our government is likely to seek an agreement to that end with any nation or nations concerned. In default of such agreement, however, the President may, on his own authority, simply proclaim the treaty at an end; or he may take such action with the support of a joint resolution of Congress. Congress itself may make any treaty's provisions of no internal legal effect by enacting legislation inconsistent with them. Although treaties are "law of the land," the Supreme Court has said that they are no more truly such than are acts passed by Congress. Invariably the Court has been reductant to construe a statute as in violation of a treaty; but when there is manifest conflict, the later in date prevails. Neither a court decision nor a statute can, however, abrogate a treaty as an international contract. Although rendered unenforceable at home, it preserves its international status until revoked by executive action. In the meantime the foreign power concerned may construe a crippling judicial decision or statute as a breach of contract entitling it to reparation through an international proceeding.

The legal status of a treaty in domestic law

Not every agreement entered into with a foreign government takes the form of a treaty and from this circumstance the President is able further to

2. Executive agreement

enlarge his influence over the conduct of foreign affairs. A very large number of legally valid agreements are "executive agreements" for which senatorial approval is neither sought nor obtained and about which the Constitution is obscure. From the earliest days, Presidents have entered such agreements usually on relatively trivial issues—boundary rectifications, private pecuniary claims against another government or its nationals, regulations of fishing rights, etc. Some have been entered into on the basis of blanket authority conferred in advance by Congress—postal conventions and trade agreements, for example. Others stem directly from the President's authority over the armed forces and relate to the conduct or stationing by agreement of American troops abroad and to the jurisdiction over offenses committed by them. Beginning, however, with McKinley, a notable expansion in their use took place. A number of understandings in this form were concluded by him, Secretary Hay, and later by Theodore Roosevelt in their management of American affairs in Cuba, the Philippines, China, Japan, and Latin America. In many cases vigorous congressional critics objected to the policies of these Presidents and might well have thwarted them if treaties had been submitted for approval. President Franklin Roosevelt carried the use of such agreements to greater lengths than any of his predecessors. In fact he used this procedure to recognize and establish relations with the Soviet Union. Out of this set of transactions two cases (U.S. *v.* Belmont, 1937 and U.S. *v.* Pink, 1946) reached the highest court in which the authority of the President was fully sustained against contrary state action. Thus vindicated, the President continued to prefer the agreement to the treaty and the famous deal (Hull–Lothian agreement) of 1940 with Britain which moved us closer to belligerency in World War II and which granted her 50 overage destroyers in exchange for ninety-nine year leases to certain bases in the British West Indies was handled in this fashion.

Strong reaction to the growing preference for avoiding treaties and thus senatorial consent occurred in the Senate during World War II. Concern first manifested itself when the State Department, under authority of the Lend-Lease Act of 1941, began concluding a series of agreements with our major allies involving relatively long-range commitments of large sums of money. When it was learned that a United Nations Relief and Rehabilitation convention involving further commitments was not to be referred to the Senate, the Secretary (Hull) was vigorously challenged. Although ultimately the UNRRA agreement was entered into without a treaty, legislative authorization of the necessary funding was provided only after the executive branch promised to be more circumspect thereafter in observing "constitutional processes." In subsequent actions Congress made it clear that admission to any world organization must be with Senate participation (that is, by treaty) and the major postwar commitments of the U.S. have been embodied in treaties. Nevertheless, a growing movement to restrict the treaty power of the President and to curtail the use of executive agreements was mounted in the early fifties and was turned back only by a

*Attack on
the
executive
agreement
system*

narrow margin in the showdown voting of 1954. Eisenhower, Kennedy, and Johnson and their respective secretaries of state have all been quite cautious in the use of the agreement procedure and no new ground has recently been occupied. In general, these agreements are now used (1) to implement legislation such as the reciprocal-trade acts and the foreign-aid authorizations; (2) to provide for U.S. membership in certain technical types of international organizations—these are usually submitted to Congress for approval by both houses; and (3) to achieve military arrangements, such as armistices, treatment of troops, and service to American military bases. A dramatic recent (1963) illustration of the use of the agreement was to provide for the installation of a "hot" teletype line between the White House and the Kremlin.

The President and the national government generally have also through the years enhanced their authority in consequence of the broadening interpretation of the scope of the treaty-making power. The question arose in Washington's time as to whether the treaty power extended only to subjects expressly assigned to the national government or whether it could be used on any matters about which two or more nations might wish to negotiate. Jefferson argued for a strict limit on the treaty authority but as in the matter of "implied powers," circumstances, subsequent Presidents, and the Supreme Court have been against him. In general, the Court has recognized that treaties may be validly entered into and then implemented by appropriate legislation on "all proper subjects" of negotiation. President Theodore Roosevelt, in 1906–1907, used the treaty power in effect to compel San Francisco to admit children of Oriental descent to its public schools. The landmark decision arose, however, out of a treaty with Great Britain authorizing agreements between the U.S. and Canada to protect migratory birds. Congress, in pursuance of the agreement, enacted strict controls over the hunting of such birds and the Supreme Court fully sustained the law despite the general belief at that time that conservation matters of this type were state responsibilities. Significantly, the Constitution requires that acts of Congress to be the supreme law of the land must be made in pursuance of the Constitution but treaties, simply "under the authority of the United States." Among other manifestations of concern over the growing network of international commitments after World War II a new attack was mounted on the treaty power. An amendment proposed by Senator Bricker (Republican of Ohio) aimed at restricting the President's authority to subjects expressly assigned to the national government by the Constitution and limiting the use of "executive agreements." The immediate impetus to the controversy of the early fifties was a proposed Covenant on Human Rights developed by the United Nations and the belief that American adherence to such an agreement might justify national regulation of race relations or economic activities heretofore believed to be solely state matters. The Bricker amendment, after many compromises of aim and language was finally rejected by one vote by the Senate in 1954 and has not been revived

The broadening scope of the treaty power

The Bricker amendment controversy

since. The Human Rights Covenant was a casualty of the struggle however. Secretary Dulles promised the Senate the United States would not subscribe to the proposed agreement and although national authority in the field of human rights has been sharply increased by subsequent legislation, the U.N. Covenant has not thus far been reconsidered.

FORMULATING AND CONTROLLING FOREIGN POLICY: THE CONGRESS

Congress controls funds and organiza- tion

However substantial the powers and resources of the President in the field of foreign affairs, he does not play a lone hand or always have his way unchallenged. Rarely can he obtain his objectives or establish lasting programs unless these are accepted and, in many cases, implemented by the Congress. Clearly, whenever funds are required, as in the cases of foreign aid, contributions to the U.N., and of support for overseas missions, Congress must supply the necessary authorizations and appropriations. In addition, whenever statutory authority is required, as in the trade agreements program, in admitting nationals of other countries to America, in distributing surplus agricultural commodities, Congress must pass the enabling legislation. The organization of the Department of State, the Foreign Service, the Agency for International Development, the United States Information Agency, and other executive branch agencies for the conduct of foreign affairs is closely regulated by statute and cannot be seriously modified without congressional consent. The need for concurrence in these aspects of foreign affairs gives to both houses of Congress or more precisely to certain congressmen (chairmen, ranking members, and subcommittee chairmen of the House Committee on Foreign Affairs and the Senate Committee on Foreign Relations, the key members of the two Appropriations Committee and the party leaders of both houses) the resources to bargain for influence over those aspects of our foreign policy which may not necessarily depend upon express legislative approval. Since the modern foreign policies of the United States require several billion dollars annually for their achievement, the role of Congress is manifestly greater than in earlier days when relatively minor sums were involved.

Congres- sional initiation in foreign policy by resolution

If the President has at times evaded the two-thirds rule for senatorial approval of treaties by the use of executive agreements, the Congress can, and has expressed its independent views on numerous international situations by simple or joint resolution. The President has been requested, for example, to bring Spain into the N.A.T.O. defense system, to investigate trade of our allies with the communist bloc, to condemn the Soviet's suppression of the Hungarian rebellion. Congress has also vigorously opposed the admission of Red China to the U.N. In these, as in many other cases, the State Department and the President would have preferred not to be so precisely instructed. Of course, presidential approval is required for joint resolutions if they are to be enacted, but such approval is hard to with-hold when the Congress is clearly reflecting popular sentiments. The joint resolution is also used, in most cases with presidential blessing, to facilitate international agreements where, for various reasons, the treaty system cannot be made to operate. Thus, for example, Texas was annexed in 1845 and Hawaii in 1898, war with Germany and the other Central Powers finally brought to an end legally in 1921 when the Treaty of Versailles failed to receive approval, and adherence to the international agreement establishing the International Labor Office achieved in 1934.

Although the concern of the House of Representatives in foreign affairs has substantially increased since World War II due to the fiscal and statutory requirements of modern foreign policy, the Senate continues to regard its participation through treaties and appointments as one of its unique responsibilities. For many years those who favored more active involvement by the United States in world affairs viewed the Senate as a stumbling block, a forum of parochial interests. From 1890 to 1940 numerous efforts to eliminate the two-thirds requirement for approval of treaties were mounted and Presidents and secretaries of state were encouraged to enlarge the use of executive agreements. The failure of Wilson's campaign to gain American adherence to the League of Nations was perhaps the high point of disenchantment with the Senate by internationally minded statesmen and scholars. Since World War II, however, with American participation in the U.N. and the unprecedented series of alliances by which we are linked to nearly half the globe, all approved by substantial majorities in the Senate, the criticism has almost completely abated. In all, from 1789 through 1963, the Senate has actually rejected only 14 treaties out of 1,357 submitted. None has been rejected outright since 1934. Serious, in several cases crippling, reservations have been attached to the Senate's approval, however, of more than 250. In perhaps a third of these, the reservations caused the President or the foreign nation to abandon efforts to reach formal agreement. Probably the most significant modern instance of this practice is the Connally reservation of 1946 to American adherence to the agreement creating the International Court of Justice. This reservation greatly modified the intentions of the authors of the agreement by reserving to the United States the right to determine which cases were essentially within our domestic jurisdiction and thus were exempt from the Court's consideration. A consular treaty negotiated in 1964 with the Soviet Union (the first bilateral treaty between the U.S. and the U.S.S.R.) authorizing consulates in some of the principal cities of each nation and an important incident in the Johnson administration's efforts to abate tensions was narrowly (66–28) approved in 1967, and only after great exertions by the White House. One reason for the Senate's willingness to accept the postwar treaty commitments of the United States has been the care manifested by Presidents and secretaries of state to involve a few of the most influential senators in the negotiations and to keep them rather fully informed on devel-

The Senate and treaties

opments. Furthermore, American adherence to the U.N. and to the tradition-breaking N.A.T.O. alliance was foreshadowed by Senate resolutions indicating Senate approval of such undertakings. In many instances, furthermore, the Senate has successfully insisted that the appointment of high level American participants in these enterprises be subject to senatorial consent. There are some, including Senator Fulbright, Chairman of the Senate Foreign Relations Committee, who now regard the twenty-five years of relative presidential–senatorial harmony on international commitments as a surrender by the Senate of its constitutional responsibilities. The Senator, partly because of his displeasure with the Viet Nam policies of President Johnson and the use of congressional resolutions and foreign-aid programs to justify American military involvement, introduced a resolution in the Senate in 1967 intended to regain for the Senate its right to participate more effectively in such commitments.

Congress lacks data

Perhaps the greatest handicap under which the Congress labors in its efforts to participate effectively in the formulation of foreign policies is the want of regular, dependable, and comprehensive information about world affairs. The small staff of the relevant committees, the small group of experts in the Legislative Reference Service, the employees of foreign missions, the staffs of interest groups, all together are few and inadequate compared with the resources of the President. Congress must largely depend upon the executive branch for the data to inform its deliberations. The Congress is also not in being for several weeks each year and every other year members are preoccupied for several weeks with electioneering. In fact, during the nineteenth century when the traditions and procedures by which foreign affairs are now conducted were being established, the Congress was out of session more than half the time. The executive branch is on duty all the time ready to meet any international situation that may arise.

Congressional leadership in foreign affairs

A determined Senate or Congress, nevertheless, may with these resources and, indeed has on a few occasions, wrested leadership in foreign affairs away from the President. War with Britain in 1812 and intervention in Cuba in 1898 were both forced upon reductant Presidents by the Congress. An unconvinced Senate may and has frustrated a President's most cherished foreign aims. Thus John Quincy Adams' Pan-American policy was thwarted as was Pierce's in Cuba and Grant's in Dominica, and Cleveland's in Hawaii. Wilson was completely routed in his League of Nations policy and Lyndon Johnson's efforts in Viet Nam were plagued by the hostility of several (not as yet a majority) key senators. The foreign-aid program has been harassed almost from its inception by congressional investigation, by statutory restrictions aimed at limiting presidential authority especially in dealing with communist-bloc or satellite states, by requirements that preference be given American products, and by junketing congressional committee whose expenses often are paid from counterpart funds.

THE ROLE OF THE COURTS

Few international controversies are settled by judicial procedures and the ones that are, are likely to be of lesser importance. The role of the courts is, therefore, distinctly a minor one in the formulation and control of American foreign policy. As in domestic matters, the courts are called upon to construe the Constitution, statutes, treaties, and executive orders and to determine the limits to the valid powers of the other branches of government and to those of the national government as a whole. In discharging their responsibility, the national courts have generally found for the President and for national power. The national power to conduct foreign affairs is not dependent solely upon the assignments of the Constitution but is an inherent power of nationality, the court has said, and presidential claims, for example, those based upon executive agreements rather than treaties, have typically been sustained when challenged. Only when the President's or Congress' policies conflict with developing concepts of civil rights as in the case of efforts to deny passports to certain American citizens to travel abroad has the court found limits to national power. The courts also are in position to give effect to international law and thus to signal to the world American adherence to certain of its principles. In a suit by the Castro government of Cuba, for example, the Supreme Court in 1964 held that the courts of the United States could not question the legality of a foreign government's expropriation of property within its own borders. The issue, said the court, must be resolved by diplomacy not by litigation.

The courts play a minor role in foreign affairs

THE ROLE OF PARTIES AND PUBLIC OPINION

Critics of democracy have argued that consistent, reliable, and stable foreign policies are impossible in a state that changes leadership frequently, encourages public discussion in the absence of information or understanding, and permits partisanship to exploit ethnic, regional, economic, or religious minority interests. Domestic policies should stop at the water's edge, say those who are strongly impressed with these difficulties. Those in power and anxious to avoid criticism of their management of foreign affairs may also usually be found urging this view upon the American people. Foreign policy, nevertheless, does spring in part from partisan competition and the contest of interest groups. The American parties have differed on numerous occasions about foreign affairs. The Whigs were critical of the continental expansionist policies of the Democrats in the eighteen-forties; the Democrats were critical of the territorial acquisitions of the Republicans in the eighteen-nineties; the Republicans assailed President Wilson's League of Nations from 1919–1920. A large measure of agreement between the

Partisanship and foreign policy

parties has, however, characterized much of the era since World War II. On adherence to the charter of the United Nations, on the formation of the European alliance, on the efforts to halt the spread of communism and communist influence, there has been strong support from leaders in both parties. Senator Vandenberg (Republican of Michigan) worked closely with the Truman Administration in developing and implementing these policies and was able to carry with him most of his own colleagues. Senator George (Democrat of Georgia) worked closely with the Eisenhower Administration in support of these same policies and was able also to carry most of his fellow Democrats with him. Major differences have occurred mainly over our policies in Asia, the vigor with which we should resist Red Chinese influence, the support which should be accorded neutralist or unaligned states, and the proper attitude to newly emerging political communities in Africa as well as Asia. These differences are likely to be emphasized during political campaigns and subdued in the interim. Presidential hopefuls nowadays feel they must exhibit wide understanding of our foreign affairs and must be critical of the policies or the arrangements of those in power. Opposition party leadership in Congress is likely also to stake out areas of disagreement with the executive branch, and within the party factions may form around established and influential congressmen. Postures thus taken by candidates and legislators are likely to influence partisan activists in the state and local apparatus and thus to mobilize a certain amount of party support for present or prospective foreign policies. The broad consensus underpinning the major postwar policies appears to break down when as in Korea in the early nineteen-fifties and in Viet Nam since 1965 extensive military engagements are undertaken largely on presidential initiative, without formal declaration of war, and without any real expectation that the enemy will or should be conquered and forced to surrender.

Interest-group interest in foreign policy is growing

In addition to the party leaders and workers, many associations, corporations, labor unions, and religious orders have foreign-policy concerns and attempt to persuade the decision-makers to adopt or to modify policies benevolent to their interests and objectives. There are, perhaps, fewer interest groups oriented mainly to international concerns than there are promoting domestic programs, but the numbers concerned in foreign affairs are nevertheless considerable and growing. It has been difficult in the past to arouse even the more active interest-group members to concerns beyond the seas but as our exports of military and economic resources have multiplied so have the range of groups and interests involved. In many respects, however, we are still parochial in our outlook and our educational system and instrumentalities of communication give relatively little time and attention to Europe and almost none to Asia, Latin America, and Africa. It is not easy to change the habits and traditions of decades and our extensive international commitments and enterprises are not closely paralleled by wide public information about or understanding of the issues and problems of foreign affairs. A close student of the subject (G. Almond) believes, however, that the decade 1950–1960 produced a marked increase in the size of the attentive public and the level of education in foreign affairs as well as a decline in the depth and breadth of regional and ethnic differences over foreign-policy goals. In spite of this growing concern, it is doubtful if the attentive public to most matters of foreign policy is as great as 10 percent of the mass and is ordinarily a great deal smaller.

CONTEMPORARY AMERICAN FOREIGN POLICIES

Swept into World War II by Japanese attack and by our own mounting concern as friendly European democracies fell one by one to the forces of dictators, Americans found they must abandon the isolation and neutrality with which they had toyed in the nineteen-twenties and nineteen-thirties. Our European and Asiatic interests were simply too strong to be silenced or repressed. We entered the European fray, however, deeply opposed to "spheres of interest," "balance of power," and "imperial needs" concepts of European international dealings. Woodrow Wilson became again our guide and mentor. We sought no continental satellites, nor territorial enclaves, and used our influence to try to prevent our allies from realizing any such ambitions. A universal moral and legal order was the *The* best hope of peace we could claim, and we applied this theory through an *attempt* international organization constructed to prevent or, failing that, to punish *to build a* aggression. In the Washington Agreement of 1942 establishing the United *world* Nations as the military union of allies against Germany, Italy, and Japan, *order* an ultimate international organization was strongly suggested. In later declarations of the major allies in Moscow, Teheran, and Yalta, such a postwar international organization became a prime goal of the alliance. Meanwhile, American opinion expressed through Congress began to form in behalf of the concept. The House of Representatives in 1943 overwhelmingly adopted the Fulbright Resolution declaring in favor of American participation in "appropriate international machinery with power adequate to establish and to maintain a just and lasting peace among the nations of the world." The Senate, on its part adopted nearly unanimously the Connally resolution carefully worded to preserve the right of that body to pass upon the agreement by which we would commit ourselves to any such arrangement but endorsing membership in an association of nations with power "to prevent aggression and preserve the peace of the world." Thus before the war ended, we and our allies were solemnly committed to the Wilsonian idea. Our active leadership in 1945 in establishing "the United Nations demonstrated our commitment to this multi-lateral approach to international affairs.

Realistic statesmen then and now have, however, felt that American *The limits* foreign interests could not be fully, probably not even mainly, served *to "one* through such a facility. While publicly skeptical of "sphere of interest" *world"* diplomacy in Europe and Asia we continued to assert special prerogatives in the Western Hemisphere as against outside powers. Our old allies, Britain and France, were not prepared completely to abandon the goals and tactics of long standing in favor of a world organ which in its earlier form (League of Nations) had failed. Our new ally, the Soviet Union, regarded its attachment to the world order as of considerably less importance than protecting its European flank against future invasion across the Polish plains and than promoting communism everywhere. Nor could the problems created by the crumbling empires of England and France and the rising economic and political expectations of subject peoples everywhere be easily resolved by the new organ. These peoples, in fact, so changed the entire balance of voting power in the international agency that in a few years it bore little resemblance to the institution we had imagined. In consequence, the United States has felt obliged to seek regional arrangements aimed at halting the spread of communist influence both in Europe and Asia. We have been constrained to take over at least some of the long-standing interests of the British Empire in the Mediterranean and in South East Asia. We have had to develop new policies and procedures to deal with the hopes of the developing world and its leaders. We have had to recognize that some of the great new states, India and Indonesia for example, are not prepared to enter arrangements with the West which might jeopardize their ability to cooperate with the Soviets or the new China. We have found it desirable, in other words, to develop policies and programs peculiar to each of the major areas of the globe even though we continue to support the idea, at least, that international peace can only be achieved by a powerful international organization capable of resolving all disputes among states. After more detailed consideration of American participation in the United Nations, we shall, therefore, consider our foreign policies in Europe, Asia, Africa, the Middle East, and Latin America.

THE UNITED STATES AND THE UNITED NATIONS

From the first, the American people and perhaps some of their leaders expected too much of the United Nations. Driven perhaps by guilt because of our desertion of its predecessor, the League of Nations, and certainly by hope, born of war-time despair, we embraced the U.N. with the fervor ordinarily exhibited by the new convert. Disappointment when the hopes were quickly revealed to be unrealistic was, therefore, widespread and excessive. Now, more than twenty years after its formation, we can, perhaps, achieve a balanced appraisal of its value.

Founding of the U.N. The Charter of the United Nations was drafted at San Francisco in 1945 at a general international conference of some 50 nations after several key problems had been resolved by the "Big Three" (Roosevelt, Churchill, Stalin) at Yalta. American adherence was approved by the Senate (July

25, 1945) by the extraordinary vote of 89 to two and the other governments acted favorably so promptly that the new organization began functioning by early 1946. Doubts about the constitutional competence of the President and senate to commit the country to the obligations of membership in such a body had troubled several senators and other opinion-leaders in 1919. These doubts seemed of little or no concern in 1945.

The great problem in creating an international body to which authority of any importance is to be entrusted is how to equate nation–states of various capacities with the realities of international power and with the notion that people as people should count for something. Represent people as such and India and China, both in the throes of upheaval, would outvote the rest. Represent nations as such and Guatemala equals Argentina, Haiti, the United States. If power or resources are to be counted, on what basis? Military? Economic? These problems were not unknown to the framers of the Constitution of the United States. The framers of the Charter of the U.N., however, faced a more formidable task in reconciling the interests and aspirations of diverse cultures, languages, races, and traditions. The resolution hit upon was to create two major organs: (1) a General Assembly in which each member nation would have the same vote as every other regardless of size or resources and endowed with mainly deliberative and advisory functions; and (2) a Security Council charged with the primary responsibility for dealing with threats to peace anywhere in the world and with the creation and management of a U.N. military force, and made up of the five most powerful nations at that time as permanent members— China, France, United Kingdom, the Soviet Union, and the United States (the allied victors of W.W.II)—plus ten (originally six, but enlarged in 1965) other states to be selected for two-year terms by the General Assembly. In order to make certain that no major power would be obligated to support by force, economic sanction, or other measures any action of which it did not approve, each of the five was required to concur in any substantive decision of the Council for it to be valid. To these central organs were added (1) an International Court of Justice composed of 15 judges elected by the General Assembly on recommendation of the Security Council, sitting at the Hague and adjudicating disputes which might be brought before it under the provisions of a separate organizing "statute"; (2) an Economic and Social Council composed of 27 (originally 18, but enlarged in 1965) member–states chosen by the General Assembly and charged with efforts to improve worldwide social and economic conditions, especially where these might be potential sources of war; (3) a Trusteeship Council of seven trustee-member–states and seven nontrustee-member–states charged with supervising the administration of trust territories including the former League of Nations mandates plus any that might thereafter be placed under U.N. jurisdiction; and (4) a Secretariat servicing the principal organs and specialized agencies and headed by a Secretary–General who could direct the implementation of U.N. decisions.

People, nations, or resources as a basis for international order

UNITED NATIONS STRUCTURE: THE PATTERN OF THE ORGANIZATION

Congo Operations

Military Staff

Disarmament Commission

Atomic Energy Agency

Security Council

Secretariat

U.N. Special Fund

U.N.'s Children's Fund

High Commissioner for Refugees

General Assembly

Economic and Social Council

International Court of Justice

Trusteeship Council

Other Subsidiary Bodies of General Assembly

Committee on Atomic Radiation

Administrative and Budgetary Committee

International Law Commission

Mid-East Emergency Force

ECONOMIC COMMISSIONS

Asia

Europe

Latin America

Africa

International Trade

Narcotic Drugs

Status of Women

Human Rights

Social

Population

Statistical

FUNCTIONAL COMMISSIONS

FAO Food and Agriculture

IDA Development Aid

IFC Financial Aid

IMCO Maritime Affairs

WHO Health

ILO Labor

UNESCO Education, Science and Culture

IBRD World Bank

IMF Monetary Fund

WMO Meteorology

ICAO Civil Aviation

ITU Tele-communications

UPU Postal Affairs

SPECIALIZED AGENCIES

SOURCE: *The New York Times*, Sept. 24, 1961.

For the central organ, the Security Council, to be effective in dealing with threatening international controversies, it is quite clear that the five permanent members must agree. With each endowed with a veto, it would be impossible for the Council to deal with any situation in which the great powers opposed one another. The Soviet Union soon discovered that its efforts to build a cordon of satellite states protecting its European frontiers from Germany or the West, regardless of the wishes of some of the national communities concerned, was regarded by the United States, Britain, and France as contrary to war-time understandings and to the spirit and purpose of the U.N. It was, in American eyes, a return to "sphere of interest" diplomacy which bred international conflict. Its determination to pursue this goal and to encourage communist activities in the weakened states of western and southern Europe ushered in the Cold War and destroyed, for a time at least, any possibility of using the Security Council as an instrument of international order at least in Europe. The United States, on its part, increasingly evolved its own program and policies outside the U.N. to meet the Soviet thrust and to protect its asserted interests.

The break-up of the "Big Five"

A great problem of international institutions has been to make provision for peaceful change. Peace cannot be kept by freezing a status quo and those satisfied by the state of affairs at any time are apt to oppose change. The U.N. has developed no effective machinery for accommodating the constant movement in the affairs of man and nature. The Charter, for example, defines China as a great power and gives it a commensurate role. But does it refer to the China of Chiang Kai-Shek and the Kuomintang, beaten, dismembered and hurled from the mainland to the island of Taiwan or that of Mao Tse-Tung, triumphant over the vast reaches and hundreds of millions of people of the ancient empire but dedicated to continuous upheaval and international revolution until every vestige of Western power in Asia is forever destroyed. It is Chiang's Taiwan China, a nation of 13 million people which occupies the seat and votes with the great powers, not Mao's China of 650 million. What of Japan and Germany? The losers of 1945 nevertheless subsequently resurgent are equal or superior in resources to France. Although Japan was finally admitted to membership, the two Germanys and Red China are still on the outside. The United States, in particular, has steadfastly refused to support admission of Mao's China. Fearful of presidential vacillation on this issue, Congress has gone on record several times against China's admission. China's absence, nevertheless, has made it impossible for the U.N. to intercede effectively in Asian controversies, since the Chinese will not recognize its jurisdiction. Should Red China take the permanent seat on the Security Council, the peace-keeping abilities of that agency might be completely lost.

The problem of providing for peaceful change

The Assembly too has been greatly transformed by the currents of international politics. Originally, there were 51 members, and the West and its friends commanded a very strong majority. The United States was particularly influential. The roll has now more than doubled (126 members

The effect of the rise of new states

Member States of the United Nations
1968

WESTERN AND EUROPEAN BLOC		LATIN AMERICAN AND CARIBBEAN GROUP	
Australia	Malta	Argentina	Guyana
Austria	Netherlands	Barbados	Haiti
Belgium	New Zealand	Bolivia	Honduras
Canada	Norway	Brazil	Jamaica
China (Formosa)	Portugal	Chile	Mexico
Denmark	Spain	Colombia	Nicaragua
Finland	Sweden	Costa Rica	Panama
France	Turkey	Cuba	Paraguay
Greece	Union of	Dominican	Peru
Iceland	South Africa	Republic	Trinidad and
Ireland	United Kingdom	Ecuador	Tobago
Italy	United States	El Salvador	Uruguay
Luxemburg		Guatemala	Venezuela

ASIAN AND MIDDLE EASTERN GROUP		AFRICAN GROUP	
Afghanistan	Kuwait	Algeria	Malagasy Rep.
Burma	Laos	Botswana	Malawi
Cambodia	Lebanon	Burundi	Mali Fed.
Ceylon	Maldive Islands	Cameroon	Mauritania
Cyprus	Nepal	Central African	Mauritius
Federation of	Pakistan	Rep.	Morocco
Malaysia	Philippines	Chad	Niger
India	Saudi Arabia	Congo (formerly	Nigeria
Indonesia	Singapore	Belgian)	Rwanda
Iran	Southern Yemen	Congo (formerly	Senegal
Iraq	Syria	French)	Sierra Leone
Israel	Thailand	Dahomey	Somalia
Japan	Yemen	Equatorial Guinea	Sudan
Jordan		Ethiopia	Swaziland
		Gabon	Tanzania
SOVIET AND SATELLITES		Gambia	Togo
Albania	Poland	Ghana	Tunisia
Bulgaria	Rumania	Guinea	Uganda
Byelorussia	Ukraine	Ivory Coast	United Arab
Czechoslovakia	U.S.S.R.	Kenya	Rep.
Hungary	Yugoslavia	Lesotho	Upper Volta
Mongolia		Liberia	Zambia
		Libya	

in 1969) by the disintegration of the British and French empires in Africa, Asia, and the Middle East. The newly established states now comprise a majority of the voting members and they feel no strong identification with the West. In fact, most try to remain unaligned as between the contestants of the Cold War. Their interest in preserving the status quo is not strong and their various trade, aid, and race problems, and economic concepts are frequently at odds with those of the United States. The Assembly can and has on occasion provided a setting for attacks on Western institutions, on white dominion in Rhodesia and South Africa, and on the remaining colonial enclaves of Portugal and Britain. American official attitudes have, in consequence, changed direction twice. Frustrated in the Security Council in its efforts to establish the international forces anticipated by the Charter and forced to battle in Korea on the basis of a legally questionable Council procedure (made possible by the temporary absence of the Soviet Union), the United States attempted to shift some of the major responsibility for peace-keeping onto the Assembly where it commanded a strong following. The "Uniting for Peace" resolution of 1950 championed and pushed by the United States authorized the assembly to halt aggression whenever the Security Council failed due to the use of the great power veto. This resolution formed the basis for the establishment of the U.N. Emergency Force in the Middle East which helped end the Suez crisis of 1956. The rapid addition of member states from Africa and Asia, however, made Assembly action less and less attractive to us and in the sixties we have looked once again to the Security Council (somewhat enlarged in 1963) to aid in resolving the conflicts of India–Pakistan (1965), Israel–Arab states (1967), Czechoslovakia (1968), and Viet Nam (since 1964).

The numerous failures of the U.N. to keep the peace in the Middle East, India, Korea, Viet Nam, the Congo, Cyprus, or to turn back aggression like those in Hungary, Czechoslovakia, Assam, Tibet, and Goa have, perhaps, overshadowed its triumphs in Indonesia, Kashmir, Palestine, Cyprus and its successes in preventing the spread of conflicts in the Congo, Cyprus, and the Middle East. Although the international army contemplated by the Charter has never been established, substantial peace-keeping forces have been created *ad hoc* and are even now still in use in several trouble spots. Russia and France, however, continue to resist efforts to force them to contribute to the maintenance of those forces used in the Congo. Perhaps the greatest successes of the U.N. have been in the promotion of human welfare through financial and technical assistance to developing societies and through efforts to promote health, trade and mutual understanding. Under its aegis, institutions of international finance like the International Bank for Reconstruction and Development (World Bank), of regional cooperation like the Lower Mekong Delta Commission, of distribution of food like the World Food Program and many others too numerous to recite here have been created and have within their means alleviated a considerable amount of human suffering. Although their efforts are frequently overshadowed by the aid programs of particular states, their benefactions are without strings and are generally welcome anywhere. They have also probably stimulated the great powers to more vigorous unilateral efforts.

Achievements of the U.N.

On balance, the U.N. continues to deserve and to receive our support. It is doubtful if a better or more acceptable organization could be created by negotiation today. It provides a forum where most grievances can be aired, even if not resolved, and where multi-lateral diplomacy can be tried whenever the leaders of the earth have the will or wit to do so. Its institutions have survived major efforts by the Soviets to undermine or remake them and our own vacillating between Council and Assembly.

THE UNITED STATES AND EUROPE: CONTAINMENT

The ties of kinship, common cultural inheritance, and economic interest have for generations related the American people to Europe more closely than to any other part of the globe. Even today when horizons have broadened, and interests extended, many of us still regard our primary international interests as maintaining close and friendly relations with the peoples of western Europe. In this century we have been drawn into terrible battles for the independence and security of our European friends. One of our recent Presidents declared himself "a Berliner" and several have placed our frontiers of interest on the Oder and the Adriatic. Earlier in this century the chief threats to our European position arose from Germany; now they arise from the Soviet Union. After the honeymoon of victory and the United Nations, we realized that the Soviet was determined to build a bloc of satellite states from the Baltic to the Mediterranean to protect its frontier from Western attack and to keep western Europe weak. Poland, Hungary, Rumania, Bulgaria, Albania, Yugoslavia were all roped to the Soviet orbit and "friendly" regimes established or supported, contrary in most cases to understandings reached at Yalta. Pressure was placed on Greece and then Czechoslovakia and the disruptive and growing Communist parties of France, Italy, and Germany were all encouraged. We felt threatened and our reaction was to take steps outside the U.N. to contain the Russian thrust, and thus began the Cold War between the two most powerful nations on earth.

Expedients for containing Russian power:

1. Aid to Greece and Turkey

The turning point in American–Soviet relations came in 1947. The Moscow Conference of foreign ministers of the "Big Four" early in that year achieved not a single important agreement and ended all hope of the "friendly" cooperation for which we had been striving since 1945. Even while the conference was in progress, President Truman took the first large step to curb Russian expansion. In a message to Congress on March 12, 1947, he called attention to northern Greece, where protracted guerrilla operations under encouragement from Moscow were threatening a coup overthrowing the Greek government the support of which, we were told, was no longer within British capabilities, and delivering the country to communism. Such a coup if successful would put Russia on the Mediterranean and place Turkey and the strategic Dardanelles in an impossible position. To avert such a disaster, he proposed that the United States at once bolster local resistance by giving both Greece and Turkey liberal aid in the form of money, goods, military supplies, and military counsel. During vigorous and prolonged discussion in Congress and outside, it was objected that by such independent action the United States would be bypassing the organization ostensibly existing for dealing with such threats to world peace and order, the U.N. The President replied that the need was too urgent to permit of waiting for the U.N. to organize measures, that the harassed countries had no place to turn except to the United States. Under an act approved quickly, the United States launched a program of assistance (an initial appropriation of $400 million was voted) to the two countries which continued for several years. Regimes friendly to the West were stabilized and the threatened subversion thwarted.

Hardly had the new idea of employing material aid to bolster war-torn nations against Soviet seduction been inaugurated before a vastly broader field opened for applying it. While Congress was still debating assistance to Greece and Turkey, the State Department published a significant study under the title of *The Development of the Foreign Reconstruction Policy of the United States.* A few weeks later Secretary of State George C. Marshall dramatized the document in a commencement address at Harvard University, outlining an ambitious scheme for cooperative but mainly American assistance in a general rehabilitation of the sagging national economies of western Europe. At the outset, the plan was not avowedly anti-Russian; on the contrary, the U.S.S.R. and its satellites were invited to participate in it. When, however, the invitation met with flat refusal, the project—promptly named by journalists the Marshall plan—was fast reoriented as a phase of the Truman program for employing American resources and power to contain, or block, the Soviet Union's aspirations. The rationale of this program was that if tired, impoverished, and despondent Western peoples could be helped to their feet and given a vision of better things under a revived economy, the strong communist parties then operating in many nations would lose their appeal. In response to a request from Washington, 16 European governments conferred on the extent of their needs and on what they and their peoples could themselves do toward meeting them, arriving in the end at a four-year rehabilitation program under which the United States (mainly) was to be asked to supply goods, money, and credit to a total for the period of $22.44 billion. Warmly supporting the project, President Truman passed it on—under the name of the European Recovery Program (E.R.P.)—to Congress, convoked in special session. After debates carrying over into the following year, he was able, on April 3, 1948, to affix his signature to a Foreign Assistance Act, embracing aid for countries outside of the 16 (for example, China), but with the major Title I designated as the Economic Cooperation Act. The legislation although limited to a single year was continued with some changes over the next four years.

Rarely has a program been so strikingly successful in achieving its aims. All told something over $29 billion has been poured into Europe and its recovery has been phenomenal. In fact, the economies of Germany and France, in particular, became strong competitors with that of America in the international market. Moderate governments have everywhere been in control and as these nations have become strong the Russian threat has become less menacing.

The communist coup in Czechoslovakia in 1948, transforming that unhappy country into a satellite of the U.S.S.R., convinced the leading

2. The Marshall plan:

a. Origin and purpose

b. Adoption

3. The Atlantic Alliance

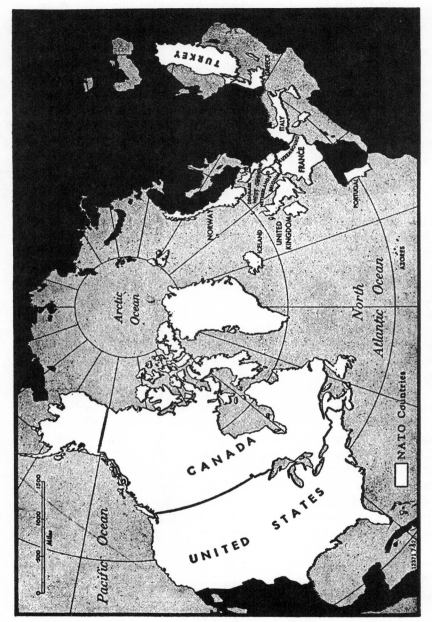

THE NORTH ATLANTIC ALLIANCE

NATO Countries

statesmen of western Europe that Russia would not be content simply to consolidate its gain of World War II but was bent on continued expansion. Great Britain, France, the Netherlands, Belgium, and Luxembourg meeting at Brussels in March of 1948 joined together in a fifty-year mutual military alliance against aggression. American support was essential if the Western bloc was to constitute an effective barrier against Russian advance. President Truman spoke out bluntly to Congress calling for American support and enlarging on the Russian menace. Led by Senator Vandenberg (Republican of Michigan), the Senate adopted by a vote of 64 to four a resolution declaring that this country should by constitutional processes seek peace and security by the "progressive development of regional . . . arrangements for . . . collective self-defense." Early in 1949, the President submitted for Senate ratification a North Atlantic Pact uniting the five nations of the Brussels Pact with seven other nations of the "Atlantic community" in a defensive military alliance. Apart from the Inter-American Pact of 1947 uniting the nations of the Western Hemisphere in resisting aggression from outside, this was the first alliance of its kind seriously considered by the United States for more than a century. After extended hearings and debates the Senate approved American adherence by a vote of 82 to 13. The North Atlantic Treaty remains a major pillar of contemporary American foreign policy in Europe. By this pact the twelve nations agreed that an armed attack on any one of them in Europe or North America is to be regarded as an armed attack against all; and if such an attack occurs, they will take action, including the use of armed force, necessary to maintain the security of the North Atlantic area. Greece and Turkey acceded to the treaty in 1952 and were added to the allied states.

The North Atlantic Treaty provides for continuing consultation among the signatories to develop ways and means, mainly military, for making the alliance formidable. A Council of Foreign Ministers of the participating nations and a Defense Committee of the Defense Ministers were specifically established in the treaty. In the fall of 1949, these organs formally began their work under the general title of North Atlantic Treaty Organization (N.A.T.O.). In 1951, General Eisenhower took command of headquarters established near Paris from which it was hoped to build a coordinated armed force of the units dedicated to N.A.T.O. by the various allies. The military forces which the United States might contribute to the joint endeavor became the subject of a lengthy debate in the Congress, largely over the question of the proper way in which the Congress ought to be involved in such a determination. The Senate, by resolution, in 1951 finally approved an increase of American divisions stationed in western Europe from two to six, but suggested that congressional consent should be obtained by the President for the sending of any more.

a. Strengthening the defense of western Europe

All efforts to reunite Germany having failed, the most difficult problem confronting the Western allies was the role to be accorded friendly West Germany. The United States strongly urged the rearmament of the Germans

b. The problem of Germany

and the inclusion of German divisions in the armed forces of the allies. The European victims of German aggression in World War II were, on the other hand, as frightened by a rearmed Germany as by an aggressive Russia. To America, the attempt to defend industrial western Europe against a Russian advance with a hostile or possibly indifferent Germany seemed unthinkable. The leaders of N.A.T.O. finally in 1952 after months of negotiations worked out a series of treaties and agreements bringing in West Germany but the French refused to agree that virtually complete independence would be accorded West Germany and that the guarantees of the Atlantic Pact would in general be extended to West Germany. France refused to ratify the key agreements and scuttled this program and a new series of accords had to be hammered out in 1954.

Under the 1954 agreements (1) West Germany was invited to become a member of N.A.T.O.; (2) Italy and West Germany were invited to accede to the Brussels Treaty of 1948; (3) a new organization of the Brussels pact states called a Western European Union was created and endowed with power to control the armaments dedicated to support of the Union; (4) full sovereignty was restored to West Germany and the allied occupation was ended; (5) a substantial military contribution to N.A.T.O. by West Germany was authorized but the size and character of this contribution was carefully limited in deference to French anxiety over a rearmed Germany; (6) West Germany was required to renounce the right to manufacture atomic and nuclear weapons. Those agreements to which the United States was a party were submitted to the Senate and ratified. The other nations, in their turn, also ratified the pacts, France finally acceding after another set of agreements between it and West Germany over the Saar were fashioned. Although the completion of the network of agreements uniting the Atlantic states in a solid bloc did not of itself create the strong military forces ultimately contemplated by the Allies, it did present the Soviet with a strong front and the Russian attitude in Europe began to change perceptibly. A peace treaty was finally concluded with Austria in March, 1955, ending the occupation and restoring its sovereignty after years of frustrating negotiations. So conciliatory grew the tone of Russian diplomacy that a top-level meeting of the "Big Four" reminiscent of the late years of World War II was held in Geneva in mid-summer of 1955. At the Geneva meeting the tone of all participants was most conciliatory. President Eisenhower went so far in an effort to find a solution for the armaments race as to propose swapping blueprints and aerial photographs of defense installations with the Russians. The important issues—the status of Germany and armaments reductions—were referred by the leaders to a conference of their foreign ministers to be held later at Geneva. This conference, held in late October and early November of 1955, ended without a single agreement of consequence between the East and West. And all subsequent negotiations including those of the Geneva Conference of Foreign Ministers of the "Big Four" in 1959, the abortive "summit" conference of the heads of state of the same powers in 1960 in Paris, and the meeting of Kennedy and Khrushchev in 1961—have also failed to produce any new accord on the status of Germany. The Soviets have strongly opposed the rearmament of West Germany and refer frequently to the danger of allowing Germany to have nuclear arms.

The most vulnerable spot in the defensive posture of the N.A.T.O. alliance is still Berlin. The capital of the former German Reich was left, by the military and political settlements of 1944–1945, an island of joint Western–Soviet responsibility in the midst of the Soviet occupation zone—later the Soviet dominated German Democratic Republic. Large sections of the city were assigned to each of the four powers and in those under Western authority a large measure of self-government with free elections was soon established. All land access to this bastion of Western strength, however, must be across territory controlled by the Soviet Union. The Russians struck quickly after the collapse of the war-time alliance and sealed off the city in 1949. The Western position and that of the citizens of West Berlin were saved only by a mammoth air lift organized by the West. Late in 1958, after efforts to weaken N.A.T.O. and prevent the rearming of West Germany had failed, the Soviet Union again sought to exploit this chink in the Western armor. In November it announced that unless negotiations looking toward a final settlement of the German question were begun in six months, it would make a separate peace with the German Democratic Republic and assign all its rights in Berlin to this satellite state. The Western powers would then be forced to negotiate with East Germany for their continued position in Berlin. The Russians indicated that in case of "trouble" they would support their puppet state. A conference of the foreign ministers of Britain, France, Russia, and the United States assembled in Geneva in mid-1959 and after prolonged discussions of the conflicting proposals for a German peace settlement adjourned without agreement. For a year, the Soviet Union pounded away at the West in soft and friendly and then in strident and belligerent tones. Khrushchev visited the United States in the fall of 1959, disavowed any ultimatum on Berlin, spoke of his hopes for amicable relationships, and promoted his country and his plan for a new "summit" conference. The conference finally occurred in May of 1960 in Paris and was dissolved almost before it began by a vigorous Russian attack on the United States and President Eisenhower for spying on the Soviet Union by means of high-flying planes, one of which was unhappily captured just prior to the conference meeting. The Russians then began to step up their pressure for a Berlin settlement on their own terms. A meeting in June, 1961 with President Kennedy in Vienna achieved no apparent results and the Russians increased their pressure.

Kennedy announced that the Soviet aim was to dislodge the West from Berlin and increased troop strength in the beleaguered city. The denouement in August 1961 was the construction of a wall sealing off the Soviet zones and virtually halting all movement between the zones. Menac-

c. Berlin: the "Achilles heel"

BERLIN AND THE TWO GERMANYS — 1967

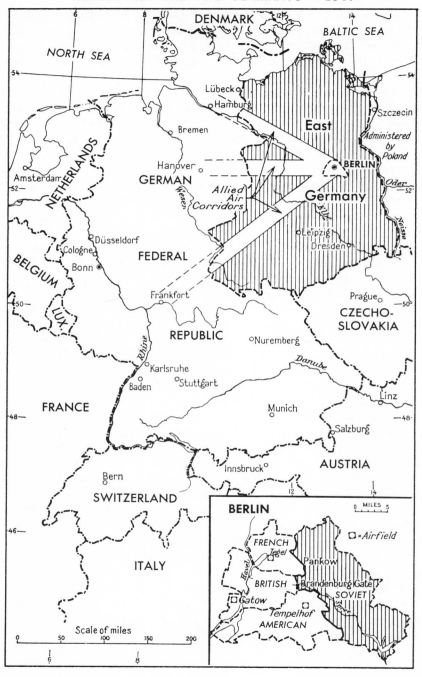

DENMARK

NORTH SEA

BALTIC SEA

NETHERLANDS

Amsterdam

Lübeck

Hamburg

Bremen

Hanover

GERMAN

East

Szczecin

Administered by Poland

BERLIN

Oder

Germany

Allied Air Corridors

Weser

BELGIUM

LUX

Düsseldorf

Cologne

Bonn

FEDERAL

Leipzig

Dresden

Elbe

Neisse

Frankfort

Prague

CZECHO-SLOVAKIA

Rhine

REPUBLIC

Nuremberg

Karlsruhe

Baden

Stuttgart

Danube

FRANCE

Munich

Linz

Salzburg

AUSTRIA

Innsbruck

Bern

SWITZERLAND

ITALY

Scale of miles

0   50   100   150   200

BERLIN

0 MILES 5 =Airfield

FRENCH

Tegel

Havel

Pankow

BRITISH

Brandenburg Gate

SOVIET

Gatow

Tempelhof

AMERICAN

ing gestures continued through 1962 and Congress responded by a resolution that "this country is determined to prevent by whatever means necessary, including the use of force," any Soviet violation of Allied rights in Berlin. In 1963, on a personal visit, President Kennedy assured the Berliners of our continued support. The Soviets finally did sign a treaty with East Germany in 1964 but it recognized Soviet rights in Berlin and was not the separate peace the leaders had threatened. Since that time the uneasy truce has continued, punctuated by occasional stoppages of traffic through East Germany by Soviet and East German officials or soldiers, probing Western responses. In 1968, East Germany began requiring visas and passports for all travel by West German's through its territory. Currency and other restrictions were also imposed.

Apart from an allusion to "mutual aid," the North Atlantic Pact obligates the United States to no program of military assistance. Such assistance, however, had been given Greece and Turkey since 1947 and Nationalist China over a longer period. No one doubted that American aid would be required by the more needy Atlantic Pact states if they were to rebuild their armies. No sooner, indeed, was the pact assured than a comprehensive and coordinated program of American assistance long in preparation was placed before Congress. President Truman was able to sign a Mutual Defense Assistance Act in October, 1949, authorizing aid for the Atlantic Pact states, but also in relatively small amounts for Greece, Turkey, Iran, Korea, the Philippines, and the "general area" of China. Thus was launched the third great program of bolstering friendly nations with American money against communist subversion or attack. By 1951, the military-aid program for western Europe far overshadowed the Marshall plan aid. Since that time $16 billion in military assistance has been provided to our European allies. *4. Military aid to friendly nations*

The Marshall plan helped make western Europe prosperous; military assistance helped make it formidable. The first great "entangling alliance" of the United States, a solid pillar of its modern foreign policy, is nevertheless in deep trouble as it approaches its twentieth anniversary. Its troubles are the consequences of its successes. Soviet adventure in western Europe is no longer feared. Repeated probings have revealed few signs of American unwillingness to defend the position of its allies. Nuclear power has reached a stalemate and Russian rockets can leap over Europe and strike America directly. The heavy commitments by the French in Algeria and Indochina have been liquidated and the blood and treasure spared for European achievements. The movement for European unity, underlying American hopes, has slowed down to a crawl after the striking successes of the Coal and Steel Community and the Common Market. France, led by de Gaulle, has embarked on an independent course aimed at (1) reducing American and British influence on the continent; (2) developing nuclear capabilities for itself; (3) regulating the nature and scope of German participation in European affairs; and (4) seeking accommodation directly with the Soviets. In pursuance of these aims, France has blocked British entrance to the *a. N.A.T.O. in the sixties*

Common Market (1963 and 1967), refused to participate in the joint-allied, multi-lateral submarine force armed with missiles and nuclear warheads (approved by England and the U.S. in 1962), driven all American troops and installations from France as well as N.A.T.O. headquarters, sharply criticized American policy in Asia especially in Viet Nam, and refused to support U.N. peace-keeping operations in Africa. On its part, Great Britain is anxious to reduce its military commitments on the continent as it already has done in Asia, largely for economic reasons. West Germany seeks its own nuclear capabilities and rapprochement with East Germany. The United States, as its involvement in Asia has grown and as threats to its currency have mounted is also anxious to reduce its troop commitments in Europe and seeks agreement with Russia to halt the further spread of nuclear weapons. The Allies are divided and the Alliance is in disarray.

b. The Soviet path also thorny   The Soviet Union, on its part, has not only had to accommodate to the resurgence of western Europe, but has found that keeping its own satellites —most of them also its allies in the Warsaw Pact, a response to N.A.T.O.— in line is not easy. Yugoslavia early, successfully asserted its independence of Moscow although it remained communist. The Hungarians, after a show of independence, had to be crushed by the Soviet Army in 1965. Albania has for sometime now sided with Red China in the international communist movement. Rumania successfully asserted a modicum of independence in 1966. Poland and East Germany experienced demonstrations of discontent which were fairly quickly restrained and in 1968, Czechoslovakia carried its efforts to liberalize its government to the point where it too was invaded by the Soviets and their Warsaw allies.

THE UNITED STATES AND ASIA

c. "Containment" not so appropriate to Asia   No such successes as have accompanied American policies in Europe characterize our postwar experience in Asia and whereas the Marshall plan, N.A.T.O., and military aid have been widely supported comparable policies in Asia have been bitterly criticized and widely condemned. The greatest setback for American hopes for political stability and economic development on Western lines in Asia, was the overturn in 1947–1949 of the Chinese government of Chiang Kai-Shek by the communists led by Mao Tse-Tung. Chiang's nationalist regime was hurled from the mainland and forced to establish itself—with much American help—on the former Japanese colony of Formosa (Taiwan). After consolidating their position, the Chinese Reds soon began pressing Western positions throughout Southeast Asia. The loss of China as an ally and the resultant decline in Western influence in Asia precipitated angry and bitter controversy in the United States. Charges of "softness on Communism," mismanagement, ineptitude, and downright disloyalty were hurled across the political lines—especially in 1952, but to some extent ever since then. Countering Chinese pressure, we have tried with indifferent results to use many of the same procedures used in Europe. Until 1962–1963, the Chinese Reds were closely and continuously supported by the Soviets and many of our policies assumed an identity of interests of the two powers as well as heavy dependence by China on Russia. A split between the two began to appear about that time, however, and it has widened steadily with virulent recrimination. The ostensible conflict is over the stated Soviet aim of "peaceful coexistence" with the West. The Chinese have placed themselves at the head of a school of communism advocating "no peace, no compromise, no deals with the West," and are at present much the most aggressively anti-American of the communist states. How to deal with their name-calling intransigence has baffled American statesmen. A vocal minority of interested citizens has steadily criticized our refusal to recognize the Red regime or to support its admission to the U.N. The attempt to isolate the Reds has been unwise and unsuccessful, they argue. We cannot however, abandon Taiwan, allow communism to spread through Southeast Asia, or ignore the nuclear capabilities the Reds are developing, respond the defenders of the present posture.

Although unable or unwilling to intervene forcefully to preserve Nationalist China, we have been unhappily obliged to abandon diplomacy for the battlefield. In Korea that effort to halt communist expansion has involved the United States—and the United Nations for the first time—in costly and divisive war. During World War II, the United States, Great Britain, China, and near the close the U.S.S.R. agreed that after the country's liberation from Japanese rule, Korea should again become a free and independent nation. As a matter of convenience Russian authorities received the surrender of Japanese forces in the Korean north and American authorities that of forces in the south; and for the purpose, an arbitrary dividing line was fixed at the 38th parallel. Before long, it became apparent that, quite contrary to American intention, the U.S.S.R. proposed to regard the division as permanent. Although Russian troops were alleged to have been withdrawn from the northern zone in 1948, every effort of the United States, supported by associates in the recent war, to bring about the creation of a free government for a united Korea was frustrated. In the north, a well-armed puppet communist regime—the Democratic People's Republic of Korea—arose under encouragement from Moscow. In the south, a Republic of Korea was established as an independent nation in 1948 after a free election held under the auspices of the United Nations—a republic promptly recognized by the United States and 31 other U.N. members, although barred by Soviet veto from membership on its own part. With the northern communist regime from the first claiming jurisdiction over the entire country, there always was danger that it would attempt by force to make its asserted authority good. On June 25, 1950, a military assault across the 38th parallel was launched with that end in view. A seven-man United Nations commission concluding investigations in the

5. Armed resistance in Korea:

a. The U.N. moves to halt aggression

country at the time testified—as was well known from other sources—that the attack was entirely unprovoked and unjustified. At the request of the United States the U.N. Security Council instantly took notice of it, insisting upon an immediate cessation of hostilities, requesting all U.N. members to refrain from aiding the aggressors, and, as the situation grew worse, calling upon all to assist in repelling the invasion. Fifty-three of the 60 U.N. members joined in condemning the North Koreans' action, and in time more than 30 pledged material assistance in stopping it.

b. The role of the United States
The military operations that ensued proved decidedly more prolonged, difficult, and costly than originally expected. With encouragement and assistance from both the U.S.S.R. and communist China, the invaders overran almost the whole of the South Korean territory. South Korea itself was not well organized or equipped for defense; the United States had withdrawn virtually all of its military forces from the country in 1949; American funds voted for Korean aid had not been fully or effectively used; for a time, poorly armed Koreans and handfuls of American occupation troops brought over from Japan could fight only delaying actions, with danger of being pushed into the sea. Calls of United Nations upon its members brought wide moral support and appreciable naval and air, with some ground, assistance. The bulk of the armed forces were supplied by the United States and with U.N. authorization were quickly thrown into action. By late autumn a successful conclusion of the operation seemed in sight— when suddenly the entire picture was changed by the entrance of communist China into the conflict; for a time gravely threatening total defeat for U.N. forces. The U.N. forces finally succeeded in driving the Chinese back north of the 38th parallel and there the battle lines were stabilized.

c. The armistice
As the Korean struggle settled into a stalemate approximately along the 38th parallel a growing rift between the Truman Administration and General MacArthur, the Commander of U.N. forces in Korea, burst into the open. The issue concerned the character and scope of American policy toward Red China. The General was anxious to push forward to complete victory in Korea by bringing military pressure on the Chinese in Manchuria and China if necessary even at the risk of an all-out war with China and perhaps with its ally, Russia. The administration, under grave pressure from its Atlantic Pact allies, was unwilling to push China too far. It feared that plunging our armies into a huge effort against the unlimited Chinese manpower would open western Europe to the Russians. On April 11, 1951, President Truman relieved MacArthur of his commands in the Far East. The General returned somewhat in the style of a conquering hero, plunging the nation and the Congress into a violent debate over the administration's Korean policy. Truman held firm in the face of the bitter controversy and the congressional efforts of his critics ended inconclusively. Persuaded by a Russian hint and by an earnest desire to have done with the Korean "police action," the United States agreed to open armistice negotiations under the U.N. banner with the North Korean leaders in July of 1951. One

train of patient negotiators after another debated over the table first at Kaesong and later at Panmunjon for month after weary month. By early 1952 agreement had been reached on all points save one—the repatriation of prisoners of war. There the truce talks bogged down for nearly a year. A new President, Eisenhower, in fulfillment of a campaign pledge visited Korea to try to end deadlock. In general, however, he gave support to the position of his predecessor. In April of 1953, the talks were resumed and, after a difficult period with the head of the South Korean Republic, Syngman Rhee, final agreements were concluded in July of 1953. A cease-fire accompanied by a withdrawal of the armies two kilometers from the battle line and a voluntary repatriation of prisoners were the highlights of the settlement. A commission of "neutral" states was created to enforce the arrangements. A meeting of the South Koreans and their U.N. defenders with the North Koreans, Chinese, and Russians in Geneva in 1954 failed to find a more permanent solution and the armistice continues. Both Chinese and U.N. forces, however, have been withdrawn in large numbers but not completely from the war-torn peninsula. The uneasy truce continues, punctuated occasionally by incursions from the North and, dramatically in 1968 by the capture by the communists of an American naval vessel (The Pueblo) and her crew, which while gathering intelligence may well have strayed too close to shore. Negotiations for the exchange of crew were completed late in 1968.

Korea dramatized the scope and nature of American concerns in the Pacific and also precipitated a vigorous and continuing controversy about the aims of America in this area and the best method to achieve them. The Republicans had seized on the loss of China to berate the Truman Administration and every single act of omission or commission was scrutinized and analyzed to show ignorance and incompetence if not willful treachery by a group which had always been "soft," as the extremists put it, toward communism. The MacArthur dismissal was a high point of the controversy, but the campaign of 1952 was filled with angry words. The election of President Eisenhower did not quiet the debate; for he soon felt obliged to part company with some of the staunchest critics of the Truman policies, including Senator Knowland, floor leader of the Republican party in the Senate. Of the many issues in this controversy, one of the major ones has been whether the gravest threat to American interests is in Europe, as the Truman Administration seemed to believe, or in Asia as the Republican critics declared. In any event, no one thought Asia could be ignored or that the communist influence could be allowed to spread throughout the peoples of this area unchallenged.

The first major move in the Pacific, after the fighting began in Korea, was to strengthen Japan as a friendly fortress against the Soviet–Chinese advance. A peace treaty bringing to an end the enemy status of Japan was negotiated throughout much of 1950 and 1951 by John Foster Dulles, later to become Republican secretary of state, in collaboration with most

6. Formation of Pacific alliances:

a. Japan

of our Allies of World War II. At a conference in San Francisco in September, 1951, the treaty was formally approved by more than 40 nations invited to participate. Russia attended the conference but refused to sign the treaty when its proposals for amendments were rejected. The treaty imposed no penalties or disabilities on the Japanese except for loss of outlying possessions which had been anticipated. Sovereignty was restored to the nation but a Security Treaty signed at the same time with the United States permitted our armed forces to remain in Japan to help maintain the peace in the Far East and the security of Japan. This right was to continue as long as necessary. Both treaties were appropriately ratified and Japan attained formal sovereignty on April 28, 1952. The next major step in the build-up of the Japanese came in 1954 when the United States concluded a mutual defense agreement with Japan providing for the progressive rearmament of Japan with American aid. The Japanese promised in return to make the "full contribution" permitted by its resources to the defense of the free world. Economic and military aid began thereafter to flow from the United States to Japan.

In 1960, the United States negotiated a new mutual security treaty with Japan to replace that of 1952. Under its terms, United States armed forces could continue to use Japanese facilities, but in accompanying notes, it was made clear that the Japanese would be consulted before any major shift in their deployment, or change in their equipment (nuclear weapons) or before they would be used in combat operations. Although this treaty was more favorable to the Japanese than the one it replaced, its ratification was accomplished in the Japanese Diet only after a prolonged crisis including riots. So grave and menacing was the crisis that the Japanese government was forced to ask President Eisenhower to cancel his proposed visit. Subsequent visits to the U.S. by Prime Ministers Ikeda in 1961 and Sato in 1967 have repaired much of the wounded feeling in this country. Sato won agreement for a return of the Bonin Islands to Japan but continued American control of Okinawa and the Ryukyus is not widely popular in Japan. Nor are American efforts to restrain a closer economic rapprochement between Japan and Red China. However, Japan continues to rely upon American arms for its own security and officially at least to support our efforts in Viet Nam.

b. Australia, New Zealand, Philippines, and Korea

Some of the victims of Japanese attacks in World War II were not anxious to build up this aggressive nation. To alleviate this anxiety the United States concluded with Australia and New Zealand a mutual defense pact. This pact, negotiated just prior to the Japanese Peace Treaty, provides (Article IV) that "an armed attack in the Pacific area on any of the parties" would be regarded by each party as "dangerous to its own peace and safety" and each party promises to "act to meet the common danger in accordance with its constitutional processes." A similar treaty was also concluded with the Philippines at the same time. South Korea demanded similar guarantees as a price for accepting the armistice and early in 1954 such a treaty was ratified by the Senate.

The Red drive, stopped at the 38th parallel in Korea, now shifted to French Indochina and after months of hostilities between communist-led northerners and French-supported southerners, four new states—one of which was frankly Red dominated—were created by international agreement at Geneva in the summer of 1954. The French were unable or unwilling to continue the struggle and America would not intervene militarily, although it gave a great deal of aid to the French regime. The American secretary of state, Mr. Dulles, now sought to create in the whole Southern Pacific area a concert of powers and resources similar to N.A.T.O. Led by India, however, a major portion of the peoples of this area were determined to remain neutral in the communist–West conflict. The best that could be achieved was a union of Pakistan and Thailand with the Philippines, Britain, France, Australia, New Zealand, and the United States. A Southeast Asia Defense Treaty was worked out by these states at Manila in September, 1954. This treaty dealt with aggression against the territory of the signatories in about the same way as had the other Pacific mutual defense treaties. It extended the area of concern, however, to include the Indochinese states of Laos, Cambodia, and South Viet Nam. It also attempted to deal with aggression by internal subversion. Threat of subversion from inside of any of the participating states is agreed to be a matter of concern for all and they promise in such a case to "consult together immediately" to agree on measures for common action. A Council (S.E.A.T.O.) and other appropriate implementing agencies were established to concert energies, resources, and policies. The United States Senate ratified the Southeast Asia Collective Defense Treaty in the spring of 1955.

c. Indochina and S.E.A.T.O.

Communist pressure in Southeast Asia, halted for a time by the Geneva settlement of 1954, resumed in mid-1960. Infiltrating Laos from communist held North Vietnam, the Reds by late 1961 controlled a substantial part of the northeastern area of the country. The S.E.A.T.O. states, assembled in Bangkok in March, 1961 pressed for a negotiated settlement. The United States believed that a cease-fire should precede negotiations and asserted that it would agree to a neutral and independent state. Negotiations begun at Geneva in late 1961 looking toward a neutralized Laos were completed in 1962 by the formation of a coalition government of the major rivals in that strife-torn land. Meanwhile in May, American troops were rushed to Thailand under S.E.A.T.O. agreements to strengthen its borders should Laos fall to the communists and some military "technicians" were loaned to the Laos central government. The Soviet Union has formally supported the neutrality declaration as did the contending parties in Laos but the struggle has not as yet ended. Massive aid, together with some military assistance was also poured into South Viet Nam.

Laos crisis 1960–1961

In 1963, the Reds of North Viet Nam, aided by Russia and China, stepped up their pressure on the weak and unstable (American-supported) regime of South Viet Nam, and in cooperation with the local communist organization, the Viet Cong, gradually extended their hold on the villages

The war in Viet Nam

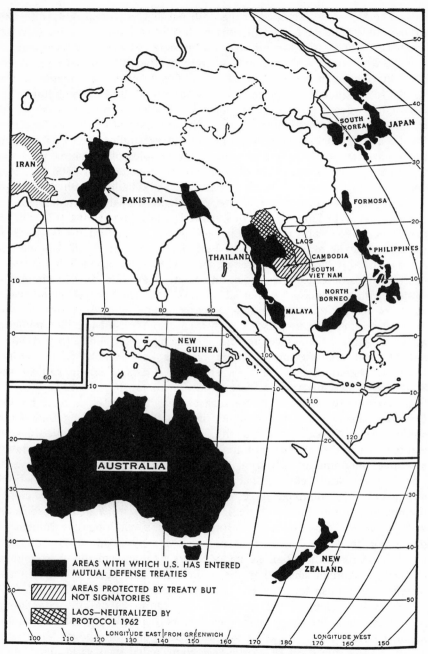

ASIATIC DEFENSIVE TREATY ARRANGEMENTS OF THE U.S.

Iraq and Iran are indirectly affiliated with the United States' defensive treaty arrangements.

490

and the countryside. The U.S. poured in heavier aid in an effort to strengthen the recognized government's will and capacity to resist. Then in August of 1964, we struck with our air force at Hanoi, capital of the North, in retaliation for reported torpedo boat attacks on American destroyers in the Gulf of Tonkin. Congress, at the President's request, backed the decision to use force by a resolution pledging "all necessary steps, including the use of armed force, to assist any member or protocol state (Laos, Cambodia, South Viet Nam) of S.E.A.T.O. requesting assistance in defense of its freedom. From then on, American military involvement has been sharply "escalated" by bombing and by the deployment of land and sea forces—more than 500,000 troops are now engaged—until our exertions and expenditures now equal or exceed those in Korea. Repeated offers to negotiate a settlement, provided the independence of South Viet Nam is assured and the people of that country are fully allowed to establish their own government, met with no acceptable response until 1968 when Hanoi agreed to meet the U.S. in Paris and begin talks. Meanwhile the American effort has been denounced by many of our allies but especially by France, criticized by the secretary general of the U.N. and vigorously condemned in America. The campaign of 1968 centered around the issue. The candidacies of Senator McCarthy (Minnesota), Senator Kennedy (New York) and then after Kennedy's assassination, Senator McGovern (South Dakota) were based upon criticism of the Johnson policy. Protests and demonstrations against the war and against the draft have been widespread. President Johnson, unable to unite his country or his party announced his retirement from the Presidency, in part so that he might more successfully negotiate a peace. In fact, the Paris talks started after Johnson announced he would not run for a new term and would halt the bombing of most of North Viet Nam. North Viet Nam demanded as a price of beginning any meaningful negotiation a complete cessation of American bombing of their territory; the U.S. replied that a complete bombing halt would expose its troops to reenforced and heavily supplied enemy units. A complete cessation of bombing in the north was finally announced by the President, Oct. 31, 1968. Rarely has an American military action provoked such a torrent of wrath at home. Alongside of those who denounce our Viet Nam actions as immoral and imperialistic and demand immediate withdrawal are an equally clamorous group of the MacArthur–Korean school who demand an end of restraint and an even more vigorous push to complete victory.

d. Nationalist China

The S.E.A.T.O. defensive arrangements still left unsettled and undefended, except by the United States, the forlorn remnant of Nationalist China on Formosa and other islands nearby. The communists of China were clearly determined to conquer this last outpost of opposition on what they, and most of the world, regarded as Chinese territory. Britain did not recognize the Nationalist regime and, therefore, could not or would not agree to aid in its defense. During the Korean "police action," President Truman had

ordered the United States Seventh Fleet to patrol the waters between Formosa and the mainland to prevent military action by either group of
Chinese against the other. President Eisenhower early directed the commander of the Seventh Fleet not to interfere with military action of the
Nationalists aimed at the communists but to continue to protect the Nationalists. There was no indication, however, that nationalist leader Chiang
Kai-shek was either willing or able to take the offensive on his own behalf
and with his own forces. With the conclusion of the Southeast Asia Treaty
some kind of decision had to be taken about the Chinese Nationalist territories. Late in 1954, therefore, the administration negotiated a mutual
defense treaty with the Republic of China embodying the same type of
guarantee as in the other Pacific treaties. The territories which were specifically recognized as within the scope of the commitments were the islands
of Formosa and the Pescadores. Several Nationalist-held islands just off
the mainland of China, including Quemoy and Matsu, were not expressly
included. The United States was given the right to station its armed forces
in and around the protected islands. The Chinese treaty was ratified by the
Senate early in 1955.

The
Formosa
Resolution
During Senate consideration of the Chinese Treaty, the Chinese communists began making menacing gestures toward the offshore, Nationalist-
held islands of Quemoy and Matsu. They also reaffirmed in belligerent
tones their intentions of conquering Formosa. This was a bold stroke aimed
at the territories whose situation was not covered by American guarantees.
Unwilling to announce the intention of the government in advance, certain
that we could not count on our European allies, especially Britain, uncertain of the real direction of the communist policy, and yet anxious to avoid
a Korea which might be charged to him alone (the Republicans had designated Korea Truman's War), President Eisenhower went to Congress. He
proposed a resolution by which Congress would authorize him to use armed
forces in accordance with the pending treaty and to include the "protection of such related positions and territories" now in friendly hands as he
felt the defense of Formosa and the Pescadores justified. Only three dissenting votes were cast in each house against the resolution. A sort of
armed truce has been in effect in the Formosa Straits since these actions.
It was broken for a short time in 1958 and occasionally since then by renewed firing on the islands but in general this area has been relatively quiet
in the sixties.

THE UNITED STATES AND THE DEVELOPING NATIONS:
SOUTH AND SOUTHEAST ASIA AND AFRICA

The rise
of new
societies
The effort of Secretary Dulles to contain China by a system of defensive alliances with virtually all of the states of South and Southeast Asia
failed in part, as we have noted, because of the unwillingness of the two

largest—India and Indonesia—as well as Burma and Ceylon to align themselves with either side in the East–West struggle. This experience suggests
that in addition to Europe and China, the U.S. has had to consider the
consequence for its policies of the rise of many new societies. The colonial
grip of England, France, and Holland in Asia and Africa has been loosened
and one after another of their former colonies have shaken off imperial
rule and sought to establish themselves as new nations and to improve the
lot of their people. India is the largest and, in many ways, the most important of these nations and its struggle for economic progress, political
stability, and national independence have stimulated many of the others.
Although Indian efforts at independence were strongly supported by the
United States as have been those of many of the other new states of Asia
and Africa, there is nevertheless some underlying suspicion of our intentions. We have also supported France in Indochina and Algeria and England in Malaysia and in some parts of Africa. We stand for the West
against which these peoples have revolted. The communist posture of
support for "people" movements to throw out the capitalist imperialists
of the West strikes many sympathetic responses. To many of those of other
races, Russia and America are both representatives of the "whites"; they
feel no affinity to either and, on the whole, wish to remain neutral or unaligned as they prefer to call it. We have noted that these new states now
command a majority in the General Assembly of the United Nations.

The major vehicle of contemporary American foreign policy toward
the developing nations is financial assistance. President Truman, in his
inaugural address in 1949 had called for a bold new program (Point Four)
of technical assistance for these nations making available to them the
benefits of our science and technology and a modest program was inaugurated during his administration. The major sums of the Marshall plan
followed by the heavy outpouring of military assistance to our allies tended
to dominate our programs, however, throughout the fifties. Gradually, as
the communists sought to spread their own influence and doctrines through
the emerging states, we began to increase our interest and our aid to help
these societies. Strong emphasis has continued on aid (economic and military) to our allies among these states, like Thailand, the Philippines, and
Pakistan and to our dependents like South Korea, Taiwan, and South Viet
Nam, but impressive sums are now going to India, Africa, and South
America. In 1961, urged by President Kennedy, Congress dropped the
mutual security framework for our aid program and assigned major responsibility for its administration to a new Agency for International Development (A.I.D.).

Assistance for economic development

Considering all forms of foreign assistance since World War II, we
find that up to 1966 the American government had spent $107 billion.
Most had been granted outright, some had been loaned directly and some
indirectly through the World Bank and the Development Banks for Asia
and Latin America. Of this total about $28 billion was spent on immediate

Foreign Economic Assistance

1948–1966
(Millions)

REGION	TOTAL	LOANS	GRANTS
Near East–South Asia	$ 9,725	$ 5,173	$ 4,552
Latin-America	3,658	2,435	1,223
East Asia–Viet Nam	9,363	780	8,583
Africa	1,852	8.30	1,039
Europe	15,229	1,876	13,553
Nonregional	2,745	21	2,724
	$42,572	$10,293.30	$31,674

postwar rehabilitation and relief and about $37 billion on military assistance. Economic assistance accounted for $42 billion and is continuing at the rate of 2 to 3 billion annually.

To sustain this continuing flow of treasure, each President has faced stern congressional critics and has had to battle vigorously for the level of support he felt essential. Rarely has he received as much as he requested or as much flexibility in administration as he thought desirable. Several of the loan and grant programs have specified that capital equipment purchased with American funds be of American manufacture. More and more insistently the Congress is urging that other prosperous nations, especially England, France, Germany, and Japan, make a larger contribution to development aids for the new states of Africa and South Asia, that wherever possible international financial institutions bear a greater share of development costs, and that aid be sharply curtailed for countries such as Yugoslavia, Ghana, and Indonesia, that show some affinity for communist doctrine. Critics also have attacked giving aid to noncapitalist countries and there are a great many of these in the developing world. The administration of foreign aid has also been repeatedly investigated and harshly criticized and has undergone numerous shifts of leadership. In the early years, foreign aid was regarded as a temporary expedient and annual extensions were necessary to keep it alive. With prime emphasis on de-

The Ten Recipients of the Largest
Amounts of Foreign Aid

1966
(Millions)

1. Viet Nam	$584.4		6. Pakistan	$114.1
2. India	308.8		7. Dominican Republic	93.8
3. Brazil	241.7		8. Chile	85.6
4. Korea	143.9		9. Colombia	75.4
5. Turkey	133.0		10. Laos	54.4

velopment aid, however, there is growing realization that we may be in this for some years and that longer-run authorizations might need to be made and more settled policies developed. Nevertheless, the program was cut to its lowest levels in twenty years by the Congress in 1968.

A special and new form of technical aid was created in 1961 by Congress on the strong recommendation of President Kennedy: the Peace Corps. A semiautonomous agency was created in the Department of State to recruit, train, and make available to underdeveloped nations for agreed upon projects a cadre of young men and women trained in various specialties (teaching, agricultural sciences, medicine, etc.) and in the language and culture of the nation to which they were assigned. These young people are to offer on the spot technical help and thus compensate for grave shortages of trained people in the new nations. In so far as possible these are to be dedicated young people who will live among the people they are to help without uniforms, high pay, or special perquisites. By mid-1967 the corps had an authorized strength of 14,000 volunteers and was engaged in projects in 46 nations.

The Peace Corps

The tremendous social, political, and economic changes associated with the revolution of the emerging peoples has not been achieved without some cost in life and treasure. Thanks to the U.N., to American foreign aid, and to the forbearance shown and the assistance frequently provided by the former colonial powers, a great deal has been and hopefully will be accomplished peacefully. In many areas the resources, economic or strategic, are considerable and it is hard to prevent communists or westerners from seeking advantage. Some emerging nations, therefore, present the contemporary battleground in which local and international factions struggle for advantage. Viet Nam is perhaps such a case, as is the Congo. The separation of India and Pakistan at the time of independence was accomplished only at the cost of terrible blood-letting, and the struggle between the two over Kashmir has precipitated extensive violence as recently as 1965. Russian mediation following a U.N. arranged cease-fire brought a temporary agreement at Tashkent in 1966. This rivalry has also caused both to devote resources desperately needed for economic development to arms and armies. India's neutrality, furthermore, has been compromised by an attack by the Red Chinese on her Assam frontier in 1962. Indonesia's gradual movement into the communist orbit in the early sixties characterized by the long, costly, and useless harassment of the Malaysian Federation, referred to as "confrontation" was ended by a military coup in 1965. Sukarno was rendered powerless, the communist party decimated and its leaders killed or imprisoned and the new government opened more friendly relations with the West. In Africa, the Congo, still patrolled by U.N. peace-keeping forces and harassed by mercenaries has achieved only a modest amount of stability. Nigeria came apart in 1968 and the Ibo's of Biafra are fighting desperately for survival against superior forces of the federal government. Rhodesia and South Africa, in which white minorities continue

The costs of independence and the revolution of rising expectations

to suppress and exploit the black masses, are potential powder-kegs by which the remnants of "white" Africa may well be exploded by *militant* black nationalists.

THE UNITED STATES AND THE MIDDLE EAST

The Middle East

The critical theater of the struggle of East and West in the mid-nineteen-fifties and then again after 1967 was undoubtedly the Middle East. A resurgent Arab nationalism led by Nasser, dictator of Egypt and encouraged by the Russians aimed its gathering strength against the remnants of European colonialism. France had been pouring out treasure and troops it could ill afford, to remain dominant in Algeria. The drains and stresses of this struggle brought down the Fourth Republic and introduced Charles de Gaulle as president of a reconstructed political system. The Suez Canal was seized by Egypt in advance of the date that the extant agreements called for its transfer. Syria and Iraq experienced upheavals which unseated governments friendly to the Western powers and Jordan and Lebanon were saved by American and British troops landed in 1958 to bolster tottering regimes.

American policy in this area was tentative and uncertain. We had encouraged but not joined mutual defense arrangements among Turkey, Iraq, Iran, Pakistan, and Great Britain concluded in 1955 at Baghdad. Despite our joining in the military planning of the Baghdad states in 1958, the bloc was rent by the pro-Nasser revolution in Iraq of that same year. We had turned against our European Allies, France and Britain, and against Israel when in 1956 they had sought by force to recapture the Suez and then had to join them in 1958 by landing troops in Lebanon while the British landed troops in Jordan.

Middle East Resolution of 1957

As in the Formosa crisis of 1955, the Eisenhower Administration sought advance approval from Congress for its movement of troops into this troubled area. Early in 1957, the President appeared before Congress and asked for a resolution authorizing him to furnish military or other aid to any nation in the general area of the Middle East threatened by communist aggression. After several weeks of debate, the Congress approved by large majorities a resolution announcing that the "United States regards as vital to the national interest and world peace the preservation of the independence and integrity of the nations of the Middle East." The President was authorized, on his own determination of necessity, to use armed force to assist any nation requesting it against armed aggression from any communist-controlled country. However, the Congress insisted that it be allowed to terminate the commitment by concurrent (not subject to veto) resolution when it saw fit. This resolution was cited in 1958 to support moving troops temporarily into Lebanon.

In general we have rather consistently sought to strengthen the role of the U.N. in mediating disputes in this area. At the time of the troop movements, the President appeared before the General Assembly and pled for a U.N. protective force and offered to withdraw our soldiers if such a force should be organized to stop raids from Nasser-held states into pro-Western territories.

The smoldering ashes of conflict erupted again in 1967 when Nasser and his allies moved to strangle Israel by blocking shipping in the Gulf of Aqaba. Western and U.N. mediation having failed, the Israelis struck quickly and virtually destroyed Nasser's army and air force together with those of Syria and Jordan in a campaign lasting only a few days. Quickly occupying the territory between the Gulf of Aqaba and the Suez Canal as well as the Syrian heights from which her territory had been shelled and raided and the rest of Jerusalem, the Israelis resisted U.N. mediation. The Soviet's deployed their fleet to restrain American intervention, increased their support and aid to the Arabs and demanded punishment of the Jewish aggressors. The U.S. has remained formally neutral, but has offered some new arms to Israel and has refused to push her into settlement. We have, however, supported as before, U.N. efforts at mediation.

The Arab–Israeli War of 1967

THE UNITED STATES AND LATIN AMERICA

The grim realities of the Cold War came closer to the American continent than ever before on July 10, 1960 when Khrushchev warned the United States that if we should attempt intervention in Cuba, the Russians would use rockets if necessary to support the regime of Fidel Castro. Until that time, most of our people supposed that Red pressure was still comfortably remote in Korea, Laos, or Tibet. True, a communist-like regime had been established briefly in Guatemala in 1954 but had rather easily been ousted without threat of American military intervention. Further signs that all was not well with our "good neighbor policy" were available: the stoning of Vice-President Nixon's car in 1958; the increasingly anti-American character of Castro's revolutionary government; the growing discontent with regimes like that of Trujillo in the Dominican Republic. These were noticed by the experts, however, Congress and the administration made no determined effort to reorient our policies or to use our foreign assistance until Russia seemed ready to perch on our very doorstep.

Cuba and Latin America

In keeping with our various Latin American professions, the immediate reaction to the Castro revolution in 1959 had been friendly and only as its anti-American aims became increasingly manifest did we take alarm. The situation in 1960 deteriorated rapidly. Agreements were negotiated between Castro and the Soviets for economic aid and for trade; Czech armaments began to appear in Cuba; with congressional authority we began to clamp down on sugar imports; we also stopped all economic aid; the Cubans nationalized large American private holdings and made menacing gestures toward our great naval base in Guantanamo Bay. Our efforts to get support from the other American republics at San Jose in order to resist the establishment of a communist-dominated state in this hemisphere revealed widespread discontent with our policies among our southern neighbors. The situation became worse in 1961 when we facilitated an invasion of Cuba by an army of Cuban refugees organized and equipped with our aid. The attack was a complete failure and the Castro regime became more admittedly pro-Russian than before. Not since the Civil War has the Monroe Doctrine been so firmly questioned and vigorously restated as in the Cuban crisis. In the late fall of 1962 we were in fact carried to the very brink of nuclear war. Aerial photography revealed the presence in Cuba of new missile bases equipped by Russia to fire nuclear rockets at the heart of our country. President Kennedy imposed a naval blockade of the island designed to halt all armament shipments into it and stated that this would be continued until all bases were dismantled. He further declared it to be our policy to regard any nuclear missile launched from Cuba as an attack on this hemisphere by the Soviet Union. Congress had earlier by resolution authorized the use of force, if necessary, to contain the Cuban regime or to prevent the use of Cuba as a base threatening the security of the United States. It had also, in response to a presidential request, authorized the call-up of portions of the Ready Reserve. In case the blockade should not be immediately effective, the President ordered preparations for invasion. Under this threat, the Russians agreed to withdraw missiles and jet bombers and dismantle the bases. Russian military "aides" remain in Cuba, however, and a strong bloc of senators continue sharply to criticize the administration's acceptance of Soviet forces in the Western Hemisphere.

The Alliance for Progress

The missile crisis safely over, the administration began to consider our relations with Latin America and now moved forward along the lines earlier marked out. Here, as in Asia and Africa, we found people struggling to throw off an *ancien régime* and to achieve rising standards of living and greater participation in the management of their affairs. Pouring out our treasure for India and Viet Nam we had overlooked the needs and hopes of our closest neighbors. A new program of financial aid had been established in 1961 under the title of the Alliance for Progress, a series of agreements at Punta del Este, Uruguay, was worked out by 1962 and reconsidered in 1967 to ensure local contributions and local efforts at economic development and to develop regional institutions for promoting trade and aid. The Organization of American States (Pan-American Union) was strengthened and reshaped to enhance its role in facilitating Latin American economic development. We noted earlier that more than $3.5 billion in aid has been spent in Latin America, most of it since 1962. Other efforts to promote peaceful progress and friendly relations include visits by President Johnson to Mexico in 1966 and to Central America in 1968; final resolution of a long-standing border conflict with Mexico stemming from a shift in the course of the Rio Grande River; and agreement with

Panama on new treaties covering the Panama Canal and other potential canals.

On the other hand, we lost some ground when in 1965 we abandoned for a time our policy of nonintervention in American states and rushed troops into the Dominican Republic. Anxious to avoid another Cuba, when revolt flared in this troubled island, President Johnson quickly landed troops, avowedly to protect American lives and property and to prevent an alleged take over of the counter-revolutionary forces by communists. Although the troops were soon withdrawn and replaced by the forces of other states under the direction of the Organization of American States, and although we got a kind of approval of our intervention from the Organization, there were many critics of our action, here and in Latin America.

PROBLEMS OF ADMINISTRATION OF FOREIGN POLICY

Conduct of the modern foreign relations of the United States has long since spilled out far beyond the organizational arrangements, traditions, and practices of the Department of State to which this function has traditionally been assigned. The review in this chapter of the modern policies and aims of the United States in international relations indicates that we are conducting affairs abroad with our money, our goods, our soldiers, our engineers, our technicians, and our publicists as well as with our diplomats. The Defense Department is as concerned with our international commitments as the State Department. The Treasury is involved in a vast array of international fiscal agencies and agreements. Commerce and Agriculture seek markets abroad, give technical counsel to friendly foreign states, and in many other ways implement our determined effort to build a strong free world. The Justice Department controls immigration. Various independent establishments have from time to time administered part or all of our postwar programs of economic, technical, and military assistance to Europe and Asia. The Hoover Commission in 1949 found no less than 46 executive agencies to be more or less concerned with foreign affairs. All of this development has raised grave problems of coordination, of multiple and thus confusing representations to foreign powers, of adjusting our policies to our military capabilities or vice versa, and of making the authority and responsibility of the President effective. Several new coordinating devices have been attempted in recent years—interdepartmental committees of many varieties, advisory councils, added staff assistance for the President. The most important of the new devices is surely the National Security Council created by the National Security Act of 1949 in the Office of the President to integrate diplomatic and military strategy. This agency is essentially a Cabinet committee to advise the President, aided by a small staff, and its operation will be described in the next chapter. None of the devices has been completely satisfactory and the search for improvement still continues.

The problem outgrows the State Department

In general, the Kennedy–Johnson policy seemed to have been to enlarge the State Department by bringing into it or associating with it other major agencies (for example, Agency for International Development, U.S. Information Agency, the Peace Corps) concerned with foreign affairs.

REFERENCES

D. Acheson, *Power and Diplomacy* (Cambridge, Mass., 1958).

G. A. Almond, *The American People and Foreign Policy* (New York, 1961).

American Assembly, *The United States and Latin America* (New York, 1959).

G. W. Ball, *The Discipline of Power: Essentials of a Modern World Structure* (New York, 1968).

R. J. Barnett and M. G. Raskin, *After Twenty Years: the Decline of N.A.T.O. and the Search for a New Policy in Europe* (New York, 1966).

N. Bentwich and A. Martin, *A Commentary on the Charter of the United Nations* (New York, 1950).

N. M. Blake and O. T. Barck, Jr., *The United States in Its World Relations* (New York, 1958).

D. S. Cheever and H. F. Haviland, Jr., *American Foreign Policy and the Separation of Powers* (Cambridge, Mass., 1952).

Committee to Strengthen the Security of the Free World (Clay Committee). *Report* (Washington, D. C., 1963).

Commission to Study the Organization of Peace, *Strengthening the United Nations* (New York, 1957).

G. Connell-Smith, *The Inter-American System* (New York, 1966).

Council on Foreign Relations, *The United States and World Affairs,* annually since 1931, usually written by R. P. Stebbins.

C. V. Crabb, Jr., *American Foreign Policy in the Nuclear Age* (New York, 1965).

D. M. Dozer, *Are We Good Neighbors?: Three Decades of Inter-American Relations, 1930–1960* (Gainesville, Fla., 1960).

T. Draper, *The Abuse of Power* (New York, 1967).

R. N. Durr, *Our Troubled Hemisphere: Perspectives on U.S. Latin American Relations* (Washington, D. C., 1967).

R. E. Elder, *The Policy Machine: the Department of State and American Foreign Policy* (Syracuse, N. Y., 1960).

R. N. Gardner, *In Pursuit of World Order: U.S. Foreign Policy and International Organizations* (New York, 1964).

J. Grange, *American Foreign Relations: Permanent Problems and Changing Policies* (New York, 1959).

L. J. Halle, *Dream and Reality; Aspects of American Foreign Policy* (New York, 1959).

R. Hilsman, *To Move a Nation* (New York, 1966).

G. F. Kennan, *Russia, the Atom and the West* (New York, 1958).

H. A. Kissinger, *The Necessity for Choice: Prospects of American Foreign Policy* (New York, 1961).

K. S. Latourette, *The American Record in the Far East, 1945–1951* (New York, 1952).

G. Lenczowski, *The Middle East in World Affairs* (Ithaca, N. Y., 1952).

C. O. Lerche, Jr., *The Foreign Policy of the American People* (Englewood Cliffs, N. J., 1958).

J. L. McCamy, *The Administration of American Foreign Affairs* (New York, 1950).

E. S. Mason, *Foreign Aid and Foreign Policy* (New York, 1955).

R. D. Masters, *The Nation is Burdened: American Foreign Policy in a Changing World* (New York, 1967).

M. F. Millikan and D. L. M. Blackmer (eds.), *The Emerging Nations: Their Growth and United States Policy* (Boston, 1961).

H. J. Morgenthau, *The Purpose of American Politics* (New York, 1960).

E. Plischke, *Conduct of American Diplomacy* (Princeton, N. J., 1961).

Don K. Price (ed.), *The Secretary of State* (Englewood Cliffs, N. J., 1960).

E. O. Reischauer, *Wanted: An Asian Policy* (New York, 1955).

H. L. Roberts, *Russia and America: Dangers and Prospects* (New York, 1956).

W. W. Rostow, *The United States in the World Arena* (New York, 1960).

W. W. Rostow and R. W. Hatch, *An American Policy in Asia* (New York, 1955).

B. M. Sapin, *The Making of United States Foreign Policy* (New York, 1964).

J. Slater, *The O.A.S. and U.S. Foreign Policy* (Columbus, Ohio, 1967).

Ronald Steel, *Pax Americana* (New York, 1967).

E. Stillman and W. Pfaff, *Power and Impotence: the Failure of American Foreign Policy* (New York, 1966).

K. W. Thompson, *Political Realism and the Crisis of World Politics: An American Approach to Foreign Policy* (Princeton, N. J., 1960).

F. O. Wilcox and C. M. Marcy, *Proposals for Changes in the United Nations* (Washington, D. C., 1955).

A. Wolfers (ed.), *Alliance Policy in the Cold War* (Baltimore, 1960).

22

DEFENDING THE NATION AGAINST ATTACK

Once a
casual
interest
Early resolution to keep out of Europe's wars did not save us as a nation from a threatened conflict with France in 1800 or an actual one with Great Britain in 1812. Nevertheless, by acquiring Louisiana and Florida we soon eliminated France and Spain as potential trouble-makers on our borders. After the final defeat of Napoleon, affairs abroad took a more peaceful turn; and for over 100 years we enjoyed a comfortable sense of national isolation and security. Wars with Mexico and Spain carried no serious threat; and although in 1917 we were drawn into the greatest armed conflict that the world to that time had known, we came off still effectively sheltered, as we thought, by our geographical location. In days which middle-aged persons can well remember, our Army numbered only 150,-000, our Navy was better developed but not top-flight, and the national temper so averse to militarism that impressive defenses hardly could be maintained at all.

Now a
paramount
concern
Then dawned a period of great change. International turmoil gripped the world; technological developments robbed us of the protection of broad oceans; mechanized global war advanced in our direction and finally in 1941 overtook us; by rapid stages, defense, long a matter of only sporadic interest, became our paramount national concern—and defense no longer confined to prudent preparedness, but actualized in deadly combat on land and sea and in the air in every quarter of the globe. And this time there was no lapsing back into an easy feeling of security after the fighting was over. As after World War I, new international machinery was set up to prevent such things happening again. But there had been failure before, and might be this time too. Besides, an ominous Cold War with the world's principal powers, the U.S.S.R. and Red China, might at any time grow hot. The new "absolute weapon" of nuclear fission and the new and spectacular thrust of rockets and missiles might presently be turned against us. In wars of the future, distance would mean little or nothing. In short, with a great

victory just won, the country had never been in so exposed a position, or so much in need of measures for protecting itself. In this situation, defense remained a paramount concern. When, in 1950, a communist assault upon the Korean Republic brought upon us undeclared but difficult and costly war, we soon found ourselves back in the atmosphere of 1940–1941— tripling military appropriations, increasing taxes, conscripting troops, imposing economic controls, and otherwise girding for an all-out international conflict which only extreme good fortune could avert. Even after a truce was patched up in Korea, the government continued to devote $35–$50 billion yearly to national security, the draft of young men for military service continued, and 3 million men stood under arms. Then with the Russian launching of the first space satellite in October, 1957, we learned how far we had fallen behind in rocketry and the dangers became even more acute. After 1964 our involvement in South Viet Nam grew steadily until by 1968 we were committing more resources than we had in Korea. All indications are that for a good while to come, defense, under a war or semiwar economy, linked to diplomacy, will be paramount among our national interests.

SOME CONSTITUTIONAL PRINCIPLES

During the Revolution and the ensuing Confederation period, lack of power of Congress to mobilize the fighting strength and material resources of the country with full effectiveness, and to deal promptly and decisively with domestic disorders, gravely imperiled the beginnings of the nation. The experience put the makers of the Constitution in a frame of mind to apply strong remedies. Into the new fundamental law they therefore wrote upwards of a dozen provisions which, taken together, provided every power at that time deemed necessary for defending the country, whether against Indian depredations, domestic uprisings, or foreign attack. Three principles of the resulting defense system require mention at the outset.

To start with, full responsibility for defense was placed where it remains today, in the national government. The states may and do maintain militia for use in enforcing their own proper authority. But unless Congress gives permission, they may not "keep troops or ships of war in time of peace . . . or engage in war unless actually invaded or in such imminent danger as will not admit of delay." Even the state militia may be called into the service of the United States, thereupon passing under supreme command of the President; and the military establishments of the states have in later times, as the National Guard, become an integral part of the war machine of the nation. In time of defense emergency, and especially of war, states, counties, cities and other jursidictions collaborate with the national government in a multitude of ways. Their efforts, however, are merely phases of an overall national effort; and full responsibility for that effort rests with the government at Washington.

1. Defense a national responsibility

A second principle is equally fundamental. While solicitous about providing for defense, the framers of the Constitution had no desire to open a way for an overweening military establishment, or for the rise of military dictatorship. True, they did not expressly enjoin in the document —as is done in all of the state constitutions except that of New York— that the military establishment should in all matters be subject to civil control. But they achieved the same end by so defining the defense and war powers of Congress and the President (civil branches of the government) as to set up safeguards against military domination. Congress alone can raise and support armies, make rules for governing them, and declare war; the President is Commander-in-Chief of all armed forces, whether in peace or in war. The principle has been buttressed by custom and by statutory elaboration. The secretary of defense must by law be a civilian; and firmly established practice makes the same requirement of the heads of the now subordinate Army, Navy, and Air Force Departments.

Finally, defense, like every other national function, must be kept within bounds constitutionally determined. Powers granted the President and Congress are broad and under stress of war tend to be stretched to their limits, if not sometimes a bit beyond. Moreover, Presidents Lincoln and Franklin D. Roosevelt plainly viewed the war power as something over and above any particular power conferred, or in fact all such powers combined. Despite occasional appearances to the contrary, however, the Constitution is not suspended in wartime. The President, as Commander-in-Chief, is no more entitled to disregard its restrictions then than in days of peace.

DEFENSE POWERS AND FUNCTIONS OF CONGRESS

To begin with, Congress has sole power to "raise and support armies" and to "provide and maintain a navy." These things it does by specifying the number and kinds of troops to be enlisted, prescribing the method of recruitment, fixing scales of pay, authorizing the building and manning of war craft, providing for auxiliary equipment such as forts, arsenals, and dockyards, and of course by raising and appropriating money for the maintenance of military, naval, and air establishments, subject to the constitutional restriction that no appropriation for raising and supporting armies may be made for a longer period than two years. There is no lack of power to take any steps considered necessary (including conscription) to safeguard the nation in time of peace and to insure vigorous and effective prosecution of hostilities in time of war.

2. Enact-
ing mili-
tary and
naval
regula-
tions

In the second place, Congress has unrestricted authority to make "rules for the government and regulation of the land and naval forces," and also "rules concerning captures on land and water." Resulting "Articles of War" for the Army and "Articles for the Government of the Navy" long were separate and subject to criticism not only for their lack of uniformity but for harsh features of the system of military justice for which they provided. Experience during World War II led to a general revision by a special committee of experts. In 1949, Congress enacted a new consolidated code, uniform for all of the armed services, and entitled "Military Laws of the United States."

Congress may provide for as large a standing army as it sees fit. Nothing is more certain than that the world situation will in future require a considerably larger one than in the past. Our earlier traditions, however, in common with those of English-speaking peoples everywhere, were opposed to any formidable army in time of peace, inclining rather, as a safeguard of freedom, to a volunteer citizens militia in each state with only such modest training and equipment as would enable it to cope with domestic disorder and to meet other relatively minor needs. All states have such militia, even though nowadays linked up, in a manner that would have shocked our ancestors, with the national defense establishment and bearing the significant name of National Guard. State contingents of the National Guard still are primarily state instrumentalities, with (so long as not drawn into national service) appointment of their officers and provision for their training expressly reserved to state authorities. Congress nevertheless is authorized to "provide for arming and disciplining the militia," to provide for calling into national service any and all portons of it required for executing the national laws, for suppressing insurrections, or for repelling invasions, and to make rules for governing such forces when "employed in the service of the United States." In pursuance of these broad powers, Congress in an Army Organization Act of 1920, gave the President permanent authority to make use of the National Guard for emergency purposes, and has enacted numerous regulations aimed at increasing the establishment's effectiveness and coordinating its organization, training, and equipment with that of the Regular Army—in addition, of course, to contributing heavily to its financial support. When, as a phase of the national defense program launched in 1940, the entire National Guard was drawn into national service and placed in cantonments for training, Congress specified that it might be used only in the Western Hemisphere and in United States territories and possessions, including the Philippines. After war came, however, the restriction was removed, and Guard units, or at any rate the men who had composed them, were sent to all overseas theaters of operation. National Guard units again were called into national overseas service in 1950 in connection with our military operations in Korea, in 1961 in connection with the Berlin crisis and such use was foreshadowed by congressional resolution in the Cuba crisis of 1962. In 1966, the Congress granted to President Johnson the power to call up members of the Ready Reserve including the National Guard without declaring a national emergency and without further reference to Congress.

3. Regulating the National Guard

He used this authority early in 1968 in connection with the Pueblo incident with North Korea.

Constitutionally, Congress alone can declare war. Hostilities may, of course, begin without a formal declaration, as in the instance of the Spanish–American War of 1898. Indeed, as illustrated by the war with Japan, Germany, and Italy starting in December, 1941, they may be forced upon us, and with an element of surprise, by aggressive action of a foreign power, leaving us no alternative. Even in such situations a declaration will normally be adopted by the two houses, as a means (if for no other purpose) of fixing, for the benefit of neutrals, an exact date from which the rights and liabilities incident to war are to be reckoned. The usual method is a joint resolution, requested and afterwards signed by the President. Many times it has been proposed by people anxious to keep the United States out of war that, except when the nation is directly attacked, the question of going to war shall in all cases be put to a countrywide popular vote. Unless the Constitution were amended, however, the decision must finally rest with Congress; and it is not clear that anything would be gained from the suggested procedure. With events moving as rapidly as they usually do, a plebiscite might not be practical; and momentary passions might make it even dangerous. The discretion of Congress in declaring war often is more theoretical than actual, not only because war may be forced upon us in spite of anything we can do, but also because the President, in conducting foreign relations, may bring the country to a point where no honorable alternative to war remains. Indeed, he may independently take steps leading to actual combat, as when President Roosevelt in 1940–1941 (before Pearl Harbor) supplied naval escorts for merchant ships carrying "lend-lease" materials to Great Britain and other countries, resulting in armed clashes between American destroyers and German submarines. On the other hand, if Congress can declare war, it also can take measures designed to avert it, a good illustration being the Neutrality Act of 1935 (later abandoned) making it unlawful, with war in progress between two or more foreign states, to ship arms and munitions to the belligerents, as entailing risk of the United States being drawn into the hostilities.

From 1950 to 1953, the United States was engaged in an armed conflict in Korea of sufficient proportions to disturb the entire national economy, yet with no war declared by Congress. We came into the operation entirely through (1) the President's bringing the communist invasion of South Korea officially to the attention of the U.N. Security Council, (2) the latter calling upon all U.N. members to assist in repelling the invaders, and (3) decision by our own executive branch to comply by military means on any necessary scale. Article 43 of the U.N. Charter, requiring U.N. members to place armed forces at the organization's disposal for maintaining peace, already had created the possibility that if such forces actually were raised and used, the United States might some day find itself in a war not declared by Congress. The Korean eruption produced precisely such a situation. To be sure, no U.N. forces had as yet been organized. But to stop a communist aggression, the U.N. Security Council asked member–states to join in military resistance. Recognizing both our interest and our moral, if not strictly legal, obligation, the President (as agent for implementing our U.N. relations) put us instantly into action. In doing so he consulted with congressional leaders but never formally asked the approval of Congress. This procedure allowed Republican statesmen, notably Senator Taft, to charge executive usurpation and to refer to Korea as "Truman's war." Moreover, as long as the U.N. serves the purpose for which it was created, the experience may be repeated. To this extent, the control of Congress over war by declaring it has been greatly reduced. From 1965 to the present (1968), we have also been involved in a substantial military effort in South Viet Nam without congressional declaration. The S.E.A.T.O. treaty described in the previous chapter and congressional resolutions have been cited as providing the legal and moral basis for the use of troops. The resolution device, described heretofore, has been growing in frequency of use and may hereafter become the predominant form of congressional participation in the opening of hostilities. Generally, however, congressmen are jealous of their constitutional prerogatives in the matter and, as we noted in the last chapter, all of the great regional defense pacts to which the United States is a party, while requiring signatories, in case of attack upon any of their number, to consult and to take individual or collective action, have been so drawn as to leave the United States (and every other signatory) free to follow the constitutional procedure. They are also growing highly critical of the resolution procedure and efforts to shape a more effective congressional role are every day more urgently needed.

There was a time when, except in case of invasion, war was of no great concern to the general mass of the people. Armies were volunteer, taxes indirect, supplies bought in the open market, sacrifice and morale demanded chiefly of the forces in the field. The vast scale on which the mechanized wars of today are waged, however, makes them of hardly less civilian than military concern. When war comes or is imminently threatened, it is, as President Wilson remarked in 1917, "not an army that we must shape and train; it is a nation." Experience gained during both world wars revealed in startling manner the lengths to which Congress may go in reorganizing and regimenting the national life for purposes of successful prosecution of, or even simply preparation for, war under twentieth-century conditions. As Commander-in-Chief of the armed forces, the President independently possesses war powers of impressive magnitude. To Congress, however, it falls, not only to provide the necessary men and money—by conscription acts, revenue acts, and appropriation acts—but to endow the Chief Executive with all the broad authority required for mobilizing industry, commerce, transportation, and even science and education. The method commonly is that of legislation delegating specified powers for the

5. Mobilizing the nation for war effort

duration of the war (or other designated period), either with or without creation by Congress of new machinery for exercising them. In each field covered, the resulting system of controls is organized and administered by the executive branch. The underlying authority comes from Congress. While the courts often have looked with disfavor upon delegations of power by one branch of the government to another, developments during the two world wars indicate that under wartime stress and excitement Congress can go almost as far as it likes with such grants. Sometimes grants are made with little hesitation; at other times, only over strong opposition and at urgent presidential request. Occasionally, indeed—as, for example, when in 1944 President Roosevelt asked for power to conscript labor, and Truman in 1950 asked for approval of his seizure of the steel mills—they are refused.

6. Regulating wartime civil liberties

Except for the provision for suspension of the writ of habeas corpus, the Constitution recognizes no distinction between civil rights in peacetime and in wartime. War, however, brings not only an intensity of military activity but a tenseness of the public mind, stimulating restrictions that would not be undertaken or tolerated in time of peace. And such restrictions, as we observed in an earlier chapter, may be imposed by the President (commonly through the Department of Justice), either under his powers as Commander-in-Chief or in pursuance of authority delegated to him by Congress. Congress itself may impose them directly by legislative act—going, indeed, to undefined lengths in restraining speech, press, assembly, and other normal rights.

7. Caring for veterans

Inheriting the practice from English and colonial usage, Congress not only has provided regular pay for soldiers and sailors, but has bestowed land, money pensions, civil service preferences, and other special benefits upon the demobilized forces after every war in which the United States has engaged from the Revolution onwards. The particularly hazardous nature of the service rendered the country by those who bear arms in its defense has always been given recognition. Persons actually incapacitated, together with their dependents, have usually been conceded to have an indisputable claim to the nation's care. However, powerful political pressure brought to bear upon congressmen by veterans' organizations often has led to grants where the obligation was considerably less clear. So generous, indeed, has been Congress where veterans are concerned that between 1792 and 1930 national outlays on money pensions alone, regardless of land allotments in earlier days and of later heavy costs of hospitalization and medical treatment, reached a total of $15 billion. Today (1968), as part of the aftercost of World War II, of Korea, and of Viet Nam the annual expenditure in behalf of 26 million veterans exceeds $6. Benefits bestowed on veterans of the recent wars in addition to the operation of regular pension, rehabilitation, and hospitalization systems, have included government aid in carrying protection originating in in-servce war-risk insurance; opportunity to acquire on favorable terms surplus war property disposed of by the government; increased preferential eligibility for employment in the civil service; continued monthly payments for a period after honorable discharge; terminal leave pay for all wartime furlough periods not actually used; generous support for high school, collegiate, and professional education; and assistance in acquiring a home, business, or farm.

DEFENSE POWERS AND FUNCTIONS OF THE PRESIDENT

The authority of Congress manifestly underlies our entire system of national defense. Without it there would be no army or navy, no money, and only imperfect means of mobilizing the nation for a defense or war effort. The central figure in defense, and especially in the conduct of war, is nevertheless the President. During its three great wars of the last hundred years, the nation had in the White House Chief Executives—Lincoln, Wilson, and Franklin D. Roosevelt—who would have loomed large in history in any event. All gained stature, however, from guiding the country's destinies amid a supreme war effort. Each of these men also added something to the concept of the office of the Presidency, partly in each case as an outgrowth of ideas of the defense powers. *The President as the central figure*

Whether in peace or in war, every President, however, has significant defense powers and functions, accruing from (1) his constitutional status as Chief Executive, (2) his constitutional role as Commander-in-Chief, and (3) grants, or delegations, by Congress. In all that he does, even under stress of war, a President is presumed to keep within limits of authority coming to him from one or more of these sources. He does not always have to be prepared to justify an action by citing any particular one of them. President Franklin D. Roosevelt rarely considered it necessary to indicate in other than very broad terms the basis of specific war powers as he exercised them, leaving it rather to others to speculate, if they chose, upon whether, in the case of any given act or order, he was relying principally upon his permanent peacetime powers as Chief Executive, or upon his status as Commander-in-Chief, or upon statutory grants; and if perchance he made allusion to the latter, he was likely not to cite chapter and verse, but merely to invoke "the statutes." *Sources of his defense powers*

In his conduct of foreign relations the President may create a situation making war virtually inevitable. In the course of stormy negotiations with Mexico in 1846, President Polk ordered American troops to advance into territory then in dispute with that country. The Mexican authorities had made it plain that such a step would be regarded as an act of war, and the soldiers were promptly fired upon. Polk then said that war existed by act of Mexico, and Congress proceeded to a formal declaration. President McKinley ordered the battleship *Maine* to Havana harbor in 1898, notwithstanding that the Spaniards were certain to regard the act as unfriendly. The vessel blew up and the Spanish–American War followed. By his han- *The President and the beginning of war* dling of relations with Berlin after the sinking of the *Lusitania* in 1915, President Wilson brought the United States to a situation where the only alternative to a declaration of war upon Germany would have been national stultification. And later, the whole course of policy and action which, over a period of years, led the United States straight to involvement in World War II, while sustained by increasing evidences of broad national support, was projected and carried forward under the sole ultimate responsibility of President Franklin D. Roosevelt. President Kennedy in 1962 brought us close to war by ordering a naval blockade of Cuba. Congress could, if it liked, declared a war to which the President was opposed, and he could attempt to avert it by interposing a veto. With the possible exception of the War of 1812, however, all of our wars have normally been declared at presidential request.

The nature of congressional participation   The extensive moral and legal obligations of the United States arising from its participation in the U.N. and from the numerous mutual defense treaties to which it is a party and the large armed forces constantly available for deployment around the world have added a new dimension to this problem of taking the nation into war. Congress, as we observed in the previous chapter, is demanding a larger share in presidential decision-making in the area of international military undertakings. The debate over the Korean police action and over the Troops for Europe Resolution in connection with N.A.T.O. revealed congressional discontent with what is called growing executive domination in these matters. A recent effort to shape an appropriate relationship between Congress and the President in committing the United States to a position which might easily result in war was the Formosa resolution of 1955, described in the previous chapter. In the course of the congressional debate over the resolution requested by President Eisenhower, a number of the Democratic leaders took the position that legally the resolution was unnecessary. The President, they said, already had the power to command the armed forces to defend Formosa or the offshore islands of Quemoy and Matsu. The resolution they regarded simply as a means of showing the Chinese communists that the nation was united in its determination to prevent their further expansion. Many other congressmen, mainly Republicans, took the position, however, that by requesting this resolution the President was acknowledging his obligation to consult Congress on such a momentous decision and was, thus, reversing the pattern of several decades. The President's message and the reports of the committees, which considered the resolution, evaded this explosive question. The fact that the President did ask for the resolution will be cited in future situations to justify congressional participation and it was alluded to in the debate on the Cuba resolution in 1962. The resolution itself, however, left the President a free hand to use force or not to defend the Nationalist-held islands. In the Middle East crisis of 1957, the same procedure was followed. In this case, the congressional resolution left the President free to determine when or where troops might be used. The Congress, however, reserved the right to terminate the commitment by its own action. In the Berlin crisis of 1961, while announcing his policy and securing congressional approval for calling up Reserve units, the President did not seek a resolution authorizing him to use troops to protect West Berlin. However, in the fall of 1962 as the Cuban situation grew menacing, the Republican leaders of Congress proposed a resolution authorizing the use of force to prevent the spread of Castro's influence in Latin America. The President, on his part, asked Congress for and received standby authority to call up part of the Ready Reserve in order to "permit prompt and effective responses, as necessary, to challenges which might be presented in any part of the free world." Congress also adopted a resolution on Cuba similar to that proposed by the Republicans and another stating the determination of the U.S. to meet its commitments in Berlin. In the Viet Nam situation in 1965 after American retaliatory air strikes, President Johnson asked for and got a resolution affirming his right to use force in the area.

Tonkin Gulf Resolution

The text of the Southeast Asia Resolution is as follows:

Resolved, etc., *Sec. 1.* That the Congress approves and supports the determination of the President, as Commander-in-Chief, to take all necessary measures to repel any armed attack against the forces of the United States and to prevent further aggression.

Sec. 2. The United States regards as vital to its national interest and to world peace the maintenance of international peace and security in Southeast Asia. Consonant with the Constitution of the United States and the Charter of the United Nations and in accordance with its obligations under the Southeast Asia Defense Treaty, the United States is, therefore, prepared, as the President determines, to take all necessary steps, including the use of armed force, to assist any member or protocol state of the Southeast Asia Collective Defense Treaty requesting assistance in defense of its freedom.

Sec. 3. This resolution shall expire when the President shall determine that the peace and security of the area is reasonably assured by international conditions created by action of the United Nations or other wise, except that it may be terminated earlier by concurrent resolution of the Congress.

In time of peace, the President performs the normal functions of chief executive in connection with defense interests and activities substantially as in relation to other government services. It is when war comes that he rises to the full stature implicit in the sources and forms of authority above described. Subject to restrictions by Congress (which almost certainly would not be imposed in the midst of conflict), he can send all branches of the armed forces anywhere that he chooses, and use them as he desires. He can take as much part as he likes in mapping out strategy and directing campaigns; indeed there is nothing to prevent him from taking the field in person if he so desires. Like any other supreme commander, he can terminate hostilities by agreeing to an armistice. He can set up military governments in conquered territory, and, directly or through appointed agents, exercise all

The President in wartime

executive powers there, and all legislative powers as well until Congress makes different arrangements. Meanwhile, availing himself of broad grants of emergency authority already on the statute book, or voted by Congress in response to White House requests unfailingly made, he can carry out sweeping programs of armed recruitment, civilian mobilization, and economic controls, authorize or issue multitudes of administrative regulations, reorganize governmental agencies and create new ones, take over plants in which labor stoppages are interfering with war production or the railroads if transportation difficulties are impeding the war effort, and do such a multitude of other things that the sum total of authority amassed and exercised almost defies comprehension. Indeed, the object in modern war being to discover and make effective all national potentialities as speedily as possible, and at the same time to break down the enemy's power of resistance, control over the use of the armed forces inevitably broadens into the general function of taking whatever measures may be found necessary to those ends. As a former secretary of war phrased it, the Commander-in-Chief's duty is nothing less than to prosecute a war "to the fullest extent." In discharging this responsibility, he, of course, must not violate the Constitution or the laws; and, to a degree, he must work in cooperation with Congress, from which much of his high authority has come and to which at least some of it will return. Outside of these limitations, however, he and his advisors, civil and military, have, and must have, virtually a free hand.

ORGANIZATION FOR NATIONAL SECURITY

Former separate defense administrations and services

Until World War II, defense organization in the United States was notoriously lacking in integration. At the top, the President as Chief Executive and Commander-in-Chief supplied a measure of unity. But the War (later Army) and Navy Departments were entirely separate; the armed services whose affairs they managed were not only separate but often uncooperative and even antagonistic. In making appropriations and enacting defense legislation, Congress rarely considered Army and Navy needs at the same time or in much relation to each other. In earlier and simpler days, the disadvantages of such disunity often were apparent but usually not serious, and little was done toward overcoming them. We emerged from our wars successfully, and the country was satisfied. Even World War I brought no significant change. World War II, however, was different. In the first place, its magnitude and complexity were unprecedented. Secondly, it demonstrated that for the attainment of objectives in such a conflict there must be a wholly new type of collaboration between land, sea, and air forces. Finally, at its end we were confronted with a world situation making it indispensable that we permanently maintain an armed establishment far larger than ever before in peacetime and organized and integrated for a maximum of efficiency at a minimum of what must in any case be stupendous cost.

From far back, there had been intermittent proposals to merge the War and Navy Departments into some form of defense department. Later the rapid development of air warfare led some people to suggest moving in the opposite direction and setting up a separate department of military (and perhaps civilian) aviation. World War II at last drove home the idea that basic reorganization must no longer be delayed and that it must be in the direction of all-around integration. After two or three years of lively bickering between the Army and the Navy, each of which had a plan of its own, and with the Truman Administration sturdily urging action, Congress eventually, in 1947, passed a comprehensive National Security Act following the Navy plan in broad outline and providing for a defense reorganization outstripping any in all our previous history. The defense set-up about to be outlined rests principally upon that piece of legislation, as amended in the direction of further coordination by two enactments: (1) the National Security Act Amendments of 1949 stemming largely from recommendations of the Hoover Commission; (2) the Defense Reorganization Act of 1958. President Eisenhower made some further changes in the structure by a reorganization order in 1953.

National Security Acts of 1947 and 1949

In pursuance of the announced objective of "integrated policies and procedures for the departments, agencies, and functions of the government relating to the national security," the Act of 1947 undertook to gather substantially everything into an administrative and advisory structure known as the National Security Organization, with a National Military Establishment as its core and a National Security Council and a National Security Resources Board on the periphery. The National Military Establishment represented a major innovation, because its creation marked the first time that the previously separate War and Navy Departments were joined under any directive authority other than that of the President. Since, however, the Departments named (with the War Department rechristened Department of the Army, and with a new Department of the Air Force added) retained most of their previous autonomy, the change was more apparent than real. An entirely new official—a secretary of defense, appointed by the President and confirmed by the Senate, and with only civilians eligible—was introduced and charged with (1) establishing general policies and programs for the National Military Establishment and for all component departments and agencies, (2) exercising "general direction, authority, and control" over such departments and agencies, (3) discovering and eliminating unnecessary duplication or overlapping in their activities, and (4) advising with the departments and agencies in the preparation of their budgets and formulating a single unified military budget for consideration by the Budget Bureau, the President, and eventually Congress. The Establishment (largely a paper affair) did not have the true character of an executive department and the secretary of defense, although seated in the Cabinet—as the heads of the three service departments were not—found himself possessed of prestige but very little else. Combined with the service departments' characteristic love of autonomy, the old traditional fear lest one man be given too much power

1. The Department of Defense

in military matters had operated to cause the secretary to be given too little. In practice, the "general" authority over the department given him very nearly evaporated. He could not appoint or dismiss (except within his own very limited staff); he could not enforce orders; he could not reorganize; even his control over budgets proved merely nominal.

Changes in 1949

The principal objective of the amending act of 1949 was to remedy this unhappy situation. The ethereal National Military Establishment was discarded, and in its place was put a single full-orbed executive department, the present Department of Defense, officially ranking second only to the Department of State. In line with this, the secretary was given powers commensurate with those of other department heads—his principal limitations being that he may not abolish any of the established functions of the Army, Navy, or Air Force or merge any portions of the armed services. Logically enough, the act also transferred the National Security Council and the National Security Resources Board to the Executive Office of the President.

Defense Reorganization Act of 1958

Demand for even greater subordination of the three services to the Secretary of Defense was a by-product of general dissatisfaction with American progress in missiles, rockets, and space exploration. Failure to keep pace with the Russians was blamed, in part, on continuing interservice rivalries and the lack of clear-cut assignments of responsibility to any service for development of the new weapons. President Eisenhower strongly urged Congress in 1958 to entrust greater authority to the Secretary of Defense, to strengthen the Joint Chiefs of Staff as professional advisors to the Secretary, and to facilitate unified command in the field. Congress responded halfheartedly. The Defense Reorganization Act of 1958 gave the Secretary power to transfer, abolish, or reassign defense functions but an order to do any of these things was made subject to congressional veto. The Secretary was given clear and specific power to assign new weapons or weapons systems among the various services and a new Director of Defense Research and Engineering was established in the Department of Defense. Power to merge any of the military departments or services or to establish a single military Chief of Staff was expressly withheld. In later spelling out the assignments of each of the services. Secretary of Defense McElroy made no major changes and avoided any resolution of the continuing controversies over their respective roles in missile development and space exploration. Major criticism of these arrangements, especially of the lack of clear decision by the Joint Chiefs, continues to be voiced by the Army leaders and, to some degree, by those of the Air Force. Under the direction of Robert McNamara (1961–1968), a centralization of control under the secretary was energetically and successfully pushed. Central agencies for intelligence, supply, organization, and management were created and the staff of the joint chiefs enlarged at the expense of those of the services. Genuine and effective central budget control based on missions and forces was established. Many of these moves were strongly criticized by some officers and by congressional spokesmen for the armed services. An effort in 1963 to

free the joint chiefs from their dependence on President and secretary prescribing four-year terms was, however, successfully resisted.

The legislation of 1949 definitely reduced the Departments of the *The*
Army, Navy, and Air Force to their present status of so-called military *military*
departments. The Department of the Army is charged with responsibility for *depart-*
organizing, training, maintaining, and equipping the United States Army, *ments*
and with various subsidiary functions such as directing the Corps of Engineers in improving waterways, formulating and executing plans for flood
control, constructing national monuments and memorials, and operating
the Panama Canal. When it shall have divested itself (as now intended) of
all insular administration, the Navy Department will have no functions not
directly connected with the Navy itself. Taking over most aeronautical functions from the War Department, the relatively new Department of the Air
Force already has developed extensive machinery concerned with substantially everything relating to not only the Regular Air Force, but to an
Air Reserve, and Air National Guard, and an Air Reserve Officers Training
Corps. All three departments undergo occasional organizational changes,
but in general operate on lines not widely different from those familiar in
the War and Navy establishments before 1947. All have the basic task of
maintaining firm central and civilian control while promoting the military
capacities and energies for which the respective—and still separate—armed
forces under them exist.

At the top level, the Defense Department is rounded out by two staff *Staff*
agencies designed for planning and policy determination: (1) the Armed *agencies*
Forces Policy Council (replacing a former War Council), advising the
secretary of defense on broad policy matters and rarely used; (2) the Joint
Chiefs of Staff, originating during World War II and having as its province
all matters pertaining to military strategy and in direct command of com-
manders of joint operations in the various theaters. The Joint Chiefs of Staff
are also military advisers of the President as well as of the Secretary of Defense. The Joint Chiefs arrangement has survived the various reorganiza-
tions and has been shored up by the development of a substantial staff under
it and separate, therefore, from the various services. It has, however, been
the object of continuing criticism for its alleged failure to provide genuine,
coordinated planning either in strategy or in budgeting and many internal
disagreements have been carried to the secretary, to the President, to Congress, and even to the public.

With the secretary of defense supplying the principal point of contact, *2. The*
the Department of Defense is the arm of the President for purposes of *National*
national security in its military, naval, and aeronautical aspects. To provide *Security*
broader basis for decisions involving defense the National Security Act of *Council*
1947 introduced two other major agencies already mentioned, the National
Security Council and the National Security Resources Board, both placed
in 1949 in the Executive Office of the President. Only the first of these has
survived. Its task is nothing less than to formulate for the President the

ORGANIZATION FOR NATIONAL SECURITY

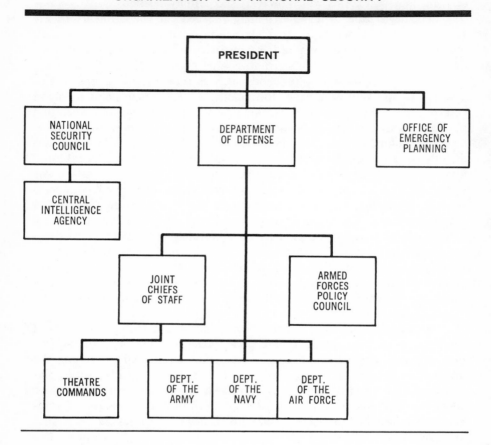

collective advice of all appropriate officers and agencies of the executive branch on the integration of domestic, foreign, and military policies in any manner touching the national security. In addition to the President as chairman, the members include the Vice President, the secretaries of state and defense, and the director of the Office of Emergncy Planning, who from their different official environments can bring together foreign policy, military, and economic viewpoints, with indeed the financial also contributed by the secretary of the treasury sitting, not as a member, but as a regular participant by presidential invitation. Meeting normally twice a month (with the President usually absenting himself in the interest of freer discussion), the Council is intended to thrash out large questions of national security and through its secretariat keep the Chief Executive currently informed on all its discussions and decisions. Under the direction of the Council is a Central Intelligence Agency (C.I.A.) to coordinate the intelligence activities of the various defense agencies and to supply the Council and the President with information necessary to their decisions. The Council does not itself determine policy. That is for the President to do, on the basis of Council advice, which, however, he is free to accept or reject, in whole or in part. If it is possible in our system—and some doubt it—to achieve high-level correlation of the nation's foreign objectives, commitments, and risks with its military and economic capacities, this is the agency designed to do so. Like the Joint Chiefs, however, it has not escaped severe censure when crises arise—as in Korea with the entrance into the fray of the Chinese, in Cuba with the abortive effort to overthrow Castro, and in the lag in rocketry and missile development—for which it has not seemed to be prepared and for which its proposed advice has not seemed clear or persuasive. It must be emphasized, however, that the final responsibility for coordination and decision falls upon just one man, the President of the United States.

Success in modern war was thought by the fathers of the present defense establishment to depend heavily upon a nation's economic preparedness, or at any rate upon the speed and effectiveness with which the economy could be converted to war production. The authors of the Security Act of 1947 provided a National Security Resources Board to investigate and plan correlating foreign and military policy with natural resources and economic capacity. The Board was replaced in 1953 with an Office of Defense Mobilization.

3. Office of Emergency Planning

The greatly increased possibilities of breaching American defenses from the air, combined with the perfection of weapons of awesome destructive power, encouraged the President and later the Congress to create a new agency of government to prepare our industrial areas for attack. The Federal Civil Defense Administration was established in 1950 first in the Office of Emergency Management in the Executive Office and later by Congress as an independent executive agency. This agency is charged with developing, in cooperation with state and local authorities, plans for the protection of our civilian population in case of enemy bombing attacks. Grants are made to states for equipment and materials for approved projects. Since 1953, this agency has also been assigned responsibilities for administering national disaster relief programs of certain types. In 1958, this agency and the Office of Defense Mobilization were merged by an executive reorganization plan into the present Office of Civil and Defense Mobilization and when in 1961 its operating responsibilities in civil defense were transferred to the Department of Defense, it was retitled the Office of Emergency Planning.

THE ARMED FORCES

Creating an effective military force has always been a troublesome problem for democratic countries, whose peoples have been suspicious of the military and of militarism. It has been especially difficult for the United

States. We have normally disavowed aggressive aims against our neighbors and, sheltered behind broad oceans, have felt no need for large or expensive forces to protect our safety. We have been unwilling to create a peacetime army of conscripts as the Europeans have preferred, but rather have relied on volunteers in peace and conscripts in war. Volunteering has proved effective only when very small forces are to be staffed. After mobilizing our people and resources for combat on a large scale in the two great wars of this century, we have demobilized them after victory as rapidly as possible. The development of nuclear weapons and of unmanned missiles to carry them, the collapse of the concert of victors after World War II, the spread of communist influence, the rise of Soviet Russia, the emergence of new states from European colonial territories, and the intransigence of Red China have all contributed to an international situation to which most of our military traditions are inappropriate. The last two decades, therefore, have witnessed not only a complete turnabout of our old military policies, and the maintenance of huge armed forces in "peacetime" backed by great stockpiles of strategic materials and armaments, but also constant changes in emphasis among the types of forces and weapons systems on which we should place our major reliance. During this period we have also become intimately involved in the deployments of our allies and have had to appraise the importance of the rapid technological developments of our potential enemies.

Change in defense policies after World War II

At the close of World War II, despite the warnings of some of our statesmen and several of our allies, under the spell of our well-established traditions we dismantled our war machine about as fast as we could and thus made it impossible to oppose Soviet adventure except by all-out war and remobilization. Deterioration of our relations with the Soviet and the loss of China to the Reds spread deep concern in high Washington circles but did not and perhaps could not at that time have convinced our people to reassemble our armed might and reverse our traditional peacetime military posture. We knew only war—full scale with all our resources mobilized —or peace with an army deployed for Indian fighting and a Navy to patrol our shores and protect the canal. Korea offered the occasion and the justification for rearmament short of total mobilization. Comfortable in our superiority in atomic weapons, no longer, unfortunately, a monopoly, we then felt that we must in concert with our European allies organize ground and sea forces large enough to halt or to delay the overwhelming ground strength of Russia. Two major policies ensued: (1) a call for Universal Military Training in the United States; and (2) the organization of substantial western European armies including those of West Germany. Both of these called for heavier peacetime military expenditures than we had ever believed to be bearable. They also assumed that given our air and atomic bomb superiority the Soviets would probably attack in Europe with their own superior ground forces.

Rearmament after Korea

The nuclear deterrent

The economic burden of these policies on the American taxpayer was a matter of grave concern to those elected to office in 1952 who feared the collapse of our economic strength upon which our military effectiveness must inevitably rest. Universal Military Training like the war in Korea was widely unpopular and was never fully implemented by Congress. Furthermore, it could legitimately be argued that any attack in Europe would have to be halted there by the troops on hand. We would not be given time to mobilize reserves in the earlier fashion and then bring them into action months after the start of hostilities. Korea and its demand for ground forces was ended by armistice. With these concerns we decided to reduce our reliance on traditional forces and to depend henceforth largely on nuclear weapons delivered from the air to break up or to prevent Soviet aggression. We brandished our nuclear warheads, talked of "massive retaliation," and curtailed ground and sea forces. The risk of these policies, as several critics pointed out, notably General Taylor, was that we might leave ourselves unable to deal with new Koreas, Quemoys, Suez Canals, or Congo revolutions except by a nuclear holocaust.

Sputnik, in 1957, virtually spelled the end of this era. Soviet technology having opened the secrets of the atom in 1949 and produced a hydrogen bomb in 1954, had now caught up and perhaps passed our own in rocketry and missiles. Russia was no longer dependent upon its ground superiority. It could now threaten, not only Europe on the ground, but also America from the air and our airplanes could not certainly stop their rockets and perhaps could not even survive a first strike in sufficient numbers to launch a counter attack. We were thus obliged to catch up in rockets and missiles at any cost. Assuming that a balance of deterrent power existed, we came back to the earlier policy of strengthening our conventional forces to deal with "crises" and to allow us to limit their spread. We continued to hedge our dependence on missiles, however, by developing faster and larger bombers and by making a beginning on an antimissile defense system, ostensibly to cope with China's as yet immature missile threat. This has proved, of course, the most costly of all our postwar military policies and seems likely to commit us to a very high level of expenditure for many years to come. Our statesmen are still wrestling with these difficult decisions. Few believe that our present posture is wholly satisfactory. Secretary McNamara argued against further investments in bombers and against a strong commitment to an antimissile system. The best defense, he said, was to strengthen our offensive missile capabilities. Others argued that the B-52 manned bomber had to be superseded and that if Russia was deploying an antimissile system, we must do so too. Meanwhile the war in Viet Nam forced our defense expenditures past $80 billion, most of the increase going to the conventional forces and weapons used on the ground and in the air in Viet Nam.

The new emphasis on conventional arms

In the democratic system, shifts in emphasis and changes in direction are rarely clean cut. Many of the dispositions, institutional arrangements, statutory authorizations, and expenditure patterns of each phase are carried on—perhaps slightly modified—into the new phase. We have, at present, therefore, a complex and not wholly consistent set of military policies and procedures on the basis of which our armed forces are recruited, trained, equipped, and deployed. Our present level of annual expenditures may be compared to $12 billion in 1948 and to $35 to $40 billion in 1953 to 1957. We have 3.5 million men under arms in various forces (about 540,000 in Viet Nam) backed up by another 950 thousand reserves in various conditions of training and readiness. These are organized into 19 army and 4 marine divisions, 136 tactical squadrons, and over 500 commissioned warships. While we do not have a full-fledged system of universal military training, we do have peacetime conscription under which young men register at age 18 and are called up for service as needed for periods up to two years. Widespread dissatisfaction with our involvement in Viet Nam has stimulated intense criticism of the draft. As operated in the mid-sixties, the draft fell heavily on the poor, the Negro, and the unskilled. College students —including, until 1968, graduate students—were generally exempted while in school, and were, therefore called, if at all, only in their mid-twenties. A Presidential Commission on Selective Service recommended replacement of the existent deferment policies by random selection among all eligible young men at age 19 and the end of student deferments. Congress in 1967 in extending the draft until 1971 refused to authorize a random selection or lottery system and continued the college student authorization but withdrew general deferment for postgraduate study. The reserve apparatus, including the national guard, has been reorganized—mainly in 1955, and to some extent in 1967—and tightened to maintain more effective control over the preparation of those in the ready or immediate reserve components. Efforts by Secretary McNamara further to consolidate the Reserves and reduce the National Guard were frustrated by the Congress in the legislation of 1967 which forbade any merger of the Army Reserve and the National Guard. Missiles of various types are rolling off production lines and numerous sites have been hardened. We maintain a string of bases—air and missile—in various friendly countries around the defense perimeter of the West and have missile-firing submarines patrolling the oceans.

NATIONAL CONTROLS IN WARTIME

Half a dozen clauses of the Constitution suggest that for carrying on a war Congress may tax, borrow, raise troops, and build ships practically without restraint, with the President exercising the broad and undefined functions accruing to him as Chief Executive and Commander-in-Chief. But they convey little idea of what this may mean either for the machinery and processes of government or for the national economy—industry, transportation, communications, labor, prices, manpower, and daily civilian life. To visualize these things, one has rather to recall what happened during two world wars, during the Korean struggle, and, in part at least, continuing right up to the present. No two wars are alike; certainly an atomic war would differ from any we have known. Up to now, however, war's impact on government and economy can best be apprehended in terms of World War II; and a word on that chapter of our experience is in order.

Fundamentally, wartime controls are exercised by the regular peacetime authorities. Congress stays in session and broadens and deepens its regulations as needs require, with little, under the circumstances, to fear from the courts. As Chief Executive, and particularly as Commander-in-Chief, the President mounts from peak to peak of directing authority, reading more and more power into his constitutional prerogatives and drawing almost equally from delegations by Congress. The executive departments and independent establishments intensify their activities in all that relates to the war effort. With new and vast specialized tasks developing, however, need arises for additional machinery, created directly by Congress or more frequently by executive order implementing some broad congressional grant. Even before we entered World War I, a top-level Council of National Defense was set up; and during that conflict a War Industries Board furnished a nucleus for new regulatory and administrative agencies. Again, the defense effort of 1940 called into existence, a year and a half before Pearl Harbor, an Office of Emergency Management, lodged in the Executive Office of the President and becoming a framework under whose broad roof were later gathered 15 major establishments concerned with wartime control, administration, and research. These agencies and others, in turn, provided hooks from which were suspended, as time went on, a maze of additional offices, boards, commissions, and the like, so numerous and so frequently reshuffled as to bewilder even the near-at-hand observer in Washington. Under stress of war, a government already big inevitably grows bigger. *Expansion of powers and agencies*

The principle is clear that the government may, insofar as it finds need, draft into its armed services able-bodied men of all ages and conditions, and women too for duties appropriate to them. Conscription was resorted to (for the first time) not only during the Civil War, but on a vast scale during World Wars I and II—in the latter instance, indeed, at a stage when war merely seemed probable. When raising forces in this way, Congress fixes age limits for men liable to induction, specifies or authorizes classifications and priorities in terms of number of dependents and occupational usefulness for war purposes, and determines exemptions. Room is left for volunteering, especially by women. But, within bounds of reason, expediency, and humanity, the government always can dig as deeply into the reservoir of potential combat and auxiliary forces as circumstances seem to it to require. *Some areas of control:*

1. Military service

Aside from a steady stream of trained men, the prime necessity in present-day war is abundant munitions and supplies. With a view to assuring ample production of these, the government may build plants (operating them directly or more often through private corporations under contract), finance the establishment or expansion of others, require plants to be turned to war production, take over and operate establishments crippled or threat- *2. Industrial production* ened by labor difficulties, curb or suspend production of nonessential consumer goods, build stockpiles of necessary raw materials, and establish priorities for funneling materials to war industries most in need of them. Largely through a major agency known as the War Production Board, all of these things actually were done during World War II.

3. Civilian life   In line with the same objective of all-out effort in prosecuting a war, the government may take any needful measures for maximum utilization of the nation's civilian manpower and womanpower, even to the extent of registering all able-bodied personnel of both sexes, imposing a work-or-fight rule, and assigning people to jobs. Although urged in some quarters to do so, Congress did not go this far during World War II. But almost immediately after Pearl Harbor the draft as already operating was broadened to require all men up to the age of 64 to register for conscription in the armed forces or for noncombatant duty; and throughout the conflict a War Manpower Commission, although without authority actually to compel men and women to work at particular jobs in particular places, promoted maximum use of personnel by measures calculated to keep people employed in jobs and places where they were most needed and to discourage moving around in quest of more congenial and better-paying positions. Strikes in industry and transportation never were expressly outlawed, and some occurred. But the conditions under which they could legally be declared and carried on were circumscribed, and heavy penalties were imposed upon labor leaders fomenting them.

4. Wages, prices, and distribution of goods   A war of any proportions instantly starts a chain of dislocations in the national economy. An upsurge of government expenditures, reenforced by augmented employment, produces a rise of prices; higher prices push up wages; higher wages, more spending power, and increasing scarcity of consumer goods stimulate further price rises. Unless brakes are applied, the spiral ends in heavy inflation, particularly devastating for people of fixed incomes but eventually disastrous for the entire economy. Speaking broadly, whatever checks are imposed must come from government; and, with various wage and price controls during World War I as precedents, an Office of Economic Stabilization early in World War II fixed wage ceilings for different industries, while an Office of Price Administration placed and kept under some restraint prices of commodities (rents also) likely to be most affected by prevailing scarcities. In connection with price controls, the O.P.A. also rationed among consumers, the country over, long lists of commodities (automobiles, tires, gasoline, fuel oil, farm machinery, shoes, coffee, sugar, meats, and many other things), demand for which was out of proportion to supply. Proposals at the beginning of the war that wages and prices be "frozen" all around never were adopted. At the end, the country was left with a considerable heritage of inflation. Matters, however, would have been far worse without the wartime stabilizations achieved.

5. Transportation   Almost as vital as the production of war materials is the transportation of them (and of troops) to places where they are needed; and here the government, with full power over interstate and foreign commerce, has especially free scope. During World War I, the railroads were taken over and operated. During World War II, no need for such a course arose. But, within the framework of preexisting transportation controls exercised by the Interstate Commerce Commission and allied agencies, an Office of Defense Transportation correlated the services of railways, inland waterways, air transport, motor transport, coastwise shipping, and pipe lines in the interest of maximum contribution to the war effort. When neighbors took to group-riding to relieve other carriers and save tires and gasoline, they were acting in the spirit of O.D.T. requests.

War is waged not only with men, munitions, and materials, but also with ideas. Every wartime government (at any rate in a democratic country) must concern itself not only with getting to the people the information it wants them to have and with cultivating a public opinion favorable to the war effort, but also with keeping from the enemy information useful to him and with preventing both the enemy and enemy sympathizers from damaging the national morale through open or secret propaganda. The story of our government's efforts during World Wars I and II—in the first instance through a Committee on Public Information and in the second through an Office of War Information—to keep the nation (and friendly peoples abroad) discreetly informed on war aims and developments would reveal a good deal of fumbling, yet reasonable attainment of the ends sought. During World War II, responsibility for guarding against dissemination of information or opinion in ways injurious to our cause was intrusted to an Office of Censorship set up almost as soon as hostilities started. Here, too, the record of achievement was generally good. On the one hand, there was literal and positive censorship, in the sense that all mail, cablegrams, long-distance telephone calls, radio messages, and other communications going out of (or in the case of mail coming into) the United States were minutely inspected, with objectionable passages deleted or even the entire message intercepted. In the case, on the other hand, of domestic publications and radio broadcasting, the milder method was employed of relying upon voluntary compliance of the press and the broadcasting companies with codes of wartime practices, telling them what they must not print or put on the air—although, of course, with no lack of power to compel obedience where not otherwise forthcoming. Closely related in wartime are, of course, laws and enforcing agencies designed to repress espionage, sabotage, and sedition, and especially to protect the armed forces against subversive influences.

6. Communications

The conduct of war is definitely a national function, but collaboration by state and local governments, and by voluntary citizen groups as well, is essential to solidarity of effort. During World War II, state and local machinery was employed in operating the Selective Service System, the rationing system, and to some extent the system of price control. Civilian defense—aimed chiefly at protecting people and property against the hazards of air raids, but later principally at promoting morale and encouraging produc-

7. Civilian defense

tiveness—was organized also largely on a state and local basis. Every state eventually set up a defense council; several thousand cities and counties did likewise: and, in all, millions of men and women rendered various voluntary services.

A new
program
of controls
instituted
in 1950

Greatly amplified after war came, the system of controls described had its beginning in 1940–1941, during days of nominal peace; and 10 years later, with the country also technically at peace, although engaged in military action in Korea, a new defense effort brought such controls again into the picture. With resolution formed in government circles to embark upon a major program of military preparedness, and with Congress and the country won to full support, President Truman, in September, 1950, stressed as three great requisites (1) production of the materials and equipment required, (2) new taxation to meet the costs involved, and (3) prevention of inflation. A special revenue act of September marked the first stage of the heavier taxation contemplated; and powers for pursuing the other objectives were supplied in a Defense Production Act conveying authority to control wages and prices and to introduce rationing; and authority also (for a year longer) to requisition materials and plants necessary to rearmament, to allocate goods in short supply, and to advance money for encouraging output. Most of the controls were discontinued after 1953 as a result of armistice in Korea and of the election of an administration pledged to reduce restrictions on the private economy. Many of the powers, however, remain in the statute books ready to be invoked should a new "emergency" occur. President Johnson refrained from declaring a national emergency over Viet Nam and sought to fight the war on a business-as-usual basis.

ATOMIC ENERGY, NUCLEAR WEAPONS, AND DISARMAMENT

On August 6, 1945, the first atomic bomb was dropped on Hiroshima, Japan, by the United States armed forces, killing 78,000 and wounding 150,000 more and introducing a new technique of destruction unparalleled in the history of the world. It is appropriate that we conclude this discussion of national defense with some notice of the consequences of this new and terrible threat to the continued existence of life on this planet.

Efforts to
achieve
inter-
national
control of
atomic
weapons

As the result of a suggestion by Albert Einstein, President Roosevelt put scientists to work early in the war to discover if the power of the atom could be unlocked for military purposes. Thousands of scientists—American, Canadian, and British—worked in this secret project for more than four years and finally achieved an explosive with the force of 20,000 tons of TNT. A successful explosion was set off at Los Alamos, New Mexico, in the summer of 1945 and, when Japan rejected the surrender ultimatum issued by the Allies at Potsdam on July 26, President Truman decided to drop the bomb. The Japanese surrender came within a few hours of the dropping of the second bomb on Nagasaki on August 9. Guided by the group of scientists, statesmen, and soldiers who had directed the successful research, the government now faced the problem of the future use of this dread weapon. Certain that they could not keep the secrets of its composition and manufacture indefinitely, fearful of the holocaust which might result from widespread use of the bomb in war, confident that peaceful uses of atomic energy of great benefit to mankind might be discovered by energetic application of many scientists, the three nations concerned, Great Britain, Canada, and the United States, proposed that the U.N. establish a commission to study and recommend a program for the control of atomic weapons and for the peaceful exploitation of the energy potential unloosed for the first time in man's history.

The U.N. created such a commission and before it the United States submitted a plan for the international control of atomic energy with an international agency equipped with inspectorial authority to enforce such controls upon the nations of the world. If such an agency should be established, the manufacture of atomic weapons should be prohibited. The Russians countered with a proposal for the outlawing of such weapons immediately, the prohibition of their manufacture in the future, and the destruction of all those in existence at the time. They would not agree to any procedure which involved inspection of their industrial operations by outsiders. Months of subsequent negotiations failed to move either major power from its central position.

Meanwhile, in the United States, President Truman seeking a more permanent arrangement for the domestic control of atomic energy research and weapons manufacture, proposed to the Congress, in late 1945, that a civilian commission be created in the executive branch for this purpose. And the Congress passed in 1946 an Atomic Energy Act creating an independent five-man commission to exercise complete control over the production of atomic energy and the research program associated with it. The Commission was assigned full ownership of all domestic uranium and other materials essential for the production of the bomb. The principal battle of civilian versus military control of atomic energy was thus largely resolved in favor of the civilians. Extremely rigid security regulations, since made even more rigid, were enacted to control virtually all phases of the Commission's operations. Many scientists have since contended that the "secrecy" requirements have inhibited effective private scientific inquiries and have thus limited the search for peaceful and constructive application of the scientific knowledge of the Commission's experts. The fact that the measure gave to a government agency complete ownership and control over a source of power which might some day replace other energy sources both at home and abroad did not at that time precipitate much controversy. Later, however, growing criticism of the atomic program on the grounds that private enterprise ought to have a larger share in the exploitation of the peaceful possibilities and that too much emphasis was placed on the military phases by the Commission paved the way for a new Atomic Energy Act of 1954. This act opened the way for

Atomic Energy Act of 1946

private industry to construct atomic furnaces and to carry on experiments of many kinds, under Commission supervision. A Joint Committee of the Congress on Atomic Energy established by the Act of 1946 provides continuing legislative oversight of the Commission's program.

The hydro-gen bomb   On the international scene, the problem of control of atomic weapons has become more and more acute in the years since 1946. The Soviet Union, in part at least through a clever spy ring and with the help of some captured scientists, acquired the secret of the bomb—an atomic explosion occurred in Russia in 1949—much sooner than the Anglo-American allies anticipated. The AEC scientists—after some bitter internal controversy—produced the hydrogen bomb, a weapon more deadly than the atom bomb and carried their researches to the very threshold of a bomb that would wipe out the entire human race. The Russians, on their part, produced a hydrogen weapon also. Thus the very real possibility that a war between the two great powers would result in extermination of life over much of the earth's surface has for more than a decade faced the nations of the world. Hoping to realize some of the constructive benefits, President Eisenhower in December, 1953, proposed to the U.N. an international pool of atomic energy resources and offered to make an American contribution to such a pool. An international conference on peaceful uses of atomic energy held in Geneva in 1955 helped to pave the way for the creation in 1957 of an International Atomic Energy Agency supported by 80 nations. Our participation, including the donation of fissionable materials, was approved by the Senate and the implementing statute by the Congress.

Nuclear test bans   Throughout these developments, the AEC scientists continued by test explosions to study the effects of various types of nuclear weapons and the administration continued to seek agreement on international control that would include inspectorial enforcement. Adlai Stevenson, in the campaign of 1956, reflected the view of a growing body of scientific opinion that fall-out of radio-active particles from the test explosions was sufficiently dangerous to life and health that testing should be halted and that America should take the lead in this matter. Our position remained, however, that until or unless international agreement could be reached containing "adequate" guarantees we must keep perfecting our knowledge. Just as we were about to launch a new series of tests early in 1958, Russia announced that it was suspending its testing and would continue to do so if the Western powers would stop also. After the completion of our test series, we also halted further testing and continued to press for international agreement. Negotiations for a permanent test ban continued thereafter for month after weary month—the Americans insisting that available long-range detecting devices were not completely reliable and that we must have neutral inspection—the Russians, that inspection was a facade for Western spying. The test suspension as a year-to-year policy continued, however, until 1961 when as an outgrowth of the Berlin crisis of that year, the Russians announced the resumption of testing and launched a series of new tests. President Kennedy then

announced that in self-defense we must resume our tests and a new series
of test explosions began in April 1962 and continued into the summer and
fall. Russia, thereafter, announced that it would also launch a new series
of tests.

Perhaps stimulated by a threatened rupture with its Chinese allies over *The test*
Soviet Cold War strategy, the Soviet leadership began in mid-1963 to take *ban treaty*
a more conciliatory tone in disarmament negotiations at Geneva. These had
been going on for many months under continuing pressure from the U.N.
General Assembly. President Kennedy announced in June a suspension of
tests pending the outcome of negotiations to be started in Moscow among
Britain, the Soviet Union, and ourselves. A limited test ban treaty was
finally agreed upon by these powers on July 25, 1963. This treaty prohibits
the signatories from conducting nuclear tests in the atmosphere, in outer
space, or on the seas. It does not apply to tests underground. Other nations
are invited to subscribe to these terms and each party reserves the right to
terminate its commitment if it decides that "extraordinary events . . . have
jeopardized the supreme interests of its country." The treaty has been approved by the Senate and signed by the President. It has now been signed
by 13 nations (not including Red China and France).

The friendly atmosphere of the test ban negotiations produced other
efforts to reduce Cold War tensions and bring some reduction, however
modest, to the mounting costs of the armaments race. The U.S., U.S.S.R.,
and U.K. reached agreement in principle in 1963 to refrain from placing
in orbit any weapons of mass destruction. The agreement was actively
sponsored by the members of the Geneva Disarmament Conference and
adopted by acclamation by the General Assembly of the U.N. It was formalized into a treaty entered into among the nuclear powers (excluding
France and Red China) in 1967. The signatories agreed not to establish
military bases or fortifications on the moon or planets and not to test weapons or conduct military maneuvers of any kind in space. The Senate unanimously ratified this treaty in April, 1967. After several years of effort,
President Johnson was also able in mid-1968 to ask the Senate to approve
a Treaty on the Non-Proliferation of Nuclear Weapons, commended by the
General Assembly of the U.N. and agreed to by Russia and the United
States. The treaty forbids the transfer of nuclear arms or explosive devices
to any nations that have no such arms and forbids the "have" nations from
assisting others to manufacture or obtain control of such arms. It also
forbids the nonnuclear states to receive such arms or assistance. An inspection, to be operated by the International Atomic Energy Agency, is set up
to insure compliance. The peaceful uses of atomic energy are to be made
available to all through the same agency. Signatories agree further to pursue negotiations leading to a cessation of the nuclear arms race and to a
treaty on general disarmament.

Red China, which exploded its first hydrogen bomb in June, 1967 and
continues its efforts to build greater capabilities, and France, still testing

in the Pacific in 1968, stand outside these efforts to overtake the global plunge to destruction.

SPACE SATELLITES

Sputnik

American complacency in our military superiority based on our advanced nuclear research, our ready fleet of great bombers, our network of bases in N.A.T.O. countries, and in our scientific and technological superiority was suddenly and devastatingly shattered in October, 1957. The Soviet Union launched the first artificial earth satellite. Scientists and military leaders appreciated that rockets with a thrust capable of hurling a 194 pound (later a 1 120 and then a 2 825 pound) device hundreds of miles into space might also hurl nuclear warheads upon Pittsburgh or Chicago with little chance of interception by man-driven airplanes. The Soviets then followed this by a successful moon-shot in 1959 and by several manned space flights each year to the present. The Soviet Union thus demonstrated that it had the capability of leaping over our protective bases and striking directly at the United States.

The lag in American rocketry

The American rocket and missile program, it appeared on subsequent investigation, had languished for some years—a victim of budgetary economies, interservice rivalries, and unwarranted satisfaction with our air-bomb retaliatory power. Congress assembled in 1958 in a mood to spare no pains and no expense to catch up scientifically and militarily to the Russians in missiles, rockets, and space explorations. The Army finally thrust a 31 pound satellite into orbit in January, 1958. This has been followed by several breathtaking thrusts into outer space and by the widely publicized orbits of several astronauts beginning in 1962 and including the moon orbit of 1968. We are now spending more on rockets than we did on the atomic bomb; we have shifted our military arrangements to lesser dependence on airpower and have increased our missile bases and rocket capabilities.

Disarmament acquires new urgency

One consequence of these frightening developments has been that our interest in international controls of nuclear weapons and in making progress in disarmament has become greater than ever and some heartening progress in this direction has, as we have seen, been made.

Debate over military policy

Another related development has been the increasing controversy about our whole military program and policies, outlined previously.

A third development has been the growing emphasis on exploration of outer space. A new Aeronautics and Space Administration created in 1958 spearheads the nonmilitary research and experimentation aimed at probing the universe. It is surely a wondrous new world when the President of the United States in 1961 soberly tells the Congress that we intend to land a man on the moon. Late in 1963, the President further proposed that the Soviet Union and the United States cooperate in their efforts to reach the moon. And in mid-1968, Johnson was able to send to the Senate for approval a treaty signed by Russia and others on assistance for astronauts in space and on the earth. Although set back by a disastrous fire in a test capsule which took the lives of the astronauts and by economies resulting from the war in Viet Nam, the Johnson Administration, nevertheless, continued to push the moon project and at Christmas 1968 was able to thrust a space capsule with three astronauts to within 70 miles of the moon.

REFERENCES

B. Brodie (ed.), *The Absolute Weapon; Atomic Power and World Order* (New York, 1946).

B. K. Chapman, *The Wrong Man in Uniform* (New York, 1967).

G. Dean, *Report on the Atom* (New York, 1953).

F. S. Dunn, *War and the Minds of Men* (New York, 1950).

R. A. Goldwin (ed.), *America Armed: Essays on United States Military Policy* (Chicago, 1963).

A. T. Hadley, *The Nation's Safety and Arms Control* (New York, 1961).

M. Halperin, *Contemporary Military Strategy* (Cambridge, Mass., 1967).

C. J. Hitch, *Decision-Making for Defense* (Berkeley, Cal., 1965).

H. L. Hoskins, *The Atlantic Pact* (Washington, D. C., 1949).

S. P. Huntington, *The Common Defense: Strategic Programs in National Politics* (New York, 1961).

E. Huzar, *The Purse and the Sword; Control of the Army by Congress Through Military Appropriations, 1933–1950* (Ithaca, N. Y., 1950).

M. Janowitz (ed.), *The New Military: Changing Patterns of Organization* (New York, 1964).

W. W. Kaufmann (ed.), *Military Policy and National Security* (Princeton, N. J., 1956).

H. A. Kissinger, *The Necessity for Choice: Prospects of American Foreign Policy* (New York, 1961).

————, *Nuclear Weapons and Foreign Policy* (New York, 1957).

K. Knorr, *On the Uses of Military Power in the Nuclear Age* (Princeton, N. J., 1966).

L. W. Koenig, *The Presidency and the Crisis* (New York, 1944), Chaps. III–V.

E. A. Kolodziej, *The Uncommon Defense and Congress, 1945–1963* (Columbus, Ohio, 1966).

M. R. Laird, *A House Divided* (New York, 1963).

R. E. Lapp, *The New Force* (New York, 1953).

E. R. May, *The Ultimate Decision: The President as Commander-in-Chief* (New York, 1960).

W. Millis, H. C. Mansfield, and H. Stein, *Arms and the State: Civil-Military Elements in National Policy* (New York, 1958).

J. R. Neuman and B. S. Miller, *The Control of Atomic Energy; a Study of its Social, Economic, and Political Implication* (New York, 1948).

President's National Advisory Commission on Selective Service, *In Pursuit of Equity: Who Serves When not All Serve?* (Washington, D. C., 1967).

T. C. Schilling and M. H. Halperin, *Strategy and Arms Control* (New York, 1961).

H. D. Smyth, *Atomic Energy for Military Purposes* (Princeton, N. J., 1945).

D. W. Tarr, *American Strategy in the Nuclear Age* (New York, 1964).

C Finances

23

FINANCING THE NATIONAL GOVERNMENT

The responsibilities of the national government, described in the preceding chapters, are heavy and the demands of the people for services are great. Sooner or later all discussions of public affairs must come to grips with the costs involved and the resources available to pay them. We, too, must turn now to the melancholy subject of paying the bills for the services the government performs. The complex structure of the national government, described in an earlier section, is obviously a costly one to sustain, and courts, Congress, and executive require millions of dollars for their effective functioning in the modern world. These costs are, however, but trifles compared with the billions required to equip and maintain our great military establishment, to sustain our allies, to uphold the economy of the farmers, to sustain the poor, the aged, and the unfortunate, to care for the veteran, to reclaim wasteland, to harness the power of our great rivers, and to penetrate outer space. Measurable changes—up or down—in our national budget result largely from changes in the services rendered and all the structural tinkering conceivable would affect the costs of government but slightly.

THE SPENDING POWER

The Congress shall have power to lay and collect taxes, duties, imposts and excises, to pay the debts and provide for the common defense and general welfare of the United States; . . .
—Art. 1, Sec. 8, cl. 1

Constitutional basis

The Constitution has rather more to say directly about raising revenue than about spending it. A government, however, that could not spend would be no government at all; and in the case of the national government, power to spend not only is expressly granted but is clearly implied in numerous provisions conferring authority to do things which could not possibly be done without spending money, for example, raise and support armies, provide and maintain a navy, establish post offices and post roads, and maintain a system of courts. If necessary, spending power could probably be deduced also from the granted powers to tax and borrow, since manifestly there would be no point to raising money if it could not be used. Only three specific restrictions are imposed: (1) that appropriations for the support of the Army shall not be "for a longer term than two years"; (2) that "no money shall be drawn from the Treasury but in consequence of appropriations made by law"; and (3) that "a regular statement and account of the receipts and expenditures of all public money shall be published from time to time."

Some broad interpre- tations

Nevertheless, throughout much of our national history the spending power of Congress has been a prolific source of constitutional controversy. Primarily, the question has been whether the power to spend is restricted to purposes connected with the exercise of *other* powers delegated in the Constitution, or whether it is a power independent of, and in addition to, other powers and properly to be exercised for *any* purpose so long as having to do with "common defense and general welfare." In early days, strict constructionists like Madison took the first view, loose constructionists like Hamilton the second. The more liberal interpretation eventually prevailed, with Congress falling into the habit of regarding its spending power as properly extending to any and all objectives rationally associated with defense or welfare. Nay, more: no appropriation made on this assumption was ever—simply as an act of spending—successfully challenged in the courts. And not only so, but the Supreme Court has gone out of its way to assert that "the power of Congress to authorize the expenditure of public moneys [or to tax] for public purposes is not limited by the direct grants of legislative power found in the Constitution," and further that such expenditure is constitutionally legitimate so long as the welfare at which it is aimed can be plausibly represented as national rather than local, with Congress the judge, subject only to judicial veto if discretion is exercised arbitrarily or unreasonably.

The matter of grants- in-aid

A good while before these principles were so securely established judicially, the spending power was brought into significant controversy by the rise of grants-in-aid. With Congress appropriating funds to states for promoting agricultural education, building roads, protecting natural resources, maintaining employment offices, and performing other functions traditionally regarded as state rather than national, taxpayers sometimes objected to diversion of their contributions to such purposes. In 1923 the Supreme Court was confronted with a case brought by a taxpayer, and also one brought by the state of Massachusetts, challenging the constitutionality of a measure of 1921 appropriating money to aid states in reducing maternal and infant mortality on the ground that the act was serving purposes not national but only local, and invading the sphere of self-government reserved to the states under the Tenth Amendment. No direct affirmation of the act's constitutionality resulted. But in a consolidated decision of the two cases the Court (1) brushed aside the contention of Massachusetts by pointing out that under the law no state was obliged to accept the grant unless it chose, and (2) set aside the taxpayer's protest on the ground that her share of the funds granted under terms of the legislation was too inconsequential to give her reasonable ground for suit. And from that day, the swelling stream of national funds flowing into the states and localities in the form of grants-in-aid has found sanction in these considerations— reinforced by the Court's later ruling that Congress has power to appropriate money for any purpose comprehended within "common defense and general [i.e., national] welfare." For a good while, national officials were fearful lest such undertakings as slum clearance and other housing activities be regarded judicially as "out of bounds"; but a decision of 1945 allayed such apprehension. So long, therefore, as a general-welfare purpose can be shown (and this usually offers little difficulty), the way for grants to states and their subdivisions seems wide open. Nor is it essential that grants be matched with state funds; and as for the regulatory power commonly going along with grants, the Supreme Court has said that it is natural and proper for the government "to regulate that which it subsidizes."

PLANNING AND CONTROLLING EXPENDITURES—
THE BUDGET SYSTEM

The role of Congress

Not a dollar of money can be expended legally except in pursuance of authorization, direct or indirect, by Congress. Voting the great appropriations becomes one of the most laborious but important tasks of the two houses at every regular session. In appropriation acts, Congress in effect instructs the Treasury to supply the executive departments and other spending agencies with stipulated sums, according to specifications set forth in great detail. Indeed, one of the chief means by which Congress exercises control over administration is this minute and itemized allocation of money, cutting off an activity here by leaving it without funds, adding an activity or agency there by makng the necessary financial provision, and in these and other ways predetermining—not always to the satisfaction of all concerned—the lines on which the government's work shall be carried on.

Loose methods of appropriation before 1921

For many years before the adoption of a budget system in 1921, appropriation bills were drafted and introduced by no fewer than nine separate House committees—the bills themselves commonly numbering 14 —and these in the Senate were handled by as many as 15 different committees. Based upon requests made by the various spending agencies, and merely swept together and transmitted to Congress in an undigested mass by the secretary of the treasury, these bills were not only framed, but considered and reported by the several committees, in little or no relation to one another—and, what was worse, in little or no relation to the condition of the Treasury or to the outlook for revenue. With no single guiding hand to exercise restraint, they were likely to emerge in even more swollen form than when they first made their appearance. Although the President might, if he chose, warn and admonish, he as a rule could do nothing in the end except affix his signature, since to do otherwise might mean halting essential government activities. Under such division of responsibility, log-rolling became a fine art, the pork-barrel an inexhaustible resource.

The Budget and Accounting Act of 1921

In the days when expenditures were relatively modest and revenues usually adequate to meet them, criticism of such haphazard procedures had little or no effect. The startling upswing of national outlays during World War I, however, lent new force to a growing demand for reform; and in 1921 a national budget system, long talked about, became a reality. The essence of a sound budget system consists in careful planning of the expenditures of a given fiscal period (usually a year) in relation to anticipated income, by a single authority, which not only will correlate income and outgo, but see that all reasonable economies are practiced. While the plan introduced by the Budget and Accounting Act of 1921 left, and still leaves, a good deal to be desired, it in general meets this basic specification.

The Bureau of the Budget

The planning and coordinating agency set up by the act is the Bureau of the Budget, originally attached loosely to the Treasury Department, although in effect an independent establishment. As supreme director of national administration, the President is, however, the logical authority to bear primary responsibility for preparing integrated programs of spending and revenue-raisings. After Franklin D. Roosevelt became Chief Executive, the Bureau was drawn into closer relations with the White House, until eventually, under authority conferred in the Reorganization Act of 1939, it was definitely placed in the new Executive Office of the President. It thereupon became and has remained the chief executive's largest and most important staff agency—his arm for all contacts and dealings with the financial side of the government.

Its expanded role

Moreover, with the passage of time there has been a remarkable expansion of functions. From an agency concerned with coordinating requests for funds in relation to anticipated revenues and putting them into coherent shape for transmission to Congress, the Bureau has developed into the principal aid to the President in planning and guiding the operations of the entire executive branch of the government. Conceptions of the budgetary process itself have been broadened to include not only the formulation in fiscal terms of the programs for the various departments and establishments, but also review of the execution of such programs, including continuous study of problems of administrative organization and business methods. Resulting in part from the enlargement of governmental activities in fighting the Depression of the thirties, the Bureau's new role arose to an even larger extent from situations created by the defense effort and war. As modern budgeting practice has moved from position and expense concerns to programmatic costs and benefits, the concern of the Bureau for agency accomplishment has grown also.

Such service the Bureau is able to render through the broad power given the director to "assemble, correlate, revise, reduce, or increase" the estimates of the several departments and agencies—a power from which flows wide discretion over the substance of department programs, not only in the planning stage but also later. After the programs have received Bureau approval, and after Congress has voted the necessary appropriations, the departments and establishments still must obtain the Bureau's approval for their financial procedures in carrying out their programs, including the periodic (usually monthly) allotment of funds and the maintenance of reasonable reserves for contingencies. In addition, since 1939 a division of legislative reference in the Bureau has examined and reported upon all measures pending in Congress which, if enacted, would impose a charge upon the public treasury or otherwise affect the President's fiscal policy, the purpose being to determine the relation of such measures to the "financial program of the Presdient"; indeed, if the Bureau does not think well of a measure passed, it may, and sometimes does, prepare a veto message and advise the President to sign it. The legislative division also acts as a central clearing house for all legislative recommendations emanating from the executive branch. All bills proposed by anyone in the executive establishments must be checked by the Bureau to see if they conform to Presidential policy.

Preparing a budget

Although the government's tax year, the year for which taxable income is computed and in which most taxes are paid, corresponds to the calendar year, and therefore starts on January 1, its fiscal year, the year for which expenditures are planned and accounts made up, opens on July 1. A fiscal year hardly begins before systematic work on the financial arrangements for the ensuing year is started. First of all, every spending agency is asked by the Budget Bureau to compile detailed estimates of the funds that it will need in the next fiscal year and to submit such estimates usually in early September. In larger agencies, this is done by special budget officers, in lesser ones by members of the staff detailed for the purpose. For many weeks conferences go on between these or other agency representatives on the one hand and Budget Bureau officials on the other—the former commonly pressing for as generous allotments as they can hope to get, the latter raising questions, offering objections, and seeking to whittle down requests regarded as extravagant or at any rate impracticable. On larger matters, the budget director is brought into the discussions; and, subject only to reversal by the President, his word is law for every department, bureau, board, and commission as to what expenditures (and in what amounts) shall be recommended to Congress and what ones shall not. Meanwhile, the Treasury Department, on its part, has been asked not only for data concerning interest charges on the national debt, but also for detailed estimates of the revenues that may be expected in the period, together with proposals for increasing such revenues in case they promise (as nowadays they almost always do) to be insufficient. Since 1947, the Council of Economic Advisors is also asked for information on the impact of spending, borrowing, and taxation on the national economy. With all the estimates and other information finally in hand (ordinarily by December 1), Bureau officials total up the amounts, and arrange data in logical order. The President must then consider in general and for specific areas the program he will propose to the Congress. Usually he has already assented to many projects in consultation with the departmental or agency head. Congress comes into regular session normally on January 3, and his budget message is due within the first fifteen days. In this message, the President presents his fiscal plan covering not only appropriations but revenues and, if necessary, proposals for deficit financing or for new taxes. At present his message is but an introduction to a comprehensive and detailed budget document in two or more volumes embracing 1200–1500 pages and setting forth in tables, charts, expository statements, and suggested appropriation language the plans he wishes the Congress to consider.

A budget before Congress   In 1920, with the adoption of a budget system imminent, the House of Representatives prepared for the new order of things by enlarging its appropriations committee to 35 (now 50) members, giving it jurisdiction over all appropriation proposals, and authorizing it to employ as many as 15 subcommittees (the present number is 13) for handling proposals relating to particular departments or agencies. Received in the House, a budget's revenue proposals are turned over at once to the committee on ways and means, and its far bulkier proposals for expenditure to the appropriations committee. With a view to more coordination of the two committees, the Legislative Reorganization Act of 1946 interposed a new procedural stage by requiring that, upon the President's proposals for a given fiscal year being received, the House committees on ways and means and appropriations and the corresponding Senate committees (on finance and appropriations), or duly authorized subcommittees thereof, should form themselves into a joint committee and, with the President's recommendations before them, work out a legislative budget fixing ceilings for expenditures and providing for any necessary borrowing, and report the results to the two houses by February 15 (or later date agreed upon) as recommendations for adoption. As tested in sessions of 1948 and 1949, however, this plan almost totally failed to yield the expected economies; ceilings tentatively established in legislative budgets were afterwards largely ignored; and in 1950 the experiment was abandoned. However, in 1967, and again in 1968, the Congress attempted to set and enforce a ceiling on total national expenditures aimed at reducing them. In 1967, an act was passed aimed at reducing expenditures by $4.1 billion and in 1968, as part of the tax increase agreement, a reduction of $6 billion was sought. The

1967 act was not fully effective; it was circumvented by subsequent deficiency appropriations. The 1968 effort, in which a ceiling of $180.1 billion on spending was fixed for 1969, has yet to be fully tested. The President, in signing the tax bill in 1968 strongly criticized the ceiling system as unwise and an evasion of congressional responsibility. The reductions voted in the various bills by the Congress, he said, will not reach the required figure, and, therefore, the executive branch will have to act.

Framing and adopting appropriation bills

Whether adhering to the President's recommendations or striking out on more or less independent lines, appropriations subcommittees in the House evolve 12 or 14 separate appropriation bills providing for departments and establishments, singly or in groups. After being approved by the main committee and passed by the House, these several measures are transmitted to the Senate. The Senate appropriations committee usually confines its activity to reviewing changes made in the President's requests by the House. Thus, the major weight in congressional review of spending is clearly in the House. Conference committees ordinarily reconcile the conflicting views of the two houses and as the session nears its end the bills go to the President. In 1950, a single-package plan was introduced under which, before appropriations finally were voted, all major ones were brought together in one bill, after the manner of the single great annual appropriation bill in the British parliament, and also of consolidated appropriation bills encountered in some of the American states. By decision of the House appropriations committee, however, the device—although warmly supported by many members of both branches as in the interest of unity and economy—was abandoned after one trial. In almost every session since 1950 supporters of the consolidated appropriation bill and of the joint committee on the budget have introduced legislation to reestablish, with some modifications, the procedures recommended in the Legislative Reorganization Act of 1946. While support for some or all of these innovations has been strong at times, the two houses have failed thus far to agree on a new procedure.

Some benefits realized

During the 40 years since the budget system went into operation, it has abundantly proved its worth. Even though we have had many years of deficit financing, no one would dream of returning to the earlier procedure. The system has imparted unity and responsibility to the spending program which otherwise would have been lacking. It opens a way for thorough and impartial review of the estimates of all spending agencies, and for reduction of those found questionable, before they are sent to Capitol Hill, and enables Congress to act with fuller information concerning spending proposals, the state of the country's finances, and the state of the national economy. It also provides the occasion for regular review of the accomplishments of the various agencies of government.

A performance budget

Efforts to improve the system are, however, constantly being made. In one of its 1949 reports, the Hoover Commission sharply criticized the budget as "an inadequate document, poorly organized and improperly designed to serve its major purpose, which is to present an understandable and workable financial plan for the expenditure of the government." Two main improvements were urged: (1) clear separation of capital outlays, for example, on public buildings, from current operating expenditures, and (2) presentation of the latter, not in terms simply of who is to get how much, department by department and bureau by bureau, but in terms rather of functions, services, and activities—in other words, of performance. Both recommendations found ready acceptance. Congress at once passed a resolution requiring the new performance principle to be applied to budgeting for the military department. The President requested all other spending departments and agencies to follow the same pattern; and the general budget for fiscal 1951, presented in January, 1950, embodied, as far as possible, the first effort at a performance budget in our history. Moreover, a Budget and Accounting Procedures Act of 1950 made the new type of budget a permanent statutory requirement. The second Hoover Commission reaffirmed the performance system for presenting budgetary data and urged continued experimentation to spread its use and to improve its effectiveness. Secretary McNamara, attempting to master, control, and simplify the enormous budget of the defense services, introduced and developed a form of performance budgeting now called "planning and programing budget system" in which existing policies for achieving declared goals are evaluated in fiscal terms against alternative methods, and cost-benefit analyses are made to determine the relative efficiencies of each method. President Johnson, impressed with the results, pushed the use of these techniques in all other agencies and much work on these lines is now going forward. The Congress, in 1958, accepted one suggestion originating with the Commission and attempted by statute to modify its method of handling, in each appropriation, obligations arising under previous legislation. The House Appropriations Committee, however, has not thus far elected to follow the procedure suggested in the law.

Executing the budget —the General Accounting Office   In its report of 1937, the President's Committee on Administrative Management criticized the Budget Bureau for concentrating too much upon the preparation of budgets and not giving enough attention to "supervision over the execution of the budget by the spending agencies." As the Committee was frank to recognize, the Bureau had never up to that time been given sufficient staff or money to enable it to perform this added task. The situation has now been measurably corrected; and much is done by way of checking up on the use actually made of funds voted and supervising the transfer of funds from one agency to another. There is need for such work, notwithstanding the existence of another establishment—the General Accounting Office. This office was created by the same act of 1921 which brought the Budget Bureau into existence, and by the Legislative Reorganization Act of 1946 is expressly declared a part of the legislative branch. In addition to auditing the accounts of spending agencies and prescribing their form, this large independent agency—particularly independent because its head, the comptroller general, is appointed by the President and confirmed by the Senate for a 15-year term and is removable only by impeachment or, for cause, by joint resolution of Congress—has as a main function the validation of payments for services, supplies, and so on, as a means of seeing that all such outlays fall within the purposes and limits of appropriations made by Congress. Without the comptroller general's approval, money for such purposes cannot be drawn from the Treasury, or, if drawn and paid over, must be refunded. After 1933, the General Accounting Office became a focus of vigorous controversy, partly because the then comptroller general, personally hostile to the New Deal, held up numerous payments in connection with New Deal enterprises as lacking proper authorization in congressional appropriations. In 1937, the President's Committee made recommendation, warmly supported by the President himself, looking to abolition of the Office, transfer of preaudits to the Treasury Department, and retention of postaudits in a new agency to be headed by an auditor general. Sharply clashing views developed, however, and no action resulted. Reverting to the subject in 1949, the Hoover Commission proposed retention of the General Accounting Office (as an agent of Congress) for purposes of postauditing, but urged the introduction of a chief accounting officer in the Treasury Department (as an agent of the executive) with the title of accountant general of the United States, to take over the administrative work of preauditing expenditures and of prescribing and enforcing day-by-day administrative accounting methods in all departments and agencies with a view to a single system of fiscal accounts, elimination of duplications, and a degree of uniformity then lacking. The Budget and Accounting Procedures Act of 1950, while it gave departments and agencies fuller accounting functions than before, nevertheless continued the system of dispersed responsibility. It directed the Treasury, Budget Bureau, and General Accounting Office to collaborate in prescribing accounting systems but left principal authority in the latter office. The Second Hoover Commission in 1955 suggested that the Budget Bureau ought to develop its accounting services for other agencies and did not grapple with the thorny problem of where ultimate authority ought to reside. The basic issue here is between the Congress and the President with the Congress reluctant to curtail the authority of its own agency.

THE GROWTH AND PRESENT PATTERN
OF NATIONAL EXPENDITURES

The tables and charts here and elsewhere in this volume tell better than words the astounding story of the growth of the expenditures of the national government since the founding of our nation. A few observations are justified. In the first place, the shift in public expenditures among the various levels of government has been pronounced. Prior to the depression

Pattern of Expenditure
National Government

(Including Trust Funds)
Fiscal 1967
(Millions)

National Defense	$ 70,092
International Affairs and Finance	4,650
Space Research and Technology	5,423
Agriculture	4,377
Natural Resources	2,132
Commerce and Transportation	7,446
Housing and Community Development	2,285
Health, Labor, Welfare	40,084
Education	4,047
Veterans Benefits and Services	6,898
Interest	12,548
General Government	2,454
Adjustments (Payments for retirement, interest of trust funds, etc.)	−4,022
TOTAL	$158,414
Public Enterprise Expenditures Covered by Receipts and Other Types of Expenses	31,759
GRAND TOTAL	$190,173

of the thirties, the national government accounted for about 35 percent of the total governmental expenditures in the United States, the states about 15 percent, and the local units about 50 percent. Today, the national government spends about 70 percent, the states about 12, and the local units 18. However, in the past two decades, the growth of expenditures for domestic services has been greater at the state and local than at the national level. In the second place, national governmental income has equaled or exceeded outgo only about half the time in our national history. Presidents Lincoln, Grant, Hayes, Garfield, Arthur, Franklin Roosevelt, Kennedy, and Johnson never experienced one year of balanced budgets during their tenures of office; and Madison, Van Buren, Tyler, McKinley, Wilson, Truman, and Eisenhower had more years of deficits than of balances. In only five years since 1930 has the government lived within its income. In the third place, the towering costs of modern government at the national level are attributable, as a noted senator has said, to the "warfare" world rather than to the "welfare" state. More than 75 percent of our national expenditures have, since 1942, steadily gone into war, its aftermath, its conduct, or preparation for it. The total national budget as outlined by the President did not until 1963 include a substantial part of the actual income and outgo. All payments into and out of trust funds like those for O.A.S.I., the long-range highway programs, and others were not included and receipts of large government enterprises like the Post Office and T.V.A. were not counted. The traditional budget has since 1963 been referred to

The Growth of National Expenditures

Administrative Budget Only
(Millions)

PERIOD	YEARLY AVERAGE
1789–1800	5.7
1801–1810	9.1
1811–1820	23.9
1821–1830	16.2
1831–1840	24.5
1841–1850	34.1
1851–1860	60.2
1861–1865	683.8
1866–1870	377.6
1871–1875	287.5
1876–1880	255.6
1881–1885	257.7
1886–1890	279.1
1891–1895	363.6
1896–1900	457.5
1901–1905	535.6
1906–1910	639.2
1911–1915	720.3
1916–1920	8,065.3
1921–1925	3,579,0
1926–1930	3,182.8
1931–1935	5,214.9
1936–1940	8,267.2
1941–1945	64,242.5
1946–1950	42,801.4
1951–1955	63,332.3
1956–1960	73,088.0
1961–1965	91,227.0

Adapted from *Statistical Abstract of the United States, 1967.*

as the "Administrative Budget" and it is this which mainly concerns the Congress. The inclusion of the income and outgo from the trust funds is called the "Consolidated Cash Budget" and the President normally discusses his requests on this basis. The total fiscal program of the government, including the receipts and expenditures in public enterprises such as the Post Office, T.V.A., and other power authorities, is referred to as the "Flow of Government-Administered Funds Budget" and as yet is presented for statistical purposes mainly. Finally, the mere size of the present national budget has overborne the laudable efforts described earlier to develop a rational procedure in the executive branch and in Congress for handling the annual tax and expenditure programs.

SOURCES OF NATIONAL FUNDS

Governments on all levels habitually live partly on borrowed money. *1. Loans* In a given year, they may take in as much as they spend and thus have the comfort of a balanced budget. But hardly ever are they out of debt; and in periods of stress their borrowings may mount to disturbing totals. Borrowings are not revenue. A man borrowing $1000 from a bank may have the money in his pocket, but he is not taxed on it as income; for of course it is *not* income. At some specified rate of interest, he may have the use of it for a while. But he will have to pay it back. Nevertheless, borrowing is a source from which for a good many years, even in peacetime, our national government has been deriving a considerable part of its current operating funds. In fact, during fiscal 1968, the national government was obliged to borrow from the public $23.1 billion to cover the largest peacetime deficit in history.

2. Nontax revenue

Most of the actual revenue commonly comes from taxes. There is, however, a good deal of nontax revenue. To begin with, the government carries on business, or quasi-business, enterprises and pockets the receipts from them as any private businessman or corporation would do. One thinks instantly of the postal service, from which in 1968 the government drew more than $6.9 billion—not *profit* certainly, but that is beside the present point. There are receipts also from the mints, the Government Printing Office, the Tennessee Valley Authority, the Alaska Railroad, the Panama Canal, the Inland Waterways Corporation, and other such diversified sources. In the second place, there is income from fees charged for services or privileges, as when a patent is applied for, a book copyrighted, or a lawyer admitted to practice before the Supreme Court. Third, there are fines levied in the courts, penalties for nonpayment of taxes, and forfeitures of property taken from transgressors, for example, liquor or tobacco on which the required excise taxes have not been paid, or liquor, jewelry, perfumes, and the like confiscated from smugglers or from importers or travelers making fraudulent declarations. There are sales of property, too—public land or surplus war equipment. President Johnson, for example, was in 1966 authorized to sell private participation in pools of national assets, such as home mortgages, acquired in loaning operations. There are rentals from grazing lands and irrigated areas. There is interest on loans to farmers and to homeowners. There are even gifts, as the National Gallery of Art in Washington (presented by the Mellon estate) eloquently testifies.

3. Taxes

Nevertheless, the national government lives principally from taxes. A major difference between the government under the Articles of Confederation and that under our present Constitution is that, whereas the former could raise money (aside from borrowings) only by making requisitions upon more or less reluctant and negligent states, the latter can reach down past the state governments to the individual citizen, levy on his business transactions, income, inheritances, and the like, and enforce payment, if necessary, by seizing and selling his possessions. Very appropriately, the long list of powers given Congress in the eighth section of the Constitution's first article starts off with the power "to lay and collect taxes, duties, imposts, and excises." Nor was it simply by chance that the Constitution's framers employed all of these different terms. To them, "taxes" meant primarily levies, like poll taxes and land taxes, falling *directly* on persons or property, and with the burden impossible to shift to other shoulders; "duties" and "imposts" denoted levies on imports and exports, respectively (what we commonly call tariff or customs duties); and "excises" were levies on the production, distribution, or use of commodities—"internal revenue," as we early fell into the habit of terming this form of tax in distinction from revenue derived from foreign trade and collected at the ports. Moreover, in contrast with "taxes," duties, imposts, and excises are *indirect,* in that, they can be, and commonly are, passed on to the consumer in the form of higher prices for goods, so that it really is he who pays the duty or excise, even though he may not realize that he is doing so. The various terms employed in the taxing clause are therefore not without significance, even though in everyday usage it is customary to lump all of the different levies together under the general heading of "taxes"—which, indeed, we shall do in the present chapter.

A tax (in the broad sense indicated) is, of course, a levy or charge imposed normally to raise money for public purposes—"an exaction," the Supreme Court has said, "for the support of the government." It may be assessed upon individuals or upon corporations or other groups. It may take any one of many forms (not all employed by the national government) —property taxes, income taxes, excise taxes, sales taxes, license taxes, inheritance taxes, poll taxes, tariff duties, and still others. It may be direct or indirect. Always, however, a tax is compulsory; one may choose whether to pay rent or wages or prices, but not whether to pay taxes. Furthermore, while justified solely as a contribution in return for government service rendered (in at least some broad sense), tax burdens necessarily are apportioned among payers according to their property, income, business transactions, and the like, and not at all on the basis of benefits individually received. It may be presumed, however, that when tax money is employed for police or military protection, for example, the big taxpayer has more to be protected and in that sense gets service in some proportion to what he pays.

THE TAXING POWER

Under the Constitution's taxing clause, Congress has general freedom to tax persons and objects within the national jurisdiction, and with nothing said about the rates that may be imposed. If the people at large think themselves taxed oppressively, they will find remedy, not in the courts, but in electing a Congress—perchance also a President—pledged, or at least predisposed, to a different tax policy. Comprehensive, however, as the taxing power is, it can be exercised only in accordance with certain express or implied restrictions.

Restrictions:

1. Purpose   To begin with, Congress is not free to levy taxes for any conceivable purpose whatsoever, but only (as the Constitution plainly says) "to pay the debts and provide for the common defense and general welfare of the United States." "Debts" and "defense" are sufficiently definite terms. "General welfare," however, is so broad that there always have been differences of opinion as to what activities and objectives may be read into it. It no longer, however, offers much of a hurdle for tax- and spending-planners to surmount.

2. Uniformity of indirect taxes   Down to World War I, the largest part of the national revenue always came from indirect taxes; and, as we shall see, a large share is still derived from that source. In laying taxes of this kind, Congress, however, is bound by the constitutional provision that "all duties, imposts, and excises shall be uniform throughout the United States." The requirement does not prevent tobacco excises, for example, from falling more heavily upon regions where tobacco products are manufactured extensively than upon others where there is little industry of the kind; it means merely that, in general, all cigars or cigarettes of a given kind or condition must be taxed at the same rate in all parts of the country. A tax may fall with very different weight on different areas, on different businesses, or on different classes of people. But—save as qualified with respect to tariff duties—it must bear with the same weight on the same objects of taxation wherever found.

3. Uniformity among ports of entry   To reinforce this principle, the Constitution further enjoins that in regulating commerce Congress shall not authorize customs duties to be collected at one rate at one port and at a different rate at another, or to be computed at different ports according to different rules. At one time, this meant absolute uniformity at all ports for any given kind or class of imports, whatever their place of origin. Under Supreme Court decisions since 1901, however, rates on commodities coming from the insular dependencies may differ from those on imports from other areas; and under the trade agreement system instituted in 1934 there is much additional variation, according to the foreign country from which given commodities are received. The constitutional restriction mentioned, however, is fully preserved; the duty on a box of cigars from Puerto Rico may differ from that on a box from Brazil, but each will be uniform at all ports.

4. Other express restrictions   The taxing power is further limited (1) by a constitutional provision forbidding duties to be imposed on exports, although Congress is authorized to regulate export trade in every way other than by taxation; and (2) by a requirement that direct taxes shall be apportioned among the several states according to population. As interpreted in earlier days, to include only poll or capitation taxes and taxes on land (and at one time slaves), direct taxes have been laid by Congress only four times in our history, most recently in 1861. Taxes on incomes laid in 1862 were held by the Supreme Court to be excise, not direct, levies. When, however, the validity of a new income tax law was challenged in the last decade of the century, the Court ruled differently. Ultimately the obvious impossibility of taxing incomes in accordance with any mathematical apportionment among the states led in 1913 to adoption of the Sixteenth Amendment, brushing aside the entire question of whether income taxes are or are not direct taxes and expressly authorizing Congress to "lay and collect taxes on incomes, from whatever source derived," without apportionment.

Finally may be mentioned restrictions nowhere specified but up to now regarded, with judicial support, as implicit in the nature of the federal union: restraints from taxing (*a*) the property or essential functions of state governments or their subdivisions, and (*b*) securities issued by such jurisdictions or incomes derived therefrom. As observed elsewhere, the restriction relating to securities probably will in time be abrogated by Congress, with Supreme Court sanction, as a similar one on the taxation of state and local salaries already has been. *5. Implied restrictions*

Most laws imposing taxation can readily be classed as revenue measures, that is, measures in which the primary, if not sole, purpose is to produce income for the government. As intimated above, some measures are tax laws in form but intended mainly or entirely for regulative purposes and, if yielding revenue at all, do so only incidentally. A good example is tariff schedules planned for the protection of American industries against foreign competition. Insofar as goods affected find their way to our ports notwithstanding heavy duties payable on them, revenue results. But high productiveness is not expected. Indeed, Congress has at times gone so far as to impose taxes with the avowed purpose of destroying a business enterprise altogether—taxing it out of existence and thereby rendering it wholly unproductive. A case in point is the act of 1865—in form a tax measure pure and simple—imposing so onerous a levy on notes issued by state banks that, as was the intention, it became unprofitable to issue them and their issuance ceased. In general, measures of the kind have been sustained whenever the courts considered that the taxing power was being used in pursuit of a purpose expressly or impliedly within the scope of congressional authority. Protective tariffs, however, have commonly been upheld, quite apart from the taxing power, on the basis of power to regulate foreign commerce. *Taxation not primarily for revenue*

Is a tax constitutional when not clearly either a revenue measure or a device for rendering effective some delegated or implied power, but rather is aimed principally or solely at promoting the general welfare of which we have spoken? This question was raised pointedly by laws of 1886 and later laying burdensome excise taxes on wholesale and retail sales of oleomargarine colored to resemble butter; by an act of 1912 taxing the manufacture of poisonous white phosphorus matches (and almost completely ending the industry); by laws of 1914 and 1919 imposing taxes on registered dealers in narcotic drugs; by the child labor law of 1919 laying a special tax on the profits of industrial establishments employing children under the age of 16; and by the Agricultural Adjustment Act of 1933 imposing levies on processors of grains, meat, cotton, and other commodities as a means of raising money for a program of curtailing agricultural production. In cases coming before it at different times, the Supreme Court up- *Taxation and the general welfare* held the oleomargarine and narcotics laws as revenue measures, refusing to inquire into the legislative intent behind them; and the constitutionality of the phosphorus match law has never been judicially tested. When, however, the child labor law was challenged, the Court fixed attention on the motive animating Congress and held the measure invalid for the reason that the tax imposed had as its sole purpose an objective—the regulation of child labor—regarded by the justices then sitting as a function reserved to the states. Similarly, the Agricultural Adjustment Act was overthrown not only because, said the justices, the processing taxes for which it provided were not true taxes in the sense of levies for general support of the government, but also because these taxes, too, were being employed to extend the national regulating arm into a field—the control of agricultural production—belonging to the states. In other words, the taxing power might not properly be invoked, even for the sake of the general welfare, when the effect would be to project national authority beyond limits constitutionally fixed, and as understood by the judges.

A changed attitude   Since these decisions were rendered, however, there have been changes. A Court with different personnel and viewpoints has broadened its concept of national power (especially under the commerce clause), as illustrated by the justices' approval of the social security taxes introduced in 1935. General welfare now can be promoted by levies which once would hardly have escaped judicial condemnation; and the presumption is that to the many occasions on which the national taxing power already has been used in advancing social and economic ends, with considerations of revenue wholly incidental, will in future be added still others of major significance. An effort to control gambling by requiring a registration tax was, however, effectively frustrated by a recent Court decision holding it to be in violation of the self-incrimination prohibitions of the Fifth Amendment. When the question is one of justifying taxing or spending on the basis of welfare, not only Congress itself but the Supreme Court as now constituted is rather more easily satisfied than before. In much of our pre-World War II income and inheritance taxation, indeed, the purpose of curbing swollen fortunes can be discerned almost as clearly as that of obtaining revenue. In messages to Congress in 1935 and on other occasions, President Franklin D. Roosevelt, pushing farther ideas advanced by Presidents Theodore Roosevelt, Wilson, and Hoover, warmly advocated such a policy, with a view to more equitable distribution of wealth and economic power. Since 1940, the problem has very nearly been taken care of automatically by tax schedules drawn to meet the heaviest demands for revenue in the country's history.

THE ENACTMENT OF TAX MEASURES

Appropriations are usually made for some specified and limited period, most commonly a year, and consequently a sheaf of appropriation bills must be passed every 12 months, with deficiency measures interspersed as needed. Measures imposing or readjusting taxation, on the other hand, are usually without time limits; a given tax once levied, or a given rate once established, continues operative as long as not repealed or amended. It is true, however, that in recent years Congress has exhibited a tendency to enact temporary or emergency taxes. Every annual budget transmitted to Congress by the President contains estimates of the revenue to be anticipated from existing sources. Along with these commonly will be submitted proposals for increasing the inflow by new or amended taxation if the yield does not promise to be sufficient, or for decreasing it if it promises to exceed needs, or perchance for maintaining the yield but redistributing tax burdens. On its part, Congress, too, may—as in the case of two tax-reduction bills killed by Presidential veto in 1947 and one passed over a veto in 1948—initiate revenue measures wholly outside of the executive's budget plans and even conflicting with them. Accordingly, tax legislation (if not in the form of a comprehensive overall revenue act, at least in that of a more or less significant amending measure) is to be anticipated with substantially the same yearly regularity as appropriation acts.

All measures for raising national revenue are required by the Constitution to originate in the House of Representatives. All portions of the President's annual budget message relating to the subject are immediately referred to the ways and means committee of that body; and to this group it falls to whip into shape a tax bill, sometimes following closely, sometimes less so, the plans and recommendations of the Chief Executive and his budget director. Working for weeks, through subcommittees when necessary, and with help from conferences with the chief executive, budget director, Treasury officials, bankers, businessmen, and others, the committee finally emerges with a measure which for further weeks absorbs much of the time and energy of the House. Passed by that body, the bill goes to the Senate, where, notwithstanding that the House was originally intended to enjoy substantial primacy in controlling the national purse, most revenue measures are more or less drastically altered, either in the finance committee or on the floor. There is, indeed, nothing to prevent the Senate from amending a House revenue bill by striking out all parts after the enacting clause and inserting an entirely new bill; and something of the sort has happened on several occasions. It is even possible for a bill which in effect, and almost in technical form, is a bill to raise revenue to be passed in the Senate before the House has taken any action at all. In any event, a major tax bill, after passing in both branches, will certainly have to go to conference. Commonly it is in the form in which it emerges from conference that the two houses finally enact it and the President signs it. Throughout the entire procedure, the country—especially the business element—watches with interest, and even anxiety, to see what new taxes will be decided upon, and what increases or other changes will be made in existing ones.

THE PATTERN OF TAXATION

Earlier situation

On the basis of incidence, that is, the point where the actual burden falls, taxes may be classified as direct and indirect—the former assessed upon and paid (as in the case of land taxes and poll taxes) by persons who cannot shift the impact to other shoulders; the latter imposed and collected commonly at some stage of production or distribution, and afterwards passed on (in the form of higher prices for commodities) to consumers. Back in the eighteenth century, the national government started off by relying almost entirely on indirect levies, principally duties on imports designed to shelter the country's developing industries as well as to yield revenue. So satisfactorily were tax needs met in this way that until the Civil War direct taxes were invoked only three times, and even excise taxes (indirect) only in two brief early periods. The exigencies of the conflict between the states, however, not only forced a temporary reversion to direct taxation, but brought excise taxes once more into use; and from then on these had a place in the tax structure. Tariff duties were, however, dominant for a good many years. Sometimes the point was made that people would be more tax-conscious, and therefore more concerned about economy and efficiency in government, if taxation were less disguised. But politicians always considered it good strategy to keep the tax burden well concealed.

Later changes

Throughout a long period of our history, the country's tax structure was thus relatively stable: state and local governments lived principally from the proceeds of the general property tax, the national government principally from the yield of customs duties. The past 50 years, however, have brought changes greatly complicating the tax picture. Mounting expenditures, increasing inadequacy of the general property tax, tempting new resources for revenue like motor cars and gasoline, and newer tax ideas and objectives, have attracted the states to numerous forms of taxation rarely or never employed before. On its part, the national government has revolutionized its tax pattern, with customs duties relegated to an insignificant position and reliance now placed mainly upon levies on incomes, the production and consumption of goods, and inheritances. The shift in the national sphere came shortly before World War I, when, with the idea growing that the nation's principal tax should be based on ability to pay as measured in terms of individual and corporate incomes, this newer (although not wholly untried) form of levy, validated by the Sixteenth Amendment, established itself promptly and firmly in our system. One of the advantages of income taxation is its flexibility—the ease with which, by juggling a few rates and brackets, it can be made to yield vastly more or vastly less as desired. Under the impact of the then unparalleled wartime expenditures of 1917–1918, the national revenue from this source rose to first place—a position which it consistently maintained until 1933. With

Receipts of the National Government

Fiscal 1967
(Millions)

Individual Income Taxes		$ 61,526
Corporate Income Taxes		33,971
Employment Taxes		27,823
Excise Taxes		13,719
Alcoholic Beverages	4,076	
Tobacco	2,080	
Manufacturers (Gasoline, oil,		
autos, home appliances)	6,129	
Retailers (Jewelry, furs, luggage,		
cosmetics, etc.)	4	
Stamp Duties	68	
Misc. (Transportation, admissions,		
communications, etc.)	1,362	
Estate and Gift Taxes		2,978
Customs Duties		1,901
Unemployment Insurance		3,652
Other Insurance, Retirement, etc.		1,853
Fees, Fines, Licenses, Sales, Rentals, etc.		2,168
TOTAL		$149,591

depression conditions deepening in the early thirties, taxes on personal and corporate incomes yielded steadily diminishing returns. Once more the bulk of national revenue began to come from customs duties and excises, even though languishing commerce and slackened business caused these also to produce less than formerly. Some measure of prosperity, however, having been regained, the income tax stream began rising again in 1937; and under wartime tax legislation after 1941 it became a torrent, quite transcending all other tax sources.

    The largest single source of revenue of the national government today is the individual income tax. As enacted in 1913, this tax fell upon only 2 or 3 million persons and at a graduated rate beginning at 4 percent on net taxable income in excess of $5500 for a married man. Under the pressure of war emergencies the rates have been revised upward quite sharply and the deductions and exemptions downward, so that 109 million persons now file returns. In other words, virtually all wage earners in the United States today pay a tax on their incomes to the national government. A large proportion of modern income tax payers pay their taxes "painlessly" through a scheme introduced in 1943 of employer withholding of a portion of their wages each pay period and transmitting the deducted portion to the government. A reckoning, of course, still occurs on April 15 when each taxpayer computes his tax liability for the previous year and pays any amount still owing or, perchance, files a claim for a refund from the total already paid for him by his employer.

    The modern income tax is a tax on net income rather than on total receipts. From the total earnings from all taxable sources, there may be

1. Income taxes:

a. Individual

subtracted: (1) personal allowance of $600 for each person dependent on the taxpayer including the taxpayer himself; (2) expenses incurred by self-employed, professional, and wage-earning taxpayers in earning the income; (3) privileged personal expenses, for example, donations for religious, charitable, or educational purposes, abnormal medical expenses, interest paid on loans, and taxes of many kinds paid to other governmental units. On the balance of the income after these allowances and deductions are taken, a graduated tax is imposed. The rate of this tax in 1968 was 20 percent on the first $2000, advancing by steps to 91 percent on net income in excess of $200,000. Beginning, however, in early 1968, a temporary surcharge of 10 percent additional on taxable income above the first $2000 for couples has been added by the Congress. The graduation or progressivity in the tax rates is designed to make larger incomes pay a proportionately larger tax on the theory that the higher the income the greater the ability of the taxpayer to support his government.

b. Corporate   A tax is also imposed on the annual net income of corporations and this ranks next to the individual income tax in the size and importance of its yield to the national government. This is undoubtedly the most complex tax used by the national government. Most of its complexities arise from an earnest effort of lawmakers to have the tax fall on the net income of corporations after allowances are made for legitimate expenses in earning the income. Others arise from various efforts to encourage plant expansion, oil deposit exploration, and other corporate practices deemed good for the national economy. The rate of tax on corporate net income is 30 percent on the first $25,000 and 52 percent on the remainder. However, a temporary 10 percent additional surcharge on corporate income for 1968 was enacted by Congress. During World War II and from 1951 to 1953, the corporation income tax was supplemented by an excess profits tax designed, in theory at least, to levy on the swollen corporate earnings of wartime so as to recapture as much of the abnormal profit as possible. In general and with numerous exceptions, the tax fell on the difference between normal earnings and those of the years in which the tax was imposed. The most recent excess profits tax, associated with the Korean combat and rearmament, was fixed at 30 percent of the abnormal earnings, but the combined corporate income and excess profits taxes could not exceed 70 percent of the net income.

2. Estate and gift taxes   On a number of occasions from the Civil War onwards, the national government imposed some form of tax on estates of deceased persons or on inheritances of portions thereof. Since 1916, an estate tax has been a regular feature of the national tax pattern. Formerly, exemptions ran as high as $100,000, and rates in lower brackets were relatively moderate, although high in upper ones. Naturally, under wartime taxation, exemptions were reduced (to $60,000) and rates stiffened. In order to reach wealth that might escape estate taxation by being given away by the possessor with that end in view, a gift tax (on a graduated scale approximately three-fourths as heavy as estate taxation) was introduced in 1924, repealed in 1926, and imposed in 1932. In order to protect existing state inheritance taxes, a credit of 25 percent against national tax liability for taxes paid to a state was inaugurated in 1924. It was increased to 80 percent in 1926. The Revenue Act of 1954 substantially reduced this credit. Estate tax rates were increased during World War II. The present rate is 3 percent on the first $5000 above the $60,000 exemption, graduated to 77 percent on estates of more than $10 million. Combined with progressive income taxes, estate and gift taxes now operate powerfully to check the growth and transmission of large fortunes.

3. Excise taxes

Everybody pays national taxes, although many people do so without realizing it. Even persons of means too modest to be reached by the income tax make their contributions when they buy articles like a package of cigarettes, priced so as to cover the excise tax due the government from the manufacturer or distributor. Traditionally, excise, or consumption, taxes have been planned to fall principally on luxury goods, and therefore to be paid chiefly by the comparatively well-to-do. The theory, however, never was completely adhered to in practice; and excises were progressively broadened during World War II until long lists of articles were covered which, for many people at all events, were everyday necessities. In 1947, existing heavy rates on tobacco, liquor, motor fuel, theater admissions, cosmetics, and scores of other articles were continued indefinitely by Congress. By 1950, however, popular demand for relief reached a point where both President and Congress became agreeable to a readjustment (the President on condition that lost revenue be made up in some other way). The Korean crisis, however, quickly turned the government's concern from remitting taxes to increasing them. It was not until 1954 that a Republican Congress was able to make a general reduction in excise taxes. A few more reductions were made in 1959, 1962, and 1968.

4. Payroll taxes

A special form of excise is a tax imposed upon employers for support of state systems of unemployment insurance under the social security program. Levied by the national government, the tax differs from others in that its proceeds are not for general government purposes; only about 10 percent of the yield actually accrues to the national government at all, the remainder being simply held by the Treasury for requisitions by the states for paying benefits. Even the 10 percent is employed in meeting administrative costs of the system. Of similar nature (although without the states involved) are payroll taxes on both employers and employes for support of the old age and survivors insurance system, including medicare.

SOME QUESTIONS OF TAX POLICY

The close of World War II and of the Korean conflict and the continuing heavy commitments in Viet Nam have made the country vitally concerned about reduction of the extraordinarily heavy tax burden. Despite some lowering of income and excise taxes before Viet Nam, such concern is still deeply felt. No one, however, pretending to any understanding of the current world situation and of America's relation to it, or of the financial implications entailed, looks forward to any substantial lowering of tax levels in the foreseeable future. The Cold War with the U.S.S.R. and Red China, preparations for eventualities if the Cold War should suddenly break into armed conflict, assistance to nations we hope to have on our side in such a situation, a huge debt largely incurred in past war, to say nothing of mounting costs of social security and other domestic services, all indicate a continuance of high levels of taxation. Barring unexpected developments, such as a Russian collapse, people and politicians will for a good while be most concerned about tax programs in terms of an immediate crisis. It should be noted that in relation to total national income, the American people are less heavily taxed than those of any other industrial nation. There is a school of thought, however, which holds that tax policy must always be concerned with economic growth and that the continued high level of unemployment accompanied by many signs of economic sluggishness make it highly desirable that taxes be cut while inflation, pressure on the dollar, and heavy deficits make it desirable that taxes be raised. These views, strongly urged by Presidents Kennedy and Johnson, have been quite influential recently and led to a sharp cut in income tax levels in 1964 and an increase in them in 1968.

Long before World War II, however, criticisms of our tax methods, policies, and objectives suggested need for general reconsideration and overhauling of our system. A few of the older long-term issues may at least be called to mind. For example: Should any new forms of taxation be introduced, for example, taxation of income from state and local securities, or fees for licenses, certificates, and other papers now issued gratis? Should the income tax base be broadened by terminating exemptions now enjoyed by a lengthy list of interests and enterprises, such as farm and consumer cooperatives, mutual insurance companies, rural electrification undertakings, surplus funds of labor unions, and even philanthropic and educational organizations in so far as engaged in business enterprises? Should the taxation of incomes be deliberately kept at levels, in the higher brackets, making accumulation of wealth difficult or impossible? How can adequate revenue be raised without unduly impairing the volume of production and the general level of national income? Should tax policies be modified to encourage plant expansion, capital investment, or accumulation of liquid reserves? How should corporate dividends and stock splits be treated for tax purposes? To what extent should tax rates be raised or lowered to curb inflation, promote economic growth, or encourage domestic industries? Should tax concessions be made to industries willing to locate in areas of chronic unemployment? And what about the time-honored issue of duplicating, or "double," taxation? A word here on this last-mentioned matter is perhaps in order.

With both nation and states reaching out in recent decades for new sources of revenue, it has come about that frequently they are found taxing the same objects. In recent years, indeed, no less than 90 percent of national and state receipts came from the same sources. To be sure, the national government leaves the general property tax entirely to the states (principally for local use) and, as we have seen, relies for the major part of its revenue upon personal and corporate income taxes, estate and inheritance taxes, and consumption taxes of different kinds. But nearly all of the objects affected are taxed by some or all of the states as well. Indeed, apart from the general property tax and customs duties, there are few if any important forms of taxation not claimed by both national and state governments, each without much regard to the other. Often (indeed almost invariably in these days) the sums collected by the national government within a state from a given tax exceed the amounts collected from that tax by the state itself. Persons finding their salaries or the gasoline they buy taxed twice sometimes harbor an idea that such double imposition is unconstitutional. In this, they are wrong. The Constitution has nothing to say against double taxation; it in effect presupposes it by leaving broad and general taxing powers to two largely independent governments, both resting directly upon the people. Even though not unconstitutional, however, the existing situation imposes handicaps on business and industry and sometimes excessive burdens on individual taxpayers, and one will not be surprised to learn that a good deal of thought has been devoted to it not only by tax experts but by business organizations, taxpayer associations, and state officials. Sometimes it is suggested that the national government withdraw from gasoline taxation (a field which it entered only in 1932), while the states give up taxing tobacco and its products; or that, in return for a monopoly of taxing liquor, the states give up taxing incomes. Often it is urged that the national government stop competing with states and localities by taxing amusements, local telephone calls, retail electrical energy, and other things. The issue is further entangled in the complexities of the grant-in-aid controversy. Those who propose the abandonment of some national aids to states, of course, expect the national government to abandon some taxes so the states can take up the burden more easily. A recent extensive staff study in the Treasury Department, however, stops short of any definite recommendations on these or related lines, as does the study of President Eisenhower's Commission on Intergovernmental Relations. In a period when all governments instinctively shy away from proposals looking to drying up sources of revenue, it is doubtful if any sources will become the exclusive property of one jurisdiction or another. More recently, proposals for sharing national income tax receipts with the states, or at least making block—unrestricted—grants to them to supplement the specific aids have been widely discussed. Critics fear a loss of equalization pressure and of national control.

"Double taxation"

BORROWING MONEY—THE NATIONAL DEBT

The bor-
rowing
power

When expenditures and revenues are approximately equal, a government is said to have a balanced budget. If, on the other hand, expenditures exceed receipts, there is a deficit, and the budget is said to be out of balance. In ordinary times, and for ordinary purposes, income derived from taxation, supplemented by receipts from nontax sources, ought to be, and much of the time has been, sufficient to meet the government's needs. In time of war or threat of war, however, or other unusual strain, for example, a depression, or to meet the cost of some special undertaking like the Panama Canal or a Marshall Plan, the government must borrow. The accumulated obligations thus incurred give rise to the national debt. Power to borrow not only is expressly conferred in the Constitution, but is one of the very few powers entirely unencumbered by restrictions—with the result that Congress may borrow from any lenders, for any purposes, in any amounts, on any terms, and with or without provision for the repayment of loans, with or without interest. Congress has tried to impose a debt limit by statute since about 1917 without, however, very striking results.

Methods
of bor-
rowing

Borrowing may take any one of several forms. By authority of Congress, the Treasury may sell notes or certificates attractive to banks and other institutions; and this is constantly done. To accelerate tax receipts, it may issue tax anticipation notes to large taxpayers, to be turned in by the corporation or individual at tax time at face value plus interest received on what has been in effect a loan. It may and does, in effect, borrow from itself; that is to say, it may arrange for interest-bearing loans out of funds accumulated and held for specific purposes by national agencies, for example, old-age, unemployment, veterans, and banks deposit insurance funds and postal savings deposits. Of far greater importance, however, is the sale of long-term interest-bearing bonds in large denominations to banks, insurance companies, administrators of trust funds, and the like, and in smaller denominations (down to $25 savings bonds) to individual savers and investors. The position of banks is such that they can virtually be compelled to purchase. In the case of private individuals, if in time of special need the investment motive, reinforced by patriotic appeals and high-pressure salesmanship, fails to bring about voluntary purchases in sufficient amounts, the government may force them by deferred-savings devices of one kind or another.

The
problem
of liqui-
dation

During the past half century, the United States has been added to the long list of countries laboring under a huge national debt. The national government, after three decades of deficit financing, now owes $1750 for each man, woman, and child in the United States. People who think seriously about such matters are by no means of one mind on how a debt of such proportions might be expected to affect the country's future. Some, comforted by the circumstance that we owed the debt to ourselves and not to

The National Debt

Selected Years, 1791–1968

YEAR	GROSS DEBT (MILLIONS)
1791	75
1801	83
1816	127
1821	90
1831	39
1840	3.5
1851	68
1861	91
1866	2,755
1871	2,322
1881	2,019
1891	1,005
1901	1,221
1911	1,154
1919	25,482
1931	16,801
1941	48,961
1946	269,422
1951	255,222
1961	289,211
1968	357,400

foreign lenders, thought that, with moderate national prosperity, the burden could be carried and the debt itself gradually reduced with no perceptible lowering of living standards. Others could not see how owing the debt to ourselves made any great amount of difference (we still *owed* it), or how the dead weight of so stupendous an obligation could fail to retard economic and social progress over a long period of years. Certain it was that generations as yet unborn would feel the impact of debt burdens which we in our time had improvidently piled up. Favored by a very high level of national prosperity, as well as by a combination of fiscal circumstances too complicated to be explained here, the government actually did contrive to shave off about $25 billion from the peak debt at the end of World War II. Rearmament, Korea, Viet Nam, and the Cold War, however, renewed deficit spending and the debt has now climbed well beyond the height reached in 1946. If the nation cannot tax itself sufficiently to pay the going expenses of the government during a period of unprecedented prosperity and high standards of living, the outlook for any significant lowering of the debt is dark indeed.

There is a school of opinion holding that we ought not to expect in our day to do much more than simply maintain the debt, paying interest scrupulously, but not making much effort to reduce principal, with the country meanwhile growing up to the debt by attaining such population and wealth that, proportionally, the burden would in time be materially reduced. Such rationalization of our current lack of progress with debt reduction (almost as fantastic in one direction as it is, in another, to expect the country ever to be literally debt-free) certainly does not appeal to many thoughtful people.

REFERENCES

F. B. Bator, *The Question of Government Spending: Public Needs and Private Wants* (New York, 1960).

R. Blough, *The Federal Taxing Process* (New York, 1952).

G. Colm with M. Young, *The Federal Budget and the National Economy: How to Make the Federal Budget a Better Tool of Fiscal Policy* (Washington, D. C., 1955).

H. M. Groves, *Financing Government* (5th ed., New York, 1960).

L. H. Kimmel, *Taxes and Economic Incentives* (Washington, D. C., 1950).

H. C. Mansfield, *The Comptroller-General; A Study in the Law and Practice of Financial Administration* (New Haven, Conn., 1939).

F. C. Mosher, *Program Budgeting* (Chicago, 1954).

F. C. Mosher and O. F. Poland, *The Costs of American Government: Facts, Trends, and Myths* (New York, 1964).

E. E. Naylor, *The Federal Budget System in Operation* (Washington, D. C., 1941).

D. S. Ott and A. F. Ott, *Federal Budget Policy* (Washington, 1965).

R. E. Paul, *Taxation in the United States* (Boston, 1956).

J. A. Pechman, *Federal Tax Policy* (Washington, 1966).

President's Commission on Budget Concepts, *Report* (Washington, 1967).

D. T. Selko, *The Federal Financial System* (Washington, D. C., 1940), Chaps. IV–X, XXIII–XXIX.

————, *The Administration of Federal Finances* (Washington, D. C., 1937).

W. J. Shultz and C. L. Harris, *American Public Finance* (New York, 1954), Chaps. VII–XXII.

A. Smithies, *The Budgetary Process in the United States* (New York, 1955).

H. Stein and J. A. Pechman, *Essays in Federal Taxation,* Prepared for the Committee on Ways and Means (New York, 1959).

A. Wildavsky, *The Politics of the Budgetary Process* (New York, 1964).

Appendix

THE CONSTITUTION OF
THE UNITED STATES OF AMERICA

We, the people of the United States, in order to form a more perfect union, establish justice, insure domestic tranquility, provide for the common defense, promote the general welfare, and secure the blessings of liberty to ourselves and our posterity, do ordain and establish this Constitution for the United States of America.

ARTICLE I

Section I

All legislative powers herein granted shall be vested in a Congress of the United States, which shall consist of a Senate and House of Representatives.

Section II

The House of Representatives shall be composed of members chosen every second year by the people of the several States, and the electors in each State shall have the qualifications requisite for electors of the most numerous branch of the State legislature.

No person shall be a Representative who shall not have attained to the age of twenty-five years, and been seven years a citizen of the United States, and who shall not, when elected, be an inhabitant of that State in which he shall be chosen.

Representatives and direct taxes shall be apportioned among the several States which may be included within this Union, according to their respective numbers, which shall be determined by adding to the whole number of free persons, including those bound to service for a term of years,[1] and excluding Indians not taxed, three fifths of all other persons.[2] The actual enumeration shall be made within three years after the first meeting of the Congress of the United States, and within every subsequent term of ten years, in such manner as they shall by law direct. The

[1] Altered by the Fourteenth Amendment.
[2] Rescinded by the Fourteenth Amendment.

number of Representatives shall not exceed one for every thirty thousand, but each State shall have at least one Representative; and until such enumeration shall be made, the State of New Hampshire shall be entitled to choose three, Massachusetts eight, Rhode Island and Providence Plantations one, Connecticut five, New York six, New Jersey four, Pennsylvania eight, Delaware one, Maryland six, Virginia ten, North Carolina five, South Carolina five, and Georgia three.[3]

When vacancies happen in the representation from any State, the executive authority thereof shall issue writs of election to fill such vacancies.

The House of Representatives shall choose their Speaker and other officers, and shall have the sole power of impeachment.

Section III

The Senate of the United States shall be composed of two Senators from each State, chosen by the legislature thereof,[4] for six years; and each Senator shall have one vote.

Immediately after they shall be assembled in consequence of the first election, they shall be divided as equally as may be into three classes. The seats of the Senators of the first class shall be vacated at the expiration of the second year, of the second class at the expiration of the fourth year, and of the third class at the expiration of the sixth year, so that one third may be chosen every second year; and if vacancies happen by resignation or otherwise during the recess of the legislature of any State the executive thereof may make temporary appointments until the next meeting of the legislature, which shall then fill such vacancies.[5]

No person shall be a Senator who shall not have attained to the age of thirty years, and been nine years a citizen of the United States, and who shall not, when elected, be an inhabitant of that State for which he shall be chosen.

The Vice-President of the United States shall be President of the Senate, but shall have no vote, unless they be equally divided.

The Senate shall choose their other officers, and also a President *pro tempore* in the absence of the Vice-President, or when he shall exercise the office of the President of the United States.

The Senate shall have the sole power to try all impeachments. When sitting for that purpose, they shall be on oath or affirmation. When the President of the United States is tried, the Chief Justice shall preside; and no person shall be convicted without the concurrence of two thirds of the members present.

Judgment in cases of impeachment shall not extend further than to removal from office, and disqualification to hold and enjoy any office of honor, trust, or profit under the United States; but the party convicted shall, nevertheless, be liable and subject to indictment, trial, judgment, and punishment, according to law.

[3] Temporary provision.
[4] Modified by the Seventeenth Amendment.
[5] Modified by the Seventeenth Amendment.

Section IV

The times, places, and manner of holding elections for Senators and Representatives shall be prescribed in each State by the legislature thereof; but the Congress may at any time by law make or alter such regulations, except as to the places of choosing Senators.

The Congress shall assemble at least once in every year, and such meeting shall be on the first Monday in December, unless they shall by law appoint a different day.[6]

Section V

Each house shall be the judge of the elections, returns, and qualifications of its own members, and a majority of each shall constitute a quorum to do business; but a smaller number may adjourn from day to day, and may be authorized to compel the attendance of absent members, in such manner, and under such penalties, as each house may provide.

Each house may determine the rules of its proceedings, punish its members for disorderly behavior, and with the concurrence of two thirds, expel a member.

Each house shall keep a journal of its proceedings, and from time to time publish the same, excepting such parts as may in their judgment require secrecy, and the yeas and nays of the members of either house on any question shall, at the desire of one fifth of those present, be entered on the journal.

Neither house, during the session of Congress, shall, without the consent of the other, adjourn for more than three days, nor to any other place than that in which the two houses shall be sitting.

Section VI

The Senators and Representatives shall receive a compensation for their services, to be ascertained by law and paid out of the Treasury of the United States. They shall, in all cases except treason, felony, and breach of the peace, be privileged from arrest during their attendance at the session of their respective houses, and in going to and returning from the same; and for any speech or debate in either house they shall not be questioned in any other place.

No Senator or Representative shall, during the time for which he was elected, be appointed to any civil office under the authority of the United States, which shall have been created, or the emoluments whereof shall have been increased, during such time; and no person holding any office under the United States shall be a member of either house during his continuance in office.

Section VII

All bills for raising revenue shall originate in the House of Representatives; but the Senate may propose or concur with amendments as on other bills.

[6] Superseded by the Twentieth Amendment.

Every bill which shall have passed the House of Representatives and the Senate shall, before it become a law, be presented to the President of the United States; if he approves he shall sign it, but if not he shall return it, with his objections, to that house in which it shall have originated, who shall enter the objections at large on their journal and proceed to reconsider it. If after such reconsideration two thirds of that house shall agree to pass the bill, it shall be sent, together with the objections, to the other house, by which it shall likewise be reconsidered, and if approved by two thirds of that house it shall become a law. But in all such cases the votes of both houses shall be determined by yeas and nays, and the names of the persons voting for and against the bill shall be entered on the journal of each house respectively. If any bill shall not be returned by the President within ten days (Sundays excepted) after it shall have been presented to him, the same shall be a law, in like manner as if he had signed it, unless the Congress by their adjournment prevent its return, in which case it shall not be a law.

Every order, resolution, or vote to which the concurrence of the Senate and House of Representatives may be necessary (except on a question of adjournment) shall be presented to the President of the United States; and before the same shall take effect, shall be approved by him, or being disapproved by him, shall be repassed by two thirds of the Senate and House of Representatives, according to the rules and limitations prescribed in the case of a bill.

Section VIII

The Congress shall have power to lay and collect taxes, duties, imposts, and excises, to pay the debts and provide for the common defense and general welfare of the United States; but all duties, imposts, and excises shall be uniform throughout the United States;

To borrow money on the credit of the United States;

To regulate commerce with foreign nations and among the several States, and with the Indian tribes;

To establish an uniform rule of naturalization, and uniform laws on the subject of bankruptcies throughout the United States;

To coin money, regulate the value thereof, and of foreign coin, and fix the standard of weights and measures;

To provide for the punishment of counterfeiting the securities and current coin of the United States;

To establish post-offices and post-roads;

To promote the progress of science and useful arts by securing for limited times to authors and inventors the exclusive right to their respective writings and discoveries;

To constitute tribunals inferior to the Supreme Court;

To define and punish piracies and felonies committed on the high seas and offenses against the law of nations;

To declare war, grant letters of marque and reprisal, and make rules concerning captures on land and water;

To raise and support armies, but no appropriation of money to that use shall be for a longer term than two years;

To provide and maintain a navy;

To make rules for the government and regulation of the land and naval forces;

To provide for calling forth the militia to execute the laws of the Union, suppress insurrections, and repel invasions;

To provide for organizing, arming, and disciplining the militia, and for governing such part of them as may be employed in the service of the United States, reserving to the States respectively the appointment of the officers, and the authority of training the militia according to the discipline prescribed by Congress;

To exercise exclusive legislation in all cases whatsoever over such district (not exceeding ten miles square) as may, by cession of particular States and the acceptance of Congress, become the seat of the Government of the United States, and to exercise like authority over all places purchased by the consent of the legislature of the State in which the same shall be, for the erection of forts, magazines, arsenals, dockyards, and other needful buildings; and

To make all laws which shall be necessary and proper for carrying into execution the foregoing powers, and all other powers vested by this Constitution in the Government of the United States, or in any department or officer thereof.

Section IX

The migration or importation of such persons as any of the States now existing shall think proper to admit shall not be prohibited by the Congress prior to the year one thousand eight hundred and eight, but a tax or duty may be imposed on such importation, not exceeding ten dollars for each person.[7]

The privilege of the writ of *habeas corpus* shall not be suspended, unless when in cases of rebellion or invasion the public safety may require it.

No bill of attainder or *ex post facto* law shall be passed.

No capitation or other direct tax shall be laid, unless in proportion to the census or enumeration hereinbefore directed to be taken.

No tax or duty shall be laid on articles exported from any State.

No preference shall be given by any regulation of commerce or revenue to the ports of one State over those of another; nor shall vessels bound to or from one State be obliged to enter, clear, or pay duties in another.

No money shall be drawn from the Treasury but in consequence of appropriations made by law; and a regular statement and account of the receipts and expenditures of all public money shall be published from time to time.

No title of nobility shall be granted by the United States; and no person holding any office of profit or trust under them shall, without the consent of the Congress, accept of any present, emolument, office, or title, of any kind whatever, from any king, prince, or foreign State.

Section X

No State shall enter into any treaty, alliance, or confederation; grant letters of marque and reprisal; coin money; emit bills of credit; make anything but gold and silver coin a tender in payment of debts; pass any bill of attainder, *ex post facto* law, or law impairing the obligation of contracts, or grant any title of nobility.

No State shall, without the consent of Congress, lay any imposts or duties on imports or exports, except what may be absolutely necessary for executing its in-

[7] Temporary provision.

spection laws; and the net produce of all duties and imposts, laid by any State on imports or exports, shall be for the use of the Treasury of the United States; and all such laws shall be subject to the revision and control of the Congress.

No State shall, without the consent of Congress, lay any duty of tonnage, keep troops or ships of war in time of peace, enter into any agreement or compact with another State or with a foreign power, or engage in war, unless actually invaded or in such imminent danger as will not admit of delay.

ARTICLE II

Section I

The executive power shall be vested in a President of the United States of America. He shall hold his office during the term of four years,[8] and together with the Vice-President, chosen for the same term, be elected as follows:

Each State shall appoint, in such manner as the legislature thereof may direct, a number of electors, equal to the whole number of Senators and Representatives to which the State may be entitled in the Congress; but no Senator or Representative, or person holding an office of trust or profit under the United States, shall be appointed an elector.

The electors shall meet in their respective States and vote by ballot for two persons, of whom one at least shall not be an inhabitant of the same State with themselves. And they shall make a list of all the persons voted for, and of the number of votes for each; which list they shall sign and certify, and transmit sealed to the seat of government of the United States, directed to the President of the Senate. The President of the Senate shall, in the presence of the Senate and House of Representatives, open all the certificates, and the votes shall then be counted. The person having the greatest number of votes shall be the President, if such number be a majority of the whole number of electors appointed; and if there be more than one who have such a majority, and have an equal number of votes, then the House of Representatives shall immediately choose by ballot one of them for President; and if no person have a majority, then from the five highest on the list the said House shall in like manner choose the President. But in choosing the President the votes shall be taken by States, the representation from each State having one vote; a quorum for this purpose shall consist of a member or members from two thirds of the States, and a majority of all the States shall be necessary to a choice. In every case, after the choice of the President, the person having the greatest number of votes of the electors shall be the Vice-President. But if there should remain two or more who have equal votes, the Senate shall choose from them by ballot the Vice-President.[9]

[8] Modified by the Twenty-second Amendment.
[9] Superseded by the Twelfth Amendment.

The Congress may determine the time of choosing the electors and the day on which they shall give their votes, which day shall be the same throughout the United States.

No person except a natural-born citizen, or a citizen of the United States at the time of the adoption of this Constitution, shall be eligible to the office of President; neither shall any person be eligible to that office who shall not have attained to the age of thirty-five years, and been fourteen years a resident of the United States.

In case of the removal of the President from office, or of his death, resignation, or inability to discharge the powers and duties of the said office, the same shall devolve on the Vice-President, and the Congress may by law provide for the case of removal, death, resignation, or inability, both of the President and Vice-President, declaring what officer shall then act as President, and such officer shall act accordingly until the disability be removed or a President shall be elected.

The President shall, at stated times, receive for his services a compensation, which shall neither be increased nor diminished during the period for which he may have been elected, and he shall not receive within that period any other emolument from the United States or any of them.

Before he enter on the execution of his office he shall take the following oath or affirmation:

"I do solemnly swear (or affirm) that I will faithfully execute the office of President of the United States, and will to the best of my ability preserve, protect, and defend the Constitution of the United States."

Section II

The President shall be commander-in-chief of the army and navy of the United States, and of the militia of the several States when called into the actual service of the United States; he may require the opinion, in writing, of the principal officer in each of the executive departments, upon any subject relating to the duties of their respective offices, and he shall have power to grant reprieves and pardons for offenses against the United States, except in cases of impeachment.

He shall have power, by and with the advice and consent of the Senate, to make treaties, provided two thirds of the Senators present concur; and he shall nominate, and, by and with the advice and consent of the Senate, shall appoint ambassadors, other public ministers and consuls, judges of the Supreme Court, and all other officers of the United States, whose appointments are not herein otherwise provided for, and which shall be established by law; but the Congress may by law vest the appointment of such inferior officers, as they think proper, in the President alone, in the courts of law, or in the heads of departments.

The President shall have power to fill up all vacancies that may happen during the recess of the Senate, by granting commissions which shall expire at the end of their next session.

Section III

He shall from time to time give to the Congress information of the state of the Union, and recommend to their consideration such measures as he shall judge necessary and expedient; he may, on extraordinary occasions, convene both houses, or either of them, and in case of disagreement between them with respect to the time of adjournment, he may adjourn them to such time as he shall think proper; he shall receive ambassadors and other public ministers; he shall take care that the laws be faithfully executed, and shall commission all the officers of the United States.

Section IV

The President, Vice-President, and all civil officers of the United States shall be removed from office on impeachment for and conviction of treason, bribery, or other high crimes and misdemeanors.

ARTICLE III

Section I

The judicial power of the United States shall be vested in one Supreme Court, and in such inferior courts as the Congress may from time to time ordain and establish. The judges, both of the supreme and inferior courts, shall hold their offices during good behavior, and shall, at stated times, receive for their services a compensation which shall not be diminished during their continuance in office.

Section II

The judicial power shall extend to all cases, in law and equity, arising under this Constitution, the laws of the United States, and the treaties made, or which shall be made, under their authority;—to all cases affecting ambassadors, other public ministers, and consuls;—to all cases of admiralty and maritime jurisdiction;—to controversies to which the United States shall be a party;—to controversies between two or more States;—between a State and citizens of another State,[10]—between citizens of different States;—between citizens of the same State claiming lands under grants of different States, and between a State, or the citizens thereof, and foreign States, citizens, or subjects.[10]

In all cases affecting ambassadors, other public ministers, and consuls, and those in which a State shall be a party, the Supreme Court shall have original jurisdiction. In all the other cases before mentioned the Supreme Court shall have appellate jurisdiction, both as to law and fact, with such exceptions and under such regulations as the Congress shall make.

The trial of all crimes, except in cases of impeachment, shall be by jury; and such trial shall be held in the State where the said crimes shall have been committed; but when not committed within any State, the trial shall be at such place or places as the Congress may by law have directed.

Section III

Treason against the United States shall consist only in levying war against them, or in adhering to their enemies, giving them aid and comfort. No person shall be convicted of treason unless on the testimony of two witnesses to the same overt act, or on confession in open court.

[10] Restricted by the Eleventh Amendment.

The Congress shall have power to declare the punishment of treason, but no attainder of treason shall work corruption of blood or forfeiture except during the life of the person attainted.

ARTICLE IV

Section I

Full faith and credit shall be given in each State to the public acts, records, and judicial proceedings of every other State. And the Congress may by general laws prescribe the manner in which such acts, records, and proceedings shall be proved, and the effect thereof.

Section II

The citizens of each State shall be entitled to all privileges and immunities of citizens in the several States.[11]

A person charged in any State with treason, felony, or other crime, who shall flee from justice, and be found in another State shall, on demand of the executive authority of the State from which he fled, be delivered up, to be removed to the State having jurisdiction of the crime.

No person held to service or labor in one State, under the laws thereof, escaping into another, shall, in consequence of any law or regulation therein, be discharged from such service or labor, but shall be delivered up on claim of the party to whom such service or labor may be due [12]

Section III

New States may be admitted by the Congress into this Union; but no new State shall be formed or erected within the jurisdiction of any other State; nor any State be formed by the junction of two or more States or parts of States, without the consent of the legislatures of the States concerned as well as of the Congress.

The Congress shall have power to dispose of and make all needful rules and regulations respecting the territory or other property belonging to the United States; and nothing in this Constitution shall be so construed as to prejudice any claims of the United States or any particular State.

Section IV

The United States shall guarantee to every State in this Union a republican form of government, and shall protect each of them against invasion, and on application of the legislature, or of the executive (when the legislature cannot be convened), against domestic violence.

[11] Made more explicit by the Fourteenth Amendment.
[12] Superseded by the Thirteenth Amendment in so far as pertaining to slaves.

ARTICLE V

The Congress, whenever two thirds of both houses shall deem it necessary, shall propose amendments to this Constitution, or, on the application of the legisatures of two thirds of the several States, shall call a convention for proposing amendments, which in either case shall be valid to all intents and purposes as part of this Constitution, when ratified by the legislatures of three fourths of the several States, or by conventions in three fourths thereof, as the one or the other mode of ratification may be proposed by the Congress, provided that no amendments which may be made prior to the year one thousand eight hundred and eight shall in any manner affect the first and fourth clauses in the ninth section of the first article,[13] and that no State, without its consent, shall be deprived of its equal suffrage in the Senate.

ARTICLE VI

All debts contracted and engagements entered into, before the adoption of this Constitution, shall be as valid against the United States under this Constitution as under the confederation.[14]

This Constitution, and the laws of the United States, which shall be made in pursuance thereof, and all treaties made, or which shall be made, under the authority of the United States, shall be the supreme law of the land; and the judges in every State shall be bound thereby, anything in the Constitution or laws of any State to the contrary notwithstanding.

The Senators and Representatives before mentioned, and the members of the several State legislatures, and all executive and judicial officers both of the United States and of the several States, shall be bound by oath or affirmation to support this Constitution; but no religious test shall ever be required as a qualification to any office or public trust under the United States.

ARTICLE VII

The ratification of the conventions of nine States shall be sufficient for the establishment of this Constitution between the States so ratifying the same.

Done in convention by the unanimous consent of the States present, the seventeenth day of September, in the year of our Lord one thousand seven hundred and eighty-seven, and of the independence of the United States of America the twelfth. In witness whereof, we have hereunto subscribed our names.
[Signed by] [15]

---

[13] Temporary clause.
[14] Extended by the Fourteenth Amendment.
[15] The signatures are omitted here.

ARTICLES IN ADDITION TO, AND AMENDMENT OF, THE CONSTITUTION OF THE UNITED STATES OF AMERICA, PROPOSED BY CONGRESS, AND RATIFIED BY THE LEGISLATURES OF THE SEVERAL STATES [OR CONVENTIONS THEREIN] PURSUANT TO THE FIFTH ARTICLE OF THE ORIGINAL CONSTITUTION:

Article I. Congress shall make no law respecting an establishment of religion, or prohibiting the free exercise thereof; or abridging the freedom of speech or of the press; or the right of the people peaceably to assemble, and to petition the government for a redress of grievances.

Article II. A well-regulated militia being necessary to the security of a free state, the right of the people to keep and bear arms shall not be infringed.

Article III. No soldier shall, in time of peace, be quartered in any house without the consent of the owner, nor in time of war, but in a manner to be prescribed by law.

Article IV. The right of the people to be secure in their persons, houses, papers, and effects, against unreasonable searches and seizures, shall not be violated, and no warrants shall issue but upon probable cause, supported by oath or affirmation, and particularly describing the place to be searched, and the person or things to be seized.

Article V. No person shall be held to answer for a capital or otherwise infamous crime, unless on a presentment or indictment of a grand jury, except in cases arising in the land or naval forces, or in the militia, when in actual service in time of war or public danger; nor shall any person be subject for the same offense to be twice put in jeopardy of life or limb; nor shall be compelled in any criminal case to be a witness against himself, nor be deprived of life, liberty, or property, without due process of law; nor shall private property be taken for public use without just compensation.

Article VI. In all criminal prosecutions the accused shall enjoy the right to a speedy and public trial, by an impartial jury of the State and district where in the crime shall have been committed, which district shall have been previously ascertained by law, and to be informed of the nature and cause of the accusation; to be confronted with the witnesses against him; to have compulsory process for obtaining witnesses in his favor, and to have the assistance of counsel for his defense.

Article VII. In suits at common law, where the value in controversy shall exceed twenty dollars, the right of trial by jury shall be preserved, and no fact tried by a jury shall be otherwise re-examined in any court of the United States, than according to the rules of the common law.

Article VIII. Excessive bail shall not be required, nor excessive fines imposed, nor cruel and unusual punishments inflicted.

Article IX. The enumeration in the Constitution of certain rights shall not be construed to deny or disparage others retained by the people.

Article X.[16] The powers not delegated to the United States by the Constitution, nor prohibited by it to the States, are reserved to the States respectively, or to the people.

Article XI.[17] The judicial power of the United States shall not be construed to extend to any suit in law or equity, commenced or prosecuted against one of the

[16] The first ten amendments took effect December 15, 1791.
[17] Proclaimed January 8, 1798.

United States by citizens of another State, or by citizens or subjects of any foreign State.

Article XII.[18] The electors shall meet in their respective States [19] and vote by ballot for President and Vice-President, one of whom, at least, shall not be an inhabitant of the same State with themselves; they shall name in their ballots the person voted for as President, and in distinct ballots the person voted for as Vice-President, and they shall make distinct lists of all persons voted for as President and of all persons voted for as Vice-President, and of the number of votes for each; which lists they shall sign and certify, and transmit sealed to the seat of the government of the United States, directed to the President of the Senate. The President of the Senate shall, in the presence of the Senate and House of Representatives, open all the certificates and the votes shall then be counted. The person having the greatest number of votes for President shall be the President, if such a number be a majority of the whole number of electors appointed; and if no person have such a majority, then from the persons having the highest numbers not exceeding three on the list of those voted for as President, the House of Representatives shall choose immediately, by ballot, the President. But in choosing the President the votes shall be taken by States, the representation from each State having one vote; a quorum for this purpose shall consist of a member or members from two thirds of the States, and a majority of all States shall be necessary to a choice. And if the House of Representatives shall not choose a President whenever the right of choice shall devolve upon them, before the fourth day of March [20] next following, then the Vice-President shall act as President, as in the case of the death or other constitutional disability of the President.

The person having the greatest number of votes as Vice-President shall be the Vice-President, if such number be a majority of the whole number of electors appointed; and if no person have a majority, then from the two highest numbers on the list the Senate shall choose the Vice-President: a quorum for the purpose shall consist of two thirds of the whole number of Senators, and a majority of the whole number shall be necessary to a choice. But no person constitutionally ineligible to the office of President shall be eligible to that of Vice-President of the United States.

Article XIII.[21] *Section* 1. Neither slavery nor involuntary servitude, except as a punishment for crime whereof the party shall have been duly convicted, shall exist within the United States or any place subject to their jurisdiction.

Section 2. Congress shall have power to enforce this article by appropriate legislation.

Article XIV.[22] *Section* 1. All persons born or naturalized in the United States, and subject to the jurisdiction thereof, are citizens of the United States and of the State wherein they reside. No State shall make or enforce any law which shall abridge the privileges or immunities of citizens of the United States; nor shall any State deprive any person of life, liberty, or property, without due process of law; nor deny to any person within its jurisdiction the equal protection of the laws.

Section 2. Representatives shall be apportioned among the several States ac-

[18] Proclaimed September 25, 1804.
[19] Modified by the Twenty-third Amendment.
[20] Superseded by the Twentieth Amendment.
[21] Proclaimed December 18, 1865.
[22] Proclaimed July 28, 1868.

cording to their respective numbers, counting the whole number of persons in each State, excluding Indians not taxed. But when the right to vote at any election for the choice of electors for President and Vice-President of the United States, Representatives in Congress, the executive and judicial officers of a State, or the members of the legislature thereof, is denied to any of the male inhabitants of such State, being twenty-one years of age, and citizens of the United States, or in any way abridged, except for participation in rebellion, or other crime, the basis of representation therein shall be reduced in the proportion which the number of such male citizens shall bear to the whole number of male citizens twenty-one years of age in such State.

Section 3. No person shall be a Senator or Representative in Congress, or elector of President and Vice-President, or hold any office, civil or military, under the United States or under any State, who, having previously taken an oath as a member of Congress, or as an officer of the United States, or as a member of any State legislature, or as an executive or judicial officer of any State, to support the Constitution of the United States, shall have engaged in insurrection or rebellion against the same, or given aid or comfort to the enemies thereof. But Congress may, by a vote of two thirds of each house, remove such disability.

Section 4. The validity of the public debt of the United States, authorized by law, including debts incurred for payment of pensions and bounties for services in suppressing insurrection or rebellion, shall not be questioned. But neither the United States nor any State shall assume or pay any debt or obligation incurred in aid of insurrection or rebellion against the United States, or any claim for the loss or emancipation of any slave; but all such debts, obligations, and claims shall be held illegal and void.

Section 5. The Congress shall have power to enforce, by appropriate legislation, the provisions of this article.

Article XV.[23] *Section 1.* The right of citizens of the United States to vote shall not be denied or abridged by the United States or by any State on account of race, color, or previous condition of servitude.

Section 2. The Congress shall have power to enforce this article by appropriate legislation.

Article XVI.[24] The Congress shall have power to lay and collect taxes on incomes, from whatever source derived, without apportionment among the several States and without regard to any census or enumeration.

Article XVII.[25] The Senate of the United States shall be composed of two Senators from each State, elected by the people thereof, for six years; and each Senator shall have one vote. The electors in each State shall have the qualifications requisite for electors of the most numerous branch of the State legislature.

When vacancies happen in the representation of any State in the Senate, the executive authority of such State shall issue writs of election to fill such vacancies: *Provided,* That the legislature of any State may empower the executive thereof to make temporary appointments until the people fill the vacancies by election as the legislature may direct.

This amendment shall not be so construed as to affect the election or term of any Senator chosen before it becomes valid as part of the Constitution.

[23] Proclaimed March 30, 1870.
[24] Proclaimed February 25, 1912.
[25] Proclaimed May 31, 1913.

Article XVIII.[26] *Section* 1. After one year from the ratification of this article the manufacture, sale, or transportation of intoxicating liquors within, the importation thereof into, or the exportation thereof from the United States and all territory subject to the jurisdiction thereof for beverage purposes is hereby prohibited.

Section 2. The Congress and the several States shall have concurrent power to enforce this article by appropriate legislation.

Section 3. This article shall be inoperative unless it shall have been ratified as an amendment to the Constitution by the legislatures of the several States, as provided in the Constitution, within seven years from the date of the submission hereof to the States by the Congress.[27]

Article XIX.[28] *Section* 1. The right of citizens of the United States to vote shall not be denied or abridged by the United States or by any State on account of sex.

Section 2. Congress shall have power to enforce this article by appropriate legislation.

Article XX.[29] *Section* 1. The terms of the President and Vice-President shall end at noon on the 20th day of January, and the terms of Senators and Representatives at noon on the 3rd day of January, of the years in which such terms would have ended if this article had not been ratified; and the terms of their successors shall then begin.

Section 2. The Congress shall assemble at least once in every year, and such meeting shall begin at noon on the 3rd day of January, unless they shall by law appoint a different day.

Section 3. If at the time fixed for the beginning of the term of the President, the President-elect shall have died, the Vice-President-elect shall become President. If a President shall not have been chosen before the time fixed for the beginning of his term, or if the President-elect shall have failed to qualify, then the Vice-President-elect shall act as President until a President shall have qualified, and the Congress may by law provide for the case wherein neither a President-elect nor a Vice-President-elect shall have qualified, declaring who shall then act as President, or the manner in which one who is to act shall be selected, and such person shall act accordingly until a President or Vice-President shall have qualified.

Section 4. The Congress may by law provide for the case of the death of any of the persons from whom the House of Representatives may choose a President whenever the right of choice shall have devolved upon them, and for the case of the death of any of the persons from whom the Senate may choose a Vice-President whenever the right of choice shall have devolved upon them.

Section 5. Sections 1 and 2 shall take effect on the 15th day of October following the ratification of this article.

Section 6. This article shall be inoperative unless it shall have been ratified as an amendment to the Constitution by the legislatures of three-fourths of the several States within seven years from the date of its submission.

[26] Proclaimed January 29, 1919.
[27] Rescinded by the Twenty-first Amendment.
[28] Proclaimed August 26, 1920.
[29] Proclaimed February 6, 1933.

Article XXI.[30] *Section* 1. The Eighteenth article of amendment to the Constitution of the United States is hereby repealed.

Section 2. The transportation or importation into any State, territory, or possession of the United States for delivery or use therein of intoxicating liquors, in violation of the laws thereof, is hereby prohibited.

Section 3. This article shall be inoperative unless it shall have been ratified as an amendment to the Constitution by conventions in the several States as provided in the Constitution, within seven years from the date of the submission hereof to the States by the Congress.

Article XXII.[31] *Section* 1. No person shall be elected to the office of the President more than twice, and no person who has held the office of President, or acted as President, for more than two years of a term to which some other person was elected President shall be elected to the office of the President more than once. But this Article shall not apply to any person holding the office of President when this Article was proposed by the Congress, and shall not prevent any person who may be holding the office of President, or acting as President, during the term within which this Article becomes operative from holding the office of President or acting as President during the remainder of such term.

Section 2. This article shall be inoperative unless it shall have been ratified as an amendment to the Constitution by the legislatures of three-fourths of the several States within seven years from the date of its submission to the States by the Congress.

Article XXIII.[32] *Section* 1. The District constituting the seat of Government of the United States shall appoint in such manner as the Congress may direct:

A number of electors of President and Vice-President equal to the whole number of Senators and Representatives in Congress to which the District would be entitled if it were a State, but in no event more than the least populous state; they shall be in addition to those appointed by the states, but they shall be considered, for the purposes of the election of President and Vice-President, to be electors appointed by a state; and they shall meet in the District and perform such duties as provided by the twelfth article of amendment.

Section 2. The Congress shall have power to enforce this article by appropriate legislation.

Article XXIV.[33] *Section* 1. The right of citizens of the United States to vote in any primary or other election for President or Vice-President, for electors for President or Vice-President, or for Senator or Representative in Congess, shall not be denied or abridged by the United States or any state by reason of failure to pay any poll tax or other tax.

Section 2. The Congress shall have power to enforce this article by appropriate legislation.

Article XXV.[34] *Section* 1. In case of the removal of the President from office or his death or resignation, the Vice-President shall become President.

Section 2. Whenever there is a vacancy in the office of the Vice-President, the

[30] Proclaimed December 5, 1933.
[31] Proclaimed March 1, 1951.
[32] Proclaimed April 3, 1961.
[33] Proclaimed February 4, 1964.
[34] Proclaimed February 23, 1967.

President shall nominate a Vice-President who shall take the office upon confirmation by a majority vote of both houses of Congress.

Section 3. Whenever the President transmits to the President pro tempore of the Senate and the Speaker of the House of Representatives his written declaration that he is unable to discharge the powers and duties of his office, and until he transmits to them a written declaration to the contrary, such powers and duties shall be discharged by the Vice-President as Acting President.

Section 4. Whenever the Vice-President and a majority of either the principal officers of the executive departments, or of such other body as Congress may by law provide, transmit to the President pro tempore of the Senate and the Speaker of the House of Representatives their written declaration that the President is unable to discharge the powers and duties of his office, the Vice-President shall immediately assume the powers and duties of the office as Acting President.

Thereafter, when the President transmits to the President pro tempore of the Senate and the Speaker of the House of Representatives his written declaration that no inability exists, he shall resume the powers and duties of his office unless the Vice-President and a majority of either the principal officers of the executive department, or of such other body as Congress may by law provide, transmit within four days to the President pro tempore of the Senate and the Speaker of the House of Representatives their written declaration that the President is unable to discharge the powers and duties of his office. Thereupon Congress shall decide the issue, assembling within 48 hours for that purpose if not in session. If the Congress, within 21 days after receipt of the latter written declaration, or, if Congress is not in session, within 21 days after Congress is required to assemble, determines by two-thirds vote of both houses that the President is unable to discharge the powers and duties of his office, the Vice-President shall continue to discharge the same as Acting President; otherwise, the President shall resume the powers and duties of his office.

REFERENCES

Department of State, *Documentary History of the Constitution of the United States of America, 1786–1870* (3 vols., Washington, D. C., 1894–1900).

The Constitution of the United States of America, Annotated to June 22, 1964, 88th Cong., 1st Sess., Sen. Doc. No. 39.

INDEX